SAULT ST MARIE
MICH.

Robert E. Lewis
3471 Ahern Dr.
Baldwin Park, CA 91706-5208

NAMESAKES 1956-1980

(REVISED AND UPDATED)

JOHN O. GREENWOOD, M.B.A.

The Sixth Book In The Namesakes Series

ISBN 0-912514-15-9

OTHER PUBLICATIONS OF FRESHWATER PRESS, INC.

Greenwood's Guide to Great Lakes Shipping (Annual)
Greenwood's & Dills' Lakeboats (Annual)
The Lakeboats Calendar
Namesakes of the Lakes - John O. Greenwood
Namesakes 1900-1909 - John O. Greenwood
Namesakes 1910-1919 - John O. Greenwood
Namesakes 1920-1929 - John O. Greenwood
Namesakes 1930-1955 - John O. Greenwood
Namesakes of the 90's - John O. Greenwood
The Fleet Histories Series - John O. Greenwood
Great Lakes Ships We Remember - Marine Historical Society of Detroit
Great Lakes Ships We Remember Vol 2 - Marine Historical Society of Detroit
Lore of the Lakes - Dana Thomas Bowen
Memories of the Lakes - Dana Thomas Bowen
Shipwrecks of the Lakes - Dana Thomas Bowen
Ghost Ships of the Great Lakes - Dwight Boyer
True Tales of the Great Lakes - Dwight Boyer
Ships & Men of the Great Lakes - Dwight Boyer
Strange Adventures of the Great Lakes - Dwight Boyer
The Lower St. Lawrence - Ivan S. Brookes
Great Lakes Fleet Identification Chart (Stack Chart)
Over 600 Ship Photographs

****** Current Catalog Available On Request ******

Soon to be released

Great Lakes Ships We Remember Vol 3 - Marine Historical Society of Detroit
History of the Ford Fleet

Copyright 1993 - John O. Greenwood, Cleveland, Ohio
Copyrighted in the United States & Dominion of Canada

Manufactured in the United States of America

All rights reserved. No part of this work covered by copyright hereon may be reproduced in any form or by any means-graphic, electronic or mechanical, including photographic, photocopying, recording, taping or information storage and/or retrieval systems - without prior written permission of Freshwater Press, Inc.

**Published by:
Freshwater Press, Inc.
1700 E. 13th Street, Suite 3 R-E
Cleveland, Ohio 44114**

IISBN 0-912514-15-9

NAMESAKES
1956-1980

(Revised & Updated)

Vessel on the Great Lakes and St. Lawrence River that were scrapped, sank or in any other way or manner left the Great Lakes trade during the quarter century between January 1, 1956 and December 31, 1980 are included in this volume. What separates this volume from the previous edition of NAMESAKES 1956-1980 is the inclusion of up-to-date or superior photographs and the inclusion of facts not previously known.

This, like all others in the NAMESAKES series is a factual, photostory of the vessels (over 100 feet in length) that delivered raw materials and finished products to and from the heartland of the North American continent.

Published by
FRESHWATER PRESS, INC.
1700 E. 13th Street, Suite 3R-E
Cleveland, Ohio 44114

This book is dedicated to a fellow historian, good friend, outstanding individual and avid Great Lakes enthusiast – Rev. Edward J. Dowling, S. J. This dedication reflects to many of us that Rev. Dowling is the "Dean of Great Lakes Historians" and one who has been a guiding light on ship research, especially the older vessels.

Edward Joseph Dowling was born in Rockford, Illinois on September 19, 1906. In 1907 he moved with his family to Chicago where he attended Loyola Academy. In 1930 he graduated from Loyola University with an A.B. degree in Classical Languages and entered the Society of Jesus (Jesuit Order) that summer. Following additional studies at Xavier University, Cincinnati University and St. Louis University, he was ordained on June 26, 1940. In 1942 he was appointed to the University of Detroit faculty where he taught Engineering Graphics until 1973. In 1977 he was awarded the honorary degree of Doctor of Humane Letters by that university. Presently, Rev. Dowling serves as curator of the University of Detroit.

For many years, Rev. Dowling served Jesuit missions in the Sault Ste. Marie, Michigan area, especially on Sugar Island where his painting skills could expand and flourish and his "boat-watching" hobby could be nurtured. Since boyhood days in Chicago, Rev. Dowling has been fascinated with Great Lakes vessels and his legacy to all of us is an unending interest in Great Lakes history and cooperation with one another in that pursuit. Indeed, it is for Rev. Dowling's extreme cooperation on my yet-to-be-published works dating from 1900 that I have chosen this time to honor him.

Rev. Dowling's numerous marine historical society memberships and accomplishments could fill several pages. Suffice here to state that he is a charter member, past Secretary and President of The Marine Historical Society of Detroit and was named its Historian of the Year in 1971. He is also an honorary life member of the Great Lakes Maritime Institute. He is the author of numerous articles and the book "Lakers of World War I." Perhaps best remembered for his editorship of *The Marine Historian*, he was also a major contributor to the award-winning publication of this Corporation, GREAT LAKES SHIPS WE REMEMBER, released in 1979. Along with four other authors, this book represents the culmination of cooperation in a Great Lakes historical work.

I am indebted to my good friend Peter B. Worden for his help in assembling material for the factual side of this dedication. He has been a personal friend of Rev. Dowling for many years and warmly accepted this task. It is my privilege to commemorate this volume in the "Namesakes Series" to Father Dowling, especially so on this anniversary of his 75th birthday!

JOHN O. GREENWOOD

EXPLANATION AND PREFACE

NAMESAKES 1956-1980 is the sixth book in "The NAMESAKES Series."

This volume compliments, and is the sequel to, NAMESAKES 1930-1955 and together with that work, the set encompasses histories of 1,050 lake vessels! Such a definitive and explanatory photo-history has never been available before now. With the two volumes, readers will have on their shelves one-half century of Great Lakes shipping history and lore!

IF A VESSEL EXISTED ON THE GREAT LAKES-ST LAWRENCE RIVER AFTER JANUARY 1, 1956 AND WAS GONE FROM THE SCENE BY THE END OF 1980, IT IS INCLUDED IN THIS VOLUME. SMALL CRAFT LESS THAN 100' IN OVERALL LENGTH AND OTHER NON-CARGO CARRYING CRAFT ARE NOT INCLUDED.

613 vessel histories are included in this volume. A cross-index of all vessel names is provided in the index, following the successful introduction of this practice with NAMESAKES 1930-1955. Photographs have been up-dated from those found in NAMESAKES II in a large measure, bringing to light for the first time the work of dedicated marine photographers that have not heretofore been published.

There are obviously many people who have brought their assistance to the fulfillment of this work. Most have contributed their photographic efforts in loaning of photos to be used herein. To these fellow historians and boat photographers, I wish to extend my sincere thanks and appreciation. These are: G. Ayoub, J. H. Bascom, J. N. Bascom, M. J. Brown, R. Campbell, Rev. E. J. Dowling, S. McLellan, D. McCormick, Rev. P. J. Van der Linden, P. B. Worden.

To all those who helped share in this production, my sincere thanks. I am sure there are some persons who have not been specifically mentioned, but please know that your help and support is most welcome and gratefully appreciated.

It is my hope that this volume will complete the most recent one-half century of Great Lakes ships and be a joy to many over the years. Thank you all for your help and support!

JOHN O. GREENWOOD

CONTENTS

FLEET	PAGE
Dedication	v
Explanation and Preface	vii
Table of Contents	ix
Algoma Central Railway	1
American Oil Company	8
Algonquin Corporation Limited	9
American Steamship Company	10
Ann Arbor Railroad Company	16
Atlantic Richfield Company	18
Bayswater Shipping Limited	19
Beaconsfield Steamships Limited	23
Bethlehem Steel Corporation/Great Lakes Steamship/Marine Division	29
The Big "D" Lines, Limited	37
Blue Heron Marine Limited	38
Blue Peter Steamships Limited	39
Branch Lines Limited	40
British-American Oil Company	50
Brooks Liquid Transport, Incorporated	51
Brown Steamship Company	52
T. H. Browning Steamship Company/Browning Lines, Incorporated	54
Buckeye Steamship Company	64
Bultema Dock & Dredge Company	76
Bultema Marine Transportation	79
John H. Bultema	80
Cambria Steamship Company	81
Canada Cement Transport Limited	83
Canada Cement LaFarge Limited	84
Canada Steamship Lines Limited/Inc	85
Canadian Coastwise Carriers Limited	133
Canadian Holiday Line	136
Canadian Pacific Railway Company	137
Cargo Carriers, Incorporated	139
Cayuga Navigation Company Limited	144
Chesapeake & Ohio Railway Company/Chessie System, Inc.	145
Chicago, Duluth & Georgian Bay Transit Company	150
Clark Oil and Refining Corporation	152
Clepro Marine Corporation	153
Cleveland-Cliffs Steamship Company	154
Cleveland Tankers, Incorporated	159
Coastalake Tankers Limited	168
Columbia Transportation Division, Oglebay Norton Company	171
Comet Enterprises Limited	189
Construction Aggregates Corporation	191
Construction Materials Corporation	192
Crystal Beach Transit Company	193
Detroit and Cleveland Navigation Company	194
Detroit Atlantic Navigation Company	198
Desgagnes Navigation Limited	199
Energy Cooperative Inc.	200
Erie Navigation Company	201
Erie Sand & Gravel Company/Esco Dredge & Fill Division	203

CONTENTS

FLEET	PAGE
Erie Sand Steamship Company	206
Escanaba Towing Company	211
Federal Motorship Corporation	212
Ford Motor Company	213
Harry G. Gamble Shipyards	214
Gartland Steamship Company	215
Gulf and Lake Navigation Company, Limited	223
Gulf Oil Corporation	225
Hall Corporation of Canada/Shipping (1969) Ltd./Shipping Ltd.	229
Hamilton Harbour Commissioners	260
Hanna Furnace Corporation	261
Hindman Transportation Company Limited	262
Imperial Oil Limited	271
Inland Steel Company	275
Interlake Steamship Company	276
Jemmig Enterprises Limited	286
Jocharanne Tugboat Corporation	287
Johnstone Shipping Limited	288
Jupiter Steamship Company	291
Kelley Island Lime and Transport Company	292
Kinsman Transit Company/Marine Transit Company	293
Labrador Steamship Company Limited	310
Lakeland Tankers, Limited	311
Lake Sand Corporation	313
La Verendrye Line, Limited	314
Law Quarries Transportation Limited	323
McAllister Towing Limited	324
T. J. McCarthy Steamship Company	326
McNamara Construction Company Limited	334
James McWilliams Blue Line, Incorporated	335
Mackinac Transportation Company	336
Marathon Corporation of Canada, Limited	337
Marine Fueling, Incorporated	338
Medusa Cement Division, Medusa Corporation	339
Michigan Atlantic Corporation	340
Highway Department, Michigan State Ferry Service	341
Michigan Tankers, Incorporated	345
Mid-Canada Transports Limited	346
Midlake Steamship Line	347
Midland Steamship Line, Incorporated	348
Scott Misener Steamships Limited/Colonial Steamships/ Misener Holdings/Misener Transportation	351
Mobil Oil Corporation	379
Mohawk Navigation Company Limited	382
National Sand and Material Company, Limited	388
National Steel Corporation	389
Neal Petroleum Company Limited	392
Nicholson Transit Company	393
Norlake Steamships Limited	408
Northern Paper Mills Limited	410
Northwest Steamships Limited	411

CONTENTS

FLEET	PAGE
Ohio Transportation, Incorporated	413
Oil Transfer Corporation	414
Ontario Northland Transportation Commission	415
Ore Navigation Corporation, Great Lakes Division	417
Owen Sound Transportation Company, Limited	418
N. M. Paterson & Sons Limited	419
Pelee Shipping Company Limited	459
Pennsylvania-Ontario Transportation Company	460
Pioneer Steamship Company	461
K. A. Powell (Canada) Limited	467
Pringle Barge Line Division, Oglebay Norton Company	469
Providence Shipping Company, Limited	471
Pyke Towing & Salvage Company Limited	473
Quebec and Ontario Transportation Company, Limited	475
Reiss Steamship Company	486
Redwood Enterprises, Limited	490
Reoch Steamship Company Limited/Transports Limited	491
Republic Steel Corporation	499
Roen Steamship Company	506
Myles J. Rosenthal	510
S. & E. Shipping Corporation	511
Saginaw Dock and Terminal Company	516
Secola Shipping Limited	517
Shasta Steamship Company	518
Shell Canada Limited	519
Silloc, Limited	522
Sinclair Refining Company	523
Socony-Mobil Oil Company	524
The Soo River Company	525
Steel Products Steamship Corporation	526
Sun Oil Company	527
Tank Truck Transport Limited	528
Texaco Canada Limited	529
Texaco, Incorporated	530
Tomlinson Fleet Corporation	531
Toth Motorship, Corporation	536
Trico Enterprises, Limited	537
Pittsburgh Steamship Division, United States Steel Corporation/Michigan Limestone Division/United States Steel Corporation Great Lakes Fleet	539
United Towing and Salvage Company Limited	564
Upper Lakes and St. Lawrence Transportation Company, Limited/Shipping Limited	565
USCAN Transport Bahamas, Limited	593
Wayne Steamship Company	594
International Cruising Company, Limited	595
Westdale Shipping Limited	596
Winona Steamships Limited	602
Wilson Transit Company/Marine Transit	603
Windsor Detroit Barge Line Limited	609
Wyandotte Transportation Company	610
Yankcanuck Steamships, Limited	611

Steamer AGAWA (2)

OWNER:	Algoma Central Railway
BUILT:	American Ship Building Company, Cleveland, Ohio - 1908
HULL NO.:	442
O. A. DIMENSIONS:	500' x 54' x 30'
FORMER DATA:	Launched as HOWARD M. HANNA, JR (1). Renamed GLENSHEE in 1915. Renamed MARQUETTE (3) in 1926. Renamed GODERICH (1) in 1927. Given last name in 1963.

During the 1968 navigation season the Steamer AGAWA (2) was sold for use as a storage grain barge at Goderich, Ontario. It was serving in that capacity under the name LIONEL PARSONS until sold for scrap in 1983. The steam whistle off this vessel was obtained by Mr. John N. Bascom of Toronto, Ontario and is now preserved as an historical artifact in the Bascom home. Mr. George Parsons, president of the current owners, provided this courtesy.

The namesake of the Steamer AGAWA (2) is the station and canyon of the same name about 115 miles north of Sault Ste. Marie, Ontario on the Algoma Central Railway. The name is Ojibwan and means "sheltered place or harbor." Originally it was a name used to describe the mouth of the Agawa River which winds along the floor of the Agawa Canyon. The river is fed by numerous waterfalls and cascades in the canyon and is very scenic.

The main line of the Algoma Central Railway follows the course of the Agawa River through the canyon providing a spectacular view of the scenery in this lush and, in many places, virgin countryside.

The Steamer AGAWA (2) is shown in this photograph on May 11, 1965 in the approach to Lock One of the Welland Ship Canal. This vessel is one of those that was wrecked in the November 9, 1913 "Great Storm" of the Great Lakes. It was considered a constructive total loss as it lay at Pointe Aux Barques, Lake Huron, but was salvaged and rebuilt at Collingwood Shipbuilding Company, Collingwood, Ontario and returned to service in 1915.

Steamer ALGOCEN (1)

OWNER:	Algoma Central Railway
BUILT:	American Ship Building Company, Lorain, Ohio—1909
HULL NO.:	368
O. A. DIMENSIONS:	524' × 54' × 30'3"
FORMER DATA:	Launched as JOHN J. BARLUM (2) Given last name in 1935.

This coal-fired Steamer ALGOCEN bears little resemblance to the current vessel in the fleet that bears the name. This steamer is shown in 1961 in the St. Mary's River. This ALGOCEN was sold for scrap in 1968.

On August 11, 1899 the Algoma Central Railway Company was incorporated. On May 23, 1901 the name was amended to Algoma Central & Hudson Bay Railway Company and this title continued until the current name was adopted in the mid-1960's.

Throughout its history the company has been the oldest continuous operation of bulk freight steamships in Canada on the Great Lakes. The firm began using parts of its corporate name in vessel names in the 1930's. Thus, this vessel is named for *ALGOMA* and *CEN*TRAL using the first two words in the railway's corporate title.

The road operates over three hundred miles of track north of Sault Ste. Marie, Ontario to Hearst, Ontario and is a large mover of commodities carried on the Great Lakes. Iron ore is a major commodity handled both by the railroad and the steamship department. It is brought to the port of Michipicoten, Ontario from the Wawa, Junction area on the railroad's mainline. Here, it is shipped over modern belt conveyor facilities to Sault Ste. Marie, Ontario and lower lake ports. Labrador iron ore is also carried up through the St. Lawrence Seaway.

Steamer ALGORAIL (1)

OWNER:	Algoma Central Railway
BUILT:	American Ship Building Company, Lorain, Ohio—1901
HULL NO.:	311
O. A. DIMENSIONS:	366' × 48' × 28'
FORMER DATA:	Launched as WILLIAM S. MACK. Renamed HOME SMITH in 1918. Given last name in 1936.

This small bulk freighter was sold for scrap in 1963, but the name is carried forward on the Great Lakes by a modern diesel-powered self-unloader of the Algoma Fleet.

The name comes from usage of parts of the corporate title, namely *ALGO* from Algoma and *RAIL* from Railway. The company adopted this method of naming its ships in the 1930's and has carried it forward. Only a few of its current vessels bear other names, different from this theme. And they mostly honor executives of the company.

The Algoma Central Railway was built northward from Sault Ste. Marie, Ontario at the turn of the century to open the door to markets of the vast supply of raw materials in the hinterland by Mr. Francis Hector Clergue, now deceased. The discovery of the Helen Mine was responsible for the steel mill being erected at Sault Ste. Marie and has been a major contributor of tonnage for the railway. It also brought into being the steamship department of the railway and is still significant in operations today.

The Steamer ALGORAIL is shown in this picture on July 22, 1954 upbound light in the Welland Ship Canal.

Steamer ALGOSOO (1)

OWNER:	Algoma Central Railway
BUILT:	American Ship Building Company, Lorain, Ohio—1901
HULL NO.:	306
O. A. DIMENSIONS:	366' × 48' × 28'
FORMER DATA:	Launched as SATURN (1). Renamed J. FRATER TAYLOR in 1913. Given last name in 1936.

The bulk freight Steamer ALGOSOO honored the owning railway with the prefix in its ship name—"ALGO." This was a common, though not universal, theme in the list of ship names of this company.

The specific namesake for this vessel is found in the suffix of the ship name—"SOO." Commonly, Sault Ste. Marie, Ontario and its sister, but smaller city in Michigan are called "Soo" for short. This ship's name could have been "ALGOSAULT," but that was reasoned to be impractical and not as easily identifiable with that famous area of the Great Lakes region.

Sault Ste. Marie, Ontario is the corporate and operating headquarters of this railway as well as being the home of the largest integrated steel plant in the Dominion of Canada. The city also contains the only Canadian lock for interlake navigation on the Upper Lakes. This lock was built and opened to traffic in 1895 at a cost of $4,000,000 because use of the United States locks was denied Canadian troops sent to supress the Riel rebellion of 1870. At that time, they had no sure passage of their own and work commenced to satisfy that demand.

The Steamer ALGOSOO continued active until being sold for scrap in 1965. It is shown below in the St. Mary's River on June 21, 1953.

Steamer ALGOSTEEL (1)

OWNER: Algoma Central Railway
BUILT: Detroit Shipbuilding Company, Wyandotte, Michigan - 1908
HULL NO.: 174
O. A. DIMENSIONS: 500' x 52' x 30'
FORMER DATA: Launched as THOMAS BARLUM. Given last name in 1935.

The bulk freight Steamer ALGOSTEEL was sold for scrap in 1967 but won at least partial reprieve in that she is ending her useful life as a breakwater in Lake Michigan.

The ship name has as its namesake for the prefix the first four letters, *ALGO*, from the company name Algoma. The suffix in the ship name is in reference to the Algoma Steel Corporation Limited located at Sault Ste. Marie, Ontario, also the headquarters city of the owners.

Over the years since the railway was begun in 1899, it has had a fine working relationship with the steel company which is a large customer of the railway. The Algoma Steel Corporation is a major steel producer of Canada.

Millions of tons of coal, iron ore and stone are brought to the plant by vessels of this fleet and others each year. In addition, thousands of tons of finished steel products are shipped out by water. These are augmented by various types of liquid cargo handled over the docks at Sault Ste. Marie.

The Steamer ALGOSTEEL is shown in one of the connecting channels on June 19, 1953. It made its maiden voyage light from Detroit to Duluth, Minnesota April 25, 1908 for the Postal Steamship Company. It was the first ship ever equipped with electric name boards on the bow. They spelled out the ship name in foot high letters.

Steamer ALGOWAY (1)

OWNER:	Algoma Central Railway
BUILT:	West Bay City Shipbuilding Company, West Bay City, Michigan—1903
HULL NO.:	608
O. A. DIMENSIONS:	376' × 50'3" × 28'
FORMER DATA:	Launched as G. WATSON FRENCH. Renamed HENRY P. WERNER in 1924. Renamed JOHN J. BOLAND, JR. (2) in 1937. Given last name in 1940.

The six thousand and fifty ton carrying capacity Steamer ALGOWAY was sold for scrap in 1963. It had fulfilled its days of usefulness on the Great Lakes, and because of its small size, was no longer an economical unit.

Since the 1930's this fleet has been using parts of its corporate title for some of its vessel names. It is a natural follow through on this theme, therefore, that brought into being this ship name.

The prefix of this ship name, ALGO, is in reference to the first word of the company title—Algoma, with the suffix of the vessel name, WAY, being the last three letters of the word Railway.

There is no current ship of the bulk freight class that carries on this name on the Great Lakes. However, the fleet does now have a very modern self-unloading vessel ALGOWAY which was commissioned in 1972 to carry on this historic name in the fleet.

The Steamer ALGOWAY is shown in this photograph on June 20, 1953 while downbound in the St. Mary's River.

Motor Vessel ROY A. JODREY

OWNER: Algoma Central Railway
BUILT: Collingwood Shipyards,
Collingwood, Ontario – 1965
HULL NO.: 186
O. A. DIMENSIONS: 640' 6" x 72' x 40'

The self-unloading Motor Vessel ROY A. JODREY is shown above while downbound in the West Neebish Channel, St. Mary's River on August 18, 1973. Little did anyone think that less than 1½ years later the ship would be a total loss.

Having cleared Seven Islands, Quebec at 6:50 AM November 18, 1974 with 20,050 gross tons of iron ore pellets for Detroit, Michigan delivery, the ship ran onto Pullman Shoal near Wellesley Island in the Thousand Islands area of the western St. Lawrence River and sank at 3:09 AM on November 21, 1974. Subsequent diving expeditions determined the ship was laying on its side in 190' of water and was unsalvageable.

Mr. Roy Adelbert Jodrey was this vessel's namesake. He was born in White Rock, King's County, Nova Scotia on December 24, 1888 and began work in growing and exporting apples from the Annapolis Valley in 1907. He worked in a wide range of jobs and managed the Avon River Power Company in 1927 and the Canadian Keyes Fibre Company in 1933. Lastly, he was president of the Minas Basin Pulp and Power Company. He was a director of the Algoma Central Railway for a number of years and at the time of his death in Halifax, Nova Scotia on August 12, 1973.

Steamer AMOCO MICHIGAN

OWNER:	American Oil Company
BUILT:	American Ship Building Company, Lorain, Ohio—1928
HULL NO.:	802
O. A. DIMENSIONS:	390'3" × 52'3" × 25'
FORMER DATA:	Launched as ROBERT W. STEWART. Given last name in 1962.

The tank Steamer AMOCO MICHIGAN was sold for off-lakes use in 1969 and ventured across the Atlantic Ocean to begin a new career as a barge in the Indian Ocean. It is shown above on September 2, 1962.

The vessel takes its name from the trade name of the oil company being AMOCO and the state of MICHIGAN. When this ship was a member of the Great Lakes fleet, the American Oil Company had a ship named for each of the surrounding four states of its corporate headquarters in Chicago, Illinois.

First permanent settlement in the state was at Sault Ste. Marie in 1668. This area is probably the most famous in the state today as the site of the world famous St. Marys Falls Canal, better known as the Soo Locks. More tonnage passes through this waterway in a short season than in most other large canals of the world on a year-round basis. This canal was first opened to traffic in 1855 and currently has four large locks.

The Steamer AMOCO MICHIGAN sailed from Lorain, Ohio on April 11, 1928 on its maiden voyage. The vessel was without cargo and destined for Indiana Harbor, Indiana.

Steamer CARDINAL (3)

OWNER: Algonquin Corporation Limited
BUILT: Furness Shipbuilding Company, Limited, Haverton Hill-on-Tees, England – 1927
HULL NO.: 115
O. A. DIMENSIONS: 256'3" x 43' x 18'
FORMER DATA: Launched as WINDSOLITE. Renamed IMPERIAL WINDSOR in 1947. Given last name in 1973.

The tanker Steamer CARDINAL (3) was acquired by Hall Corporation Shipping Ltd. early in 1973 and immediately was placed in this subsidiary firm for corporate operating purposes. It, thus, did not have a name in keeping with the usual set of theme names in the Hall fleet.

This ship name was chosen at random from the past early history of the Hall fleet. The name was applied to a wooden steam barge in 1905. The unit had been built in 1875 at Montreal and served until it was broken up in 1917.

The specific namesake of both that early unit and this tank vessel was the small community of 2,000 population known as Cardinal, Ontario. It was given the name by Loyalists in 1784 because of the great abundance of the red bird known as the cardinal which the settlers found in the area.

During the early days of navigation Cardinal was located on the Galops Canal. When the new Seaway was built, the town was literally moved north. This vessel is shown on May 10, 1973 shortly after going into operation in this fleet. After a collision near Point Pelee, Lake Erie on May 21, 1974, the ship was sold for scrap after having been declared a constructive total loss.

Steamer BEN W. CALVIN

OWNER: American Steamship Company
BUILT: American Ship Building Company,
Lorain, Ohio - 1911
HULL NO.: 388
O. A. DIMENSIONS: 557' x 58' x 31'
FORMER DATA: Launched as the bulk freighter WILLIAM C. AGNEW. Renamed GEORGE F. RAND (1) in 1926. Converted to a self-unloader at American Ship Building Company, Lorain, Ohio in 1936. Given last name in 1954.

The self-unloading Steamer BEN W. CALVIN sailed on its maiden trip April 24, 1911, departing Ashtabula, Ohio with a cargo of coal for Duluth, Minnesota delivery. The vessel was active until being sold for scrap early in 1974 and is shown outbound at Cleveland, Ohio on June 16, 1967.

Mr. Benjamin Willis Calvin was the namesake of this vessel. He was born at Topeka, Kansas February 20, 1896 and attended the University of Illinois prior to joining the U.S Air Force during World War I. In 1919 he joined the Universal Atlas Cement Company in Chicago, Illinois, then left to work in the wholesale merchandising business in Kentucky and Michigan.

He re-entered the cement business in 1927, joining General Portland Cement at Jackson, Michigan. He rose to become sales director by 1936 at which time he left to assume duties as vice president and general manager of Aetna Portland Cement Company at Bay City, Michigan. Elected president in 1937. His namesake's original owner was the Buffalo and Susquehanna Steamshp Company.

Steamer FONTANA (2)

OWNER: American Steamship Company
BUILT: Great Lakes Engineering Works, Ecorse, Michigan—1904
HULL NO.: 1
O. A. DIMENSIONS: 377' × 50' × 28'3''
FORMER DATA: Launched as the bulk freighter R. W. ENGLAND. Renamed FRANK SEITHER (1) in 1919. Given last name in 1923. Converted to a self-unloader at Leatham D. Smith Dock Company, Sturgeon Bay, Wisconsin in 1924.

The self-unloading Steamer FONTANA is shown above in the Eastern Gap of Toronto, Ontario harbor outbound into Lake Ontario on one of its many voyages from that harbor. It continued active until it was sold for scrap in 1960.

This vessel took this name when it became the property of the Fontana Steamship Company in 1923. This company was one of many managed by, and a subsidiary of, Cleveland-Cliffs Iron Company. The parent firm had a Barge FONTANA earlier in this century that was towed by their Steamer KALIYUGA. This was, then, the second usage of the ship name in Cleveland-Cliffs history. Subsequent owners never saw fit to change the name.

Fontana was the name originally suggested by Mrs. William G. Mather for the earlier barge. The name referred to Mr. Domenico Fontana, famous Italian architect of the 17th century. He was born in Lombardy, Italy in 1543 and died in 1607. He was in Rome during the lifetime of Michelangelo and was a protege of Cardinal Montalto, later Pope Sixtus V. During this Pope's reign, Fontana was pontifical architect at the Vatican. Many of his masterpieces are visible today and Mrs. Mather felt very strongly in favor of his work when she suggested this name to her husband who was then chief executive of Cleveland-Cliffs.

Steamer EDMUND P. SMITH

OWNER: American Steamship Company
BUILT: Great Lakes Engineering Works, Ecorse, Michigan—1907
HULL NO.: 32
O. A. DIMENSIONS: 500' × 54' × 30'
FORMER DATA: Launched as JACOB T. KOPP. Renamed G. N. WILSON (2) in 1928. Renamed CONSUMERS POWER (1) in 1931. Renamed HARRY YATES (2) in 1934. Given last name in 1939.

The namesake of this bulk freighter was an enterprising coal merchant named Mr. Edmund Peter Smith. He was born in Azalea, Michigan on January 4, 1883 and was educated in the public schools. Upon graduation from high school he began working for the Ann Arbor Rail Road in their office at Toledo, Ohio. He became agent at that office in 1905.

Mr. Smith then moved to Menominee, Michigan in 1906 and was the agent there for the railroad. At this time he saw the opportunity of handling coal on a local basis and began bringing in carloads of coal and reselling it on a consignment basis.

In 1907 he formed and became president of the Central West Coal Company with dock facilities at Menominee, Michigan. This firm did a considerable business with this vessel's owners by reason of their delivery of coal to Mr. Smith's dock. The owners christened this vessel in his honor in 1939 in recognition of that customer relationship. Mr. Smith continued to head the coal company until selling it on April 1, 1941 to North Western Fuel Company. Concurrently, he formed the Limestone Products Company at Menominee in 1931 and headed it until its sale in 1958. He then retired. Both of his former firms were sold to The C. Reiss Coal Company on July 1, 1965.

Mr. Smith died at Green Bay, Wisconsin in 1968 and his namesake was sold for scrap in 1963. It is shown below being unloaded of a grain cargo at the Concrete-Central Elevator at Buffalo, New York in 1952.

Steamer HARRIS N. SNYDER

OWNER: American Steamship Company
BUILT: Great Lakes Engineering Works, Ecorse, Michigan - 1907
HULL NO.: 31
O. A. DIMENSIONS: 526' x 54' x 30'
FORMER DATA: Launched as the bulk freighter JOHN J. BOLAND (1). Lengthened 26' and converted to a self-unloader at American Ship Building Company, Lorain, Ohio in 1936. Renamed THUNDER BAY QUARRIES (2) in 1939. Given last name in 1953.

Mr. Harris Noble Snyder was the namesake of this vessel. He was born at Bloomville, Ohio on May 13, 1889 and was educated in the public schools. Following several years' work in various jobs, Mr. Snyder joined the Buffalo Slag Company, Incorporated and rose through its ranks to become president and treasurer of the firm in 1913. He remained active in the post until his death in 1972.

In addition to his connection with Buffalo Slag, he was a director of Federal Crushed Stone Corporation, Buffalo Gravel Corporation and Bituminous Products Company. His namesake was active through the 1973 season and was sold for scrap in 1974.

The Steamer HARRIS N. SNYDER is shown above while downbound with limestone in Pelee Passage, Lake Erie, on September 1, 1970.

Steamer UNITED STATES GYPSUM (2)

OWNER: American Steamship Company
BUILT: Great Lakes Engineering Works, St. Clair, Michigan—1910
HULL NO.: 78
O. A. DIMENSIONS: 524' × 56' × 30'
FORMER DATA: Launched as the bulk freighter THEODORE H. WICKWIRE, JR. Converted to a self-unloader at American Ship Building Company, Lorain, Ohio and renamed THUNDER BAY QUARRIES (1) in 1932. Given last name in 1939.

The self-unloading Steamer UNITED STATES GYPSUM was named for the United States Gypsum Company with headquarters at Chicago, Illinois. For many years this fleet has transported many millions of tons of commodities for this firm and had, as a result, named this vessel in the firm's honor.

The company was originally incorporated in New Jersey in 1901 and took its present name on August 26, 1920 after a number of mergers and acquisitions. The firm operates throughout the United States and Canada with its main Great Lakes operation at Alabaster, Michigan. There, the dock facility is at the end of a 6,800 foot tramway from the western shore of Lake Huron. Vessels are loaded at this facility by means of buckets-to-hopper crib via the tramway.

The United States Gypsum Company markets, through its own name and subsidiaries, various products used in construction and industry. Some of these include plaster bases, gypsum wallboard products, sheeting, lime products and associated items.

The maiden trip of this vessel began August 8, 1910 from St. Clair, Michigan when it proceeded upbound, light to load iron ore at Superior, Wisconsin. The freighter was sold for scrap in 1972 after having run in a restricted trading zone. It is shown above at Detroit River light on May 2, 1972.

Steamer JOSEPH S. YOUNG (2)

OWNER: American Steamship Company
BUILT: Great Lakes Engineering Works, Ecorse, Michigan - 1907
HULL NO.: 28
O. A. DIMENSIONS: 579' x 58' x 32'
FORMER DATA: Launched as the bulk freighter WILPEN. Renamed DAVID P. THOMPSON in 1927. Converted to a self-unloader at Fraser-Nelson Shipbuilding and Dry Dock Company, Superior, Wisconsin in 1957. Given last name in 1969.

Originally in the Shenango Furnace fleet, this ship was built with a pipe organ in the guest's lounge. No other Great Lakes freighter has ever been so equipped.

Namesake of this vessel is Mr. Joseph Samuel Young who was born June 15, 1898 in Allentown, Pennsylvania. He graduated from Princeton University in 1919 with a B.A. degree and from Columbia University in 1923 with an Ll.B. degree. He entered employment of the Lehigh Portland Cement Company that same year and has spent his entire business career there.

Mr. Young became vice president and assistant to the president in 1926 and served in that capacity until becoming president in 1932. He remained as president until 1963 when he became chairman of the board and of the executive committee. He retained that title until retiring but is still a director of Lehigh. Mr. Young is also a director of Armstrong Cork Company, Bell Telephone Company and other firms.

The ship is shown while downbound in the West Neebish Channel, St. Mary's River on July 18, 1976. It was sold for scrap in 1979 after 2½ years of idelness.

Steamer ANN ARBOR NO. 5

OWNER: Ann Arbor Railroad Company
BUILT: Toledo Shipbuilding Company, Toledo, Ohio—1910
HULL NO.: 118
O. A. DIMENSIONS: 377'9" × 56'3" × 21'

The carferry Steamer ANN ARBOR NO. 5 had a carrying capacity of 26 railroad cars and 100 passengers in topside staterooms. This vessel is shown above entering Kewaunee, Wisconsin on August 1, 1946. The ship remained in service until being sold in 1966 for trade-in purposes. In the following year it was sold for non-transportation use and was engaged in breakwall use at South Haven, Michigan until 1969. In 1970 the hull was sold for scrap.

The numerical reference in this ship name was merely an internal designation of the lines vessels. This was the fifth such vessel to be named. The specific namesake was the owner's name itself, referring to the interesting history of the rail line.

The Ann Arbor Railroad is an outgrowth of several predecessor railroads. In 1872 the State Line Railroad Company was chartered in Ohio to build a steam railroad from Elm Street in Toledo to the connection with the Detroit, Canada Southern and Toledo Company at Alexis, Ohio. After various mergers, the Toledo, Ann Arbor and Northeastern Railroad was organized in 1878 and built a line to Pontiac, Michigan. In 1892 various south-to-north and vice versa lines were merged to form the present Ann Arbor Railroad and two carferries were built and put into service to reach northern Michigan ports. On September 21, 1895 the present corporation was organized in the state of Michigan and has operated continuously since. Though the line still operates, it is now owned by the Detroit, Toledo & Ironton Railroad, having been sold by the parent Wabash Railroad to this firm on August 31, 1963.

Steamer CITY OF GREEN BAY (2)

OWNER: Ann Arbor Railroad Company
BUILT: Toledo Shipbuilding Company,
Toledo, Ohio – 1927
HULL NO.: 177
O. A. DIMENSIONS: 380' x 58'3" x 25'
FORMER DATA: Launched as WABASH. Given last name in 1963.

Namesake of this carferry was the city of Green Bay, Wisconsin which is the seat of Brown County and the second largest trade and shipping center in the state of Wisconsin.

Green Bay is located at the mouth of the Fox River and is at the southern point of a body of water called Green Bay, Lake Michigan. The population of the metropolitan area is about sixty-five thousand persons.

In the 1600's it was a meeting point for the men who developed the Mississippi Valley and is in Winnebago Indian country. Jean Nicolet came into the area in 1634 and Claude Allouez, a Jesuit priest, set up a mission in Green Bay in 1669. It became a village in 1829 and the first newspaper in Wisconsin was begun there in 1833. It is fitting, therefore, that a large paper and paper products industry is centered in Green Bay today.

This vessel was sold for overseas scrapping in the spring of 1974.

Motor Vessel GREAT LAKES

OWNER: Atlantic Richfield Company
BUILT: Ingalls Iron Works Company, Incorporated, Decatur, Alabama—1963
HULL NO.: 1577
O. A. DIMENSIONS: 340' × 50' × 22'
FORMER DATA: Launched as SINCLAIR GREAT LAKES. Renamed GREAT LAKES in 1972.

The tank Motor Vessel GREAT LAKES is shown above while downbound in Lake St. Clair on August 15, 1974.

Since this ship was built specifically for Great Lakes service, the owners thought that a name taking into consideration the entire trading area of the vessel would be appropriate. Hence, the name is in reference to the freshwater seas known as The Great Lakes, comprised of Lakes Superior, Michigan, Huron, Erie and Ontario.

From the level of Lake Superior to the level of Lake Ontario, commerce descends 357 feet. The total area of the Great Lakes is 94,710 square miles.

This tanker sailed on its maiden voyage May 15, 1963 with 37,797 barrels of gasoline from East Chicago, Indiana to Milwaukee, Wisconsin. It was sold for off-Lakes use in 1976 following sale of the firm's only Great Lakes area refinery.

Steamer BAYANNA

OWNER: Bayswater Shipping Limited
BUILT: Detroit Dry Dock Company, Wyandotte, Michigan—1896
HULL NO.: 123
O. A. DIMENSIONS: 256' × 42' × 17'3"
FORMER DATA: Launched as the bulk freighter ARAGON. Converted to a self-unloading sandsucker at Canadian Vickers Limited, Montreal, Quebec in 1927. Converted to a self-unloader at Muir Brothers Dry Dock Company, Limited, Port Dalhousie, Ontario in 1942. Given last name in 1946.

The Steamer BAYANNA was sunk in 1962, subsequently raised and later sold for scrap after laying idle at Kingston, Ontario for two years.

When this fleet was founded in 1946 by Mr. George Davidson, this became his first ship. The firm was active in the sand and salt trades into Georgian Bay ports at the time and Mr. Davidson chose the name for the company in relation to the many bays and their waters of the area he was then serving. A few years later, however, the main base of operations was in the bays and waters of Lake Ontario. The name of the firm was still apropos, only the background for selecting the firm name was blurred and many people have thought the name came from this later service area of the fleet.

The specific namesake of this ship was Mr. Davidson's mother, the former Anna McKinnon who was born and lived along the Ottawa River. She was the mother of twelve children.

The vessel is shown above on November 26, 1961 while unloading. Note the profuse emission of smoke that would be severely criticised today.

Steamer BAYFAIR

OWNER:	Bayswater Shipping Limited
BUILT:	Furness Shipbuilding Company Limited, Haverton Hill-on-Tees, England—1928
HULL NO.:	134
O. A. DIMENSIONS:	258' × 43'3'' × 25'
FORMER DATA:	Launched as COALHAVEN. Given last name in 1962.

Together with the common fleet shipname prefix, this self-unloader honored Mr. Albert Fairfield McGaw as its namesake. The first four letters of his middle name form the suffix of the shipname. This vessel was active until sold for scrap in 1968.

Mr. McGaw was born in Toronto, Ontario on June 24, 1908 and graduated with honors from the University of Toronto. In 1926-27 he was a clerk with Manufacturers Life Insurance Company and in 1927-28 was a laboratory and testing assistant with the Spruce Falls Paper Company. Following this he worked briefly for the H. G. Stanton & Company firm in 1929-30 and Aird Macleod & Company in 1931-32 prior to joining F. P. Weaver Coal Company Limited as a scale clerk and dispatcher in 1932.

He became associated with the accounting department of the firm in 1934 and served as cashier in 1936-38 before being named traffic manager in 1939. Mr. McGaw held this position until being named vice president in 1951. In 1961 he became president of the Empire-Hanna Coal Corporation on its reorganization and held this post until December 31, 1969. Business and friendly relationships between this man and Mr. George Davidson brought his name to the bow of this ship.

The Steamer BAYFAIR is shown in the photograph above on arrival in Toronto Harbour on August 25, 1963. Note the "deckload" of coal rising above the hatch combings. The maiden voyage of this vessel commenced July 8, 1928 from Haverton Hill-on-Tees, England light for Montreal, Quebec.

Steamer BAYGEORGE

OWNER:	Bayswater Shipping Limited
BUILT:	Caledon Shipbuilding and Engineering Company, Limited, Dundee, England - 1912
HULL NO.:	226
O. A. DIMENSIONS:	343'8" x 42'6" x 25'6"
FORMER DATA:	Launched as the tanker IOCOMA. Renamed IMPERIAL WHITBY in 1947. Converted to a self-unloader and deepened 7' at St. Lawrence Dry Docks Limited, Montreal, Quebec and renamed GEORGE S. CLEET in 1951. Lengthened 86'6" at Kingston Shipyards, Kingston, Ontario in 1965.

Following the demise of this company in 1968, this ship was sold for scrap. It is shown here outbound at the Eastern Gap of Toronto, Ontario harbour on August 15, 1962.

The prefix of this ship name is in reference to the owning company and all vessels in the fleet had the same name beginning. The suffix, therefore, of each name is the specific namesake. This vessel was the largest to be operated in this fleet and was the flagship. Aptly, it was named for Mr. George McKinnon Davidson, president of the company.

He was born at Ottawa, Ontario on February 23, 1905 and began sailing on the oceans in 1921. In the early 1930's he returned to Canada to sail the Great Lakes and was a mate in the Canada Steamship Lines fleet in 1937-1938. He then took the position of office manager for Coal Carriers Limited at Brockville, Ontario, serving until 1946 when he founded and became president of Bayswater Shipping Limited. He headed the firm at the time of his death on March 19, 1964. Mr. Davidson was well-liked and respected in the marine fraternity.

Steamer BAYQUINTE

OWNER: Bayswater Shipping Limited
BUILT: American Ship Building Company, Cleveland Ohio—1912
HULL NO.: 456
O. A. DIMENSIONS: 208' × 37' × 16'
FORMER DATA: Launched as the sandsucker FRANK C. OSBORN. Converted to a self-unloading sandsucker at American Boiler Works, Erie, Pennsylvania in 1940. Converted to a self-unloader and lengthened 41' at Muir Brothers Dry Dock Company, Limited, Port Dalhousie, Ontario in 1942. Renamed BAYFAX in 1943. Given last name in 1956.

The namesake of this vessel is the long and irregularly shaped inlet of Lake Ontario known as the Bay of Quinte. It lies between the peninsula of Prince Edward County, Ontario and the mainland of Ontario in the area of Belleville.

The length of the bay is about fifty miles and it has a width varying from six to twelve miles. The bay and Lake Ontario are joined at the western end by the Murray Canal which cuts across an isthmus less than two miles wide. At the eastern end the bay opens out into Lake Ontario by the Long and Adolphus reaches, commonly called "The Narrows."

The Bay of Quinte has a number of smaller bays within its confines and receives water from the Trent, Moira, Salmon and Napanee Rivers. The bay name is derived from the Indian village of Kenté but the word is pronounced as though it were spelled "kwintee" in modern times. This vessel traded with great regularity into the Bay of Quinte ports. It is shown in the picture above near Deseronto, Ontario, a port on the Bay of Quinte of Lake Ontario. The date was October 24, 1956. The ship was sold for scrap in 1967.

Motor Vessel REDCLOUD

OWNER: Beaconsfield Steamships Limited
BUILT: Canadian Vickers Limited, Montreal, Quebec—1930
HULL NO.: 115
O. A. DIMENSIONS: 260' × 43'6" × 20'
FORMER DATA: Launched as a barge. Converted to a powered bulk freighter at Les Chantiers Manseau Limitee, Sorel, Quebec in 1933.

The Motor Vessel REDCLOUD was one of four sister ships to operate in this fleet until they were phased out of operation in 1962. A total of six barges were built in 1930 for what was known as the Red Barge Line, but two were disposed of and lived out their lives in other fleets.

The ships shared a common name prefix, *RED*, which was in reference to the company title. It was also germane as a fleet prefix because the ship hulls were painted red in color. The owners have stated that no specific significance is or was attached to the various suffixes in the ship names. Some parallel in meaning can be found in the four names, however, since all relate to things either above the water, such as this suffix, *CLOUD*, or names that can generally be found near the water as later suffix names will show.

The Motor Vessel REDCLOUD is shown while light in Lock Two at Cascades, Ontario in the Soulanges Canal of the old St. Lawrence Seaway system on October 21, 1958. It had the honor of bringing the first cargo of zinc ever delivered into Cleveland, Ohio on June 14, 1940. The cargo was loaded at Quebec City, Quebec.

Motor Vessel REDFERN

OWNER: Beaconsfield Steamships Limited
BUILT: Canadian Vickers Limited, Montreal, Quebec—1930
HULL NO.: 113
O. A. DIMENSIONS: 260' × 43'6" × 20'
FORMER DATA: Launched as the barge REDSTAR. Given last name in 1930. Converted to a powered bulk freighter at Les Chantiers Manseau Limitee, Sorel, Quebec in 1934.

The common prefix in ship names applies to this vessel as explained for the previous ships and the specific namesake of this bulk carrier is the fern, a family of leafy perenial spore-bearing plants with slender horizontal, stout roots.

The fern family is very large and of widely differing habit and structure existing among over seven thousand species belonging to one hundred-seventy genera scattered all over the world. Nineteen genera with some eighty-three species are native to Canada. These plants are frequently found near the water, be it along a lake shoreline or in boggy land far from a lake or river.

The Motor Vessel REDFERN was decommissioned in 1962 and was sold for off-lakes use in 1963. It was converted to fish processing barge and saw service in Newfoundland and Labrador, as ZENAVA, until it was lost on April 28, 1971. It is shown here on July 15, 1952 in the Welland Ship Canal.

Motor Vessel REDRIVER

OWNER:	Beaconsfield Steamships Limited
BUILT:	Les Chantiers Manseau Limitee, Sorel, Quebec—1930
HULL NO.:	B-14
O. A. DIMENSIONS:	260' × 43'6" × 20'
FORMER DATA:	Launched as a barge. Converted to a powered bulk freighter at Les Chantiers Manseau Limitee, Sorel, Quebec in 1934.

The Motor Vessel REDRIVER ceased operations in 1962 as a result of competitive pressures and was subsequently sold for scrap in 1965.

This ship has the familiar name prefix and specifically honors the rivers and river systems of the world as her namesake. Since man first travelled by other than foot, rivers have been important arteries for commerce and pleasure the world over.

Rivers usually start far up in mountains or hills or may have their origin from a small spring or lake. Some rivers are very short, being only a few miles long, while others such as the Nile River travel a distance of 4,132 miles. The Nile is the longest river in the world, with the Amazon River of South America in second place with 3,900 miles. The longest river in North America is the Mackenzie of Canada which is 2,635 miles in length.

The Motor Vessel REDRIVER is seen here approaching the tie-up wall below Lock One of the Welland Ship Canal at Port Weller, Ontario on November 5, 1955.

Motor Vessel REDWOOD

OWNER: Beaconsfield Steamships Limited
BUILT: Canadian Vickers Limited, Montreal, Quebec—1930
HULL NO.: 114
O. A. DIMENSIONS: 260' × 43'6" × 20'
FORMER DATA: Launched as the barge REDWING (1). Given last name in 1930. Converted to a powered bulk freighter at Les Chantiers Manseau Limitee, Sorel, Quebec in 1934.

Like her sisterships, the Motor Vessel REDWOOD was a familiar sight on the St. Lawrence River. All carried iron ore inbound once the Iron Ore Company of Canada loading facility was opened in 1954 and this vessel had the distinction of bringing the first Labrador iron ore into the port of Erie, Pennsylvania. That event occurred on July 5, 1955.

Also like her sisterships, this carrier was laid-up following the 1962 season and was sold for scrap in 1965. The specific namesake of this carrier is the woodland that surrounds much of the Great Lakes country. The woods are beautiful to behold and serve useful purposes as protection from winds and adverse weather conditions as well as campsites, logging operations sources and untold other uses.

The wood of trees is generally classed as either soft wood, like that of pine, fir, and other coniferous trees, or hard wood such as oak, elm, birch or that of other angiospermous trees.

The Motor Vessel REDWOOD is seen in this picture being lowered in Lock Four of the Welland Ship Canal on July 15, 1952.

Motor Vessel SANDLAND

OWNER: Beaconsfield Steamships Limited
BUILT: Swan, Hunter & Wigham Richardson Limited
Wallsend-on-Tyne, England - 1925
HULL NO.: 1273
O. A. DIMENSIONS: 259' x 42'9" x 18'6"
FORMER DATA: Launched as a self-unloading sandsucker. Convented to a bulk freighter and lengthened 45'9" at Muir Brothers Dry Dock Company, Limited, Port Dalhousie, Ontario in 1943.

The Motor Vessel SANDLAND had no specific namesake aside from the sand beds over which she worked from the beginning of her career in 1925 when she performed work for the Harbour Brick Company of Toronto, Ontario, digging water-washed sand for the manufacture of bricks.

During the late 1920's and through the 1930's, sandsucking bulk carriers flourished on the Great Lakes. Many landfill projects were authorized and these vessels provided the cheapest means of accomplishing the tasks at hand. This business is significant even today, but the number of vessels has diminished and their size and carrying capacity has increased.

The quality of sand taken from lake and river bottoms is so high that it is very much in demand. It is nearly pure in the state in which it is pumped aboard the vessels and little refining is required before its end use. The Motor Vessel SANDLAND honored all such operations and succeeded in that effort its' earlier sister ship in the fleet of the original owners, OVERLAND.

The Motor Vessel SANDLAND is shown in this photograph in the Welland Ship Canal on October 31, 1953 at Port Weller, Ontario. It was active on the Great Lakes until being sold for off-lakes use in 1961.

Steamer WILLIAM C. WARREN

OWNER:	Beaconsfield Steamships Limited
BUILT:	Napier & Miller Limited, Glasgow, Scotland—1925
HULL NO.:	249
O. A. DIMENSIONS:	263' × 43'3" × 20'

Namesake of this canal-sized bulk freighter was Mr. William Candee Warren who was born on August 4, 1859 in Buffalo, New York. He received a Ph.B. degree from the Sheffield Scientific School, Yale University in 1880 and was a descendent of Mr. Richard Warren, one of the passengers on the "Mayflower."

He and his half-brother formed a partnership known as James D. Warren's Sons to manage what became the Buffalo newspaper "Commercial" in 1886. From 1892 to 1907 Mr. Warren was sole managing editor. When the partnership was dissolved in 1907, and a corporation formed, he became president and held that post until the company was sold in 1918 at which time he retired from the newspaper business.

Mr. Warren did not retreat from business life, however, and was a director of the Eastern Steamship Company which built this vessel. He was also a director of the Eastern Grain Corporation which firm was an affiliate of the vessel line. In addition, he was a director of Buffalo financial institutions.

The unusual photograph of his namesake shown here was taken on November 17, 1956 from the lock wall above Lock Seven, but looking north to below Lock Seven of the Welland Ship Canal. This vessel outlived its namesake, who died at Buffalo, New York on November 27, 1935. It was sold for scrap in 1965.

Steamer WILLIAMSPORT

OWNER:	Bethlehem Steel Corporation
BUILT:	American Ship Building Company, Lorain, Ohio—1908
HULL NO.:	362
O. A. DIMENSIONS:	400' × 50' × 28'
FORMER DATA:	Launched as JOHN A. DONALDSON. Renamed J. H. MACOUBREY in 1933. Given last name in 1951.

The small bulk freight Steamer WILLIAMSPORT was sold for scrap in 1955 and met that fate at Buffalo, New York in 1957. It was chartered to Midland Steamship Line, Inc. in its last years of operation and is shown below in their colors while upbound in Little Rapids Cut, St. Mary's River on August 6, 1953.

Bethlehem Steel gave this ship a name in keeping with other ship names of the day in their fleet. This was for the steel manufacturing plant owned and operated by Bethlehem at Williamsport, Pennsylvania. The plant is devoted exclusively to the manufacture of wire rope, slings and strand and is the largest wire rope plant under one roof in the United States.

Williamsport was first settled in 1795 and was granted a charter as a borough in 1806. It was granted status as a city in 1866. Today, it has a population of about 43,000 persons. The city is located in north-central Pennsylvania on the west branch of the Susquehanna River.

It is the seat of Lycoming County and is about eighty-five miles north of Pittsburgh, Pennsylvania. For a time in the 1860's it was the center of the lumber industry in the United States as the huge forests of the county were harvested.

Steamer CAMBRIA (3)

OWNER:	Bethlehem Steel Corporation, Marine Division
BUILT:	Detroit Shipbuilding Company, Wyandotte, Michigan—1910
HULL NO.:	184
O. A. DIMENSIONS:	524' × 54' × 30'
FORMER DATA:	Launched as the bulk freighter E. H. UTLEY. Given last name in 1925. Converted to a crane ship at American Ship Building Company, Lorain, Ohio in 1955.

The crane-equipped Steamer CAMBRIA was active on the Great Lakes through 1970. Late that year it was sold for use as a floating scrap iron and transfer ship in Milwaukee, Wisconsin. It is shown above in the St. Mary's River. The ship had sailed on its maiden voyage June 25, 1910 with a cargo of coal from Lorain, Ohio to Milwaukee, Wisconsin.

This vessel took its name from the Cambria Iron Company which was part of the original Bethlehem Steel Corporation group. It was located as a separate entity at Johnstown, Pennsylvania but became part of Bethlehem and is now known as the Johnstown plant, formerly called the Cambria Works.

Mr. John Fritz, one of the steel industry's leading innovators and later a world famous steelmaster, came to Bethlehem, Pennsylvania from the Cambria Iron Company in 1860 to construct and operate the new plant being built in the city. The word "cambria" is Latin for Wales, England and the residents of Wales still refer to themselves by that name.

After serving at Milwaukee, Wisconsin on a "spare unit" basis, this vessel was sold in mid-1973 for off-lakes, non-transportation use at Norfolk, Virginia.

Steamer WILLIAM H. DONNER

OWNER: Bethlehem Steel Corporation, Marine Division
BUILT: Great Lakes Engineering Works, Ashtabula, Ohio—1914
HULL NO.: 134
O. A. DIMENSIONS: 524' × 54' × 30'
FORMER DATA: Launched as a bulk freighter. Converted to a crane ship at American Ship Building Company, Lorain, Ohio in 1956.

Mr. William Henry Donner was the namesake of this steamer. He was born at Columbus, Indiana on May 21, 1864 and graduated from Hanover College in 1882. Mr. Donner began is career with the Donner Milling Company of Columbus, Indiana and served as its manager from 1885 to 1894.

He became treasurer and manager of the National Tin Plate Company in 1894 and held that post until 1899. In 1894, he was a founder of Monessen, Pennsylvania and, in 1899 he helped found Donora, Pennsylvania, part of which city name honors him.

He served as president of the Union Steel Company of Donora from 1899 to 1903 and was instrumental in the development of several steel enterprises from 1903 to 1912 when he became president of the Cambria Steel Company. He served in that capacity until 1916 and from 1914 to 1916 was also chairman of the board of the Pennsylvania Steel Company. He became president of Donner Steel Company in 1916 and served until retirement in 1929.

Mr. Donner's namesake is shown outbound at Cleveland, Ohio on July 12, 1969. It was sold for use as a floating scrap iron barge and transfer ship at Milwaukee, Wisconsin in 1970. It had sailed on its maiden voyage July 8, 1914 from Toledo, Ohio with coal for Superior, Wisconsin delivery.

Steamer ELBA

OWNER:	Bethlehem Steel Corporation, Marine Division
BUILT:	American Ship Building Company, Cleveland, Ohio—1907
HULL NO.:	440
O. A. DIMENSIONS:	440' × 52' × 28'6"
FORMER DATA:	Launched as a bulk freighter. Converted to a crane ship at American Ship Building Company, Buffalo, New York in 1950.

The crane vessel Steamer ELBA was originally built and operated by Pickands, Mather & Company of which Mr. Jay C. Morse was a partner. He was a classical-minded man who had ardently toured the Mediterranean area of the world. Many of the line's vessels were given names that reflected his deep attachment to this area.

The specific namesake of this ship was the island of Elba. It is the largest island of Tuscan Archipelago in the Tyrrhenian Sea of Italy. Elba is only eighteen miles long and twelve miles wide, but the area in which it is located is industrially important in that it produces ninety percent of Italy's iron ore.

A secondary namesake of this ship was the Elba Mine located at Gilbert, Minnesota on the Mesabi Range. This mine also took its name from the island of Elba. Pickands, Mather & Company was agent for this mine. The mine was opened in 1898 and shipped iron ore through 1926, forwarding a total of 3,481,872 gross tons during the period. Minnesota Iron Company operated the Elba Mine, shipping Bessemer ore during its years of production.

The steamer ELBA was active on the Great Lakes until being sold for trade-in and later use as a floating warehouse in 1968. It is shown above in Mud Lake, St. Mary's River on June 20, 1956.

Steamer BETHLEHEM (2)

OWNER: Bethlehem Steel Corporation, Great Lakes Steamship Division
BUILT: Great Lakes Engineering Works,
Ashtabula, Ohio – 1917
HULL NO.: 167
O.A. DIMENSIONS: 600' x 60' x 32'
FORMER DATA: Launched as MIDVALE. Given last name in 1925.

The bulk freight Steamer BETHLEHEM was named in honor of the Bethlehem Works plant of this owner located in Bethlehem, Pennsylvania. It has an ingot production capacity of 5,000,000 tons annually and is one of the largest single plants in the country. It was the steel firm's first plant on formation in 1905.

The city of Bethlehem, Pennsylvania has a population of 77,000 and many of these are directly or indirectly affiliated with the plant and its related functions or with the company headquarters also located there. The city is in both Northampton and Lehigh counties and is the industrial center of the Lehigh Valley. On completion of the Lehigh Canal in 1829, traffic in coal began in the area and, in 1855, the Lehigh Valley Rail Road began operations in the area. The community formed its present boundaries in 1917.

This vessel commenced its maiden trip July 3, 1917 when it departed Ashtabula, Ohio light for Duluth, Minnesota to load iron ore. It remained active until delivering itself to overseas buyers for scrap late in the fall of 1973 at Montreal, Quebec. It is shown below while upbound, light abreast Port Huron, Michigan on October 6, 1973.

Steamer LEBANON

OWNER:	Bethlehem Steel Corporation, Great Lakes Steamship Division
BUILT:	Great Lakes Engineering Works, Ecorse, Michigan—1907
HULL NO.:	33
O. A. DIMENSIONS:	552' × 56' × 31'
FORMER DATA:	Launched as JOSIAH G. MUNRO. Renamed EFFINGHAM B. MORRIS in 1916. Given last name in 1925.

The Bethlehem Steel Corporation plant at Lebanon, Pennsylvania is the namesake of this former bulk freighter. The plant specializes in the production of industrial fasteners such as bolts, nuts, spikes, tie-rods, high-strength structural bolts, rivets, studs and other fasteners for high-temperature, high-pressure service and special fasteners of all kinds, including mineroof bolts, galvanized pole-line accessories, aluminum-coated products, and sucker rods for oil-field pumping operations.

Lebanon is the county seat of Lebanon County and is 86 miles northwest of Philadelphia, Pennsylvania. It is known for its manufacture of boilers, shoes, clothes, lime, chemicals and pharmaceuticals as well as for iron and steel. The area was first settled by Germans in the 1720's, but it was not until 1750 that the town was laid out. It was incorporated as a borough in 1821 and as a city in 1868. Today's population of Lebanon is about 32,000. It is served by the Reading Railroad and is in the heart of the fertile Lebanon Valley.

The Steamer LEBANON was active on the Great Lakes until it was sold for scrap in 1967. It is shown in the photograph below while upbound, light for cargo, at Port Huron, Michigan on April 24, 1966.

Steamer LEONARD C. HANNA

> OWNER: Bethlehem Steel Corporation, Great Lakes Steamship Division
> BUILT: American Ship Building Company, Cleveland, Ohio—1905
> HULL NO.: 425
> O. A. DIMENSIONS: 524' × 54' × 30'

This vessel was sold for trade-in and scrapping in 1965 and had been in lay-up status for several years prior to that at Erie, Pennsylvania.

Namesake of this ship was Mr. Leonard Colton Hanna who was born on November 30, 1850 at New Lisbon, Ohio. He attended the public schools and Holbrook Military School, graduating in June, 1867.

His first important business experience was in the oil industry associated with Hanna, Doherty & Company. He sailed on the Steamer NORTHERN LIGHT in 1871 and in January, 1872 went to St. Paul, Minnesota, residing there until November, 1874 when he returned to Cleveland, Ohio to take an active interest in the business affairs, with his brother, in the management of the M. A. Hanna Company. He took upon himself a large amount of the detailed management of the company. He retired on December 31, 1904.

He was a director of Hanna, Great Lakes Towing Company, Republic Iron & Steel Company, Kelley Island Lime & Transport Company, Cleveland Railway Company and other firms. Mr. Hanna died at Cleveland, Ohio on March 22, 1919.

The bulk freight Steamer LEONARD C. HANNA is shown below in the St. Clair River on June 10, 1956.

Steamer POWELL STACKHOUSE

>   OWNER: Bethlehem Steel Corporation, Great Lakes
>   Steamship Division
>   BUILT: Detroit Shipbuilding Company,
>   Wyandotte, Michigan—1905
>   HULL NO.:   160
> O. A. DIMENSIONS: 524' × 54' × 30'

This vessel was sold for trade-in in 1965 and was scrapped the following year. Its namesake is Mr. Powell Stackhouse who was born at Philadelphia, Pennsylvania on July 16, 1840. He attended school until 1855 and that year joined the Cambria Iron Company at Johnstown, Pennsylvania.

Mr. Stackhouse's career was interrupted by several periods of military service in the Civil War. After the war he returned to Cambria Iron and, in 1866, was made superintendent of the subsidiary Johnstown Manufacturing Company. In 1868 he became assistant superintendent of Cambria Iron Company and was general agent of the Republic Iron Company at Marquette, Michigan in 1874-76.

He was named acting general manager of Cambria Iron in 1878, comptroller in 1880, vice president in 1884 and became president of the firm in 1892. In 1898 he became president of Cambria Steel Company which took over the former firm and was one of the foremost independent steel manufacturers in the United States. He resigned this post in 1910 and died at St. Petersburg, Florida on February 4, 1927. He had been identified with Cambria Iron interests for 71 years and had been married four times.

This ship loaded the initial cargo of iron ore pellets at the Picton, Ontario facility of Marmoraton Mining Company on May 10, 1955 destined for Lackawanna, New York delivery. It is shown below in the process of taking on an iron ore cargo at Allouez, Wisconsin on August 11, 1940.

Barge ALFRED CYTACKI

OWNER: The Big "D" Lines, Limited
BUILT: Swan, Hunter & Wigham Richardson, Limited, Newcastle-on-Tyne, England — 1932
HULL NO.: 1426
O. A. DIMENSIONS: 260' x 43'6" x 17'6"
FORMER DATA: Launched as the powered tanker LAKESHELL (1). Renamed JOHN A. McDOUGALD in 1933. Renamed EASTERN SHELL (1) in 1950. Renamed FUEL MARKETER (1) in 1969. Renamed WESTERN SHELL in 1970. Converted to a barge at Herb Fraser & Associates, Port Colborne, Ontario and given last name in 1971.

The Barge ALFRED CYTACKI is shown above at Port Colborne, Ontario November 7, 1971. It went to the Sarnia, Ontario area for use as a barge, but was found to be unsuited in its proposed trade. After months of idleness at Erieau, Ontario, the vessel was sold for scrap late in 1973.

Namesake of this vessel was Mr. Alfred Walter Cytacki, president of the Enterprise Oil and Gas Company of Detroit, Michigan, which firm had put together the concept of use for this hull. Mr. Cytacki was born in Detroit on December 24, 1918 and attended Wayne State University before joining his father's firm, the Enterprise Heat & Power Company. He rose to become vice president in 1946 and president in 1948. The firm has grown to become one of the few large independent oil marketers in the state of Michigan.

Motor Vessel S. M. DOUGLAS

OWNER:	Blue Heron Marine Limited
BUILT:	W. C. White, Montreal, Quebec – 1897
HULL NO.:	None assigned.
O. A. DIMENSIONS:	160' 6" x 25' 6" x 10'
FORMER DATA:	Launched as the passenger vessel WHITE STAR (2). Shortened 9' 1" at Oliver Gillespie Company, Cornwall, Ontario in 1905. Converted to a bulk freighter at James Sowards Company, Kingston, Ontario in 1927. Given last name in 1949. Converted to a self-unloading sandsucker at Simpson Sand Company, Limited, Brockville, Ontario and lengthened 2' 5" in 1950.

Mr. Stuart Meighen Douglas was this vessel's namesake. He was born in Smith's Falls, Ontario on August 16, 1916 and graduated from the local schools. He began his career as a draftsman in 1924, working in the logging industry until 1929. At this time he went into the construction industry and worked at successively important jobs until 1944 when he opened his own manufacturing business in Smith's Falls in the field of tools and dies.

In 1948, he and Messrs. Wells Simpson and D. E. Beggs joined together to form the Simpson Sand Company to produce and sell concrete sand from a pit on Grenadier Island, Lake Ontario, between Gananoque and Kingston, Ontario. This vessel was an integral part of the operation, but laid inactive from 1970 until it was sold for partial demolition and sinking as a breakwall in 1973 at Larue Mills Cove, Ontario. It is shown above in the finer days of operation.

Motor Vessel BLUE LAKER

OWNER: Blue Peter Steamships Limited
BUILT: Higgins Industries, Inc.,
New Orleans, Louisiana – 1945
HULL NO.: 97
O. A. DIMENSIONS: 179'9" x 32'6" x 14'3"
FORMER DATA: Launched as FS-231. Renamed ZEBRULA in 1948. Given last name in 1960.

The package freight Motor Vessel BLUE LAKER began its career as a unit of the United States Government, operated by the U. S. Army Corps of Engineers. As World War II hostilities faded, it became excess capacity and was sold to Canadian owners. Operated into the Great Lakes largely with frozen fish through most of the life under its second name, the vessel was sold to these Newfoundland owners in 1960. They operated the ship on the Great Lakes for 1½ seasons and withdrew her in 1961 for off-lakes use.

The Motor Vessel BLUE LAKER took its name from the first word of these owner's corporate name, BLUE, and the fact that they intended it for use on the Great Lakes as opposed to several other ships which they owned which traded strictly coastwise. When purchased, these owners also inherited a fish delivery contract which provided the ship must service its former regular Great Lakes trade through 1960. The Newfoundland-based concern decided on this name as a result. When the contract expired they tried a new concept for future delivery of fish, but it did not prove successful, causing the withdrawal of this unit from Great Lakes service.

The vessel is shown above in the Welland Ship Canal on July 10, 1960.

Barge APPLEBRANCH

OWNER:	Branch Lines Limited
BUILT:	Marine Industries Limited, Sorel, Quebec – 1945
HULL NO.:	146
O. A. DIMENSIONS:	341' x 54' x 27'
FORMER DATA:	Launched as an uncompleted Landing Ship, Tank hull with no name. Converted to a bulk freight barge at Marine Industries Limited, Sorel, Quebec and named M.I.L. 461 in 1949. Given last name in 1956.

The bulk freight Barge APPLEBRANCH was utilized in the pulpwood trade of the lower St. Lawrence River until the early 1960's. It was then laid-up and was sold for scrap in 1966.

Namesake of this barge is the apple, a fruit dating back to antiquity. It is grown nearly throughout the temperate zones of the earth and has been multiplied in varieties by grafting to other living trees and cross-breeding into a thousand or more varieties.

The apple was introduced into the American Colonies in Massachusetts in 1630. Its cultivation has spread from the East Coast to the Pacific and south to Virginia. Canada produces many varieties from Nova Scotia through Ontario and also in British Columbia. Fine orchards of apples can be found in the area of Quebec along the south shore of the St. Lawrence River nearby the headquarters of this owning vessel firm. The second part of the ship name honored the owners themselves as is still typical in the fleet for the older ships.

Barge BAYBRANCH

OWNER: Branch Lines Limited
BUILT: Marine Industries Limited, Sorel, Quebec – 1945
HULL NO.: 974
O. A. DIMENSIONS: 341' x 54' x 27'
FORMER DATA: Launched as an unnamed Landing Ship, Tank Vessel. Converted to a bulk freight barge at Marine Industries Limited, Sorel, Quebec and named M. I. L. 462 in 1949. Given last name in 1956.

The Barge BAYBRANCH has a hull number out of sequence for this yard because it was, in fact, begun as a hull at Canadian Vickers' yard in Montreal, Quebec. When World War II ended, the partially-finished hull was purchased by Marine Industries who completed the hull work and left it idle until the conversion noted above. The vessel served in the pulpwood trade until being sold for scrap in 1966.

With the second part of this ship name in reference to the corporate wording of the owner's title, this barge specifically honored the group of trees and shrubs which more or less resemble the laurel or Victor's laurel. This group of laurels is also known as sweet bay. The name bay once applied exclusively to the fruit of the trees and shrubs but is now more casually used in a broader meaning.

Housewives usually are familiar with bay leaves which are very aromatic leaves used to flavor various cooked dishes. In earlier times, garlands or crowns were made of bay or laurel leaves and were given as a prize for excellence.

Motor Vessel ELMBRANCH

OWNER:	Branch Lines Limited
BUILT:	Collingwood Shipyards, Collingwood, Ontario—1944
HULL NO.:	124
O. A. DIMENSIONS:	329' × 43'9" × 22'6"
FORMER DATA:	Launched as NORWOOD PARK. Given last name in 1945. Lengthened 70' and deepened 2'6" at Marine Industries, Limited, Sorel, Quebec in 1960.

The Motor Vessel ELMBRANCH takes its name from the family of large graceful deciduous trees or shrubs which are found in widely dispersed regions of the northern hemisphere. Elms have small flowers and unequal-sided leaves. Thirteen genera and about one hundred-fifty species are known.

The elm is a hardwood tree which is useful in certain kinds of crafts. The white elm is the most common and the most useful. It grows to approximately one hundred-twenty five feet in height and seven feet in diameter and is prominent along the entire Great Lakes area.

Slippery elm is the smallest of the group and is found from Quebec to Lake Superior. The rock elm is found along the southern part of the Great Lakes region and grows to a height of about seventy feet. Having served its usefulness on the Lakes, this ship was sold for off-Lakes use in 1977.

Motor Vessel FIRBRANCH

OWNER: Branch Lines Limited
BUILT: Marine Industries, Limited, Sorel, Quebec—1944
HULL NO.: 143
O. A. DIMENSIONS: 259' × 43'9" × 20'3"
FORMER DATA: Launched as MILLICAN PARK. Given last name in 1945.

The tank Motor Vessel FIRBRANCH served the last four years of its existance in semi-retirement as a floating storage hull and was finally scrapped in 1970. Like its sister ships in this fleet, it bore the familiar fleet suffix BRANCH in reference to the first word of the owning company's corporate title.

The specific namesake of this tanker was the fir tree. Actually, this name is applied to many coniferous trees of the genus Abies. The name fir has often been used to embrace all the evergreen coniferous trees that have short, rigid leaves, occuring singly and scattered over the stems as distinguished from the pines whose leaves are long and usually occur in bundles of two to five or more.

There are about 25 species of fir found throughout the cooler regions of the north temperate zone. Often these are in extensive tracts to the almost entire exclusion of other species. Some of these fir, such as the Douglas and Oregon fir, grow to 300 feet in height and as much as ten feet in diameter.

This vessel is shown above at Toronto, Ontario's Eastern Gap harbor entrance in July, 1952.

Steamer OLIVEBRANCH

OWNER: Branch Lines Limited
BUILT: S. O. S. Welding Corporation, Brooklyn, New York- 1928
HULL NO.: 1
O. A. DIMENSIONS: 120' x 20'1" x 7'7"
FORMER DATA: Launched as PIONEER (3). Renamed SUPERTEST in 1928. Given last name in 1957.

The tank Steamer OLIVEBRANCH was sold for off-lakes use in 1969 after some time in lay-up status with this owning company. It had, prior to its lay-up, been used in the Ottawa River trade and in servicing smaller St. Lawrence River and Maritime ports with only shallow draft capability.

The namesake of this tanker was the olive tree. The more encompassing definition refers not only to the tree, but to olive shrubs and woody climbers with opposite or very rarely alternate pinnate or simple leaves lacking stipules. The fruit of all of these is a drupe, berry, capsule or samara. The family of twenty genera and about four hundred species is widely distributed, however concentration is mostly in Asia.

Olive oil, by far the most important of all food oils, is obtained from the fruits of "Olea europaea," a small tree native to the Mediterranean region where it has been cultivated for more than 3,000 years. Perfume oil is extracted from the flowers of "Jasminum officinale." These flowers are perfect or rarely unisexual, regular and mostly four-merous, in axillary or terminal panicles or cymes.

The Steamer OLIVEBRANCH is shown above in one of the rarest photographs in this book while outbound from Sorel, Quebec just after having been renamed in 1957.

Barge PALMBRANCH

OWNER: Branch Lines Limited
BUILT: Marine Industries Limited, Sorel, Quebec – 1945
HULL NO.: 976
O. A. DIMENSIONS: 341' x 54' x 27'
FORMER DATA: Launched as an unnamed Landing Ship, Tank vessel. Converted to a bulk freight barge at Marine Industries Limited, Sorel, Quebec and named M. I. L. 464 in 1950. Given last name in 1955.

The bulk freight Barge PALMBRANCH was like the BAYBRANCH in that it was a purchased hull from Canadian Vickers Limited after World War II and was completed by the Sorel yard. They left it idle, however, until conversion to a pulpwood barge in 1950. Usefulness ended in the 1960's and the barge was sold for scrap in 1966.

With the second part of the ship name honoring the owners' name, the specific namesake of this barge was the palm tree fruit commonly known as the coconut. The owners felt, however, that "coconutbranch" was too cumbersome a name and, instead, settled for the tree name.

The palm tree group has about fifteen genera and these are found almost exclusively in the tropical regions of the world. They form a striking part of the vegetation wherever they are found, with lofty clusters of wide branches and the coconut fruit in evidence in season. The coconut palm grows in almost any kind of soil ranging from dry and sandy to wet and swampy and is often found in dense forests. They may grow singly in otherwise barren soil or may be found in groups covering huge areas.

Barge PEACHBRANCH

OWNER: Branch Lines Limited
BUILT: Marine Industries Limited, Sorel, Quebec — 1945
HULL NO.: 147
O. A. DIMENSIONS: 341' x 54' x 27'
FORMER DATA: Launched as an uncompleted Landing Ship, Tank hull with no name. Converted to a bulk freight barge at Marine Industries Limited, Sorel, Quebec and named M. I. L. 465 in 1955. Renamed PEACHBRANCH in 1956.

The bulk freight pulpwood-carrying Barge PEACHBRANCH was the last of the "LST quartet" to be converted. It was also the only one to survive the scrap torch in the 1960's. When its sisters were sold for scrap in 1966, the Barge PEACHBRANCH was not. Instead, it was sold for off-lakes use in 1967.

The namesake of this barge was the desiduous orchard fruit tree believed to have come to North America from Chinese origin. The peach tree is of moderate stature, tends to spread its branches and is deep-rooted. There are nearly 300 varieties of peaches in North America and these have been classified into five races, each with its own characteristics, ripening season and uses.

Principal peach growing states are Georgia, Delaware, Maryland, Virginia, Pennsylvania and New Jersey. The states of Florida and Texas also produce peaches, but mostly to fill the winter needs when the more northern states' production is dormant. In the west, California, Oregon, Washington and Colorado are the producing regions. Totally, about fifty million bushels are harvested in the United States annually.

Steamer PINEBRANCH

OWNER: Branch Lines Limited
BUILT: Chicago Shipbuilding Company, Chicago, Illinois—1895
HULL NO.: 13
O. A. DIMENSIONS: 259' x 40' x 25'
FORMER DATA: Launched as the barge MALTA. Renamed THUNDER BAY (1) in 1912. Cut in two at Collingwood Shipbuilding Company, Collingwood, Ontario in 1918. Re-assembled at Canadian Vickers Limited, Montreal, Quebec in 1918. Cut in two, shortened 54' and converted to powered bulk freighter at Davie Shipbuilding and Repairing Company, Limited, Lauzon, Quebec in 1921. Renamed PINEBRANCH in 1937. Converted to a tanker at Marine Industries, Limited, Sorel, Quebec in 1940. Renamed EMPIRE STICKLEBACK in 1941. Given last name, for the second time, in 1946.

The tank Steamer PINEBRANCH was owned by this company until it was sold for sinking as a breakwater in 1960. The ship bore the usual ship name suffix, "BRANCH," of the fleet and took the pine tree as its specific namesake.

The pine tree is beautiful in appearance and fragrant in scent. Anyone who has experienced a visit to a forest knows the unique way in which the pine tree rustles in the wind, like the sound of an onrushing train. Some kinds of pine are: Norway pine, Jack pine, White pine, Red pine and Ponderosa pine.

This vessel is shown entering Toronto, Ontario harbor in July, 1951.

Motor Vessel SPRUCEBRANCH

OWNER:	Branch Lines Limited
BUILT:	Marine Industries, Limited, Sorel, Quebec - 1944
HULL NO.:	141
O. A. DIMENSIONS:	329' x 43'9" x 22'6"
FORMER DATA:	Launched as OTTERBURN PARK. Given last name in 1946. Lengthened 70' and deepened 2'6" at Marine Industries, Limited, Sorel, Quebec in 1960.

The Motor Vessel SPRUCEBRANCH was named for the spruce tree which is an evergreen of the pine family found across Canada and in the United States. This coniferous tree has cone-shaped crowns and sharp needles on its branches. The cones drop off when they are mature.

Spruce wood is light and soft and is excellent for pulpwood and for woodworking of finished products. Of course, many families around the world are familiar with the spruce as making a lovely Christmas tree in the home.

The red spruce is the most common along the St. Lawrence and Ottawa River Valleys. Other types of spruce found in Canada include white spruce, black spruce, Englemann spruce, western white spruce and the Sitka spruce. Of these, the Sitka spruce is the largest, growing to about two hundred-twenty feet in height and having a diameter of twelve feet. This vessel was sold for off-Lakes use in August, 1974. It is shown above in the Welland Ship Canal.

Motor Vessel WILLOWBRANCH (2)

OWNER:	Branch Lines Limited
BUILT:	Marine Industries, Limited, Sorel, Quebec—1950
HULL NO.:	185
O. A. DIMENSIONS:	291' × 43'6" × 20'
FORMER DATA:	Lengthened 30' at Marine Industries, Limited, Sorel, Quebec in 1966.

With the fleet name for the suffix of this ship name, the Motor Vessel WILLOWBRANCH takes its name from the willow tree which is a member of the family of dioecious trees or shrubs with deciduous leaves.

Three genera and over three hundred species of willow are found in the temperate and arctic-alpine parts of the northern hemisphere. They grow well even when under water for extended periods and are very useful for flood control and erosion control.

Of the twenty species existing in Canada, the following are treelike: black willow, peachleaf willow, pacific willow and arctic willow. Some trees grow to one hundred feet in height. Willows are valued for their wood, osiers and tanbark. Cricket bats are also frequently made from their stock.

The Motor Vessel WILLOWBRANCH is seen in this photograph at Toronto, Ontario in 1972. The ship was sold and cut down to a barge for off-Lakes use in 1978.

Steamer MEXOIL (2)

OWNER:	British-American Oil Company
BUILT:	Alabama & New Orleans Transportation Company, Violet, Louisiana—1918
HULL NO.:	23
O. A. DIMENSIONS:	258'7" × 37'9" × 19'

Though this vessel was not specifically built for the Pure Oil Company, it became part of that firm's subsidiary fleet and operated on the Great Lakes for a large part of its life. It was sold for off-lakes use in 1948, later returned to partial use on the Great Lakes from the Atlantic Coast, and finally disappeared from the Great Lakes scene in 1957 when it was scrapped as a member of this fleet.

Like its sister ship, the Steamer PANOIL, this vessel took a country south of the United States border as its namesake. Mexico was this vessel's specific namesake, with the suffix in the ship name in reference to the second word of the owner's corporate title.

Mexico is a Latin-American republic whose capital and largest city is Mexico City, with a current population of about 3,400,000. The country occupies an area of 761,602 square miles, bounded on the west by the Pacific Ocean and on the east by the Gulf of Mexico and the Caribbean Sea. To the north is the United States and to the south is Central America.

This was the first steel vessel built south of Newport News, Virginia and was built on the Isherwood design. It is shown above in the Welland Ship Canal at Thorold, Ontario on November 1, 1952.

Steamer DANIEL PIERCE

OWNER:	Brooks Liquid Transport, Incorporated
BUILT:	Bethlehem Shipbuilding Corporation Limited, Wilmington, Delaware—1921
HULL NO.:	3476
O. A. DIMENSIONS:	391'6" × 53' × 28'
FORMER DATA:	Launched as E. W. SINCLAIR. Renamed DANIEL PIERCE in 1941. Renamed SHIKELLAMY in 1943. Given last name, for the second time, in 1946.

The tank Steamer DANIEL PIERCE was sold in 1963 for off-lakes use after having been sold by Sinclair Refining Company to the above owners who never operated her on the lakes.

Mr. Daniel Thompson Pierce was born at Washington, D.C. on March 22, 1875 and graduated from the George Washington University law school. He was admitted to the Bar of the District of Columbia and became editor of the magazine "Public Opinion" in 1895. He continued in this activity until 1905 and then was a private advisor on public relations in Washington, D.C. Among his clients were the Pennsylvania Railroad and Bethlehem Steel Corporation.

He became associated with the oil industry and joined Continental Oil Company in 1930 as assistant to the chairman of the board. By 1947 he had taken a similar post with Sinclair Refining Company and held that position when he died on February 16, 1952. He was also a director of both of the above oil companies and had acquired a reputation of knowing his way around Washington. He had many influential friends and associates both in and out of government.

The Steamer DANIEL PIERCE is shown above outbound, light in the Toronto Ship Channel at Toronto, Ontario on August 24, 1956.

Steamer J. J. H. BROWN

OWNER: Brown Steamship Company
BUILT: American Ship Building Company, Lorain, Ohio - 1908
HULL NO.: 358
O. A. DIMENSIONS: 452' x 52' x 28'3"

Mr. James Jeremiah Hezekiah Brown was this bulk freighter's namesake. He was born at Cleveland, Ohio on February 9, 1838. At the age of twelve he left the city with his father and sailed around the world on merchant vessels and had experience on whalers by the time he was twenty.

From 1858 he sailed on the Great Lakes rising to the position of master of the Schooner SCOTIA in 1873. In 1878 he entered partnership with Captain Daniel Rodgers in the vessel agency business at Buffalo, New York. In 1885 when Capt. Rodgers died, he associated with Mr. Edward Smith under the firm name Brown & Company. He headed that firm until his death at Buffalo, New York on June 10, 1912.

Captain Brown was an active man and engaged in every movement for the betterment of the port of Buffalo. He was also president of Lake Carriers' Association in 1896-97 and a director of that organization upon his death. His namesake was sold for scrap in 1965 after a useful life in the grain and bulk trades of the Great Lakes.

This ship made its maiden voyage on May 14, 1908 when it left Buffalo, New York with a cargo of coal for Duluth, Minnesota. It is shown below in the St. Clair River on August 26, 1961.

Steamer JAMES E. McALPINE

OWNER:	Brown Steamship Company
BUILT:	American Ship Building Company, Lorain, Ohio—1908
HULL NO.:	361
O. A. DIMENSIONS:	452′ × 52′ × 28′3″
FORMER DATA:	Launched as WILLIAM H. TRUESDALE. Given last name in 1934.

Mr. James Ernest McAlpine was the namesake of this bulk freighter. He was born at Buffalo, New York on January 23, 1878 and was a graduate of the Bryant & Stratton Business College. In 1896 he began work for the vessel agency firm of Brown & Rodgers as an office boy at Buffalo, New York.

He was admitted to partnership in the firm in 1912 and through faithful service in the accounting and traffic departments, rose to become president of the firm in 1930 on the death of Mr. Joseph B. Rodgers. Mr. McAlpine was also president of the Shasta Steamship Company and a vice president of the Grain Handling Company, Incorporated, both of Buffalo, New York.

Mr. McAlpine retained the presidency of Brown Steamship Company and the aforementioned firms at the time of his death at Buffalo on March 26, 1946. His namesake was sold for scrap in 1965.

The bulk freight Steamer JAMES E. McALPINE is shown below at the Frontier Elevator of General Mills, Incorporated at Buffalo, New York in 1952. It had arrived the day before with a full cargo of wheat from Duluth, Minnesota. This ship was a regular caller at this grain facility during its latter days on the Great Lakes.

Steamer L. D. BROWNING

OWNER:	T. H. Browning Steamship Company
BUILT:	Globe Iron Works, Cleveland, Ohio—1896
HULL NO.:	64
O. A. DIMENSIONS:	432' × 48' × 28'
FORMER DATA:	Launched as the bulk freighter CORALIA. Converted to an automobile carrier at Great Lakes Engineering Works, River Rouge, Michigan in 1927. Converted to a combination automobile carrier and bulk freighter at Great Lakes Engineering Works, River Rouge, Michigan in 1941. Re-converted to a bulk freighter at G. A. Henrickson Company, Cleveland, Ohio in 1942. Renamed TROY H. BROWNING (2) in 1949. Given last name in 1952.

The Steamer L. D. BROWNING honored Mr. Lorenzo Dowl Browning as its namesake. He was born in Knoxville, Tennessee on July 13, 1914 but moved to Detroit in 1922 and completed his education in that city.

Mr. Browning worked at various jobs during the Depression and sailed on the Great Lakes beginning in 1938. In 1942 he attained his 2nd Mate's license and went to the oceans to sail in 1943. Following World War II he returned to Detroit and became active in operations of the Nicholson-Universal Steamship Company in 1946. He served as vice president—operations of that firm and was also charter manager of this owning company when this vessel took his name. He is now active as president of the Bob-Lo Company operating two passenger ferries on the Detroit River.

His namesake is shown here in the St. Mary's River on August 27, 1953. It was the largest ship on the Great Lakes in 1896 and loaded 4,869 net tons of iron ore at Escanaba, Michigan on its first trip to establish a new Great Lakes cargo record. The ship was sold in 1955 as a storage barge and for scrap in 1962.

Steamer FRED L. HEWITT (2)

OWNER: T. H. Browning Steamship Company
BUILT: West Bay City Shipbuilding Company, West Bay City, Michigan - 1903
HULL NO.: 610
O. A. DIMENSIONS: 436' x 50'3" x 28'
FORMER DATA: Launched as the bulk freighter SONOMA. Renamed DAVID S. TROXEL in 1924. Converted to an automobile carrier at Great Lakes Engineering Works, River Rouge, Michigan and renamed SONOMA, for second time, in 1928. Re-converted to a bulk freighter at Nicholson Terminal and Dock Company, River Rouge, Michigan in 1942. Given last name in 1947.

Mr. Fred Lincoln Hewitt was born on April 14, 1880 in South Weymouth, Massachusetts and received his Ll.B degree from Boston University in 1903. He practiced corporate law during his early years and was a senior partner in the firm of B. J. Baker & Co. on February 7, 1924 when Nicholson-Universal Steamship Company was formed.

On February 19, 1927 Mr. Hewitt furthered his career in Great Lakes shipping by arranging the purchase of all of the stock in Nicholson-Universal by the Universal Carloading & Distributing Company. In April, 1932 with Mr. Hewitt as head technician, this firm formed the Overlakes Freight Corporation which became the parent company of several lake and ocean steamship and terminal operations including Nicholson-Universal Steamship Company and Newtex Steamship Company among others. Mr. Hewitt became head of these firms and chairman of the board of the Newtex organization.

He was active in business circles until his death at Stuart, Florida on January 30, 1968. His namesake was used as a storage grain barge from 1955 unitl being scrapped in 1962.

Steamer D. A. MOLONEY

OWNER:	T. H. Browning Steamship Company
BUILT:	Superior Shipbuilding Company, West Superior, Wisconsin—1902
HULL NO.:	504
O. A. DIMENSIONS:	438' × 48' × 28'
FORMER DATA:	Launched as G. J. GRAMMER. Lengthened 72' at American Ship Building Company, Cleveland, Ohio in 1905. Renamed ADAM E. CORNELIUS, JR. in 1937. Renamed TROY H. BROWNING (1) in 1942. Given last name in 1944.

The bulk freight Steamer D. A. MOLONEY was active until being sold for use as a grain storage hull at Buffalo, New York in 1955. It was subsequently sold for scrap in 1965.

This vessel's namesake was Mr. Denis Aloysius Moloney who was born at Troy, New York on September 13, 1873. He was educated in the local schools and began his career in 1894 when he joined the Pacific Mail Steamship Company as an accounting clerk. In 1918-19 when with United States Lines he was instrumental in arranging overseas travel for the Gold Star's Mothers Movement in his capacity of joint operating manager.

Mr. Moloney became associated with Mr. Fred L. Hewitt, his longtime friend, as president and part owner of Newtex Steamship Company in 1932. Mr. Moloney served for a time during World War II as assistant port director at New York City but returned to his presidency at Newtex Steamship on March 5, 1944 and served until his retirement in 1949. He died at Flushing, New York on March 21, 1957.

When this vessel took his name this ship was controlled in ownership by his friend Mr. Hewitt. The ship is shown below in the St. Mary's River on June 20, 1953.

Steamer CARL W. MEYERS

OWNER:	T. H. Browning Steamship Company
BUILT:	Chicago Shipbuilding Company, Chicago, Illinois—1897
HULL NO.:	25
O. A. DIMENSIONS:	420' × 48' × 28'
FORMER DATA:	Launched as the bulk freighter CRESCENT CITY. Converted to an automobile carrier at Great Lakes Engineering Works, River Rouge, Michigan in 1928. Re-converted to a bulk freighter at Nicholson Terminal and Dock Company, River Rouge, Michigan in 1942. Given last name in 1950.

The bulk freight Steamer CARL W. MEYERS was sold for use as a storage grain barge at Buffalo, New York in 1955 and was sold for scrap in 1959.

This carrier was last named for Mr. Carl Wilhelm Meyers who was born in Youngstown, Ohio on June 2, 1891. He was educated in the public schools and began his career as a switchboy at the Carnegie Steel Company in 1907. He held various positions in the firm until 1923 when he was named superintendent of the McDonald Mills. In 1931 he left the company to join Republic Steel Corporation as superintendent of rolling mills at Chicago, Illinois.

Mr. Meyers held posts as rolling engineer, Cleveland assistant district manager and manager of the central alloy district for Republic before leaving the firm in 1946 to become president of the Colorado Fuel and Iron Corporation. In 1952 he was elected vice chairman of the board and a director and served in this capacity until his death at North Madison, Ohio on April 10, 1960.

During this last tenure he was instrumental in arranging floating agreements between his firm and this steamship line. It was in this vein that this ship bore his name.

Steamer SPARKMAN D. FOSTER

OWNER:	Browning Lines, Incorporated
BUILT:	Great Lakes Engineering Works, Ecorse, Michigan—1905
HULL NO.:	6
O. A. DIMENSIONS:	524' × 54'3" × 30'
FORMER DATA:	Launched as the bulk freighter HOOVER & MASON. Converted to a self-unloader at American Ship Building Company, Lorain, Ohio and renamed E. M. YOUNG in 1928. Renamed COLONEL E. M. YOUNG in 1929. Re-converted to a bulk freighter at Erie Boiler Works Division, T. H. Browning Steamship Company, Ashtabula, Ohio and given last name in 1954.

The bulk freighter shown here was named in honor of Mr. Sparkman Deats Foster who was born at Fostoria, Alabama on November 19, 1897. He received an Ll.B. degree from the Detroit College of Law in 1922 and was admitted to the Michigan Bar the same year.

Mr. Foster began practice in Detroit and through the years became known as the "dean" of Great Lakes admiralty attorneys. He handled the legal affairs and was general counsel for many Great Lakes companies including Browning Lines, Incorporated, of which predecessor firm he was president in 1943, Bob-Lo Company, Erieau Shipbuilding & Drydock Company, Roen Steamship Company, McQueen Marine Limited and others. He was senior partner in the firm of Foster, Meadows & Ballard of Detroit, Michigan when he died on January 15, 1967. His namesake had been sold for scrapping in 1963.

The ship is shown in this photograph upbound at Port Huron, Michigan on July 5, 1961. The maiden voyage of this ship was light from Detroit, Michigan to Duluth, Minnesota to load iron ore on July 24, 1905.

Steamer NORMAN W. FOY

OWNER:	Browning Lines, Incorporated
BUILT:	Superior Shipbuilding Company, West Superior, Wisconsin—1907
HULL NO.:	516
O. A. DIMENSIONS:	552' × 56' × 31'
FORMER DATA:	Launched as SHELDON PARKS. Renamed EDWARD A. UHRIG in 1914. Renamed DAVID M. WEIR in 1931. Given last name in 1955.

The bulk freight Steamer NORMAN W. FOY was sold for scrap in 1964. Mr. Norman Ward Foy who was born at Baltimore, Maryland on July 25, 1895 is the namesake of this ship. He was educated in the local schools and began his career in the sales departments of the Carnegie Steel Company in 1912.

In 1917 he entered the U.S. Army and served for one year in Washington, D.C. In 1918 Mr. Foy became associated with the Philadelphia, Pennsylvania sales office of the Republic Iron and Steel Company and by 1930 had headed the sales offices of the company in several other cities. When the firm became part of Republic Steel Corporation in 1930, he was named district sales manager in Chicago, Illinois.

From 1937 to 1953, with periodic leaves for government work, he served Republic as general manager of sales. He was elected vice president—sales in 1953, a director in 1956, and continued as vice president until 1961 and a director until 1962 when he retired. He was director of several other firms and a member of the American Iron & Steel Institute. These owners honored him with this namesake because of their iron ore floating affiliation with Republic Steel Corporation.

The Steamer NORMAN W. FOY is shown below in the St. Mary's River on June 18, 1955, downbound with a cargo of iron ore.

Steamer W. WAYNE HANCOCK

OWNER:	Browning Lines, Incorporated
BUILT:	American Ship Building Company, Lorain, Ohio—1906
HULL NO.:	344
O. A. DIMENSIONS:	552' × 56' × 31'
FORMER DATA:	Launched as J. Q. RIDDLE. Renamed J. J. TURNER in 1914. Renamed GEORGE R. FINK (1) in 1931. Renamed THOMAS E. MILLSOP (1) in 1952. Given last name in 1955.

The Steamer W. WAYNE HANCOCK was sold for scrap in 1962 after having served several owners as an iron ore carrier. Mr. William Wayne Hancock is this ship's namesake. He was born near Washington, Pennsylvania on April 3, 1886 and educated at California State Teachers College, California, Pennsylvania, graduating in 1902. He also attended the University of Michigan in 1905-06.

Mr. Hancock was assistant cashier at the Bank of Donora from 1902 to 1905 and was clerk and accountant in a real estate and utility office from 1906 to 1913 when he joined Cambria Steel Company as executive assistant. He became secretary of the firm the same year, serving until 1916 when he became secretary and vice president of the Donner Steel Company. He held that post when it became part of Republic Steel Corporation in 1930 and was named assistant secretary of the enlarged firm. He rose to become vice president—finance of Republic in 1941 and was also named a director. He held these posts until retirement in 1960. Mr. Hancock was also a member of the American Iron & Steel Institute.

The bulk freight Steamer W. WAYNE HANCOCK is shown in this photograph passing through Little Rapids Cut, St. Mary's River, on June 21, 1955.

Steamer JOHN C. HAY

OWNER:	Browning Lines, Incorporated
BUILT:	Great Lakes Engineering Works, Ecorse, Michigan—1905
HULL NO.:	8
O. A. DIMENSIONS:	524' × 54' × 30'
FORMER DATA:	Launched as PETER WHITE. Given last name in 1959.

Mr. John Clement Hay was born at Detroit, Michigan on October 8, 1904 and received his education at the Acme Business College and the University of Detroit, graduating in 1924. He began working for several area banks in various minor capacities but on February 27, 1934 joined the Capital National Bank in Lansing, Michigan as commercial teller.

He progressed through the positions of collection teller, note teller, assistant cashier, assistant vice president and vice president at this bank until October, 1947 when he transferred to the Saginaw, Michigan office of Michigan National Bank as a vice president in the loan department. In 1952 he returned to the Lansing headquarters and remained there until resigning to take the position of president of the Michigan Bank on December 22, 1955. He served in this capacity until retiring on May 31, 1962.

It was in the latter connection that he came to the association of this ship's owners as friend and business associate. Mr. Hay's namesake was sold for scrap in 1961. When in the Cleveland-Cliffs fleet, it was a ship of distinctive markings in that the name was written out in longhand on the bow instead of being in the usual block letters. This vessel left Detroit, Michigan on September 25, 1905 on its maiden voyage. The upbound trip was light for Marquette, Michigan and a cargo of iron ore.

Steamer ERNEST R. JOHNSON

OWNER: Browning Lines, Incorporated
BUILT: West Bay City Shipbuilding Company, West Bay City, Michigan—1908
HULL NO.: 625
O. A. DIMENSIONS: 524' × 55' × 30'2"
FORMER DATA: Launched as ALEXIS W. THOMPSON. Renamed W. H. BECKER in 1921. Renamed EDWARD N. SAUNDERS, JR. (2) in 1933. Given last name in 1955.

The bulk freight Steamer ERNEST R. JOHNSON was sold for storage grain usage as a barge in 1959 and was later scrapped. Namesake of the ship is Mr. Ernest Raymond Johnson who was born at Chicago, Illinois on December 25, 1899. He received a B.S. degree and an M.S. degree in engineering from the University of Michigan in 1921 and 1922 respectively.

Mr. Johnson began his career as a helper in various jobs at Central Steel Company and in 1929 was named assistant chief metallurigcal engineer. He continued in this post and was appointed chief metallurgical engineer for Republic Steel Corporation's central alloy steel district in 1944. In this capacity and for a time previous, he was involved with wartime production affairs.

He was named manager of the above district in 1946 and in May, 1953 was named assistant vice president of operations for Republic Steel. In October, 1954 he was elected vice president of operations and in May, 1960 was made assistant president, a member of the board of directors and first vice president of Republic Steel. He retained these titles until retirement.

This vessel is shown here downbound in the St. Mary's River on June 17, 1956.

Steamer L. S. WESCOAT

OWNER:	Browning Lines, Incorporated
BUILT:	Chicago Shipbuilding Company, Chicago, Illinois—1898
HULL NO.:	32
O. A. DIMENSIONS:	420' × 48'3" × 28'
FORMER DATA:	Launched as the bulk freighter WILLIAM R. LINN. Converted to a tanker and given last name at Great Lakes Engineering Works, River Rouge, Michigan in 1940.

This tanker remained active on the Great Lakes until 1964 when it was sold for overseas scrapping. The large construction of pipelines for the Pure Oil Company, original owners of the vessel as a tanker, during the 1960's made the further operation of this ship on the Great Lakes unnecessary.

Namesake of this ship was Mr. Leon Stadler Wescoat who was born on January 19, 1889 at Bridgeton, New Jersey. He was a graduate of Peirce School of Business Administration in Philadelphia, Pennsylvania in 1908 and began his career with an industrial real estate firm in 1909.

Mr. Wescoat spent several years in the oil fields of Louisiana for this firm and met and became friends with a Mr. Daws who was later to head the Pure Oil Company. In 1915 he left the South and went with Fisher Body Company in Detroit, Michigan as a real estate appraiser and manager. In 1920 he joined Horn & Hardart Company in Chicago, Illinois, again in real estate, but left that firm to join Pure Oil Company as vice president and general manager in 1925. He was named vice president and secretary in 1932 and president of the firm in 1947. Mr. Wescoat continued as president until being named chairman of the executive committee in 1954. He retired in 1961. He was active in business affairs of Chicago, Illinois and also served on numerous boards of other companies.

His namesake is shown here at Sault Ste. Marie, Michigan on June 18, 1959.

Steamer SIR WILLIAM FAIRBAIRN

OWNER:	Buckeye Steamship Company
BUILT:	Detroit Shipbuilding Company, Wyandotte, Michigan—1896
HULL NO.:	124
O. A. DIMENSIONS:	436' × 45'6" × 28'

Sir William Fairbairn was born at Kelso, Roxburghshire, England on February 19, 1789 and is the namesake of this former bulk freighter.

He was afforded scant schooling and at the age of fourteen went to work on a farm his father was managing. He was apprenticed to a millwright in 1804 and in 1811 became a fully accredited millwright.

He built a nail machine and a sausage machine before going to Zurich, Switzerland in 1824 to erect two water mills. He became a member of the Institution of Civil Engineers in 1830 and began to work with iron in the construction of ships. He built ships in pieces in 1835 and in 1842 took out patent number 9409 for improvements he had made in vessels. Sir William Fairbairn also built bridges and is accredited with other mechanical and engineering breakthroughs. He died on August 18, 1874.

His namesake was sold for grain storage use in 1959 and was subsequently scrapped. The Steamer SIR WILLIAM FAIRBAIRN is shown in this photograph outbound at Duluth, Minnesota in October, 1938. The ship is heading into a real " 'Noreaster"! Even in these piers the waves are nearly washing on deck.

Steamer HARVARD

OWNER:	Buckeye Steamship Company
BUILT:	Detroit Shipbuilding Company, Wyandotte, Michigan—1900
HULL NO.:	134
O. A. DIMENSIONS:	474' × 50' × 28'6"

The bulk freight Steamer HARVARD retained its original name for its entire sixty year career on the Great Lakes. This ship was sold for scrap in 1960.

Built for Carnegie interests and merged into the United States Steel fleet in 1901, this ship was one of several known as the "college boats." These ships each honored a different prominent college or university in the United States.

The namesake of this vessel was Harvard University, the oldest institution of higher learning in the United States. It was founded as a college at Cambridge, Massachusetts in 1636 and was named in honor of Reverend John Harvard who was a Puritan. During the Colonial period the aim of Harvard was "the education of the English and Indian youth in knowledge and godliness," mainly with a view to their entering the Puritan ministry.

Since the administrations of Charles W. Eliot (1869-1909) and A. Lawrence Lowell (1909-1933) Harvard has ranked with the leading universities of the world.

This steamer is shown below at the coal loading dock in Cleveland, Ohio in the 1950's.

Steamer HARRY Wm. HOSFORD

OWNER:	Buckeye Steamship Company
BUILT:	Jenks Ship Building Company, Port Huron, Michigan—1903
HULL NO.:	26
O. A. DIMENSIONS:	530' × 50' × 28'
FORMER DATA:	Launched as F. B. SQUIRE. Lengthened 96' at Toledo Shipbuilding Company, Toledo, Ohio in 1921. Given last name in 1936.

Mr. Harry William Hosford is the namesake of this vessel. He was born on January 9, 1886 at Watertown, New York and worked on farms in the area as a young boy. At the age of twelve he became a messenger for the Western Union Company at Syracuse, New York and later the same year went to Buffalo, New York as a messenger. There he delivered a message to a Great Lakes freighter and became interested in sailing.

He sailed on the Great Lakes until 1905 at the close of navigation when he arrived in Cleveland, Ohio on December 9th. He went to work as an office boy in 1906 with C. E. Dennison & Company, real estate brokers and bond salesmen. In 1912 he left that employ to join Spitzer-Rorick & Company as a bond salesman and did such a successful job selling around the State of Ohio that he left the company in 1916 to set up business on his own.

Mr. Hosford was eminently successful in his field and became a multi-millionaire by the early 1940's. He died in Cleveland, Ohio on July 13, 1955. He had shunned the public spotlight even though many of his endeavors involved civic and patriotic acts.

This ship was sold for scrap in 1961. It is shown in this photograph at Sault Ste. Marie, Michigan on June 18, 1956.

Barge MAGNA

OWNER:	Buckeye Steamship Company
BUILT:	Chicago Shipbuilding Company, Chicago, Illinois—1896
HULL NO.:	22
O. A. DIMENSIONS:	366' × 44' × 26'

The bulk freight Barge MAGNA was originally built for the Minnesota Steamship Company, one of the major companies merged into Pittsburgh Steamship Company on its formation in 1901. Minnesota Steamship Company named its ships and barges for places and things that had some relation to mineral deposits, developments and the like. But when no place could be found that suited this criteria and that began with the letter "M" and ended in the letter "A", as did their own firm name, other more general names were picked to keep the theme alive in their ship names.

This barge took its name from Magna, Utah. This town of 6,500 population is located twelve miles southwest of Salt Lake City, Utah at an altitude of 4,278 feet. The town is the dividing line between cultured fields and structures of industry.

Prior to 1906 men lived in tents and shanties near the ore smelters of Magna. Larger concentrating plants were erected in 1906, however, and better living accommodations were made available. The first plant was the Magna Concentration Mill which treated gold, silver, lead, copper and other minerals before smelting. The huge Arthur Concentration Mill prepares iron ore for smelting.

The barge remained active until being sold for use as a breakwater in 1956. It was later raised and scrapped at Ashtabula, Ohio in 1962. The barge is shown above on June 15, 1956 in the St. Mary's River.

Barge MAIA

OWNER: Buckeye Steamship Company
BUILT: Chicago Shipbuilding Company, Chicago, Illinois—1898
HULL NO.: 33
O. A. DIMENSIONS: 390' × 48' × 26'

This vessel carried forward the theme in ship names of its original owners, the Minnesota Steamship Company. As pointed out previously in this book, these owners were inclined to christen their ships and barges with names starting with "M" and ending with "A" just as their own company name began and ended in those letters.

The namesake of this barge was the tiny village of Maia on the island of Tau, the chief island in the Manua group of islands forming Samoa East, American Samoa in the southern Pacific Ocean. Maia is located at 14.14 degrees south latitude and 169.25 degrees west longitude.

Quiet tranquillity surrounds this village and the whole island. The scent of white ginger on moon-drenched evenings, naked children playing in the surf, massive forests of breadfruit and coconut trees all are part of the past and current scene of Tau.

Inasmuch as this vessel was a barge, making no power sounds, the name of MAIA proved quite applicable. This barge was used in the bulk freight trades of the Great Lakes until being sold for use as a breakwater in 1956. It was later raised and scrapped at Ashtabula, Ohio in 1962.

The Barge MAIA is shown above in the St. Mary's River on June 15, 1956.

Barge MANILA

OWNER: Buckeye Steamship Company
BUILT: Chicago Shipbuilding Company, Chicago, Illinois—1899
HULL NO.: 36
O. A. DIMENSIONS: 450'7" × 50' × 28'7"

Manila, Utah is the namesake location of this bulk freight barge. It is located at 40.59 degrees north latitude and 109.44 degrees west longitude at the foot of the Unita Mountains near the Utah-Wyoming border.

This small town of three hundred and fifty population is on Utah highway #44 in Lucerne Valley which runs east and west along the Utah-Wyoming state boundary line. The area was first surveyed in 1898 and was believed to contain valuable mineral deposits at that time. This survey occurred at the time of Admiral Dewey's successful capture of the Philippine capital of the same name and the town was named in honor of that event in American history.

Little actual development of those supposed resources has occurred and the area is not industrialized today. This vessel was another that was originally constructed for the Minnesota Steamship Company and was given a name in keeping with the theme of ship names in that fleet.

The bulk freight Barge MANILA was sold for off-lakes use in 1956. It is shown in the above photograph downbound with a cargo of iron ore destined for Lake Erie delivery on June 19, 1953.

Barge MARSALA

OWNER:	Buckeye Steamship Company
BUILT:	Chicago Shipbuilding Company, Chicago, Illinois—1900
HULL NO.:	39
O. A. DIMENSIONS:	450'7" × 50' × 28'6"

The bulk freight Barge MARSALA was also built for the Minnesota Steamship Company and shared the theme of ship names common to that fleet. It was active on the Great Lakes until being sold for off-lakes use in 1956.

The namesake of this barge was the city of Marsala, Sicily which is located at 37.48 degrees north latitude and 12.27 degrees east longitude. It is eighteen miles southwest of Trapani and twelve miles northwest of Mazara on Sicily's westernmost point of land, Cape Boeo.

Marsala is a fortified seaport. Garibaldi and volunteer forces landed there on May 11, 1860 to begin the successful expedition against the Bourbons. Today, the port is most famous for its exports. Chief among these is Marsala Wine, first manufactured there in 1773. Other exports include grain, salt and soda.

In ancient times, the city of Marsala, now 65,000 in population, was the site of Lilybaeum which was founded by Hililco of the Carthagenians in 396 B.C.

The Barge MARSALA is shown in the above photograph passing downbound in the Detroit River in tow of its lake steamer consort headed for Lake Erie with a cargo of iron ore.

Steamer SIMON J. MURPHY (2)

OWNER:	Buckeye Steamship Company
BUILT:	Detroit Shipbuilding Company, Wyandotte, Michigan—1900
HULL NO.:	135
O. A. DIMENSIONS:	451' × 51'6" × 28'

Sold for scrap in 1960, the Steamer SIMON J. MURPHY honored as its namesake Mr. Simon Jones Murphy. He was born on April 22, 1815 at Windsor, Maine and was educated in the public schools.

In 1833 he went to work in the lumber works at Milford, Maine and by 1840 he formed a partnership with James Thissell for the purpose of lumbering for their own account. He had worked in every phase of the cutting, processing and selling of lumber. After several successes and a scarce setback, he became interested in the lumber industry of Michigan. This was in 1852 and he moved to Michigan in 1865. Mr. Murphy bought large blocks of pine land and in 1886 organized the S. J. Murphy Lumber Company and built a saw mill at Green Bay, Wisconsin.

All his operations were quite successful and he gradually had holdings in iron ore, railroads, copper mining, electric power, finance, manufacturing and oil. He formed the Murphy Oil Corporation which still is active in Great Lakes commerce. He was a director or officer in innumerable firms and was also responsible for the construction of both the old and present Penobscot Buildings at Detroit, Michigan. Mr. Murphy died at Detroit on February 1, 1905.

The Steamer SIMON J. MURPHY is shown below while upbound, light in the St. Mary's River on August 18, 1955. It is headed for Duluth, Minnesota to take on a cargo of iron ore.

Steamer PRINCETON

OWNER:	Buckeye Steamship Company
BUILT:	American Ship Building Company, Lorain, Ohio—1900
HULL NO.:	302
O. A. DIMENSIONS:	474' × 50' × 28'6"

The bulk freight Steamer PRINCETON was active on the Great Lakes until 1963 when it was sold for use as a breakwater. It was raised and re-sunk several times until its final sinking as a breakwater at Burns Harbor, Indiana in 1966.

This vessel was one of the ships in the "college fleet" of ships which was absorbed into Pittsburgh Steamship Company in 1901. It was sold to these owners in 1945.

Princeton University was the namesake of this ship. The university is located at Princeton, New Jersey and is an institution of higher learning for men. It grew out of the Synod of Philadelphia which had been formed in 1739 owing to the success of a Scotsman, William Tennant, in a school of Pennsylvania known as Log College. This Synod split in 1742 and the membership of the New York section obtained a charter to found a new college in 1746. It began operations at Princeton, New Jersey in 1756. Several name changes until the present name was adopted in 1896.

A graduate school was made a permanent addition to the University in 1913 and a school of architecture was opened in 1920. In 1921 the school of engineering was added and, in 1930, a school of public and international affairs was founded. The non-sectarian institution now has an enrollment of over 4,000 and operates on the semester system.

The Steamer PRINCETON is shown below at the former lower dock of the Central Furnace Company in Cleveland, Ohio.

Barge JOHN SMEATON

OWNER: Buckeye Steamship Company
BUILT: American Steel Barge Company, West Superior, Wisconsin—1899
HULL NO.: 143
O. A. DIMENSIONS: 461' × 50' × 29'6"

The Barge JOHN SMEATON held the honor of being the largest tow-barge ever constructed on the Great Lakes. In modern times larger barges have come into existence, but these have generally been of the type that was pushed rather than being towed as was common in former practice. This vessel was in the above fleet until being sold for off-lakes use in 1956.

Mr. John Smeaton was born in Austhorpe, England on June 8, 1724. He was educated in the public schools and learned the art of mathematical instrument making in London, England. He became a Fellow in the Royal Society in 1753 as a result of his accomplishments.

In 1755, on a tour of rivers and canals, he became very much interested in things of a marine nature. He built the third lighthouse on Eddystone Reef opposite Plymouth, England in 1759 and established widespread recognition for himself. Mr. Smeaton also built the Forth and Clyde Canal, various bridges at Perth, Banff and Coldstream and completed the harbor at Ramsgate. One of his capstone achievements was the building of a boring mill at Carron Iron Works concurrent with perfection of the Newcomen engine. He continued active in his various affairs until his death at Austhorpe, England on October 28, 1792.

His namesake barge is shown above on July 20, 1953 in the St. Mary's River.

Steamer GEORGE STEPHENSON

OWNER:	Buckeye Steamship Company
BUILT:	F. W. Wheeler & Company, West Bay City, Michigan—1896
HULL NO.:	116
O. A. DIMENSIONS:	432' × 48' × 28'3"

The Steamer GEORGE STEPHENSON honored Mr. George Stephenson, inventor and acknowledged father of the steam locomotive. This vessel was sold for grain storage use in 1959 and was subsequently scrapped.

Mr. George Stephenson was born at Wylam, England on June 9, 1781. He enjoyed little formal education and began working very young as a herder of cows. By 1798 he had worked at several jobs and was a plugman at a colliery. While on this job he began to read a great deal and to attend night school. He became interested in engineering and railways.

In 1808 he worked on engines at the Killingworth mine and weekly took the machines apart to familiarize himself with their every detail. He invented a safety lamp for miners in 1815 and built and ran a successful steam locomotive on July 25, 1814. This led to a series of triumphs culminating on October 6, 1829 when his "Rocket" rolled down British railway tracks, proving that genius and mechanical ability had conquered the former difficulties in railroading progress. Mr. Stephenson died on August 12, 1848 after an illustrious career. This ship honored his contributions to industry and all railroads serving the Great Lakes shipping industry.

This bulk freighter is shown passing upbound at the Ambassador Bridge in the Detroit River on August 23, 1951.

Steamer ANDREW S. UPSON

OWNER: Buckeye Steamship Company
BUILT: American Ship Building Company, Cleveland, Ohio—1909
HULL NO.: 444
O. A. DIMENSIONS: 400' × 52' × 28'1"

The bulk freight Steamer ANDREW S. UPSON was sold for bulk grain storage in 1959 and eventually was scrapped. It was named in honor of Mr. Andrew Seth Upson who was born at Burlington, Connecticut on June 16, 1835. He was educated in the public and private schools of the area and went to work at the age of eighteen for Dwight Langdon in a manufacturing operation at Farmington, Connecticut.

In 1855 he became a travelling salesman for the firm and in 1860 was named manager of the company. He then formed a partnership for the manufacture of nuts and bolts under the name Upson & Dunham which was incorporated on July 14, 1864 as The Upson Nut Company.

The firm had its main factory in Connecticut and a branch plant in Cleveland, Ohio. It became the largest producer of nuts in the world and Mr. Upson presided over the operation from Cleveland as the firm's president. He continued active until his death in 1911. He had spent the last twenty-two years of his life as a resident of Cleveland and had come into contact with a number of Great Lakes vessel owners who became his friends. He was a member of various boards of directors, including those of some steel companies.

His namesake is shown in this photograph downbound in the Lower St. Mary's River below Sault Ste. Marie, Michigan on June 15, 1956.

Steamer GRAND RAPIDS

OWNER:	Bultema Dock & Dredge Company
BUILT:	Manitowoc Shipbuilding Company, Manitowoc, Wisconsin - 1926
HULL NO.:	226
O. A. DIMENSIONS:	360' x 56'3" x 21'6"

The carferry Steamer GRAND RAPIDS was named in honor of the city of Grand Rapids, Michigan which is the seat of Kent County and frequently called the "Furniture Capital of America." Much quality furniture is manufactured in the city which is located on the Grand River at the southern end of the great Michigan pine forests.

The city is thirty miles east of Lake Michigan and has a population of about 180,000. It serves as the center of the wholesale trade in western Michigan. It was founded by Louis Campau in 1826 when he had a fur trading post there. In 1916 Grand Rapids was the scene of the establishment of the first junior college in the state of Michigan.

Grand Rapids is also the seat of several religious bishops. And it has about seven hundred manufacturing companies in its metropolitan area.

This carferry had a capacity of 26 rail cars and 16 passengers and was a tribute to the city on the rail line of the Grand Trunk Western Railroad Company. It laid idle from 1970 until being sold for non-transportation use to these owners in mid-summer 1975, then was sold for scrap in 1989.

Barge HILDA (2)

OWNER: Bultema Dock & Dredge Company
BUILT: American Ship Building Company, Cleveland, Ohio – 1903
HULL NO.: 418
O. A. DIMENSIONS: 350' x 56' x 19'6"
FORMER DATA: Launched as the powered carferry PERE MARQUETTE 19. Converted to a barge at Manitowoc Shipbuilding Company, Manitowoc, Wisconsin and given last name in 1941.

The Barge HILDA (2) is shown above at the Rock Cut, West Neebish Channel, St. Mary's River on September 11, 1974. It is loaded with steel from Sault Ste. Marie, Ontario destined to Burns Harbor, Indiana and has the tug JOHN McLEAN on the forward end and the tug MUSKEGON guiding the stern. The barge had been substantially cut down in the summer and made only a few trips before being sold for off-lakes use in 1975.

Namesake of this unit was Mrs. Hilda Asher, daughter of the late Captain John Roen. She was born January 10, 1919 at Charlevoix, Michigan and was awarded a B.S. degree from Michigan State University in 1940. While at the university, she met Mr. Charles Asher whom she married on August 24, 1940.

After living in Brighton, Michigan where Mr. Asher coached football and after service in the U.S. Navy, the family moved to Green Bay, Wisconsin where they operated a 33-unit motel and supper club. In 1948 this was sold and they moved to Sturgeon Bay, Wisconsin where Captain Roen was in business, and they formed Roen Salvage Company to engage in marine construction work. As this vessel changed hands several times in its last Great Lakes years, none of the owners saw fit to remove Hilda Asher's name from its bow.

Steamer MADISON

OWNER: Bultema Dock & Dredge Company
BUILT: Manitowoc Shipbuilding Company, Manitowoc, Wisconsin - 1927
HULL NO.: 227
O. A. DIMENSIONS: 360' x 56'3" x 21'6"

Namesake of the carferry Steamer MADISON was the capital of the State of Wisconsin. Madison, Wisconsin is located in a surrounding of beautiful lakes and moderately hilly terrain. It, in turn, is named in honor of Mr. James Madison, fourth president of the United States.

It is seventy-six miles due west of Milwaukee, Wisconsin and has a population of about 130,000 persons. The land area was first purchased by Messrs. Doty and Mason in 1831 as a speculation. They later were able to convince the government to establish its headquarters there and, in 1848, Madison became the state capital. It was granted city status by a charter in 1856.

The Steamer MADISON is shown in the photograph above leaving Muskegon, Michigan harbor on February 26, 1974. It is on a regular run and bound for the firm's terminal at Milwaukee, Wisconsin. The vessel laid idle for about four years until sold to the owners in mid-1979 for non-transportation use, then was sold for scrap in 1989.

Barge MAITLAND NO. 1

         OWNER: Bultema Marine Transportation
         BUILT: Great Lakes Engineering Works,
                         Ecorse, Michigan—1916
     HULL NO.:   129
O. A. DIMENSIONS: 350' × 56' × 20'6"
  FORMER DATA: Launched as a powered carferry. Converted to a barge at Great Lakes Engineering Works, Ashtabula, Ohio in 1942 and at Sturgeon Bay Shipbuilding Company, Sturgeon Bay, Wisconsin in 1943.

The crane-equipped bulk carrying Barge MAITLAND NO. 1 retains its original name even though it probably has never been into Port Maitland, Ontario since it ceased operations as a Lake Erie carferry. This barge was a steamer until its engine, auxiliaries and some deck equipment was removed by the United States Government during World War II at Ashtabula, Ohio. The new owners purchased the balance of the ship and towed it to Sturgeon Bay, Wisconsin in December, 1942 and finished the conversion work the following spring.

This barge replaced the Roen Steamship's Barge TRANSPORT which sank in Lake Superior in 1942, and that firm operated it until the late 1960's.

Port Maitland, Ontario, the namesake of this ship, is a small community of about 1,200 population at the mouth of the Grand River on Lake Erie's northern shore.

The barge is shown above in the Welland Ship Canal on June 26, 1976 with a cargo of beer vats destined for Genesee Brewing Company, Oswego, New York. It was sold for off-lakes use in November, 1980.

Barge MANISTEE (2)

OWNER: John H. Bultema
BUILT: Globe Iron Works,
Cleveland, Ohio — 1898
HULL NO.: 75
O. A. DIMENSIONS: 318' x 52'3" x 18'6"
FORMER DATA: Launched as the powered carferry ANN ARBOR NO. 3. Lengthened 48'9" and deepened 3'3" at Manitowoc Shipbuilding Company, Manitowoc, Wisconsin in 1922. Converted to a barge at Bultema Dock & Dredge Company, Manistee, Michigan and given last name in 1965.

This vessel was originally built as a railroad carferry for trans-Lake Michigan service, operating out of Frankfort, Michigan. After its conversion to a barge, these owners used it for shuttling railroad cars across the Straits of Mackinac. Thereafter, it was taken to Detroit, Michigan and was intended to be used for cross-river movement of containers, however, this did not come about. The unit was finally sold for off-lakes use as a moored dock front at Peoria, Illinois late in 1974. It is shown above at Detroit, Michigan on August 8, 1972.

The namesake of this barge was the hometown of its last Great Lakes owner, Mr. John H. Bultema. Manistee, Michigan is the seat of Manistee County and is situated on the eastern shore of Lakes Michigan and Manistee. While the channel into Manistee Lake is not suitable for very large lake steamers, once in the lake smaller commercial and pleasure craft find excellent refuge. The city was first settled in 1841 and salt deposits were discovered there in 1882.

Steamer DANIEL J. MORRELL

OWNER: Cambria Steamship Company
BUILT: West Bay City Shipbuilding Company, West Bay City, Michigan—1906
HULL NO.: 619
O. A. DIMENSIONS: 600' × 58' × 32'

This steamer is shown about a week before it met with great misfortune and sank on Lake Huron with a loss of twenty-eight lives. The freighter was caught in a severe storm while proceeding upbound without cargo and broke in two on November 29, 1966.

Namesake of this vessel was Mr. Daniel Johnson Morrell who was born at North Berwick, Maine on August 8, 1821. He was educated in the public schools and began working as a clerk in a counting room of a mercantile enterprise in Philadelphia, Pennsylvania in 1837. He continued in this line of endeavor until 1855 when he moved to Johnstown, Pennsylvania to become manager of the Cambria Iron Company which he and Mr. C. S. Wood had leased under the firm name of Wood, Morrell & Company.

They refinanced the company and by 1865 saw the plant producing 1,000 tons of steel per week. It was one of the first places to substitute Bessemer steel for iron in the manufacture of rails in 1871. Mr. Morrell retained this managership capacity until his death on August 20, 1885.

The Cambria Iron Company was later to become an affiliate of the Bethlehem Steel Corporation who built and operated this ship.

Steamer EDWARD Y. TOWNSEND

OWNER: Cambria Steamship Company
BUILT: Superior Shipbuilding Company, Superior, Wisconsin—1906
HULL NO.: 515
O. A. DIMENSIONS: 602' × 58' × 32'

Mr. Edward Young Townsend was this bulk freighter's namesake. He was born in West Chester, Pennsylvania on October 4, 1824 and was educated in the public schools. In 1842 he entered the employ of Wood, Abbott & Company, drygoods merchandisers in Philadelphia, Pennsylvania. He was a salesman and traveled on horseback across large areas. He eventually became a partner in the firm and stayed on until the firm acquired a large interest in the Cambria Iron Company of Johnstown, Pennsylvania in 1855.

With the organization of Wood, Morrell & Company as creditors of the Cambria Iron Company, which had failed twice, Mr. Townsend became one of three active managers of the business. In 1861 he became vice president of Cambria Iron Company on its reorganization. He was named its president in 1873 and served in that capacity until his death on November 5, 1891 at Bryn Mawr, Pennsylvania. During his presidency he succeeded in working down the large debt of the firm and he placed the company on sound financial footing.

His company later became a fundamental ingredient of Bethlehem Steel Corporation. Mr. Townsend was one of the original members of the American Iron & Steel Institute and his namesake survived as an active carrier until being sold for trade-in and scrap in 1968. It is shown in this photograph upbound in the St. Mary's River on August 26, 1966.

Steamer BULKARIER

OWNER:	Canada Cement Transport Limited
BUILT:	Furness Shipbuilding Company Limited, Haverton Hill-on-Tees, England—1929
HULL NO.:	147
O. A. DIMENSIONS:	331' × 43'3" × 25'
FORMER DATA:	Lengthened 73' at Canadian Vickers Limited, Montreal, Quebec in 1961.

The Steamer BULKARIER was the first ship owned by this company and one of the first operated by any Canadian concern for the movement of cement in bulk.

The namesake relates to the ship's designated service. Since it was built to carry cement in bulk, the obvious choice for the firm was to have that fact noted in the ship name. Thus, the prefix of the ship name "BULK." The balance of the ship name also relates to the fact that the vessel was engaged in transportation as a carrier of bulk commodities. Instead of the usual word spelling, however, the Canada Cement Company Limited (now Canada Cement Lafarge Limited) determined to drop one "r" from the word carrier and complete the ship name by coupling the two words together, without the "c" to end up with the spelling as it appears in this ship name. It was a novel combination and spelling for the theme presented.

This ship saw service until being sold for off-lakes use in 1968. It was to have been a processing vessel, but never saw activity in that role. In 1971 it was sold to the consortium dredging Quebec Harbour approaches and renamed SABLE ISLAND and became a bottom-dump barge.

The Steamer BULKARIER is seen in the above picture at a lay-by berth at Toronto, Ontario on July 30, 1958.

Electric Motor Vessel CEMENTKARRIER

OWNER: Canada Cement LaFarge Limited
BUILT: Furness Shipbuilding Company, Limited, Haverton Hill-on-Tees, England—1930
HULL NO.: 175
O. A. DIMENSIONS: 307'6" × 43'3" × 20'
FORMER DATA: Lengthened 49'6" at Davie Shipbuilding Limited, Lauzon, Quebec in 1960.

The Canada Cement Firm owned and operated the E. M. V. CEMENTKARRIER for the private carriage of its Portland cement. The vessel was a boom-equipped self-unloader, allowing it to discharge itself at the several Company port terminals along the Great Lakes-Seaway system.

There is no record of any particular meaning or history behind the name of the ship itself or of the spelling of the name. Logically, it can be assumed that the name comes from the type of service in which the vessel is engaged and that the usual "c" was interchanged for a "k" in the name as a touch of individuality.

Canada Cement Company Limited was incorporated October 22, 1927 as a successor to a firm of the same name formed in 1909. It has plants throughout Canada. The Bath, Ontario cement plant near Kingston on Lake Ontario is its major Great Lakes loading facility. This ship is shown at Toronto, Ontario on October 1, 1972. The ship was too small to compete in the 1970's and was sold for off-lakes use as a barge in 1978.

Steamer ACADIAN (2)

OWNER: Canada Steamship Lines Limited
BUILT: North of Ireland Shipbuilding Company, Londonderry, Ireland - 1913
HULL NO.: 55
O. A. DIMENSIONS: 256'6" x 42'6" x 20'6"
FORMER DATA: Launched as GLENMAVIS. Given last name in 1927.

The bulk freighter shown below was unique on the Great Lakes in that it was built to specifications of the British self-trim design. A sister ship was built for Great Lakes service but left for ocean service in World War I and never returned.

The Steamer ACADIAN is shown at Lock Four of the Soulanges Canal on October 21, 1958. It was subsequently sold for scrap in 1959 after the opening of the St. Lawrence Seaway.

Namesake of this ship was the original name given to natives of what is now Nova Scotia. Residents of Acadie or Acadia were called Acadians. Nova Scotia was an area victimized by external forces many times in its history. First the area belonged to France and then to the British before becoming part of the Dominion of Canada.

The new era began for Nova Scotia and Acadians when Edward Cornwallis arrived in 1749 with 2,500 English Colonists and a plan to build a fortress at Halifax. This fort was to counter the French stronghold at Louisburg. The territory became British in 1763 when France relinquished all of its claims on the area.

This vessel was the first carrier built by this shipyard in the 20th century. The yard laid idle for well over a decade before commencing work on this hull.

Steamer ASHCROFT

OWNER: Canada Steamship Lines Limited
BUILT: Midland Shipbuilding Company Limited, Midland, Ontario—1924
HULL NO.: 12
O. A. DIMENSIONS: 560'6" × 60' × 32'
FORMER DATA: Launched as GLENIFFER (2). Given last name in 1926.

The bulk freight Steamer ASHCROFT was sold for scrap in 1969 and was the last smaller unit of this bulk freight class to be sold by the owners.

This vessel was one of many in the fleet that had names in reference to places in Canada. Ashcroft, British Columbia is a village of about one thousand population on the south bank of the Thompson River about two hundred miles northeast of Vancouver, British Columbia.

Ashcroft is on the main lines of both the Canadian Pacific and Canadian National Railways and is at the junction of the Trans-Canada and Cariboo highways. It is the main entry point to the Cariboo country. The town received its name after the building of the Canadian Pacific Railway past the point and in reference to the English manor home of the Cornwall family whose ranch continued to be the principal congregating point in the area for many years after the founding of the town. Ashcroft was incorporated in 1952 and is now in the lumbering, ranching and mining district of the province.

The namesake of this small, but important village is shown below on August 24, 1968 in the St. Mary's River below the famous St. Mary's Falls Canal at Sault Ste. Marie, Michigan. This vessel was the first in excess of 500 feet in overall length to pass through the Welland Ship Canal and did so on July 6, 1932 with a cargo of grain from Fort William, Ontario for Kingston, Ontario delivery.

Steamer BARRIE

OWNER: Canada Steamship Lines Limited
BUILT: Collingwood Shipbuilding Company Limited, Collingwood, Ontario—1925
HULL NO.: 76
O. A. DIMENSIONS: 261' × 43' × 19'9"
FORMER DATA: Launched as ROBERT P. KERNAN. Given last name in 1927.

The bulk freight Steamer BARRIE was sold for scrap in 1960, one year after the new St. Lawrence Seaway made ships of her size uncompetitive.

The namesake of this ship is the city of Barrie, Ontario which is the county seat of Simcoe County and is located fifty miles north of Toronto, Ontario. It is situated at the head of Kempenfelt Bay on Lake Simcoe and is a division point on the Canadian National Railways. Preliminary survey of the area was made in 1812 and the first structure was erected as a government depot at the eastern terminus of Nine Mile Portage. The first settlers came in 1833. It was incorporated as a town in 1851, became the official seat of the area in 1852, and was granted city status in 1959.

Barrie is believed to have been named in honor of Commodore Barrie who led the squadron at Kingston, Ontario in early Canadian days. Small industries are located at Barrie but the area is mainly noted for its fine recreational facilities. Golfing, hunting, boating and fishing are the key summertime activities and ice fishing, skiing, curling and winter carnivals provide pleasurable activities for winter visitors. Barrie is a city of 22,000 population and is the capital of the Lake Simcoe region.

The Steamer BARRIE is seen here at Toronto, Ontario on July 4, 1958.

Steamer BATTLEFORD

OWNER: Canada Steamship Lines Limited
BUILT: Swan, Hunter & Wigham Richardson Limited, Wallsend-on-Tyne, England—1925
HULL NO.: 1275
O. A. DIMENSIONS: 261' × 43'6" × 25'6"
FORMER DATA: Launched as the bulk freighter GLENROSS. Lengthened 95' at Collingwood Shipbuilding Company Limited, Collingwood, Ontario in 1926. Shortened 95' at Collingwood Shipbuilding Company Limited, Collingwood, Ontario in 1939. Converted to a package freighter at Davie Shipbuilding Limited, Lauzon, Quebec in 1939. Renamed BATTLEFORD in 1941.

The Steamer BATTLEFORD has had an involved history. When it was commissioned it was known to the owners that she was destined to be in service in a lengthened capacity. This vessel carried, as ballast, its midbody which was inserted at the Canadian yard shown the year following its christening. When package freight needs predominated the company interests, this vessel adopted a new role and served in that career the balance of its Great Lakes life.

The Steamer BATTLEFORD is shown in this photograph above Lock One of the Welland Ship Canal on June 23, 1951. This ship was sold for off-lakes use and renamed REAL GOLD in 1966.

Battleford, Saskatchewan and, by pre-declaration, Battleford, Ontario, the site of the battle between Canadian and United States forces, is the namesake of this vessel. Battleford is a site on the North Saskatchewan River which was first established as an outpost of Hudson's Bay Company in 1876. The area was incorporated as a village in 1899 and as a town in 1910.

Steamer BEAVERTON (2)

OWNER: Canada Steamship Lines Limited
BUILT: Robert Stephenson & Company, Limited, Hebburn-on-Tyne, England—1908
HULL NO.: 118
O. A. DIMENSIONS: 256′ × 42′6″ × 23′6″

The package freight Steamer BEAVERTON is shown in the photograph above being unloaded of a grain cargo at Toronto Elevators at Toronto, Ontario on August 25, 1952. Occasionally, on downbound trips these package freighters carried grain cargoes when full cargoes of package freight were not available. This trip of the ship is one of those occasions.

The namesake of this vessel is the village in Ontario on Lake Simcoe's east shoreline at the mouth of the Beaver River. That site is some sixty-four miles north of Toronto, Ontario and is on the Canadian National Railways System.

Beaverton was first settled in the period from 1820-1835 by British immigrants. The first public performance of Alexander Muir's "The Maple Leaf Forever" was given at Beaverton, Ontario in 1871.

The town has a population of about 1,200 persons and is a favorite among tourists to the region of Lake Simcoe. It is a toy manufacturing center, but the chief interests relate to tourists and resort industry activities. These provide the most impetus to local business.

The namesake town of this vessel was honored on the Great Lakes for over fifty-two years until the ship was sold for scrap in 1960, one year after the opening of the St. Lawrence Seaway proved this size vessel to be uneconomical.

Steamer BURLINGTON (3)

OWNER: Canada Steamship Lines Limited
BUILT: Cleveland Shipbuilding Company, Lorain, Ohio - 1899
HULL NO.: 34
O. A. DIMENSIONS: 464' x 50'3" x 28'3"
FORMER DATA: Launched as HENRY W. OLIVER. Renamed S. H. ROBBINS in 1915. Given last name in 1948.

The bulk freight Steamer BURLINGTON was active in Great Lakes commerce until being sold for scrap in 1967. It is shown here in the St. Mary's River.

Burlington, Ontario is the namesake town of this ship. It is situated on the western shore of Burlington Bay, Lake Ontario in Halton County and takes its name from the bay. It was first settled in 1810 when the area was purchased from an estate. It was known as Wellington Square at that time.

In 1873 it was incorporated as a village and took the present name. It was granted town status in 1914 and has a population of fifty thousand today.

There are over one hundred industries in the area including steel products manufacturing, household goods, chemicals and shoes. Little waterborne commerce is carried on in the town but there is a great deal of heavy industrial and general cargo waterborne commerce in the bay on the Hamilton, Ontario piers.

The name is thought to have come from Bridlington, a watering place in Yorkshire, England which had a fine sand beach similar to that found on Burlington Bay.

Steamer CALGARIAN (2)

OWNER: Canada Steamship Lines Limited
BUILT: Caledon Shipbuilding & Engineering Company, Dundee, Scotland - 1905
HULL NO.: 183
O. A. DIMENSIONS: 256' x 43'3" x 27'3"
FORMER DATA: Launched as GLENELLAH. Given last name in 1926.

The package freight Steamer CALGARIAN is shown in this photograph as it approaches Lock One of the Welland Ship Canal in May of 1955. It served in commercial traffic patterns until being sold for scrap in 1960.

This canal-sized freighter was one of many in the fleet that took placenames as their namesakes. The residents of the city of Calgary, Alberta singularly and collectively are the namesakes of this vessel.

Calgary, Alberta is a city of about 275,000 population located on the main transcontinental line of the Canadian Pacific Railway. It is 832 miles west of Winnipeg, Manitoba, 642 miles east of Vancouver, British Columbia and 138 miles north of the United States border. It is at the junction of the Bow and Elbow Rivers and is the chief urban center of southern Alberta.

The Steamer CALGARIAN left Toronto, Ontario on its maiden voyage October 4, 1905 for Fort Williams, Ontario. The ship had run across the Atlantic Ocean in ballast. On May 22, 1958, it became the first merchant vessel to pass upbound in the new Iroquois Lock at Cardinal, Ontario in the newly created St. Lawrence Seaway at 1510 hours.

Steamer CANADIAN (2)

OWNER:	Canada Steamship Lines Limited
BUILT:	William Dobson & Company, Limited, Newcastle-on-Tyne, England—1907
HULL NO.:	154
O. A. DIMENSIONS:	255'3" x 43' x 26'6"

The package freight Steamer CANADIAN was one of the first of full pre-Seaway size ships to be operated in the general cargo trade by this line. This vessel remained in operation until being sold for scrap in 1959.

The namesake of this vessel is its registry country and all the inhabitants of Canada. Though it was built in the United Kingdon, as were many sister ships both for this and other early Canadian lines, the country of registry was Canada and this was a Canadian ship.

The name was fitting also in the sense that it took into consideration part of the corporate title of the owning company in later years. As a country Canada is the second largest in area in the world with 20,000,000 population and an area of 3,851,809 square miles.

The Steamer CANADIAN is seen in the photograph above at Sault Ste. Marie, Michigan on August 18, 1955. The vessel carried a name throughout its career with a familiar suffix—that of "IAN" which was shared by many vessels of the Canadian Interlake Line, a company which was merged into this owning firm in 1913. Many of the acquired ships, like this one, retained their original names.

Steamer CITY OF HAMILTON (2)

OWNER: Canada Steamship Lines Limited
BUILT: Midland Shipbuilding Company Limited, Midland, Ontario—1927
HULL NO.: 18
O. A. DIMENSIONS: 250' × 38' × 23'

Late afternoon shadows grace the bow of the package freight Steamer CITY OF HAMILTON in this photograph showing the vessel approaching Lock One of the Welland Ship Canal on November 10, 1956. The ship remained active in Great Lakes commerce until 1959 and was sold for scrap in 1961.

This vessel had cleared its namesake port and package freight terminal dock at the foot of Wellington Street about three hours before this picture was taken. Hamilton, Ontario is known as the steel-making capital of Canada, but it is also a major general cargo port for this line and for overseas commerce.

Hamilton is the seat of Wentworth County and has a population of 400,000 persons. It was named in honor of Mr. George Hamilton who bought a tract of land there in 1813. The harbor at Hamilton is excellent and serves not only the busy port activities, but also as a refuge for ships when Lake Ontario storms preclude their passage on the lake. Entrance and exit from the harbor is by means of a canal cutting across Burlington Beach which acts as the barrier of protection for the harbor.

Hamilton is known as a city of parks, gardens and beautiful hinterland. The hillsides surrounding the city provide an excellent view of the harbor area below and of Lake Ontario beyond. The city is at the western tip of Lake Ontario and is served by major roads and rail systems of Canada. Its location justly deserves the title "The Pittsburgh of Canada."

Steamer CITY OF KINGSTON

OWNER: Canada Steamship Lines Limited
BUILT: Davie Shipbuilding & Repairing Company Limited, Lauzon, Quebec—1926
HULL NO.: 490
O. A. DIMENSIONS: 250' × 38' × 23'

Kingston, Ontario, seat of Frontenac County, is the namesake of this package freighter. The city of 70,000 population is located on the north shore of Lake Ontario at the mouth of the Cataraqui River and terminus of the Rideau Canal. The Kingston Grain Elevator Division of this fleet is located there and, formerly, large transit sheds used to serve in the general cargo traffic of the port.

In 1673 the area served as the first meeting place between the Iroquois Indians and Governor Frontenac. In 1783 it was occupied for settlement by United Empire Loyalists from New York state led by Captain Gross. The first session of the Executive Council for Upper Canada was held in Kingston in 1792. Kingston was incorporated as a town in 1838 and as a city in 1846.

The harbor at Kingston was once a focal point of grain trans-shipments to the Lower St. Lawrence River ports, but the 1959 opening of the St. Lawrence Seaway changed all that. Now, only small amounts of grain are trans-shipped through Kingston and most of the receipts of the port are for local consumption and processing.

The package freight Steamer CITY OF KINGSTON is shown here on June 23, 1951 at Port Huron, Michigan. The Point Edward package freight dock at Sarnia, Ontario can be seen in the background. This vessel had just left that dock and is proceeding downbound in the St. Clair River. The ship continued active until being sold for scrap in 1961.

Steamer CITY OF MONTREAL (2)

OWNER: Canada Steamship Lines Limited
BUILT: Midland Shipbuilding Company Limited, Midland, Ontario—1927
HULL NO.: 19
O. A. DIMENSIONS: 250' × 38' × 23'

The canal-size package freight Steamer CITY OF MONTREAL is shown in this picture passing through the Eastern Gap of Toronto, Ontario harbor in July, 1955. This passage could be used by vessels which were not drawing much water. As can be seen in the photograph, this ship easily falls into that category.

The namesake city of this vessel is the largest city in Canada and the second largest French-speaking city in the world. It is located on Montreal Island at the confluence of the St. Lawrence and Ottawa Rivers. Mount Royal, at the center of the island, rises 769 feet above sea level and can be seen from miles around.

On May 17, 1642 a mission station was founded at Montreal by Jeanne Mance. The American Revolution led to an unsuccessful attack on Montreal in 1775 by Ethan Allen and to the city's abandonment by Sir Guy Carleton. When Upper and Lower Canada reunited in 1840, Montreal became the capital for a short time. At Confederation in 1867, Montreal was already the metropolitan city of Canada.

Steamer CITY OF TORONTO

OWNER: Canada Steamship Lines Limited
BUILT: Davie Shipbuilding & Repairing Company Limited, Lauzon, Quebec—1926
HULL NO.: 489
O. A. DIMENSIONS: 250' × 38' × 23'

The package freight Steamer CITY OF TORONTO is shown in the above photograph at Toronto, Ontario in July, 1955. It continued to be an active steamer on the Great Lakes until being sold for scrap in 1961.

Toronto, Ontario is the namesake city of this ship. It has been the capital of the Province of Ontario since 1867 and is the second largest city in Canada with a population of 2,500,000 persons. Its boroughs of Etobicoke, North York, East York, York and Scarborough, plus the city of Toronto, comprise the Municipality of Metropolitan Toronto covering 270 square miles.

Toronto is a name of Indian origin meaning "place of meeting." The Seneca Indian village of Teiaigon was located at the mouth of the Humber River in the 17th century. The area was first visited by white men in 1615 when Etienne Brule arrived and was first settled by white men in 1672 with the establishment of a trading post by priests. Fort York was established in the area in 1793.

The city was the first in the Dominion of Canada to have a subway and is among the most cosmopolitan areas in North America. The package freight terminal of this line used to be located directly in Toronto Harbour at the foot of Bay Street, but is now located in the western suburb of Port Credit, Ontario.

Steamer CITY OF WINDSOR (3)

                OWNER: Canada Steamship Lines Limited
                BUILT: Davie Shipbuilding & Repairing Company Limited,
                        Lauzon, Quebec—1929
             HULL NO.: 501
    O. A. DIMENSIONS: 250'9" × 40'3" × 24'6"

The package freight Steamer CITY OF WINDSOR was active on the Great Lakes until being sold for scrap in 1961. Up to that time it had served in the various Canadian trade routes of the owning company and served admirably. The onset of newer and faster, large package freight vessels in the fleet proved to be too much for this little vessel to bear, and it soon became uneconomical to operate.

The Steamer CITY OF WINDSOR is shown in the photograph above entering Toronto harbour in July of 1955.

This vessel has a namesake that is borne in the ship name quite obviously. Windsor, Ontario is the seat of Essex County and is across the Detroit River from Detroit, Michigan. Much of the activity of Windsor is as the counterpart of American activity at Detroit. Distilling at Hiram Walker, manufacturing at Ford Motor Company of Canada and other similar related activities testify to this.

The city has a background of its own, however, and this is told in the fact that the area was named in 1836, incorporated as a village in 1854, as a town in 1858 and as a city in 1892.

Over four hundred-fifty different industries are represented in the city of Windsor, Ontario and this locale has become the focal point of southwestern Ontario.

Steamer COLLIER (3)

OWNER: Canada Steamship Lines Limited
BUILT: Vickers Limited,
Barrows-in-Furness, England - 1924
HULL NO.: 610
O. A. DIMENSIONS: 258' x 43'2" x 20'9"
FORMER DATA: Launched as COLLIER NO. 1. Given last name in 1928.

The Steamer COLLIER (3) was the first self-unloading ship in the Canada Steamship Lines fleet. Subsequent to her proving to be successful, other vessels were built for the self-unloader trade. Some of those in the fleet today are among the largest in carrying capacity on the entire Great Lakes-Seaway system.

The vessel was sold for scrap in 1959 after other conversions to self-unloading ships had alleviated the need of this owner to operate such small tonnage in a specialized trade.

A definition of a collier is "a ship employed in transporting coal." That transportation of coal from United States ports to users in Canada was the prime activity of this vessel. It thus was aptly named in honor of its predetermined function as a member of the fleet.

Since most of industrial Canada's coal is imported from fields in the United States a large fleet of Canadian ships has now been built-up to almost totally serve in this movement. Compared to this vessel's capacity of less than 3,000 net tons, current self-unloaders in the coal trade regularly carry more than 32,000 net tons.

The Steamer COLLIER (3), with the typical all-black hull, is shown in this photograph at Toronto, Ontario on October 7, 1954. Note the unusual deck apparatus for the self-unloading rig.

Steamer COLLINGWOOD

OWNER: Canada Steamship Lines Limited
BUILT: Collingwood Shipbuilding Company Limited, Collingwood, Ontario—1907
HULL NO.: 17
O. A. DIMENSIONS: 406' × 50' × 28'
FORMER DATA: Launched as a bulk freighter. Converted to a package freighter at Midland Shipyards, Limited, Midland, Ontario in 1950.

The package freight Steamer COLLINGWOOD was active on the Great Lakes until the last days of the older vessels in that trade. It was finally sold for scrap in 1968. The Steamer COLLINGWOOD is shown in the above photograph downbound at Clayton, New York in the St. Lawrence River in August, 1960. It is being met near the Gananaque-Clayton International Bridge by a yacht enroute from Montreal to Buffalo, New York on which the author was a guest.

Collingwood, Ontario is the namesake town of this ship. It has been, for many years, the scene of great ship launchings and in the recent past has been the building place of record-breaking steamers and motor vessels for this line. The Collingwood Shipyards Division of Canadian Shipbuilding & Engineering Limited has produced many of today's lake giants.

Collingwood's first settler was Mr. George Carney in 1835. He settled in the swampy country of the Tobacco Indians and named the town in honor of Admiral Collingwood who was Nelson's second-in-command at Trafalgar. The first industry in the area was a sawmill erected in 1853. This was followed in 1855 by the site being made the northern terminus of what is now part of the Canadian National Railways. Collingwood was granted town status in 1858.

Steamer DONNACONA (2)

OWNER: Canada Steamship Lines Limited
BUILT: Western Dry Dock & Shipbuilding Company Limited, Port Authur, Ontario—1914
HULL NO.: 12
O. A. DIMENSIONS: 625' × 59'3" × 32'9"
FORMER DATA: Launched as W. GRANT MORDEN. Given last name in 1926.

When put into commission, the Steamer DONNACONA was the largest ship ever built for the Canadian Great Lakes trade. It had extremely high cubic measurements to enable it to be a competitive carrier until its last days in the grain trade. The vessel was sold for scrap in 1969.

On April 30, 1947 this vessel cleared Fort William, Ontario for Kingston, Ontario with the largest cargo of barley ever loaded in the world, up to that time. It consisted of 589,844 bushels. Today's record for the Great Lakes is in the area of 1,100,000 bushels and the record for the world is about twice that figure.

Namesake of this ship is the Indian chief whom Jacques Cartier met on this continent and took back to France with him in 1535. A town is also named Donnacona in honor of the chief. It is located in Portneuf County, Quebec about 31 miles southwest of Quebec City. It was incorporated as a village in 1915 and as a town in 1920. The Donnacona Paper Company is the prime source of livelihood in the town with its large mill. The Jacques Cartier River is used for log floating to the mill and also provides hydro-electric power for the mill and the town. The town has a current population of 5,000 persons.

The maiden trip of this vessel, with iron ore, commenced June 15, 1914 from Escanaba, Michigan with the cargo destined for Port Colborne, Ontario delivery. The ship is shown below upbound in the Welland Ship Canal on September 4, 1965.

Steamer EDMONTON

OWNER:	Canada Steamship Lines Limited
BUILT:	Robert Stephenson & Company, Limited,
	Hebburn-on-Tyne, England—1906
HULL NO.:	110
O. A. DIMENSIONS:	256′ × 42′6″ × 23′

The package freight Steamer EDMONTON's namesake is the capital city of Alberta located on the banks of the North Saskatchewan River. It was first settled in 1795 when Hudson's Bay Company set up a fur-trading post there and called it Fort Edmonton. It received that name from its namesake town, a suburb of London, England. Many of the Canadian towns took their names from those of the Mother England.

In 1874 the North West Mounted Police arrived at this place and the Canadian Pacific Railway passed through in 1891. The site was incorporated as a town in 1892 and as a city in 1904. Edmonton was given a great push towards modern development in 1898 when the gold rush to the Klondike was on.

Today, Edmonton is the western terminus of the Interprovincial Pipe Line Company. This firm's line extends eastward to Sarnia, Ontario and provides that province with the raw materials needed to supply the demands of the areas and provinces bordering Ontario. Sarnia is the heart of the "chemical valley" of Ontario.

The Steamer EDMONTON is shown in this photograph at the Allanburg Bridge in the Welland Ship Canal on May 21, 1955. It is downbound for a Lake Ontario port before continuing its journey towards Montreal. This vessel was active on the Great Lakes until being sold for scrap in 1961.

Steamer ELGIN

OWNER:	Canada Steamship Lines Limited
BUILT:	Swan, Hunter & Wigham Richardson Limited, Newcastle-on-Tyne, England—1923
HULL NO.:	1144
O. A. DIMENSIONS:	261' × 42'6" × 20'6"
FORMER DATA:	Launched as GLENGELDIE. Given last name in 1927.

Sold for scrap in 1963, the Steamer ELGIN is seen in this photograph inbound at Toronto's Eastern Gap harbor entrance on July 16, 1958. Its deckload of pipe was manufactured in Europe and transferred to this vessel at Montreal, Quebec. The pipe was used for construction of the Trans Canada Pipeline.

This vessel took Elgin, Manitoba as its namesake. This town of 400 population is located one hundred-seventy miles southwest of the city of Winnipeg, Manitoba on the Canadian National Railways System. It is in the heart of a rich grain-growing region and it is this fact that led it to be chosen as this bulk freighter's namesake.

It was named in honor of Mr. James Bruce, 8th Earl of Elgin and Governor General of Canada from 1847 to 1854. He was born in London, England on July 20, 1811 and died in Dharmsala, India on November 20, 1863.

Elgin was first settled as a townsite when the branch of the Northern Pacific Railway from Belmont to Hartney was finished in 1898. It had about forty buildings in 1899 and by 1901 also had three grain elevators to service the growing region around it and a number of commercial stores and services. It also could boast a newspaper of its own.

Steamer FAIRMOUNT (2)

OWNER:	Canada Steamship Lines Limited
BUILT:	Ayrshire Dockyard Company, Irvine, Scotland—1923
HULL NO.:	492
O. A. DIMENSIONS:	261' × 43' × 19'
FORMER DATA:	Launched as METCALFE. Given last name in 1927.

The bulk freight Steamer FAIRMOUNT (2) was sold in 1961 for scrap, but under subsequent agreement was reduced to a salvage barge by Marine Industries, Limited, finally being scrapped in 1970. It is shown in this photograph downbound in the lower Detroit River on September 2, 1952.

Fairmount Station, Saskatchewan is the namesake town of this ship. It is exactly located at 51.24 north latitude and 109.16 west longitude. This site is about one hundred miles west southwest of Saskatoon, Saskatchewan on the Canadian National Railway System.

In and of itself it is not a primary point of interest or of historic importance. However, it was a main railroad junction point in the early days of the westward movement in the Dominion of Canada and, thus, was chosen to be honored when this vessel took the name FAIRMOUNT.

The town has a population of about two hundred people today and is a typical prairie town in the vast wheat growing province of Saskatchewan. One would hardly notice passing through the area if driving along the main highway. Yet, in its day of importance, the town of Fairmount worthily deserved to have a Great Lakes vessel take its name as its namesake.

Steamer FERNIE

OWNER:	Canada Steamship Lines Limited
BUILT:	Midland Shipbuilding Company Limited, Midland, Ontario—1929
HULL NO.:	23
O. A. DIMENSIONS:	258'9" × 42'9" × 26'6"

Sold for scrap in 1963 and meeting that fate at Hamilton, Ontario in 1964, the package freight Steamer FERNIE is shown in the above photograph on August 10, 1956 at the Eastern Gap of Toronto, Ontario harbor. The ship is inbound from Montreal, Quebec with a deck load of general cargo as well as holds full of general cargo.

This package freighter was named in honor of a small town in British Columbia located at 49.30 north latitude and 115.0 west longitude. Fernie, British Columbia is situated on the Elk River and the Canadian Pacific Railway. It is thirty-five miles southwest of the locally famous Crow's Nest Pass and about sixty miles north of the United States border. Fernie has become important as the center of vast coal deposits of the province. Its development has been almost totally related to the concurrent development of those deposits.

Fernie has a current population of about 2,700 persons. It was named for Mr. William Fernie who obtained information from local Indians as to the location of the coal deposits in 1887. About eighty per cent of British Columbia's coal production comes from these deposits. When these deposits were first made known, the area around Fernie was only slightly developed. It thus was a "pioneer" town of the Canadian West and was chosen as a namesake of this freighter by the owners because of its historic significance.

Steamer GLENELG

OWNER:	Canada Steamship Lines Limited
BUILT:	Midland Shipbuilding Company Limited, Midland, Ontario—1923
HULL NO.:	11
O. A. DIMENSIONS:	259' × 43' 26'6"
FORMER DATA:	Launched as a self-unloader. Converted to a bulk freighter at Kingston Shipyards, Kingston, Ontario in 1955. Converted to a self-unloading cement carrier at Kingston Shipyards, Kingston, Ontario in 1958.

The cement carrying Steamer GLENELG has a name with a singular distinction. It could be spelled either forwards or backwards with equal appropriateness. To this writer's knowledge, this was the only name ever borne on the bow of a Great Lakes ship that could make that claim.

The Steamer GLENELG is shown in this excellent photograph at the Rochester Portland Cement Company's dock at Rochester, New York. The unloading pipes and connections onboard can be clearly seen.

Glenelg, Scotland is located at 57.13 north latitude and 5.37 west longitude on the Sound of Sleat about 25 miles northeast of the city of Mallaig. Glenelg is a very small town with about 2,000 population. A ferry crosses the Sound from the town to the Island of Skye. The area is abounding in "Glen" names such as Glenloyne, Glengarry, Glenshiel and Glenaffric. This steamer continued active until the fall of 1965 and was scrapped at Hamilton, Ontario in 1966.

Motor Vessel GRAINMOTOR

OWNER: Canada Steamship Lines Limited
BUILT: Davie Shipbuilding & Repairing Company, Limited, Lauzon, Quebec—1929
HULL NO.: 503
O. A. DIMENSIONS: 257′ × 43′ × 25′7″
FORMER DATA: Deepened 5′1″ at Davie Shipbuilding Limited, Lauzon, Quebec in 1961.

Sold for off-lakes use in 1966, the Motor Vessel GRAINMOTOR was among the last "canaller" size vessels operated by this fleet. It is shown in the photograph below in the Lachine Canal at Montreal, Quebec.

The bulk freighter discussed here was built for the carriage of grain from Lake Superior directly through to Montreal and other Quebec grain receiving ports. It was designed to provide maximum cargo hold cubic measurement and for as much speed as was practical in a ship of its size.

From its first trip, it could be seen that the builders had done a commendable job. The fact that this vessel operated as long as any canaller in the fleet also testifies to this. Diesel power for Great Lakes vessels was becoming more commonplace by 1929, but this carrier was the first to be so equipped for the St. Lawrence River trade and to be successful.

Vessels that are powered by diesel engines are classed as "motor vessels" or "motor ships." It was the marriage of the trade for which this vessel was designed—GRAIN, and the type of propulsion system that it used—MOTOR that brought about the namesake. The owners felt that no more apropos name could be chosen that would be as meaningful as GRAINMOTOR since it tied together the trade of the ship and its type.

Steamer HAGARTY

OWNER:	Canada Steamship Lines Limited
BUILT:	Collingwood Shipbuilding Company, Limited, Collingwood, Ontario—1914
HULL NO.:	42
O. A. DIMENSIONS:	550' × 58'3" × 31'3"
FORMER DATA:	Launched as J. H. G. HAGARTY. Given last name in 1926.

The namesake was Sir John Hawkins Grassett Hagarty who was born in Dublin, Ireland on December 17, 1816. He was educated at Trinity College and went to Canada to settle in Toronto, Ontario in 1835. He was called to the bar of Upper Canada in 1840 and in 1856 was raised to the bench as a puisne judge of the court of Common Pleas. He was appointed a judge of the court of Queen's Bench in 1862, chief justice of Common Pleas in 1868, chief justice of Queen's Bench in 1878 and president of the Court of Appeal with the title Chief Justice of Ontario in 1884. He retired in 1897 and died at Toronto, Ontario on April 26, 1900. His namesake was sold for scrap in 1968.

During his many years as a prominent jurist he came into contact with powers of the Great Lakes shipping industry in Canada. His astute judgment and findings proved beneficial in many respects to the eventual large build-up of vessels in the Canadian fleet. He was also one of the principal owners of the St. Lawrence and Chicago Steam Navigation Company for whom this vessel was built.

This vessel is shown below while downbound with a cargo of grain from Thunder Bay, Ontario in the upper St. Mary's River. The maiden voyage of this ship was from Collingwood, Ontario on July 28, 1914, light for Detroit, Michigan where she went on drydock at Great Lakes Engineering Works to repair twenty-two damaged plates that were distorted during the launch.

Steamer HASTINGS

OWNER:	Canada Steamship Lines Limited
BUILT:	North of Ireland Shipbuilding Company, Londonderry, Ireland—1923
HULL NO.:	102
O. A. DIMENSIONS:	261' × 42'3" × 20'6"
FORMER DATA:	Launched as GLENCALVIE. Given last name in 1927.

The bulk freight canal-sized Steamer HASTINGS took its name from a small town of one thousand population in Northumberland County, Ontario. This town is located on the banks of the Trent River which was a major thoroughfare in the pioneer days of Canada's exploration. It is about thirty miles northeast of Cobourg, Ontario and twenty-five miles east of Peterborough, Ontario.

Hastings was first settled in 1795 by United Empire Loyalists and Missisauga Indians continued to inhabit the area until 1818. The Irish settlers came in the period between 1830 and 1840. In 1852 it dropped the former name of Crooks' Rapids and adopted the current name in honor of the Countess of Lowden, wife of the first Marquis of Hastings.

Today the primary income to the town and its residents comes from the tourist trade that is very prevalent in the summer. Boating on the famous Trent Canal and River provides many callers to the town and its nearby water-related service facilities.

The Steamer HASTINGS is seen in this picture with a full load of pulpwood upbound in the Welland Ship Canal, at the old Homer Wharf, on November 10, 1956. This vessel remained active in Great Lakes commerce until being sold for scrap in 1963.

Steamer KENORA

OWNER:	Canada Steamship Lines Limited
BUILT:	A. McMillan & Sons, Limited, Dumbarton, Scotland—1907
HULL NO.:	420
O. A. DIMENSIONS:	256' × 42'7" × 23'

The package freight Steamer KENORA was built to carry general cargo and continued to do so until being sold for scrap in 1959. It is shown in this photograph above Lock Twenty of the Cornwall Canal on September 1, 1957. The sideports which were typical ingredients of early package freighters can be seen along the ship side, particularly at the side lettering of the words "Lines" and the last part of the word "Steamship."

Kenora, Ontario is the namesake town of this vessel. It is the seat of the Kenora District of Ontario and the main Canadian center of commerce on Lake of the Woods. It is one hundred-twenty-five miles east of Winnipeg, Manitoba.

Kenora has a population of about 11,000 persons and is named from a combination of words. The *KE* in the name comes from the Indian word "Keewatin," a former trading territory to the north. The *NO* comes from "Norman," the name of an adjoining community. And the *RA* is credited to the original townsite name—Rat Portage.

This ship ran across the Atlantic Ocean in ballast and loaded its maiden cargo at Montreal, Quebec. It was a cargo of sugar, loaded November 26, 1907, for Hamilton, Ontario.

Steamer KINMOUNT (2)

OWNER: Canada Steamship Lines Limited
BUILT: Collingwood Shipbuilding Company Limited, Collingwood, Ontario—1923
HULL NO.: 72
O. A. DIMENSIONS: 261' × 43' × 19'9"
FORMER DATA: Launched as DALRYMPLE. Given last name in 1927.

The bulk freight Steamer KINMOUNT was launched on April 30, 1923 and served until 1927 for its original owners, The Main Transit Company. In 1927 it was sold to this fleet and renamed as indicated. The vessel was built to the maximum dimensions of the old St. Lawrence River canal system, as known in 1923. Slightly larger vessels were built in the 1950's which were deeper and had larger cubic measurements.

This stern view of the Steamer KINMOUNT shows her as she appeared at Port Colborne, Ontario, upper end of the Welland Ship Canal, on October 4, 1958. Within two years the vessel was reduced to scrap, having been sold for that end use in 1960 to the Steel Company of Canada at Hamilton, Ontario.

The namesake of this bulk freighter was the small town of four hundred population located in Victoria County, Ontario. It lies on the Burnt River about thirty-eight miles northeast of Lindsay, Ontario. Kinmount is largely a lumbering town today. Its exact position is 44.46 degrees north latitude and 78.40 degrees west longitude.

Steamer LEMOYNE (1)

```
         OWNER:  Canada Steamship Lines Limited
         BUILT:  Midland Shipbuilding Company Limited,
                 Midland, Ontario - 1926
       HULL NO.: 16
O. A. DIMENSIONS: 633' x 70'3" x 29'3"
   FORMER DATA: Launched as GLENMOHR. Given last name in 1926.
```

The bulk freight Steamer LEMOYNE (1) was the first seventy-foot beam vessel on the Great Lakes and the largest ship ever constructed for Great Lakes service when it was launched on June 23, 1926. On its maiden voyage it loaded 15,415 net tons of coal at Sandusky, Ohio August 19th and, on September 21st, took onboard a record cargo of wheat at Fort William, Ontario amounting to 518,000 bushels. On July 29, 1942 the Steamer LEMOYNE (1) set a new Great Lakes iron ore record when it departed Superior, Wisconsin for Hamilton, Ontario with 17,253 gross tons of ore.

This vessel is shown at Welland, Ontario in the Welland Ship Canal on May 1, 1965. It had passed this point literally hundreds of times during its career. That career ended when the ship was sold for overseas scrapping in 1968.

The namesake of this ship was the summer residence of Mr. William H. Coverdale who was president of Canada Steamship Lines when the vessel was built. The home was located near Portsmouth Bay just west of Kingston, Ontario. It had a name which referred to the Governor of Montreal from 1724 to 1729, Mr. Charles LeMoyne, 1st Baron de Longueuil.

Steamer LETHBRIDGE

OWNER: Canada Steamship Lines Limited
BUILT: Furness Shipbuilding Company Limited, Haverton Hill-on-Tees, England—1924
HULL NO.: 69
O. A. DIMENSIONS: 258' × 42'9" × 26'6"

Built for use through the old St. Lawrence River system of locks and canals, the Steamer LETHBRIDGE survived only two years after the opening of the large St. Lawrence Seaway and was sold for scrap in 1961. It is shown in the above photograph on August 31, 1958 at the Eastern Gap entrance to Toronto harbor.

This package freighter was named for the city of Lethbridge, Alberta, a city of 39,000 population located on the Oldman River about one hundred and forty miles southeast of Calgary, Alberta. It is on the Canadian Pacific Railway.

Lethbridge was originally known as Coalbanks when it was first settled in 1870 by Mr. Nicholas Sheran. The present name was adopted in 1885 in honor of Mr. William Lethbridge who was the first president of the North West Coal and Navigation Company which built the first narrow-gauge railroad from the town to supply Canadian Pacific Railway and United States buyers of coal.

Note the variety of general cargo on deck of this vessel. Automobiles, barrels, cable drums and packaged goods can be seen. Other smaller types of cargo are stowed below deck.

Steamer MAPLEHEATH

OWNER: Canada Steamship Lines Limited
BUILT: Swan, Hunter & Wigham Richardson Limited, Newcastle-on-Tyne, England—1911
HULL NO.: 840
O. A. DIMENSIONS: 261' × 42'6" × 19'10"
FORMER DATA: Launched as TOILER (1). Given last name in 1920.

Called in the Lake Carriers' Association Report for 1911, "the strangest looking vessel to visit the lake region during the year," this ship was originally built with two four-cylinder, 180 brake horsepower reversible Diesel oil engines of the two-cycle type. These were experimental engines and were replaced by conventional steam power in 1913 at Kingston, Ontario. The advent of this ship in Great Lakes service brought into being use of Diesel power which now had proven itself quite handsomely. An interesting original feature of this ship is that fuel oil was carried in the double bottom in place of water ballast, thus saving space in the hull and providing area for better cubic-oriented payloads such as grain.

The Steamer MAPLEHEATH was active on the Great Lakes until being sold for use as a salvage barge in 1959. It is shown below at the Eastern Gap entrance to Toronto, Ontario harbor on July 28, 1951. As can be seen, besides a full cargo in her holds, she is also transporting a full deckload of new English automobiles, including a Rolls-Royce in the left foreground.

The namesake of this vessel specifically related to the suffix in the ship name—HEATH, which refers to the heath family of shrubs to which maple brush belongs. These are found in 1,500 species, with 21 genera and 63 species native to Canada. The prefix of this ship name was a common fleet vessel name prefix in the early days of this firm and related to the national symbol, the maple leaf.

Steamer MARTIAN (2)

OWNER: Canada Steamship Lines Limited
BUILT: American Ship Building Company, Lorain, Ohio - 1901
HULL NO.: 305
O. A. DIMENSIONS: 366' x 48' x 28'
FORMER DATA: Launched as the bulk freighter NEPTUNE. Converted to a crane-equipped bulk freighter at American Ship Building Company, Lorain, Ohio in 1925. Reconverted to a bulk freighter at American Ship Building Company, Cleveland, Ohio and renamed WILLIAM M. CONNELLY in 1937. Given last name in 1948. Converted to a package freighter at Midland Shipbuilding Company Limited, Midland Ontario in 1950.

The package freight Steamer MARTIAN (2) is shown in this photograph being unloaded of a grain cargo at Humberstone, Ontario during the last years of its operation. It was retired from service in 1966 and sold for overseas scrapping in 1969.

The namesake of this ship was the supposed inhabitant of the planet Mars. The name was not new to the Great Lakes when it was placed on the bow of this vessel in 1948. In the 1920's and previously there existed a Steamer MARTIAN, but that ship had passed from the roles when this ship took up the name in 1948. This vessel was just carrying on a long tradition in the Canadian fleet of a ship named in reference to the planet Mars.

The first vessel was so named because of the high degree of speculation at the turn of this century that life existed on Mars. In stories and tales of adventure, Martians were envisioned visiting Earth. This was in the day that travel to the Moon seemed to be a farfetched possibility.

Steamer MEAFORD (2)

OWNER: Canada Steamship Lines Limited
BUILT: Collingwood Shipbuilding Company Limited, Collingwood, Ontario—1925
HULL NO.: 74
O. A. DIMENSIONS: 261' × 43' × 19'9"
FORMER DATA: Launched as ROBERT J. BUCK. Given last name in 1927.

The canal-size Steamer MEAFORD was sold for scrap in 1959, but the name was carried on by a bulk freighter of another fleet in later years.

Namesake of this bulk freighter is the town of Meaford, Ontario located in Nottawasaga Bay at the southern end of Georgian Bay and at the mouth of the Big Head River. The town of some 4,000 population is a terminus of the Canadian National Railways System and was originally named Stephenson's Landing. It was renamed for Meaford Hall, the Staffordshire estate of Admiral Sir John Jervis, Earl St. Vincent. The location was first settled in 1840 and was incorporated as a town in 1874.

There is no commercial vessel activity in the port today except for fishing operations, but in years when this ship was operating, sizable tonnages of coal and other commodities were received at the port facilities. It is a town from which many mariners have come over the years and this is a reason for its selection as a namesake of the Great Lakes ship. The town was also identified with the Playfair interests who originally built the ship.

The Steamer MEAFORD is shown in the photograph below between Locks One and Two of the Soulanges Canal at Cascades. At 2:00 PM on September 16, 1929, this vessel opened traffic at Lock Eight of the Welland Ship Canal, leading a parade of vessels to the interest of between 4,000 and 5,000 onlookers lining the banks at Ramey's Bend at Port Colborne, Ontario.

Steamer MIDLAND PRINCE

OWNER: Canada Steamship Lines Limited
BUILT: Collingwood Shipbuilding Company Limited, Collingwood, Onatario—1907
HULL NO.: 9
O. A. DIMENSIONS: 484' × 55' × 31'
FORMER DATA: Launched as a bulk freighter. Converted to a self-unloader at Midland Shipbuilding Company, Limited, Midland, Ontario in 1929.

The self-unloading Steamer MIDLAND PRINCE is shown above at Lock Eight of the Welland Ship Canal, at Port Colborne, Ontario on October 8, 1960. The vessel survived on the Great Lakes longer than most vessels of small size in this fleet and was finally sold for scrap in 1968.

Several ships were built in the 1905-10 era that had the city of Midland, Ontario as the reference in the first word of their shipname. All bore reference to nobility or members of a royal family in the second word of the shipname.

This ship was the last survivor in the group and honored all male members of royal families, with no one specific individual being honored. The first word of the shipname honored the city of Midland as mentioned above. Midland is a grain receiving port and point of entry in Georgian Bay. It is located in Simcoe County and is thirty-two miles northwest of both Barrie and Orillia, Ontario.

It was originally named Midland Harbour and was the terminus of the Midland Railway in 1872. It was incorporated as a village in 1878 and as a town in 1887. The current population of Midland is about 9,000 persons. The shipyard mentioned at the top of this page has been closed, but considerable vessel activity still abounds in the port in the grain, coal and quartzite trades.

Steamer PENETANG

OWNER:	Canada Steamship Lines Limited
BUILT:	Collingwood Shipbuilding Company Limited, Collingwood, Ontario—1925
HULL NO.:	75
O. A. DIMENSIONS:	261' × 43' × 19'9"
FORMER DATA:	Launched as WALTER B. REYNOLDS (1). Given last name in 1927.

The bulk freight Steamer PENETANG is shown here above Lock One of the Welland Ship Canal on October 11, 1958. It was sold the following year for scrap and met that fate in 1960 at Hamilton, Ontario.

Like so many of the early ships of this line, the Steamer PENETANG was named for a small town of pioneer or historic importance in the settlement of the Dominion of Canada. The town namesake of this ship is actually Penetanguishene, Ontario, but it is now commonly referred to as merely Penetang.

Penetang is an Indian word meaning, literally, "where the sand slides down the bank." The area was originally occupied by Ojibwa Indians but they relinquished their right to the Penetang Peninsula by a treaty in 1798. The town is located on an arm of Georgian Bay and is the terminus of the Canadian National Railways System in the area. It is thirty-three miles northwest of Barrie, Ontario.

Penetang was first visited by Etienne Brule in 1610 and was then visited by Champlain and Father Le Caron in 1615. In 1793 Governor Simcoe selected the site as his naval headquarters which was active in the War of 1812. The first permanent house was built there in 1828 by Dedin Revolte. Penetang was incorporated as a village in 1875 and as a town in 1882.

Steamer R. O. PETMAN

OWNER:	Canada Steamship Lines Limited
BUILT:	Canadian Shipbuilding Company, Bridgeburg, Ontario—1908
HULL NO.:	1
O. A. DIMENSIONS:	510' × 56' × 31'
FORMER DATA:	Launched as the bulk freighter E. B. OSLER. Renamed OSLER in 1926. Converted to a self-unloader at Collingwood Shipbuilding Company, Collingwood, Ontario in 1940. Given last name in 1954.

Mr. Robert Osmond Petman was this vessel's namesake. He was born August 1, 1886 at Toronto, Ontario and received his education in the public schools and Upper Canada College. From 1907 to 1910 he worked as a salesman for the Crescent Coal Company. In 1911 he was with Underhill Coal Company as a salesman and that same year joined the Weaver Coal Company.

In 1918, Mr. Petman was elected vice president of the Weaver Coal Company Limited, serving until 1926 when he became vice president of Canada Coal Corporation. In 1931 he became that firm's president and continued in that capacity until retirement in the early 1950's. He died at Bradenton, Florida on January 14, 1970.

Mr. Petman was also president of the Crespey Slate Products Company and was active in numerous other business and civic affairs. His namesake is shown in this picture at Toronto, Ontario on September 27, 1958. It continued in service on the Great Lakes until being sold for scrap in 1968. During its career as a collier, it transported literally millions of tons of coal.

Steamer PRESCOTT (2)

OWNER: Canada Steamship Lines Limited
BUILT: Detroit Shipbuilding Company, Wyandotte, Michigan - 1903
HULL NO.: 115
O. A. DIMENSIONS: 508' x 50'3" x 28'3"
FORMER DATA: Launched as WESTERN STAR. Renamed GLENISLA in 1918. Lengthened 72' at Collingwood Shipbuilding Company, Limited, Collingwood, Ontario in 1924. Given last name in 1926.

The Steamer PRESCOTT (2) is shown in its last days on the Great Lakes as a bulk freighter. May 5, 1962 was the date of this picture taken at Port Weller, Ontario as the ship was proceeding towards Lock One of the Welland Ship Canal with a cargo of iron ore. Later that year it was sold for scrap.

Prescott, Ontario is the namesake town of this vessel. That city of 5,400 is located in Grenville County on the St. Lawrence River, opposite Ogdensburg, New York. A bridge connects the two cities. Prescott is sixty-two miles south of Canada's capital, Ottawa, Ontario and it is sixty-one miles northeast of Kingston, Ontario.

Prescott is at the head of the rapids in the St. Lawrence River and was, before the opening of the St. Lawrence Seaway, the farthest east port which was reachable by large bulk freighters from Upper Lakes ports. As such, it was a tremendously busy trans-shipment port and could boast of the fastest unloading grain elevator on the Great Lakes.

The man for whom the town is named is Mr. Robert Prescott, later General Prescott, Governor-in-Chief of Canada from 1797 to 1807. He was born in Lancashire, England, April 22, 1725 and died at Rosegreen, England on December 21, 1815.

Steamer RENVOYLE (2)

OWNER:	Canada Steamship Lines Limited
BUILT:	Swan, Hunter & Wigham Richardson Limited, Wallsend-on-Tyne, England—1925
HULL NO.:	1271
O. A. DIMENSIONS:	390'6" × 44'3" × 27'
FORMER DATA:	Launched as GLENLEDI. Lengthened 126' at Collingwood Shipbuilding Company, Limited, Collingwood, Ontario in 1925. Given last name in 1926.

The package freight Steamer RENVOYLE had the distinction of carrying its own midbody addition in its holds as ballast on the maiden trans-Atlantic crossing from England to the Great Lakes. On arrival in the Lakes, the ship proceeded to Collingwood for the lengthening job. Pre-Seaway lock dimensions prevented her from coming into the Lakes in the 390'6" dimension. This ship served as an active vessel until being sold for scrap in 1968.

The namesake of this vessel is both obscure and unusual. There is no place in the world with a spelling exactly like that on this former ship's bow. The most extensive research proved that it was not a given name, but a place name which had been altered slightly by these owners for ease of pronouncing the name.

Like so many ships of her day, placenames from the British Isles were used since many management people of Canadian lines had their ancestry in that part of the world. Renvyle, Republic of Ireland was this vessel's namesake town. The letter "O" was inserted between the "V" and "Y" in the name for clarity of pronunciation. Renvyle is a locale of great beauty located on Killary Harbour below Clew Bay on the west coast of Ireland.

The vessel is seen in the picture above on October 27, 1956 at the northern end of the Welland Ship Canal.

Steamer RICHELIEU (2)

OWNER:	Canada Steamship Lines Limited
BUILT:	Harlan & Hollingsworth Corporation, Wilmington, Delaware—1913
HULL NO.:	420
O. A. DIMENSIONS:	340' × 48' × 21'6"
FORMER DATA:	Launched as NARRAGANSETT. Given last name in 1922.

The passenger Steamer RICHELIEU is shown here arriving at Murray Bay, Quebec on the St. Lawrence River in August, 1957. This vessel name is carried on today in the fleet on the bow of a maximum-size bulk freighter.

Richelieu County, Quebec is the namesake for this vessel. It borders to the north along the south shore of the St. Lawrence River and has a population of 41,000 residents. The name was given to the area in 1642 by Governor Montmagny in honor of Cardinal Richelieu who served there from 1582 through 1642.

The Richelieu River flows northward through the county, being the outlet from Lake Champlain in New York State, into Lake St. Peter which is a widening of the St. Lawrence River at Sorel, Quebec. The river varies from one thousand feet to one and one-half miles in width along its course.

This passenger ship was sold for scrap in 1965. Along with its sister ships, it was in the last remaining cruise trade on the St. Lawrence River.

Steamer ST. LAWRENCE (2)

OWNER: Canada Steamship Lines Limited
BUILT: Davie Shipbuilding and Repairing Company Limited, Lauzon, Quebec—1927
HULL NO.: 495
O. A. DIMENSIONS: 349'10" × 68' × 20'3"

This twin-stacked passenger vessel was named for the St. Lawrence River, a body of water on which it was built and through which it sailed for all of its days.

The St. Lawrence is one of the great rivers of the world. It is the final link in the water system that includes the Great Lakes and the St. Louis River extending 2,440 miles from Belle Isle, at the entrance to the Atlantic Ocean, to the heart of the state of Minnesota.

The river drains an area of 498,494 square miles and flows northeastward from Lake Ontario into the Gulf of St. Lawrence at the west end of Anticosti Island, Quebec. The river name comes from the fact that Jacques Cartier entered Pillage Bay on August 10, 1535 which is the Feast of St. Lawrence. He named the river in honor of that saint.

The Steamer ST. LAWRENCE is shown in this picture passing under the Jacques Cartier bridge at the eastern end of Montreal Harbor where the St. Lawrence Seaway now joins the river below Lachine Rapids. The fine passenger ship cruised the St. Lawrence and Saguenay Rivers until its disposition for off-lakes use in 1965.

Steamer SASKATOON (2)

OWNER: Canada Steamship Lines Limited
BUILT: Midland Shipbuilding Company Limited, Midland, Ontario - 1927
HULL NO.: 20
O. A. DIMENSIONS: 254'3" x 42'9" x 26'

The canal-sized package freight Steamer SASKATOON (2) was sold for partial scrapping in 1961 and was re-sold for use as a breakwater several years later. It is shown in this photograph on November 21, 1959 in the Welland Ship Canal.

Namesake of this vessel was the city of 120,000 population located on the South Saskatchewan River one hundred-seventy miles southwest of Regina and in the center of population of the province of Saskatchewan. Saskatoon is the second largest city in the province and is served by both the Canadian National Railways and the Canadian Pacific Railway Company. It is sometimes known as the "Hub City" because of the excellent transportation routes to and from the area.

The city name comes from the Cree Indian word "missasktoomina" which was a name given an edible berry found in abundance in the area. Saskatoon was first settled in 1883 and had a sawmill, store, school and ferry service on the river by a year later. It was incorporated as a village in 1901 and as a town in 1903. In 1906 Saskatoon and the neighboring communities of Nutana and Riverdale were amalgamated as the city of Saskatoon.

Today, Saskatoon has important industries in the fields of grain milling and meat packing. In fact, the largest independent meat-packing operation in Western Canada is located in the city.

Steamer SELKIRK (3)

OWNER: Canada Steamship Lines Limited
BUILT: Davie Shipbuilding & Repairing Company, Limited, Lauzon, Quebec—1926
HULL NO.: 494
O. A. DIMENSIONS: 261' × 42'9" × 26'6"

The 3,000 gross ton capacity package freight Steamer SELKIRK is shown entering Toronto, Ontario harbor through the Eastern Gap on September 8, 1956 in the above photograph. It continued to serve in this line until being sold for scrap in 1964.

Namesake of this vessel was the city of ten thousand population located on the west bank of the Red River in Manitoba. It is twenty-three miles north of the capital city of Winnipeg and is the head of deepwater navigation from Lake Winnipeg. It is the inland port for fishing and freight vessels going to and coming from northern Manitoba ports on Lake Winnipeg. The city is served by the Canadian Pacific Railway Company and several good highways.

Selkirk was first settled in 1767 when two independent fur-traders set up business in the area. In the 1830's St. Peter's Indian mission was established. Gradual further development occurred until the town was incorporated in 1882. It was named for Mr. Thomas Douglas, 5th Earl of Selkirk who was a colonizer and philanthropist. He was born June 20, 1771 on St. Mary's Isle, Scotland and died at Pau, France on April 8, 1820.

Since 1917 the main industrial activity in Selkirk has been steel. Manitoba Rolling Mills and Manitoba Steel Foundry are the largest employers and economic mainstays of the city. The hinterland area has some agricultural activity, but not to the extent that it is found in areas south and west of Winnipeg.

Steamer SIMCOE (1)

OWNER:	Canada Steamship Lines Limited
BUILT:	Swan, Hunter & Wigham Richardson Limited, Wallsend-on-Tyne, England—1923
HULL NO.:	1195
O. A. DIMENSIONS:	261' × 42'6" × 20'6"
FORMER DATA:	Launched as GLENCORRIE. Given last name in 1927.

The canal-sized bulk freight Steamer SIMCOE was sold from this fleet in 1961 and was turned into a drill barge operating in the natural gas fields of Lake Erie on the Canadian side of that lake until sold for scrap in 1974.

Simcoe County, Ontario which is located north of Toronto, near Georgian Bay, is the namesake of this ship. The county consists largely of inland lakes and many wooded environs which attract tourists in large numbers during the summertime.

The county was named in honor of Mr. John Graves Simcoe, first Lieutenant Governor of Upper Canada, in 1829. It was first settled by white men before the end of the eighteenth century and had a population of about 145,000 according to the last census figures.

The area is noted for fine fishing, water sports and leisure woodsmen's activities. Dairying, farming of several crops, light industry, tourism and lumbering are the chief activities.

The Steamer SIMCOE is shown here below Lock Two of the Welland Ship Canal on November 12, 1955.

Steamer STARMOUNT

OWNER:	Canada Steamship Lines Limited
BUILT:	Dunlop, Brenner & Company Limited, Port Glasgow, Scotland—1923
HULL NO.:	348
O. A. DIMENSIONS:	259' × 43' × 19'
FORMER DATA:	Launched as PABJUNE. Renamed STARMOUNT in 1927.

The bulk freight Steamer STARMOUNT actually existed on the Great Lakes for two years after having been sold in 1961. It had been sold to Diesel Sales & Service, Limited and was converted to a barge by that firm and renamed GOOD STAR. When liquidation of the firm took place in April, 1962, this hull was sold for scrap at auction. As a going steamer, the STARMOUNT is shown in this photograph at Humberstone, Ontario in the Welland Ship Canal on October 26, 1957.

Canada Steamship Lines renamed four freighters in 1927, all with a common suffix in the ship name—MOUNT. These were: FAIRMOUNT, KINMOUNT, ROSEMOUNT and STARMOUNT. All of these ships took places as their namesakes except this vessel. The suffix MOUNT was used to carry out the theme of common name endings in that year which suffix was inherited in this fleet in 1920 from ships it acquired from the Montreal Transportation Company. The specific namesake of this vessel was the North Star or Polaris, which has guided mariners throughout the world since the beginning of time.

Wherever one may be in the northern latitudes, the direction north may be found by reference to this star. Polaris can easily be located because the two stars Merak and Dubhe, in Ursa Major, also known as the Big Dipper or Great Bear, always point towards it. Polaris is the brightest star in the constellation Ursa Minor, or Little Bear. The name of the star is derived from the Greek language and means, literally, "center of attraction."

Steamer TADOUSSAC (3)

```
        OWNER:    Canada Steamship Lines Limited
        BUILT:    Davie Shipbuilding and Repairing Company Limited,
                  Lauzon, Quebec—1928
      HULL NO.:   496
O. A. DIMENSIONS: 370' × 70' × 21'
```

The twin-stacked passenger Steamer TADOUSSAC is shown in this photograph in the St. Lambert Lock in 1959 on one of its Seaway cruises that year. The vessel was sold for overseas use in 1965 and has begun a new career as a floating hotel for immigrant workers at Copenhagen, Denmark.

This name is carried on today on the bow of the modern self-unloader, also equipped with two stacks, which began service in 1969.

Tadoussac, Quebec is the namesake of this vessel. It is the oldest settlement in Canada, having been visited by Jacques Cartier on September 1, 1535. It is now the seat of Saguenay County and is located about one hundred-four miles northeast of Quebec City on the north shore of the St. Lawrence River where the Saguenay River joins the St. Lawrence.

In 1615 Recollet Jean Dolbeau built the first mission to the Indians at this site which was taken over by the Jesuits in 1641. Tourist traffic dates from 1853 and has had much to do with development in the area. This passenger ship used to call at the site on regular schedules, bringing hundreds of people to visit the town.

Steamer TEAKBAY

OWNER: Canada Steamship Lines Limited
BUILT: Smith's Dock Company, Limited, South Bank-on-Tees, England—1929
HULL NO.: 870
O. A. DIMENSIONS: 259' × 43'9" × 20'6"

The canal size bulk freighter shown here was originally built to the order of Tree Line Navigation Company, Limited which had a common theme of vessel names. Ships had the common suffix BAY and specifically were named for various types of trees or wood as denoted by the prefix of the ship name. These last owners carried the ship name forward when they acquired the vessel in 1945.

The Steamer TEAKBAY was active until being sold for scrap in 1964. It is shown in this picture on October 26, 1956 in the Cardinal Canal of the former St. Lawrence River system.

Teak is a tree of the verbena family coming from southeast Asia, primarily India, Burma and Thailand. The wood of the teak tree is highly valued for shipbuilding and for furniture manufacturing. It resembles coarse mahogany and is strong and durable and water resistant, making it ideal for decking on power and sail boats.

The trees grow to an average height of one hundred feet and in groups with other trees. The leaves often grow to two feet in length and are about one and one-half feet in width. Teak trees also grow in Africa. Though their wood is valuable also, it is not as durable as Asian teak and, hence, is not used so prevalently in the pleasure boat construction business.

Steamer WESTMOUNT (2)

        OWNER: Canada Steamship Lines Limited
        BUILT: Collingwood Shipbuilding Company Limited,
                              Collingwood, Ontario—1917
    HULL NO.:   48
O. A. DIMENSIONS: 550' × 58'3" × 31'3"

The bulk freight Steamer WESTMOUNT honored the English-speaking suburb of the City of Montreal, Quebec in its name. Many of the executives of this fleet and other Canadian shipping firms live in Westmount, Quebec which is a city of fine homes and parks.

Westmount is totally surrounded by Montreal and is in a real sense a city within a city. It was originally known as Notre Dame de Grace when just a village. In 1873 the area was granted status as a town and the present name was in use. Westmount became a city in 1908. Over 26,000 residents call this pleasant city "home."

The Steamer WESTMOUNT is shown in the picture below while being unloaded at the C. S. L. grain elevator at Midland, Ontario on August 20, 1956. The vessel served as a bulk freighter all of its life, but was adapted to the carriage of new automobiles on deck for part of a season in the early 1960's. Slats were placed between the hatches to form a solid wooden platform on which to carry the vehicles. This carriage was primarily upbound with the vessel again returning to the usual bulk trades for the downbound trips.

After fifty years of service, this ship was sold for overseas scrapping in 1967. This ship was one of the first to be sold for scrap of the larger vessels in this fleet with the trend towards total utilization of maximum-size vessels in full swing.

Steamer WEYBURN

OWNER: Canada Steamship Lines Limited
BUILT: Midland Shipbuilding Company Limited, Midland, Ontario—1927
HULL NO.: 21
O. A. DIMENSIONS: 261' × 42'9" × 26'6"

Sold for off-lakes use in 1963, the package freight Steamer WEYBURN is shown in the photograph above in the Soulanges Canal on October 21, 1958.

Weyburn, Saskatchewan is the namesake of this ship. The city of ten thousand residents is located sixty-eight miles southeast of Regina, Saskatchewan and is an important rail center for international business, being situated on both the Canadian Pacific Railway and the Soo Line Rail Road.

It is also well connected by land routes with highways #13, #35 and #39 intersecting at the site. The Souris River flows past the city and provides water for industrial and domestic uses. The area was first settled in 1892 and was incorporated as a village in 1900. It was granted town status in 1903 and formally became a city in 1913. Weyburn is a marketing and distribution center for the large grain producing area which surrounds it.

The name of the city is believed to have come from early Scottish settlers who described the river as "wee burn." Interestingly enough, a brand of Scotch whiskey is also known by this name today. This ship is among those in the fleet of Canada Steamship Lines which were named for towns and cities throughout the Dominion. All of these locales were important to varying degrees in the pioneering development of Canada.

Steamer WINNIPEG (3)

OWNER: Canada Steamship Lines Limited
BUILT: Davie Shipbuilding & Repairing Company, Limited, Lauzon, Quebec - 1926
HULL NO.: 493
O. A. DIMENSIONS: 261' x 42'9" x 26'6"

The package freight Steamer WINNIPEG (3) is shown above in the Welland Ship Canal on September 7, 1959. Note the deck kingposts for the handling of cargo. The ship was sold for scrap in 1964 after newer and much faster vessels were brought into service.

Namesake of this ship is the capital of the Province of Manitoba. Winnipeg is a city of 500,000 persons located at the junction of the Assiniboine and Red Rivers some sixty miles north of the United States border. It is the largest population center between central Canada and the West Coast.

The city name comes from the Cree Indian word "win-nipiy" which means murky water. The waters in the rivers at the point where first settlers made camp in 1811-12 undoubtedly were reflective of the Indian name. Vast areas of prairie surround Winnipeg and are the growing regions for massive tonnages of grain.

Winnipeg was incorporated as a city in 1873 and in 1887 the Winnipeg Grain Exchange was formed. This body of traders, shippers and brokers is the heart of all Canadian grain activity and is the scene of daily deals in grain involving millions of dollars. It is one of the great grain marketing centers of the world. No less than seven Canadian Great Lakes fleets have special brokerage offices in Winnipeg to facilitate the chartering of their vessels in the grain trade.

Motor Vessel ESKIMO

OWNER:	Canada Steamship Lines Inc.
BUILT:	Davie Shipbuilding, Limited, Lauzon, Quebec - 1959
HULL NO.:	617
O. A. DIMENSIONS:	360' x 51' x 30'
FORMER DATA:	Launched as a bulk freighter. Converted to a package freighter at Davie Shipbuilding, Limited, Lauzon, Quebec in 1964.

The package freight Motor Vessel ESKIMO has a name out of keeping with the rest of the package freight fleet of this company. The name was so designated because this carrier was originally constructed to operate in the Arctic to supply northern bases. After several years of that operation, however, it was converted to its present class. It is similar in many ways to the "Fort" class ships, except that the original name is retained.

Eskimos are the people occupying all of the northern coasts of America from Greenland and Labrador in the east to the Bering Sea in the west. They number approximately fifty-five thousand today. The Eskimos are divided into five chief groups which are: Labrador Eskimos, Central Eskimos, Caribou Eskimos, Copper Eskimos and Mackenzie Eskimos.

After three years of nominal lay-up and operation, this ship was sold for off-lakes use in June, 1980, however, in 1985 it returned to the Great Lakes, and appears in NAMESAKES OF THE '90'S."

Steamer TRANSLAKE

OWNER: Canadian Coastwise Carriers Limited
BUILT: Societe Anciens Etab. Henri Satre, Arles-sur-Rhone, France—1921
HULL NO.: 11
O. A. DIMENSIONS: 229'6" × 34'3" × 14'9"
FORMER DATA: Launched as the bulk freighter PIENTRE. Renamed BIESSARD in 1921. Renamed POPLARBAY in 1923. Converted to a tanker at Muir Brothers Dry Dock Company, Limited, Port Dalhousie, Ontario and renamed TRANSLAKE in 1937.

The Steamer TRANSLAKE was laid-up for a short while prior to its disposition for off-lakes use in 1962 as the barge HALFUELER at Halifax, Nova Scotia. Its name honors the operating company in the prefix of the ship name, namely, TRANS as short for Transit Tankers and Terminals Limited.

The suffix of the shipname is the specific namesake and in it all the lakes of the world are honored. No particular lake, but all in general as bodies of water are included.

On August 30, 1950 this vessel departed Humberstone, Ontario for Montreal, Quebec with a deck load of 50 tons of flour in bags. This was the first instance of a Canadian tanker transporting a deck cargo in addition to its usual liquid cargo in the ship tanks.

The Steamer TRANSLAKE is shown in the above photograph above Lock One of the Welland Ship Canal on November 8, 1952.

Steamer TRANSRIVER

OWNER: Canadian Coastwise Carriers Limited
BUILT: Societe Anonyme de Travaux Dyle & Bacalan, Bordeaux, France—1920
HULL NO.: 1
O. A. DIMENSIONS: 229'6" × 34' × 14'9"
FORMER DATA: Launched as the bulk freighter GRÉEUR. Renamed SOTTEVILLE in 1922. Renamed MAPLEBAY in 1923. Converted to a tanker at Les Chantiers Manseau Limitee, Sorel, Quebec and given last name in 1937.

The Steamer TRANSRIVER is shown here entering Toronto Harbor in its last colors on the Lakes. The ship was sold for off-lakes use in 1964 after having laid idle for several years in Montreal, Quebec.

The prefix of this ship name refers to the operating company title and a shortening of the first word in that title as previously explained.

The suffix of the ship name is the specific reference and is to all the world's rivers. No particular river, but all of them in general are honored. Since man first traveled by other than foot, rivers have been important arteries for commerce and pleasure the world over.

Rivers usually start far up in mountains or hills or may have their origin from a small spring or large lake. The forks of a river, called tributaries, together with the river itself are known as a river system. Large areas of land are drained by such systems throughout the world.

Steamer TRANSTREAM

OWNER:	Canadian Coastwise Carriers Limited
BUILT:	Horton Steel Works Limited, Fort Erie, Ontario—1935
HULL NO.:	2513
O. A. DIMENSIONS:	250' × 34'3" × 15'8"
FORMER DATA:	Launched as TRANSITER. Lengthened 32' at Les Chantiers Manseau Limitee, Sorel, Quebec in 1937. Lengthened 41'6" at Muir Brothers Dry Dock Company, Limited, Port Dalhousie, Ontario and renamed TRANSTREAM in 1942.

The Steamer TRANSTREAM was sold for off-lakes use in 1970 and made the journey to the Caribbean Sea late in May of that year as the Steamer WITSUPPLY. It had previously been idle at Montreal, Quebec for several years.

Like some other ships in the fleet operated by Transit Tankers and Terminals Limited, this vessel had the common fleet prefix, *TRANS*, as part of the ship name. The suffix *STREAM*, minus the second "s," is the specific namesake of this tanker. This name carries on the theme of specific names of ships for water-related things or objects in the fleet.

A stream may be defined as "a body of running water, such as a creek or brook, flowing on the surface of the earth." It may also refer to a beam of light and a continuous moving procession, as in a line of cars. However, the stream meaning which is relevant to this ship bears only upon the word meaning in reference to the subject of water and its flow.

The Steamer TRANSTREAM is shown above in the Port Weller, Ontario approach to Lock One of the Welland Ship Canal on June 13, 1964.

Steamer NORTH AMERICAN

OWNER: Canadian Holiday Line
BUILT: Great Lakes Engineering Works, Ecorse, Michigan—1913
HULL NO.: 107
O. A. DIMENSIONS: 291' × 47'10" × 18'3"

This passenger ship was named for the continent on which it served-North America. North America is the northern part of the land mass comprising the Americas of the Western Hemisphere, which comprises the continental United States, Canada, Mexico and the countries and islands of the Caribbean area.

North America is bounded on the north by the Arctic Ocean, on the west by the North Pacific Ocean and Bering Sea, on the east by the North Atlantic Ocean with the Caribbean Sea and the Gulf of Mexico to the south. It is separated in the northeast from Greenland by Baffin Bay.

Canada and the United States are outstandingly rich in natural resources and both possess highly industrialized economies. The Great Lakes area, in which this ship sailed, is at the heart of the North American continent.

This ship served actively until being sold in 1963 at auction. In 1964 it operated for a short time in the Canadian Holiday Line but when this failed it changed hands several times until being bought for off-lakes use in the fall of 1967. It sank in four hundred feet of water at 40 degrees, 46 minutes north latitude and 68 degrees, 53.02 minutes west longitude enroute to its destination in the Atlantic Ocean. The vessel is shown above leaving Toronto, Ontario on its last trip on June 11, 1964.

Steamer ASSINIBOIA

OWNER:	Canadian Pacific Railway Company
BUILT:	Fairfield Shipbuilding & Engineering Company, Limited, Govan, Scotland—1907
HULL NO.:	452
O. A. DIMENSIONS:	346' × 43'9" × 23'6"
FORMER DATA:	Cut in two at the Government Drydock, Lauzon, Quebec in 1907. Re-assembled at Buffalo Dry Dock Company, Buffalo, New York in 1907.

The combination passenger-package freight Steamer ASSINIBOIA was one of the last regularly scheduled ships to operate on the Great Lakes. Along with its sister ship, it plyed the Georgian Bay-Thunder Bay route for its entire career on the Great Lakes. It is shown in the above photograph at Sault Ste. Marie, Ontario on August 27, 1966 in the freight-only service which she maintained from cessation of passenger service in 1965 until her retirement in 1967. It was sold and taken from the Lakes in 1968 and burned at its pier in Philadelphia, Pennsylvania in 1969.

Assiniboia is a rich agricultural district of Saskatchewan, Canada served by the railroad which owned this vessel. This district was absorbed into the Dominion of Canada by an act of 1905. Its southern border ran to the United States. This district was formerly in the Northwest Territories with a land area of 88,879 square miles.

A town still exists with the name. It is 67 miles southwest of Moose Jaw, Saskatchewan and is a junction point of the Canadian Pacific. In very early times, Assinboin Indians inhabited the Red River Settlement of Lord Selkirk. This area had the name Assiniboia as its official name.

Steamer KEEWATIN (2)

OWNER: Canadian Pacific Railway Company
BUILT: Fairfield Shipbuilding & Engineering Company, Limited, Govan, Scotland—1907
HULL NO.: 453
O. A. DIMENSIONS: 346' × 43'9" × 23'6"
FORMER DATA: Cut in two at the Government Drydock, Lauzon, Quebec in 1907. Re-assembled at Buffalo Dry Dock Company, Buffalo, New York in 1907.

This ship, with the ASSINIBOIA, was the partner on the Georgian Bay-Thunder Bay run for many years. Serving in the passenger-package freight trade for all but the last years of its life, the Steamer KEEWATIN was known for its fine accommodations and good speed. It is shown in this photograph at Sault Ste. Marie, Ontario on August 18, 1957. It was a fitting end that met this vessel. Running actively until the fall of 1965, it was sold for use as a museum at Saugatuck, Michigan in 1966 and was brought to that port in the summer of 1967.

Like its sistership, this vessel was given a name in honor of one of the districts of western Canada. Keewatin is the most easterly district of the three divisions of the Northwest Territories. It is bounded on the east by Hudson Bay and Foxe Channel, on the west by the district of Mackenzie and on the south by the province of Manitoba. It has an area of 228,160 square miles.

Most of the area is tundra with frequent rock outcrops and many lakes and marshes. It is sparsely forested and populated. Keewatin is a Cree Indian name meaning "the north wind."

Steamer CALUMET

OWNER: Cargo Carriers, Incorporated
BUILT: Detroit Shipbuilding Company, Wyandotte, Michigan—1907
HULL NO.: 171
O. A. DIMENSIONS: 440' × 52' × 28'

Shown below entering Lock Seven of the Welland Ship Canal in May of 1956, the bulk freight Steamer CALUMET was one of three ships operated steadily in the Upper Lakes to Lower Lakes bulk trades of this owning company until the firm ceased Great Lakes operations of United States flag vessels in 1958. This ship was sold for scrap in 1960.

Namesake of this freighter was the Calumet Mine of the Menominee Range which was managed by Pickands Mather & Company, long-time owners of this vessel through the Interlake Steamship Company. The Calumet Mine shipped 5,847 gross tons of hard, red, siliceous iron ore during its first year of production in 1882.

The property was not a large producer and shipped only 175,917 tons of ore, intermittently, before its closing in 1913. The name Calumet comes from the popular Indian name for the ceremonial pipe. The Indians had pipes of various shapes and sizes made of clay, stone or bone, but the ceremonial pipe was usually of larger size and made of red catlinite from the pipestone quarry in Minnesota. The stem was made long, of wood or reed ornamented with feathers and porcupine quills. Native tobacco, mixed with willow bark or sumac leaves was used for the smoking material. Although frequently referred to as "the peace pipe," the ceremonial pipe was, in fact, used in ratification of all solemn engagements, of both war and peace.

Motor Vessel CARPORT/G1

OWNER:	Cargo Carriers, Incorporated
BUILT:	Christy Corporation, Sturgeon Bay, Wisconsin—1950
HULL NO.:	367
O. A. DIMENSIONS:	300' × 43'6" × 21'

On February 21, 1950 this firm signed the contract for construction of this integrated unit of a tug and barge. It called for construction of the first tank barge ever built on the Great Lakes exclusively for the transportation of food products. The concept was to carry soybean oil from Chicago, Illinois to New York City via the New York State Barge Canal and return to the Great Lakes with molasses.

This unit was only marginally successful in practice, not because of its design, but because of the changing trade patterns and labor difficulties in manning. It is shown above while upbound in the St. Mary's River heading towards Lake Superior to take on a cargo of grain. It remained on the Great Lakes until it was sold for off-lakes use in 1962. The tug-barge unit cleared South Chicago, Illinois November 11, 1950 with corn and soybean oil for Buffalo, New York and New York City on its maiden voyage.

It is interesting to note that the tug-barge concept is now regaining favor and that this design pre-dated the current concepts by 20 years!

The namesake of this power unit, CARPORT, was the terminal of Cargill, Incorporated located at Savage, Minnesota and known as Port Cargill. The prefix of the name was common to all power units in the Cargill/Cargo Carriers fleets. The barge designation G1 merely followed in the letter and numbering sequency of the owning company.

Steamer HEMLOCK

OWNER: Cargo Carriers, Incorporated
BUILT: West Bay City Shipbuilding Company, West Bay City, Michigan—1907
HULL NO.: 624
O. A. DIMENSIONS: 440' × 52' × 28'

This vessel was one of several in the fleets managed by, and later owned and managed by, Pickands Mather & Company which was named for a mining property. The last owners never saw fit to rename this ship when they acquired it in 1955. It remained active on the Great Lakes until being sold for scrap in 1960.

The Hemlock Mine at Amasa, Michigan was the namesake of this bulk freighter. The mine was located on the Chicago & Northwestern Railway on the Menominee Range and was opened in 1891. In that year it shipped 35,531 gross tons of iron ore. The mine forwarded iron ore each year through 1919, except 1894 and 1917. This tonnage amounted to 2,125,756 of hard, red, high phosphorus ore.

The Hemlock Mine was officially closed in 1938 after a clean-up tonnage of only 75 tons was shipped to Escanaba, Michigan for the lower lakes.

In this fleet the Steamer HEMLOCK carried iron ore, coal and grain, but was primarily purchased to insure the dependable and low-cost delivery of grain for the parent firm, Cargill, Incorporated. In the photograph below, the vessel is shown while the ship was downbound in the St. Mary's River on August 28, 1957.

Steamer HARRY R. JONES

OWNER:	Cargo Carriers, Incorporated
BUILT:	Superior Shipbuilding Company, Superior, Wisconsin—1903
HULL NO.:	509
O. A. DIMENSIONS:	468' × 52' × 28'
FORMER DATA:	Launched as D. G. KERR (1). Given last name in 1916.

This bulk freighter ran aground in the lower Detroit River in November, 1958 and, though capable of grain storage use at Buffalo, New York, it was never repaired for service. It was finally sold for overseas scrapping in 1960.

Mr. Harry Ross Jones was the namesake of this ship. He was born at Youngstown, Ohio on June 27, 1869 and graduated from Rayon High School in 1888. Mr. Jones first employment was with the Youngstown Bridge Company as a draftsman in 1889. In 1892 he joined the Variety Iron Works of Cleveland, Ohio. He remained with that firm until 1899 except for two years, 1893-94 when he was with the Columbus Bridge Company at Columbus, Ohio.

Mr. Jones and Mr. Harry M. Geiger organized Geiger, Jones & Company as a security and financial house to assist the steel firms and other afflicted industries in 1904 at Canton, Ohio. They were most successful in this and on reorganization in 1914, Mr. Jones became president of a firm known as United Alloy Steel Corporation. He held this post until retiring in 1921 to devote his time to banking and finance. He was chairman of the board of the Union Metal Manufacturing Company and the First Trust and Savings Bank when he died on December 4, 1936 at Canton, Ohio.

Mr. Jones' namesake is shown on August 12, 1957 while upbound in the Welland Ship Canal after having discharged grain at Oswego, New York.

Steamer JUPITER (2)

OWNER:	Cargo Carriers, Incorporated
BUILT:	American Ship Building Company, Lorain, Ohio - 1901
HULL NO.:	308
O. A. DIMENSIONS:	366' x 48' x 28'
FORMER DATA:	Launched as a bulk freighter. Converted to a crane-equipped bulk freighter at American Ship Building Company, Lorain, Ohio in 1927. Re-converted to a bulk freighter at American Ship Building Company, Cleveland, Ohio in 1937.

The small bulk freight Steamer JUPITER (2) ran for only a very short time in this fleet in 1957 and was then relegated to use as a floating grain storage hull at South Chicago, Illinois until it was sold for scrap in 1958. It met that fate at Hamilton, Ontario in 1959. The ship is shown in the photograph below on one of the few trips it made under Cargo Carriers' colors in the St. Mary's River below Sault Ste. Marie, Michigan. It had the distinction of delivering the first cargo of quartzite ever brought to Lorain, Ohio, doing so on August 21, 1946 when it arrived from Little Current, Ontario.

The namesake of this ship was the planet Jupiter, largest planet in the solar system. This vessel was originally managed by the Gilchrist Transportation Company and was one of several ships taking their names from planets of the earth's solar system.

Jupiter has a huge mass, being nearly three times as great as the combined masses of all the other planets in the solar system. Its orbit is about five and one-fifth times as far from the sun as that of the earth, or at a mean distance of 483,300,000 miles. Its mean distance from the earth when in opposition is about 390,000,000 miles, and it moves around the sun in eleven years and 314.92 days. Jupiter's mean diameter is about 86,500 miles.

Steamer CAYUGA (1)

OWNER:	Cayuga Navigation Company Limited
BUILT:	Canadian Shipbuilding Company, Toronto, Ontario—1906
HULL NO.:	100
O. A. DIMENSIONS:	317'6" × 36'6" × 15'

The passenger Steamer CAYUGA began service in 1907 between Toronto, Ontario and the Niagara River across Lake Ontario. It continued active in this run until Canada Steamship Lines Limited announced abandonment of the service on January 25, 1952. The vessel was sold to these owners in 1953. This firm floated a successful new issue of stock which brought in $140,000 for the purpose of restoring the ship to class and beginning operations. The first sailing under the new arrangement was on June 5, 1954.

The Steamer CAYUGA is shown above at the Eastern Gap of Toronto, Ontario harbor on September 3, 1956. It was sold for scrap in 1960 and met that fate at Toronto, Ontario in 1961.

The namesake of this vessel was the Cayuga Indian tribe of the Iroquois federation which formerly occupied the shores of Lake Cayuga in New York State. The tribe's local council was composed of four clans and this structure became the pattern of the confederation of the Five Nations of the Iroquois.

The Cayuga fought on the side of the British during the American Revolution and at the close of the war numbered little more than one thousand in population. Since that time the tribe has intermixed in marriage with whites and other Indians and it has lost all of its identity.

Steamer CITY OF SAGINAW 31

OWNER: Chesapeake and Ohio Railway Company
BUILT: Manitowoc Shipbuilding Company, Manitowoc, Wisconsin – 1929
HULL NO.: 246
O. A. DIMENSIONS: 381'6" x 57' x 22'6"

The passenger and freight carferry Steamer CITY OF SAGINAW 31 suffered fire damage in 1971 which was never repaired. It was sold for scrap early in 1973 and was towed overseas to meet that fate. It is shown above departing Milwaukee, Wisconsin in July, 1964.

The number 31 in this ship name designates this carferry as being powered by a turbo-electric engine. It thus carries on the numbering sequence for this fleet for power plant class. The railway used this naming theme for various classes of vessels in the fleet.

The specific identifiable namesake of this vessel was the city of Saginaw, Michigan. Saginaw is a manufacturing center of about 140,000 population located on the Saginaw River off Saginaw Bay, Lake Huron. It was settled in 1820 when Fort Saginaw was established on the west bank of the river. In 1849 East Saginaw was formed on the opposite bank, and in 1889, the two settlements merged into one community as the city of Saginaw.

Farms near the city produce large crops of sugar beets and volumes of these find their way into Great Lakes export commerce. Grain, general cargo, bulk cargo and petroleum products are also handled in the modern day port.

Steamer PERE MARQUETTE 14

OWNER: Chesapeake and Ohio Railway Company
BUILT: Detroit Shipbuilding Company, Wyandotte, Michigan—1904
HULL NO.: 156
O. A. DIMENSIONS: 350' × 52' × 21'

Like other carfloat vessels in this fleet, the Steamer PERE MARQUETTE 14 took its name from the railroad line that originally built it and the number 14 behind that name was merely a sequence numbering of ships in the general category of river car floats. This was an internal designation and bore no specific reference to anything outside the line.

The Steamer PERE MARQUETTE 14 was active until it was sold for scrap in 1957. It is shown here with a full deck load of freight cars at Windsor, Ontario in 1950.

The Pere Marquette Railroad Company operated as a separate entity serving the lower part of the state of Michigan and parts of Ontario until it was merged into the Chesapeake and Ohio Railway Company. The last owners of this vessel and its sisterships kept the first two words in the ship names because of the historical significance of them.

Father Jacques Marquette was honored both in the name of the railroad and in its fleet of ships. The French word for father is "Pere" and this company name reflected that national word usage.

Steamer PERE MARQUETTE 18 (2)

OWNER: Chesapeake and Ohio Railway Company
BUILT: Chicago Shipbuilding Company, Chicago, Illinois—1911
HULL NO.: 77
O. A. DIMENSIONS: 350' × 56' × 20'6"

The Steamer PERE MARQUETTE 18 (2) was a trans-Lake Michigan unit of this fleet. It carried automobiles and passengers as well as freight cars of the railroad. It is shown above at Milwaukee, Wisconsin. This vessel remained in service until it was sold for scrap in 1957.

This vessel was constructed in 100 days and was built to replace a ship of the same name that was sunk in 1910. It sailed from Chicago, Illinois on January 27, 1911 for Ludington, Michigan to join the fleet and was placed in service from that port on January 30, 1911 when it departed for Milwaukee, Wisconsin.

As in the case of other units in this fleet, the number following the PERE MARQUETTE name designated this vessel's class. The number assigned in this case was in a sequence of numbers which were used to designate larger trans-lake ships. These numbers ran from 15 to 22.

The two newest vessels in this fleet are the BADGER and SPARTAN. When these units were placed in service in 1953 and 1952, respectively, smaller and older units such as this vessel were found to be both uneconomical and unnecessary to maintain fleet operations. In due course the decision was made to scrap this vessel and that occurred as noted above.

Steamer PERE MARQUETTE 21

OWNER: Chessie System, Inc.
BUILT: Manitowoc Shipbuilding Company, Manitowoc, Wisconsin – 1924
HULL NO.: 209
O. A. DIMENSIONS: 400' x 56' x 21'6"
FORMER DATA: Lengthened 40' at Manitowoc Shipbuilding, Incorporated, Manitowoc, Wisconsin in 1954.

The Steamer PERE MARQUETTE 21 was a carferry which had a capacity for passengers of 132. It plied regularly on the lines of the railroad across Lake Michigan until being laid up at Ludington, Michigan. Following a few years in this status it was sold in July, 1973 for off-lakes use. Having been cut down at Milwaukee, Wisconsin for this purpose, it cleared the lakes for the Caribbean late in 1974. The ship is shown above outbound at Ludington, Michigan late in the 1960's.

The number "21" was used in this ship name in reference to class of vessel as explained fully on the following page. The first part of the ship name, PERE MARQUETTE, came from the railroad which originally owned the ship and that name, in turn, honored Father Jacques Marquette, "Pere" being the French word for father.

Father Marquette was born June 1, 1637 at Laon, France and became a famous explorer and Jesuit missionary. He traveled down the Mississippi River with Louis Jolliet in 1673 and founded many missions in what is now upstate Michigan. He died on May 18, 1675 at the river which now bears his name. It flows into Pere Marquette Lake at Ludington, Michigan.

Steamer PERE MARQUETTE 22

OWNER: Chessie System, Inc.
BUILT: Manitowoc Shipbuilding Company, Manitowoc, Wisconsin — 1924
HULL NO.: 210
O. A. DIMENSIONS: 400' x 56' x 21'6"
FORMER DATA: Lengthened 40' at Manitowoc Shipbuilding, Incorporated, Manitowoc, Wisconsin in 1953.

The 205-passenger capacity carferry Steamer PERE MARQUETTE 22 took its name from the original owner, Pere Marquette Railroad Company, as did its sistership on the preceding page. The number "22" was the specific namesake as used by the railroad and designated vessels in the fleet numbered 15 through 22 whose power plant consisted of steam driven engines. This numbering system was purely an internal matter and was used simply to differentiate one class of carferry from another.

This fleet of carferries was and is operated mostly on Lake Michigan, with headquarters at Ludington, Michigan. From this Michigan railhead, cars and railroad equipment as well as passengers are carried to the western shore of the lake into various Wisconsin ports.

This vessel was idle for several years before being sold for off-lakes use in July, 1973. It was removed late that fall and was cut down for use as a barge in the Caribbean. The ship is shown above leaving Milwaukee, Wisconsin on July 20, 1968.

Steamer ALABAMA

OWNER:	Chicago, Duluth & Georgian Bay Transit Company
BUILT:	Manitowoc Shipbuilding and Drydock Company, Manitowoc, Wisconsin—1910
HULL NO.:	36
O. A. DIMENSIONS:	275' × 45'6" × 26'

Launched on December 18, 1909, the icebreaking passenger Steamer ALABAMA was to serve in many lines before being reduced to a barge for use in the marine construction field in 1964. She now serves in that capacity out of Bay City, Michigan. The ship was retired from service in this line in 1947. It is a tribute to the builders that her hull was useful enough after many years of sailing service to carry on in her present capacity. The ship is shown above leaving Mackinac Island in 1939.

The namesake of this vessel, when built for the Goodrich Transit Company, was the state of Alabama because the line had a policy of naming many ships in the fleet for states of the Union whose names ended in the letter "A." Various other states were chosen for their namesakes as well.

Alabama was the 22nd state to be admitted to the Union and that event took place on December 14, 1819. The state has 51,609 square miles of area, of which 549 square miles is inland water. It was first settled when Fort Louis was established by Hernando de Soto in 1702. Previously, it had been explored by others in 1540.

The port of Mobile is the only major waterborne commerce city in Alabama. However, numerous other towns are involved in the varied barge-river trades of the state. Iron ore, coal, limestone and a host of other products abound in the state and Birmingham is the center of heavy industrial activity. Total current population of Alabama is about 3,700,000 persons.

Steamer SOUTH AMERICAN

OWNER:	Chicago, Duluth & Georgian Bay Transit Company
BUILT:	Great Lakes Engineering Works, Ecorse, Michigan—1914
HULL NO.:	133
O. A. DIMENSIONS:	321' × 47'10" × 18'3"

The passenger Steamer SOUTH AMERICAN was the last of the large regularly scheduled cruise ships to be operated on the Great Lakes. Because of this, it has a fond recollection in the minds of many, many Lakes minded people yet today.

This ship sailed a number of voyages through the St. Lawrence Seaway in the Canadian centennial year of 1967 to Montreal's Expo '67. It is seen in the photograph above in the Welland Canal on June 30th of that year enroute to Montreal, Quebec. Later that year it was sold for off-lakes use as a floating classroom on the United States East Coast.

This line used the names of the two sister continents as namesakes of their ships which were regarded as the finest passenger cruise vessels on the Great Lakes. South America was the namesake of this ship. It is the fourth largest of the continents in the world and is located between 34 degrees and 82 degrees west longitude and 13 degrees north and 55 degrees south latitude. It has an area of approximately 6,879,000 square miles, or about thirteen percent of the earth's surface.

Motor Vessel CLARK MILWAUKEE

OWNER:	Clark Oil and Refining Corporation
BUILT:	Ingalls Shipbuilding Corporation, Decatur, Alabama—1941
HULL NO.:	290
O. A. DIMENSIONS:	235' × 35' × 14'6"
FORMER DATA:	Launched as MINNEAPOLIS HUSKY. Renamed REPUBLIC-PITTSBURGH in 1944. Converted to a special purpose oil carrier at Jeffersonville Boat & Machine Company, Jeffersonville, Indiana in 1952. Given last name in 1954.

The Motor Vessel CLARK MILWAUKEE was active on the Great Lakes for approximately one decade and was sold for off-lakes use in 1964. It is shown at the Municipal Dock, Milwaukee, Wisconsin in 1955.

The namesake of this ship was two-fold. The first word of the shipname paid tribute to the owning company. Clark Oil and Refining Corporation was incorporated in Wisconsin on July 12, 1934 as Petco Corporation. The current name was adopted on March 31, 1954. This company refines petroleum products and distributes them at wholesale and retail, including their own service stations in the Midwest. The firm has, within the last decade, entered the petrochemical industry and is now producing various products in that field.

The second word of the shipname honors the major city of the state of the firm's incorporation. Milwaukee is the largest city in Wisconsin with a current population of about 1,350,000 in the metropolitan area. It was founded by Soloman Juneau as a trading post in 1818. Milwaukee was laid out as a city in 1848 with Mr. Juneau being the first mayor. This gentleman is a direct relative of this writer.

Barge PETER REISS

OWNER: Clepro Marine Corporation
BUILT: Superior Shipbuilding Company, Superior, Wisconsin – 1910
HULL NO.: 522
O. A. DIMENSIONS: 524' x 54'3" x 30'
FORMER DATA: Launched as a bulk freighter. Converted to a self-unloader at Manitowoc Shipbuilding Company, Manitowoc, Wisconsin in 1949. Converted to a barge at Hans Hansen Welding Company, Toledo, Ohio in 1972.

The self-unloading Barge PETER REISS was converted to serve in the coal trades of Lake Erie and the Detroit River. Unfortunately, this unit saw very little service, the owning firm noted here went out of business and this barge was sold for scrap late in 1972. It had sailed as a steamer on its maiden voyage May 27, 1910 with a cargo of iron ore from Duluth, Minnesota to Ashtabula, Ohio.

The namesake of this vessel throughout its life was Mr. Peter Reiss who was born on January 17, 1857 at Pigeon River, Wisconsin. He rose from the position of grocery clerk at the age of 14 to become one of the early giants in the coal industry. Peter Reiss started in business with a dock at Sheboygan, Wisconsin from which he shipped lake coal to points in Minnesota, Wisconsin and upper Michigan. The business flourished and, in time, he was one of the most extensive miners shipping over the former Wheeling and Lake Erie Railroad.

His shipping interests began with the purchase of the Steamers BRAZIL and AMERICA. Later the Reiss Steamship Company was formed in 1916. Mr. Reiss died at Sheboygan Falls, Wisconsin on September 4, 1926. The barge is shown at Toledo, Ohio on April 8, 1973 just prior to scrapping.

Steamer FRONTENAC (4)

OWNER: Cleveland-Cliffs Steamship Company
BUILT: Great Lakes Engineering Works, River Rouge, Michigan — 1923
HULL NO.: 244
O. A. DIMENSIONS: 603'9" x 60' x 32'

This bulk freighter had a name in keeping with the explorer theme of ship names in this fleet. The Steamer FRONTENAC (4) took its name from Louis de Buade Frontenac et Palluau, architect of French expansion in the New World.

Frontenac founded Fort Frontenac on Lake Ontario in 1673 and shortly after became associated with Sieur de La Salle who secured royal consent to continue explorations of Louis Jolliet down the Mississippi River to its mouth. He was one of the more skilled and colorful persons in North American history.

The maiden trip of this ship began July 9, 1923 from Detroit, Michigan upbound, light, for Marquette, Michigan to load iron ore. On October 23, 1923 it became the first 600-foot vessel to dock at the Ford Motor Company plant at River Rouge, Michigan. The ship is shown here while downbound in the St. Mary's River on May 30, 1977. Following a grounding just off Silver Bay, Minnesota on November 22, 1979, the ship was found to be a constructive total loss and was moored at the CLM dock in Superior, Wisconsin on December 13, 1979. The hull was sold for scrap in 1980.

Steamer GRAND ISLAND (2)

OWNER:	Cleveland-Cliffs Steamship Company
BUILT:	Craig Shipbuilding Company, Toledo, Ohio—1905
HULL NO.:	106
O. A. DIMENSIONS:	500' × 52' × 30'
FORMER DATA:	Launched as EUGENE ZIMMERMAN. Given last name in 1916.

The bulk freight Steamer GRAND ISLAND is shown below downbound in the connecting channels of the Great Lakes. This vessel continued active on the Great Lakes until being sold for trade-in and scrap in 1963.

Grand Island, Alger County, Michigan is the namesake of this ship. It amounts to the largest island on the southern shore of Lake Superior and is very scenic. It is approximately eight miles long and three miles wide. Indian legend holds that Grand Island and the hills of Munising, Michigan are the remains of huge giants created by the Great Spirit during his leisure moments as a pastime. The beauty of Pictured Rocks and Grand Island was first described in 1657 by the French explorer Pierre Radisson.

The Cleveland-Cliffs Iron Company purchased huge tracts of land in Alger County and on Grand Island in 1901. This was done by Mr. William Gwinn Mather, Cliffs' chief executive according to a plan to preserve the great beauty of the island. Also, cottages were erected and a game preserve established and stocked with elk and moose. Some of the trees on the island have been and are being cut down and taken to the mainland for the firm's forestry division, but always, the replanting goes on so that the island's scenic beauty may be preserved.

Steamer JOLIET (2)

OWNER:	Cleveland-Cliffs Steamship Company
BUILT:	American Ship Building Company, Lorain, Ohio—1916
HULL NO.:	717
O. A. DIMENSIONS:	524' × 54' × 30'3"
FORMER DATA:	Launched as HERBERT F. BLACK. Given last name in 1930.

The bulk freight Steamer JOLIET began its career on the Great Lakes when it sailed from Lorain, Ohio on October 14, 1916 on its maiden voyage. The ship proceeded upbound, light to Duluth, Minnesota for iron ore. During its career this ship carried a record cargo of newsprint, leaving Thorold, Ontario on April 24, 1932 bound for the Chicago Tribune dock at Chicago, Illinois where it arrived on April 29th.

Namesake of this vessel was Mr. Louis Jolliet who was born at Quebec City, Quebec on September 21, 1645. He was educated at Jesuit College and went to France for special additional studies in 1667. In 1668 he returned to Canada and set out with Mr. Jean Péré in 1669 to search for copper mines near Lake Superior. While on the trip they engaged in fur-trading and gathered information about the hinterlands of their journey.

In 1672 Jolliet was appointed by Frontenac to determine into what ocean the Mississippi River emptied. Jolliet left Michilimackinac on May 17, 1673 and reached the Mississippi on June 17th, passing through Illinois Indian country via Illinois City. Jolliet reached 33 degrees latitude and 40 degrees longitude on July 17, 1673 and returned homeward, being convinced the Mississippi River did not enter the Pacific Ocean.

This ship continued active on the Great Lakes until being sold for scrap in 1963. It is shown here in Little Rapids Cut, St. Mary's River, downbound on August 10, 1959.

Steamer MARQUETTE (2)

OWNER:	Cleveland-Cliffs Steamship Company
BUILT:	Great Lakes Engineering Works, Ecorse, Michigan—1906
HULL NO.:	24
O. A. DIMENSIONS:	440' × 52' × 28'
FORMER DATA:	Launched as E. L. WALLACE. Given last name in 1916.

The bulk freight Steamer MARQUETTE served faithfully in the carriage of iron ore and coal until it became an uneconomical unit and was sold for scrap in 1963.

Namesake of this ship is Father Jacques Marquette who was born on June 1, 1637 at Laon, France. He became a Jesuit missionary and a famous explorer. This fleet has a history in its vessel names of honoring men who helped explore and open up the Great Lakes area.

Father Marquette travelled down the Mississippi River with Jolliet in 1673 and founded many missions along the way and in the area that is now upstate Michigan. A river bears his name and so does the lake at Ludington, Michigan. This was the sight of his death when he died on May 18, 1675.

This vessel was one of a large number that were built between 1905 and 1910, all having similar dimensions. They formed the backbone of the fleet of ore vessels for many years and were also active in the coal and grain trades. The Steamer MARQUETTE is shown on July 21, 1945 taking on the first cargo of iron ore from the Steep Rock Mine at Port Arthur, Ontario.

Motor Vessel RAYMOND H. REISS

OWNER:	Cleveland-Cliffs Steamship Company
BUILT:	American Ship Building Company, Lorain, Ohio—1916
HULL NO.:	715
O. A. DIMENSIONS:	600' × 60' × 32'
FORMER DATA:	Launched as EMORY L. FORD. Given last name in 1965.

The Isherwood design Motor Vessel RAYMOND H. REISS is named in honor of Mr. Raymond Henry Reiss who was born at Chicago, Illinois on June 29, 1897. He received a B.S. degree from Georgetown University in 1919, a Ph.D. degree in 1933 and an Ll.D. degree from Fordham University in 1938.

Since graduating in 1919 Mr. Reiss has been with Ronthor-Reiss Corporation. He was elected vice president in 1924, executive vice president in 1928 and president and chairman of the board in 1955, which post he currently holds.

Mr. Reiss is a member of the board of the C. Reiss Coal Company, Irving Trust Company, Schering Corporation and is chairman of the President's Council of Georgetown University. He continues to live in New York City.

This bulk freighter sailed from Lorain, Ohio August 26, 1916 light to Marquette, Michigan for a cargo of iron ore on its maiden voyage. It is shown here entering Cleveland, Ohio's Cuyahoga River with iron ore on September 27, 1973. In late 1980 the ship was sold for scrap.

Steamer COMET

OWNER:	Cleveland Tankers, Incorporated
BUILT:	American Ship Building Company, Lorain, Ohio – 1913
HULL NO.:	705
O. A. DIMENSIONS:	332' x 43' x 25'
FORMER DATA:	Launched as COMET. Renamed COMETA in 1927. Renamed COMET, for the second time, in 1934. Lengthened 72' at Great Lakes Engineering Works, River Rouge, Michigan in 1940.

The tank Steamer COMET sailed from Lorain, Ohio July 18, 1913 for Montreal, Quebec on its maiden voyage. The trip was made without cargo. It remained active until being sold for scrap on July 5, 1973 and is shown in the photograph above outbound off Cleveland, Ohio on May 22, 1961.

The namesake of this tanker was the celestial body known as the comet. No particular comet, but all of them in general were honored by this ship name.

A comet looks much like a star with a tail. Most have three parts: a nucleus, a head, and a tail. The bright center may be in excess of seven thousand miles in diameter. The head surrounding it may be as much as one hundred thousand miles in diameter, and the tail streaking behind the comet can be up to one hundred million miles in length.

The most famous comet known currently is Halley's Comet which appears every 77 years and is due to appear next in 1986.

Steamer MERCURY (2)

OWNER: Cleveland Tankers, Incorporated
BUILT: American Ship Building Company, Lorain, Ohio – 1912
HULL NO.: 396
O. A. DIMENSIONS: 390'3" x 52' x 25'
FORMER DATA: Launched as RENOWN. Renamed BEAUMONT PARKS in 1930. Given last name in 1957.

The tank Steamer MERCURY (2) made its maiden voyage beginning July 19, 1912 when it departed Cleveland, Ohio with a cargo of fuel oil for delivery to Port Arthur, Ontario. It served regularly on the Great Lakes and, most recently, worked the winter runs on Lake Michigan. Age took its toll, however, and the veteran tanker was sold for scrap in 1975. It is shown above while underway on Lake Erie in the early 1970's.

The namesake of this steamer was the smallest planet in our solar system, and the one nearest the Sun. It was named for the sleek, fast-footed messenger of the ancient gods of Roman mythology. Mercury had more duties than any other god and was a favorite of Jupiter.

The planet orbits the Sun once every 88 days at an average distance of thirty-six million miles. Estimates as to its external temperature range as high as 770 degrees Fahrenheit.

Mercury passes directly between Earth and the Sun at intervals from three to thirteen years and these passes are called "transits."

Steamer METEOR (2)

OWNER:	Cleveland Tankers, Incorporated
BUILT:	American Steel Barge Company, Superior Wisconsin—1896
HULL NO.:	136
O. A. DIMENSIONS:	380' × 45' × 26'
FORMER DATA:	Launched as the bulk freighter FRANK ROCKEFELLER. Renamed SOUTH PARK in 1928. Converted to an automobile carrier at Great Lakes Engineering Works, River Rouge, Michigan in 1936. Converted to a combination automobile carrier and bulk freighter at American Ship Building Company, Superior, Wisconsin in 1941. Re-converted to a bulk freighter at American Ship Building Company, Superior, Wisconsin in 1942. Converted to a tanker at Manitowoc Shipbuilding Company, Manitowoc, Wisconsin and given last name in 1943.

This tank vessel has now become an historic landmark and is a museum piece having been given for that purpose by these owners in 1972 to the city of Superior, Wisconsin.

This class of vessel was designed and pioneered on the Great Lakes by Mr. Alexander McDougall between 1888 and 1896.

The vessels in this fleet all take their names from celestial bodies or things related thereto. In this case, all meteors are the namesakes of this vessel.

Motor Vessel ORION (3)

OWNER: Cleveland Tankers, Incorporated
BUILT: Great Lakes Engineering Works, River Rouge, Michigan—1931
HULL NO.: 276
O. A. DIMENSIONS: 300' × 43' × 20'
FORMER DATA: Launched as the New York State Barge Canal-type bulk carrier EDGEWATER. Converted to a tanker at Bethlehem Steel Company, Staten Island, New York in 1947. Given last name in 1949.

The Motor Vessel ORION is shown above heading into Lake Ontario via Toronto, Ontario harbour's Eastern Gap on July 29, 1957. Shortly afterwards the vessel was laid up at Cleveland, Ohio and remained there until being sold for scrap in 1964. In 1965 it was converted to a sand barge after partial demolition and finally sank in Lake Erie in 1968.

Namesake of this tanker was the constellation Orion, named for the Greek mythological son of Hyreius or Poseidon who was a mighty hunter of great beauty and strength. Orion is one of the most conspicuous constellations in the sky. It contains many bright stars.

Several varying accounts of the death of Orion prevail. One holds that he was killed by Artemis with her arrows when he fell in love with her daughter Eos, the goddess of dawn. Another holds that Orion was killed by Artemis by mistake when she was tricked into shooting him by the angry Apollo who had discovered her love of Orion. After his death, by all accounts, he was changed into the constellation now bearing his name.

This ship sailed from River Rouge, Michigan on August 17, 1931 on its maiden voyage to Green Island, New York and Edgewater, New Jersey with auto parts.

Steamer PLEIADES

OWNER: Cleveland Tankers, Incorporated
BUILT: Staten Island Shipbuilding Company, Mariners Harbor, New York—1921
HULL NO.: 725
O. A. DIMENSIONS: 361'6" × 43' × 26'
FORMER DATA: Launched as FRANKLIN. Renamed MAINE (2) in 1933. Lengthened 105'9" at Great Lakes Engineering Works, River Rouge, Michigan in 1934. Given last name in 1956.

The tank Steamer PLEIADES was active on the Great Lakes until 1966 when it was sold to Atlantic coast interests. It was later re-sold several times, finally to the United States Maritime Commission for trade-in and non-transportation use in 1968 and was finally dismantled in 1972. The ship is shown above in the Ship Channel at Toronto, Ontario on June 23, 1956.

This vessel, like others in this fleet, took a celestial namesake. Pleiades is a star cluster known in mythology as the seven daughters of Atlas and Pleione, and sisters of Hyades.

The stars are located in the constellation Taurus. They are referred to in the Old Testament of the Bible in the Book of Job. According to legend, the daughters were changed to stars because of their grief at the death of their sisters and at the suffering of their father. In another account of mythology, the Pleiades and their mother met Orion who persued them for five years through the woods until Zeus translated all of them, Pleione and her daughters and Orion and his dog, to the sky.

Various interpretations of these tales have come down through the centuries. But all of the stories relate to the positions of the constellations in the sky.

Motor Vessel POLARIS

OWNER: Cleveland Tankers, Incorporated
BUILT: Bethlehem Shipbuilding Company, Hingham, Massachusetts - 1945
HULL NO.: 3453
O. A. DIMENSIONS: 327'9" x 50' x 25'3"
FORMER DATA: Launched as the LST-type ship LST 1063. Converted to a tanker and given last name at Moore Drydock Company, Oakland, California in 1949.

This was the first Landing Ship, Tank vessel (LST) to be converted to a tanker to remain under American registry. After conversion it sailed with a cargo to Central America, through the Panama Canal and up the Mississippi River system. It cleared East Chicago, Indiana May 22, 1949 with a cargo of gasoline for Bay City, Michigan for its maiden voyage on the Great Lakes. It is shown in 1972.

The Motor Vessel POLARIS was named for the star Polaris, better known as The North Star. It has been used for centuries by navigators in determining their location. Wherever one may be in the northern latitudes, the direction north may be found by reference to this star.

Polaris can easily be located because the two stars Merak and Dubhe, in Ursa Major, also known as the Big Dipper or Great Bear, always point towards it. It is the brightest star in the constellation Ursa Minor, or Little Bear. The name is of Greek derivation. The Greek word *cynosura,* with the English translation being *cynosure,* meaning "center of attraction," is the form and reference basis for Polaris' meaning. The vessel operated through 1976 and was sold for scrap in June, 1977.

Steamer ROCKET (2)

OWNER: Cleveland Tankers, Incorporated
BUILT: American Ship Building Company, Lorain, Ohio – 1913
HULL NO.: 701
O. A. DIMENSIONS: 359' x 43' x 25'
FORMER DATA: Launched as RADIANT. Renamed GENERAL MARKHAM in 1933. Lengthened 101' at Great Lakes Engineering Works, Ashtabula, Ohio in 1942. Given last name in 1943.

Reference in use of this name is the fast moving vehicle now known to be an integral part of moving towards the universe.

Some scientists believe the Chinese invented rockets since their historians describe "arrows of flying fire" being used in wars in 1232 A.D. In the War of 1812, the British used Sir William Congreve's rockets during the siege of Fort McHenry, and our National Anthem refers to "the rockets' red glare."

The maiden voyage of this tanker began September 8, 1913 when the ship left Lorain, Ohio light for Montreal, Quebec. The vessel was sold for scrap in the spring of 1974 and is shown above while downbound, light, in the West Neebish Channel, St. Mary's River on September 5, 1973.

Motor Vessel TAURUS (2)

OWNER: Cleveland Tankers, Incorporated
BUILT: Sun Shipbuilding and Dry Dock Company, Chester, Pennsylvania—1924
HULL NO.: 76
O. A. DIMENSIONS: 260' × 40' × 14"
FORMER DATA: Launched as OSWEGO SOCONY. Rebuilt with new midbody at Bethlehem Shipbuilding Corporation, Sparrows Point, Maryland in 1936. Given last name in 1950.

The small tank Motor Vessel TAURUS was named within the fleet theme of ship names. These were, as noted earlier for the fleet, along the lines of celestial body names. In this case, this vessel bore the name of the constellation Taurus.

Taurus is known as The Bull, both astronomically and astrologically, because of the grouping of its stars in the form of a bull.

A v-shaped cluster of stars called Hyades forms the bull's face. The star Aldebaran forms the right eye and two stars at the end of the v-shape are the horn tips. The loose cluster of six stars, visable to the average eye, is known as Pleiades and forms the bull's shoulder.

This ship was purchased near the time the owners acquired a larger vessel they named Pleiades. They felt it appropriate to christen this smaller ship TAURUS, because the star cluster Hyades in the constellation is smaller than the cluster Pleiades.

This tanker operated quite regularly until the late 1960's. It laid idle for several seasons before being sold for scrap in 1972. It is shown above while underway upbound with a full cargo at Port Huron, Michigan in 1966.

Motor Vessel VENUS (2)

OWNER: Cleveland Tankers, Incorporated
BUILT: American Ship Building Company, Lorain, Ohio – 1928
HULL NO.: 803
O. A. DIMENSIONS: 344'9" x 51' x 18'6"
FORMER DATA: Launched as MARTHA E. ALLEN. Given last name in 1967.

The medium-sized tank Motor Vessel VENUS (2) was active through the 1974 navigation season on the Great Lakes and was sold for scrap in 1975 after it had been determined that further operation of her would be uneconomic due to costly repairs and possible pollution control problems. The vessel is shown in operation in the Welland Ship Canal, at Port Robinson, Ontario, on September 8, 1973.

This vessel had the distinction of bringing in the first cargo to the Shell Oil Company's new dock at Toledo, Ohio on May 21, 1930. The cargo consisted of 32,000 barrels of fuel oil loaded onboard at East Chicago, Indiana.

The planet Venus is the most brilliant in our solar system and was the namesake of this tanker. Venus, of course, had been named for the goddess of beauty and love in ancient Greek mythology.

When this vessel was commissioned it was named for a lady. These owners felt it apropos and in keeping with their own theme of vessel names to rename it VENUS. The coincidence between the planet name and the motor vessel originally being named for a lady was unique on the Lakes at the time.

Steamer COASTAL CASCADES

OWNER:	Coastalake Tankers Limited
BUILT:	Forg. & Chile de la Mediterranee, La Seyne, France—1919
HULL NO.:	1124
O. A. DIMENSIONS:	230' × 34'3" × 14'9"
FORMER DATA:	Launched as the bulk freighter CHARPENTIER. Renamed VERNON in 1922. Renamed CEDARBAY in 1923. Renamed JOAN VIRGINIA in 1936. Converted to a tanker at Muir Brothers Dry Dock Company Limited, Port Dalhousie, Ontario in 1937. Given last name in 1952.

The Steamer COASTAL CASCADES was sold for scrap in 1961 after serving in this fleet for a number of years. Its double name first of all honors the corporate title in the word COASTAL, being a shortening of the first title word.

The second word of the ship name, CASCADES, is the specific namesake of this vessel. As in other ship names of the fleet, various names of bodies of water or things relating thereto form the subject genera for the names on the bow.

A cascade may be defined as "a steep, usually small, fall of water." Or, "something falling or rushing in quantity." Cascades of water, though none in particular, are the background of this name.

The Steamer COASTAL CASCADES is shown entering Toronto, Ontario harbor with a full load of petroleum products during the latter days of her career.

Steamer COASTAL CLIFF

OWNER:	Coastalake Tankers Limited
BUILT:	Horton Steel Works Limited, Fort Erie, Ontario—1935
HULL NO.:	2512
O. A. DIMENSIONS:	257'4" × 30' × 16'3"
FORMER DATA:	Launched as the tank barge BRUCE HUDSON. Converted to a powered tanker, lengthened 7' and deepened 5' at Muir Brothers Dry Dock Company, Limited, Port Dalhousie, Ontario in 1939. Lengthened 40' at Muir Brothers Dry Dock Company, Limited, Port Dalhousie, Ontario in 1944. Renamed COASTAL CLIFF in 1952. Lengthened 36'4" at St. Lawrence Dry Docks Limited, Montreal, Quebec in 1957.

The tank Steamer COASTAL CLIFF was sold for off-lakes use in 1970 and left the Lakes that spring as the Steamer WITCROIX. On July 13, 1935, with only 18 inches of freeboard, this vessel turned over and was towed into Toronto, Ontario harbor upside down. None of her 1,800 barrels of oil was lost as the decks were secured.

This vessel's first ship name honored the owning company as noted above, using the shortened prefix of the corporate title's first word. Other ships in this fleet used the same first ship name word.

The specific namesake of this tanker was CLIFF, though none in particular. Since cliffs are quite often found in nature along bodies of water, the theme of water-related names is furthered in this ship name which refers to the cliffs of the Great Lakes and St. Lawrence River in general.

This ship is shown above in the Galops Lock near Cardinal, Ontario while under charter to Liquifuels Limited on October 31, 1957.

Steamer TRANSBAY

OWNER: Coastalake Tankers Limited
BUILT: Manitowoc Shipbuilding and Drydock Company, Manitowoc, Wisconsin - 1912
HULL NO.: 49
O. A. DIMENSIONS: 206'9" x 36' x 16'
FORMER DATA: Launched as the sandsucker E. GUNNELL. Renamed PETER KOENIG in 1926. Renamed AMHERST in 1940. Converted to a tanker and given last name at St. Lawrence Dry Docks Limited, Montreal, Quebec in 1943. Lengthened 30' at St. Lawrence Dry Docks Limited, Montreal, Quebec in 1952.

The Steamer TRANSBAY served in interlake commerce on the Great Lakes until the late 1960's when it was relegated to fueling service in Montreal Harbour. The vessel is shown in the above photograph while underway at Toronto, Ontario on September 8, 1957.

After serving actively as a fueling vessel at Montreal, Quebec until 1970, this ship became semi-retired and was used in that capacity only occasionally. In mid-summer 1972 the ship was chartered for use as an asphalt storage barge at Havre St. Pierre, Quebec. But, while enroute to that port, under tow, the vessel foundered in Seven Islands Bay, Quebec in seven hundred feet of water, its asphalt cargo hardening to become and underwater paved surface.

This ship took a name that was in keeping with the theme of names in the fleet which were given in honor of water-related things or places. The prefix, TRANS, bore reference to the operating firm's first word in the corporate title - TRANSit Tankers and Terminals Ltd. The specific namesake of this vessel was not one single bay, but all bays of the Great Lakes and St. Lawrence River area combined.

Steamer BUCKEYE (1)

OWNER: Columbia Transportation Division, Oglebay Norton Company
BUILT: Detroit Shipbuilding Company, Wyandotte, Michigan—1901
HULL NO.: 138
O. A. DIMENSIONS: 428′ × 51′6″ × 28′
FORMER DATA: Launched as the bulk freighter D. M. WHITNEY. Renamed DAVID MARSHALL WHITNEY in 1901. Renamed DAVID M. WHITNEY in 1908. Renamed EDWIN L. BOOTH in 1913. Renamed G. N. WILSON (1) in 1921. Renamed THOMAS BRITT (2) in 1928. Converted to a crane ship at Fairport Machine Shop, Fairport, Ohio and given last name in 1943.

The Steamer BUCKEYE is shown while upbound at Sault St. Marie in 1962. The ship was sold for overseas scrapping in 1968 after having been idle for several seasons.

The namesake of the vessel was the State of Ohio whose nickname is "The Buckeye State" and whose championship football team of Ohio State University is also known as the Buckeyes. The state is the headquarters location of the owning company noted above for this ship.

Ohio ranks thirty-fourth in physical size of the United States with a land area of 40,972 square miles and a water area of 250 square miles.

This vessel was the first to pass downbound in the Welland Ship Canal on June 15, 1931 when that canal was first opened to ships up to 450 feet in overall length.

Steamer JAMES DAVIDSON

OWNER: Columbia Transportation Division, Oglebay Norton Company
BUILT: Detroit Shipbuilding Company, Wyandotte, Michigan — 1920
HULL NO.: 288
O. A. DIMENSIONS: 600' x 60' x 32'

Mr. James Davidson was born at Buffalo, New York on August 12, 1841 and was orphaned when he was eleven years old. He was raised by an aunt at Ashtabula, Ohio and attended a commercial college at Buffalo, New York.

In 1860 he sailed before the mast and by his nineteenth birthday had received his master's papers. Captain Davidson returned to the Great Lakes in 1865 and sailed on vessels in the commercial trades.

Captain Davidson became interested in the building of lake ships and leased a parcel of land along the Saginaw River on which to build ships. There he built his first wooden schooner, the LAURA BELLE in 1870. This vessel was of 600 tons capacity and was 138 feet long. Over the course of the years, Captain Davidson completed no less than 115 ships at his yard in West Bay City, Michigan. He sailed on some of these himself and sold others to operators. He met Mr. G. A. Tomlinson during this time and the founding of the Tomlinson Fleet Corporation was begun. Captain Davidson died at Bay City, Michigan on February 5, 1929.

His grandson, Mr. Edward Cobb Davidson of Bay City, Michigan was the last chief executive of the Tomlinson Fleet and presided over its sale of vessels to this owning firm and the liquidation of the company in 1971. The ship is shown below in the St. Mary's River on August 10, 1969. It was sold for scrap in 1974.

Steamer HARRY T. EWIG

OWNER:	Columbia Transportation Division, Oglebay Norton Company
BUILT:	Chicago Shipbuilding Company, Chicago, Illinois—1902
HULL NO.:	52
O. A. DIMENSIONS:	366' × 48' × 28'
FORMER DATA:	Launched as the bulk freighter W. W. BROWN. Renamed BALTIC (3) in 1920. Renamed JOHN W. AILES in 1922. Given last name in 1926. Converted to a crane vessel at Fairport Machine Shop, Fairport, Ohio in 1939.

The Steamer HARRY T. EWIG was sold for scrap in 1963 and was later cut down to form two storage barges at Sturgeon Bay, Wisconsin.

The namesake of this vessel is Mr. Harry Thomas Ewig who was born on the family farm near West Newton, Pennsylvania on July 25, 1888. After completing his high school education in 1906 he began working in the coal mines of western Pennsylvania and continued serving in various jobs in the mines until enlisting in the U.S. Army in 1917. Upon release from the service in 1919 he moved to Cleveland, Ohio to join the Valley Camp Coal Company. Cleveland was the headquarters office of the firm and Mr. Ewig began in the general office and accounting departments.

In 1930 he was named treasurer of Valley Camp Coal Company and served in that capacity until 1940 when he was elected the firm's president, in which capacity he served until retiring in 1965.

The crane vessel HARRY T. EWIG is shown in the above photograph in the connecting channels of the Great Lakes system on August 22, 1952.

Steamer EDMUND FITZGERALD

OWNER: Columbia Transportation Division, Oglebay Norton Company
BUILT: Great Lakes Engineering Works,
River Rouge, Michigan – 1958
HULL NO.: 301
O. A. DIMENSIONS: 729' 3" x 75' x 39'

Shown below on May 10, 1972 upbound in the St. Mary's River, the bulk freight Steamer EDMUND FITZGERALD began its career on the Great Lakes September 22, 1958 when it cleared Detroit, Michigan on its maiden voyage, light to Silver Bay, Minnesota to take on iron ore pellets. A disaster befell the ship, however, on November 10, 1975. While downbound with pellets from Superior, Wisconsin and destined for Detroit, Michigan, she foundered and sank suddenly about 7:20 PM taking with her all 29 crewmen aboard. Site of the sinking was about 15 miles north of Whitefish Point in Lake Superior where the depths range to 500 feet. Severe seas were running with waves up to 25 feet and wind gusts to 75 m.p.h. The vessel had been a record-setter, being the first Great Lakes ship to carry more than 26,000 and 27,000 gross tons.

Mr. Edmund Fitzgerald was chairman of the board of Northwestern Mutual Life Insurance Company when the vessel took his name. His firm actually owned the ship and long-term chartered it to Columbia. He was born in Milwaukee, Wisconsin on March 1, 1895 and was educated at Yale University, receiving a Ph.B. degree in 1916. After service in World War I, Mr. Fitzgerald was secretary of the Northwestern Malleable Iron Company from 1920 to 1927. In 1928 he was secretary of the Combined Locks Paper Company. He served as vice president of the Second Wisconsin National Bank and other financial institutions until joining Northwestern Mutual in 1933 as a vice president. In 1947 he was elected president and became chairman in 1958. After retiring in 1960 he continued to work in civic affairs in the city of Milwaukee, Wisconsin.

Steamer HOWARD M. HANNA, JR. (2)

OWNER:	Columbia Transportation Division, Oglebay Norton Company
BUILT:	American Ship Building Company, Cleveland, Ohio—1914
HULL NO.:	458
O. A. DIMENSIONS:	524' × 54' × 30'

The namesake of this bulk freighter was Mr. Howard Melville Hanna, Jr. who was born at Cleveland, Ohio on December 14, 1877. He was a graduate of the University School and attended Sheffield Scientific School of Yale University for three years.

In 1901 he began his career as a clerk on the C. & P. Dock in Cleveland, Ohio. In 1902 he was named assistant to the manager of the Pennsylvania ore docks and for two years was secretary of the Boomer Coal & Coke Company before entering the coal sales department of M. A. Hanna Company in 1904.

In 1906 he organized the iron ore mining department at Hanna and became its manager. Mr. Hanna became a partner of the firm in 1911 and was the company's first president on corporate reorganization in 1922. From 1929 until he died, he served as the chairman of the board of M. A. Hanna Company.

He was also a director of National Steel Corporation, Howe Sound Company and the National Biscuit Company. He died on March 17, 1945.

The maiden trip of this vessel was commenced July 8, 1914 with a cargo of coal from Ashtabula, Ohio to Milwaukee, Wisconsin. It is shown below in the St. Mary's River on August 16, 1956. It was sold for scrap in 1968.

Steamer HURON (4)

OWNER: Columbia Transportation Division, Oglebay Norton Company
BUILT: Great Lakes Engineering Works, Ecorse, Michigan—1914
HULL NO.: 132
O. A. DIMENSIONS: 439'3" x 56' x 30'

The self-unloading Steamer HURON had a name chosen by its former owners, Wyandotte Chemical Company. The name was picked because the Huron Indians called themselves by the name "Wendat" which later became Wyandotte in English translation. It had a reverse meaning, therefore, for the name of the Company.

The Hurons were a hybrid group thought to be a mixture of several Indian stocks. They were Iroquoian speaking and lived in Ontario, Canada between Georgian Bay and Lake Simcoe. Samuel de Champlain encountered them on his early travels into the Great Lakes region and chose them as being the strongest and most populous tribe in his efforts to extend French influence in Canada. He sought to win their friendship and partially succeeded. Many followed him and his leaders back to Quebec in the seventeenth century. The Hurons are largely fragmented today.

The maiden trip of this ship began April 23, 1914, upbound light from Detroit, Michigan for Alpena, Michigan where it loaded a cargo of limestone. This ship is shown above in Lake St. Clair on July 8, 1967.

Steamer O. S. McFARLAND

OWNER: Columbia Transportation Division, Oglebay Norton Company
BUILT: Craig Shipbuilding Company, Toledo, Ohio - 1903
HULL NO.: 94
O. A. DIMENSIONS: 381'6" x 50' x 28'
FORMER DATA: Launched as the bulk freighter KENSINGTON. Renamed M. A. REEB in 1916. Given last name in 1928. Converted to a crane ship at Fairport Machine Shop, Fairport, Ohio in 1940.

This crane ship was named in honor of Mr. Orin Sumner McFarland who was president of the Wisconsin Great Lakes Coal & Dock Company. He was born in New Castle, Pennsylvania on December 26, 1885 and was educated in the schools of that area and in Tampa, Florida. He joined the above coal firm as a dock foreman and in 1906 became dock superintendent of all facilities of the firm around the Great Lakes.

On April 1, 1917 he was named general manager of the company and also served a short while as vice president before being elected president on the firm's incorporation in 1921. He continued as chief executive officer until his retirement in 1953. He died at Milwaukee, Wisconsin on May 21, 1958.

The Steamer O. S. McFARLAND was sold for scrapping in 1970 and is shown above while discharging cargo. When it was converted in 1940 it had the largest magnets, 77 inches, of any crane ship on the lakes. Following default of the purchasers for scrap in 1970, this vessel was re-sold at auction in July, 1971 to the Escanaba Towing Company for use as a barge lighter but proved incapable in that service and was re-sold for scrap in 1972.

Steamer E. G. MATHIOTT (2)

OWNER: Columbia Transportation Division, Oglebay Norton Company
BUILT: Chicago Shipbuilding Company, Chicago, Illinois—1902
HULL NO.: 51
O. A. DIMENSIONS: 366' × 48' × 28'
FORMER DATA: Launched as the bulk freighter A. G. BROWER. Renamed SARGENT in 1920. Renamed C. B. NIENABER in 1922. Renamed S. B. WAY (1) in 1923. Converted to a self-unloader at Leatham D. Smith Dock Company, Sturgeon Bay, Wisconsin in 1927. Renamed HOWARD P. EELS, JR. in 1931. Renamed D. E. CALLENDER (2) in 1934. Given last name in 1937.

The Steamer E. G. MATHIOTT was named in honor of Mr. Edward George Mathiott who was born at Pittsburgh, Pennsylvania on July 12, 1895. He was educated in the local schools and moved to Cleveland with his family in the early 1900's. He began his working career with the Wheeling and Lake Erie Rail Road where he had accepted a job as an office boy in 1909.

During the course of his work with the railroad he became acquainted with Mr. Herman Griggs of Lake Carriers' Association and, in 1921, this association led Mr. Mathiott to the Valley Camp Coal Company where he began as a junior clerk. His promotions came rapidly and by 1928 he was vice president of sales. He continued in this capacity until becoming president of the subsidiary Valley Camp Coal Company of Canada in 1937. He retained this post until 1942 and then returned to Cleveland, Ohio to become officer in charge of retail operations until retiring in 1950.

His namesake was sold for scrap in 1960 and is shown here in the harbor of Toronto, Ontario on August 29, 1955.

Steamer J. CLARE MILLER

OWNER: Columbia Transportation Division, Oglebay Norton Company
BUILT: American Ship Building Company, Lorain, Ohio – 1906
HULL NO.: 342
O. A. DIMENSIONS: 545' x 55' x 31'
FORMER DATA: Launched as HARVEY D. GOULDER. Given last name in 1937.

Namesake of this bulk freighter was Mr. James Clare Miller who was born at Madison Furnace, Ohio on February 2, 1874. After completing his education he began his business career with Columbus Iron and Steel Company in 1900 as a stenographer.

In 1901 he joined Armco Steel Corporation. This was a short time after that company was founded. In 1907 he was named general manager of blast furnace operations at the company's Middletown, Ohio plant. Mr. Miller was transferred in 1922 to the newly acquired Ashland, Kentucky Works of Armco as works manager.

In 1937, Mr. Miller returned to the Middletown headquarters of Armco Steel Corporation as vice president of raw materials. He served in that capacity until retiring in 1946. In that capacity he was largely responsible for the development of close working relationships between Armco and Oglebay Norton Company and he served on the board of directors of Columbia Transportation Company. He died on January 3, 1962 at Cincinnati, Ohio. His namesake is shown on August 16, 1969 in the St. Mary's River. It was sold for scrap in 1973.

Steamer R. E. MOODY

OWNER: Columbia Transportation Company
BUILT: Buffalo Dry Dock Company, Buffalo, New York- 1903
HULL NO.: 205
O. A. DIMENSIONS: 375' x 48'6" x 28'1"
FORMER DATA: Launched as the bulk freighter P. P. MILLER. Renamed COLLIER (2) in 1920. Renamed JOHN Mc CARTNEY KENNEDY in 1922. Converted to a self-unloader at Leatham D. Smith Dock Company, Sturgeon Bay, Wisconsin in 1926. Given last name in 1937.

The self-unloading Steamer R. E. MOODY honored the man for whose utility company in Milwaukee, Wisconsin the ship carried many coal cargoes. Mr. Ralph Edmund Moody was born in Milwaukee, Wisconsin on April 19, 1890. He graduated from the University of Wisconsin in 1913 with a B.S. degree in electrical engineering.

He began his career as a general clerk for the Milwaukee Electric Railway & Light Company in 1913. In 1915 he was named a statistician, in 1917 a valuation engineer, in 1919 assistant research engineer, in 1921 research engineer and in 1929 executive assistant. Mr. Moody became assistant to the president in 1932 and served as vice president of Appleton and Racine, Wisconsin subsidiary firms from 1935 until 1940 when he left to become a vice president and director of North American Companies in New York City. In 1941 he moved to St. Louis, Missouri as vice president of operations of the Union Electric Power Company. He was elected chairman of the board of that firm in 1954 and served until retirement in 1956. Mr. Moody died at Bellaire Beach, Florida on March 28, 1970. His namesake was sold for scrap in 1958 and is shown above at Toronto, Ontario on April 8, 1957.

This vessel was the first large ship to pass through the Welland Ship Canal and did so when she locked down at Port Colborne, Ontario at 11:45 AM on October 29, 1930 with coal for Lake Ontario delivery.

Steamer DAVID Z. NORTON (2)

OWNER:	Columbia Transportation Division, Oglebay Norton Company
BUILT:	American Ship Building Company, Cleveland, Ohio—1906
HULL NO.:	431
O. A. DIMENSIONS:	500' × 52' × 30'

Mr. David Zadock Norton is the namesake of this bulk freighter. He was born at Cleveland, Ohio on June 1, 1851 and was educated in the public schools. Mr. Norton began as a messenger at the Commercial National Bank of Cleveland on April 1, 1868 and rose to the position of cashier in 1873. He held that post until 1890 when he resigned to join with Earl W. Oglebay to organize Oglebay Norton Company to engage in the iron ore trade. The Columbia Transportation Company was eventually formed as the transportation arm of the Oglebay Norton Company.

With banking and mining as the basis of his career, he assumed many varied and important financial interests in the course of time. For several years he was president of Citizens Savings & Loan Association and, in 1903, upon its consolidation to become Citizen Savings & Trust Company, he became vice president, holding that post until being elected president on January 1, 1910. He retired in 1919 and died on January 6, 1928.

Mr. Norton's namesake was sold for scrapping in 1964 after a number of years of idleness at Toledo, Ohio. It was one of a formerly large group of carriers on the Great Lakes with identical dimensions.

The carrier is shown here downbound in Lake St. Clair.

Steamer CRISPIN OGLEBAY (1)

OWNER: Columbia Transportation Division, Oglebay Norton Company
BUILT: Great Lakes Engineering Works, Ecorse, Michigan - 1908
HULL NO.: 41
O. A. DIMENSIONS: 556'9" x 58' x 31'
FORMER DATA: Launched as the bulk freighter WILLIAM LIVINGSTONE. Renamed S. B. WAY (3) in 1936. Converted to a self-unloader at American Ship Building Company, Lorain, Ohio and given last name in 1948.

Mr. Crispin Oglebay was born at Wheeling, West Virginia on October 10, 1876 and received a B.A. degree from Yale University in 1900. He began as a clerk with Swift Packing Company in 1901 at Kansas City, Missouri and came to Cleveland in 1903 as secretary of Hoffman Hinge & Foundry Company. In 1906 he became president of Ferro Machine and Foundry Company and in 1920 became its chairman. He was elected president of Columbia Transportation in 1921, and was with Oglebay Norton Company and its various divisions since 1924, serving as president until becoming chairman of the board in 1949 shortly before his sudden death in Gates Mills, Ohio on October 23, 1949.

He was one of Cleveland's prominent citizens and was a director of some twenty-three corporations. He was also an ardent horse fancier and steeds from his stables were entered in many important races at the nation's leading tracks. His namesake is shown above while downbound in the St. Clair River on May 22, 1971. It was sold for scrap in 1973.

Steamer W. C. RICHARDSON (2)

OWNER:	Columbia Transportation Division, Oglebay Norton Company
BUILT:	Detroit Shipbuilding Company, Wyandotte, Michigan—1908
HULL NO.:	175
O. A. DIMENSIONS:	440' × 52' × 28' 6"
FORMER DATA:	Launched as the bulk freighter WAINWRIGHT. Given present name in 1916. Converted to a crane ship at American Ship Building Company, Chicago, Illinois in 1950.

A former dean of Great Lakes vessel managers is the namesake of this vessel. Captain Wesley Cunningham Richardson was born in Unionville, Ohio on June 10, 1840 and attended school in Ashtabula, Ohio. When he was sixteen years old he decided to become a lake sailor and shipped before the mast on a sailing vessel. He studied navigation while onboard the sailing ship and in 1863 held chief mate's papers. In 1865 he and his brother Chauncey bought the schooner TRANSPORT.

He accepted a position with Briggs, Hathaway & Garrison, wholesale grocers, in 1880 and remained in that employ for a number of years. His earlier love of the water came to the fore again and Captain Richardson joined the firm of H. J. Webb & Company, vessel brokers and managers. After Mr. Webb's death the firm became W.C. Richardson & Company.

The fleet of ships he managed became the nucleus of the Columbia Transportation Company, later a division of Oglebay Norton Company, after his death on October 2, 1919. His namesake is shown discharging stone at Milwaukee, Wisconsin September 21, 1974. It was sold for non-transportation use as a dock front at Toledo, Ohio in mid-1977.

Steamer SIERRA

OWNER:	Columbia Transportation Divison, Oglebay Norton Company
BUILT:	Toledo Shipbuilding Company, Toledo, Ohio—1906
HULL NO.:	108
O. A. DIMENSIONS:	461′ × 52′ × 28′
FORMER DATA:	Launched as a bulk freighter. Converted to a self-unloader at Leatham D. Smith Dock Company, Sturgeon Bay, Wisconsin in 1929.

The self-unloading Steamer SIERRA was active on the Great Lakes until being sold for scrap in 1964. It had a name which followed a pattern of the original owner and manager of the ship, Mr. G. A. Tomlinson. He had a penchant for naming his ships for areas, places or things that started with the letter "S" and ended with the letter "A." In keeping with that theme, this freighter got its name.

The Sierra Nevada range of mountains in California, forming the eastern boundary of the Great Central Valley, is the namesake area of this vessel. These mountains extend from the northwest to the southeast for about 400 miles. The breadth of the range varies from 40 to 80 miles.

The spectacular scenery of the Yosemite Valley is in this range as is the world-famous Donner Pass, at altitude 7,017 feet, which is used today by the Southern Pacific Railway and U.S. Highway # 40.

Steamer WILLIAM F. STIFEL

OWNER:	Columbia Transportation Division, Oglebay Norton Company
BUILT:	Great Lakes Engineering Works, St. Clair, Michigan—1908
HULL NO.:	39
O. A. DIMENSIONS:	441'3" × 52' × 28'
FORMER DATA:	Launched as NORMANIA. Given last name in 1916.

The bulk freight Steamer WILLIAM F. STIFEL honored a family name that was prominent in the industrial world for decades. That name continued to be honored until 1960 when this vessel was scrapped.

Mr. William Frederick Stifel was this ship's namesake. He was born August 12, 1840 in Wheeling, West Virginia and was educated in Linsly Institute. In 1855 he joined the family concern which had been started in Wheeling by his father in 1835. He was at first an apprentice in the woolen mills of the firm, but in 1859 joined with his brother, Mr. L. C. Stifel, to form a partnership with his father in the firm of John L. Stifel & Sons, Incorporated.

From this time onward the firm expanded greatly. About fifty people were employed in the making of calico textiles. Mr. Stifel grew in influence in the firm and after serving for several years as general manager, was elected president of the company in 1881. He continued in the family business until his death at Wheeling, West Virginia on February 19, 1930.

Mr. Stifel was a prominent citizen of his native city and was an original member of the board of directors of Wheeling Steel Corporation. His namesake is shown below in the St. Mary's River on August 10, 1957.

Steamer BEN E. TATE

OWNER:	Columbia Transportation Division, Oglebay Norton Company
BUILT:	Chicago Shipbuilding Company, Chicago, Illinois—1902
HULL NO.:	56
O. A. DIMENSIONS:	376' × 50' × 28'
FORMER DATA:	Launched as the bulk freighter PANAY. Renamed WILLIAM NELSON in 1928. Converted to a self-unloader at Leatham D. Smith Dock Company, Sturgeon Bay, Wisconsin in 1930. Given last name in 1936.

Mr. Benjamin Ethan Tate was the namesake of this small self-unloader. He was born at Mount Vernon, Illinois on September 4, 1890 and was a graduate of Vanderbilt University in 1910.

Mr. Tate's career began in small coal firms located in the coal-mining regions of the United States where he served as an office worker and accountant. During World War I he joined United Collieries, Inc. as vice president and was elected that firm's president in 1920.

Mr. Tate also held offices or directorships in other companies including, Diamond Elkhorn Coal Company, Raymond City Coal and Transportation Company, Continental Collieries, Inc. and United Mineral Development Company. He died at Cincinnati, Ohio on March 15, 1968. This was the same year his namesake was sold for scrap.

The vessel is shown in the above photograph in the Welland Ship Canal on November 12, 1960. This ship is the last on which this author worked during the summer college vacation of 1957.

Steamer G. A. TOMLINSON (2)

OWNER:	Columbia Transportation Division, Oglebay Norton Company
BUILT:	Great Lakes Engineering Works, Ecorse, Michigan—1907
HULL NO.:	29
O. A. DIMENSIONS:	556'9" × 58' × 31'
FORMER DATA:	Launched as the bulk freighter D. O. MILLS. Converted to a self-unloader at Fraser-Nelson Shipbuilding and Dry Dock Company, Superior, Wisconsin and given last name in 1960.

Mr. George Ashley Tomlinson who was born at Lapeer, Michigan on January 26, 1869 is the namesake of this ship. He was educated in the public schools of Detroit, Michigan and spent two years after graduation in Wyoming as a cowboy. There he was captured and tortured by Indians. He then returned to Michigan and worked on newspapers in Detroit and on the New York Sun, later becoming managing editor of the Detroit Times.

In 1893 Mr. Tomlinson moved to Duluth, Minnesota and set up a vessel agency. This gradually led him to the belief that his future lay in ships and in 1901 he became a ship owner when the Steamer SULTANA was delivered for his account. The fleet grew to eighteen vessels at its zenith.

He was president of the Duluth Steamship Company, Superior Steamship Company, Globe Steamship Company and the Inter Ocean Steamship Company and was a member of the executive committee of Lake Carriers' Association. In the late 1930's he was also chairman of the board of Missouri Pacific Railroad. Mr. Tomlinson died on January 24, 1942 in Pasedena, California. His namesake is shown above at Cleveland, Ohio on October 24, 1979. It was sold for scrap later in 1979.

Steamer WYANDOTTE (4)

OWNER: Columbia Transportation Division, Oglebay Norton Company
BUILT: Great Lakes Engineering Works, Ecorse, Michigan - 1916
HULL NO.: 155
O. A. DIMENSIONS: 439'3" x 56' x 30'
FORMER DATA: Launched as CONNEAUT (2). Given last name in 1963.

The self-unloading Steamer WYANDOTTE (4) took its name in reference to the former owner of the vessel, Wyandotte Chemicals Corporation, which is headquartered in Wyandotte, Michigan, a suburb of Detroit. It came into this fleet in 1966 along with other ships the firm owned.

The chemical firm sells mostly to large customers and is a leading producer of basic heavy chemicals and of cleaning and sanitizing products for industrial and institutional use. Plants are located throughout the North American continent.

The firm was incorporated under the above name on December 30, 1942 as a consolidation of Michigan Alkali Company and J. B. Ford Company, both founded in the 1890's by the late Mr. J. B Ford. The company is now a subsidiary of an international organization and is known as BASF Wyandotte.

The Steamer WYANDOTTE (4) made its maiden voyage July 12, 1916 departing Ecorse, Michigan light for Conneaut, Ohio to load coal. After several years in lay-up it was sold for scrap in 1973. It is shown above in Rouge River at Detroit, Michigan.

Steamer OUTARDE (2)

OWNER: Comet Enterprises, Limited
BUILT: Superior Shipbuilding Company, Superior, Wisconsin – 1906
HULL NO.: 513
O. A. DIMENSIONS: 545' x 55' x 31'
FORMER DATA: Launched as ABRAHAM STEARN. Renamed EDWARD N. SAUNDERS, JR. (1) in 1914. Renamed JOHN C. WILLIAMS in 1931. Renamed MICHAEL K. TEWKSBURY in 1956. Given last name in 1963.

The Steamer OUTARDE (2) was named after Riviere-aux-Outardes, a river in Saguenay County, Quebec which provided power for the building of the city of Baie Comeau, Quebec and the Quebec North Shore Paper Company plant there.

The river is two hundred-seventy miles in length and flows southward from its origin to join the St. Lawrence River about fifteen miles west of Baie Comeau at Pointe-aux-Outardes. Its name is derived from the French word for geese - Outardes. Numerous wild geese are frequently found along the river and the region is an ideal hunting area. In 1937 a 70,000 horsepower hydro-electric plant was built on the river to harness its flow and produce power for area development.

The bulk freight Steamer OUTARDE (2) is shown below downbound in Lake St. Clair on June 11, 1968. It remained active for this fleet until being sold for scrap late in 1973.

Steamer THOROLD (3)

OWNER:	Comet Enterprises Limited
BUILT:	American Ship Building Company, Lorain, Ohio - 1917
HULL NO.:	722
O. A. DIMENSIONS:	550' x 58' x 31'
FORMER DATA:	Launched as CARMI A. THOMPSON. Given last name in 1963.

The oil-fired bulk freight Steamer THOROLD (3) is shown below in the approach to the Iroquois Lock of the St. Lawrence Seaway System on May 26, 1968. It is upbound towards its namesake port with a full cargo of pulpwood from Baie Comeau, Quebec. This vessel was active until the end of the navigation season in 1971 and was sold for scrap and for December, 1971 delivery for that fate at Port Colborne, Ontario. On docking, the "LD" was deleted from the ship name so that the name THOROLD could be re-used in the active fleet in the future.

This vessel was the flagship of the fleet until its demise. The namesake of this vessel was the town of Thorold, Ontario which is the corporate headquarters of the Ontario Paper Company, parent owners of this vessel and the fleet. The area also served as operating headquarters for the fleet.

Thorold is situated on the Welland Ship Canal in Welland Country, Ontario and was chosen by the Ontario Paper Company as its primary site because of the access to the inland waterways to move its goods.

This fleet handled everything from paper machines to needles for the parent firm from 1914 until ceasing operation at the end of 1983. Annual cargoes ran 700,000 tons of newsprint, pulpwood, pig iron, salt and clay plus 20,000,000 bushels of grain.

Steamer AMERICAN

OWNER: Construction Aggregates Corporation
BUILT: Manitowoc Shipbuilding Company,
Manitowoc, Wisconsin - 1921
HULL NO.: 201
O. A. DIMENSIONS: 255' x 42' x 20'
FORMER DATA: Lengthened 40' at Manitowoc Shipbuilding Company, Manitowoc, Wisconsin in 1946.

The Steamer AMERICAN was a self-unloading suction sand dredge named for the country of her registry. This vessel last operated in 1956 and is shown above at Milwaukee, Wisconsin on June 22nd of that year. The vessel was then laid-up and remained that way until sold for non-transortation use at South Chicago, Illinois in 1980. It was sold for scrap in 1983.

Construction Aggregates Corporation has been involved with Great Lakes shipping for over fifty years and employed this vessel in the sand trade to deliver that product to its docks and that of its customers on Lake Michigan. Extensive landfill projects became a boon to the firm and equated to boom times. Likewise, when projects were not so active, slack times for them and this vessel happened. The stellar project was in 1929-1931 in preparation for the Chicago World's Fair of 1932. Literally millions of tons of sand and lake bottom material were moved into place at Jackson Park on the south side of Chicago, Illinois for this event.

Steamer ALGONAC

OWNER: Construction Materials Corporation
BUILT: Detroit Dry Dock Company, Wyandotte, Michigan—1884
HULL NO.: 70
O. A. DIMENSIONS: 258'9" × 38'6" × 18'
FORMER DATA: Launched as the package freighter SYRACUSE (1). Converted to a combination package freight and passenger vessel at Reid Dry Dock Company, Port Huron, Michigan and renamed LAKEWOOD (1) in 1912. Re-converted to a package freighter at Toledo Shipbuilding Company, Toledo, Ohio in 1915. Converted to a bulk freighter and shortened 21'3" at Detroit Shipbuilding Company, Wyandotte, Michigan in 1919. Converted to a sandsucker at Buffalo Dry Dock Company, Buffalo, New York in 1925. Converted to a self-unloading sandsucker at Nicholson Engineering Works, River Rouge, Michigan and renamed K. V. SCHWARTZ in 1947. Given last name in 1953.

The venerable freight Steamer ALGONAC is shown above at Windsor, Ontario on June 14, 1962. It remained active on the Great Lakes until it was sold in 1962 for reduction to a barge. It subsequently sank, was raised and was scrapped.

During its last years, this vessel dredged actively in the area of its namesake town—Algonac, Michigan. Algonac is a town of about 4,000 population near the mouth of the St. Clair River at its southern end. Algonac means, literally, "place of the Algonquins."

Steamer CANADIANA

OWNER:	Crystal Beach Transit Company
BUILT:	Buffalo Dry Dock Company, Buffalo, New York—1910
HULL NO.:	215
O. A. DIMENSIONS:	216' × 45' × 18'10"

This day excursion Steamer CANADIANA was delivered to its owners on June 18, 1910. It was sold to these owners in 1934 and subsequently has sustained a fitful life. From 1958 onward it has changed hands several times, though never as an operating ship, and is now moored at Collision Bend on the Cuyahoga River at Cleveland, Ohio awaiting its current restaurant owner's conversion to a cusine "flotilerry."

In the glorious days of this vessel it sailed on Lake Erie much as it is seen in the above photograph—full of decks of happy faces enjoying an old-fashioned "steamboat ride." This photograph was taken on one of the occasions of the vessel's appearance in the Detroit River.

There was an amusement park at Crystal Beach and it was a favorite spot for Buffalonians to "get away." On peak holiday runs this vessel would be literally filled to capacity with patrons. When the automobile came into its own and travelers began to prefer setting their own departure times by using their own vehicles, patronage of the steamer began its downward trend. Finally, the service was abandoned both for lack of business and because of the ever-higher costs to maintain and operate a ship for what amounted to a very short period of utilization. It is a credit to the memory of this fine vessel and its former service, however, that to this day the dock area where she formerly came is still called the Crystal Beach dock.

Steamer CITY OF CLEVELAND III

OWNER:	Detroit and Cleveland Navigation Company
BUILT:	Detroit Shipbuilding Company, Wyandotte, Michigan—1908
HULL NO.:	168
O. A. DIMENSIONS:	402' × 54' × 22'
FORMER DATA:	Launched as CITY OF CLEVELAND (4). Given last name in 1908.

Shown under way in the Detroit River on July 11, 1947, the Steamer CITY OF CLEVELAND III was one of the fine palatial passenger liners of this firm's fleet. It also carried package freight for most of its career but this was dropped after World War II when trucks captured a much larger share of inter-city traffic in this field than they had held prior to World War II.

This vessel was equipped with paddle wheels for its propulsion and these can be detected amidships in this photograph, churning up the water. The extreme breadth over these paddle wheel boxes was 91 feet. This ship suffered damage in a collision in 1950 and was retired from service. It was sold for scrap in 1956 after having been partially dismantled for use as a barge in 1954. That project never saw fulfillment and the hull was scrapped.

The namesake of this liner was Cleveland, Ohio. This city of 1,519 square miles in metropolitan area and 2,000,000 population was founded in 1796 when Mr. Moses Cleaveland chose the site as the capital for the Western Reserve.

This ship sailed on its maiden voyage June 4, 1908 from Detroit, Michigan to Sault Ste. Marie, Michigan.

Steamer CITY OF DETROIT III

OWNER:	Detroit and Cleveland Navigation Company
BUILT:	Detroit Shipbuilding Company, Wyandotte, Michigan—1912
HULL NO.:	187
O. A. DIMENSIONS:	470' × 55'4" × 22'
FORMER DATA:	Launched as CITY OF DETROIT. Given last name in 1912.

The passenger Steamer CITY OF DETROIT III was one of the palatial overnight liners of the inland seas operated by this company until 1956 when it was finally sold for scrap. After partial dismantling that year, the hull was subsequently scrapped at Hamilton, Ontario in 1957.

This fine steamer is shown in the above photograph on June 22, 1941. The maiden trip of this vessel was made from Detroit, Michigan on June 12, 1912 with a group of earlier-day folk of the Detroit Board of Commerce who had chartered this ship for a trip into Lake Huron and the Upper Lakes and return to Detroit.

This steamer was one of several of its day with paddle-wheel propulsion. The wheels are barely visible in this picture, but the churning water can be detected amidships. The dimension given above is moulded breadth. The total breadth of this ship including the outside of the paddle-wheel boxes was 93'.

Other ships of this line were named CITY OF DETROIT and all had that city as their namesakes. Known throughout the world as the motor capital of the world, this city of nearly 4,500,000 population in the metropolitan area, is the largest and most important port in the state of Michigan. It was the home city of these owners also.

Steamer EASTERN STATES

OWNER:	Detroit and Cleveland Navigation Company
BUILT:	Detroit Shipbuilding Company, Wyandotte, Michigan—1902
HULL NO.:	144
O. A. DIMENSIONS:	360′ × 45′6″ × 19′6″

The passenger Steamer EASTERN STATES is shown above while under way in the Detroit River on one of its many visits to that city from Lake Erie during its fifty-four year career. This venerable ship was sold for scrap in 1956 and totally met that fate at Hamilton, Ontario in 1957 after the superstructure had been intentionally burned off on Lake St. Clair.

Like its sister ship WESTERN STATES, this was a paddle wheel steamer and measured 80 feet in total width over the paddle boxes. In conjunction with this same sister ship, this vessel took as its namesake the eastern two-fifths of the continental United States.

The eastern states area is generally regarded to be that area lying east of the Mississippi River. It begins in the state of Wisconsin at the north and extends southward through Illinois, Kentucky, Tennessee and Mississippi to the Gulf of Mexico.

This area of the United States was the first colonized by early settlers and, of course, bears much historic importance in its past character and activities. It is the most densely populated area of this country today and has within its boundaries the most advanced manufacturing centers in the western world. It is also prominent for nearly totally encompassing the entire Great Lakes region.

Steamer GREATER DETROIT

OWNER: Detroit and Cleveland Navigation Company
BUILT: American Ship Building Company, Lorain, Ohio—1923 and Great Lakes Engineering Works, Ecorse, Michigan—1924
HULL NO.: 785
O. A. DIMENSIONS: 535' × 58'3" × 23'7"

This vessel was primarily built at Lorain, Ohio but was towed to Detroit, Michigan October 8, 1923 for finishing of the vessel's interior and wood decorations. It sailed from that port on its maiden voyage August 28, 1924 for Buffalo, New York. The ship is shown leaving Mackinac Island in 1949, her last year of operation.

When placed in commission, this vessel and its sister ship, GREATER BUFFALO, were the largest side wheel passenger steamers in the world. It continued active in the Great Lakes trade of these owners until being sold for scrap in 1956. The men who bought her, however, had plans to rehabilitate the ship and return her to operation. When these failed to materialize it was decided to junk the ship and the hull was cut up at Hamilton, Ontario in 1957.

The namesake of this vessel was the total area and hinterland of the owners. Greater Detroit has an area of 1,965 square miles and a current population of about 4,500,000 persons. It is the fifth largest center of population in the United States and was for the duration of this fleet's operations the headquarters city of the line.

Steamer JACK DALTON

OWNER:	Detroit Atlantic Navigation Company
BUILT:	Great Lakes Engineering Works, River Rouge, Michigan—1952
HULL NO.:	296
O. A. DIMENSIONS:	360'2" × 73'6" × 25'3"
FORMER DATA:	Launched as VACATIONLAND. Renamed JACK DALTON in 1960.

This vessel was originally built for the State of Michigan for service in the Straits of Mackinac. It was sold when the Mackinaw Bridge did away with the need for ferries and, after a short tenure in this firm, was sold for off-lakes use in 1961. It is shown above at Cleveland, Ohio on its maiden voyage to that city on May 5, 1960.

The namesake of this ship was Mr. Carson Elwood "Jack" Dalton who was born in Manistique, Michigan on November 9, 1904. He was educated at the University of Notre Dame from which he graduated in 1927 with a B.A. degree, majoring in foreign commerce. In that year he joined Chrysler Corporation in the Detroit, Michigan headquarters where he worked in the international division.

Mr. Dalton joined Ford Motor Company in its international division in 1950. In 1958 he was elected a vice president of operations at Toronto, Ontario for Ford. He returned to Detroit the following year. In 1960, with the Browning interests of Detroit, he was instrumental in the short-lived operations of this vessel in the above named owning firm. The purpose of the operation between Detroit and Cleveland was to move cross-country tractor trailors. But, after a few months' operation, the idea was dropped and this vessel was sold.

Mr. Dalton resumed business activities with Goodbody & Company in the investment field and was with that firm when he died at Birmingham, Michigan on June 24, 1966. He was an avid gardner and enjoyed the outdoors.

Motor Vessel JEAN-TALON

OWNER: Desgagnes Navigation Limited
BUILT: Swan, Hunter & Wigham Richardson, Limited, Wallsend-on-Tyne, England—1936
HULL NO.: 1517
O. A. DIMENSIONS: 259' × 43'9" × 22'
FORMER DATA: Launched as FRANQUELIN (2). Renamed PRINCE UNGAVA in 1964. Given last name in 1967.

Jean Baptiste Talon is the man for whom this vessel was named. He was born at Chalons Sur Marne, France in 1619 and was educated at Jesuit College, Paris, France. Following his education he joined the civil service of his country and was appointed commissary of war in Turenne's army in 1653.

In 1655 he became intendant of the province of Hainant and of New France on March 23, 1665. He was the first administrator of New France from this time until returning to France in 1668 and served again from 1670 to 1672 before returning to France for the last time.

He is credited with taking the first census in Canada and with organizing a selective and growing immigration, importing skilled craftsman in all trades and with building the first dry dock and ships at Quebec City. He also founded the first brewery in that city. His know-how was responsible for the foundation of the colony being built upon sound economic ground. Jean-Talon died on November 24, 1694.

His namesake still appears on the Lakes, but only occasionally since it was put into lower St. Lawrence River and Maritime trades in 1964. It is shown below with a full cargo of pulpwood in the lower St. Lawrence River.

Motor Vessel GARY

OWNER:	Energy Cooperative, Inc.
BUILT:	Sun Shipbuilding & Dry Dock Company, Chester, Pennsylvania – 1931
HULL NO.:	138
O. A. DIMENSIONS:	201'3" x 34' x 12'
FORMER DATA:	Launched as WHITE FLASH. Renamed BERT REINAUER (1) in 1944. Renamed CHARLES McCARREN in 1951. Renamed SINCLAIR POWER in 1953. Renamed SINCLAIR GARY in 1955. Given last name in 1972.

The tank Motor Vessel GARY was used as a bunkering ship in the Chicagoland area of lower Lake Michigan for over twenty years and laid idle during 1978-79 because of its age and condition. Finally, in early 1980, it was sold to a Peoria, Illinois resident for off-lake use as a storage hull on the inland waterways. The ship is shown above at East Chicago, Indiana on November 30, 1978.

The namesake of the ship was the city of Gary, Indiana. The city of 185,000 population is named in honor of Judge Elbert Henry Gary, a steel industrialist and lawyer who helped form United States Steel Corporation in 1901.

Gary was planned in 1903 and was rapidly built up by the United States Steel Corporation from barren sand dunes and marsh wasteland into what was for many years the largest steel-making facility in the world.

Motor Vessel CEMICO-ERIE

OWNER: Erie Navigation Company
BUILT: John W. Sullivan Company, Elizabeth, New Jersey - 1921
HULL NO.: 83
O. A. DIMENSIONS: 198' x 28'6" x 12'6"
FORMER DATA: Launched as SYRACUSE SOCONY. Lengthened 40' at New York Shipbuilding Corporation, Camden, New Jersey in 1924. Renamed FRANKLIN REINAUER in 1946. Renamed K. H. DUNBAR in 1950. Renamed DU-VAL in 1952. Renamed CEMICO-ERIE in 1954.

The tank Motor Vessel CEMICO-ERIE had two namesakes in that it honored the home port headquarters of the owning company–Erie, Pennsylvania–and it also honored the early beginnings of the last Great Lakes owning firm. The vessel was sold for off-lakes use on December 5, 1958 and left the lakes in the spring of 1959.

The first word of this ship name is its most prominent namesake. The word CEMICO is taken from the first two letters of the company name Cement Mix Company. This firm was in operation years ago as a subsidiary of the Erie Sand & Gravel Company and was a ready-mix trucking company.

In 1951 the Cemico Oil Company was formed in the state of Pennsylvania, as a subsidiary of the Erie Sand & Gravel Company, to distribute heating oils in the Erie County area of the state. When deciding upon a name for the new corporation, management cast back to the trucking firm noted above and picked letters from that corporate name for the new firm name.

This vessel served in bringing to Erie the various types of oils that were to be distributed inland. The Cemico Oil Company was sold to United Refining Company of Warren, Pennsylvania in 1968. This tanker is shown above while upbound in the Detroit River abreast Ojibway, Ontario.

Motor Vessel PEERLESS (2)

OWNER:	Erie Navigation Company
BUILT:	Manitowoc Shipbuilding Company, Manitowoc, Wisconsin – 1926
HULL NO.:	223
O. A. DIMENSIONS:	152' x 33'6" x 15'
FORMER DATA:	Launched as the cement carrier DANIEL McCOOL. Renamed J. B. JOHN (2) in 1951. Converted to a self-unloader at Breckling Concrete Corporation, Cleveland, Ohio and renamed A. G. BRECKLING in 1965. Reconverted to a cement carrier at Erie Navigation Company, Erie, Pennsylvania and renamed PEERLESS in 1969.

Namesake of this diminutive bulk vessel was the Peerless Cement Division, American Cement Corporation. The firm was incorporated in Delaware on April 10, 1928 as Riverside Cement Company. Through the years since then several acquisitions were made and on December 31, 1957 Hercules Cement Corporation and Peerless Cement Corporation were merged and the name changed to American Cement Corporation with headquarters in Los Angeles, California.

This ship shuttled between Detroit's Peerless plant and the Cleveland, Ohio silo facility briefly in 1969. Economics of the movement did not prove satisfactory and, after laying idle for six seasons, the ship was sold for off-lakes use in 1976. It is shown in this photograph underway in 1969 in the Detroit River.

Steamer HYDRO

OWNER:	Erie Sand & Gravel Company
BUILT:	Manitowoc Shipbuilding Company, Manitowoc, Wisconsin—1913
HULL NO.:	59
O. A. DIMENSIONS:	185' × 40'6" × 19'

The self-unloading sandsucker Steamer HYDRO ended its career as a partially demolished ship which was sunk at Erie, Pennsylvania to form part of a dock extension on the property of the owning company. This occurred in 1962.

During the life of the ship it helped construct many areas by providing landfill which was dredged up from the lake and river bottoms. Perhaps none of these activities was so important to the ship name as the activity in which the vessel was engaged when first brought out.

For a number of years the Steamer HYDRO was engaged in providing landfill to assist in the building of the great power dams now in evidence near Niagara Falls, New York. These are hydro-electric installations and it was in consort with the development of these facilities that this vessel came into being.

It is fitting, therefore, that the name chosen for this ship by its former owners, the Kelley Island Lime and Transport Company, be in honor of the trade and purpose for which the vessel was mainly employed after its construction.

The Steamer HYDRO is shown in this photograph at Cheboyganning Creek, Saginaw River, Michigan on June 16, 1959.

Motor Vessel ROCKWOOD

OWNER:	Erie Sand & Gravel Company
BUILT:	F. W. Wheeler & Company, West Bay City, Michigan—1899
HULL NO.:	127
O. A. DIMENSIONS:	240' × 40' × 16'3"
FORMER DATA:	Launched as the bulk carrier JESSE SPAULDING. Renamed MOOREMACK in 1916. Renamed VINDAL in 1921. Renamed CORDOVA (1) in 1923. Converted to a self-unloading sandsucker at Great Lakes Engineering Works, Ecorse, Michigan and renamed JAY A. PEARSON in 1925. Given last name in 1935.

The Motor Vessel ROCKWOOD was sold for scrap in 1963 and is shown in the above photograph at Cleveland, Ohio on June 24, 1959. It was shortly after this that the owners sold the ship for scrapping in Ashtabula, Ohio.

Throughout the history of sand ships on the Great Lakes a common suffix has been attached to the names of many of them. Thus, the suffix "WOOD" in this ship name had been carried forward from the heyday of sand dredging on the Great Lakes until the ship's demise.

The prefix "ROCK" was related to the namesake of this vessel. No specific rock or group of rocks were thought of when the ship name was decided upon, but rather the name was picked by former owners of the ship because of that word's relation to sand and sand dredging.

Motor Vessel LIL' ROCK

OWNER: Erie Sand & Gravel Company, Esco Dredge & Fill Division
BUILT: Manitowoc Shipbuilding Company, Manitowoc, Wisconsin – 1942
HULL NO.: 338
O. A. DIMENSIONS: 120' x 32' x 6'
FORMER DATA: Launched as the Landing Craft, Tank vessel L C T 516. Given last name in 1947. Converted to a sandsucker by Toth Transportation Company, Toledo, Ohio in 1948.

Shown above at Milwaukee, Wisconsin on September 21, 1974 as it lay awaiting a role for its new tasks as a non-transportation use vessel in erosion and flood control, the diminutive ship was active as a sandsucker until sold to the environmental firm early in 1974. The LIL' ROCK was operated for the purpose of pumping sand from lake bottoms and filtering it through its machinery, depositing only sand in the hold and discharging the excess overboard from 1948 until 1974.

The ship name was carried forward by the above owners from Mr. Michael Toth who formerly owned the ship and had it converted for the sandsucking purpose. No specific namesake was intended, except for the fact that the ship operated in waters where "big rocks were separated from little rocks" for the purpose of bringing sand pebbles to the aggregate businesses that wanted this product.

Rocks generally may be separated into three catagories. These are igneous, metamorphic and sedimentary, which are believed to have been formed by heat, pressure and sedimentation.

Steamer ALPENA (1)

OWNER: Erie Sand Steamship Company
BUILT: Detroit Shipbuilding Company, Wyandotte, Michigan - 1909
HULL NO.: 177
O. A. DIMENSIONS: 376' x 47'3" x 26'3"
FORMER DATA: Launched as ALPENA. Renamed SIDNEY E. SMITH, JR. (1) in 1968. Renamed ALPENA (1), for the second time, in 1972.

When this self-unloader was built for the account of the Michigan Alkali Company it was the second ship of this type ever built on the Great Lakes. It is the eldest ship on the Great Lakes that was built as a self-unloader.

This vessel was originally named in honor of Alpena, Michigan and served in its last days under that name also. For the duration of four years it bore its second name. When this firm acquired a larger ship the SMITH, JR. name was given to that and this vessel was retired, taking its original name again.

The city of 16,000 population is situated on Thunder Bay, an arm of Lake Huron and the largest industry is the cement plant. Also made in the city, however, is machinery, automobile trim, hardboard, paper and hydraulic cylinders. The community is a summer and winter resort, with an annual winter carnival, and good hunting and fishing areas within easy reach. It was first settled in 1835 as a trading post. It was laid out in 1853 and incorporated as a city in 1871.

This vessel is shown above at Humberstone, Ontario on October 28, 1967. It was sold for scrap in 1972, never seeing operation under its original name for the second time.

Steamer J. F. SCHOELLKOPF, JR.

OWNER: Erie Sand Steamship Company
BUILT: American Ship Building Company, Lorain, Ohio—1907
HULL NO.: 349
O. A. DIMENSIONS: 557' × 56' × 31'
FORMER DATA: Launched as the bulk freighter HUGH KENNEDY. Given present name in 1930. Converted to a self-unloader at American Ship Building Company, Lorain, Ohio in 1933.

Mr. Jacob Frederick Schoellkopf, Jr. was the namesake of this self-unloader. He was born in Buffalo, New York on May 3, 1883 and received a B.A. degree from Cornell University in 1905 and his Ph.D. in chemistry in 1908.

At this time he joined Schoellkopf, Hartford & Hanna Company as a chemist and became secretary of Schoellkopf Aniline &Chemical Works in 1912. When that firm merged with National Aniline & Chemical Company, Inc., in 1917 he served until 1918 as vice president and director of manufacturing. During 1919 he visited the Orient to study conditions in China and Japan. Upon returning he helped organize the investment house of Schoellkopf, Hutton & Company and became its first vice president in 1922.

Mr. Schoellkopf became president of Niagara Shares Corporation in 1930 and retained that post until retiring on October 23, 1950. He died at Buffalo, New York on December 16, 1952. Among other directorships, he was on the board of American Steamship Company, former owners of this vessel. This ship is shown unloading at the United States Gypsum dock, River Rouge, Michigan on August 20, 1978. The ship was sold for scrap in 1980.

Motor Vessel JOSEPH S. SCOBELL

OWNER:	Erie Sand Steamship Company
BUILT:	Cleveland Shipbuilding Company, Cleveland, Ohio—1891
HULL NO.:	12
O. A. DIMENSIONS:	284' × 38'6" × 24'
FORMER DATA:	Launched as the bulk freighter GRIFFIN (1). Converted to a crane ship at American Ship Building Company, Superior, Wisconsin in 1918. Re-converted to a bulk freighter at Buffalo Dry Dock Company, Buffalo, New York in 1929. Converted to a self-unloading sandsucker at Erie Sand Steamship Company, Erie, Pennsylvania and given last name in 1938.

When finally sold for scrap in 1970, this ship was the oldest bulk freight vessel on the Great Lakes. It is shown in the photograph above in the Cuyahoga River at Cleveland, Ohio.

Mr. Joseph Spurway Scobell was this vessel's namesake. He was born in Kingston, Ontario on February 12, 1854 and was the son of the governor of the Provincial Prison at Kingston. After completing his education, he went to Erie, Pennsylvania in 1874 as a railroad telegrapher and worked his way up to become superintendent of the Renova Division of the Pennsylvania Railroad.

In 1898 Mr. Scobell went with a group of Erie people in organizing what is now the Erie Sand & Gravel Company. He became president of the firm and continued in that capacity until his death on December 18, 1927.

Steamer SIDNEY E. SMITH, JR. (2)

OWNER:	Erie Sand Steamship Company
BUILT:	Detroit Shipbuilding Company, Wyandotte, Michigan—1906
HULL NO.:	161
O. A. DIMENSIONS:	500' × 52'3" × 30'
FORMER DATA:	Launched as the bulk freighter W. K. BIXBY. Renamed J. L. REISS in 1920. Converted to a self-unloader at Manitowoc Shipbuilding Company, Manitowoc, Wisconsin in 1933. Given last name in 1972.

The namesake of this self-unloading bulk freighter was Mr. Sidney Errington Smith, Jr. who was born at Buffalo, New York on October 15, 1925. He was educated in the Nichols School at Buffalo and graduated from the Oxford School of Business Administration in Boston, Massachusetts in 1948. Mr. Smith had sailed during the summers of his college days and upon graduation sailed the balance of the 1948 season on the Great Lakes.

In March, 1949 he went to work in the marine department of the Erie Sand Steamship Company and became marine manager of that firm in 1951. Mr. Smith was elected vice president of the company in 1956 and became president of the organization in 1964.

This vessel is shown above on June 4, 1972 in the Detroit River. On June 5, 1972, at 0150 hours, it was struck by the Steamer PARKER EVANS abreast Port Huron, Michigan and sunk. On June 21, 1972 it was abandoned and has since been demolished.

Steamer JACK WIRT

OWNER: Erie Sand Steamship Company
BUILT: American Ship Building Company, Cleveland, Ohio—1910
HULL NO.: 448
O. A. DIMENSIONS: 524' x 54' x 30'
FORMER DATA: Launched as the bulk freighter A. M. BYERS. Converted to a self-unloader at American Ship Building Company, Toledo, Ohio in 1955. Renamed CLEMENS A. REISS (2) in 1959. Given last name in 1970.

The self-unloading Steamer JACK WIRT began its career on June 17, 1910 when it sailed on its maiden trip with a cargo of coal from Toledo, Ohio to Duluth, Minnesota. The vessel was active until being sold for scrap late in 1973 and is shown above in Cleveland, Ohio on July 10, 1973.

Namesake of this vessel was Mr. Jack Wirt who was born in New York, New York April 6, 1917. He was educated in schools in Detroit, Michigan and the University of Detroit and moved to Bay City, Michigan in 1940. In 1942 he began a transport company with two dump trucks. In 1944 he opened the Martin Street dock at Bay City and 10 years later the Crow Island dock in Saginaw, Michigan. Mr. Wirt is president of Wirt Transport Company and Wirt Stone Docks.

When the Boland and Cornelius group acquired this ship in 1970 they gave it this name. When it was then sold to these owners on July 27, 1972, Erie Sand management kept the name on the boat.

Barge WILTRANCO

OWNER: Escanaba Towing Company
BUILT: Toledo Shipbuilding Company, Toledo, Ohio – 1917
HULL NO.: 137
O. A. DIMENSIONS: 585' x 60' x 32'
FORMER DATA: Launched as the powered bulk freighter HORACE S. WILKINSON (2). Converted to a barge and shortened 15' at Fraser-Nelson Shipbuilding & Dry Dock Company, Superior, Wisconsin in 1963. Renamed WILTRANCO I in 1963. Given last name in 1970.

This bulk freight unit was the object of an experiment in 1963 and 1964 when the steamer hull was shortened and notched in the stern for use with a high-powered tug. The idea was to make commodity movement more economical by use of fewer crew and less costly machinery. But the vessel took too long for round trip voyages and never lived up to expectations. It finally grounded outside Buffalo, New York, laid there for over a year, was salvaged and partially repaired for service, and began to operate for these owners.

Though intermittently successful, a series of mishaps proved too much to cope with and the hull was sold for scrap in 1973. It is shown above being pushed by the tug OLIVE L. MOORE in the St. Mary's River on August 12, 1970.

The Roman numeral "I" was dropped from the name when these owners took over in 1970. When the concept was initiated this unit was to be one of many, thus the designation "I." The balance of the name came from <u>Wil</u>son Marine <u>Trans</u>it <u>Co</u>mpany, founders of the concept.

Motor Vessel BUCKEYE STATE (2)

OWNER:	Federal Motorship Corporation
BUILT:	St. Lawrence Marine Repair Dock Corporation, Ogdensburg, New York—1930
HULL NO.:	2
O. A. DIMENSIONS:	260' × 43'6" × 18'

The New York State Barge Canal-type Motor Vessel BUCKEYE STATE was active on the Great Lakes and through the New York State Barge Canal until being sold for off-lakes in 1956.

The namesake of this vessel was the thirteenth state to be admitted to the Union. Ohio gained statehood on March 1, 1803 and was the first state carved out of the Northwest Territory. It is called the "Mother of Presidents" since so many of the nation's leaders have come from Ohio.

The state has an area of 41,222 square miles of which 250 square miles are inland water. It is the largest iron ore receiving and coal shipping state on the Great Lakes and has been the state of the most shipbuilding activity on the Great Lakes.

The nickname "Buckeye State" originated because of the plentiful supply of buckeye , or horse chestnut, trees that once grew on Ohio's hills and plains. Many of these trees still can be found, but they are not as plentiful as when the state was less densely populated. Current population of Ohio is about ten million, two hundred-thousand inhabitants.

The Motor Vessel BUCKEYE STATE is shown below on one of its typical voyages in the connecting channels of the Great Lakes system.

Steamer ROBERT S. Mc NAMARA

OWNER: Ford Motor Company
BUILT: Great Lakes Engineering Works, Ecorse, Michigan—1909
HULL NO.: 66
O. A. DIMENSIONS: 500' × 56' × 30'
FORMER DATA: Launched as STADACONA (1). Renamed W. H. McGEAN in 1921. Given last name in 1962.

Mr. Robert Strange Mc Namara was born in San Francisco, California on June 9, 1916 and received a B.A. degree from the University of California in 1937 and an M.B.A. degree from Harvard University in 1939. He joined the accounting firm of Price, Waterhouse & Company in 1939 and taught at Harvard University in the period 1940-1943.

Mr. Mc Namara then went to England as a civilian consultant for the War Department and subsequently served in the United States Air Force. He was discharged in 1946 with the rank of lieutenant colonel. At this time he joined the Ford Motor Company as manager of the planning and financial analysis office. In 1949 he was named controller, in August, 1953 he was named assistant general manager of the Ford Division, and in January, 1955, he was elected a vice president and general manager of that division.

Mr. Mc Namara became a group vice president in 1957 and served as Ford's president from November 9, 1960 until January 1, 1961 when he resigned to become Secretary of Defense of the United States. He left that post November 29, 1967 to become president of the World Bank.

His namesake is shown below with a full cargo of coal for the Ford plant on the Rouge River on August 13, 1967. It was sold in 1972 for use as a dockface on the Rouge River and for scrap in 1973.

Barge ERIE (2)

OWNER:	Harry G. Gamble Shipyards
BUILT:	Detroit Dry Dock Company, Wyandotte, Michigan – 1894
HULL NO.:	119
O. A. DIMENSIONS:	210' x 32' x 12'6"
FORMER DATA:	Launched as the powered passenger vessel PENNSYLVANIA (1). Renamed OWANA in 1902. Renamed ERIE in 1927. Converted to a bulk freight barge at Nicholson Terminal and Dock Company, Ecorse, Michigan and renamed T. A. IVEY in 1934. Renamed ERIE, for the second time, in 1964.

The bulk freight Barge ERIE once sailed Lake Erie proudly carrying passengers on enjoyable cruises. It would be interesting to hear the comments from former passengers if they could have seen the vessel as shown above at Port Dover, Ontario on August 19, 1964. Likely, no one would recognize the hull.

As a barge the unit was towed between Erie, Pennsylvania and Port Dover, carrying coal for fuel in the Ivey greenhouse power stations. This stopped when natural gas became the fuel in 1964. After ten years of only occassional use, the vessel was sold for sinking as a breakwall in 1975.

Namesake of the Barge ERIE was Erie, Pennsylvania, the only Great Lakes port of the state of Pennsylvania. It is a city of 145,000 population today handling mostly stone, sand and oil cargoes in addition to general cargo. The former coal, ore and grain docks are no longer in use. Gone also is the once-flourishing lumber and pulpwood trade. The current major new industry is the Litton shipyard known as Erie Marine, Inc.

Steamer RALPH S. CAULKINS

OWNER: Gartland Steamship Company
BUILT: American Ship Building Company, Lorain, Ohio—1902
HULL NO.: 317
O. A. DIMENSIONS: 434' × 50' × 28'3"
FORMER DATA: Launched as J. M. JENKS. Renamed R. R. RICHARDSON in 1916. Given last name in 1942.

The bulk freight Steamer RALPH S. CAULKINS is shown in this photograph downbound with a cargo of grain on August 8, 1960. The ship was sold for scrap in 1963.

Mr. Ralph Stone Caulkins was born at Grosse Pointe, Michigan on May 20, 1923 and received his education at Yale University, graduating with a B.S. degree in metallurgical engineering in 1943. He joined the Canadian Furnace Company at Port Colborne, Ontario that year and worked in the capacity of his degree. In 1949 he left that firm to return to the United States and take the position of vice president of the Waterways Navigation Company at Detroit, Michigan. The firm was headed by his father Mr. H. L. Caulkins and it formerly owned this ship.

Since 1960 Mr. Ralph Caulkins has lived in Fort Lauderdale, Florida and continues as vice president of the Waterways Navigation Company. Before that company acquired the ship in 1941 plans were announced by the Minnesota-Atlantic Transit Company to convert this ship to a package freighter. These plans, however, did not materialize and she remained a bulk freighter in the iron ore, stone and grain trades.

Steamer W. E. FITZGERALD

OWNER: Gartland Steamship Company
BUILT: Detroit Shipbuilding Company, Wyandotte, Michigan—1906
HULL NO.: 167
O. A. DIMENSIONS: 440' × 52'3" × 28'6"
FORMER DATA: Launched as a bulk freighter. Converted to a self-unloader at Boom Electric Welding Company, Cleveland, Ohio in 1928.

The namesake of this self-unloader was Mr. William Edmund Fitzgerald who was born at Milwaukee, Wisconsin on September 27, 1859. He was educated in the local schools and in 1878 began his business career with his father, Mr. John Fitzgerald, who owned the Milwaukee Dry Dock Company of Milwaukee, Wisconsin.

The younger Fitzgerald stayed in the firm until it was acquired by the American Ship Building Company on that firm's beginning in 1900. He then became a director of the parent company and also a member of the executive committee as well as assistant general manager. The yard was headed at that time by Mr. James C. Wallace.

Mr. Fitzgerald served only a short time in this capacity. He was killed by a gas explosion at the family home near Milwaukee, Wisconsin on July 7,1901. His friend and business associate, Captain Denis Sullivan of Chicago, Illinois, named this vessel in memory of Mr. Fitzgerald in 1906. The ship was sold for scrap in 1971 and, though Gartland Steamship vessels carried Boland and Cornelius fleet colors after their merger, this vessel never operated in the Boland managed fleet and is thus shown in her Gartland colors, upbound in the St. Mary's River.

Steamer HENNEPIN (2)

OWNER: Gartland Steamship Company
BUILT: West Bay City Shipbuilding Company, West Bay City, Michigan – 1905
HULL NO.: 614
O. A. DIMENSIONS: 524' x 54' x 30'3"
FORMER DATA: Launched as the bulk freighter SOCAPA. Renamed GEORGE G. BARNUM in 1915. Given last name in 1937. Converted to a self-unloader at American Ship Building Company, Lorain, Ohio in 1957.

The self-unloading Steamer HENNEPIN is shown above while downbound on Lake Huron on July 5, 1972. It defied the scrapper's torch on two occasions before finally bowing out of the Great Lakes scene when it was sold for scrap in 1975.

The namesake of this vessel was Father Jean Louis Hennepin who was born in Ath, Belgium in 1640. He entered Recollet Order Seminary in 1658 and was ordained a priest in 1666. For eight years he visited Italy and Germany and served as an army chaplain. In 1675 he was sent to Canada as a missionary and was stationed at Fort Frontenac on Lake Ontario. In 1678, Father Hennepin joined La Salle's expedition in search of the Mississippi River.

Enroute on this search, Father Hennepin was captured by Indians and later was rescued by Sieur Dulhut in 1680. He returned to Europe in 1681 and never again returned to North America.

Steamer HENRY R. PLATT, JR. (1)

OWNER: Gartland Steamship Company
BUILT: Chicago Shipbuilding Company, Chicago, Illinois - 1901
HULL NO.: 50
O. A. DIMENSIONS: 450' x 50' x 28'8"
FORMER DATA: Launched as FREDERICK B. WELLS. Renamed OTTO M. REISS (1) in 1916. Renamed SULLIVAN BROTHERS (1) in 1934. Given last name in 1957.

This bulk freighter operated only one season under its last name. It was the victim of the severe ice congestion on Lake Erie in December, 1958 and was declared a constructive total loss and never repaired for service as a steamer. The days of usefullness were not lost, however, since it was sold to The Pillsbury Company and used as a floating grain storage unit at Buffalo, New York as PILLSBURY BARGE until being sold for scrap in 1966.

The shipname was carried on in the fleet by another carrier until that unit also was scrapped. Namesake of both vessels was Mr. Henry Russell Platt, Jr. who was born at Chicago, Illinois on November 22, 1897. He was educated at Williams College and joined the Continental Illinois National Bank & Trust Company as a clerk. He rose to the post of vice president by 1952 when he left to become treasurer of the Truax-Traer Coal Company.

Mr. Platt retired from active affiliation in 1962 and devoted his time to the private investment business at Chicago, Illinois. He enjoys golf as his favorite form of recreation.

The steamer that bore this gentleman's name is shown in the picture below at Victory Soya Mills, Toronto, Ontario in July 11, 1958.

Steamer HENRY R. PLATT, JR. (2)

OWNER:	Gartland Steamship Company
BUILT:	American Ship Building Company, Lorain, Ohio—1909
HULL NO.:	370
O. A. DIMENSIONS:	524' × 54' × 30'
FORMER DATA:	Launched as G. A. TOMLINSON (1). Given last name in 1959.

The bulk freight Steamer HENRY R. PLATT, JR. did not operate since this company became a wholly-owned subsidiary of the American Steamship Company. It, therefore, never received the familiar Boland & Cornelius stack colors. The ship was sold for scrap in 1970 and was resold for sinking in a breakwall project in 1971 and sunk in Hamilton, Ontario harbor.

Mr. Henry Russell Platt, Jr. was honored when this ship took his name in 1959. He was born in Chicago, Illinois on November 22, 1897 and graduated from Williams College in 1919 with a B.A. degree. After one year in the United States Air Force, he joined the Continental Illinois National Bank & Trust Company at Chicago, Illinois as a clerk. In due course he progressed through the ranks and held the post of vice president when he left the bank in 1952 to join Truax-Traer Coal Company as treasurer.

This vessel was of the standard "504" size except that it had exceptionally good cubic dimensions in its holds. This fact allowed it to be a competitive carrier in the grain trade for several seasons after its sister ships were retired. The ship is shown at Dain City, Ontario while in the Welland Ship Canal on June 4, 1966.

Steamer SULLIVAN BROTHERS (2)

OWNER:	Gartland Steamship Company
BUILT:	American Ship Building Company, Lorain, Ohio—1910
HULL NO.:	380
O. A. DIMENSIONS:	524' × 54' × 30'
FORMER DATA:	Launched as JOSEPH WOOD. Given last name in 1957.

This vessel was sold for scrap in 1967 following a grounding accident late in 1966. It was one of the first American bulk freighters to utilize the new St. Lawrence Seaway regularly in the early 1960's.

The namesakes of this steamer were the five sons of Captain Denis Sullivan. These are, in order of birth, Frank J. Sullivan, Ralph G. Sullivan, Arthur C. Sullivan, Harry J. Sullivan and Paul D. Sullivan. These men were born in 1879, 1880, 1881, 1884 and 1892 respectively and died as follows, in order: 1941, 1955, 1948, 1950 and 1961.

Messers. Arthur, Harry, Frank and Paul Sullivan were partners in D. Sullivan & Company which was the managing firm of Gartland Steamship Company until 1939, at which point the first three men became officers of Gartland as follows: Arthur—president, Harry—vice president and treasurer and Paul—secretary. Frank Sullivan was vice president of the office in Cleveland, Ohio.

Mr. Ralph Sullivan never came into the family business, but went to the west coast as a young man where he became a vice president of Norton Lilly & Company in charge of stevedoring.

The maiden voyage of this bulk freighter was commenced May 25, 1910. The trip was without cargo from Lorain, Ohio to Two Harbors, Minnesota for a cargo of iron ore. The vessel is shown below in the St. Mary's River on August 19, 1957.

Steamer FRANK E. TAPLIN

OWNER:	Gartland Steamship Company
BUILT:	American Ship Building Company, Lorain, Ohio—1908
HULL NO.:	356
O. A. DIMENSIONS:	440' × 52'3" × 28'6"
FORMER DATA:	Launched as CHARLES W. KOTCHER. Given last name in 1920.

The bulk freight Steamer FRANK E. TAPLIN is shown below upbound in the Welland Ship Canal, near Humberstone, on November 12, 1968. It is returning to Lake Erie after discharging grain at Oswego, New York. The ship was sold for scrap in 1968 and had sailed on its maiden voyage on April 11, 1908 from Lorain, Ohio to Ashland, Wisconsin with a cargo of coal.

Mr. Frank Elijah Taplin was this vessel's namesake. He was born on October 28, 1875 in Cleveland, Ohio and was educated in the local schools. He began working as an office boy at the Standard Oil Company in 1892. In 1898 he joined Morgan, Moore & Baine Coal Company as a salesman and stayed on in that capacity when the firm was taken over by Pittsburgh Coal Company in 1899.

From 1901 to 1912 Mr. Taplin was sales manager of the Youghiogheny & Ohio Coal Company. He resigned to form the Cleveland & Western Coal Company in 1912 and was the largest individual shipper of cargo coal on the Great Lakes by 1925. In 1926 he founded and became president of the North American Coal Corporation which took over his former company and other affiliated firms.

Mr. Taplin was active in civic and social circles and founded the Cleveland Institute of Music prior to his death on June 7, 1938.

Steamer WILLIAM H. WOLF (2)

OWNER:	Gartland Steamship Company
BUILT:	American Ship Building Company, Lorain, Ohio—1908
HULL NO.:	360
O. A. DIMENSIONS:	524' × 54' × 30'

The bulk freighter shown below in the St. Mary's River on August 19, 1955 honored Mr. William Henry Wolf as its namesake. This ship continued to serve on the Great Lakes until being sold for trade-in and scrap in 1966.

Mr. Wolf was born August 7, 1828 in Wendelsheim, Germany and came to the United States in 1836. He first visited Milwaukee, Wisconsin in 1849. He worked in several lesser positions before becoming a foreman in the J. M. Jones shipyard at Milwaukee in 1853. When that firm failed in the panic of 1857, Mr. Wolf formed a shipbuilding partnership with Mr. Theodore Lawrence in 1858 and they continued this venture at Milwaukee until the business was sold to Ellsworth and Davidson in 1863.

From this time until 1868, Mr. Wolf was in the shipbuilding and lumber business at Green Bay, Wisconsin and built over a dozen vessels. He returned to Milwaukee in 1868 and purchased Ellsworth's interest and the new firm of Wolf and Davidson was born. Mr. Wolf headed this firm until it was sold to the Milwaukee Dry Dock Company in 1890. He retired at that time and died at Milwaukee, Wisconsin on January 28, 1901.

This ship departed Lorain, Ohio with a cargo of coal for Milwaukee, Wisconsin on June 6, 1908 for its maiden voyage. It was the first vessel to load a cargo at the Rail to Water Transfer Corporation facility in South Chicago, taking 8,300 net tons of coal on July 2, 1938.

Steamer BIRCHTON

OWNER:	Gulf and Lake Navigation Company, Limited
BUILT:	A. McMillan and Sons, Dumbarton, Scotland—1924
HULL NO.:	489
O. A. DIMENSIONS:	261' × 43'9" × 22'6"
FORMER DATA:	Deepened 2'6" at Muir Brothers Dry Dock Company, Limited, Port Dalhousie, Ontario in 1950.

The bulk freight Steamer BIRCHTON was active on the Great Lakes and St. Lawrence River until shortly after the opening of the new St. Lawrence Seaway and was sold for scrap in 1962. The ship did not meet that fate, however, and was later bought for use as a drydock. This plan did not go through, however, and the hull was scrapped between 1968-1977.

This vessel retained the suffix "TON" which was given it by the original builders, Mathews Steamship Company of Toronto, Ontario. This firm went into receivership and sold its vessels to various fleets. The Gulf and Lake Navigation Company never saw fit to rename any of the vessels it bought from this line.

The birch tree was the namesake of this vessel, with the suffix being the common ending of each ship name. The birch is of the genus Betula and is usually light in color and of thin foliage with the outer bark separable into thin paper layers. This bark has historically been used in the making of canoes. The French Canadian explorers made huge canoes up to 60 feet long and capable of carrying several hundred tons from this bark.

The Steamer BIRCHTON is shown below at Thorold, Ontario in the Welland Ship Canal.

Steamer CEDARTON

OWNER:	Gulf and Lake Navigation Company, Limited
BUILT:	A. McMillan and Sons, Dumbarton, Scotland—1924
HULL NO.:	488
O. A. DIMENSIONS:	261' × 43'3" × 22'6"
FORMER DATA:	Deepened 2'6" at George T. Davie and Sons Limited, Lauzon, Quebec in 1951.

The bulk freight Steamer CEDARTON was active in Great Lakes commerce until being sold for scrap in 1962. This ship was also one of those purchased from the original Mathews Steamship Company fleet and, like others in the fleet, it bore a name which ended in the Mathews fleet suffix, "TON."

The specific namesake of this freighter was the cedar tree. This name is actually applied to several species of coniferous evergreen trees, as well as to the wood of a number of trees in no way related to the conifers. The name properly belongs to the genus cedrus, of which there are three species generally recognized. These are: Cedrus libani-the Cedar of Lebanon, Cedrus deodara-the deodar tree of India and Cedrus atlantica-the tree of the mountains of North Africa.

The white cedar of North America probably was picked as the exact namesake of this ship from the various cedar trees around the world. It is usually up to 90 feet high and is found in swampy places from Maine to Mississippi. The wood is excellent for durability and is used in the making of chests for storage of valuables where moisture should not penetrate. It is also very fragrant wood and is used in scenting areas used for semi-permanent storage of clothes.

This vessel is shown at Toronto, Ontario on July 27, 1953.

Motor Vessel HARMONY

OWNER:	Gulf Oil Corporation
BUILT:	Bethlehem Steel Corporation Limited, Sparrows Point, Maryland—1931
HULL NO.:	4280
O. A. DIMENSIONS:	219' × 38' × 13'9"

The Motor Vessel HARMONY was one of the Gulf Oil tankers which traded on the Great Lakes via the New York State Barge Canal during the navigation season on the Lakes and on the east coast during the winter months when the Great Lakes were frozen over. It remained in the Gulf fleet until 1961 when it was sold to the Elizabeth Graham Company of Gladwyn, Pennsylvania for off-lakes use.

The namesake of this vessel was in keeping with the theme of inland waterway ships of the day in the Gulf fleet and had reference to the internal company name applied to their brand name for a premium grade of lubricating oil which the firm formerly produced. HARMONY was the name given to the product produced throughout the United States in Gulf Oil refineries which was marketed as a specialty oil primarily designed to be of service in diesel engines.

This premium lubricating oil was brought into production about the time this ship was ordered but was discontinued in the 1950's. It was a product well known to marine men and was used by many fleet engineers in the lubricating systems, especially on the inland waterways of the United States.

The ship is shown above underway in Delaware Bay without cargo in 1960.

Motor Vessel PARATEX

OWNER:	Gulf Oil Corporation
BUILT:	Pennsylvania Shipyards, Incorporated, Beaumont, Texas—1938
HULL NO.:	131
O. A. DIMENSIONS:	293'6" × 43'9" × 17'6"
FORMER DATA:	Lengthened 36' at American Ship Building Company, Toledo, Ohio in 1961.

The tank Motor Vessel PARATEX is named for a base product for lubricating oils produced by the Gulf Oil Corporation. It is an internal word in origin and was applied in the naming of this ship in a theme of such names for inland waterway vessels owned by the company.

Gulf Oil Corporation is one of the principal oil enterprises in the United States. It has recently been seen extensively on television with its advertising and sponsorship of space spectacular reports on the National Broadcasting Company.

The firm has an extensive ocean marine fleet and a large fleet on the inland waterways for the movement of its crude oil and finished products. The Motor Vessel PARATEX was the last vessel regularly operated on the Great Lakes by the Gulf Oil Corporation (U.S.). The firm now charters outside tonnage as required. This vessel was sold for off-Lakes use in 1975 and is shown above at Cleveland, Ohio on November 3, 1973.

Motor Vessel REGENT

OWNER: Gulf Oil Corporation
BUILT: Bethlehem Shipbuilding & Drydock Company, Sparrows Point, Maryland—1934
HULL NO.: 4291
O. A. DIMENSIONS: 256' × 40' × 14'6"

Following a theme of ship names in the Gulf inland fleet in reference to the company's products, the Motor Vessel REGENT was named for a lubricating oil that was produced by Gulf Oil Corporation when this ship was commissioned. That product is no longer manufactured in the current production processes.

The Motor Vessel REGENT was not a vessel that operated solely on the Great Lakes. Rather, it came into the Great Lakes via the New York State Barge Canal for operation in the summer months. It served with regularity in this partial service until the end of the 1970 naviagation season. At that time, it was permanently removed from Great Lakes service by the owners who now employ the ship strictly in East Coast operations.

Completion of large pipelines in the area of the Great Lakes brought about the cessation of operations in this field of this vessel. It is shown in the photograph above in the St. Clair River on August 4, 1961.

The Gulf Oil Corporation still maintains service on the Great Lakes with the Motor Vessel PARATEX which serves totally in Great Lakes service. It is the lone ship on the Great Lakes in Gulf's service. All of the firm's Great Lakes vessels seem tiny in comparison to the huge ships of the ocean fleet. The firm was the first to take delivery of the super 300,000 gross ton capacity ocean tankers on the run from the Persian Gulf to Bantry Bay, Ireland.

Motor Vessel SUPREME

OWNER:	Gulf Oil Corporation
BUILT:	Bethlehem Steel Corporation Limited, Sparrows Point, Maryland—1931
HULL NO.:	4281
O. A. DIMENSIONS:	219′ × 38′ × 13′9″

The Motor Vessel SUPREME had a name which also followed the theme of ship names in this fleet at the time when those ships were largely employed on the inland waterways of the nation as opposed to being ocean-going carriers. This carrier served in combination Great Lakes and off-lakes use in the fleet until it was sold for permanent off-lakes use in 1960.

The theme of honoring various grades of lubricating oils was carried on in the name of this motor vessel. SUPREME is an internal brand name applied to a medium grade of lubricating oil which is manufactured by the company even today. It is used primarily as a motor oil but has other applications as well.

Of all the ship names in the fleet that served on the Great Lakes, this vessel had a name which still relates to a final product still marketed by the organization on a national basis. Other ship names related to final products that have since ceased to exist, at least under the names originally given them when these vessels were placed in commission.

The tank Motor Vessel SUPREME is shown above while fully loaded in a fall mist on Lake Erie.

Steamer BAY TRANSPORT (1)

OWNER:	Hall Corporation of Canada
BUILT:	Furness Shipbuilding Company, Limited, Haverton Hill-on-Tees, England—1932
HULL NO.:	212
O. A. DIMENSIONS:	258' × 43'3" × 18'
FORMER DATA:	Launched as BRITAMLUBE. Given last name in 1959.

This name is carried forward in the present Hall fleet by a motor vessel. The Steamer BAY TRANSPORT was sold for off-lakes use in 1964.

As for all Hall tankers, this vessel had the second word of the ship name in the theme for the fleet tankers which all end in TRANSPORT. The first word, in this case, refers to a body of water.

A bay is commonly referred to or defined as an indentation of land that borders a lake or ocean. Some bays are called estuaries or fiords or rias.

There is no specific bay for which this ship was named, but all bays in general. The Bay of Fundy probably comes closest to being the namesake of this ship, however, because it is in the trading territory where the ship formerly operated. Other famous bays on the North American continent include: Chesapeake Bay, Delaware Bay and San Francisco Bay. Whitefish Bay of Lake Superior is probably the best known of any in the Great Lakes system.

The Steamer BAY TRANSPORT is shown above near Lock Two of the Welland Ship Canal.

Steamer COALFAX

OWNER:	Hall Corporation of Canada
BUILT:	Furness Shipbuilding Company Limited, Haverton Hill-on-Tees, England—1927
HULL NO.:	125
O. A. DIMENSIONS:	259' × 43'3" × 25'

The self-unloading Steamer COALFAX is shown in this photograph at Marblehead, Ohio, taking on a stone cargo. It was active until being sold for scrap in 1965.

This ship was constructed for Coal Carriers Corporation of Brockville, Ontario. That firm was headed at the time by Mr. Nelson Howard, son of the one-time president of Hall Corporation Mr. John C. Howard of Ogdensburg, New York. The younger Mr. Howard coined the suffix which was borne by all vessels in his fleet. FAX was used as a play on the word "facts," denoting usage as in reference to realism, truth, etc. Thus, COALFAX referred to the facts of coal handling and moving. It was also a play on the slang term "cold facts" which was much in use at that time. The phrase meant "hard truth."

When this vessel was acquired by Hall Corporation in 1951, it brought into being the suffix FAX to that fleet. To the present day, all self-unloaders in the fleet bear that suffix in their name as an identification of the ship class. It is interesting to note that this vessel served the last years of its life in the Hall fleet, a fleet once headed by Mr. Howard whose son built the ship.

The Steamer COALFAX was appropriately named since the majority of its trade related to the carriage of coal into Lake Ontario and St. Lawrene River ports of Canada. The firm which originally built it passed out of the vessel business in the 1950's.

Steamer ISLAND TRANSPORT (1)

OWNER: Hall Corporation of Canada
BUILT: Furness Shipbuilding Company Limited, Haverton Hill-on-Tees, England—1931
HULL NO.: 199
O. A. DIMENSIONS: 258′ × 43′3″ × 18′
FORMER DATA: Launched as BRITAMOIL. Given last name in 1959.

In keeping with the class names for tankers, the Steamer ISLAND TRANSPORT carried the same second word in its ship name as all tankers in the fleet. The specific namesake of this ship, therefore, is the first word in the ship name—ISLAND.

The fleet has named many tankers for bodies of water. An island is not a body of water, but is a natural name for the theme of ships since it must be surrounded by a body of water.

One definition of an island is "a tract of land surrounded by water and smaller than a continent." There are, of course, many such islands in the Great Lakes and Seaway system, notably the Thousand Islands of New York and Ontario through which all traffic on the Seaway passes.

While no specific island is referred to in this ship name, it is plausible that the primary reference might be to the Island of Montreal on which, in the city of Montreal, Quebec, the headquarters of this fleet's operation are located. This tanker was sold for off-lakes use in 1963.

The tank Steamer ISLAND TRANSPORT is shown in the photograph above in the Welland Ship Canal on May 19, 1960.

Steamer LEECLIFFE HALL (2)

OWNER: Hall Corporation of Canada
BUILT: Fairfield Shipbuilding & Engineering Company, Limited Glasgow, Scotland - 1961
HULL NO.: 811
O. A. DIMENSIONS: 730' x 75' x 39'9"

The bulk freight Steamer LEECLIFFE HALL (2) was an active carrier and carried several record cargoes of bulk commodities before its untimely ending in 1964. On September 5, 1964 this vessel collided with the Greek Steamer APPOLONIA about sixty miles east of Quebec City in the St. Lawrence River and was sunk. It had an inbound cargo of iron ore at the time in its holds. This disaster, resulting in the loss of life, was the first incident involving the destruction of a maximum-size Great Lakes bulk carrier capable of transiting the St. Lawrence Seaway.

The namesake of this vessel was Mrs. Frank A. Augsbury, Jr., the former Miss Lavinia Lee Andrews. She was born in Manhasset, New York on November 21, 1925 and was educated at Green Mountain College in Poultney, Vermont. It was this lady's middle name that was taken as the namesake word for this bulk freighter.

In due course Miss Andrews and Mr. Augsbury, Jr. met and were married. They lived in Ogdensburg, New York where she was active in civic and family affairs. She served as a trustee of Green Mountain College and of the United Helpers Home of Ogdensburg, New York. Mrs. Augsbury was also a member of the advisory board of Mater Dei College of Ogdensburg, New York. She died in Watertown, New York August 25, 1986.

Her namesake is shown in this photograph while downbound with a cargo of grain from the Canadian Lakehead in the St. Mary's River on June 14, 1962.

Steamer OIL TRANSPORT

OWNER: Hall Corporation of Canada
BUILT: Ingalls Iron Works Company, Chickasaw, Alabama—1936
HULL NO.: 171
O. A. DIMENSIONS: 258' × 43' × 16'3"
FORMER DATA: Launched as TRANSOIL. Renamed OIL TRANSPORTER in 1951. Given last name in 1959.

When these owners acquired the assets and ships of Gayport Shipping Limited in 1959, they inherited a sizeable fleet of tankers, all of which bore the same second word in their ship names. That word was TRANSPORTER. It was at that time that Hall Corporation decided to designate a common suffix to all vessels in any given carrier class in their fleet. They dropped the "ER" on these ship names and carried forward the word TRANSPORT for all classes of tanker names in the fleet.

This steamer paid tribute in the first word of its name to the fact that it was built to carry oil and petroleum products. It did so for its entire life up until being sold for off-lakes use as a fresh water storage vessel in 1968.

The oil industry has been a constant source of employment for ships in the Hall fleet since 1959. Petroleum products and by-products account for millions of tons and nearly a billion barrels of commodities moved on the Great Lakes each year. This fleet thought it most fitting to continue this recognition of the industry that has provided so much cargo and livlihood for it and other tanker fleets on the Great Lakes.

The Steamer OIL TRANSPORT is seen above underway in the St. Mary's River in 1964.

Steamer ROBERT J. PAISLEY (2)

OWNER:	Hall Corporation of Canada
BUILT:	Superior Shipbuilding Company, Superior, Wisconsin—1901
HULL NO.:	502
O. A. DIMENSIONS:	414′ × 48′ × 28′
FORMER DATA:	Launched as the bulk freighter CHRISTOPHER. Renamed THOMAS BRITT (1) in 1924. Renamed J. E. SAVAGE in 1928. Converted to a self-unloader at Sturgeon Bay Dry Dock Company, Sturgeon Bay, Wisconsin in 1929. Given last name in 1932.

Mr. Robert John Paisley was born in Ashtabula, Ohio on May 26, 1900 and was educated in the local schools and an eastern academy. He served in the Marines during World War I and moved to Cleveland, Ohio in 1920 to begin his business career. He joined the Valley Camp Coal Company and assisted his father in the managing of the Great Lakes vessels of that firm.

When the coal company sold its fleet in 1935, Mr. Paisley began operating steamers for his own account. He became president of the Morrow Steamship Company and the J. A. Paisley Steamship Company and continued as head of these firms until his death at Cleveland, Ohio on March 10, 1951.

Mr. Paisley was a director of the Columbia Transportation Company, Oglebay Norton Company and also of Lake Carriers' Association upon his death. His namesake is shown at Rochester, New York in the photograph above. The vessel served under Canadian registry for the last five years of its life until being sold for scrap in 1969.

Steamer JOHN H. PRICE

OWNER:	Hall Corporation of Canada
BUILT:	Smith's Dock Company Limited, South Bank-on-Tees, England—1927
HULL NO.:	832
O. A. DIMENSIONS:	259' × 43'3" × 20'

Mr. John Herbert Price is the namesake of this bulk freighter which foundered at Ste. Anne des Monts, Quebec in 1951. It was restored to service in 1952 and sold for scrap in 1961. He was born at Quebec City, Quebec on August 5, 1898 and was educated at Bishops' Collegiate School and the Royal Military Academy. He served with "A" Battery, 70th Brigade of the R.A.F. and was wounded and later received the Military Cross in 1918.

He came from a prominent family. Sir William and Lady Blanche Price were his parents and he entered the family business upon leaving the service of his country. By 1925 he was president of Price Brothers & Company Limited. This firm was established in 1817 and was prominent in the newsprint and woodlands business of Quebec.

In addition to serving in the above firm, Mr. Price was president of the Gravel Lumber Company Limited, Quebec Investment Company Limited, Jonquiere Pulp Company and, later, the J. H. Price & Associates Limited of Montreal, Quebec.

The canal sized bulk freight Steamer JOHN H. PRICE is shown in the photograph below on October 29, 1960 in the Welland Ship Canal. This vessel delivered the first cargo of Labrador iron ore to Buffalo, New York, arriving at the Republic Steel docks August 9, 1954.

Steamer WAVE TRANSPORT

OWNER:	Hall Corporation of Canada
BUILT:	Furness Shipbuilding Company Limited, Haverton Hill-on-Tees, England—1931
HULL NO.:	200
O. A. DIMENSIONS:	258′ × 43′3″ × 18′
FORMER DATA:	Launched as BRITAMOLENE. Given last name in 1959.

The Steamer WAVE TRANSPORT was sold for off-lakes use in 1963 after thirty-two seasons on the Great Lakes in the service of moving petroleum products.

The namesake of this tanker is a wave, commonly defined as "a moving ridge or swell on the surface of a liquid." In steamship parlance, of course, a wave is thought of as something that one may see or experiences on a body of water. It is in this context that the ship was named, for the Hall fleet has had a theme of naming tank vessels after bodies of water or things related thereto.

The second word in the ship name indicates that she is a tanker since the Hall fleet ends all its tanker names with the word TRANSPORT.

Naturally, no one wave or series of them can be considered to be specific namesakes of this ship. It is the general characteristic of waves and their relation to any ship navigation that provides the germane meaning to this ship name.

This tanker is shown in the photograph above at Toronto harbour's Eastern Gap on September 5, 1960. The ship is inbound for a cargo of fuel oil.

Motor Vessel CREEK TRANSPORT

OWNER: Hall Corporation (Shipping) 1969 Ltd.
BUILT: Sunderland Shipbuilding Company Limited, Sunderland, England - 1910
HULL NO.: 256
O. A. DIMENSIONS: 258' x 42'6" x 18'6"
FORMER DATA: Launched as the bulk freighter SASKATOON (1). Renamed ROSEMOUNT (2) in 1927. Converted to a tanker at Marine Industries, Limited, Sorel, Quebec and renamed WILLOWBRANCH (1) in 1940. Renamed EMPIRE TADPOLE in 1945. Renamed BASING CREEK in 1947. Renamed COASTAL CREEK in 1950. Renamed CREEK TRANSPORT in 1968.

The Motor Vessel CREEK TRANSPORT was sold for use as a scow in 1971 in the Quebec Harbor project after several years in lay-up status. It had the same suffix common to all tankers in the Hall fleet, that being the word TRANSPORT which is the class name for this fleet's tankers. On sale for the Quebec project, however, it took the name I'LE DE MONTREAL as a non-operating vessel, then was sold for scrap in 1979.

The first word of the ship name, therefore, is the distinguishing namesake of this vessel. The word creek may be defined as "a small inlet or bay narrower and extending farther inland than a cove" and also "a natural stream of water normally smaller than and often tributary to a river." The name follows along with the theme in the fleet for naming some tankers for bodies of water.

Motor Vessel EASTCLIFFE HALL

OWNER:	Hall Corporation (Shipping) 1969 Ltd.
BUILT:	Canadian Vickers Shipyards, Limited, Montreal, Quebec—1954
HULL NO.:	262
O. A. DIMENSIONS:	349' × 43'9" × 24'6"
FORMER DATA:	Lengthened 90' and deepened 3'9" at Canadian Vickers Shipyards, Limited, Montreal, Quebec in 1959.

The bulk freight Motor Vessel EASTCLIFFE HALL was one of three former canal-sized vessels that were made into more competitive carriers by the lengthening process when the St. Lawrence Seaway was opened in 1959. It met its ending when it ran aground and sank at Chrysler Shoal on the St. Lawrence River on July 14, 1970 with a loss of nine lives.

This ship had the regular first word suffix and the common second word for bulk freighters in the Hall fleet. The prefix of the first word in the ship name was its specific namesake and stood for the direction East. Along with three other ships in the Hall fleet, this vessel name came from one of the four directions.

East is the direction commonly referred to as being towards the eldest area where civilization appears. Hence, the Middle East is the area known from Biblical times as the location of the works of Creation. The Far East, on the other hand, encompasses Asian countries such as Japan, Korea, Cambodia, Burma and so on.

East, in world geographic terms, is the general direction of all sunrises and also is, therefore, the exact opposite of the direction West.

Steamer FUEL TRANSPORT

```
      OWNER:      Hall Corporation (Shipping) 1969 Ltd.
      BUILT:      Furness Shipbuilding Company, Limited,
                  Haverton Hill-on-Tees, England—1930
    HULL NO.:     177
O. A. DIMENSIONS: 258' × 43'3" × 24'6"
  FORMER DATA:    Launched as CYCLO-CHIEF. Renamed TEXACO
                  CHIEF (1) in 1947. Renamed FUEL TRANS-
                  PORTER in 1955. Given last name in 1959.
```

The tank Steamer FUEL TRANSPORT remained on the Great Lakes until it was sold for off-lakes use in 1970. For two years prior to that it saw very little service or was laid-up. It is shown above at the Iroquois Lock of the St. Lawrence Seaway system on November 19, 1967.

This ship's name came directly from the fact that fuel and fuel products consituted the largest part of its cargoes. The Hall Corporation felt it apropos to have a ship name in the fleet directly in reference to the fuel trade which is such a major part of the liquid cargo movement of its ships.

Since the name prior to its last name was not too unlike its last name, they kept it, dropping the "er" to hold the theme of Hall tankers having a common second word of the ship name, namely, TRANSPORT.

The fuel trade on the Great Lakes is a sub-division of the total tanker trade and consists of the movement of commodities such as gasoline, fuel oil, jet fuel, kerosene, naptha and diesel fuel.

Steamer GULF TRANSPORT

OWNER:	Hall Corporation (Shipping) 1969 Ltd.
BUILT:	Furness Shipbuilding Company, Limited, Haverton Hill-on-Tees, England—1932
HULL NO.:	209
O. A. DIMENSIONS:	258' × 43'3" × 18'
FORMER DATA:	Launched as BRITAMOCO. Given last name in 1959.

The tank Steamer GULF TRANSPORT was active in the Hall fleet until being sold for off-lakes use in 1970. It is shown above on its last trip on the lakes, at Port Colborne, Ontario on October 24, 1970.

This ship took its name from the generic term gulf and referred to no one particular gulf, but all the gulfs of the world in general. The second word in the ship name identifies the ship as a tanker in this fleet.

Gulfs vary in size from small, like Greece's Gulf of Corinth, to enormous, like the Gulf of Mexico. They are formed when a portion of the earth's crust is depressed below sea level or when a fractured part of that crust slips below sea level.

Well-known gulfs include: Gulf of Aden, Gulf of California, Gulf of Mexico and Gulf of St. Lawrence. While none of these are specific namesakes of this ship, the Gulf of St. Lawrence comes closest to being a specific namesake. This ship traded not only on the Great Lakes, but also to ports along the St. Lawrence River and in the Gulf of St. Lawrence. It, thus, was familiar to that gulf while it never saw service in other gulf areas until it was sold for off-lakes use.

Motor Vessel HUTCHCLIFFE HALL

OWNER:	Hall Corporation (Shipping) 1969 Ltd.
BUILT:	Canadian Vickers Shipyards, Limited, Montreal, Quebec—1954
HULL NO.:	261
O. A. DIMENSIONS:	349' × 43'9" × 24'6"
FORMER DATA:	Launched as the bulk freighter HUTCHCLIFFE HALL. Lengthened 90' and deepened 3'9" at Davie Shipbuilding, Limited, Lauzon, Quebec in 1959. Renamed, as a scow, I'LE AUX COUDRES in 1971.

The namesake of this bulk freight vessel was Mr. Albert Hutchinson who was born at Aycliffe, England on September 4, 1889. He received his higher education in England and came to Canada in 1912.

Mr. Hutchinson began working in Canada for the engineering firm of Hall Engineering Company at Montreal, Quebec and in time was vice president of the company. When that firm sold its marine interests to the Oka Sand and Gravel Company of Montreal, he went to work for the buyers and headed the operations under the direction of Mr. Frank Ross.

In the early 1920's Mr. Hutchinson left to become manager of Hall Corporation interests in Montreal and, on incorporation of the Hall Corporation of Canada in April, 1927, was elected secretary of the company. He became vice president in 1936, president in 1945 and chairman of the board in 1951. Mr. Hutchinson held this post at his death on May 25, 1952 in Montreal, Quebec.

The Motor Vessel HUTCHCLIFFE HALL was active through the 1970 season and was sold in October, 1971 for use as a piece of floating dredging equipment in the channel deepening project at Quebec City, Quebec.

Motor Vessel OREFAX

OWNER:	Hall Corporation (Shipping) 1969 Ltd.
BUILT:	Canadian Vickers Limited, Montreal, Quebec—1947
HULL NO.:	231
O. A. DIMENSIONS:	341' × 43'9" × 23'6"
FORMER DATA:	Launched as the bulk freighter SOUTHCLIFFE HALL. Lengthened 82', deepened 2'9" and converted to a self-unloader at Canadian Vickers Limited, Montreal, Quebec in 1959. Renamed OREFAX in 1961. Renamed, as a scow, ISLE ROYALE (2) in 1971.

The Motor Vessel OREFAX was active on the Great Lakes in usual commercial trades until 1970. It then laid idle for several months and did not run in 1971. In that year it was sold, in October, to a consortium of firms engaged in the vast project of deepening the navigation channel to fifty feet upstream in the St. Lawrence River as far as Quebec City.

The name of this former self-unloader was given in honor of the major commodity moving in Great Lakes commerce—iron ore. The suffix on the ship name, -FAX, was used in this fleet as a common name ending for self-unloading ships to easily designate them as that class of ship. The usage of this suffix was derived from the former usage of it in the fleet of an earlier acquisition of this fleet, as explained on page 297 under COALFAX.

The Motor Vessel OREFAX is shown above in Pelee Passage, Lake Erie, on September 1, 1970.

Motor Vessel SEA TRANSPORT (1)

OWNER: Hall Corporation (Shipping) 1969 Ltd.
BUILT: St. John's River Shipbuilding Company, Jacksonville, Florida—1945 and Todd Shipyard Corporation, Brooklyn, New York—1951
HULL NO.: 93
O. A. DIMENSIONS: 325'3" × 48'3" × 21'6"
FORMER DATA: Launched as TELLICO. Renamed TRANSEA in 1951. Renamed SEA TRANSPORTER in 1956. Given last name in 1959.

Together with the common second word in all tanker names of the Hall fleet, this ship's namesake was the sea itself. A sea is a body of water usually smaller than an ocean that may be either connected to an ocean or be a large inland area of water.

Sea or ocean waters cover seven-tenths of the surface of the earth. Literally millions of tons of food products have already been taken from the oceans and, with new efforts being taken in oceanograhy for useful purposes, it is likely that even greater benefits will occur in the future.

The largest sea in the world is the Mediterranean Sea between Europe and Africa. No one sea in particular, but all seas in general are the namesakes of this tanker.

This vessel was partially completed at the end of World War II and remained in that state until acquired for ocean duty and taken to Brooklyn, New York by the new owners. It is for this reason that two building yards are shown above.

The Motor Vessel SEA TRANSPORT remained active until the end of the 1970 season on the Great Lakes and was sold for off-lakes use in 1971. The vessel is shown above in the Welland Ship Canal.

Steamer STONEFAX

OWNER:	Hall Corporation (Shipping) 1969 Ltd.
BUILT:	West Bay City Shipbuilding Company, West Bay City, Michigan—1903
HULL NO.:	609
O. A. DIMENSIONS:	441' × 50' × 28'
FORMER DATA:	Launched as the bulk freighter SINALOA. Renamed WILLIAM F. RAPPRICH in 1924. Converted to a self-unloader at Leathem D. Smith Dock Company, Sturgeon Bay, Wisconsin and renamed SINALOA, for second time, in 1928. Converted to a self-unloading sandsucker at Leathem D. Smith Dock Company, Sturgeon Bay, Wisconsin in 1931. Re-converted to a self-unloader at Manitowoc Shipbuilding Company, Manitowoc, Wisconsin in 1942. Given last name in 1960.

Together with the class suffix common to all self-unloaders in this fleet, the Steamer STONEFAX was named in reference to stone, a word most generally used to describe a piece of rock or the earth's solid crust.

Stone is widely used as a building material and this vessel was utilized in the Hall fleet to transport many kinds of stone cargoes from the time the ship was acquired in 1960 until it was sold for scrapping in Europe in 1971. This ship had one of the most involved histories of major changes in its construction of all Great Lakes ships.

This vessel is shown above while docking at Rochester, New York to receive a coal cargo. When converted in 1931, this ship was the only vessel in the world equipped with self-sorting equipment onboard for the purpose of classifying material brought aboard by size so that it might be ready for classified unloading when the ship got into port. This onboard sorting alleviated much delay in the delivery of cargoes when the products were consigned to different customers.

Motor Vessel BAFFIN TRANSPORT

```
       OWNER:  Hall Corporation Shipping Ltd.
       BUILT:  Smith's Dock Company, Limited,
               Middlesbrough, England—1955
    HULL NO.:  1233
O. A. DIMENSIONS:  529' × 69'9" × 38'
 FORMER DATA:  Launched as FOSNA. Renamed EUROCHEMIST in
               1967. Renamed CABATERN in 1970. Given last
               name in 1973.
```

The tanker Motor Vessel BAFFIN TRANSPORT had a name in keeping with the theme of vessel names in this fleet for tank vessels which specifically honor northern bay areas in the Arctic region. This ship was classed for service into such areas and served equally well on the Great Lakes or in deep-sea service.

Baffin Bay was the specific namesake of this vessel. It is the body of water between Baffin Island and Greenland connected with the Atlantic Ocean by the Davis Strait. The bay is 800 miles long and 280 miles wide with depths ranging from 200 to 1,500 fathoms. Outlets to the Arctic Ocean are via Lancaster, Jones and Smith Sounds. The bay is navigable in summer and closed to traffic in the heavy winter periods. The coastline of the bay is barren, mountainous and deeply indented.

William Baffin, navigator, is the man for whom Baffin Bay is named. He served as a pilot of an expedition to Greenland from Europe in 1612 and was killed at the siege of Ormuz, Persia on January 23, 1622. Before this, in 1615, Baffin returned to this area as pilot of the DISCOVERY under Captain Robert Bylot on a mission for the Muscovy Company to seek the northwest passage. His name was not given to the bay until 1821 by Parry. This tanker is shown on June 26, 1973 in the Welland Ship Canal. It was sold for scrap in 1978.

Motor Vessel BAY TRANSPORT (2)

OWNER: Hall Corporation Shipping Ltd.
BUILT: McDougall-Duluth Shipbuilding Company, Duluth, Minnesota—1921
HULL NO.: McDougall—#53, St. Lawrence—#555
O. A. DIMENSIONS: 259'3" × 43'6" × 17'6"
FORMER DATA: Launched as the barge canal freighter I. L. I. 104. Renamed ALDEN BARNES FIERTZ in 1936. Rebuilt and converted to a tanker by lengthening 1'11", widening 12'6" and deepening 3'6" at St. Lawrence Dry Docks, Limited, Montreal, Quebec in 1950. Renamed COASTAL CARRIER in 1950. Given last name in 1968.

This tanker is shown above in the Thousand Islands, Lake Ontario in 1973. It was sold for scrap in November, 1976.

As for all Hall tankers, the Motor Vessel BAY TRANSPORT has the second word of its ship name in theme with its class of vessel. The first word, in this case, refers to a body of water. It will be noted that bodies of water have formed the basis for several other first names of ships in this class.

A bay is commonly referred to or defined as an indentation of land that borders a lake or ocean. Some bays are called estuaries or fiords or rias.

Famous bays on the North American continent include the Bay of Fundy, Chesapeake Bay and Delaware Bay. Fiords are more usually thought of in reference to the deep and narrow features of Norway or Alaska. The Bay of Fundy probably comes closest to being the namesake of this ship because it is in the trading territory of the vessel.

Steamer CAPE TRANSPORT

OWNER: Hall Corporation Shipping Ltd.
BUILT: Canadian Vickers Limited, Montreal, Quebec—1947
HULL NO.: 230
O. A. DIMENSIONS: 259'3" × 43'9" × 20'6"
FORMER DATA: Launched as the bulk freighter NORTHCLIFFE HALL (1). Converted to a tanker at Canadian Vickers Limited, Montreal, Quebec in 1957. Given last name in 1961.

As for other Hall tankers, the second word in the ship name indicates the tanker class. It is explained elsewhere for all Hall tank vessels.

Namesake of the Steamer CAPE TRANSPORT is a point of land, headland or cliff that projects prominently into a lake, sea or ocean and is called a cape. Capes are also known by similar meaning terms such as point, head or promontory.

All capes, in general, as opposed to any specific cape form the basis for choosing this name in the fleet. There are many such capes in the areas served by the fleet and the choice appeared reasonable for this name. Capes may be formed in several ways.

This vessel is shown in the Welland Ship Canal on September 15, 1971. It laid idle for several seasons until being sold for off-lakes use in 1977.

Motor Vessel CONISCLIFFE HALL (3)

OWNER: Hall Corporation Shipping Ltd.
BUILT: Davie Shipbuilding, Limited,
Lauzon, Quebec — 1957
HULL NO.: 611
O. A. DIMENSIONS: 259' x 43'10" x 22'6"

The canal-size bulk freight Motor Vessel CONISCLIFFE HALL (3) served in coal, pulpwood and general cargo trades until the early 1970's. It laid idle in 1972 and 1973 at Kingston, Ontario and was sold late in 1973 for non-transportation use and conversion at Port Colborne, Ontario to a drillboat for use on Lake Erie in the oil and gas drilling industry. The ship is shown below in the Welland Ship Canal.

With the usual bulk freighter theme of names in this fleet, the specific namesake of the vessel was the town of Conisbrough, England which is located 140 miles northwest of London. It is in the county of Nottinghamshire whose area is 540,017 acres.

Conisbrough has a population of about 8,500 and is located on the River Don, about 55 miles inland from the northeast coast of England. It is near Doncaster and Barnsley and is only 13 miles distant from the coal mining city of Sheffield.

The river on which Conisbrough is located flows into the Trent River at Blacktoft, England where the two form the Humber River which is the navigable outlet to the sea. Coal mining and hoisery manufacturing predominate in the area.

Steamer COVE TRANSPORT

OWNER: Hall Corporation Shipping Ltd.
BUILT: Canadian Vickers Limited, Montreal, Quebec—1947
HULL NO.: 228
O. A. DIMENSIONS: 259'3" × 43'6" × 20'6"
FORMER DATA: Launched as the bulk freighter LEECLIFFE HALL (1). Converted to a tanker at George T. Davie & Sons, Limited, Lauzon, Quebec in 1956. Given last name in 1961.

This tank vessel shares the common fleet suffix for tankers and also shares in the theme of some ships being named for bodies of water.

The Steamer COVE TRANSPORT's namesake is no specific cove, but all coves in general. Coves are small sheltered bays or inlets off larger bodies of water. In a sense, this is an appropriate name for this tanker, since it is smaller than most in the fleet, but yet is of the same class and carries the same types of cargoes.

Coves are also known as sea inlets, recesses, caves or chasms. The latter usage primarily applies to coves found on land, however, rather than on water.

Many small coves and inlets can be seen dotting the shores of the St. Lawrence River. This is familiar territory to this carrier and to the fleet. This vessel is shown above in the Welland Ship Canal on October 29, 1966. It was sold in 1977 for off-Lakes use after several years of inactivity.

Motor Vessel EAGLESCLIFFE HALL (2)

OWNER: Hall Corporation Shipping Ltd.
BUILT: Grangemouth Dockyard Company, Limited, Grangemouth, England — 1956
HULL NO.: 520
O. A. DIMENSIONS: 259' x 43'9" x 22'6"

Shown below while upbound between Cote St. Catherine and Beahournois Locks, St. Lawrence Seaway on September 18, 1964, the Motor Vessel EAGLESCLIFFE HALL (2) was a bulk freighter with a name which carried on the theme of bulk freighter names in this fleet. The vessel laid idle at Kingston, Ontario for several years prior to being sold for off-lakes use late in 1973.

The specific namesake of this ship was the small town of 3,500 population in northeastern England called EAGLESCLIFFE. This town is in the area where Mr. Hutchinson, once president of this firm, grew up prior to coming to the North American continent.

Eaglescliffe is located outside Middlesbrough, England and is nearby Stockton-on-Tees and Thornaby-on-Tees. It is on the west side of the River Tees about 15 nautical miles from its mouth on the North Sea. While always relatively busy with commercial vessel traffic, the town of Eaglescliffe and its surrounding ports are now caught up in the swirl of new excitement surrounding the discovery of natural gas and oil in the North Sea. Inland, however, largely fertile farmland abounds and lends a quiet atmosphere to the hinterland area.

Motor Vessel INLAND TRANSPORT

OWNER: Hall Corporation Shipping Ltd.
BUILT: Federal Shipbuilding and Dry Dock Company, Kearney, New Jersey – 1926
HULL NO.: 83
O. A. DIMENSIONS: 258′3″ x 42′9″ x 20′
FORMER DATA: Launched as the barge canal freighter STEEL CHEMIST. Renamed THE INLAND in 1946. Converted to a tanker at Port Weller Dry Docks, Limited, St. Catharines, Ontario in 1948. Renamed TRANS-INLAND in 1949. Given last name in 1968.

The Motor Vessel INLAND TRANSPORT took its name from a series of former names with the exception of the second word, TRANSPORT, which is common to Hall fleet tankers.

When Hall took over this carrier in 1968 it did so with a short-range purpose in mind. It was to serve as a stop-gap carrier until delivery of more modern tonnage was made. It remained in service longer than originally planned due to increased tanker demand. However, it suffered severe bottom damage in a Georgian Bay grounding late in 1972 and was sold for scrap in 1976. The ship is shown above while inbound at Toronto, Ontario in August, 1969.

Since the ship's former names were congruous with the fact that it sailed mainly on inland waters of the Great Lakes, its last owner decided to carry on the tradition. The vessel originally became THE INLAND when owned by Inland Steel Company.

Steamer LAKE TRANSPORT (2)

OWNER: Hall Corporation Shipping Ltd.
BUILT: Furness Shipbuilding Company, Limited, Haverton Hill-on-Tees, England — 1930
HULL NO.: 178
O. A. DIMENSIONS: 258'9" x 43'3" x 24'3"
FORMER DATA: Launched as CYCLO-WARRIOR. Renamed TEXACO WARRIOR (1) in 1947. Renamed LAKE TRANSPORT in 1969.

The tank Steamer LAKE TRANSPORT followed the theme for its class of names and was named for a body of water. In this case it is a lake, defined as "a body of water surrounded by land."

The greatest number of lakes are in areas once covered by glaciers. Glaciers tend to cut deep valleys in the earth as they travel and the deposits of them act as a dam. When the glaciers melt, the water often collects in these pockets and lakes are formed. Naturally, many years are required for this process.

Minnesota is the state which is most noted for lakes and, in fact, a state motto is "Land of 10,000 Lakes." Actually, there are probably closer to eleven thousand lakes in that state.

This vessel is shown while underway with a cargo of gasoline in the Thousand Island area of Lake Ontario in October, 1973. The ship ran for about 3 months in 1974 and was then sold for off-lakes use.

Motor Vessel NORTHCLIFFE HALL (2)

OWNER: Hall Corporation Shipping Ltd.
BUILT: Canadian Vickers Limited, Montreal, Quebec – 1952
HULL NO.: 255
O. A. DIMENSIONS: 259' x 43'9" x 24'6"
FORMER DATA: Launched as FRANKCLIFFE HALL (1). Deepened 3'9" at Canadian Vickers Limited, Montreal, Quebec in 1959. Renamed NORTHCLIFFE HALL in 1962. Renamed ROLAND DESGAGNES in 1976.

Namesake of this pre-Seaway canal-sized bulk freighter was the direction North, with the vessel name suffix utilizing the theme for bulk freighter names in the Hall fleet.

Perhaps the North as a section of our country has always had the most indefinite boundaries. In Colonial times a distinction was made at the Potomac River. This river served as the boundary line between northern and southern mainland settlements of British America. Over the course of history, and differing among peoples on all continents, north has most usually been referred to as meaning the opposite of south, whether referring to a specific direction or in general usage.

The Motor Vessel NORTHCLIFFE HALL is shown below at the Iroquois Lock, St. Lawrence Seaway with a full cargo of pulpwood for Waddington, New York delivery. It had been loaded at Godbout, Quebec. The date was September 12, 1965. This ship was in lay-up for several years before being sold in 1974 for off-lakes use.

Motor Vessel RIVER TRANSPORT

OWNER: Hall Corporation Shipping Ltd.
BUILT: St. John's River Shipbuilding Company, Jacksonville, Florida and Maryland Dry Dock Company, Baltimore, Maryland – 1947
HULL NO.: 90
O. A. DIMENSIONS: 325'3" x 48'3" x 21'9"
FORMER DATA: Launched as QUINNEBAUG. Renamed TRANSPAN in 1948. Given last name in 1960.

The medium-sized Motor Vessel RIVER TRANSPORT was active on the Great Lakes and Seaway through most of its career in the Hall fleet until the 1970's. It then spent considerable time on the East Coast and lower St. Lawrence River. Following this service at the end of 1974 management decided that the tanker was no longer needed in the fleet and it was sold for off-lakes use early in 1975.

This vessel had a name in the Hall fleet theme for tanker names related to a body of water, in this case, the rivers of the world. No particular river, but all rivers in general are thus honored. Since man first travelled by other than foot, rivers have been important arteries for commerce and pleasure the world over.

The longest river in the world is the Nile at 4,132 miles. In second place is the Amazon at 3,900 miles. The longest river in North America is Canada's Mackenzie measuring 2,635 miles in length. The Motor Vessel RIVER TRANSPORT is shown above in the Welland Ship Canal in the late 1960's.

Motor Vessel SCOTIACLIFFE HALL

OWNER:	Hall Corporation Shipping Ltd.
BUILT:	Canadian Vickers Limited, Montreal, Quebec – 1958
HULL NO.:	271
O. A. DIMENSIONS:	580'4" x 72'4" x 42'6"
FORMER DATA:	Launched as AVERY C. ADAMS. Renamed CYPRESS in 1964. Renamed UNION in 1968. Renamed FREJA in 1969. Given last name in 1972.

When the bulk Motor Vessel SCOTIACLIFFE HALL was built it was intended to serve in both the Great Lakes-Seaway system and on saltwater, year-around. After only several trips, however, the original owners chartered the vessel to California operators for strictly deep-sea voyages because it was deemed too small to effectively compete in Great Lakes-Seaway traffic patterns.

With fuller development of grain trading between Canadian lake ports and the Maritimes by 1972, the Hall fleet management decided to purchase this vessel and try their hand at making the ship pay its way. Unfortunately, she was found to be unworkable at many of the iron ore docks because of ballast capacity and depth. Thus, the vessel was again sold for off-lakes use at the end of the 1974 navigation season. It is shown below upbound in the Welland Ship Canal on its maiden Great Lakes trip bearing this name, in September, 1972.

The namesake of this vessel in the Hall fleet was the province of Nova Scotia to which she regularly traded from the Canadian Lakehead.

Motor Vessel SEA TRANSPORT (2)

OWNER:	Hall Corporation Shipping Ltd.
BUILT:	Burntisland Shipbuilding Company, Limited, Burntisland, Scotland—1966
HULL NO.:	416
O. A. DIMENSIONS:	366'7" × 47'8" × 26'11"
FORMER DATA:	Launched as OLAU MARK. Renamed SEA TRANSPORT (2) in 1971.

The tank Motor Vessel SEA TRANSPORT (2) replaced the fleet's original ship of this name. It has a capacity of 40,000 barrels of gasoline at mid-summer draft and is classed for service into the deep Arctic. The photograph of the ship shown above was taken in late August, 1973 by the captain of the vessel at Bjorne Landing which is off Eureka Sound on Ellsmere Island in the Arctic.

Since there are no docks in this vast area of tundra and ice, vessels must "moor" to the shore. In the photograph above the SEA TRANSPORT has its bow in the fine sand of the area to secure a safe berth and discharge its cargo of petroleum products. The area is in the Arctic gas and oil drilling region and tankers such as this are used to deliver the very staples of life to the industrial work going on in the field. This particular locale is directly north of Cleveland, Ohio 2,200 miles as the frozen Arctic tern flies!

Besides carrying on the theme of tanker names, this vessel honored as its namesake the very sea in which she is pictured here. The vessel was active in the fleet until sold for off-Lakes use in 1977.

Steamer SHIERCLIFFE HALL

OWNER: Hall Corporation Shipping Ltd.
BUILT: Canadian Vickers Limited, Montreal, Quebec - 1950
HULL NO. 248
O. A. DIMENSIONS: 259' x 43'9" x 23'6"
FORMER DATA: Deepened 2'9" at Canadian Vickers Limited, Montreal, Quebec in 1959.

The small canal-size bulk freight steamer SHIERCLIFFE HALL is shown in this picture in lock nineteen of the old Cornwall Canal. This bulker laid idle at Toronto, Ontario for four years before being sold for scrap early in 1973.

First word suffix and the second word of the ship name apply as designating this vessel's class. The namesake of this steamer, shown by the first word prefix, was Shiermoor, England, a small town five miles north of Wallsend-on-Tyne, England.

The large town of Newcastle-upon-Tyne, England is not far distant and is the main shipbuilding and manufacturing center of the area at the mouth of the Tyne River.

Background of the town names comes from an early geographical division in England in which "shiers" had about the same boundaries as modern counties. They were first formed in early Anglo-Saxon states made up of a number of small districts called "hundreds."

Steamer STERNECLIFFE HALL

OWNER:	Hall Corporation Shipping Ltd.
BUILT:	Canadian Vickers Limited, Montreal, Quebec – 1947
HULL NO.:	229
O. A. DIMENSIONS:	259'3" x 43'9" x 23'6"
FORMER DATA:	Deepened 2'9" at Canadian Vickers Limited, Montreal, Quebec in 1959.

The canal-sized bulk freight Steamer STERNECLIFFE HALL followed the fleet theme for ship names in her class, but specifically honored the late wife of Mr. Frank Augsbury, Sr. who was the founder of this company.

Mrs. Augsbury was the former Bessie Sterne. She was born on September 28, 1887 at Charlotte, North Carolina and married Mr. Augsbury in 1920 at Charlotte, North Carolina. In a short time the family moved north where the business interests of Mr. Augsbury were under development and flourishing.

Mrs. Augsbury did not take an active part in the business affairs of the family, but was a good wife and homemaker. The Augsburys had one son, Frank Jr., who continues as the chairman of the board of this fleet and numerous other firms. She died on November 26, 1961 at Ogdensburg, New York. Her namesake was sold for scrap in 1973 after laying in idleness four years at Toronto, Ontario. It is shown below leaving Dickinson's Landing while upbound in the Cornwall Canal on June 8, 1958.

Motor Vessel WESTCLIFFE HALL (2)

OWNER: Hall Corporation Shipping Ltd.
BUILT: Grangemouth Dockyard Company, Limited, Grangemouth, England — 1956
HULL NO.: 519
O. A. DIMENSIONS: 259' x 43'9" x 22'6"

The bulk freight Motor Vessel WESTCLIFFE HALL (2) was one of the smallest existing vessels on the Great Lakes when it was sold late in 1973 for off-lakes use. Originally built to the maximum dimensions suiting the old St. Lawrence River canals, it retained those size limits while on the Great Lakes. They proved to be too small for economic operation of the ship and its sisters by the early 1970's however, once shallow draft ports into which it once traded ceased to provide waterborne commerce.

The ship name carried on the theme of names for bulk freighters in the fleet and the specific namesake of the vessel was the direction West. West is a term applied to geographic locations and to a socio-economic condition. This ship was one of four in the Hall fleet originally named for each of the four major directions.

Because settlement began on the eastern rim of this continent and, in most cases, expanded in a westerly direction, the West was both a place farther out towards the setting sun and a place where men were beginning over again the creation of a new society. This vessel is shown above Lock 7, Welland Ship Canal, on September 6, 1965.

Steamer LADY HAMILTON

OWNER: Hamilton Harbour Commissioners
BUILT: Great Lakes Engineering Works, River Rouge, Michigan – 1928
HULL NO.: 260
O. A. DIMENSIONS: 170′6″ x 66′ x 17′9″
FORMER DATA: Launched as CADILLAC (3). Renamed ARROWHEAD in 1942. Renamed CADILLAC for the second time, in 1946. Given last name in 1952.

After serving on the cross-river route between Detroit, Michigan and Windsor, Ontario for fourteen years, this vessel was requisitioned by the United States Government in 1942 for World War II use in the Coast Guard. Upon returning to civilian use it passed through several ownerships and worked the last ten years in Canada. In 1962 this vessel was sold for scrapping in Hamilton, Ontario.

The modern look of this old vessel belies her age. The "rebirth" took place during wartime use and was carried onward during the ship's return to the Great Lakes. The vessel is shown above at Port Weller, Ontario enroute to the drydock just above Lock One on the Welland Ship Canal on August 15, 1960.

As a passenger and excursion vessel out of Hamilton, Ontario harbor, this vessel carried people on pleasure cruises on the western end of Lake Ontario. The namesake of the vessel was Hamilton, Ontario in which Mr. George Hamilton located in 1813. The site was incorporated as a town in 1833 and as a city in 1846. The first word of the ship name referred to the fact that most vessels, especially those carrying passengers, are referenced in the feminine gender.

Steamer GEORGE R. FINK (2)

OWNER: Hanna Furnace Corporation
BUILT: Toledo Shipbuilding Company, Toledo, Ohio – 1923
HULL NO.: 174
O. A. DIMENSIONS: 600' x 60' x 32'
FORMER DATA: Launched as WORRELL CLARKSON. Renamed ERNEST T. WEIR (1) in 1936. Given last name in 1952.

The namesake of this vessel was Mr. George Rupert Fink who was born November 1, 1886 in Brackenridge, Pennsylvania. He began his career in the steel business as a steel mill worker with Allegheny Steel Corporation and later became a steel salesman.

Mr. Fink was closely identified with steel making in Detroit. Consumption of steel in the automotive industry led to plants in that area and Mr. Fink was on hand for the job. He organized and operated the Michigan Steel Corporation and Great Lakes Steel Corporation located on Zug Island and in Ecorse, Michigan along the Detroit River.

After Great Lakes Steel Corporation was merged into, and became a subsidiary of, National Steel Corporation, Mr. Fink progressed through the ranks of top management, becoming National Steel Corporation president. After retirement, he lived in the suburb of Grosse Pointe Farms, Michigan until his death.

The Steamer GEORGE R. FINK is shown here loading the only grain cargo it ever carried for these owners, at Superior, Wisconsin. The vessel was sold for scrap in 1973.

Barge DELKOTE

OWNER:	Hindman Transportation Company Limited
BUILT:	Chicago Shipbuilding Company, Chicago, Illinois—1897
HULL NO.:	26
O. A. DIMENSIONS:	366' × 44' × 26'
FORMER DATA:	Launched as CARRINGTON. Renamed CORDOVA (2) in 1927. Given last name in 1939.

The bulk freight Barge DELKOTE honored a product of the Detroit Sulphite Paper Company as its namesake. This parent firm owned the three barges noted herein through its subsidiary firm in Canada, the Driftwood Lands & Timber Company Limited until they were sold to the Hindman Transportation Company in 1954.

With the barges went a floating contract for pulpwood to be delivered primarily to the Detroit, Michigan plant. These owners kept the names given these vessels by the former owners in recognition of their continuing business relationship.

Delkote was a brand name applied to a very heavy, high-quality paper which was manufactured by the Detroit Sulphite Paper Company. This paper had a glossy finish and sheen, closely resembling typical enameled paper stock of today.

This fine paper was manufactured in various colors to conform with the firm's customers' wishes and specifications. It was usually produced in one hundred pound weight and was of bonded strength. Delkote paper ranked among the highest quality paper products in the industry.

The Barge DELKOTE remained active in the pulpwood trade until being sold for scrap in 1967. It is shown above in the St. Mary's River on July 10, 1963.

Steamer BLANCHE HINDMAN (2)

OWNER:	Hindman Transportation Company Limited
BUILT:	Great Lakes Engineering Works, Ecorse, Michigan—1909
HULL NO.:	56
O. A. DIMENSIONS:	464' × 56' × 28'
FORMER DATA:	Launched as THEODORE H. WICKWIRE. Renamed HARRY YATES (3) in 1939. Given last name in 1960.

The small bulk freight Steamer BLANCHE HINDMAN was the first entry of this fleet into the larger size of vessels that became known in the Great Lakes trade as "mediums."

The former Edith Blanche Proctor was born at Walkerton, Ontario on November 23, 1893 and received her education in that locale. She married Captain George Hindman March 17, 1914 in Owen Sound, Ontario and was a helpmate, wife and homemaker to him for the rest of his life.

She was the daughter of an officer of the Keenan Lumber Company, on whose tug her husband-to-be was employed in 1914. After they were married, the young family moved to Sarnia, Ontario where Captain Hindman was employed by the Reid Towing & Wrecking Company. In 1919 they moved back to Owen Sound and made that city their residence for the balance of their lives. Mrs. Hindman never took an active part in the family business, but remained a steadfast mother and wife during the careers of her husband and offsprings.

Her namesake was active in the fleet until being sold for scrap in 1968. It is shown here in the Welland Ship Canal in 1963.

Motor Vessel ELIZABETH HINDMAN

OWNER:	Hindman Transportation Company Limited
BUILT:	Midland Shipbuilding Company Limited, Midland, Ontario - 1921
HULL NO.:	9
O. A. DIMENSIONS:	259' x 42'6" x 21'
FORMER DATA:	Launched as GLENCLOVA. Renamed ANTICOSTI in 1927. Renamed RISACUA in 1948. Renamed GEORGE HINDMAN (2) in 1953. Given last name in 1962.

The Motor Vessel ELIZABETH HINDMAN was sold for scrap in 1970 after over a year of inactivity. It had served in the transport of pulpwood and grain during its later years and at one time was painted in four different colors which made it readily identifiable.

Namesake of this vessel was one of the daughters of Mr. Howard Hindman, president of the company. Mary Elizabeth Hindman was born at Owen Sound, Ontario on April 22, 1946 and was educated at Toronto Teacher's College, Toronto, Ontario. She graduated in 1967 and is currently teaching in the elementary school system of London, Ontario. She was married on August 17, 1968.

This motor vessel was the last of the canal-sized units to be operated by this fleet. It survived longer than most canallers of her age because of the relatively modern power plant that was installed onboard in 1955. Carrying capacity was not significantly increased by this improvement, but speed was and that additional speed made the life of the vessel about six years longer than it would have been without the improved power plant. The vessel is shown upbound in the St. Mary's River on June 1, 1963.

Steamer GEORGE HINDMAN (3)

OWNER:	Hindman Transportation Company Limited
BUILT:	American Ship Building Company Lorain, Ohio—1914
HULL NO.:	710
O. A. DIEMNSIONS:	524' × 54' × 30'
FORMER DATA:	Launched as WILLIAM D. CRAWFORD. Renamed BAIRD TEWKSBURY in 1953. Given last name in 1962.

After a grounding accident at Clayton, New York in 1967, this bulk freighter was sold for scrap after having served for five years in the Hindman fleet.

Captain George Hindman, founder of the fleet and long time head of it, was the namesake of this vessel. He was born at Hepworth, Ontario on July 7, 1888 and moved to Owen Sound, Ontario with his family the next year.

He began sailing as wheelsman in 1904 and by 1911 was a mate on the steam tug KEENAN. He obtained his master's papers later that year. He continued to sail on a number of different ships and in 1922 bought property on Manitoulin Island to mark the beginning of the Hindman Timber Company Limited. A series of developments led the Captain to form the Lakehead Transportation Company in 1936 and other subsequent predecessor companies to the Hindman Transportation Company. Captain Hindman continued active in all these ventures until his death in Florida on February 27, 1969.

His namesake is shown while being loaded at the National Harbours Board Elevator in Prescott, Ontario, for downriver shipment. The maiden trip of this ship was with coal from Sandusky, Ohio on May 19, 1914 for Milwaukee, Wisconsin discharge.

Steamer HOWARD HINDMAN (2)

OWNER: Hindman Transportation Company Limited
BUILT: American Ship Building Company, Lorain, Ohio - 1910
HULL NO.: 374
O. A. DIMENSIONS: 524' x 54' x 30'
FORMER DATA: Launched as A. A. AUGUSTUS. Given last name in 1961.

The bulk freight Steamer HOWARD HINDMAN (2) suffered damage early in the 1969 navigation season and was sold for overseas scrapping later that year. It marked the passing of a carrier that had traded on the Great Lakes and Seaway for this fleet for nine years in the movements of coal, grain, iron ore and pulpwood.

Namesake of the vessel is Mr. Howard Hindman who was born at Toronto, Ontario on October 28, 1916. He attended Pickering College, Newmarket, Ontario and began working on properties of the family-owned Hindman Timber Company Limited on Manitoulin Island, Ontario in 1937. Mr. Hindman became superintendent of the operations in a short time and also assisted his father and others in the family in various affairs of their companies.

In 1945 he moved to Owen Sound, Ontario as general manager of the Hindman interests. He was elected president of the Hindman Transportation Company Limited and affiliated enterprises in 1960.

His namesake vessel is shown below leaving the Cote Ste. Catherine Lock on the St. Lawrence Seaway as viewed on October 19, 1967. It sailed on its maiden voyage from Cleveland, Ohio on April 12, 1910 with a cargo of coal for Green Bay, Wisconsin delivery.

Steamer RUTH HINDMAN

OWNER:	Hindman Transportation Company, Limited
BUILT:	Toledo Shipbuilding Company, Toledo, Ohio - 1910
HULL NO.:	115
O. A. DIMENSIONS:	524' x 58' x 30'
FORMER DATA:	Launched as NORWAY (2). Given last name in 1965.

Mrs. Ruth Hindman was the former Ruth McKay of Owen Sound, Ontario. She was born at Owen Sound, Ontario on June 25, 1917 and was educated in the schools of that city and Toronto, Ontario.

In 1938 she married the only son of company founder Captain George Hindman, Mr. Howard Hindman. After a short time in Toronto, the couple moved back to Owen Sound and Mrs. Ruth Hindman became involved in the family business and in being a homemaker and mother to four children.

Mrs. Hindman's husband, Howard, was the president of Hindman Transportation Company and had been a guiding force in its development until the fleet was sold in 1978.

Hobbies of Mrs. Ruth Hindman were curling and various civic responsibilities until she died in the winter of 1978. The Steamer RUTH HINDMAN honored her contributions to the success of the family concern.

Her namesake is shown in the St. Mary's River, unbound on August 14, 1972. It was sold for scrap in 1975.

Barge MITSCHFIBRE

OWNER:	Hindman Transportation Company Limited
BUILT:	Chicago Shipbuilding Company, Chicago, Illinois—1895
HULL NO.:	12
O. A. DIMENSIONS:	318'6" × 40' × 24'6'
FORMER DATA:	Launched as MARCIA. Given last name in 1924.

The bulk freight Barge MITSCHFIBRE was also given a namesake which was a brand name of a paper product of the Detroit Sulphite Paper Company. This name means, literally, fibers of wood pulp manufactured by the process developed by Mr. Jonathan Mitscherlich.

Mr. Mitscherlich came to the United States in the nineteenth century from his native Sweden. He possessed knowledge of a new chemical process he had developed which became the basis for expansion of the sulphite method of pulpwood processing in the United States and Canada. He oversaw construction of pulpwood mills at Detroit and Alpena, Michigan and at Appleton, Wisconsin.

One of the prime ingredients in this process was fine spruce trees. They were sought because of their low resin content. As these trees became harder to find in quantity in later years, this method of production slowly waned.

Mitschfibre was known in the paper industry as a brand of paper representing the strongest type of paper that was made. This brand name is no longer in use, having given way to more modern terminology in the paper and paper products industry.

This barge remained in the Hindman fleet until being sold for scrap in 1966. It is shown above at Detroit, Michigan on July 4, 1958.

Barge SWEDEROPE (2)

OWNER: Hindman Transportation Company Limited
BUILT: Globe Iron Works, Cleveland, Ohio—1897
HULL NO.: 68
O. A. DIMENSIONS: 378' × 44' × 26'
FORMER DATA: Launched as SIDNEY G. THOMAS. Given last name in 1940.

Swederope was a brand name used by the Detroit Sulphite Paper Company, and later by the Scott Paper Company, to identify its heavy paper for use in office filing materials. It was a product name that could be appropriately applied today in reference to the commonly called "manila" envelopes and storage filing folders.

The Swederope brand of paper ranged in weight from fifty to one hundred pounds. The name originated out of honor to Mr. Jonathan Mitscherlich who largely developed the methods by which this paper was produced. The prefix of this name honored his native land—Sweden.

It is of interest to note that the sulphite process developed by Mr. Mitscherlich was one of three processes used in the paper industry. By this process, wood pulp is made by cooking chips of wood in a solution of calcium, magnesium or ammonium bisulfite and an excess of sulfur dioxide under pressure and at a raised temperature. This method differed from the soda and sulfate process, also called the Kraft process, and the semi-chemical process in which both mechanical and chemical means were utilized in producing wood pulp. The long cooking period, 24 hours, has diminished the number of plants still using this process in modern times.

The bulk freight Barge SWEDEROPE was active on the Great Lakes until its sale for scrap in 1967. It is shown here in the St. Mary's River on August 17, 1956, downbound with a load of pulpwood for Detroit, Michigan.

Barge VIGILANT

OWNER: Hindman Transportation Company Limited
BUILT: Polson Iron Works,
Toronto, Ontario – 1904
HULL NO.: 70
O. A. DIMENSIONS: 185' x 22' x 14'3"
FORMER DATA: Launched as an armoured Fisheries Department cruiser. Converted to a bulk freight barge at Port Colborne Iron Works, Limited, Port Colborne, Ontario in 1935. Converted to a crane-equipped bulk freight barge at Hindman Transportation Company Limited, Owen Sound, Ontario in 1944.

The Barge VIGILANT served these owners in the pulpwood trade for twelve years before being sold for scrap in 1956. The vessel is shown above while underway on August 20, 1952. The lines of the hull indicate the "pencil-like" form remained in the barge from its first days in service as a government cruiser. This made the unit a fine vessel to tow because the fine lines did not create much water resistance. However, the barge was awkward to handle in heavy weather and, coupled with its very narrow beam and small capacity, by the mid-1950's the end was in sight for the barge.

The namesake of the barge was found in the meaning of the word VIGILANT. That is, "alertly watchful, especially to avoid danger." When this vessel was completed in 1904, it was almost an inland Navy ship. The purpose was to patrol Canadian shoreline areas and international waters of the Great Lakes for possible illegal crossing of the border and to intercept illegal fishing by aliens in Canadian waters. The little craft performed this service well, but was replaced by more modern equipment in the early 1930's.

Steamer IMPERIAL HAMILTON

OWNER: Imperial Oil Limited
BUILT: Collingwood Shipbuilding Company Limited, Collingwood, Ontario—1916
HULL NO.: 47
O. A. DIMENSIONS: 258' × 43' × 18'
FORMER DATA: Launched as SARNOLITE. Renamed IMPERIAL SARNIA (1) in 1947. Given last name in 1948.

The Steamer IMPERIAL HAMILTON was sold for use as a breakwater in 1963 and now is serving that purpose at Kewaunee, Wisconsin.

The namesake of this tanker is twofold. First name of the ship name refers to the owning company whose headquarters are in Toronto, Ontario. The second word of this ship name refers to the city of Hamilton, Ontario which is nearby Toronto and at the western tip of Lake Ontario.

Hamilton is a city of about 400,000 population and is the industrial heart of Canada. It is named in honor of Mr. George Hamilton who bought a tract of land at the site in 1813. He subdivided the area and named its streets for members of his family. Hamilton was incorporated as a village in 1816, as a town in 1833 and as a city in 1846.

The Steamer IMPERIAL HAMILTON is seen above in the Eastern Gap entrance to Toronto, Ontario harbour in August, 1958.

Steamer IMPERIAL LA HAVE

OWNER:	Imperial Oil Limited
BUILT:	Furness Shipbuilding Company, Limited, Haverton Hill-on-Tees, England—1930
HULL NO.:	173
O. A. DIMENSIONS:	181' × 35' × 13'
FORMER DATA:	Launched as OTTAWALITE. Renamed IMPERIAL OTTAWA (1) in 1947. Given last name in 1965.

Though not exactly a Great Lakes ship, this tank vessel was operated out of the owner's headquarters in Toronto, Ontario and did, on occasion, run into the Great Lakes. Its primary trade, however, was from the firm's large refinery at Montreal East past intermediate points on the Ottawa River to Ottawa and Hull, Quebec. It served under this last name only a short while, being sold for scrap in 1966.

The namesake of this tanker was the small community of 300 population, La Have, Nova Scotia. The current population belies the importance of this place in history, however, for it was here that many battles were waged and that countries sought to hold forth.

The place was called Cape La Have, or Cap de la Have, when visited in 1604 by Monts and Champlain. France and Britain controlled it through the years and, in 1701, it was used as a fort by pirates against New Englanders. It was burned in 1705 by Boston privateers.

Steamer IMPERIAL SIMCOE

OWNER: Imperial Oil Limited
BUILT: Furness Shipbuilding Company, Limited, Haverton Hill-on-Tees, England—1930
HULL NO.: 171
O. A. DIMENSIONS: 258' × 43' × 18'
FORMER DATA: Launched as SIMCOLITE. Given last name in 1947.

The tank Steamer IMPERIAL SIMCOE is shown in the photograph above approaching Lock One of the Welland Ship Canal on May 26, 1962. This steamer continued to serve on the Great Lakes until being sold for scrap in 1965.

This vessel was typical of the canal-sized tankers operated by this fleet until after the opening of the St. Lawrence Seaway in 1959. After this date, the fleet gradually enlarged their Great Lakes vessels to provide enlarged former "canallers" and ships of greater beam and length than could have ever maneuvered the former size locks.

The first word of this ship name was common to all the ships and stood for the name of the owning company. The second word of the ship name was the specific namesake. Simcoe, Ontario was this namesake. It is a town in Norfolk County on the Lynn River 24 miles south of Brantford, Ontario. It was first settled in the 18th century and was named in honor of John Graves Simcoe, the first Lieutenant Governor of Upper Canada.

Known as a model town and a center of the flue-cured tobacco industry, Simcoe is in a district also noted for its canning crops, apples and other fruits, as well as dairying and general farming. It is naturally picturesque and has fine parks and playgrounds, including beautiful Lake George and Lynn River Park where Governor Simcoe camped in 1795.

Steamer IMPERIAL WELLAND

OWNER: Imperial Oil Limited
BUILT: Collingwood Shipbuilding Company, Collingwood, Ontario—1916
HULL NO.: 45
O. A. DIMENSIONS: 258' × 43' × 18'
FORMER DATA: Launched as ROYALITE. Given last name in 1947.

The namesake of this tank vessel was one through which it passed literally hundreds of times during its Great Lakes career. That namesake was the Welland Ship Canal, together with the town of Welland, Ontario which is located on that canal.

The Welland Ship Canal provides navigational passage from Lake Erie to Lake Ontario and vice versa for vessels up to and including overall dimensions of: length 730', beam 75' and depth which is virtually unlimited so long as the draft of the ship in the canal does not exceed 26'.

The first canal was built by private funds of the Welland Canal Company at a cost of $7,700,000. This was opened to traffic in 1829. This 8-foot deep canal connected Port Dalhousie with Port Robinson on Chippawa Creek which gave access to the Niagara River. In 1833 the canal was extended to Port Colborne, Ontario on Lake Erie.

Additonal improvements were made through the years, always allowing for larger tonnage and the present canal was opened to traffic in 1932. Many further developments have been made to speed passage and a ten mile straight section of the canal around Welland, Ontario has just been opened to traffic which allows safer passage and prompter vessel accommodation between the southern and northern ends of the canal.

This vessel is shown in Toronto, Ontario Harbour's Eastern Gap on September 5, 1963. It was sold for scrap in 1965.

Steamer CLARENCE B. RANDALL (2)

OWNER: Inland Steel Company
BUILT: American Ship Building Company, Cleveland, Ohio - 1907
HULL NO.: 439
O. A. DIMENSIONS: 552' x 56' x 31'
FORMER DATA: Launched as J. J. SULLIVAN. Given last name in 1962.

Mr. Clarence Balden Randall is the namesake of this vessel. He was born on March 5, 1891 at Newark Valley, New York and received a B.A. degree from Harvard University in 1912 and an Ll.B. degree from that school in 1915. He was admitted to the Michigan Bar in July, 1915.

Mr. Randall practiced law at Ishpeming, Michigan from 1915 to 1925 when he joined Inland Steel Company in August as assistant vice president–raw materials. He served in that capacity until 1930 when he became vice president. He held that post until becoming president of Inland Steel on April 27, 1949 and its chairman of the board in 1953. Mr. Randall retired for age in April, 1956. He had served as a director of the company since 1935 and died on August 4, 1967.

He was active in civic affairs and a trustee of two colleges. He was awarded the Medal of Freedom in 1963 for his work in governmental affairs under three Presidents. He was a spokesman of the steel industry and of business in general. His namesake is shown below while downbound in the West Neebish Channel, St. Mary's River on May 24, 1975. The ship is light because the port to which it was destined became struck-bound May 23rd and the RANDALL returned light to Port Inland. The ship was sold for scrap November 18, 1976. It was subsequently sold in 1980 for use as a grain storage hull and then, in 1986, for scrap.

Steamer ADRIATIC (2)

OWNER: Interlake Steamship Company
BUILT: American Ship Building Company, Lorain, Ohio - 1907
HULL NO.: 354
O. A. DIMENSIONS: 440' x 52' x 28'6"

The bulk freight Steamer ADRIATIC (2) was one of several in the fleet which had mines and place names as their namesakes. This ship was sold for scrap in 1962.

The Adriatic mine on the Missabe Range at Mesaba, Minnesota was one of those of which Mr. Joseph Sellwood picked up control for Pickands, Mather & Company in 1906. It was one of a large number of mines acquired by Pickands, Mather and other firms when the Missabe Range was coming into full early development. Mr. Sellwood and Pickands, Mather & Company each shared equally in the ownership of the Adriatic mine which shipped 1,167,731 gross tons of non-bessemer ore by its closing in 1918.

The namesake of the mine and this ship, in retrospect, is the Adriatic Sea of Europe. This is a small sea in comparision to other more prominent seas of the world. It lies between Italy on the west and Yugoslavia and Albania on the east. It is a sea that is, in reality, an arm of the Mediterranean Sea. Coming from the inward portion of the Adriatic Sea, however, one must pass through a body of water known as the Ionian Sea before coming into the main body of the Mediterranean Sea.

The Steamer ADRIATIC (2) is shown in this photograph upbound in Lake St. Clair on August 21, 1951.

Steamer ARCTURUS

OWNER:	Interlake Steamship Company
BUILT:	West Bay City Shipbuilding Company, West Bay City, Michigan—1906
HULL NO.:	616
O. A. DIMENSIONS:	534' × 54' × 31'3"
FORMER DATA:	Launched as JAMES B. WOOD. Given last name in 1913.

The bulk freight Steamer ARCTURUS is shown in the photograph below downbound in the St. Clair River with a full cargo of iron ore destined for Cleveland, Ohio on July 16, 1959. The vessel was sold for scrapping overseas in 1961 but foundered enroute to Europe.

The namesake of this vessel was the Arcturus Mine at Marble, Minnesota. It was also the brightest star in the northern hemisphere which is called Arcturus. The dual nature of the namesake is interesting.

The star is so called because, according to mythology, Arcas, son of Lycaon, King of Arcadia, was killed by his father as a sacrifice to Zeus but was later restored to life and afterwards turned into a star.

At the time this ship took its last name, the mine of the same name as the star was one of the brightest prospects for enriched iron ore known on the Mesabi Range. The property was managed by the Oliver Iron Company and was a producer of high grade natural iron ore.

Steamer FAYETTE BROWN (2)

OWNER:	Interlake Steamship Company
BUILT:	American Ship Building Company, Lorain, Ohio—1910
HULL NO.:	378
O. A. DIMENSIONS:	524' × 54' × 30'3"
FORMER DATA:	Launched as CHARLES L. HUTCHINSON (1). Given last name in 1917.

Mr. Fayette Brown was born on December 17, 1823 near Bloomfield, Ohio and was educated in the schools of Jefferson and Gambier, Ohio. In 1841 he began working as a clerk in his eldest brother's wholesale dry goods business in Pittsburgh, Pennsylvania. He was later a partner in that firm until going to Cleveland, Ohio in 1851.

In Cleveland he entered partnership with the Honorable George Mygatt in the firm of Mygatt & Brown in the field of banking. This firm closed at the outbreak of Civil War in 1861 and Mr. Brown served as paymaster in the army until 1862. He returned to Cleveland in that year and became actively associated with iron and steel interests as general agent for the Jackson Iron Company.

He remained with Jackson Iron until December, 1887. Mr. Brown was associated with many Cleveland firms and was president of the Brown Hoisting Machinery Company, Union Steel Screw Company, National Chemical Company and G. C. Kuhlman Car Company. He also was chairman of the board of Stewart Iron Company and H. H. Brown & Company, large iron ore sellers. He died in Cleveland on January 20, 1910 and his namesake was sold for scrap in 1963. It never reached its destination, being run on the rocks in the Lower St. Lawrence River on Anticosti Island in a wild fall storm. The ship is shown in the picture below at Little Rapids Cut, St. Mary's River while downbound from the Soo Locks in 1955.

Steamer CRETE (2)

OWNER:	Interlake Steamship Company
BUILT:	American Ship Building Company, Lorain, Ohio—1907
HULL NO.:	352
O. A. DIMENSIONS:	500' × 52' × 30'

The bulk freight Steamer CRETE took the Crete Mining Company and the island of Crete as its dual namesake. The mining company was active on the Mesabi Range of Minnesota and was a property managed by Pickands Mather & Company and eighty percent owned by Youngstown Sheet and Tube Company.

The island of Crete is the fourth largest in size among the islands of the Mediterranean Sea. As was the case with other early ships in this fleet, they were given names by Mr. Jay C. Morse who was particularly partial to locations in the Mediterranean area.

Crete is one hundred and fifty miles southeast of Greece and has an area of 3,195 square miles. The island is one hundred and sixty-one miles in length and varies from seven to thirty-four miles in width. It is traversed by mountains, the highest peaks being Mount Theodoros at 8,103 feet and Mount Ida at 8,061 feet. Several nations have occupied Crete in history. In 66 B.C. the Romans were there. From 823 A.D. onward, until it was united with Greece in 1913, the island was governed by Mohammedans, The Crusaders, The Latin Empire, The Ottoman Empire and Turkey.

The Steamer CRETE was sold for scrap in 1962 and is shown below in the St. Clair River while downbound for Lake Erie with a cargo of iron ore.

Steamer COLONEL JAMES PICKANDS

OWNER: Interlake Steamship Company
BUILT: American Ship Building Company, Lorain, Ohio – 1926
HULL NO.: 791
O. A. DIMENSIONS: 600' x 60' x 32'

Colonel James Pickands was born at Akron, Ohio on December 15, 1839 and came to Cleveland, Ohio while in his teens to work as a clerk in a mercantile house. At the outbreak of the Civil War he was active in organizing regiments of volunteers in Cleveland. He accepted a commission in 1862 and rose to the rank of colonel by 1865 when he was discharged from the Union Army.

He then went to work in the Cleveland office of Brown & Company, but shortly thereafter moved to Marquette, Michigan to form his own hardware, coal and general merchandise business. He later built a coal dock at Marquette in conjunction with his coal business.

He came back to Cleveland, Ohio in 1881 and, with Messers. Samuel Mather and Jay C. Morse formed Pickands Mather & Co. in 1883. Colonel Pickands' close connection with the varied interests which were important factors in the building of Cleveland made him one of the most important, honored and representative citizens of the city. His name carried weight in both financial and industrial circles and was reknowned in mining areas. Colonel Pickands died July 14, 1896. His namesake remained active until being sold for scrap in 1974 for the highest price yet ever achieved! It is shown here on one of its last trips, upbound in the St. Clair River on June 24, 1974.

Steamer JOSEPH SELLWOOD

OWNER:	Interlake Steamship Company
BUILT:	American Ship Building Company, Lorain, Ohio—1906
HULL NO.:	340
O. A. DIMENSIONS:	545' × 55' × 31'

Mr. Joseph Sellwood was born at Cornwall, England on December 5, 1846. He received little formal education and set out for the United States in 1865.

He first went to the copper mining area of upper Michigan and remained there until August 1, 1870. It was at this time that he foresaw the vast possibilities of a developing iron range in Minnesota as well as the iron ranges of upper Michigan. He worked for various mining firms in the region until being sent to open the Colby mine on the Gogebic Range by Mather, Morse & Company in 1885.

In 1886 he bought the Chandler mine on the Vermilion Range for the Chicago & Minnesota Ore Company for $26,000 and divided his time between the two ranges until mid-1888. He then spent his time wholly on the Minnesota ranges and in November, 1892 went to work as an acquirer of Mesabi Range properties for the Minnesota Iron Company. In 1898 he took over the management of American Steel & Wire Company properties. He continued active in mining and financial affairs until his death on February 24, 1914. The Mitchell fleet named this ship in his honor and the last owners kept the name in honor of a great pioneer. The ship was sold for scrap in 1961.

The Steamer JOSEPH SELLWOOD is shown departing Superior, Wisconsin.

Steamer AMASA STONE

OWNER: Interlake Steamship Company
BUILT: Detroit Shipbuilding Company, Wyandotte, Michigan—1905
HULL NO.: 158
O. A. DIMENSIONS: 545' × 55' × 31'

Sold for scrap in 1964 and later sunk as a breakwater foundation, the Steamer AMASA STONE honored Mr. Amasa Stone who was born at Charlton, Massachusetts on April 27, 1818. He was educated in the public schools and worked as a carpenter in the period 1835-38.

He then went to work with his brother-in-law, William Howe, in constructing bridges. The Howe Truss Bridge was later patented by the firm. Mr. Stone secured a contract to build the first railroad bridge over the Connecticut River at Springfield in 1840.

In 1844, Mr. Stone became superintendent of the New Haven, Hartford & Springfield Railroad. In 1849 he was associated with the Cleveland, Columbus & Cincinnati Railroad and later was its president. In 1869 he became managing director of the Lake Shore Railroad Company and continued active in consulting design work in bridge building in the Northwest. He served on numerous committees and boards of directors and his daughter married the late Samuel Mather, original member of the company which owned this ship for its lifetime.

Mr. Stone died in Cleveland, Ohio on May 11, 1883. His namesake is shown in this photograph being overtaken by another freighter in the St. Clair River in the summer of 1952. It had loaded coal at Toledo, Ohio for Superior, Wisconsin on its maiden voyage, departing Toledo on May 10, 1905.

Steamer JAMES C. WALLACE

OWNER:	Interlake Steamship Company
BUILT:	American Ship Building Company, Lorain, Ohio—1905
HULL NO.:	334
O. A. DIMENSIONS:	552' × 56' × 31'

Namesake of the bulk freighter Steamer JAMES C. WALLACE was Mr. James Chase Wallace who was born on May 23, 1865 at Cleveland, Ohio. He was educated in the public schools and went to work in 1881 as a machinist's apprentice in his father's Globe Iron Works at Cleveland, Ohio. He also sailed on the lakes for a season.

He returned to Cleveland, Ohio in 1887 as an employee of the Cleveland Shipbuilding Company which was then being organized and continued to work for that firm until the incorporation of American Ship Building Company on March 16, 1899. This was done by his father, Mr. Robert Wallace and other associates, and Mr. J. C. Wallace became general manager of the new firm. The new company amalgamated the Cleveland Shipbuilding Company, Globe Iron Works, Ship Owners' Dry Dock Company and several other yards at Chicago, Milwaukee, West Superior, Detroit and Buffalo into one unit. Mr. Wallace was named president in 1904 and continued in that post until 1914. He died on October 31, 1916 and his namesake was sold for scrap in 1961.

The Steamer JAMES C. WALLACE is seen in this photograph passing upbound in the St. Mary's River. Its maiden voyage was commenced April 26, 1905 from Lorain, Ohio light to Duluth, Minnesota for a cargo of iron ore.

Steamer HARRY W. CROFT

OWNER:	Interlake Steamship Company, A Division of Pickands Mather and Co.
BUILT:	Toledo Shipbuilding Company, Toledo, Ohio—1908
HULL NO.:	112
O. A. DIMENSIONS:	524' × 58' × 30'
FORMER DATA:	Launched as FRED G. HARTWELL (1). Given last name in 1917.

This steamer was sold for scrap in 1969 and was towed overseas late in that year. Namesake of the ship is Mr. Harry William Croft who was born on December 12, 1865 at Allegheny City, Pennsylvania. He was educated in the public schools and at Iron City College in Pittsburgh, Pennsylvania.

Mr. Croft began as a bookkeeper at Livingston Foundry Company in 1881 and worked there until 1887 when he went with the Woodland Fire Brick Company Limited. This was a company controlled by Harbison-Walker Company. He became manager of the Woodland plant in 1895 and general works manager of Harbison-Walker in 1898. He was promoted to vice president and general manager in 1899 and became the firm's president in 1907. He was elected chairman of the board in 1921 and retired from that post in 1938. Mr. Croft died at Greenwich, Connecticut on February 25, 1947.

He was active on the boards of other companies including Koppers Company, Mellon National Bank, Republic Steel & Iron Company, Mack Trucks, Incorporated and Metropolitan Life Insurance Company.

The bulk freight Steamer HARRY W. CROFT is shown below on June 20, 1960 at Central Furnace Works, Cleveland, Ohio.

Steamer HENRY G. DALTON

OWNER:	Interlake Steamship Company, A Division of Pickands Mather & Company
BUILT:	American Ship Building Company, Lorain, Ohio—1916
HULL NO.:	713
O. A. DIMENSIONS:	600' × 60' × 32'

The Steamer HENRY G. DALTON has held a Great Lakes cargo record longer than any other vessel, past or present. That record is for the largest cargo of anthracite coal ever moved on the Great Lakes. It was loaded on September 3, 1920 at Lackawanna, New York for delivery to Duluth, Minnesota and totaled 14,614 net tons. It is the only vessel ever to be retired while still holding a recognized Great Lakes cargo record.

Mr. Henry George Dalton was born on October 3, 1862 in Cleveland, Ohio and abandoned school at the age of 14 to take a boy's job on the Nypano Dock in Cleveland. He became clerk of the dock 7 years later and joined Pickands, Mather & Company on June 15, 1883. He rose rapidly in the firm becoming its fourth member in 1893. From that point he was prominent in the widespread influence of the firm in industrial affairs. Mr. Dalton became senior partner in 1931. At the time of his death on December 26, 1939 he was the last surviving member of the original founders of the firm.

In addition to being Pickands, Mather & Company's senior partner, he was also president of Interlake Steamship Company and chairman of the board of Youngstown Sheet and Tube Company from 1932 onward.

His namesake was sold for scrap in 1972 and is shown below while upbound in Lake Nicolet on June 30, 1970. This vessel commenced its maiden voyage May 21, 1916 with a cargo of coal from Toledo, Ohio for Duluth, Minnesota delivery.

Steamer H. J. Mc MANUS

OWNER:	Jemmig Enterprises Limited
BUILT:	Earle's Shipbuilding & Engineering Company Limited, Hull, England—1925
HULL NO.:	647
O. A. DIMENSIONS:	261' × 43'3" × 20'
FORMER DATA:	Launched as JUDGE KENEFICK. Given last name in 1961.

This vessel served for a very short time in this fleet, having been acquired in 1960 and sold for scrap in 1961. It was later reduced to a barge.

Mr. Henry Joseph Mc Manus is the namesake of this vessel. He was born at St. Thomas, Ontario on July 9, 1907 and received his education at the Collegiate Institute, St. Thomas, Ontario.

He served in several capacities before attaining the presidency of Imperialle Fuels Limited in 1934. He has been active in numerous companies and organized and controlled Mc Manus Petroleums Limited in 1938, holding control until 1946. He later was vice president of St. Catharines Fuel Oils Limited, Husband International (Ontario) Transport Limited, and president of Hotel London Limited, Northcrest Investments Limited, Wildron Investments, Harmony Finance Corporation Limited and Apex Auto Leasing Limited.

Mr. Mc Manus served as a director of the Automotive Transport Association of Ontario, London Chamber of Commerce and was one of the directors and investors in this ship-owning company in the early 1960's. His namesake is shown in the photograph on May 13, 1961. It had begun its maiden voyage April 3, 1925 from Swansea, Wales with a cargo of coal for Toronto, Ontario.

Motor Vessel LIO

OWNER:	Jocharanne Tugboat Corporation
BUILT:	New York Shipbuilding Corporation, Camden, New Jersey—1924
HULL NO.:	292
O. A. DIMENSIONS:	260' × 40' × 14'
FORMER DATA:	Launched as BOSTON SOCONY. Given new midbody at Federal Shipbuilding and Dry Dock Company, Kearny, New Jersey in 1935. Renamed J. L. LATIMER in 1954. Given last name in 1957.

Until sold for off-lakes use in 1964, the Motor Vessel LIO was in use on the Great Lakes and the eastern seaboard via the New York State Barge Canal. It was a tank vessel of usual size for this trade and its name corresponded with many small tankers of the day in that the name stemmed from the theme of vessel names in reference to heavenly bodies.

The preferred spelling of this name in literature is LEO and the name refers to the fifth sign of the zodiac, or The Lion. This in turn refers to the constellation which appears in the sign of Virgo.

LIO, or Leo, is one of the oldest constellations and was described as a lion in the oldest known zodiac. Its brightest star is of the first magnitude and is named Alpha Leonis, or Regulus. It is sometimes called Cor Leonis because it marks the heart of the lion. Spectacular showers of meteors emanated from this constellation in 1799, 1833 and 1866.

The Motor Vessel LIO is shown above in open lake on June 17, 1962.

Motor Vessel CONGAR (1)

OWNER:	Johnstone Shipping Limited
BUILT:	Canadian Vickers Limited, Montreal, Quebec—1930
HULL NO.:	112
O. A. DIMENSIONS:	260' × 43'6" × 20'
FORMER DATA:	Launched as the barge REDHEAD. Converted to a powered bulk freighter at Muir Brothers Dry Dock Company, Limited, Port Dalhousie, Ontario and renamed BLUE CROSS in 1934. Converted to a tanker at Muir Brothers Dry Dock Company, Limited, Port Dalhousie, Ontario in 1940. Renamed LAKE TRANSPORT (1) in 1959. Given last name in 1966.

The Motor Vessel CONGAR is named in honor of two members of the Rod W. Smith family of Toronto, Ontario. Mr. Smith is the manager of this fleet and also operates a ship repair business in Toronto.

Prefix of this ship name is in reference to the former Constance Johnstone, now Mrs. Rod Smith. The "CON" in CONGAR stands for her first name. Mrs. Smith was born on July 8, 1929 and married Mr. Smith in 1947.

The suffix of the vessel name is in reference to the son of this couple, Garry Smith. "GAR" is the shortened usage of his first name. He was born at Toronto on December 16, 1952 and has embarked on a career of his own.

This vessel was sold for off-lakes use late in 1969, but the ship name is carried forward by a larger tanker in the fleet. It is shown in this photograph in the Welland Ship Canal on December 14, 1968 while loaded with a cargo of fuel oil.

Motor Vessel CONGAR (2)

OWNER: Johnstone Shipping, Limited
BUILT: Sir James Laing & Sons Limited, Sunderland, England—1946
HULL NO.: 766
O. A. DIMENSIONS: 357'7" × 48'4" × 26'9"
FORMER DATA: Launched as EMPIRE MALDON. Renamed IMPERIAL HALIFAX in 1946. Given last name in 1970.

The tank Motor Vessel CONGAR is named in honor of two members of the Rod W. Smith family of Toronto, Ontario. Mr. Smith is the manager of this fleet and also operates a ship repair business in Toronto.

Prefix of this ship name is in reference to the former Constance Johnstone, now Mrs. Rod Smith. The "CON" in CONGAR stands for Constance. Mrs. Smith was born on July 8, 1929 and married Mr. Rod Smith in 1947. She is president of Johnstone Shipping, Limited.

The suffix of the vessel name is in reference to the son of this couple, Gary Smith. "GAR" is the shortened usage of his first name. He was born at Toronto on December 16, 1952.

Mrs. Smith is a homemaker and mother, primarily, and devotes most of her time to those pursuits. The name of this ship is a fine testimony to a family business.

After two years in retirement this vessel was sold for scrap in 1977.

Motor Vessel RIVERSHELL (3)

OWNER: Johnstone Shipping, Limited
BUILT: Swan, Hunter & Wigham Richardson, Limited, Wallsend-on-Tyne, England—1933
HULL NO.: 1485
O. A. DIMENSIONS: 179' × 34' × 15'
FORMER DATA: Launched as the tank barge PETER G. CAMPBELL. Converted to a powered tanker at Canadian Vickers Limited, Montreal, Quebec in 1935. Renamed RIVERSHELL (1) in 1950. Renamed GOOD HOPE in 1960. Renamed B. A. SENTINEL in 1962. Renamed GULF SENTINEL in 1969. Given last name in 1974.

The small bunkering vessel shown above was given its previous name, after consideration of several other names, in May, 1974. It is noted here, for historical purposes, as RIVERSHELL (3), although under any other set of circumstances it would be denoted simply as RIVERSHELL. This is because, although this was the first ship originally to be named RIVERSHELL, a later ship in the Shell fleet was the second ship to be so named. And rather than say that this vessel was still RIVERSHELL (1), which outlived RIVERSHELL (2) by several years at least, it has been noted as shown above.

This vessel was the first all-welded oil carrying vessel built in the British Empire. It has served in many trades and is shown here at Corunna, Ontario in May, 1974. It was sold for scrap in 1966.

The name was apropos in that it was operating under charter to Shell Canada Limited and used in the St. Clair River area for a short while.

Steamer CORNELL

OWNER: Jupiter Steamship Company
BUILT: Chicago Shipbuilding Company, Chicago, Illinois—1900
HULL NO.: 42
O. A. DIMENSIONS: 474' × 50' × 28'6"

The bulk freight Steamer CORNELL continued active on the Great Lakes until 1961 when it was sold for scrap. In the last decade of its existence, it largely remained active in the domestic grain trade.

For most of its life this ship served as an iron ore carrier in the United States Steel Corporation fleet. It was one of several ships built at the turn of the century that were given names of eastern colleges. This group of ships were popularly known as "The College Boats."

The namesake of this ship was Cornell University, a non-sectarian institution for higher education of men and women at Ithaca, New York. It was founded in 1865 by Mr. Ezra Cornell and Andrew Dickson White with the assistance of the Federal Government and the State of New York. The university now consists of fifteen coeducational and non-sectarian schools, eleven of which are endowed. Enrollment currently averages about 14,500 students.

There are ten specialized centers in operation at Cornell. These are: Material Science Center, Statistical Center, Water Resources Center, Housing & Environmental, International Studies, Radio & Physics, Space Research, Applied Mathematics, Aviation Safety and Research in Education Laboratories. In addition, the Cornell Laboratory of Nuclear Studies operates a federally financed 10 billion electron volt synchronton.

Steamer KELLEY ISLAND

OWNER: Kelley Island Lime and Transport Company
BUILT: American Ship Building Company, Lorain, Ohio—1914
HULL NO.: 711
O. A. DIMENSIONS: 186' × 38' × 16'
FORMER DATA: Launched as a sandsucker. Converted to a self-unloading sandsucker at American Ship Building Company, Lorain, Ohio in 1936.

The small steamer KELLEY ISLAND is shown above on August 29, 1951. It was subsequently passed into two other fleets for parts of the sailing season and, in 1961, reduced to a barge now in service on Lake Michigan as OHIO. Its maiden trip was made June 25, 1914 from Lorain, Ohio to Pelee Island, Lake Erie to dredge sand.

This vessel's namesake is one of the highly fertile islands of western Lake Erie around which it spent much of its time. Kelley Island was first inhabited by a Frenchman by the name of Cunningham in 1808 and, until legislative action gave it its present name, it was known as Cunningham's Island.

The extensive stone quarries on the south side of Kelley Island were activated in 1848 by Messrs. Webb, Kelley and Huntington. On visiting the site in 1872, Mr. M. C. Younglove of Cleveland, Ohio saw the potential of further development of the excellent limestone areas on the island, and he backed the formation of Kelley Island Lime and Transport Company. The quality of the limestone was remarkable, being 91% carbonate of lime, 8-1/2% magnesia and 1/2% moisture.

Steamer LA BELLE

OWNER:	Kinsman Transit Company
BUILT:	American Ship Building Company, Lorain, Ohio—1909
HULL NO.:	367
O. A. DIMENSIONS:	524' × 54' × 30'3"

The bulk freight Steamer LA BELLE is shown here upbound with a load of coal in the St. Mary's River. This ship remained in service on the Great Lakes until being sold for scrap in 1962.

Originally this vessel was owned by the La Belle Steamship Company. It was decided by the men who planned to build this ship that if Mr. William Howard Taft was elected President of the United States in the then upcoming election, they would proceed with construction. Mr. Taft was elected President on November 3, 1908 and this group formed La Belle Steamship Company on November 18, 1908. Messrs. J. S. Ashley, S. W. Folsom, A. B. Kern, C. W. Morris and G. H. Warner were the incorporators and original shareholders of the firm. They divided nearly equally the 1,500 outstanding shares.

These men were prominent on the Great Lakes and some worked for the M. A. Hanna Company. That firm had a relationship with Wheeling Steel Corporation and floated much of its iron ore. An affiliate of Wheeling Steel was the La Belle Iron Works of Steubenville, Ohio. It was from this firm's name that the steamship company and the vessel took their names.

By 1910, 798 of the 1,500 shares of stock in the La Belle Steamship Company were owned by the La Belle Iron Works. Wheeling is now known as Wheeling-Pittsburgh Steel Corporation and annually floats in excess of one million tons of iron ore on the Great Lakes.

Steamer Mac GILVRAY SHIRAS

OWNER:	Kinsman Transit Company
BUILT:	American Ship Building Company, Cleveland, Ohio—1904
HULL NO.:	420
O. A. DIMENSIONS:	440' × 50' × 28'
FORMER DATA:	Launched as UMBRIA. Given last name in 1916.

This bulk freighter served from 1916 until 1944 in the fleet of the United States Steel Corporation and bore, until its sale for scrap in 1959, the name of one of that firm's executives. It is shown in this picture in the St. Mary's River.

Mr. William Mac Gilvray Shiras was born at Sharon, Pennsylvania on July 16, 1872 and was educated in the local high school. He began working as a chemist for the Aschman Steel Casting Company in 1890 and from 1891 to December 31, 1892 worked for the Wheeler Furnace Company as a chemist. He joined Carnegie Steel Company in 1893 in the same capacity. In 1897 he became a blast furnace burden clerk at the Duquesne Works of the company but left the company on October 13, 1900 to become blast furnace superintendent of the Dominion Iron and Steel Company at Sydney, Nova Scotia.

He rejoined Carnegie Steel on July 1, 1900 and served as assistant ore agent at Pittsburgh, Pennsylvania until becoming ore agent in 1910. He held this post until October 29, 1935 when he was promoted to director of raw materials at the Carnegie-Illinois Steel Company headquarters office in Pittsburgh. Mr. Shiras retired on December 31, 1940. He spent a good deal of his time, once retired, at his country home near Ligonier, Pennsylvania and died at that home on November 8, 1959.

Steamer BUCKEYE MONITOR

OWNER: Kinsman Marine Transit Company
BUILT: American Ship Building Company, Lorain, Ohio – 1913
HULL NO.: 708
O. A. DIMENSIONS: 550' x 58' x 31'
FORMER DATA: Launched as ALTON C. DUSTIN. Renamed J. A. CAMPBELL in 1916. Given last name in 1965.

The Hutchinson & Company name had been around the Great Lakes for nearly one hundred years when this ship was purchased by the former Buckeye Steamship Company, which was largely owned and formerly run by Mr. John T. Hutchinson, a descendent of the original Hutchinson family.

In 1861, the original Mr. John T. Hutchinson, purchased a scow called the MONITOR to mark the initial entry into Great Lakes transportation for the family. When this vessel was purchased in 1965, it appeared fitting to the new owners to use the company name at that time, Buckeye, and couple it with the name of the original boat in the fleet of Hutchinson & Company, that being the scow MONITOR.

The name Buckeye comes from the fact that operating headquarters were in Ohio – The Buckeye State, thus the name of this ship. It held that name until being sold for scrap late in 1973 and is shown here downbound in the West Neebish Channel, St. Mary's River on August 18, 1973. It had sailed on its maiden voyage from Fairport, Ohio to Sheboygan, Wisconsin with coal on July 18, 1913.

Steamer JAMES E. FERRIS

OWNER: Kinsman Marine Transit Company
BUILT: Great Lakes Engineering Works, Ecorse, Michigan - 1910
HULL NO.: 71
O. A. DIMENSIONS: 465' x 56' x 30'
FORMER DATA: Launched as ONTARIO (4). Renamed F. R. HAZARD in 1915. Given last name in 1924.

The little bulk freighter shown below while upbound with salt in the Middle Neebish Channel, St. Mary's River, on June 30, 1970, began its Great Lakes career by departing with coal from Fairport, Ohio on April 19, 1910 destined for Escanaba, Michigan. The vessel remained active until late Ocotber, 1974 when it was sold for scrap after having delivered its last cargo of 309,183 bushels of wheat taken aboard at Duluth, Minnesota for Cleveland, Ohio and Buffalo, New York delivery on October 4, 1974.

Namesake of this vessel was Mr. James Edward Ferris who was born in Cleveland, Ohio on September 12, 1870 and graduated from the University of Michigan in 1892. He began his career as an accountant with Corrigan-McKinney Steel Company in Cleveland, Ohio and progressed through the ranks until coming to the attention of Mr. Price McKinney, head of the firm, who was impressed with his drive and acumen. He rose through various posts until becoming treasurer, vice president and secretary when he retired in 1928.

Mr. Ferris died suddenly at Cleveland, Ohio on February 27, 1936 after having led an active life in business and civic affairs. His namesake had long since his death been acclaimed by boat-watchers as one of the most "artistically-built" lake freighters ever to ply the Inland Seas.

Steamer KINSMAN INDEPENDENT (1)

OWNER: Kinsman Marine Transit Company
BUILT: Chicago Shipbuilding Company, Chicago, Illinois – 1907
HULL NO.: 72
O. A. DIMENSIONS: 605'9" x 60' x 32'
FORMER DATA: Launched as WILLIAM B. KERR. Renamed FRANCIS E. HOUSE in 1911. Given last name in 1966.

When this ship was acquired by this fleet in 1966, Mr. Henry G. Steinbrenner picked this name for the vessel as best fitting its new role in their fleet as the last "INDEPENDENT" bulk carrier on the U. S. Great Lakes. As time wore on, however, economics of reality set in and, after a damage in the Rock Cut in August, 1973, it was determined that repairs to this old vessel could not be warranted. Thus, it was sold for scrap in the spring of 1974. It is shown below while upbound in the St. Mary's River enroute for a cargo of iron ore in the summer of 1973.

The first word of the vessel name referred to the owning company's corporate title. Originally, when formed in the last century, the firm was merely Kinsman Transit Company. The name was changed in the 1960's to the above noted corporate name on reorganization of the company and to clearly identify it with marine oriented activities.

After a surge of vessel buying in the early 1970's, management of the company decided that economics of the times were soon to overtake the operation of smaller, older ships. Vessels such as this could no longer compete with the 50,000 tonners!

Steamer KINSMAN VENTURE

OWNER: Kinsman Marine Transit Company
BUILT: West Bay City Shipbuilding Company, West Bay City, Michigan—1906
HULL NO.: 617
O. A. DIMENSIONS: 534' × 54' × 31'
FORMER DATA: Launched as JOHN SHERWIN (1). Renamed SATURN (3) in 1958. Renamed GEORGE M. STEINBRENNER (1) in 1959. Given last name in 1969.

The bulk freight Steamer KINSMAN VENTURE was the last carrier on the Great Lakes to operate with these overall dimensions. It had the general characteristics of the famous "504" class of ship, but was ten feet longer in overall length and had a greater carrying capacity.

The name of this ship is two-part. The first reference, KINSMAN, was to the owning company name. This name is of long standing on the Great Lakes.

The second part of the ship name is in reference to the definition of the word venture. It may be defined as "an undertaking involving chance or danger," or "a speculative business enterprise." For a time it appeared that this ship's days were very numbered and that it would no longer operate. However, strong demand for iron ore and Great Lakes vessel space in 1969 caused the owning firm to operate this ship the whole season to meet industry's needs, even though it may not have appeared profitable to do so. In that sense, it was a VENTURE.

The vessel was sold for use as a breakwater at Nanticoke, Ontario in 1970. It is shown in this photograph downbound in the St. Mary's River in 1969.

Steamer KINSMAN VOYAGER

OWNER: Kinsman Marine Transit Company
BUILT: Superior Shipbuilding Company, Superior, Wisconsin — 1907
HULL NO.: 519
O. A. DIMENSIONS: 560' x 56' x 30'
FORMER DATA: Launched as H. P. BOPE. Renamed E. A. S. CLARKE (2) in 1916. Given last name in 1970.

The bulk freight Steamer KINSMAN VOYAGER is shown below at the Little Rapids Cut, St. Mary's River in the summer of 1970. The ship operated only slightly between then and the sale for scrap late in 1974.

The namesake of this freighter was two-fold. The first name was in reference to the family firm, long existant on the lakes, Kinsman Transit (Marine) Company. Having its founding in the last century, this was the last of the independent lines to serve in general commerce. It eventually became a subsidiary of The American Ship Building Company.

The second part of the ship name was specific in its reference to "the voyager." A voyager is one who partakes in exploration and discovery. As old as man himself, the term has been applied to those on expeditions and adventures of discovery. While thought in 1970 that this ship name would be apropos and that the vessel would be successful in its career with Kinsman, economics soon dictated that the name belied the day of reality and the vessel was soon found to be uneconomic to operate and maintain. Therefore, judicious management sold the ship to a better purpose — making of new steel for other industrial endeavours.

Steamer HENRY LaLIBERTE

OWNER: Kinsman Marine Transit Company
BUILT: Great Lakes Engineering Works, Ecorse, Michigan – 1908
HULL NO.: 42
O. A. DIMENSIONS: 552' x 56' x 31'
FORMER DATA: Launched as JAMES CORRIGAN. Renamed ARTHUR E. NEWBOLD in 1916. Renamed MARYLAND in 1925. Given last name in 1954.

The well-known resident of Duluth, Minnesota for whom this ship was named was Mr. Henry LaLiberte who was born in Minneapolis, Minnesota on September 19, 1885. He was educated in the public schools and began working as a salesman for the Superior Manufacturing Company, a lime producer in Minneapolis, in 1902.

Through the course of his progress he became general manager of the firm, then resigned in March, 1913 to go to Duluth, Minnesota and take the same post with Cutler-Magner Company which had salt and stone processing and receiving facilities at both Duluth and across the harbor at Superior, Wisconsin. Mr. LaLiberte was named president in 1931 and chairman of the board in 1959. He died at Duluth on July 3, 1963.

Through the association as a major head-of-the-lakes vessel cargo receiver, Mr. LaLiberte was honored when this boat took his name. The vessel was sold for scrap in 1973 and is shown below while in the St. Mary's River on August 9, 1972. This was the first bulk freighter to have a Skinner Uniflow engine installed in May, 1946.

Steamer LACKAWANNA (2)

OWNER:	Kinsman Marine Transit Company
BUILT:	Great Lakes Engineering Works, Ecorse, Michigan—1908
HULL NO.:	43
O. A. DIMENSIONS:	552' × 56' × 31'
FORMER DATA:	Launched as DANIEL B. MEACHAM. Renamed EDWIN E. SLICK in 1916. Given last name in 1925.

The Steamer LACKAWANNA carried into the Kinsman Fleet a name the hull had borne for forty-five years. This was a name honoring the Lackawanna, New York Steel plant of Bethlehem Steel Corporation, owners of this ship since 1925. The bulk freighter is shown below in the St. Mary's River on August 15, 1969.

The Lackawanna plant is located near Buffalo, New York at the eastern end of Lake Erie and ranks as the fourth largest steel mill in the United States. Until 1969, it was the only steel plant located directly on any of the Great Lakes of Bethlehem Steel. This plant became the property of Bethlehem in 1922.

It is a modern facility employing about 19,500 people with an annual payroll of some 165 million dollars.

The Steamer LACKAWANNA remained active on the Great Lakes until being sold for use as a breakwall in 1970. It had made its maiden voyage from Ashtabula, Ohio on July 25, 1908 with a cargo of coal destined for Superior, Wisconsin delivery.

Steamer PHILIP MINCH (2)

OWNER: Kinsman Marine Transit Company
BUILT: American Ship Building Company, Lorain, Ohio—1905
HULL NO.: 335
O. A. DIMENSIONS: 500' × 52' × 30'

Shown in this photograph on June 18, 1959 in the St. Mary's River, the bulk freight Steamer PHILIP MINCH honored Mr. Philip Minch as its namesake. He was born on May 14, 1820 at Blankenheim, Germany and was educated in the local schools and learned the trade of a shoemaker. He followed that trade until coming to the United States in 1840.

Mr. Minch located at Vermilion, Ohio and soon became interested in ship building. His first ship was the Scow LINDEN, capable of fourteen cords of stone carriage. He subsequently built many other ships at his yard in Vermilion. He moved to Cleveland, Ohio in 1875 and was interested in the building of the Steamer ONOKO, the first steel ore boat on the Great Lakes. Mr. Minch was a managing partner in its ownership which he held until death.

Mr. Minch helped found the Cleveland Shipbuilding Company on land of the former Cuyahoga Steam Furnace Company in Cleveland, Ohio in 1886 and was also instrumental in the beginnings of the Kinsman Transit Company which later built this vessel.

Captain Philip Minch died on June 20, 1887 and this vessel was sold for scrap in 1969.

Steamer JOE S. MORROW

OWNER: Kinsman Marine Transit Company
BUILT: American Ship Building Company, Lorain, Ohio—1907
HULL NO.: 350
O. A. DIMENSIONS: 440' x 52' x 28'

The bulk freight Steamer JOE S. MORROW was the smallest bulk freighter operating under United States flag on the Great Lakes when it was sold for scrap at the end of the 1973 navigation season.

The namesake of this vessel was Mr. Joseph Sellwood Morrow who was born at Duluth, Minnesota on April 8, 1890. He was the only child of Mr. John Paul Morrow and Elizabeth Sellwood Morrow and was the grandson of Captain Joseph Sellwood and Ophelia Matthews Sellwood.

He was educated in the public schools of Duluth and Hill School at Pottstown, Pennsylvania. Unfortunately, his life was a short one and he died before beginning a business or other career on December 25, 1911 at Duluth, Minnesota.

The Sellwood family was prominent in the Duluth area in the early days of iron ore mining and relatives continue to live in the community today.

In 1937 the vessel was sold to the Red Arrow Steamship Company which was a Reiss family corporation of Sheboygan, Wisconsin. When this firm acquired the ship in 1972, it did not see fit to rename this vessel. The ship is shown in Cleveland, Ohio on August 27, 1972.

Steamer PEAVEY PIONEER

OWNER:	Kinsman Marine Transit Company
BUILT:	American Ship Building Company, Lorain, Ohio—1905
HULL NO.:	336
O. A. DIMENSIONS:	500' × 52' × 30'
FORMER DATA:	Launched as STEPHEN M. CLEMENT. Renamed UNITED STATES GYPSUM (1) in 1931. Renamed JOHN J. BOLAND (2) in 1939. Renamed NIAGARA MOHAWK in 1953. Given last name in 1965.

The bulk freight Steamer PEAVEY PIONEER is shown below in one of the few photographs taken of this ship operating in Kinsman colors. It shows the vessel on May 22, 1966 at Point Edward, Ontario. The vessel sustained bottom damage shortly thereafter and was sold for scrap the same year. It had made its maiden voyage from Lorain, Ohio on June 24, 1905 with a cargo of coal for Duluth, Minnesota delivery.

This vessel honored the founder of The Peavey Company, Mr. Frank Hutchinson Peavey who was born at Eastport, Maine on January 20, 1850. After being educated in the local schools, he moved to Chicago, Illinois in 1865 to join the grain firm of Hinkley, Handy & Company as a messenger and clerk. After locating in several places he settled at Sioux City, Iowa and founded the Peavey Company in 1874.

Under Mr. Frank Peavey's direction, the firm grew steadily to become one of the major grain merchandising firms in the nation. Mr. Peavey died at Minneapolis, Minnesota on December 30, 1901.

Steamer PETER ROBERTSON (2)

OWNER: Kinsman Marine Transit Company
BUILT: Detroit Shipbuilding Company, Wyandotte, Michigan – 1906
HULL NO.: 163
O. A. DIMENSIONS: 569' x 56' x 31'
FORMER DATA: Launched as HARRY COULBY (1). Renamed FINLAND in 1927. Renamed PETER ROBERTSON (2) in 1969. Renamed MARINSAL in 1978.

Namesake of this ship until sold for scrap in 1975 was Mr. Peter Robertson who was born in Glasgow, Scotland on September 5, 1907. He came to the United States in 1924 and began work with the General Electric Company. After taking additional college courses he joined Republic Steel Corporation in 1934 as an industrial engineer. He was named manager of the Truscon Division in 1944. In 1954 he advanced to the post of vice president in charge of research and planning. Mr. Robertson retired from this post on January 31, 1971.

While his namesake was sold for scrap in 1975, it survived the cutting torch because of the depressed state of the scrap market. Moored at Port Colborne, Ontario it was readily available for its non-transportation task as a "dead ship" in the experimental use of shunters in the Welland Canal. The St. Lawrence Seaway Authority chartered the hull from Marine Salvage Limited in 1978 for the beginning of the tests. The shunters are like scows, only they move sideways and are affixed, one each, to the bow and stern to aid maneuverability. On completion of the tests the vessel was towed overseas for scrapping in 1980. The ship is shown below downbound at Sault Ste. Marie, Michigan on May 25, 1973.

Steamer GEORGE E. SEEDHOUSE

OWNER: Kinsman Marine Transit Company
BUILT: Great Lakes Engineering Works,
Ecorse, Michigan - 1910
HULL NO.: 74
O. A. DIMENSIONS: 604' x 58' x 32'
FORMER DATA: Launched as WILLIAM J. OLCOTT. Given last name in 1970.

This bulk freight vessel was named for a native Clevelander who worked throughout his life in the interests of youth and their betterment. Mr. George Edward Seedhouse was born in Cleveland, Ohio on March 24, 1906 and received his B.S. degree from Ohio University in the field of education in 1930.

He began his career as an athletic coach at Struthers, Ohio in 1930. In 1933 he moved back to Cleveland and joined the Cleveland Public School system where he served as athletic director, physical education instructor and coach until 1946 when he joined the Joint Recreation Board.

Mr. Seedhouse was promoted to manager of all boys physical education programs in the city of Cleveland in 1953 and, in 1955, he was named chief of playgrounds and community centers for the city. He retired from this post on July 31, 1971 and died in Cleveland, Ohio December 3, 1976.

Mr. Seedhouse's namesake is shown in the photograph below while upbound at Port Huron, Michigan on July 3, 1971. It sailed on its maiden voyage from Detroit, Michigan on September 7, 1910, upbound light for Two Harbors, Minnesota for a cargo of iron ore. It was sold for non-transportation use as a floating storehouse at Sturgeon Bay, Wisconsin in 1975.

Steamer GEORGE M. STEINBRENNER (2)

OWNER: Kinsman Marine Transit Company
BUILT: West Bay City Shipbuilding Company, West Bay City, Michigan—1907
HULL NO.: 76
O. A. DIMENSIONS: 569' × 56' × 31'
FORMER DATA: Launched as ARTHUR H. HAWGOOD. Renamed JOSEPH BLOCK in 1912. Given last name in 1969.

Mr. George Michael Steinbrenner was born at Cleveland, Ohio on November 2, 1880 and graduated from the local high school system. His grandfather was Captain Philip Minch, one of the earliest of Cleveland area shipbuilders in the picturesque steamer and wooden schooner days.

Mr. Steinbrenner went into business with his father in 1901 and devoted his lifetime to developing lake shipping interests. He eventually became president of Kinsman and was responsible for the building of the company's fleet of Great Lakes ships. He was also keenly interested in matters relating to vessel personnel and served as chairman of the Lake Carriers' Association welfare committee from 1922 until 1941. He was a director of Lake Carriers' from 1914 until his death on August 6, 1949 at Lakewood, Ohio.

The Steamer GEORGE M. STEINBRENNER is shown here underway in the Detroit River. It was sold for scrap in 1978.

Steamer UHLMANN BROTHERS (2)

OWNER:	Kinsman Marine Transit Company
BUILT:	American Ship Building Company, Lorain, Ohio – 1906
HULL NO.:	341
O. A. DIMENSIONS:	545' x 55' x 31'
FORMER DATA:	Launched as LOFTUS CUDDY. Renamed C. S. ROBINSON in 1916. Given last name in 1965.

Two men who head the Standard Milling Company were honored as the namesakes of this bulk freighter.

Mr. Hugh (Pat) Uhlmann was born in Kansas City, Missouri on March 17, 1916 and is a graduate of Dartmouth University where he received his B.A degree in 1937. He began working in the family-owned Uhlmann Grain Company and then worked in the Midland Flour Mill. After military service in World War II he joined Valley Grain Company in 1946 serving as vice president until 1951. He then joined Standard Milling Company as a vice president, and in 1966, became president of that firm.

Mr. Paul Uhlmann, Jr. was born on November 14, 1920 in Kansas City, Missouri and received his B.A. degree from Dartmouth University in 1942. After military service he was in the investment business from 1946 until 1952. At that time he joined Standard Milling Company as a vice president and serves in that capacity currently.

This fleet carried nearly all of Standard Milling's requirements of grain to Buffalo, New York for many years and honored that association with this ship. It was sold for scrap in 1973 and is shown below in Little Rapids Cut, downbound with a grain cargo on August 8, 1970.

Steamer R. E. WEBSTER

OWNER:	Kinsman Marine Transit Company
BUILT:	Chicago Shipbuilding Company, Chicago, Illinois – 1905
HULL NO.:	66
O. A. DIMENSIONS:	569' x 56' x 31'
FORMER DATA:	Launched as ELBERT H. GARY. Given last name in 1964.

One of the few Great Lakes vessels in modern times named in honor of a woman, the Steamer R. E. WEBSTER honored the late Miss Ruth Ellen Webster who was born on September 2, 1893 in Grand River, Ohio.

Miss Webster was one of the extremely small group of women who have held executive positions in lake shipping. She was a graduate of Spencer Business College at Cleveland, Ohio in 1918 and joined the Kinsman Transit Company in that year. For 45 years she was associated with the Kinsman organization and handled all phases of book work. There was, in the words of her employer at the time, "no finer example of loyalty or devotion to duty than her." Miss Webster had made over 20 lake voyages and was widely known.

She retired in 1964 as assistant secretary of the firm and died on August 9, 1964 at Cleveland, Ohio. Her namesake is shown below while downbound in the St. Mary's River on August 17, 1970 with a cargo of grain for Buffalo, New York. This ship was the largest ever built on the Great Lakes when it was launched on April 8, 1905. It was also the largest ship ever to negotiate the kinky Cuyahoga River at Cleveland, Ohio to the Central Furnace Works when it arrived there on October 6, 1946. The vessel laid idle in 1972 and was sold for scrap in 1973.

Steamer AUGUSTUS B. WOLVIN

OWNER: Labrador Steamship Company Limited
BUILT: American Ship Building Company, Lorain, Ohio—1904
HULL NO.: 330
O. A. DIMENSIONS: 560' × 56' × 32'

On its maiden voyage in June, 1904, this bulk freighter took aboard a Great Lakes record iron ore cargo of 10,694 net tons at Two Harbors, Minnesota for lower lakes delivery. It was the largest ship ever built on fresh water in the world and was nicknamed "The Yellow Kid" because of the original color of her hull.

Mr. Augustus Benjamin Wolvin, who built the ship for his own account, is the namesake of the vessel. He was born at Cleveland, Ohio on October 16, 1857 and became a cabin boy on Great Lakes ships at the age of ten.

He received his master's papers at the age of 21 and sailed on the Lakes until 1883 when he decided to enter the produce business at Pecatonica, Illinois. In 1888 he went to Duluth, Minnesota as a member of LaSalle & Company in the general vessel commission business. In 1895 he built five large ships under the flag of his Zenith Transit Company and in 1901, when Pittsburgh Steamship Company was formed to bring 116 vessels together under one fleet, he became vice president and general manager of the fleet. In 1904 he left that firm and became president of Zenith Furnace Company until retirement. Capt. Wolvin died at Duluth, Minnesota March 31, 1932 and his namesake was scrapped in 1967.

His namesake is shown here upbound in the St. Mary's River on July 4, 1966.

Motor Vessel LUBROLAKE

OWNER: Lakeland Tankers, Limited
BUILT: Pennsylvania Shipyards, Incorporated, Beaumont, Texas—1937
HULL NO.: 116
O. A. DIMENSIONS: 258' × 43' × 16'6"
FORMER DATA: Launched as MERCURY (1). Given last name in 1948.

The tank vessel shown here was active until 1967 when it was sold for off-lakes use as a bunkering barge for Maritime District fishing tugs. It was enroute to that duty when it broke loose from its tug and stranded on the shore of Cape Breton Island and subsequently was abandoned in December, 1967. The vessel is viewed in this photograph on August 31, 1957 while entering Toronto harbour.

This ship's namesake was of two parts, both directly connected with its activities. The prefix "LUBRO" stood for the many varied kinds of lubricants and petroleum products that it carried. Lubricants are generally classed in five categories. These are: petroleum or mineral oils, animal oils, synthetic lubricants, solid lubricants and greases. Petroleum products which are produced from crude oil, are the most used forms of liquid bulk cargoes on the Great Lakes. Over sixty-five large ships are currently engaged in the regular transport of such cargoes currently on the Great Lakes.

The suffix in the ship name, "LAKE," stood for both the area on which this vessel served and the main theme of the owning firm's corporate title. Lakeland Tankers was a subsidiary of Cleveland Tankers, Incorporated of Cleveland, Ohio.

Steamer MAKAWELI

OWNER:	Lakeland Tankers, Limited
BUILT:	Great Lakes Engineering Works, Ashtabula, Ohio—1919
HULL NO.:	503
O. A. DIMENSIONS:	261' × 43'6" × 27'6"
FORMER DATA:	Launched as the dry bulk carrier COWEE. Given last name in 1922. Converted to a tanker at Bethlehem Shipbuilding Corporation, San Francisco, California in 1937.

The tank Steamer MAKAWELI was given its last name by owners other than those shown above. After World War I Matson Navigation Company acquired this vessel and gave it a two-part name in honor of both a place and an Indian tribe which had gained fame along the West Coast for its seamanship and excellent canoe building.

The small town of about six hundred population on the island of Kauai, Hawaii was honored by the name "Makaweli." This place is located along the Kaulakahi Channel on the northernmost island of the Hawaiian group. It is very scenic and was passed frequently by vessels of the Matson Line.

The Makah Indians are the last of the warlike tribes and are a branch of the Nootka. Their main reservation now is at Neah Bay, Washington. The last owners of this ship had only an hour to decide on a re-name before closing registration of this ship in 1946. No unanimous name could be found and they decided to let the former name prevail in this fleet.

This tanker was sold for scrap in 1967 and is shown above in the Welland Ship Canal on November 12, 1955. On April 21, 1951 this vessel loaded the initial cargo, consisting of 25,000 barrels of crude oil, at the new Superior, Wisconsin terminal of the Interprovincial Pipe Line Company.

Steamer GILBERT

OWNER: Land Sand Corporation
BUILT: Sturgeon Bay Dry Dock Company, Sturgeon Bay, Wisconsin - 1924
HULL NO.: 5
O. A. DIMENSIONS: 202' x 42'6" x 18'6"
FORMER DATA: Launched as a sandsucker. Deepened 4' at Calumet Shipyard and Dry Dock Company, Chicago, Illinois in 1937. Converted to a self-unloading sandsucker at Calumet Shipyard and Dry Dock Company, Chicago, Illinois in 1946.

The small sandsucking Steamer GILBERT was active only intermittently in the 1950's and was eventually abandoned by these owners in December, 1959. The vessel is shown in this photograph at the company dock on the Calumet River at 95th Street in May, 1955. Plans to convert the hull to a barge by Vindof Marine Salvage Company never materialized.

This ship was named in honor of a man who presided over a Wisconsin firm which provided the financing for the ship's construction. Mr. William Markley Gilbert was born in Philadelphia, Pennsylvania on July 25, 1852 and attended Northwestern University until he entered the paper merchandising concern owned by his father in 1872. He was trained in various departments of the Chicago, Illinois firm, but left the company in 1882 to begin his own paper-making business at Menasha, Wisconsin in partnership with George A. Whiting. The firm was known as the Gilbert & Whiting Company.

In 1887 he sold his interest to Mr. Whiting and began what was to become the Gilbert Paper Company at Menasha, Wisconsin. It was the first firm to use sulphite wood pulp for the making of letter paper and soon attained a reputation for excellent products. He died at Neenah on January 6, 1926.

Steamer KEYBAR

OWNER:	La Verendrye Line, Limited
BUILT:	Smith's Dock Company Limited, South Bank-on-Tees, England—1923
HULL NO.:	778
O. A. DIMENSIONS:	261' × 42'6" × 19'9"

The canal-size bulk freight Steamer KEYBAR was one of the more attractive vessels in this fleet as can be seen in this photograph of the ship taken on October 22, 1958 while the vessel was passing through the Soulanges Canal of the old St. Lawrence River System.

Some of the vessels of this fleet were sold to the Hall Corporation of Canada in 1961 while others were sold for scrap the same year. Since only one of the fleet of nine ships ever saw any service with the Hall Corporation, the story of these vessels and the photographs of them will discuss and show them as they were for all but a small fraction of their lives.

The original owning company was known as Keystone Transports Limited. That name was changed to the corporate title shown in 1958. Common to all vessels in the fleet was the prefix KEY in the ship name. This stood in reference to the original name of the fleet.

The suffix in all the fleet's ship names was the specific namesake of the vessel. Some of these referred to persons, but most referred to water-related objects or places. In the case of this vessel, the namesake is the water-related item of a sandbar which is a commonly found ridge or bank of sand that becomes built up by settling of sand particles such as at the mouths of rivers. This vessel remained on the Lakes until being sold for scrap in 1963.

Steamer KEYBELL

OWNER:	La Verendrye Line, Limited
BUILT:	Collingwood Shipbuilding Company Limited, Collingwood, Ontario—1912
HULL NO.:	37
O. A. DIMENSIONS:	261' × 42'6" × 20'3"

The bulk freight Steamer KEYBELL is shown in this picture as it approaches Lock One of the Welland Ship Canal at Port Weller, Ontario on November 8, 1950. This time was prior to the westbound movement of iron ore in the St. Lawrence River System and these vessels, typically, returned to Lake Erie ports from Montreal, Quebec in ballast. On reaching their destination, they loaded coal for the Montreal utility.

The Steamer KEYBELL was sold for scrap at Kingston, Ontario in 1961. It had begun its maiden voyage October 12, 1912 from Fort William, Ontario to Montreal, Quebec with a cargo of wheat.

The specific namesake of this ship is the bell. Not all bells in general, but those that relate to water activity are honored by this ship name. Bells have been associated with navigation on seas all over the world for centuries. Ship's bells ring out every half hour from the bridges of vessels. On Great Lakes vessels every four hours the series of varied numbers of rings begins over again. This is to coincide with the changes of the watches onboard.

Bells also have a place of prominence on some buoys which mark channel lanes. These gong as the clapper strikes the side of the bell which is suspended on the buoy. As the buoy bobs around in the water due to the currents and wave action, the bell rings out signalling to passing ships. Thus, in daylight and in night time passing vessels are notified of the buoy's placement at the side of the channel or reef.

Steamer KEYDON

OWNER:	La Verendrye Line, Limited
BUILT:	Cowpen Dry Docks & Shipbuilding Company, Limited, Blyth, England—1927
HULL NO.:	238
O. A. DIMENSIONS:	261' × 42'6" × 21'
FORMER DATA:	Launched as SWIFTWATER. Given last name in 1939.

Shown in this picture at Allanburg, Ontario in the Welland Ship Canal on April 21, 1956, the canal size bulk freight Steamer KEYDON saw service on the Great Lakes until being sold for scrap at Kingston, Ontario in 1961.

This steamer arrived at Toledo, Ohio on August 9, 1954 with the initial cargo of Lakes' bound iron ore from the Seven Islands, Quebec facility of Iron Ore Company of Canada. The same day another canal-sized freighter arrived at Buffalo, New York with the second such cargo.

Namesake of this vessel was Mr. Donald Gordon Munroe who was born in Baldwinsville, New York on Feburary 27, 1890. He received a B.A. degree from Cornell University in 1912 and joined Koppers Company the same year in the New York City office. Mr. Munroe was transferred to the Pittsburgh, Pennsylvania headquarters of the firm in 1920 and was active in the traffic and planning departments.

In 1927 he went to Canada and was associated with various construction projects in various locations. In 1930 he joined the Montreal Coke and Manufacturing Company as vice president. He became president of that firm in 1937 and retained that position until his death at Montreal, Quebec on October 7, 1950. Since this Montreal firm was a very large receiver of coal from this line's ships, Mr. Munroe was honored with the DON in this name.

Steamer KEYNOR

OWNER:	La Verendrye Line, Limited
BUILT:	North of Ireland Shipbuilding Company, Limited, Londonderry, Ireland—1914
HULL NO.:	58
O. A. DIMENSIONS:	261' × 42'6" × 20'6"

Shown here in Lock Five of the Welland Ship Canal on November 8, 1958, the bulk freight Steamer KEYNOR takes Mr. John Stewart Norris as its specific namesake. The prefix in the vessel name refers to the original name of the owning company as previously explained.

Mr. Norris was born on January 6, 1874 in Montreal, Quebec and was educated at Royal Arthur School and Bishop's College before beginning his career as an office boy with the Guarantee Company of North America in Montreal, Quebec in 1888. He stayed with that firm until joining Bell Telephone Company in 1891 as a general office hand and mailroom clerk. In 1896 he saw an advertisement in the newspaper for an accountant and shorthand job and decided to apply. Though he had neither talent at the time, his ambition and convincing manner won him the job. He became secretary to Sir Herbert Holt, president of the Montreal, Light, Heat and Power Consolidated and a new career was launched.

Advancing rapidly, he was elected secretary-treasurer in 1906 and general manager in 1910. He was this fleet's first president since the vessel firm was a jointly-owned subsidiary of the utility. Mr. Norris was named president of Montreal Light, Heat & Power Consolidated in 1932 and retained that post until 1944. Mr. Norris also held other executive positions concurrently and he was active in numerous civic and charitable affairs until his death in Montreal, Quebec on June 26, 1956. His namesake survived him by only five years, being sold for scrap in 1961. The suffix, NOR, bore proud tribute to one of Canada's leading industrialists.

Steamer KEYPORT

OWNER: La Verendrye Line, Limited
BUILT: Swan, Hunter & Wigham Richardson Limited, Newcastle-on-Tyne, England—1909
HULL NO.: 816
O. A. DIMENSIONS: 261' × 42'6" × 21'

The bulk freight Steamer KEYPORT was one of those ships in this fleet which was sold to Hall Corporation of Canada in 1961. It never ran under Hall colors though and was sold for scrap in 1963.

The vessel is shown in this picture in the Welland Ship Canal above Lock One on a bright day in October, 1953.

Together with the prefix reference in the shipname to the original owning company, this vessel specifically honored its ports of call in the suffix of its name. Actually the ports of call mentioned were not singularly related to this vessel, but to all the ships in the fleet.

These ports were places where the vessels were loaded and unloaded in their various trade routes. Ports such as Toledo, Sandusky, Lorain, Cleveland, Ashtabula and Fairport, Ohio were very familiar loading ports of call for this coal-carrying line. The port of Montreal, Quebec was perhaps the most common destination for the fleet since all its eastbound coal was delivered to the utility based there. Other common ports of call included these in the lower St. Lawrence River: Shelter Bay, Godbout, Baie Trinite, Clarke City, Three Rivers, Quebec City, Franquelin, Riviere-du-Loup and Batiscan, Quebec. This ship made its sea trials May 18, 1909. The keel had been laid on February 18, 1909.

Steamer KEYSHEY

OWNER: La Verendrye Line, Limited
BUILT: Smith's Dock Company, Limited,
South Bank-on-Tees, England - 1928
HULL NO.: 838
O. A. DIMENSIONS: 258' x 42'3" x 21'3"
FORMER DATA: Launched as CLEARWATER. Renamed TRENORA in 1928. Given last name in 1949.

Shown here in the Welland Ship Canal in 1962, the bulk freight Steamer KEYSHEY took its name from members of the family of Mr. Severe Godin, second president of this fleet. The ship was sold for scrap in 1963. In 1962 the vessel was operating under charter to the Hall Corporation of Canada.

The usual shipname prefix refers to the original name of the owning company. The suffix provides insight to the specific namesakes. Captain James A. Milne, then operating manager of the fleet, suggested this shipname to Mr. Godin and he approved. In order, the letters of the suffix refer to: Mr. *S*evere Godin, Mr. *H*ubert Godin, Mrs. *E*udora Godin and *Y*olande Godin. The second name is that of the son in the family and the fourth is that of the daughter. Mrs. Godin was the former Eudora Boucher.

Respective birth dates and places are: Severe–Ste. Anne de Bellevue, Quebec on November 22, 1889; Eudora–Montreal, Quebec on December 5, 1893; Yolande–Montreal, Quebec on April 13, 1917; Hubert–Montreal, Quebec on January 29, 1924.

Mr. Severe Godin began his career as a secretary in the office of Sir Herbert Holt, president of the Royal Bank of Canada and Montreal Light, Heat & Power Company in 1906. He was Sir Herbert's personal secretary by 1915 and a vice president of the power company and manager of this fleet by 1929. He was president of the fleet from 1946 until 1962.

Steamer KEYSTATE

OWNER:	La Verendrye Line, Limited
BUILT:	Smith's Dock Company Limited, South Bank-on-Tees, England—1927
HULL NO.:	777
O. A. DIMENSIONS:	261' × 42'6" × 19'9"

Shown in this photograph in the Lachine Canal on August 31, 1957, the canal-size bulk freight Steamer KEYSTATE remained active on the Great Lakes until being sold for scrap in 1961.

The State of Pennsylvania was the specific namesake of this carrier. That state was chosen because it was the headquarters state of one of the joint-venture firms that owned this fleet. Koppers Company, Incorporated of Pittsburgh, Pennsylvania was the United States partner in the fleet.

Pennsylvania is known as "The Keystone State" because it was the corner or keystone of the 'arch' formed by the original thirteen American states. It has only one port on the Great Lakes which is Erie. This port has recently been in the news as the site of construction and commissioning of the first one thousand foot freighter ever built for Great Lakes service.

Pennsylvania has an area of 45,333 square miles including 326 square miles of inland water. It has a population in excess of twelve million people and was the second state to be admitted to the Union on December 12, 1787. It leads the nation in the production of pig iron and steel and is also a leading food processing area. The highest point in the state rises 3,213 feet above sea lever at Mount Davis in Somerset County.

Steamer KEYVIVE

OWNER: La Verendrye Line, Limited
BUILT: Smith's Dock Company Limited, Middlesborough, England—1913
HULL NO.: 551
O. A. DIMENSIONS: 261' × 42'6" × 20'3"

The bulk freight Steamer KEYVIVE is shown in the picture below at the Montreal, Quebec facility of Quebec Natural Gas Corporation in the former Lachine Canal on August 31, 1957. This vessel was sold for scrap in 1962.

The vessel discussed on this page was the first ship to load Iron Ore Company of Canada ore at the Seven Islands facility for the destination of Cleveland, Ohio. A civic celebration including television and radio coverage announced the arrival of this vessel at Cleveland on September 4, 1954.

The vessel took as its namesake, the English derivation of the French saying "Qui—Vive," meaning "who goes there". Mrs. Godin, wife of the second president of Keystone Transports Limited, the predecessor owning company of this firm, suggested this name since the fleet was relatively new on the Lakes and was subject to the usual critical question of "who goes there?"

Since the "Qui" rhymed with the English "KEY" it was a natural marriage of the founding name of the firm with the suggested suffix of this vessel name that brought the shipname about. Mrs. Godin did not know, perhaps, that her specific namesake would prove to be a venerable competitor in the Great Lakes trade and last until it died a scrapper's death in 1962 after having served as a most successful bulk carrier for forty-nine years.

Steamer KEYWEST (2)

OWNER:	La Verendrye Line, Limited
BUILT:	Cowpen Dry Docks & Shipbuilding Company, Limited, Blyth, England—1927
HULL NO.:	239
O. A. DIMENSIONS:	261' × 42'6" × 20'6"
FORMER DATA:	Launched as SUREWATER. Given last name in 1949.

The bulk freight Steamer KEYWEST (2) is shown in this photograph in the canal system of the Great Lakes on November 25, 1956. It was active on the Great Lakes until being sold for scrap in 1961.

This vessel had the common fleet prefix in its name and took the direction West as its specific namesake. West is the term applied to geographic locations and to a socio-economic condition. Because settlement began on the eastern rim of this continent and, in most cases, expanded in a westerly direction, the West was both a place farther towards the setting sun and a place where men were beginning over again the creation of a new society.

This ship received its last name in 1949, a year in which another vessel in the fleet also received its name. A series of names in the fleet began with suffixes in alphabetical order. This was the last ship to be named in 1949 and the last ship to have no namesake relating to a person. Since the fleet had already used this name in the past and since all prominent persons in executive positions had been previously honored by ship names, management in 1949 drew upon their own history and chose this name for this ship.

Steamer DOLOMITE

OWNER:	Law Quarries Transportation Limited
BUILT:	Cleveland Shipbuilding Company, Cleveland, Ohio—1897
HULL NO.:	28
O. A. DIMENSIONS:	425' × 48' × 28'
FORMER DATA:	Launched as the bulk freighter EMPIRE CITY. Converted to a self-unloader at American Ship Building Company, Lorain, Ohio and renamed SUMATRA in 1929. Given last name in 1962.

The Steamer DOLOMITE was the oldest self-unloader operating when it was sold for scrap in 1968. It had seen more service and carried more cargo in its seventy-one years than any other vessel of comparable size.

The last owners of this ship have a quarry at Port Colborne, Ontario and also a shipping dock at Humberstone, Ontario on the Welland Canal. The vessel was acquired to help them merchandise their stone. In looking for a name for the vessel the name DOLOMITE was chosen because that most nearly fit the product name of material being delivered from the quarry.

Dolomite is the double carbonate of calcium and magnesium. Like calcite it has perfect rhombohedral fracture and commonly occurs in crystals. When pure it is white or of yellow cast in color and has a glassy lustre. It is present to some extent in all limestones and deposits of dolomite generally have the same structural features as calcium limestone. Dolomite is quarried most prominently at Haley, Ontario and is processed for the production of magnesium metal.

Barge INTERNATIONAL (2)

OWNER: McAllister Towing Limited
BUILT: John Smith, Fort Erie, Ontario – 1872
HULL NO.: None assigned
O. A. DIMENSIONS: 220' x 40' x 12'8"
FORMER DATA: Launched as a powered carferry. Converted to a crane-equipped bulk freight barge at Montreal Dry Docks Limited, Montreal, Quebec in 1938.

This iron vessel was sold for non-transportation use in 1966 and is shown above in Montreal, Quebec harbor on August 11, 1964. Following sale in 1966, the hull was further cut down at Sorel, Quebec and in 1980 was still afloat as McAllister No. 4.

This vessel was originally built for service between Canada and the United States on the Niagara River. Its namesake was for that purpose of being international in its service. The hull was fabricated at Palmer Company, Yarrow-on-Tyne, England and then taken in sections to Fort Erie for assembly. In July 1872, it went into service for the Grand Trunk Railway between Sarnia, Ontario and Port Huron, Michigan. It made two trips per hour. Due to its smaller size in comparison to its competitors in the 1920's, it was largely used as a "spare" boat, being pressed into service only upon demand. The iron hull of this vessel has successfully passed the test of time. As this is being written, the hull, in one form or another, has existed on these waters for 110 years!

Barge LONDONDERRY

OWNER:	McAllister Towing Limited
BUILT:	Carrier-Laine Company, Levis, Quebec – 1901
HULL NO.:	None assigned
O. A. DIMENSIONS:	215' x 40' x 14'6"
FORMER DATA:	Launched as the schooner-barge QUEBEC (1). Given last name in 1930. Converted to a crane-equipped bulk freight barge at Montreal Dry Docks Limited, Montreal, Quebec in 1934.

The Barge LONDONDERRY was sold for non-transportation use as a scow in 1966. It was equipped with a 9-ton walking crane for use in handling cargo or in salvage operations since this firm took control of the vessel. The 1,100 gross ton capacity of the hull made it ideal for such service in salvage work or for light-draft port deliveries.

This composite-hulled vessel was named for the maritime county of Londonderry, North Ireland in historic Ulster Province on Lough Foyle, an arm of the Atlantic Ocean. A city by the same name came into headlines around the world in the 1970's for the revolutions there between Roman Catholics and Protestant factions. Much bloodshed was seen. The city has a population of 52,000, the county 131,000.

The Barge LONDONDERRY is seen above at Victoria Pier, Montreal, Quebec on April 19, 1965. It is the outboard vessel in view.

Steamer DENMARK

OWNER:	T. J. McCarthy Steamship Company
BUILT:	Toledo Shipbuilding Company, Toledo, Ohio—1909
HULL NO.:	114
O. A. DIMENSIONS:	460' × 56' × 28'

This bulk freighter was built for the account of one of the individual ship companies later merged into Great Lakes Steamship Company. Unless named for a primary investor in the fleet of ships, the vessels took names of Baltic countries.

Denmark is the smallest of the three Scandinavian states, comprising the peninsula of Jutland, with its adjacent islands in the Baltic Sea. These Faroe Islands are now a part of Schleswig as a result of the plebiscite of 1920 under the terms of the Treaty of Versailles. Iceland is a free sovereign state, but is united with Denmark under the King of Denmark who is also head of the Government of Iceland.

Denmark's capital city is Copenhagen. This fine city of 1,500,000 population lies across the Ore Sound on the island of Sjaelland. It is the country's major seaport and the scene of constant harbor activity.

The land area of Denmark is 16,575 square miles including the Faroe Islands. Most of the country area is a continuation of the plains of North Germany. Agriculture is of primary importance due to the lack of coal, iron and other natural resources.

This bulk ship was active on the Great Lakes until it was sold for scrap in 1961. It is shown below at Lorain, Ohio on August 30, 1961 being loaded with a ballast cargo of scrap prior to its last departure from the Great Lakes.

Steamer J. F. DURSTON

OWNER:	T. J. Mc Carthy Steamship Company
BUILT:	Superior Shipbuilding Company, Superior, Wisconsin—1908
HULL NO.:	521
O. A. DIMENSIONS:	452' × 52' × 28'

The bulk freighter shown here was named in honor of Mr. James Franklin Durston who was a director and investor in the former Great Lakes Steamship Company and predecessor companies. When that line was sold in 1957 this vessel passed into the hands of this owner who continued to operate the ship until selling it for scrap in 1961.

Mr. Durston was born in Syracuse, New York on October 21, 1842 and received his education in the public schools. He began his working experience as a teacher in the school system, but gave that up to join his father in boat building at the Durston Dry Dock Company located on the Erie Canal, in 1861. On the death of his father on May 6, 1863, he took over the shipyard and built many barges and boats of different kinds. He also erected the Durston and Howlett Buildings during this period.

In 1874 he retired from this business and became associated with the Durston Book Store as its manager. In 1891 he joined Lefever Arms Company as its president and under his management the firm prospered, gradually turning into other lines including gear manufacturing. As the manufacture of guns decreased, the making of gears increased and the firm became Durston Gear Company with Mr. Durston as vice president until 1917 when he retired. He was also president of the Sanford Motor Truck Company and the Salt Springs Solar Salt Company. In addition, he held trusteeships in various other businesses. Mr. Durston died in Syracuse, New York on November 16, 1921.

This steamer is shown below in the St. Mary's River on June 19, 1958.

Steamer GEORGE H. INGALLS

OWNER:	T. J. McCarthy Steamship Company
BUILT:	Chicago Shipbuilding Company, Chicago, Illinois - 1901
HULL NO.:	47
O. A. DIMENSIONS:	452' x 50'3" x 28'6"
FORMER DATA:	Launched as the bulk freighter WILLIAM L. BROWN. Given last name in 1924. Converted to an automobile carrier at Nicholson Engineering Works, Detroit, Michigan in 1936. Re-converted to a bulk freighter at American Ship Building Company, Buffalo, New York in 1942. Re-converted to an automobile carrier at Ranahan-McCarthy Marine Terminal, Buffalo, New York in 1946.

The automobile carrier GEORGE H. INGALLS is shown in this photograph downbound in the Detroit River on June 16, 1953. Its namesake was Mr. George Hoadly Ingalls who was born at Boston, Massachusetts on July 28, 1872. He graduated from Harvard University in 1893 with a B.A. degree.

Mr. Ingalls began his career as a clerk in the office of the general manager of the Chesapeake & Ohio Railway at Richmond, Virginia in 1893 and progressed through several posts until being named assistant to the president in 1896. He served in that capacity until 1900 when he became assistant freight agent.

From November 1, 1919 until his death on June 14, 1931, Mr. Ingalls was vice president of freight and passenger traffic of the New York Central. This vessel was sold for trade-in and scrap in 1965.

Steamer ROBERT N. JOYNT

OWNER:	T. J. Mc Carthy Steamship Company
BUILT:	Toledo Shipbuilding Company, Toledo, Ohio—1907
HULL NO.:	110
O. A. DIMENSIONS:	458' × 52' × 28'
FORMER DATA:	Launched as SMITH THOMPSON. Given last name in 1959.

The namesake of this bulk freighter was Mr. Robert Nicholas Joynt who was born in Detroit, Michigan on January 23, 1907. He attended the local schools and began working for his father in the R. Joynt & Sons Company in 1925. This firm was engaged in the custom building of various types of automotive equipment and vehicles for the Detroit automobile industry. As his skills grew, Mr. Joynt became an expert tool and die designing engineer.

In 1934 he married Margaret Mc Carthy who was the daughter of the founder of this steamship company. He continued to work for R. Joynt & Sons however until joining Excello Corporation in 1941 as a machine designer at Cadillac, Michigan. After World War II he became associated with Mc Carthy-Root Company, one of the Mc Carthy family enterprises as design superintendent. In the early 1950's he worked for a subsidiary division of the above firm known as the Schwartz Tool Company as its design chief. Mr. Joynt was engaged in this activity when he died at Detroit, Michigan on April 29, 1955.

Among his contributions to the steamship business was the colorful funnel design on the Mc Carthy fleet of ships. He namesake served most of its life in another fleet and took his name posthumously. It was sold for scrap in 1961 after its size became obsolete in Great Lakes trading of bulk cargoes.

This vessel is shown below in the Middle Neebish Channel of the St. Mary's River on June 19, 1960.

Steamer T. J. Mc CARTHY

OWNER:	T. J. Mc Carthy Steamship Company
BUILT:	Chicago Shipbuilding Company, Chicago, Illinois—1901
HULL NO.:	48
O. A. DIMENSIONS:	452' × 50'3" × 28'6"
FORMER DATA:	Launched as the bulk freighter MARY C. ELPHICKE. Renamed MORRIS S. TREMAINE in 1924. Converted to an automobile carrier at Ranahan-Mc Carthy Marine Terminal, Buffalo, New York in 1936. Given last name in 1941. Re-converted to a bulk freighter at Ranahan-McCarthy Marine Terminal, Buffalo, New York in 1942. Re-converted to an automobile carrier at Nicholson Engineering Works, Detroit, Michigan in 1946.

Flagship of the fleet, this automobile carrier is shown in the picture above just after docking in Erie, Pennsylvania on May 29, 1963 with a capacity load of 500 cars. It was sold for scrap in 1965.

Namesake of this vessel was Mr. Timothy Joseph Mc Carthy who was born at Erie, Pennsylvania on March 31, 1884. He completed his high school education and went to work as a salesman for the Tropical Paint & Oil Company of Cleveland, Ohio in 1902.

In 1922-23, Mr. Mc Carthy pioneered what is known as "fishy-back" service. This was successful in the transport of truck trailers and he was made traffic manager before leaving in 1930 to become a freight solicitor for the Detroit & Cleveland Navigation Company. In 1935 he organized and became president of this fleet and the Automotive Trades Steamship Company. He died at Detroit on November 22, 1961.

Steamer GEORGE W. MEAD

OWNER:	T. J. McCarthy Steamship Company
BUILT:	American Ship Building Company, Cleveland, Ohio—1905
HULL NO.:	424
O. A. DIMENSIONS:	401' × 50'3" × 28'6"
FORMER DATA:	Launched as the bulk freighter FRANCIS L. ROBBINS. Converted to a special-purpose paper carrier and given last name at Manitowoc Shipbuilding Company, Manitowoc, Wisconsin in 1928. Converted to a combination paper carrier and automobile carrier at Manitowoc Shipbuilding Company, Manitowoc, Wisconsin in 1929. Re-converted to a bulk freighter at Nicholson Terminal & Dock Company, River Rouge, Michigan in 1942. Re-converted to an automobile carrier at Ranahan-McCarthy Marine Terminal, Buffalo, New York in 1946.

The Steamer GEORGE W. MEAD is shown in the above picture abreast Ecorse, Michigan on August 24, 1951. It was active until being sold for scrap in 1965.

This automobile carrier honored Mr. George Wilson Mead. He was born in Chicago, Illinois on February 22, 1871 and received his B.A. degree from the University of Wisconsin in 1894. He began his career in the furniture business at Rockford, Illinois but moved to Wisconsin Rapids, Wisconsin in 1902 to assist in managing the new facilities of the Consolidated Water, Power & Paper Company. Mr. Mead quickly assumed leadership roles in the firm and was elected president in 1916. He continued active until retirement in September, 1950 and died October 2, 1961 at Wisconsin Rapids, Wisconsin. For a short time this vessel was owned by the Consolidated firm.

Steamer HURLBUT W. SMITH

OWNER:	T. J. McCarthy Steamship Company
BUILT:	American Ship Building Company, Lorain, Ohio—1903
HULL NO.:	322
O. A. DIMENSIONS:	434' × 50'2" × 28'1'

The bulk freight Steamer HURLBUT W. SMITH was sold for scrap in 1958 following a grounding accident in which it became a constructive total loss.

Namesake of this carrier was Mr. Hurlbut William Smith who was born at Centre Lisle, New York on June 24, 1865. He was educated at Lisle Academy and was a graduate of Syracuse University in 1921 with an M.A. degree. He was one of four brothers which founded the L. C. Smith & Brothers Typewriter Company at Syracuse, New York in 1903, but prior to that began working in the manufacture of guns at L. C. Smith Manufacturing Company. He later was with Premier Typewriter Company as treasurer until the 1903 organization of L. C. Smith & Brothers Typewriter Company.

He became a director of the new firm and was concurrently president of the Syracuse Industrial Gas Company and vice president of Smith-Lewis Fibre Can Company. In addition, he was a director of the Syracuse Trust Company, Toledo Shipbuilding Company and a director and treasurer of the Great Lakes Steamship Company which firm owned this vessel until 1957. He became president, chairman of the board and director of the L. C. Smith & Corona Typewriter Company in 1937, continuing in that capacity until his death on December 16, 1951.

This bulk freighter is shown below in the St. Mary's River on August 18, 1957.

Steamer SWEDEN

OWNER:	T. J. McCarthy Steamship Company
BUILT:	West Bay City Shipbuilding Company, West Bay City, Michigan—1902
HULL NO.:	606
O. A. DIMENSIONS:	434' × 50' × 28'
FORMER DATA:	Launched as L. C. SMITH. Given last name in 1916.

The bulk freight Steamer SWEDEN served in Great Lakes commerce until it was sold for scrap in 1961. It was originally built for the United States Transportation Company, which was one of the companies in which Mr. Horace S. Wilkinson and his friends held a majority of the stock. As such, it fell into the category of ships with names in reference to Baltic countries.

Sweden occupies the eastern and largest part of the Scandinavian peninsula. It extends from 55 degrees, 20 minutes to 69 degrees north latitude and from 11 degrees to 24 degrees east longitude and covers an area of 173,347 square miles. Much of this area is in fine fertile, level land which has been adopted to support the population of the country.

The northern half of Sweden is sparsely populated and is called Norrland. The southern half, Svealand and Gotland, is where the concentration of population exists. The country contains large stores of iron and copper and lesser quantities of silver, manganeese, nickel, zinc and cobalt. Exports into foreign markets of much of the production of these fields keeps Sweden's balance of payments quite favorable.

This vessel is shown below being discharged of a grain cargo at Victory Soya Mills, Toronto, Ontario harbor, on May 7, 1957.

Steamer SIDNEY M.

OWNER:	McNamara Construction Company Limited
BUILT:	J. & K. Smits, Kinderdijk, Holland—1900
HULL NO.:	4
O. A. DIMENSIONS:	165' × 33' × 12'6"
FORMER DATA:	Launched as NEREUS. Renamed RESTIGOUCHE (2) in 1912. Renamed O'CONNOR DICK in 1923. Given last name in 1940.

The little sandsucking Steamer SIDNEY M. is shown in the above photograph at Toronto, Ontario. It was active until being sold for scrap in 1960.

This vessel first of all honored Mr. Sidney John Bird as its namesake. He was born in Norfolk, England on November 19, 1892 and took engineering courses at Cambridge University for one year before coming to Canada and settling in Toronto, Ontario in 1907. He began working for the Canadian Government in the area of Matheson, Ontario and was settlement officer in this lumbering and mining district in 1914 when he joined the Royal Canadian Engineers and served in the 6th Canadian Railway Troops.

During his service years he came to know Messrs. Howard D. and George A. McNamara with whom he served and the three men formed McNamara Construction Company Limited in 1920, with Mr. Bird serving as general manager. He became secretary-treasurer in 1923, vice president in 1940 and president in 1952, serving in that post until retiring in 1955. Mr. Bird then formed the Ontario Marine and Dredging Limited and headed the firm at the time of his death on April 10, 1964 at Toronto, Ontario.

The letter "M" in the ship name was in reference to the owning company and was a commonly used name ending of waterborne craft in the fleet.

Motor Vessel BLUE COMET

OWNER:	James McWilliams Blue Line, Incorporated
BUILT:	Sun Shipbuilding & Dry Dock Company, Chester, Pennsylvania—1923
HULL NO.:	65
O. A. DIMENSIONS:	253'9" × 37'6" × 14'
FORMER DATA:	Launched as TROY SOCONY. Given last name in 1946.

The New York State Barge Canal-type tank Motor Vessel BLUE COMET took the common first name of the fleet in its ship name. Blue was the predominant color on all ships and barges of this fleet and, as can be noted, was a part of the corporate title of the owning company. All vessels in the fleet bore this same first name.

The specific namesake was in reference to heavenly bodies known as comets. Other celestial names were borne by other members of this fleet.

A comet looks much like a star with a tail. Most have three parts; a nucleus, a head and a tail. The bright center may be in excess of seven thousand miles in diameter. The head surrounding it may be as much as one hundred thousand miles in diameter, and the tail streaking behind the comet can be up to one hundred million miles long.

Only theories exist as to the origin or composition of comets. They travel in eliptical orbits around the sun and some have fairly regular orbital times. The most famous, Halley's Comet, will appear again in 1986.

This vessel remained in service on the Great Lakes and to the East Coast until being sold for scrap in 1964. It is shown above while upbound in the Detroit River on July 5, 1951.

Steamer SAINTE MARIE (2)

OWNER: Mackinac Transportation Company
BUILT: Toledo Shipbuilding Company,
Toledo, Ohio - 1913
HULL NO.: 127
O. A. DIMENSIONS: 266' x 62'3" x 25'

The railroad carferry Steamer SAINTE MARIE (2) was a regular in the early ice-breaking operations at the Straits of Mackinac and the St. Mary's River. Its twin propellers aft and single propeller forward provided excellent flexibility in ice and the vessel was regularly chartered by Lake Carriers' Association, representing Great Lakes vessel owners, in the annual spring test of strength with the ice in breaking open navigable channels for the iron ore carriers.

This hearty vessel remained active until 1961 when it was sold for scrap. It met that fate at Ashtabula, Ohio in 1962. It had sailed from Toledo, Ohio on March 13, 1913 on its maiden voyage to St. Ignace, Michigan to begin its regular run across the Straits of Mackinac.

The namesake of this venerable carferry was the city of Sault Ste. Marie, Michigan which was named by Father Marquette in 1668 for the Virgin Mary. This area passed through French and British hands until 1820 when it became a United States possession. Sault Ste. Marie was incorporated as a village in 1879 and was chartered as a city in 1887.

Today, Sault Ste. Marie, Michigan and its larger sister city Sault Ste. Marie, Ontario hold the key to commerce on the upper Great Lakes. Through the world-famous locks of both cities pass over one hundred million tons of commerce annually. There are four major locks on the Michigan side and one on the Canadian side. All of these arteries of commerce are kept busy for the nine month navigation season.

Steamer NORCO

OWNER:	Marathon Corporation of Canada, Limited
BUILT:	Great Lakes Engineering Works, Ecorse, Michigan—1915
HULL NO.:	149
O. A. DIMENSIONS:	258'6" × 38'2" × 18'
FORMER DATA:	Launched as INCA. Given last name in 1938.

The bulk freight Steamer NORCO was active on the Great Lakes until rail and truck transportation of pulpwood became more economical for these owners and this vessel was sold for off-lakes use in 1957. It is shown below near Sault Ste. Marie, Michigan on June 26, 1953 with a full cargo of pulpwood bound for the parent company's plant at Green Bay, Wisconsin.

The owner shown on this page is the current corporate name of an outgrowth of mergers and acquisitions which included the Northern Paper Mills Limited, of Canada, and its parent firm, Northern Paper Mills Company of Green Bay, Wisconsin. When this vessel was renamed in 1938, it took portions of the parent corporate name to form the vessel name. *NOR* stood for the first three letters in the word "northern" and *CO* stood for the first two letters in the word "company."

Northern Paper Mills utilized this vessel in transporting pulpwood loaded at Michipicoten, Ontario to the processing plant at Green Bay, Wisconsin.

Both American and Canadian operations of Northern Paper Mills were merged into Marathon Corporation in 1953. This firm had been incorporated in Wisconsin on February 6, 1909. This merged firm was, in turn, acquired by The American Can Company of New York, New York and is now part of that organization.

Motor Vessel MARINE FUEL

OWNER: Marine Fueling, Incorporated
BUILT: William Cramp & Sons Ship and Engine Building Company, Philadelphia, Pennsylvania—1911
HULL NO.: 378
O. A. DIMENSIONS: 103'6" × 24' × 9'
FORMER DATA: Launched as POLING BROS., NO. 10. Renamed VIRGINIA in 1950. Renamed CEMICO in 1954. Given last name in 1956.

The bunkering tank Motor Vessel MARINE FUEL is shown above at its dock in Cleveland, Ohio during the period of its use in that port. The vessel was sold for scrap in 1968.

This vessel took its name from that of the owning company whose headquarters are in the Terminal Tower at Cleveland, Ohio. The firm began as a small bunkering service and is now the largest oil marine fueling operation of the Great Lakes with service via ships and tank barges at Duluth/Superior, Two Harbors, Silver Bay, Taconite Harbor, Toledo, Lorain and Cleveland.

Marine Fueling, Incorporated was chartered in the state of Wisconsin on January 25, 1952 for the purpose of providing bunkers to vessels plying the Great Lakes. There were facilities for fueling vessels in Canada, but up to that time none existed on the United States side of the Great Lakes for oil bunkering.

The typical bunkering operation is carried on while the larger ships are either loading or unloading. These small tankers merely tie-up to the shipside of the larger vessel and perform their bunkering functions.

Steamer C. H. Mc CULLOUGH, JR.

OWNER: Medusa Cement Division, Medusa Corporation
BUILT: Superior Shipbuilding Company, Superior, Wisconsin—1907
HULL NO.: 518
O. A. DIMENSIONS: 550' × 56' × 30'
FORMER DATA: Launched as WARD AMES. Given last name in 1916.

Mr. Charles Henry Mc Cullough, Jr. is the namesake of this bulk freighter. He was born at Philadelphia, Pennsylvania on December 25, 1868 and graduated from Stevens Institute of Technology with an M.E. degree in 1891.

He joined Illinois Steel Company at Chicago, Illinois after graduation and stayed with that firm in various positions until 1905 when he resigned to become vice president and general manager of Lackawanna Steel Company at Buffalo, New York. Mr. Mc Cullough was second vice president of Illinois Steel at the time of his resignation.

On January 1, 1919 he became president of Lackawanna Steel Company and held that post when he died in Baltimore, Maryland on April 3, 1920. He was a director of Lackawanna Steel and also Consolidated Steel Corporation, American Iron & Steel Institute, Manufacturers & Traders National Bank, Pierce-Arrow Motor Car Company, Morris Plan Bank and the Clark Equipment Company.

His namesake is shown below upon arrival at the NYPANO dock in Cleveland, Ohio with a cargo of iron ore on July 26, 1973. Sold for scrap in 1980 after 5 years of idleness at South Chicago, Illinois.

Motor Vessel MICHIGAN (6)

OWNER: Michigan Atlantic Corporation
BUILT: McDougall-Duluth Shipbuilding Company, Duluth, Minnesota—1921
HULL NO.: 54
O. A. DIMENSIONS: 254' × 36' × 14'
FORMER DATA: Launched as the barge canal freighter INTERWATERWAYS LINE INCORPORATED 105. Renamed I.L.I. 105 in 1932. Converted to a caustic soda tanker at Great Lakes Engineering Works, River Rouge, Michigan in 1935. Given last name in 1936.

The tank Motor Vessel MICHIGAN is shown in the photograph above in the Welland Ship Canal. It is enroute to Detroit, Michigan with a cargo of liquid caustic soda from the East Coast, having passed into the Great Lakes via the New York State Barge Canal at Oswego, New York. This vessel remained active until the following year on this trade route. It was sold for off-lakes use in 1961.

The namesake of this vessel was the state of Michigan which state name also provided the first word of the owning firm's corporate title. Much of the trade of this vessel had to do with the state whose ports received a large percentage of the liquid caustic soda cargoes brought into the Great Lakes area by this vessel. Unless eastbound cargoes could be found that were suited to the specialized tanks of this carrier, the ship would return light to the East Coast.

Steamer CITY OF CHEBOYGAN

OWNER: Highway Department, Michigan State Ferry Service
BUILT: American Ship Building Company, Cleveland, Ohio—1906
HULL NO.: 436
O. A. DIMENSIONS: 270' × 52' × 19'
FORMER DATA: Launched as the railroad carferry ANN ARBOR NO. 4. Converted to an automobile carferry at Manitowoc Shipbuilding Company, Manitowoc, Wisconsin and Lund Brothers, Cheboygan, Michigan in 1937. Renamed CITY OF CHEBOYGAN in 1938.

The Steamer CITY OF CHEBOYGAN was in regular use across the Straits of Mackinac until the completion of the new bridge connecting Mackinaw City and St. Ignace, Michigan in 1957. The ship is shown above on one of its typical voyages in the Straits. It was sold for use as a potato processing hull in 1958 and named EDWARD H. ANDERSON. In 1973 the hull was sold for scrap.

During the time this vessel served in the service of the Highway Department it had a carrying capacity of 85 automobiles. It was named for a small city on Lake Huron near the Straits of Mackinac. Cheboygan, Michigan has a population of about 6,000 and is at the mouth of the Cheboygan River. It is not a major port in terms of annual commerce, but does have several dock facilities for dry bulk and liquid cargo which do accommodate large lake ships.

The Steamer CITY OF CHEBOYGAN had begun its service in the Straits on August 8, 1937 when it was commissioned by these owners following its conversion.

Steamer CITY OF MUNISING

OWNER: Highway Department, Michigan State Ferry Service
BUILT: American Ship Building Company, Cleveland, Ohio—1903
HULL NO.: 419
O. A. DIMENSIONS: 350' × 56' × 19'6"
FORMER DATA: Launched as the railroad carferry PERE MARQUETTE 20. Converted to an automobile carferry at Manitowoc Shipbuilding Company, Manitowoc, Wisconsin and given last name in 1938.

The Steamer CITY OF MUNISING is shown above on one of its typical voyages in the Straits of Mackinac before its retirement in 1958. It served as a potato warehouse at Washington Island, Wisconsin until sold for scrap in 1973.

This vessel was engaged in a strange service in 1943 when it was not needed by the State of Michigan because of World War II's restrictions on gasoline usage and that reflected decreased automobile traffic in the Straits of Mackinac. The ship, along with its sistership CITY OF PETOSKEY, was chartered to the Trucker Steamship Company of Detroit, Michigan. This firm, a Browning enterprise, tried to float truck trailors between Detroit and Cleveland, Ohio in an effort to save gasoline and rubber wear on the highways. Unfortunately, few teamsters officials agreed and the service was abandoned in the fall of 1943.

The namesake of this vessel was Munising, Michigan which was founded by white men in 1850. A dock was completed for lake shipping in 1870 and a furnace, blacksmith's shop and sawmill were erected in that era. In 1895 Mr. Timothy Nestor started work on clearing some land and plotting a town and the village of Munising was incorporated in 1896. The village was granted status as a city in 1915. The city has a current population of 5,000 persons.

Steamer CITY OF PETOSKEY

```
        OWNER:  Highway Department, Michigan State Ferry Service
        BUILT:  American Ship Building Company,
                Cleveland, Ohio - 1901
      HULL NO.: 406
O. A. DIMENSIONS: 350' x 56' x 19'6"
  FORMER DATA:  Launched as the railroad carferry PERE MARQUETTE
                17. Converted to an automobile carferry at Manitowoc
                Shipbuilding Company, Manitowoc, Wisconsin in 1940
                and at Great Lakes Engineering Works, River Rouge,
                Michigan in 1941. Given last name in 1941.
```

The Steamer CITY OF PETOSKEY was given its last name on May 26, 1941 when an Indian princess, Miss Virginia Chingwa of Petoskey, Michigan smashed the traditional bottle of champagne on the vessel's bow. The ship then proceeded into service in the Straits of Mackinac. It continued to serve until being sold for scrap in 1961, though it had lain idle since completion of the Mackinaw Bridge in the fall of 1957. The vessel is shown above while underway in the Straits of Mackinac on a typical voyage.

The namesake of this vessel was the city of Petoskey, Michigan. It is the seat of Emmet County and is located at the mouth of the Bear River on the south shore of Little Traverse Bay, an inlet of Lake Michigan. The main industry of Petoskey was a large cement plant of Penn-Dixie Cement Company located just outside the city at Bayshore. It is now dismantled.

The area was first settled in 1872 by white traders and missionaries and was incorporated in 1879. It was chartered as a city in 1895 and has a current population of 7,000. The area is a year-around tourist retreat and is known for its scenic beauty, especially during the fall when the tree colors are outstanding.

Steamer THE STRAITS OF MACKINAC

OWNER: Highway Department, Michigan State Ferry Service
BUILT: Great Lakes Engineering Works, River Rouge, Michigan—1928
HULL NO.: 261
O. A. DIMENSIONS: 202'11" × 48' × 16'6"

The automobile and passenger carferry Steamer THE STRAITS OF MACKINAC is shown in the photograph above on one of its typical runs across the Straits of Mackinac with a full load of tourists and automobiles. This service by the State of Michigan ended with completion of the giant suspension bridge connecting St. Ignace and Mackinaw City, Michigan in 1957. The ship operated for a few years by Straits Transit, Incorporated in the same area, but was sold for use as a storage vessel at Sturgeon Bay, Wisconsin in 1968 and currently lies at that port.

This vessel had a namesake which was fully identified in its name. The Straits of Mackinac is the modern name applied to this area of Michigan formerly known by the Algonquin name "Michilimackinac." The strait is the connecting link between Lakes Huron and Michigan and, due to the narrower channels in them, has also been the scene of many accidents in the history of Great Lakes commerce.

Nicolet discovered the straits in 1634 and the area was an important one in the fur trade. The first settlement was begun in 1668 on the north shore at what is now St. Ignace. During the following years the site changed hands between governments several times, but the United States took possession of it permanently in 1815.

Motor Vessel DETROIT (2)

OWNER: Michigan Tankers, Incorporated
BUILT: His Majesty's Dockyard, Chatham, England - 1914
HULL NO.: None assigned.
O. A. DIMENSIONS: 255'6" x 34'3" x 15'2"
FORMER DATA: Launched as the powered tank vessel H.M.S. SERVITOR. Renamed PULOE BRANI in 1923. Renamed B. B. Mc COLL in 1927. Converted to a tank barge at St. Lawrence Marine Railway Company, Ogdensburg, New York and renamed A. J PATMORE in 1929. Reconverted to a powered tank vessel at Interlake Engineering Company, Cleveland, Ohio in 1930. Renamed ROTARY in 1942. Renamed A. J. PATMORE for the second time in 1945. Renamed PEGGY REINAUER in 1946. Given last name in 1955. Lengthened 45'6" at Manitowoc Shipbuilding, Incorporated, Manitowoc, Wisconsin in 1959.

The small tanker DETROIT (2) took its name from the "Motor City" of Michigan in which operating headquarters of this fleet were situated until the mid-1960s. They were then moved to Park Ridge, Illinois and, lastly, to Findlay, Ohio where the parent firm, Marathon Oil Company is headquartered. Detroit, Michigan was founded in 1701 by Antoine de la Mothe Cadillac and was incorporated as a city in 1815.

The Motor Vessel DETROIT (2) is shown above while downbound in Lake Huron in 1973. It was sold for non-transportation use in August, 1975. This vessel is among those having the most involved histories in its background of any that ever sailed the Great Lakes.

Steamer SCOTT MARK

OWNER:	Mid-Canada Transports Limited
BUILT:	Furness Shipbuilding Company, Limited, Haverton Hill-on-Tees, England—1923
HULL NO.:	43
O. A. DIMENSIONS:	261' × 43'3" × 20'
FORMER DATA:	Launched as the bulk freighter WILLIAM H. DANIELS. Converted to a crane-equipped bulk carrier at Western Engineering Service, Fort William, Ontario in 1965. Re-converted to a bulk freighter at Western Engineering Service, Fort William, Ontario and given last name in 1966.

The canal sized bulk freighter shown here retained its last name only for a short time and was sold for scrap in 1967.

The namesake of this ship was two-fold. The first name, SCOTT, referred to Master Robert Scott Bennett, grandson of one of the principals in ownership of this firm. Young Scott was born in Ottawa, Ontario on March 15, 1966 and is now living with his parents and attending grade school in Calgary, Alberta.

The second part of this vessel's name was in honor of Mr. Timothy MARK Rand, the son of one of the other principals in ownership of this vessel. Mr. Rand was born in London, Ontario on October 21, 1957 and is now attending school in that city. His hobbies are outdoor activities such as building construction and pleasure boating.

Steamer WALLACEBURG

OWNER: Midlake Steamship Line
BUILT: Earle's Shipbuilding & Engineering Company, Limited, Hull, England - 1923
HULL NO.: 643
O. A. DIMENSIONS: 261' x 43'3" x 20'
FORMER DATA: Launched as JOHN J. RAMMACHER. Given last name in 1956.

The canal-size bulk freight Steamer WALLACEBURG took its name from a town in Kent County, Ontario situated on the Sydenham River and the Chesapeake and Ohio Railway. The former owners of this vessel carried a large portion of the grain products that were shipped from the small elevator at Wallaceburg and felt it apropos to christen this vesel in honor of that port.

This ship is shown in this photograph in Little Rapids Cut, St. Mary's River on October 10, 1965. The following year it was sold for scrap.

Wallaceburg, Ontario is located seventeen miles north of Chatham, Ontario and was originally known as The Forks. It was named Wallaceburg by Hugh McCallum, the First Postmaster, in honor of Sir William Wallace who was the champion of Scottish independence.

Today, the town has a population of 12,500 people and is the center of the southwestern Ontario canning region. Large crops of vegetables and fruit are processed there. In addition, the main industry is glassmaking. The Sydenham River flows past Wallaceburg and joins the Chenal Ecarte River to the west and south respectively. What waterborne traffic still exists in the port reaches and leaves the area by way of the Sydenham River branch that flows into the St. Clair River.

Steamer ANGELINE

OWNER:	Midland Steamship Line, Incorporated
BUILT:	Detroit Shipbuilding Company, Wyandotte, Michigan—1899
HULL NO:	132
O. A. DIMENSIONS:	437' × 50' × 28'

The small bulk freight Steamer ANGELINE was originally constructed for the Presque Isle Transportation Company which was an affiliate of the Cleveland-Cliffs Iron Company. This firm was very active in the developing iron ore properties of the Marquette Range and are even more so today.

When it came to choose a name for this ship before it was launched on July 2, 1899, the owners conferred and decided to choose a name that directly bore relation to their Marquette Range activities and settled upon this name.

The namesake of this vessel was the Angeline Mine located on the Marquette Range which was opened by Cleveland-Cliffs Iron Company in 1864. It shipped iron ore each year through 1922 except 1916 and 1921. It is now inactive. Large quantities of soft, red Bessemer ore were forwarded during production years.

The mine was actually owned by another affiliate, the Pittsburgh and Lake Angeline Iron Company and was managed by the Cleveland-Cliffs organization.

This steamer was active on the Great Lakes until being sold for grain storage use at Buffalo, New York in 1955. It was sold to Continental Grain Company in that year but returned to service in 1956 for these owners. The ship is shown below at Cleveland, Ohio on September 11, 1956. It ran also in 1957 and was sold for scrap in 1965.

Steamer MICHAEL GALLAGHER (2)

OWNER:	Midland Steamship Line, Incorporated
BUILT:	Detroit Shipbuilding Company, Wyandotte, Michigan - 1907
HULL NO.:	170
O. A. DIMENSIONS:	524' x 54' x 30'
FORMER DATA:	Launched as CHARLES O. JENKINS. Renamed JOHN W. DAVIN in 1943. Given last name in 1956.

Mr. Michael Gallagher was born in Latrobe, Pennsylvania on September 3, 1870 and was educated in the public schools. He began his career in the local coal fields in 1893 and became associated with the Hanna Mining Company in the late 1890's. By 1911 he had attained the post of head of bituminous coal mining with Hanna. He held this post until resigning on August 1, 1926 to make a general survey of the coal industry for the Van Sweringen brothers.

During this period he became aware of the collapse of the Becker Fleet and, through various banking associations, simultaneously became associated with the founding of this fleet. Mr. Gallagher was a board member of Midland Steamship Line from 1930 until retiring in 1955. During this period, his son-in-law, Mr. Baird Tewksbury became associated with the firm as its president and, later, chairman of the board.

Mr. Gallagher believed in hard work and saw little point in retirement. In addition to his steamship interests, therefore, he became associated with the Nickel Plate Railroad in 1941 and served until 1955 as assistant to the president. He died at Cleveland, Ohio on August 27, 1956.

This steamer is shown below taking its last fueling at Cleveland, Ohio in 1961 prior to departing for scrap.

Steamer W. G. POLLOCK

OWNER:	Midland Steamship Line, Incorporated
BUILT:	American Ship Building Company, Cleveland, Ohio—1906
HULL NO.:	434
O. A. DIMENSIONS:	440' × 52' × 28'6"

The Steamer W. G. POLLOCK was sold for grain storage use in the port of Buffalo, New York in 1955 and served in that capacity for over a decade. It was subsequently resold for scrap.

The namesake of this vessel was Mr. William Granville Pollock who was born at Youngstown, Ohio on September 20, 1847. He was educated in the local schools and began his business career in various jobs in his hometown. In 1865 he moved to the city of Cleveland, Ohio to seek his further business opportunities.

He became associated with parties in the iron ore brokerage business and it proved to be his forte. From 1875 he was associated with the W. H. Becker interests who were involved with both iron ore mining and Great Lakes shipping. Mr. Pollock became manager of the iron ore mine in Michigan and the dock activities at Ashtabula, Ohio and by 1900, was secretary-treasurer of the Pittsburgh & Lake Angeline Iron Company, a subsidiary firm. Mr. Pollock was named president of the Pollock, Becker & Company, iron ore merchants and Great Lakes vessel operators in 1912 and continued to serve in that capacity until his retirement. He was also secretary of the Presque Isle Transportation Company.

He was an ardent horseman and owned and even rode trotters in his younger days. Mr. Pollock died at Cleveland on March 2, 1925.

Motor Vessel WALTER INKSTER

OWNER:	Colonial Steamships Limited
BUILT:	William Doxford & Son, Limited, Sunderland, England - 1895
HULL NO.:	234
O. A. DIMENSIONS:	258' x 45' x 26'10"
FORMER DATA:	Launched as the bulk freighter TURRET CAPE. Converted to a barge at Muir Bros. Dry Dock Company, Port Dalhousie, Ontario in 1935. Re-converted to a powered bulk freighter at Davie Shipbuilding and Repairing Limited, Lauzon, Quebec in 1941. Converted to a sandsucker at Sprostons Limited, Georgetown, British Guiana in 1943. Renamed SUNCHIEF in 1947. Re-converted to a bulk freighter at E. G. Marsh, Limited, Port Colborne, Ontario and given last name in 1949.

The namesake of this canal-sized bulk freighter was Captain Walter Inkster. He was born on September 9, 1866 in Burra, Shetland Islands, Scotland and had little formal education before becoming an apprentice seaman on square-rigged sailing ships in 1880. He learned his trade quickly and received his master's papers in 1896.

Captain Inkster sensed the flurry of Great Lakes activity and decided to come to Canada where he settled at Sault Ste. Marie, Ontario. He moved to Collingwood, Ontario in 1907 and established a navigation school and also had a practice in compass adjusting. He had met Mr. R. Scott Misener at Sault Ste. Marie and the two became great friends. Captain Inkster was senior advisor on maintenance with Misener's from 1922-1950.

Captain Inkster died at Ottawa, Ontario January 22, 1954 and his namesake was sold for scrap in 1956.

Steamer ACTON

OWNER:	Scott Misener Steamships Limited
BUILT:	Smith's Dock Company, Limited, South Bank-on-Tees, England—1928
HULL NO.:	847
O. A. DIMENSIONS:	259' × 43'9" × 21'3"
FORMER DATA:	Launched as CONISCLIFFE HALL (1). Given last name in 1955.

The canal size bulk freight Steamer ACTON was one of a number of "canallers" in this fleet which was named for a town in the province of Ontario, Canada. Management of the fleet considered keeping the inherited suffix "TON" on these ship's names.

This vessel was active in the Misener Fleet until being sold for scrap in 1961. It is shown in the photograph below at Port Colborne, Ontario in May of 1955.

Acton, Ontario is a town of 4,000 population in Halton County about 45 miles west of Toronto, Ontario and 35 miles north of Hamilton, Ontario. It is situated on the mainline between Toronto and Sarnia, Ontario of the Canadian National Railways.

Acton was first settled in 1821 and was known then as Danville and later Adamsville. In 1844 Robert Swan, the first postmaster, named it for Acton, England. It was incorporated as a village in 1873 and was granted town status in 1950. Industries include tanning, wool-combing, glove making, flour milling, machine-making and the production of engineering and factory equipment, knitted products, plastics, electrical, ceramic and wood products.

Steamer C. A. ANSELL

OWNER:	Scott Misener Steamships Limited
BUILT:	Barclay, Curle & Company, Limited, Glasgow, Scotland—1929
HULL NO.:	633
O. A. DIMENSIONS:	259' × 43'3" × 20'9"
FORMER DATA:	Launched as FAIRLAKE. Renamed RALPH S. MISENER (1) in 1944. Given last name in 1954.

Mr. Charles Arthur Ansell was the namesake of this bulk freighter. He was born at Ventwor, Isle of Wight, England on June 17, 1899 and came to Canada with his parents in 1902 to settle in the Niagara Falls area.

In 1920 he joined the Muir Brothers Dry Dock Company Limited at Port Dalhousie, Ontario as a junior clerk and his career in the shipbuilding and repair business was launched. By 1929 he had progressed through various positions to become the yard's general superintendent and in the 1930's he pioneered and experimented with numerous innovations in ship repair and construction. In 1938 he became general manager of Muir Brothers Dry Dock Company and held that position when he left in 1946 to form Port Weller Dry Docks Limited.

Mr. Ansell was not an engineer nor a naval architect, but he had tremendous vision and drive. He became a good friend of the Scott Misener organization and their large new vessels of the 1950's were built at his yard. He continued as president of Port Weller Dry Docks Limited until his death in St. Catharines, Ontario on November 7, 1957.

His namesake was active in Great Lakes commerce until being sold for scrap in 1959. It is shown in this picture at Thorold, Ontario on December 8, 1956. This ship began its maiden voyage from Glasgow, Scotland on May 30, 1929, light for Montreal, Quebec.

Steamer DAVID BARCLAY

OWNER:	Scott Misener Steamships Limited
BUILT:	Smith's Dock Company Limited,
	South Bank-on-Tees, England—1928
HULL NO.:	846
O. A. DIMENSIONS:	258'6" × 43'3" × 20'6"
FORMER DATA:	Launched as EAGLESCLIFFE HALL (1). Given last name in 1955.

The canal-size bulk freight Steamer DAVID BARCLAY honored a man who spent most of his working life with the Misener organization.

Mr. David Barclay was born on September 24, 1890 at Dundee, Scotland. On completing his education he began sailing on the oceans of the world with the British India Steamship Lines. His voyages took him to every seabordering country of the world except China and Chile. His shipboard time was spent as an engineer in various progressive stages of rank.

In 1926 he went to Canada and became guarantee chief engineer with the Canadian Government. In this role he took the government vessels CHESTERFIELD and N. B. McLEAN to Hudson Bay. In 1929 he sailed on the Great Lakes as chief engineer in the Canada Steamship Lines fleet. In 1931 he became acquainted with Captain R. Scott Misener who persuaded him to join his organization. After sailing on numerous vessels in the fleet, he was named Commodore Engineer and held that title when he retired. Mr. Barclay died at Collingwood, Ontario on September 29, 1969. His namesake had been sold for off-lakes use in 1959.

The Steamer DAVID BARCLAY is seen below taking on a transfer cargo of grain at the Prescott, Ontario elevator of National Harbours Board on October 31, 1957.

Steamer BAYTON

OWNER:	Scott Misener Steamships Limited
BUILT:	American Ship Building Company, Cleveland, Ohio - 1904
HULL NO.:	421
O. A. DIMENSIONS:	436' x 50' x 28'
FORMER DATA:	Launched as FRANCIS WIDLAR. Given last name in 1921.

The bulk freight Steamer BAYTON is shown in this picture above Lock Three of the Welland Ship Canal on April 4, 1964. It was active on the Great Lakes for only two more seasons and was sold for scrap in 1966. Final disposition of the hull was that of being sunk for a breakwater late in 1966 at Burns Harbor, Indiana.

This vessel had the distinction of being the only ship to carry a coal cargo downbound through the Soo Locks up to the recent advent of Western Canada coal moving in the eastbound direction from Thunder Bay, Ontario and Superior, Wisconsin. Late in June, 1904 a mistake in the orders received by the vessel sent the ship to Duluth, Minnesota with coal instead of the proper discharge port of Sheboygan, Wisconsin. When it was determined that no one at Duluth was willing to accept the cargo, the ship returned back over its track, downbound throught the locks and to the correct port.

The Misener organization kept this name on the bow when they acquired the vessel in 1933. Formerly owned by Mathews Steamship Company of Toronto, Ontario, the vessel bore that fleet's theme suffix, "TON." The prefix of the ship name, "BAY," was in reference to the bays of the Great Lakes and St. Lawrence River areas.

Steamer C. A. BENNETT

OWNER:	Scott Misener Steamships Limited
BUILT:	American Ship Building Company, Lorain, Ohio—1908
HULL NO.:	357
O. A. DIMENSIONS:	500′ × 52′ × 30′
FORMER DATA:	Launched as B. F. BERRY. Renamed BERRYTON in 1922. Renamed VISCOUNT BENNETT in 1942. Given last name in 1954.

Mr. Clifford Arnold Bennett is the namesake of this bulk freighter which was sold for scrap in 1968. He was born on August 8, 1895 at Port Rowan, Ontario and attended the University of Toronto as an undergraduate.

After completing his schooling he joined the Federal Department of Railways and Canals in July, 1914. He served in various operational and maintenance capacities until September, 1930 when he was appointed superintendent. From this time until July, 1958 he served in the same capacity under the Department of Transport and National Harbours Board.

On August 1, 1958 he was appointed to the post of elevator advisor, National Harbours Board and served in this capacity until his retirement in August, 1960. Mr. Bennett died in December, 1965. He was active in social organizations and the United Church of Canada and was respected as an astute business man and a gentleman by his fellow associates.

The Steamer C. A. BENNETT is seen in this picture entering Port Weller, Ontario harbor with a load of iron ore for Lake Erie discharge on October 22, 1966.

Steamer NIXON BERRY

OWNER:	Scott Misener Steamships Limited
BUILT:	Detroit Shipbuilding Company, Wyandotte, Michigan—1920
HULL NO.:	287
O. A. DIMENSIONS:	600' × 60' × 32'
FORMER DATA:	Launched as MERTON E. FARR. Given last name in 1966.

The bulk freight Steamer NIXON BERRY was named in honor of Mr. Nixon Berry, attorney at Toronto, Ontario and a director of this owning company.

Mr. Berry was born on October 15, 1905 at Caledonia, Ontario and received a B.A. degree in 1928 from the University of Toronto. In 1931 he graduated from the Osgoode Hall Law School and was admitted to the Bar.

After six years of private practice he joined the predecessor firm to his current association. From that time, 1937, to the present, he has practiced law in Ontario. He was appointed to the Queen's Council in 1946 and is presently a partner in the firm of McMillan, Binch, Berry, Dunn, Corrigan & Howland in Toronto, Ontario.

Mr. Berry is also a director of Catalytic Construction of Canada Limited, Channel 7 Television Limited, L. McBrine Company Limited and enjoys fishing as a hobby. His namesake was sold for overseas scrapping in the spring of 1970 and is shown below in the St. Lawrence River.

Steamer BRAMPTON

OWNER:	Scott Misener Steamships Limited
BUILT:	Swan, Hunter & Wigham Richardson Limited, Sunderland, England—1927
HULL NO.:	1315
O. A. DIMENSIONS:	261' × 43'3" × 20'
FORMER DATA:	Launched as WELLANDOC (1). Given last name in 1947.

The town of Brampton, Ontario was the namesake of this canal-sized bulk freighter. Brampton, a town of 19,000 population, is located in Peel County, Ontario on the Canadian Pacific Railway and highways #7 and #10, about twenty miles northwest of Toronto, Ontario.

In 1830 power from the Etobicoke River was utlizied for a small grinding and chopping mill. A pot ashery and distillery were also built. In 1834 Mr. John Elliott plotted the lots of the site and named the village for his home town of Brampton, England. The area was incorporated as a village in 1852 and as a town in 1873.

Brampton has present industry which includes the manufacture of footwear, furniture and optical goods. Another industry is horticulture with large greenhouses which belong to the famous rose growers, the Dale Estate.

The Steamer BRAMPTON is shown in the Lachine Canal at Montreal, Quebec on August 31, 1957. This picture was taken before the opening of the St. Lawrence Seaway and at a time when literally hundreds of these "canallers" were used to transport iron ore and other products through the old St. Lawrence River canal system. This ship remained in the fleet until being sold for scrap in 1961.

Steamer FRANK H. BROWN

OWNER: Scott Misener Steamships Limited
BUILT: North of Ireland Shipbuilding Company, Londonderry, Northern Ireland – 1924
HULL NO.: 105
O. A. DIMENSIONS: 261' × 42'6" × 20'6"
FORMER DATA: Launched as DRUMAHOE. Given last name in 1944.

This canal-sized bulk freighter was sold for scrap in 1961. It was named in honor of Mr. Frank Herbert Brown who was born at Birmingham, England on April 26, 1894. He was a graduate of Queen's University, Belfast, Ireland and became a naturalized Canadian citizen in 1911.

He began his career in Canadian industry with the Canadian Bank of Commerce in 1911 and served in various jobs in western Canada until 1926 when he was appointed inspector at the head office in Montreal, Quebec. In the late 1920's he served as deputy to the assistant general manager and then worked in the field of business reorganization for the bank until 1936 as assistant corporate executive. He was superintendent of the Montreal office from 1939 until 1941.

He joined the Department of Munitions and Supply as director of General Munitions Contracts in 1941, was a deputy minister and financial advisor in 1942 and head of finance and contracts until 1946 when he left to take a post in the Department of National Defense. Since 1948, Mr. Brown has been advisor to large industries in finance and management and since 1951 has been president of the White Pass & Yukon Corporation. He has served as director of many Canadian firms including Scott Misener Steamships Limited and Canadian Vickers Limited, both Great Lakes area firms.

The Steamer FRANK H. BROWN is shown in this photograph in the Cardinal Canal of the St. Lawrence River system on October 26, 1956.

Steamer GEORGE M. CARL (1)

OWNER:	Scott Misener Steamships Limited
BUILT:	Swan, Hunter & Wigham Richardson Limited, Newcastle, England—1928
HULL NO.:	1290
O. A. DIMENSIONS:	259' × 43'6" × 20'
FORMER DATA:	Launched as SCOTT MISENER (1). Given last name in 1950.

This vessel was sold for scrap in 1959, but the name was carried forward on a larger ship for more than a decade.

Mr. George Mansfield Carl is the namesake of this vessel. He was born at Welland, Ontario on April 7, 1915 and was educated in the local schools and St. Catharines Business College, graduating in 1933.

He joined Sarnia Steamships Limited and Colonial Steamships Limited, predecessor firms to Scott Misener Steamships Limited, as an accountant in 1934. Mr. Carl was named treasurer of the company in 1951 and traffic manager in 1964. He became comptroller of the firm in 1969.

Mr. Carl is one of the longest service employees of the present company and this ship and the one bearing his name in later years were christened in his honor in recognition of that service to the Misener organization.

This Steamer GEORGE M. CARL was one of a number such sized ships in the fleet that were found to be uneconomical upon the opening of the St. Lawrence Seaway and all were eventually phased out of operation.

His first namesake is shown below on October 22, 1958 in the Soulanges Canal of the old St. Lawrence River route to the sea.

Steamer CLAYTON

OWNER:	Scott Misener Steamships Limited
BUILT:	Swan, Hunter & Wigham Richardson Limited, Newcastle-on-Tyne, England—1929
HULL NO.:	1356
O. A. DIMENSIONS:	259' × 43'3" × 20'
FORMER DATA:	Launched as FARRANDOC (1). Given last name in 1947.

The canal size bulk freight Steamer CLAYTON was active until the opening of the new St. Lawrence Seaway in 1959. It was sold for scrap in 1960 and met that fate at Humberstone, Ontario. The ship is shown in this photograph above Lock Three in the Welland Ship Canal on November 12, 1955.

The namesake of this ship was the town of about two thousand persons located in Jefferson County, New York. It is located directly on the American side of the St. Lawrence River about midway between Lake Ontario and Alexandria Bay, New York and for many years was an important fueling stop for bunker coal for ships traveling in the St. Lawrence River.

Coal was brought into the bunkering terminal by rail on the New York Central System from eastern mines. Various grades of coal were kept in reserve for supplying the varying needs of ships that might call. With the cost of running the operation rising and with coal usage in Seaway ships diminishing, the facility was abandoned in the late 1960's. During its day, however, this ship and many of her sisters regularly fueled at Clayton.

This area of upper New York is very scenic, being directly in the famous Thousand Islands of the St. Lawrence River.

Steamer EVERETTON

OWNER:	Scott Misener Steamships Limited
BUILT:	Great Lakes Engineering Works, Ecorse, Michigan—1908
HULL NO.:	38
O. A. DIMENSIONS:	482' × 52'3" × 30'3"
FORMER DATA:	Launched as the bulk freighter M. A. BRADLEY. Converted to an automobile carrier at Great Lakes Engineering Works, River Rouge, Michigan and renamed GRAHAM C. WOODRUFF in 1929. Renamed FRED L. HEWITT (1) in 1941. Re-converted to a bulk freighter at Fairport Machine Shop, Fairport, Ohio in 1942. Given last name in 1947.

Until this bulk freighter was sold for scrap in 1968, it carried a name on its bow for the last twenty-one years of its existence which honored the father of the late Captain R. Scott Misener, founder and president until his death of this owning company and its predecssor firms. The ship is shown in this photograph above Lock Two in the Welland Ship Canal on April 25, 1964.

Mr. Everett Wilson Misener was the namesake of this vessel. He was born on a farm near Lyndon, Ontario on November 30, 1857 and was educated in the local schools. He began working for the Burtis Lumber Company at Brucefield, Ontario in 1875 and moved to Providence Bay, Manitoulin Island, Ontario in 1880 where he acquired timber limits. Mr. Misener worked these lands until selling them to McFadden Lumber Company in 1886 and he joined that firm as assistant mill foreman. In 1891 he associated with Diamond Lumber Company as mill superintendent and retained that capacity until 1916. At this time he moved to Port Dalhousie, Ontario and took up farming. He died in that city on March 23, 1929.

Steamer DONALD F. FAWCETT

OWNER:	Scott Misener Steamships Limited
BUILT:	North of Ireland Shipbuilding Company, Londonderry, Northern Ireland—1924
HULL NO.:	104
O. A. DIMENSIONS:	261' × 42'6" × 20'6"
FORMER DATA:	Launched as CHEMONG. Given last name in 1950.

The canal-sized bulk freight Steamer DONALD F. FAWCETT was one of the several in this fleet which honored long-time Misener organization employees as its namesake. Mr. Donald Francis Fawcett was born on March 22, 1905 at Owen Sound, Ontario.

He attended the local public schools and graduated from the University of Toronto in 1926 with a B.A. degree in commerce and finance. Mr. Fawcett worked in several accounting positions after college prior to joining Colonial Steamships Limited in 1934 as a clerk in the accounting department. Colonial was one of the forerunner firms of the Misener organization.

Mr. Fawcett worked diligently for the steamship line and was named chief accountant in 1948. He had served with the line continuously except for four years during World War II when he was the accounting officer with the Canadian Ordinance Corps. He was active in his last position with the Misener organization when he died at Port Colborne, Ontario on May 1, 1966.

His namesake served until after the St. Lawrence Seaway was opened. It met its fate at the hands of the scrapper's torch at Deseronto, Ontario in 1961. It is shown below above Lock Two of the Welland Ship Canal on November 22, 1956.

Steamer J. G. IRWIN

OWNER:	Scott Misener Steamships Limited
BUILT:	Swan, Hunter & Wigham Richardson Limited, Wallsend-on-Tyne, England—1929
HULL NO.:	1369
O. A. DIMENSIONS:	259' × 43'6" × 20'
FORMER DATA:	Launched as JOHN O. McKELLAR (1). Given last name in 1952.

The canal size bulk freighter on this page was named in honor of Mr. John Gerald Irwin who was born on December 21, 1900 in Londonderry, Ireland. He was educated at Ebrington Public School and Foyle College, graduating in 1921 with background training in engineering.

Mr. Irwin was interested in sailing on the high seas and took up that pursuit following his schooling. Concurrently, he worked towards a Board of Trade marine engineer's certificate and was awarded the certificate in 1923. He continued to sail until 1925 when he moved to Canada and became interested in a career on the Great Lakes. Mr. Irwin took up the operation of a garage in Buffalo, New York in 1926 while he studied further in the field of marine engineering. He also continued sailing.

Concurrently, he took courses at Queen's University, Kingston, Ontario leading to a degree in electrical engineering. He was marine superintendent of the fleet from 1932 until his retirement in 1958. Mr. Irwin died in Port Colborne, Ontario on October 7, 1960.

His namesake was active until 1959 when it was sold for scrap. It is shown below on October 21, 1958 in the Soulanges Canal of the St. Lawrence River system.

Steamer LAKETON (1)

OWNER: Scott Misener Steamships Limited
BUILT: American Ship Building Company, Cleveland, Ohio - 1903
HULL NO.: 416
O. A. DIMENSIONS: 436' x 50' x 28'
FORMER DATA: Launched as SAXONA. Given last name in 1917.

The bulk freight Steamer LAKETON (1) was active on the Great Lakes until being sold for off-lakes use as a grain storage hull at St. John's, Newfoundland in 1965. It was later sunk in the Atlantic Ocean enroute to Italy for scrapping in 1968. It is shown below on May 13, 1961 at Thorold, Ontario in the Welland Ship Canal.

This vessel was part of the Mathews Steamship Company of Toronto, Ontario until bought by the Misener organization. The last owners never saw fit to rename the ship which had a ship name relevant to trading on the Great Lakes. The suffix TON was common to all Mathews Fleet ships and represented the city of the owning company–Toronto, Ontario.

The specific namesake of this vessel was the inland body of water commonly known as a lake. No one lake, but all lakes in general, and the Great Lakes in particular, typify the namesake of this vessel.

This ship was the first Canadian carrier to load iron ore at a United States port after emergency regulations were passed in 1941 to allow foreign ships to carry United States commerce between United States ports. It loaded a cargo of ore at Duluth, Minnesota on July 19, 1941 for the C & P Dock at Cleveland, Ohio.

Steamer J. N. Mc WATTERS (1)

OWNER:	Scott Misener Steamships Limited
BUILT:	Swan, Hunter & Wigham Richardson Limited, Wallsend-on-Tyne, England—1929
HULL NO.:	1393
O. A. DIMENSIONS:	259' × 43'3" × 20'
FORMER DATA:	Launched as LOCKWELL. Renamed J. N. Mc WATTERS (1) in 1944. Given last name in 1960.

This vessel write-up differs from others in this book in that the namesake discussed is not the last name that the vessel officially bore, but the second last. This has been done because the name CARDINAL was only hand-scrawled upon the bow and the ship never ran under that name. Any photograph, therefore, does not show the ship at its best, but as a laid up hull prior to sale for scrap in 1961. The current ship bearing this name when launched in 1960 required that another name be chosen for this ship. Since the vessel was laid-up at Cardinal, Ontario, that was the name given. Cardinal was one of the towns partially relocated when the new St. Lawrence Seaway was opened in 1959.

Mr. John North Mc Watters was the namesake of this ship. He was born on May 23, 1908 at Watford, Ontario and was educated in the public schools and attended Queen's University. He began his business career with Canada Steamship Lines in 1927 and in 1928 worked in the offices of the Canadian National Railways. In March, 1929 he joined the company now known as Scott Misener Steamships Limited as a bookkeeper.

He became assistant secretary of the firm in 1934, secretary and a director in 1942 and vice president in 1945. Mr. Mc Watters achieved the presidency of the firm in the fall of 1970. He was named vice chairman of the Board in 1973. His first namesake is shown in this picture on May 18, 1957 above Lock One of the Welland Ship Canal.

Steamer PAUL MANION

OWNER: Scott Misener Steamships Limited
BUILT: Swan, Hunter & Wigham Richardson Limited, Wallsend-on-Tyne, England—1929
HULL NO.: 1371
O. A. DIMENSIONS: 259' × 43'3" × 20'
FORMER DATA: Launched as C. H. HOUSON. Given last name in 1949.

The bulk freight Steamer PAUL MANION was sold for scrap in 1961 as one of a great number of such size vessels to be withdrawn from service after the opening of the St. Lawrence Seaway.

Mr. Paul Desaulniers Manion was born at Fort William, Ontario on November 20, 1908 and attended McGill University at Montreal, Quebec for two years. While a student, he had a job broadcasting bi-lingual stock market reports on a local radio station. He was an excellent linguist.

In 1928 he decided to take up work as a lumberjack and in 1930 he was busily engaged as a gold prospector. He continued this pursuit until 1933 when he joined Sarnia Steamships Limited in the accounting department. He moved into the traffic department in 1948 and became traffic manager in 1952.

Mr. Manion held the post of traffic manager when he died on May 31, 1962 at Montreal, Quebec. His hobbies included painting in oils, and stamp and coin collecting. He was a well-liked individual, both by members of the Misener organization and many friends in the Great Lakes shipping community.

The Steamer PAUL MANION is shown here on May 14, 1955 above Lock Three of the Welland Ship Canal.

Steamer R. H. MARSHALL

OWNER:	Scott Misener Steamships Limited
BUILT:	Swan, Hunter & Wigham Richardson Limited, Wallsend-on-Tyne, England—1929
HULL NO.:	1375
O. A. DIMENSIONS:	259' × 43'3" × 20'
FORMER DATA:	Launched as JOSEPH P. BURKE. Given last name in 1952.

Mr. Robert Hamilton Marshall was born at Clinton, Ontario on May 8, 1907 and was educated in the public schools and the University of Toronto. Upon graduation he moved to Port Colborne, Ontario in 1935 and operated the Quality Dairy there for several years, until 1938.

Mr. Marshall then worked as truck driver for the Wallace Transport Company before joining the Sarnia Steamships Limited organization, predecessor company to Scott Misener Steamships Limited, in the accounting department in 1938.

He was made assistant traffic manager of the fleet in 1952 and traffic manager in June, 1962. Ill health forced him to retire in 1963 from this position and he died on December 31, 1965 at Port Colborne, Ontario.

Mr. Marshall enjoyed curling as his favorite sport. He was active as a member of the Welland Curling Club and several other civic organizations. His namesake was sold for scrap in 1961. It is seen in the photograph below upbound in the Welland Ship Canal in 1959. The vessel is laden with grain for Montreal, Quebec. This is one of the few good photographs taken of this canaller underway.

Steamer MATHEWSTON

OWNER: Scott Misener Steamships Limited
BUILT: Port Arthur Shipbuilding Company, Port Arthur, Ontario—1922
HULL NO.: 47
O. A. DIMENSIONS: 550' × 58'3" × 31'
FORMER DATA: Launched as MATHEWSTON. Renamed RALPH S. MISENER (2) in 1954. Given last name, for the second time, in 1967.

The bulk freight Steamer MATHEWSTON was one of two ships in the modern fleet of Scott Misener Steamships which were originally built for the Mathews Steamship Company of Toronto, Ontario. This vessel was active on the Great Lakes until its sale for overseas scrapping in the spring of 1970. It is shown in this photograph below the Iroquois Lock of the St. Lawrence Seaway system on July 28, 1968.

The specific namesake of this bulk freighter was Mr. Alfred Ernest Mathews who became a second-generation shipowner of the Great Lakes. He was born in Toronto, Ontario on April 29, 1871 and was educated in the public schools. He began his business career at the age of fifteen when he went to work for Mr. James Carruthers and Company, grain brokers. In 1886 he founded A. E. Mathews and Company.

The *TON* suffix in the ship name was a common suffix in the fleet and is believed to have always referred to the city of Toronto, Ontario, which this fleet's operating headquarters.

Steamer F. W. MOORE

OWNER:	Scott Misener Steamships Limited
BUILT:	Smith's Dock Company Limited, South Bank-on-Tees, England—1929
HULL NO.:	869
O. A. DIMENSIONS:	258' × 43'9" × 20'6"
FORMER DATA:	Launched as GEORGE L. EATON (2). Given last name in 1955.

The Steamer F. W. MOORE was sold for scrap in 1961 after the opening of the St. Lawrence Seaway had proven that ships of this old canal size were no longer competitive in Great Lakes bulk cargo trades.

The namesake of this bulk freighter is Mr. Francis William "Dinty" Moore who was born at Toronto, Ontario on October 29, 1900. He graduated from St. Michael's College in 1918 and began playing amateur hockey for the Toronto Canoe Club team in 1919 and 1920.

In 1921 he moved to Port Colborne, Ontario and worked in the bag department of Maple Leaf Mills Limited until going to work at the National Harbours Board elevator in 1922 as a timekeeper. He then served in various jobs at Canada Cement Company in Port Colborne until joining the Milwaukee Athletic Club hockey team for the 1923-24 season. On August 1, 1924 he rejoined National Harbours Board at Port Colborne, working on the distribution line. He became assistant superintendent in 1930 and superintendent in 1959. Mr. Moore moved to Montreal, Quebec, in 1962 as general superintendent of all Montreal elevators for the National Harbours Board and retired on July 31, 1966. His namesake is shown on April 26, 1958 in the Welland Ship Canal.

Steamer PICTON (3)

OWNER:	Scott Misener Steamships Limited
BUILT:	Smith's Dock Company, Limited, South Bank-on-Tees, England—1929
HULL NO.:	868
O. A. DIMENSIONS:	258' × 43'9" × 20'6"
FORMER DATA:	Launched as MEADCLIFFE HALL. Given last name in 1955.

The canal-sized bulk freight Steamer PICTON was named after one of the most scenic spots on the semi-inland waters of Lake Ontario. Picton, Ontario is the seat of Prince Edward County and is located on Picton Bay, an arm of the Bay of Quinte on the Canadian National Railways.

Today, this is a port of major iron ore shipments of the Marmoraton Mining Company, a subsidiary of Bethlehem Steel Corporation. The largest ships capable of navigating the Seaway regularly call here to load iron ore, most of it destined for Buffalo, New York.

Picton was founded in 1786 following the arrival of the Loyalists led by Messrs. Andrew and Henry Johnson. It was first known as Hallowell, but was later named by the local Church of England rector in honor of Sir Thomas Picton, a major-general in the Napoleanic Wars. The settlement was incorporated in 1837 and is now the hub of the county's business life. In addition to the iron ore shipments noted above, the locale has been the scene of shipments of manufactured cement by the Canada Cement LaFarge Limited for many years.

The Steamer PICTON is shown in the photograph below at Lock 22, Farrans Point, of the old St. Lawrence Canal System on October 26, 1956. It remained in the Misener fleet until being sold for off-lakes use in 1959.

Steamer QUEENSTON

          OWNER: Scott Misener Steamships Limited
          BUILT: Swan, Hunter & Wigham Richardson Limited,
                         Sunderland, England—1927
       HULL NO.:   1311
O. A. DIMENSIONS: 261' × 43'3" × 20'
    FORMER DATA: Launched as LACHINEDOC (1). Given last name
                         in 1947.

Queenston, Ontario is the namesake town of this vessel. It is a small community located on the west shore of the Niagara River, below Niagara Falls, Ontario in Lincoln County. The town name is believed to have originated from Governor Simcoe's regiment, the Queen's Rangers, which was stationed at Niagara Landing in 1792. This is the current site of the town.

Founded by Mr. Robert Hamilton, Queenston was the center of hotly contested territory in the War of 1812. General Sir Isaac Brock's monument is located in Queenston Heights Park while nearby is the site of Brock's death and Vrooman's battery. Among historic buildings in Queenston are the homes of the Hamilton Family, Laura Secord and William Lyon Mackenzie.

The canal-sized bulk freight Steamer QUEENSTON is shown below in the Galops Canal on October 31, 1957. The vessel was decommissioned in 1961 and was taken to Bois Blanc Island, Ontario at the mouth of the Detroit River where cabins were cut away and the hull sunk to form an extension to the ferry dock on the island. The hull form is visible today to ships passing upbound in the Amherstburg Channel and to visitors to the Bob-Lo Island amusement park.

The Steamer QUEENSTON sailed from Sunderland, England on May 5, 1927 light for Montreal, Quebec on its maiden voyage.

Steamer TRENTON

OWNER:	Scott Misener Steamships Limited
BUILT:	Smith's Dock Company, Limited, South Bank-on-Tees, England—1927
HULL NO.:	832
O. A. DIMENSIONS:	261' × 43'3" × 20'
FORMER DATA:	Launched as WALTER B. REYNOLDS (2). Given last name in 1955.

This canal size bulk freighter was named in honor of Trenton, Ontario, a town of 14,000 population located in Hastings County, Ontario on the Bay of Quinte, Lake Ontario.

Trenton was first settled in 1790 with the influx of people to that end of Lake Ontario. Originally, it was called Trent Port, then Trent Town, and finally, Trenton. It is the site of the southern end of the famous and beautiful Trent Canal which winds its way north and westward towards scenic territory. Not far from Trenton, the Murray Canal serves small craft in cutting through the Prince Edward County isthmus, affording quick access to Lake Ontario.

This port used to be quite active in receipt of coal and other lake-borne commodities, but today is very seldom used as a Great Lakes port by large ships. Among the town's manufactured products are structural steel, machinery, lumber, paper, creosote, copperage, clothing and flour.

The Steamer TRENTON is shown below approaching Lock One of the Welland Ship Canal at Port Weller, Ontario on November 5, 1955. It is upbound with a cargo of iron ore for Cleveland, Ohio delivery from the port of Seven Islands, Quebec. This ship continued to exist in this fleet until being sold for scrap in 1961.

Steamer J. S. WALTON

OWNER:	Scott Misener Steamships Limited
BUILT:	Smith's Dock Company Limited, South Bank-on-Tees, England—1928
HULL NO.:	841
O. A. DIMENSIONS:	258'6" × 44' × 20'6"
FORMER DATA:	Launched as ROCKCLIFFE HALL (1). Given last name in 1955.

Mr. James Stuart Walton is the namesake of this canal-size bulk freighter. He was born at Ladysmith, Ontario on March 10, 1898 and was educated in the public schools.

He began working as a deckhand on the Steamer ROSEDALE in 1916 and worked his way up through the ranks, becoming first mate on the Steamer GLENBRAE in 1922. He took the required courses and wrote for his master's papers and took his first command in the Steamer EDWARD L. STRONG in 1925.

He joined the Misener organization in 1932 as mate on the Steamer BERRYTON and assumed command of the Steamer PORTWELL in the fleet in 1935. He remained a sailing captain until coming ashore in 1954 as assistant marine superintendent. Captain Walton became marine superintendent in 1962 and held that post upon his retirement on June 30, 1966.

It is interesting to note that Captain Walton brought out each of the first three modern ships in the fleet in 1951, 1952, and 1954. He enjoys retirement and is busily occupied at Port Colborne, Ontario. His namesake was sold for off-lakes use in 1959 but never saw service off the lakes. Instead, this ship was scrapped at Hamilton, Ontario in 1961.

The Steamer J. S. WALTON is shown below in the Galops Canal of the old St. Lawrence River waterway on October 25, 1956.

Steamer FRANK WILKINSON

OWNER:	Scott Misener Steamships Limited
BUILT:	Barclay, Curle & Company Limited, Glasgow, Scotland—1929
HULL NO.:	635
O. A. DIMENSIONS:	259' × 43'3" × 20'
FORMER DATA:	Launched as FAIRRIVER. Given last name in 1944.

The bulk freight steamer shown here took Mr. Frank Wilkinson as its namesake. He was born on February 21, 1899 at Superior, Wisconsin and moved to Midland, Ontario in 1905 when his father became general manager of the Midland Shipbuilding Company. He received his education in Midland and at Osgoode Hall Law School, graduating in 1920. He was admitted to the Bar of Ontario the same year.

Mr. Wilkinson joined the firm run by Colonel Towers at Sarnia, Ontario in 1920, but moved to Toronto, Ontario in 1922 when Col. Towers joined the firm of Galt, Gooderham & Towers. He left that law firm in 1926 to join Wright & McMillan at Toronto and stayed on through his death. He became a partner in 1939. By the time of his death at Toronto, Ontario on December 27, 1950, the firm name had become McMillan, Binch, Wilkinson, Berry & Wright.

This law firm acted as general counsel for Scott Misener Steamships Limited and its predecessor companies since their formation. Mr. Wilkinson was a director of the line and also its chief counsel. Other members of the firm were similarly honored with namesakes on the Great Lakes through the years.

His namesake was sold for scrap in 1959 and is shown in this photograph at Port Weller, Ontario in October, 1953.

Steamer H. L. WYATT

OWNER:	Scott Misener Steamships Limited
BUILT:	Swan, Hunter & Wigham Richardson Limited, Wallsend-on-Tyne, England—1929
HULL NO.:	1391
O. A. DIMENSIONS:	259' × 43'3" × 20'
FORMER DATA:	Launched as PORTWELL. Renamed LT. JOHN MISENER in 1944. Given last name in 1954.

This canal-sized bulk freighter was sold for scrap in 1960, one year after the opening of the large St. Lawrence Seaway.

Namesake of this vessel is Mr. Harold Lynn Wyatt who was born at Sault Ste. Marie, Ontario on May 23, 1906. He was educated at Sault Ste. Marie Collegiate and began his career as an office boy in the general manager's office at the Spanish River Pulp & Paper Mills at Sault Ste. Marie. This company was later absorbed by the Abitibi Paper Company Limited and Mr. Wyatt moved to the Montreal, Quebec office of the firm, working there from 1927 until the headquarters was removed to Toronto, Ontario in 1930.

He remained with Abitibi until 1933 and had worked in the accounting, traffic and purchasing departments. In 1933 he joined the Rochester & Pittsburgh Coal Company (Canada) Limited as office manager. He became traffic manager in 1937, general traffic manager in 1947 and was elected vice president of traffic in 1958. He held this post on retirement on May 31, 1970.

The Steamer H. L. WYATT is shown here while upbound, light at Thorold, Ontario on April 26, 1958. The ship commenced on its maiden voyage May 24, 1929 from Wallsend-on Tyne, England, light to Montreal, Quebec.

Steamer WHEATON

OWNER:	Misener Holdings Limited
BUILT:	Smith's Dock Company, Limited, South Bank-on-Tees, England—1928
HULL NO.:	840
O. A. DIMENSIONS:	259' × 43'9" × 21'
FORMER DATA:	Launched as WESTCLIFFE HALL (1). Given last name in 1955.

The canal-sized bulk freight Steamer WHEATON was an operating unit of Scott Misener Steamships Limited but was the lone vessel in this particular subsidiary for internal policy reasons. It is shown below on May 4, 1957 below Lock Four of the Welland Ship Canal. It continued in the fleet until being sold for scrap in 1963.

This vessel had the theme suffix on its name—"TON." This was a carry forward from the Mathews Steamship Company days when all vessels bore that name ending. The specific namesake of the ship was the grain wheat. Throughout its history this fleet has been closely identified with the Canadian wheat trade. When a new name was being selected in 1955, management decided to honor that grain by this ship name.

Wheat is the most valuable of all the cereal grains and is grown in terms of hundreds of millions of bushels annually in Canada and the United States. This grain was introduced to North America, in Mexico, in 1530 and was first planted in New England in 1602. Many varieties of wheat are grown today. The most widely harvested include red wheat, white wheat, spring wheat and durum.

Steamer ROYALTON (1)

OWNER: Misener Transportation Limited
BUILT: Collingwood Shipbuilding Company, Limited
Collingwood, Ontario - 1924
HULL NO.: 73
O. A. DIMENSIONS: 550' x 58'3" x 31'

The bulk freight Steamer ROYALTON (1) is shown in the photograph below while downbound in the West Neebish Channel, St. Mary's River with a cargo of iron ore for Indiana Harbor, Indiana delivery on July 2, 1977. This ship name remained unchanged since it was built for the Mathews Steamship Company. That fleet had a common suffix "TON" for all its ship names. It is believed this was done to honor the headquarters city of the fleet, that being Toronto, Ontario.

The prefix in this ship name was in reference to the fact that when it was built it was the Canadian Queen of the Lakes, so far as modern equipment and hull form were concerned. It capped the fleet's "ROYAL" achievement on the Great Lakes.

The Steamer ROYALTON (1) was the only ship built in Canadian Great Lakes yards in 1924. With a carrying capacity of 12,200 gross tons at mid-summer draft, it was a hard-working, profitable vessel for over fifty years, but economics of the late 1970's caught up with her. After only a very brief period of service in 1979, then idleness until November, it was sold for scrap late in 1979.

Motor Vessel MOBIL ALBANY

OWNER:	Mobil Oil Corporation
BUILT:	United Dry Docks, Incorporated, Mariners Harbor, New York—1934
HULL NO.:	823
O. A. DIMENSIONS:	289'3" × 40' × 18'
FORMER DATA:	Launched as PLATTSBURGH SOCONY. Lengthened 29'4" and given new midbody at Avondale Marine Ways, Incorporated, Avondale, Louisiana in 1956. Given last name in 1962.

The New York State Barge Canal-type tank Motor Vessel MOBIL ALBANY continued in use until being sold for scrap in 1968. It honored the owning company in the first word of the ship name and a primary port at the eastern end of the New York State Barge Canal in the second word of the name. Ships of this fleet were given common first names in 1962 to identify them with the other product names and services of this company.

The specific namesake of this unit was the city of Albany, capital of the state of New York. Albany is situated on a hill on the west bank of the Hudson River. It is a deep-water port and a major trans-shipping point for railroads, trucks, barges and saltwater vessels.

Albany was visited by Mr. Henry Hudson in 1609, ending his exploration of the river that later bore his name. In 1614 the Dutch built Fort Nassau at the site and, in 1624, they built Fort Orange. This fort was captured by the British in 1664 and they renamed it Albany.

Motor Vessel MOBIL CHICAGO

OWNER: Mobil Oil Corporation
BUILT: Todd-Houston Shipbuilding Corporation, Houston, Texas – 1953
HULL NO.: 117
O. A. DIMENSIONS: 300' x 43'3" x 19'3"
FORMER DATA: Launched as CHICAGO SOCONY. Given last name in 1962.

The tanker Motor Vessel MOBIL CHICAGO's name was changed when the Socony portion of the owning firm's title was corporately changed. The "MOBIL" in this ship name identified it as a part of the worldwide Mobil Oil fleet.

Chicago, Illinois was the specific namesake for this tanker. It is widely known as the greatest transportation center in the world and has many other titles to its credit. It is the world's largest grain market with trading headquartered in the Board of Trade. It is also the Midwest finance center and its O'Hare International Airport is the world's busiest.

The Port of Chicago, if one includes the lower Lake Michigan coastline port areas, handles nearly 48,000,000 tons of shipments and receipts annually. Steel making and oil refining are very large commercial factors in the industrial complex at Chicago.

The city was founded in 1803 and was incorporated in 1837. This vessel was active on the Great Lakes until late 1973 when these owners took her to the East Coast for off-lakes use.

Motor Vessel MOBIL NEW YORK

OWNER: Mobil Oil Corporation
BUILT: United Dry Dock, Incorporated, Richmond, New York—1934
HULL NO.: 824
O. A. DIMENSIONS: 289'4" × 40' × 18'
FORMER DATA: Launched as POUGHKEEPSIE SOCONY. Lengthened 29'4" and given new midbody at Avondale Marine Ways, Incorporated, Avondale, Louisiana in 1957. Renamed MOBIL NEW YORK in 1962.

The tank Motor Vessel MOBIL NEW YORK is shown in the above photograph in the Welland Ship Canal while upbound for Lake Erie with a full cargo of gasoline for Cleveland, Ohio delivery. This vessel was sold very late in 1971 for off-lakes use and was subsequently renamed CAPTAIN SAM.

While on the Great Lakes this vessel honored these owners with its name derived from the corporate firm name, and the fact that those corporate headquarters are located in New York City.

Mobil Oil Corporation ranks as one of the major producing, refining and marketing organizations in the United States and it engages prominently in the world petroleum trades. Indeed, the company as a whole owns a large number of ships and barges on the high seas and the inland waterways.

Originally incorporated in New York on August 10, 1882, this firm acquired Vacuum Oil Company in 1931 and a number of other firms in the intervening period. The name was changed to Mobil Oil Corporation on May 17, 1966 from Socony-Vacuum Oil Company, Incorporated.

Motor Vessel BELVOIR (2)

OWNER:	Mohawk Navigation Company Limited
BUILT:	E. B. McGee Limited, Port Colborne, Ontario—1955
HULL NO.:	1
O. A. DIMENSIONS:	349' × 43'6" × 25'6"
FORMER DATA:	Lengthened 90' and deepened 3'6" at Canadian Vickers, Limited, Montreal, Quebec in 1959.

The Motor Vessel BELVOIR had the distinction of being the first vessel, and only vessel to date, built at Port Colborne, Ontario. These builders have since gone out of business. The ship continued active on the Great Lakes until being sold for off-lakes use in 1968. The ship is shown below passing Welland, Ontario on the Welland Ship Canal, on December 3, 1966.

The name Belvoir was used on a new ship built for these owners in 1925 and when it came time to christen this ship, they reached into their past for re-use of this ship name. The name stems from England where Mr. Robert de Belvoir founded and dedicated the Belvoir Priory to the Virgin Mary in 1545. It was of the Order of Black Monks of St. Albans and was in Leicestershire County. Not long after, Belvoir Castle was erected and became a repository for historical records.

Belvoir Castle is located on the summit of a hill nearby the Priory. By permission of His Grace the Duke of Rutland I, the library of the castle was opened June 30, 1869 to selective public examination of more than 4,000 manuscripts, most dating from the 12th, 13th, 14th, and 15th centuries.

Because of the historical significance of Belvoir Castle and Belvoir Priory, the *Pindarick Ode upon Belvoir-Castle, the Seat of the Earls of Rutland* was written in the year 1679. The Ode contains sixty-six verses.

Barge ALFRED KRUPP

OWNER: Mohawk Navigation Company Limited
BUILT: Chicago Shipbuilding Company, Chiago, Illinois—1896.
HULL NO.: 24
O. A. DIMENSIONS: 365' × 44'3" × 27'3"

After running in regular service for many years, the bulk freight Barge ALFRED KRUPP was relegated to storage grain usage and was finally sold for sinking as a breakwater in 1967 and was sold for scrap late in 1973.

This was another of the many barges built during the 1890's that took the name of a famous steel pioneer as its namesake. Because of the early significance of these men, their names prevailed on the hulls until they were scrapped.

Mr. Alfred Krupp was born at Essen, Germany on April 26, 1812 and was educated in the local schools. He was heir to the famous Krupp steel works at the age of fourteen when his father died. His father left him the secret of making high-quality cast steel that he had developed and the son literally took over the operation at his tender age. In 1830 he enlarged production to include manufacture of steel rolls and also designed modern machinery for household goods production.

In 1851 he exhibited the largest steel ingot ever cast at the World Exhibition in London, England. It weighed 4,300 pounds. His works grew fantastically and was called "The Arsenal of the Reich" as a result of its superior weapons production in 1871. Mr. Krupp took active part in civic and welfare activities of his workers and was beloved by them when he died at Essen, Germany on July 14, 1887.

This barge is shown above underway, under tow, downbound in the Detroit River on July 10, 1960.

Steamer F. V. MASSEY

OWNER:	Mohawk Navigation Company Limited
BUILT:	Smith's Dock Company, Limited, South Bank-on-Tees, England—1929
HULL NO.:	873
O. A. DIMENSIONS	259' × 43'9" × 20'6"

This steamer was named in honor of a banker who was instrumental in arranging financing of the ship when Captain J. B. Foote sought such help in the late 1920's.

Mr. Frederic Vernon Massey was born in Montreal, Quebec on October 27, 1882 and was educated at Feller Institute, Grand Linge, Quebec. Upon graduation he entered the employ of The Bank of Ottawa in June, 1899 as a junior clerk in the Montreal office. His first transfer took him to Shawinigan Falls in December, 1903 and the following June he was moved to the Ottawa office. He was appointed accountant at Pembroke in December, 1906 and his first managerial job was at Maxville, Ontario, dating from December, 1908. In May, 1911 he was appointed manager at Alexandria and in Decmber, 1915 he moved to the head office as an inspector.

In April, 1920 Mr. Massey was appointed manager of The Bank of Nova Scotia at the King and Victoria Streets Branch in Toronto, Ontario. This is one of the Bank's more important locations to this day. He was manager of the branch until his retirement on January 31, 1940. Mr. Massey died at Toronto, Ontario on November 1, 1966 and outlived his namesake.

This bulk freighter was sold for scrap in 1961. It is shown in this photograph below Lock One of the Soulanges Canal at Cascades on October 22, 1959.

Steamer MOHAWK DEER

OWNER:	Mohawk Navigation Company Limited
BUILT:	F. W. Wheeler & Company, West Bay City, Michigan—1896
HULL NO.:	112
O. A. DIMENSIONS:	470'3" × 46'6" × 28'
FORMER DATA:	Launched as L. C. WALDO. Lengthened 72' at Craig Shipbuilding Company, Toledo, Ohio in 1905. Renamed RIVERTON in 1916. Given last name in 1944.

The bulk freight Steamer MOHAWK DEER was sold for scrap in 1967 and was subsequently towed across the Atlantic Ocean for demolition. The scrappers were foiled, however, as this ship was wrecked enroute.

When the Mohawk Navigation Company Limited acquired this vessel in 1944, they decided to use the first word of the corporate title in the ship name. Thus, *MOHAWK* refers to the owning company in this name.

The second word of the ship name came into being because when the ship was acquired it had a reputation as being a fast steamer. Since the deer is a fleet-footed animal, the owners chose that logical connection in deciding upon the second word of the ship name. It proved, however, not to be as fast a steamer as originally believed. Nonetheless, the name remained on the bow until the end of the vessel's life.

Several close calls with disaster accompanied this vessel during its lifetime, including being nearly broken in two at least twice by storms or accidents. During its career on the Great Lakes, millions of bushels of grain were transported in its holds. The vessel is shown in this photograph in the St. Mary's River on July 31, 1962.

Motor Vessel CAPTAIN C. D. SECORD

OWNER:	Mohawk Navigation Company Limited
BUILT:	Superior Shipbuilding Company, West Superior, Wisconsin—1900
HULL NO.:	144
O. A. DIMENSIONS:	557' × 50' × 33'6"
FORMER DATA:	Launched as CHARLES R. VAN HISE. Deepened 4'6" at Lake Shipbuilding Company, Buffalo, New York in 1918. Cut into two sections and rolled on shipsides at Buffalo Dry Dock Company, Buffalo, New York in 1918. Renamed A.E.R. SCHNEIDER in 1919. Reassembled and lengthened 96' at Great Lakes Engineering Works, Ashtabula, Ohio in 1920. Renamed S. B. WAY (2) in 1931. Renamed J. M. OAG in 1936. Given last name in 1936.

This bulk freighter was the largest commandeered by the United States Government in 1918 for salt water service. By the time it was cut into two sections for the trip to saltwater, World War I was over and the ship never saw ocean service. After its rebuilding it remained active on the Great Lakes until being sold for scrap in 1968. It is shown in this picture in the Welland Ship Canal on October 22, 1955.

Namesake of this vessel was Captain Carleton Dace Secord who was born in Niagara-on-the-Lake, Ontario on February 11, 1857. He began sailing in 1874 as a lamp boy on the Steamer JAPAN and progressed through the ranks in both the Anchor Line and American Barge Line. His first command was the Steamer JOSEPH L. COLBY on May 10, 1899.

Captain Secord became superintendent of freight for Canada Steamship Lines at Toronto, Ontario in April, 1914. In 1922 he became partners with Mr. Robert A. Campbell in forming International Waterways Corporation with offices at Cleveland, Ohio. He was an officer of this firm on his death at Cleveland on May 7, 1938.

Steamer SIR THOMAS SHAUGHNESSY

OWNER:	Mohawk Navigation Company, Limited
BUILT:	Detroit Shipbuilding Company, Wyandotte, Michigan—1906
HULL NO.:	164
O. A. DIMENSIONS:	500' × 52'3" × 30'

Namesake of this bulk freighter, which was sold for scrap in 1969, was Sir Thomas George Shaughnessy who was born at Milwaukee, Wisconsin on October 6, 1853. He was educated in the public schools and began working for the Milwaukee & St. Paul Railway in their purchasing department in 1869.

Mr. Shaughnessy became general storekeeper of the Chicago, Milwaukee & St. Paul Railway in 1879 and served that system until 1882. In that year he joined the Canadian Pacific Railway. He was general purchasing agent there until 1884 and then progressed into management ranks. By 1885 he was assistant general manager and from 1889 to 1891 served as assistant to the president. He was named vice president and a director in 1891 and took over as the railroad's third president on June 12, 1898. He was knighted in 1901, again recognized by the Crown in 1907 and was created Baron Shaughnessy in 1916.

A quote in his time said, "As an operator of railways (he) probably has not a superior on this continent, which is equivalent to saying that he has not an equal in this line in the world." He was active on the boards of a number of companies and was considered among less than a dozen men as the basis of Canadian finance. Lord Shaughnessy died in Montreal. Quebec on December 9, 1923 and retained the railroad's presidency at that time.

The ship is shown on October 29, 1966 in the Welland Ship Canal.

Steamer CHARLES DICK

OWNER: National Sand and Material Company, Limited
BUILT: Collingwood Shipyards,
Collingwood, Ontario—1922
HULL NO.: 71
O. A. DIMENSIONS: 258'6" × 43'3" × 20'

The self-unloading sandsucker Steamer CHARLES DICK is named for Mr. Charles Dick of Welland, Ontario, whose father headed this company when the vessel was constructed. Mr. Dick had the unusual pleasure, for such a young boy, of christening his namesake. He was six years old at the time.

Mr. Dick was born on February 16, 1916 at Welland, Ontario and graduated from the University of Toronto in 1939 with a B.A.Sc. degree. He enlisted in the Air Force and served during some of World War II. In 1942 he formed and became president of Dick Construction and Engineering Company Limited in Welland, Ontario. The firm is active in the Niagara Frontier and west-central portions of Ontario. Mr. Dick died August 4, 1977 at St. Catharines, Ontario.

When this ship was commissioned, it was the largest of its kind on the Great Lakes. It is still unique in the form of machinery it has onboard. The cargo hold is divided into two large hoppers, each capable of holding 2,000 cubic yards of sand and gravel. A specially fitted "A" frame device runs the length of the hoppers and is used for unloading onto a short boom for overside discharge. It is shown above at Sandusky, Ohio on September 5, 1971. The vessel was sold for scrap late in 1976.

Steamer CARLE C. CONWAY

OWNER: National Steel Corporation
BUILT: Chicago Shipbuilding Company, Chicago, Illinois—1907
HULL NO.: 75
O. A. DIMENSIONS: 552' × 56' × 31'
FORMER DATA: Launched as WILLIAM A. HAWGOOD. Renamed R. L. AGASSIZ in 1911. Given last name in 1934.

Shown here downbound at Port Huron, Michigan on June 18, 1960, the Steamer CARLE C. CONWAY was named in honor of Mr. Carle Cotter Conway who was born at Oak Park, Illinois on December 19, 1877. He graduated from the Sheffield Scientific School, Yale University in 1899 and began that year with the W. W. Kimball Company in Chicago, Illinois.

The Kimball firm was involved with making pianos. He remained in that employ until moving to New York, New York in 1908 where he became associated with Hallet & Davis Piano Company as vice president and treasurer. He formed a company of his own called Conway Company of New Jersey and headed it concurrently upon going with the Continental Can Company in 1917 as a member of the executive committee. In 1923 he was vice president of Continental Can and was elected president of the firm in 1926. Mr. Conway became chairman of the board in 1934 and continued in that capacity until his death.

He was a director of many national concerns including the National Steel Corporation. His namesake was sold for scrap in 1963.

Steamer EDMUND W. MUDGE

OWNER:	National Steel Corporation
BUILT:	American Ship Building Company, Lorain, Ohio—1911
HULL NO.:	389
O. A. DIMENSIONS:	524' × 54' × 30'
FORMER DATA:	Launched as QUINCY A. SHAW. Given last name in 1931.

Mr. Edmund Webster Mudge who was born at Philadelphia, Pennsylvania on January 12, 1870 is the namesake of this bulk freighter. He was educated at Friend's School and Woods Town Academy before beginning work in Pittsburgh, Pennsylvania in 1887 in the iron and steel business.

In 1905 he founded Edmund W. Mudge & Company. This enterprise became prominent in the dealings of the pig iron and coke business. Mr. Mudge was president of this firm from 1905 until it was dissolved in the mid-1920's.

Among his positions was the vice presidency of National Steel Corporation who honored him when this ship took his name. The vessel was sold for scrap on the Great Lakes in 1963 after many years of profitable service.

This steamer was the second to be built on the Great Lakes on the Isherwood longitudinal design system. Mr. J. R. Isherwood came to Lorain, Ohio from his native England to witness the launch on May 17, 1911. The vessel made its maiden voyage with coal from Toledo, Ohio to Duluth, Minnesota on June 19, 1911. It is shown below in the St. Mary's River on August 29, 1953.

Steamer NATIONAL TRADER

OWNER: National Steel Corporation
BUILT: American Ship Building Company, Lorain, Ohio – 1920
HULL NO.: 778
O. A. DIMENSIONS: 600' x 60' x 32'
FORMER DATA: Launched as H. H. PORTER. Renamed YOUNGSTOWN in 1925. Renamed WALTER E. WATSON in 1957. Given last name in 1974.

The bulk freight Steamer NATIONAL TRADER sailed on its maiden voyage September 3, 1920, leaving Lorain, Ohio light to load iron ore at Two Harbors, Minnesota. It remained in operation in the bulk cargo trades until the end of 1973 when it was sold to these owners. Their purpose in acquiring the ship was to convert it to a crane vessel. This did not happen due to a change in the economics in their movement of steel coils. The vessel lay idle at South Chicago, Illinois until sold for scrap in April, 1976 and never ran under this name. It is shown in this rare photograph at Chicago on August 6, 1974.

Namesake of this ship was the original intended purpose of the acquisition, that is, to be a TRADER for NATIONAL Steel. The concept in 1973 was to use this vessel between Detroit, Michigan and the firm's new plant at Burns Harbor, Indiana in the transportation of coils and other finished products. Cranes to put aboard the ship were not available then so the conversion was postponed. By 1976 it became apparent that the economics of such a conversion were adverse.

National Steel Corporation is America's third largest producer of raw steel and was incorporated on November 7, 1929.

Steamer GOLDEN SABLE

OWNER: Neal Petroleum Company Limited
BUILT: Furness Shipbuilding Company, Limited, Haverton Hill-on-Tees, England—1930
HULL NO.: 170
O. A. DIMENSIONS: 256'3" × 43' × 18'
FORMER DATA: Launched as ACADIALITE. Renamed IMPERIAL CORNWALL in 1947. Given last name in 1971.

The tank Steamer GOLDEN SABLE existed for only a short while under this name and, in fact, made only one trip under this name before it was determined that she was unfit for the carriage of "clean" petroleum products after having been in use in the transportation of crude oil for so many years.

This vessel was sold in May, 1971 by Imperial Oil Limited to Penn Shipping Limited of Guelph, Ontario. She made two trips for this company as IMPERIAL CORNWALL then laid-up. In July, 1971 the ship was sold at auction to this firm which is allied with the Golden Eagle Refining Company whose new refinery at St. Romuald, Quebec was commissioned in the summer of 1971. The ship made one round trip from Quebec City, Quebec to Buffalo, New York as GOLDEN SABLE and is shown in the above photograph just prior to making that round-trip voyage. It was her last and the ship was sold for off-lakes non-transportation use in 1972.

This ship had a two-part namesake. The word GOLDEN in the ship name referred to the oil company noted above. The second word, SABLE, referred to Cape Sable Island, Nova Scotia which is located at the southernmost tip of that province.

Steamer CANOPUS

OWNER:	Nicholson Transit Company
BUILT:	Great Lakes Engineering Works, St. Clair, Michigan—1905
HULL NO.:	11
O. A. DIMENSIONS:	484' × 50' × 28'
FORMER DATA:	Launched as the bulk freighter GEORGE H. RUSSEL. Given last name in 1913. Converted to a combination bulk freighter and automobile carrier at Nicholson Terminal and Dock Company, River Rouge, Michigan in 1946. Converted to an automobile carrier at Nicholson Terminal and Dock Company, River Rouge, Michigan in 1950.

This veteran ship was sold for scrap in 1961 when it became apparent that the dwindling business of carrying new automobiles across Lake Erie could not support its further operation. The vessel is shown above at Ecorse, Michigan on August 24, 1951.

At the time this ship was sold out of the Gilchrist fleet and into Interlake Steamship Company, the new name was given in a theme of vessel names having to do with heavenly bodies. Canopus was one of these.

Canopus is the principle star in the constellation Carina, a part of the older constellation Argo Navis. It is never visible above 37 degrees latitude and is believed to be in excess of 100 light years distant from Earth. Canopus is a yellow-white star which is the second brightest in the sky.

Steamer CHARLES DONNELLY

OWNER: Nicholson Transit Company
BUILT: Detroit Dry Dock Company, Wyandotte, Michigan - 1898
HULL NO.: 128
O. A. DIMENSIONS: 410' x 47' x 28'
FORMER DATA: Launched as the package freighter TROY (2). Given last name in 1926. Converted to a combination bulk and automobile carrier at Nicholson Engineering Works, Ecorse, Michigan in 1946. Converted to an automobile carrier at Nicholson Engineering Works, Ecorse, Michigan in 1948.

This automobile carrying vessel was named in honor of Mr. Charles Donnelly who was born at Wisconsin Rapids, Wisconsin on November 9, 1869 and who was a graduate of George Washington University in 1896 with a Ll.B. degree.

He began his career as a railroad man in 1903 when he joined the legal department of the Northern Pacific Railway Company at St. Paul, Minnesota. He had previously served in partnership with Mr. William A. Lancaster in Minneapolis, Minnesota after having passed the Bar in 1896. Mr. Donnelly worked at the Helena, Montana office of the railway until 1908 when he transferred back to St. Paul and was named assistant general counsel and served in that post until 1918.

He was general solicitor until 1919 and was then named executive vice president in 1920. Later that year he became the line's president and served until his death in St. Paul, Minnesota on September 4, 1939. He was also an officer or director of affiliated railway interests and of several banks. His namesake was sold for scrap in 1961 and is shown here in the Detroit River, upbound for another load of autos, on August 25, 1953.

Steamer FELLOWCRAFT (2)

OWNER:	Nicholson Transit Company
BUILT:	Detroit Shipbuilding Company, Wyandotte, Michigan—1903
HULL NO.:	152
O. A. DIMENSIONS:	255' × 41'2" × 18'9"
FORMER DATA:	Launched as ALBERT M. MARSHALL. Renamed BRIGNOGAN in 1921. Given last name in 1929.

The canal-sized bulk freight Steamer FELLOWCRAFT carried on a name originally given to a former wooden bulk carrier in the Nicholson fleet. Captain William Nicholson owned a ship of this name when he started out in business. It was a good vessel for him and when he acquired this ship in 1929, he desired to have the ship name carried on.

Background of this name is interesting and not obvious, for it was derived from two last names of famous Americans who were prominent in Michigan history and close personal friends as well. Messrs. Henry Wadsworth Longfellow and Henry Rowe Schoolcraft were these men. The vessel name combined the "fellow" from Longfellow's name and the "craft" from Schoolcraft's name.

Longfellow's *Song of Hiawatha* was based on Schoolcraft's collection of Indian lore when it was published in 1855. Mr. Schoolcraft was an explorer, writer and lecturer, having made extensive expeditions into Michigan territory in 1820 and beyond.

The Steamer FELLOWCRAFT is shown below while upbound, light, near Amherstburg, Ontario on July 20, 1952.

Steamer IRONWOOD

OWNER: Nicholson Transit Company
BUILT: Craig Shipbuilding Company, Toledo, Ohio—1902
HULL NO.: 88
O. A. DIMENSIONS: 219′ × 40′9″ × 16′
FORMER DATA: Launched as the bulk carrier CHARLES BEATTY. Renamed USONA in 1916. Renamed BAYUSONA in 1917. Renamed PORT DE ST. MALO in 1920. Renamed BAYUSONA, for second time, in 1922. Renamed ROSLYN in 1922. Renamed USONA, for second time in 1923. Converted to a self-unloading sandsucker at Great Lakes Engineering Works, Ecorse, Michigan in 1926. Given last name in 1936. Converted to a bulk freighter at Nicholson Terminal & Dock Company, River Rouge, Michigan in 1942.

The bulk freight Steamer IRONWOOD had a very complex series of name changes. It was idle for some time prior to its sale for use as a barge at Toledo, Ohio in 1961. Various parts of the ship were gradually taken and what is almost unrecognizable as the original hull is in use as a derelict scow around the lower lakes region.

When this vessel became a sandsucker it took a name it had borne previously, but when it came into this fleet it was given a name in keeping with other sandsuckers of the day. These bore a common suffix in their name—WOOD. The prefix, therefore, was the specific namesake.

The Great Lakes fleet is predominantly involved in the movement of iron ore. As other sandsuckers of the day honored the oak forests and the lakes on which the ships moved, this vessel honored the iron ore products themselves, and in addition, the town of Ironwood, Michigan which is located on the Gogebic Range, one of the early iron mining regions near Lake Superior.

Steamer ADRIAN ISELIN

OWNER:	Nicholson Transit Company
BUILT:	Detroit Shipbuilding Company, Wyandotte, Michigan—1914
HULL NO.:	194
O. A. DIMENSIONS:	257' × 43' × 23'6"
FORMER DATA:	Launched as a bulk freighter. Converted to a crane-equipped bulk freighter at Nicholson Terminal & Dock Company, River Rouge, Michigan in 1940. Reconverted to a bulk freighter at Nicholson Terminal & Dock Company, River Rouge, Michigan in 1942.

This small canal-sized bulk freighter was sold for non-transportation use in 1961. Its namesake was Mr. Adrian Iselin who was born in New York, New York on October 14, 1846. He was born into a well-known New York City family which was active in many financial affairs.

After completing his education, he became a member of the family firm of A. Iselin & Company, investment bankers, on December 1, 1868. He was destined to be engaged in banking and financial matters all his business life. When his father died, Mr. Iselin took over as head of the company.

He was also president of Helvetia Realty Company, Neptune Realty Company and Cowanshannock Coal & Coke Company. Mr. Iselin was a director of many firms including the Lackawanna Steel Company of Buffalo, New York. It was in the pig iron trade to and from this plant that this ship mostly traded. Mr. Iselin was honored when this ship took his name because of this relationship and that similar relationship with George Hall Corporation. He died on January 29, 1935.

This bulk carrier is shown below on June 16, 1953 in the connecting channels system of the Great Lakes.

Steamer MATAAFA

OWNER: Ranahan-McCarthy Terminal Company
BUILT: Cleveland Shipbuilding Company,
Lorain, Ohio - 1899
HULL NO.: 33
O. A. DIMENSIONS: 450' x 50' x 28'6"
FORMER DATA: Launched as the bulk freighter PENNSYLVANIA (2). Given last name in 1899. Converted to an automobile carrier at Nicholson Engineering Works, River Rouge, Michigan in 1946.

This auto- carrying vessel served only part of its latter days in the fleet. During the winding-down operations at Nicholson, the ship was chartered to T. J. McCarthy Steamship Company. It is shown in this photograph on July 11, 1962 in the Detroit River when operated under charter to McCarthy Steamship Company. This ship was sold for scrap in 1964.

The Steamer MATAAFA was originally in the Minnesota Steamship Company fleet. This line had a practice of beginning their ship names with the letter "M" and ending them with "A." In the same year this ship was launched the line took possession of another bulk freighter. Both this and the other ship were given names relative to the Samoan Islands.

Mataafa was the reigning and popular soverign on Samoa in 1889 when Malietoa returned from his two years in exile. Both were jealous of the other prior to the Lackawanna Agreement of 1881, but Mataafa was to win the long-term personal battle for importance on the island group. Mataafa entered into a competition of generosity with Malietoa in 1889 and won the loyalty and respect of the countrymen.

Steamer PENOBSCOT (2)

OWNER: Nicholson Transit Company
BUILT: F. W. Wheeler & Company, West Bay City, Michigan - 1896
HULL NO.: 108
O. A. DIMENSIONS: 466' x 44'6" x 26'9"
FORMER DATA: Launched as a bulk freighter. Lengthened 96' at Toledo Shipbuilding Company, Toledo, Ohio in 1906. Converted to a combination automobile carrier and package freighter at Great Lakes Engineering Works, River Rouge, Michigan in 1926. Converted to a combination automobile carrier and bulk freighter at American Ship Building Company, Buffalo, New York in 1942.

The Steamer PENOBSCOT (2) suffered extensive damage when it collided with the tank barge MORANIA - 130 in Buffalo, New York harbor on October 29, 1951 but was restored to service and served in Great Lakes commerce until being sold for use as a grain storage barge at Buffalo, New York in 1955. It was sold for scrap in 1963 and is shown in this photograph in the Detroit River on August 17, 1954.

The namesake of this bulk freighter was the Penobscot Indian tribe which is of the Algonquin strain. The name Penobscot means, literally, "it forks on the white rocks" or, "it flows on the white rocks." This applies directly to the falls at Oldtown, Maine.

It is interesting to note that this was the first ship on the Great Lakes to be lengthened as much as 96', others of the day were only being lengthened 72 feet. This vessel also carried her engine and boilers amidships when originally built.

Steamer PERSEUS

OWNER: Nicholson Transit Company
BUILT: Great Lakes Engineering Works, St. Clair, Michigan—1905
HULL NO.: 12
O. A. DIMENSIONS: 484' × 50' × 28'
FORMER DATA: Launched as the bulk freighter FRANK J. HECKER. Given last name in 1913. Converted to a combination automobile carrier and bulk freighter at Nicholson Terminal and Dock Company, River Rouge, Michigan in 1946.

The Steamer PERSEUS was active on the Great Lakes in the automobile and grain trades until being sold for scrap in 1961. It is shown in the above photograph downbound in the St. Mary's River with a full load of wheat for Buffalo, New York delivery. The ship had sailed from St. Clair, Michigan on October 18, 1905 on its maiden voyage, light to Duluth, Minnesota to load iron ore.

The namesake of this vessel was the constellation Perseus. This constellation of the northern hemisphere is named for the hero of Greek mythology who was the slayer of the Gorgon Medusa and rescuer of Andromeda from the sea monster. The Interlake Steamship Company named this vessel in 1913 in keeping with a current theme at the time for heavenly bodies and beings as the background for ship names.

The legend of Perseus in Greek mythology holds that as a lad he was cast into the sea in a box with his mother by her father Acrisius, king of Argas, to whom it had been prophesied that he would be killed by his grandson.

Steamer PIONEER (2)

OWNER: Nicholson Transit Company
BUILT: Detroit Shipbuilding Company,
Wyandotte, Michigan - 1907
HULL NO.: 169
O. A. DIMENSIONS: 524' x 54' x 30'3"
FORMER DATA: Launched as J. H. BARTOW. Given last name in 1918.

Before the Steamer PIONEER (2) was sold to its last owners, it served for many years as an iron ore and coal carrier for the Cleveland-Cliffs Steamship Company which gave it this name. The vessel was sold for scrap in 1961 when this owning company ceased vessel operations.

The theme of naming vessels, for the most part, after explorers and Indian chieftains is one that has a long tradition in the former owner's fleet. Such names as Pontiac, Cadillac, Frontenac, Champlain, Marquette, Peter White and Joliet were famous in history as early pioneers.

The Steamer PIONEER (2) honored all of these men and many more in its name and has a vast collection of namesakes. Two definitions of a pioneer are "one of the first to settle in a territory" and "a person or group that originates or helps to open up a new line of thought or activity or a new method of technical development." Since the Great Lakes region was "pioneered" by sheer determination and skill, it is most apropos that a lake ship should have borne this name to honor all those who have gone before us and brought this area into economic fulfillment.

This largest vessel ever operated in the Nicholson Fleet is shown below in the St. Clair River on June 11, 1960.

Steamer SONORA (2)

OWNER:	Nicholson Transit Company
BUILT:	Superior Shipbuilding Company, West Superior, Wisconsin—1902
HULL NO.:	505
O. A. DIMENSIONS:	366' × 48' × 28'
FORMER DATA:	Launched as a bulk freighter. Converted to a combination package freighter and automobile carrier at Great Lakes Engineering Works, Ecorse, Michigan in 1924. Re-converted to a bulk freighter at Great Lakes Engineering Works, River Rouge, Michigan in 1937. Converted to a crane vessel at Nicholson Terminal and Dock Company, River Rouge, Michigan in 1953.

The crane-equipped Steamer SONORA was active on the Great Lakes until it was sold for scrap in 1961. It is shown in the above photograph on August 18, 1955 in the St. Mary's River.

This vessel was originally in the fleet of Mr. G. A. Tomlinson who, it will be recalled, named his ships for places, things or objects that began with the letter "S" and ended with the letter "A." This theme of ship names continued for the early years of his fleet.

The namesake of this vessel was the northwest state of Mexico. Sonora has an area of 71,403 square miles and a current population of about 800,000 residents. It is bounded on the north by the United States, on the east by Chihuahua and on the south by Sinaloa. The Gulf of Lower California lies to the west.

Steamer STEEL KING (2)

OWNER: Nicholson Transit Company
BUILT: Union Dry Dock Company, Buffalo, New York—1897
HULL NO.: 80
O. A. DIMENSIONS: 342' × 44' × 28'
FORMER DATA: Launched as the package freighter STARUCCA. Renamed DELOS W. COOKE in 1912. Converted to a bulk freighter at Nicholson Terminal and Dock Company, Ecorse, Michigan in 1940. Given last name in 1941. Converted to a crane ship at Nicholson Terminal and Dock Company, Ecorse, Michigan in 1945. Re-converted to a bulk freighter at Nicholson Terminal and Dock Company, Ecorse, Michigan in 1951.

This unit was originally purchased by Nicholson Transit Company for conversion to a crane ship. With the outbreak of World War II, however, they used her as a bulk freighter but renamed her in reference to her later trade since they still counted on the conversion to move finished steel products.

To this company the ship represented the utmost in their crane ship fleet and was the "KING" of their "STEEL" hauling business. They thus define their choice of this ship name.

When it became evident that better ships were around for the crane ship business, this vessel was again converted back to a bulk freighter and served out its days as such until it was sold in 1954. The forward portion of the hull was scrapped and the after portion was retained as a cut down deck barge, appropriately named AFT. It was finally sold for scrap in 1971, but defied that fate by sinking in Lake Erie enroute to Port Colborne, Ontario.

Steamer SULTANA

OWNER:	Nicholson Transit Company
BUILT:	Superior Shipbuilding Company, West Superior, Wisconsin—1902
HULL NO.:	503
O. A. DIMENSIONS:	366′ × 48′ × 28′
FORMER DATA:	Launched as a bulk freighter. Converted to a combination package freighter and automobile carrier at Great Lakes Engineering works, River Rouge, Michigan in 1924. Converted to a combination bulk freighter and automobile carrier at Great Lakes Engineering Works, River Rouge, Michigan in 1937.

The Steamer SULTANA is shown in this photograph while unloading grain at Cleveland, Ohio, It remained active in the grain and automobile trades until 1961 when it was sold for scrap. It was subsequently partially demolished, but 300 feet of its hull existed as a dry cargo deck barge used in the rock-hauling trade until it was sold for scrap late in 1973.

This vessel was originally built for Mr. George Ashley Tomlinson's Duluth Steamship Company. It was given a name in 1902 following the theme of ship names chosen by Mr. Tomlinson which called for the first letter of the name beginning with "S" and the last letter of the name being "A." Due to this theme, ship names often came from places or things far removed from Great Lakes shipping.

The namesake of this ship was the oldtime favorite house plant that has now become a fine garden flower as well. The sultana is an annual and is especially well suited to part-shade or fully shaded areas. The plant usually grows to between 6 and 12 inches in height and flowers bloom in a variety of shades. It is part of the balsam family and of the genus impatiens.

Steamer TAMPICO

OWNER: Nicholson Transit Company
BUILT: Craig Shipbuilding Company, Toledo, Ohio—1900
HULL NO.: 77
O. A. DIMENSIONS: 256' × 42' × 25'
FORMER DATA: Launched as a bulk freighter. Converted to a sandsucker at Great Lakes Engineering Works, River Rouge, Michigan in 1924. Converted to a crane vessel at Nicholson Engineering Works, Ecorse, Michigan in 1938. Re-converted to a bulk freighter at American Ship Building Company, Buffalo, New York in 1942.

The canal-sized bulk freight Steamer TAMPICO retained its original name throughout its rather extensive career as a bulker, sandsucker, crane ship and, again, a bulker. It was active on the Great Lakes until being sold for scrap in 1961. This, however, could not daunt this vessel. It subsequently served as a barge and, finally, as a partial breakwater.

This vessel was originally built for interests on the East Coast and they had a policy of naming ships for ports in Mexico and Central and South America. Tampico is a city and leading port of Mexico on the Panuco River about six miles from the Gulf of Mexico. It is almost surrounded by lagoons and swampy lands. The eastern end of the city is situated on low ground but the western end rises to 150 feet higher. Tampico has excellent, modern facilities and is built largely of brick and stone.

This steamer is shown below in August, 1952 with a load of pig iron in the lower Detroit River.

Steamer JAMES WATT

OWNER: Nicholson Transit Company
BUILT: Cleveland Shipbuilding Company, Cleveland, Ohio—1896
HULL NO.: 26
O. A. DIMENSIONS: 427' × 48' × 28'3"
FORMER DATA: Launched as a bulk freighter. Converted to a combination automobile carrier and bulk freighter at Nicholson Terminal and Dock Company, River Rouge, Michigan in 1937.

The auto carrying bulk freight Steamer JAMES WATT was sold for scrap in 1961 after having served as an iron ore carrier, automobile transport and a regular in the domestic grain trade. It is shown above with a full load of new automobiles bound for Duluth, Minnesota. The ship is upbound in the Detroit River on July 14, 1951.

Namesake of this venerable carrier was Mr. James Watt who was born in Greenock, Scotland on January 19, 1736. He went to London, England in 1754 to learn the trade of an instrument maker and returned to Scotland in 1756 to establish himself with Glasgow University the following year. There he met two friends, Joseph Black and John Robison, who discussed with him the possibilities of improving his steam engine.

He received other patents as the machine was finally improved. His successes made the steam engine quick in working and a powerful and efficient machine. Many further improvements were needed, of course, but it is fitting that there should have been a Great Lakes vessel named in honor of the man who so richly contributed his work to the eventual major form of 20th century propulsion for Great Lakes ships. Mr. Watt continued active until his death on August 19, 1819.

Steamer J. P. WELLS

OWNER:	Nicholson Transit Company
BUILT:	American Ship Building Company, Lorain, Ohio—1906
HULL NO.:	345
O. A. DIMENSIONS:	440' × 52' × 28'6"
FORMER DATA:	Launched as the bulk freighter JOSHUA W. RHODES. Renamed FRANK SEITHER (2) in 1923. Renamed HAZEN BUTLER in 1933. Converted to a combination automobile carrier and package freighter and given last name at Manitowoc Shipbuilding Company, Manitowoc, Wisconsin in 1946. Converted to a combination automobile carrier and bulk freighter at Nicholson Terminal and Dock Company, River Rouge, Michigan in 1951.

This vessel honored Mr. Joseph Pee Wells as its namesake.

Mr. Wells was born in Sheffield, England on March 24, 1852 and was educated in the public schools. He worked at various jobs until coming to Canada in 1870, settling at Dresden, Ontario, and took up sailing.

In 1900 Mr. Wells joined the Detroit & Cleveland Navigation Company as chief engineer. He brought out many vessels on their maiden voyages and was chief engineer of the Steamers GREATER BUFFALO, CITY OF CLEVELAND and EASTERN STATES before coming ashore in 1908 as fleet engineer. In 1914 he was named superintendent of hulls and machinery and retained that title until retiring in 1932. He died in Detroit, Michigan on July 8, 1933. D & C managers honored his memory in 1946.

His namesake was active in the automobile and grain trades until being sold for scrap in 1961 and is shown here upbound at Port Huron, Michigan in June, 1960.

Steamer ALEXANDER LESLIE

OWNER:	Norlake Steamships Limited
BUILT:	American Ship Building Company, Cleveland, Ohio—1901
HULL NO.:	405
O. A. DIMENSIONS:	366' × 48' × 28'
FORMER DATA:	Launched as J. T. HUTCHINSON. Renamed H. A. ROCK in 1923. Given last name in 1927.

Mr. Alexander Leslie was born at Toronto, Ontario on October 3, 1864 and was educated at the Model School, Toronto, Ontario. He began his career as an office boy at the Toronto, Grey & Bruce Railway Company offices in 1880. In 1883-84 he was cashier of the Ontario Division of the Canadian Pacific Railway and from 1884 to 1886 served as cashier of the system in Montreal headquarters.

In 1886, Mr. Leslie became general auditor of the Lake Erie and Detroit River Railway, serving until 1903 when he became associated with the Lake Erie Coal Company Limited. He possessed talents that were quickly apparent and by 1919 he was general manager of the firm and served in that capacity until 1929 when he was elected president and general manager.

He was also president and general manager of the Lake Erie Navigation Company and Bessemer Navigation Company. The company he headed owned this vessel until its last few years on the Great Lakes. Mr. Leslie's hobbies included farming and golf and he enjoyed them to the fullest until his final days.

His namesake was sold for scrap in 1969 and is shown in this photograph passing downbound in the St. Mary's River bound for a Georgian Bay port with a typical cargo of Canadian wheat on August 15, 1969.

Steamer MANITOBA (2)

OWNER: Norlake Steamships Limited
BUILT: American Ship Building Company, Lorain, Ohio—1907
HULL NO.: 355
O. A. DIMENSIONS: 500' × 52' × 30'
FORMER DATA: Launched as VERONA. Renamed HENRY STEINBRENNER (2) in 1959. Renamed UHLMANN BROTHERS (1) in 1965. Given last name in 1965.

The bulk freight Steamer MANITOBA was active in the Canadian fleet on the Great Lakes until being sold for scrap in 1969. It is shown in this photograph on August 17, 1966 above Port Huron, Michigan on Lake Huron.

The province of Manitoba, Canada was the namesake of this vessel. It is the easternmost prairie province with Winnipeg, the heart of the Canadian grain trade, as the capital. It is because of this capital city that this vessel was so named. During its career in this fleet, after having been an American ship for fifty-eight years, its primary assignment was to carry Canadian wheat to Georgian Bay ports and, occasionally, down the St. Lawrence River.

The province of Manitoba is bounded by the Keewatin District in the north, Hudson Bay in the northeast, Ontario in the east and the states of North Dakota and Minnesota in the south. Saskatchewan borders it on the west. The area of the province is mostly low level with a large number of lakes and rivers, all of which drain to Hudson Bay. Wheat is the primary agricultural product of the area. Large mineral deposits in the province are only slightly developed.

Barge NORMIL

OWNER: Northern Paper Mills Limited
BUILT: Detroit Dry Dock Company, Wyandotte, Michigan - 1893
HULL NO.: 114
O. A. DIMENSIONS: 250' x 38'6" x 13'6"
FORMER DATA: Launched as the passenger vessel CITY OF ALPENA (2). Renamed CITY OF ALPENA II in 1912. Renamed CITY OF SAUGATUCK in 1922. Renamed SAUGATUCK in 1939. Converted to a crane-equipped bulk freight barge, shortened 25', reduced in depth 1'6" and renamed LEONA at Sturgeon Bay Shipbuilidng and Dry Dock Company, Sturgeon Bay, Wisconsin in 1941. Converted to a bulk freight barge at Northern Paper Mills Limited, Marathon, Ontario and given last name in 1946.

The bulk freight Barge NORMIL was acquired by these owners from Captain John Roen on July 13, 1945 for $26,250. They operated the vessel in the carriage of pulpwood from Lake Superior and Manitoulin Island ports to the Green Bay, Wisconsin area until selling the barge for scrap in 1957. The barge had a capacity of 700 cords of pulpwood and is shown above at Green Bay, Wisconsin on November 10, 1954.

The namesake of this vessel is found in the first three letters of the first word of the corporate name, NORthern, and the first three letters of the third word, MILls. The company headquarters is located at Green Bay, Wisconsin. The firm was incorporated on February 6, 1909 and a series of mergers and name changes followed through the years. Now, firm is known as part of The American Can Company.

Steamer A. A. HUDSON

OWNER:	Northwest Steamships Limited
BUILT:	Swan, Hunter & Wigham Richardson Limited, Wallsend-on-Tyne, England—1924
HULL NO.:	1241
O. A. DIMENSIONS:	261' × 43' × 25'
FORMER DATA:	Launched as RAHANE. Given last name in 1939.

This package freighter was named in honor of Mr. Arthur Archibald Hudson who was born on Arthur's Island, Georgian Bay, near Midland, Ontario on June 26, 1887. He was educated in the public schools and began his career as a cabin boy on the tugs serving the Georgian Bay area in the early 1900's.

He rose through the ranks from deckhand to master, receiving his first command in 1912 aboard the Steamer GEORGE A. GRAHAM. He also served in other ships and was with the James Playfair fleet from 1915 until 1923 when he joined the N. M. Paterson & Sons fleet. Captain Hudson was shore captain of this fleet in 1929 when he left to found the Northwest Transportation Company to handle package freight on the Upper Great Lakes.

He and his brother, Captain Dalton Hudson, ran this business successfully with each man serving as master during this period. In 1938 Captain A. A. Hudson purchased this vessel to assist in handling the volume of business the firm had built up. He brought the ship out as the newest member of the newly organized Northwest Steamships Limited fleet. Captain Hudson did not live to see the further developments of his business, however, as he died of a heart attack at Toronto, Ontario on November 25, 1939. His namesake was sold for off-lakes use in 1965.

A tribute for him was given in Goderich, Ontario in the 1930's and it was stated "In all his sailing career, while he had many 'close shaves,' he holds the remarkable record of never having suffered an accident." His namesake is seen above on an early spring run at Sault Ste. Marie, Michgan.

Steamer SUPERIOR (2)

OWNER:	Northwest Steamships Limited
BUILT:	Globe Iron Works, Cleveland, Ohio—1889
HULL NO.:	27
O. A. DIMENSIONS:	260' × 38'3" × 23'
FORMER DATA:	Launched as PARKS FOSTER. Shortened 14' at Great Lakes Engineering Works, Ecorse, Michigan in 1921. Given last name in 1929.

The package freight Steamer SUPERIOR was named for Lake Superior, the largest body of fresh water in the world. After this vessel was acquired by Mr. A. A. Hudson and his brother in 1934, Captain Dalton Hudson sailed this ship for a number of years through its namesake waters. The vessel was sold for scrap in 1960 after having served its usefulness for well over a half century.

Lake Superior is the highest in elevation and the most western of the Great Lakes. Its greatest length is 420 miles from Duluth, Minnesota to Sault Ste. Marie, Michigan. It has a breadth of 167 miles, at the widest point, and a total area of about 31,500 square miles. The deepest sounding taken in the lake is in excess of 1,300 feet off Stannard Rock Light.

Lake Superior receives no rivers of great importance, but literally hundreds of smaller rivers and streams pour themselves into the lake. The two largest of these rivers are St. Louis from Minnesota and Nipigon from Ontario.

The Steamer SUPERIOR is shown in the above photograph upbound in the Detroit River in August, 1954.

Steamer MALIETOA

OWNER: Ohio Transportation, Incorporated
BUILT: Cleveland Shipbuilding Company, Lorain, Ohio—1899
HULL NO.: 36
O. A. DIMENSIONS: 474' × 50' × 28'6"

The Samoan Islands provided names for at least two Great Lakes bulk freighters. This ship was one of them. The vessel was active on the Great Lakes until it was sold for scrap in 1963.

In the Samoan Islands of the last century two tribal families predominated political life. The Tupua was one and the Malietoa was the other. Actually, Malietoa was taken as a last name by tribal appointed chieftains and their normal last name was then used as the first name, once this honor was bestowed. Thus, there could be several "Malietoa" at one time.

The Malietoa referred to as the namesake of this ship was a chief known as Laupepa Malietoa, given governorship of Samoa by the Lackawanna Agreement of July 12, 1881 which was signed in peace by British, German and United States representatives. The idea was to give local rule but Laupepa Malietoa ruled badly and by the fall of 1884, Samoan life was in disarray. Malietoa was a disinterested protagonist who shielded himself from outside affairs. He was deposed and exiled in 1887, but returned in 1889 to find his opponent for power strongly in control with German and British aide. Little is known about his final demise, but he never again attained stature in the country. His name was chosen from history because it had meaning in the theme of the Minnesota Steamship Company practice of naming ships. The vessel is shown below in the St. Mary's River on August 19, 1957.

Motor Vessel OTCO BAYWAY

OWNER:	Oil Transfer Corporation
BUILT:	Todd Galveston Dry Docks, Incorporated, Galveston, Texas—1944
HULL NO.:	110
O. A. DIMENSIONS:	249'6" × 37' × 14'6"
FORMER DATA:	Launched as ROYSTON. Renamed SEQUATCHIE in 1944. Lengthened 28'6" at Bethlehem Steel Company, Incorporated, Staten Island, New York and renamed A.O.G. 21 in 1948. Renamed OTCO BAYWAY in 1948.

The tank Motor Vessel OTCO BAYWAY is shown above in the East River in New York City in 1956. It served occasionally on the Great Lakes and on the East Coast running via the New York State Barge Canal until it was sold for permanent off-lakes use in 1961.

The namesake of this tanker was twofold. The first word of the ship name used the first letter of each of the first two words in the company title, *Oil Transfer*, and the *CO* of the word corporation. This was a common fleet prefix word and recognized the privately-held firm that was organized in the state of New York in 1923 for the purpose of owning and operating tugs and barges for the carriage of petroleum products and chemicals on the eastern seaboard.

The second word of the ship name referred to Bayway, New Jersey's large refinery of Esso Standard Oil Company, from which this tanker carried many cargoes to northern seaboard destinations. This refinery is still among the largest in the United States, but when this ship took its name in 1948, it was the largest in the world.

Motor Vessel NORGOMA

OWNER: Ontario Northland Transportation Commission
BUILT: Collingwood Shipyards,
Collingwood, Ontario—1950
HULL NO.: 145
O. A. DIMENSIONS: 188' × 37'6" × 22'6"
FORMER DATA: Launched as a package freighter. Converted to a carferry at Collingwood Shipyards, Collingwood, Ontario in 1964.

The Motor Vessel NORGOMA had the common fleet prefix which is "NOR" and which stands for the direction north. The last syllable of this ship name, "GOMA," is in reference to the Algoma District of Ontario of which Manitoulin Island, a major base for fleet operations, is a part.

The Algoma District in northern Ontario is a land area of 19,320 square miles. It lies north of Lake Huron and the St. Mary's River between the districts of Sudbury on the east and Thunder Bay on the west. Cochrane District borders it to the north.

There are four hundred seventy-five townships in the Algoma District and Sault Ste. Marie, Ontario is the district seat. The name Algoma stems from Henry Rowe Schoolcraft, an American explorer and adventurer, who advocated its use in naming Lake Superior. He coined it in recognition of the Ojibwa Indian claim to Lake Superior as the Algonkin Sea. Derivation is AL from Algonkin and GOMA which is a varient of gum-ee, meaning waters. This vessel was sold for use as a museum and civic center in 1975 and now reposes at a municipal dock in Sault Ste. Marie, Ontario. This photo was taken at Kagawong, Ontario on Manitoulin Island on June 21, 1971.

Steamer NORISLE

OWNER:	Ontario Northland Transportation Commission
BUILT:	Collingwood Shipyards, Collingwood, Ontario – 1946
HULL NO.:	136
O. A. DIMENSIONS:	215'9" x 36'3" x 16'

The Steamer NORISLE was the first modern Great Lakes passenger vessel to be completed. It went into service on September 16, 1946 and was the first Canadian passenger ship commissioned since the Steamer NORONIC in 1913. It was a coal-fired ship, however, and this caused its eventual downfall.

Concurrent with commissioning of a very large, by comparison, new carferry-passenger vessel in 1974, the smaller NORISLE was deemed to be unnecessary for future use primarily because the price of coal for fuel had sky-rocketed threefold in twelve months! It was thus sold in 1975 to the town of Manitowaning, Ontario for conversion to a museum and eating place.

The namesake of this vessel was two-fold. The "NOR" was a common ship prefix in the Owen Sound Transportation Company fleet, referring to the direction north. The second syllable of the name - "ISLE," referred to Manitoulin Island, Ontario. It was to and from Manitoulin Island and adjacent islands that the fleet traded during the mainline days of operation. Thousands of tourists and their automobiles were annually shuttled between the lower Bruce Peninsula and the island by this vessel and its sister ships.

Steamer LAGONDA

OWNER:	Ore Navigation Corporation, Great Lakes Division
BUILT:	F. W. Wheeler & Company, West Bay City, Michigan—1896
HULL NO.:	115
O. A. DIMENSIONS:	393' × 45'10" × 28'3"
FORMER DATA:	Launched as a bulk freighter. Converted to a crane ship at Toledo Shipbuilding Company, Toledo, Ohio in 1926.

The crane-equipped Steamer LAGONDA remained active on the Great Lakes until being sold for scrap in 1958. Throughout its sixty-two years of service, it carried the same name on its bow.

This name was chosen by the original builders of the ship, The Cleveland Steamship Company, and honored a small community in Washington County, Pennsylvania. Lagonda, Pennsylvania currently has a population of about 100 people and is a suburb of Washington, Pennsylvania, the county seat some 28 miles southwest of Pittsburgh, Pennsylvania.

Lagonda is located on Chartiers Creek and is in the heart of an industrialized area. Jessop Steel Company and Washington Steel Corporation are located nearby. In addition, the surrounding area includes heavy activity in oil, clay, limestone, sand, tin plating and glass manufacture. To the south of Lagonda, fine, rich agricultural land abounds.

The area was originally known as Catfish's Camp and was a Delaware Indian village. Some of the Mitchell family, managers of Cleveland Steamship Company, originated in this part of Pennsylvania. Because of this and the close proximity of Lagonda to steel interests, this ship name was chosen.

This vessel is shown above in the St. Clair River on August 25, 1951.

Steamer NORMAC

OWNER:	Owen Sound Transportation Company, Limited
BUILT:	Jenks Shipbuilding Company, Port Huron, Michigan—1902
HULL NO.:	19
O. A. DIMENSIONS:	124'6" × 25' × 18'
FORMER DATA:	Launched as the fire tug JAMES R. ELLIOTT. Converted to a combination passenger and package-freight vessel at Georgian Bay Shipbuilding Company, Limited, Midland, Ontario and given last name in 1931.

The namesake of this vessel was Captain Norman McKay who was born at North Capreol, Ontario on October 10, 1887. He was largely self-educated and grew up with his five brothers and six sisters at Lion's Head, Ontario. He went aboard Great Lakes vessels at an early age as a cabin boy and rose rapidly through the ranks, becoming a captain at the age of twenty-eight. This was in the Canada Steamship Lines fleet where he sailed on the Saguenay River.

In 1926 Captain McKay left Canada Steamship Lines to found the Owen Sound Transportation Company. He personally went to Detroit, Michigan to take possession of this vessel and sail it to Georgian Bay. The vessel name is derived from the first three letters of his first name, "NOR," and the first two letters of his last name plus an "A" for ease of spelling and pronunciation. Captain McKay was president of the line during these times. He continued so until going down with another ship, the Steamer HIBOU, on November 21, 1936 when he lost his life.

Steamer ALTADOC (2)

OWNER:	N. M. Paterson & Sons Limited
BUILT:	Chicago Shipbuilding Company, Chicago, Illinois—1896
HULL NO.:	21
O. A. DIMENSIONS:	425' × 48'3" × 28'
FORMER DATA:	Launched as MARICOPA. Renamed JOHN P. GEISTMAN in 1937. Renamed E. E. JOHNSON in 1941. Given last name in 1945.

The bulk freight Steamer ALTADOC ended its sailing days in 1962 when it was sold to the Goderich Elevator & Transit Company of Goderich, Ontario for use as a grain storage hull at that port. It subsequently was renamed D. B. WELDON and was in Goderich harbour until sold for scrap in 1974.

The namesake of this venerable ship was the province of Alberta, Canada. Like many other ships of the Paterson fleet, cities of importance in the Dominion and provinces of the Dominion of Canada were used in the ship names. The beginning letters of the Dominion of Canada, in fact, are used as the nearly universal ship name suffix in this fleet.

Alberta has an area of 255,285 square miles including 6,485 square miles of freshwater lakes. It is the most westerly of the three prairie provinces and is a vast plateau comprising, roughly, the third steppe of the Great Plains of Canada. Edmonton is the capital city and has a current population of about 350,000 persons.

This vessel had the honor of delivering the first cargo to the new Robin Hood Flour Mill elevator at Humberstone, Ontario on August 7, 1940. It consisted of 210,000 bushels of wheat from Fort William, Ontario. The ship is shown below in the St. Mary's River above the Soo Locks on April 18, 1956.

Steamer BRICOLDOC

OWNER:	N. M. Paterson & Sons Limited
BUILT:	Superior Shipbuilding Company, West Superior, Wisconsin—1902
HULL NO.:	506
O. A. DIMENSIONS:	424' × 50' × 27'
FORMER DATA:	Launched as JAMES H. HOYT. Lengthened 48' at Superior Shipbuilding Company, Superior, Wisconsin in 1910. Given last name in 1926.

The 7,800 gross tons carrying capacity Steamer BRICOLDOC took the province of British Columbia as its namesake. The ship also used the familiar Paterson Fleet suffix "DOC," on the ship name. This carrier is shown here downbound at Sault Ste. Marie, Michigan with a load of grain for Georgian Bay delivery. It remained in the fleet until being sold for scrap in 1968.

British Columbia is the westernmost province of Canada and ranks third largest in area with 366,255 square miles of which 6,976 square miles is water. It has a current population of about two million people and its focal point for industry is Canada's third largest city—Vancouver.

The province entered Confederation on July 20, 1871. Its history precedes that date by many years, however, since the coast line of British Columbia was first visited by Juan Perez who was on a coastal expedition from Mexico in 1774. He conducted the first general exploration. It remained largely wilderness country until the gold rush days of the nineteenth century.

Today, British Columbia produces about ten percent of all of Canada's goods with mining, forest products, fisheries, agriculture, furs and manufacturing being the leading industries.

This vessel is shown below in the St. Mary's River on July 18, 1966.

Motor Vessel CALGADOC (2)

OWNER: N. M. Paterson & Sons Limited
BUILT: Collingwood Shipyards,
Collingwood, Ontario – 1956
HULL NO.: 156
O. A. DIMENSIONS: 259' x 43'9" x 22'6"

This vessel was one of the last built to dimensions of the old canal locks of the pre-Seaway canals in eastern Canada. At the time of its sale for off-lakes use, it was also one of the last of this canal size existant on the Great Lakes. It was sold for use in off-lakes service in 1975 and is shown below while downbound in the St. Mary's River, on August 1, 1972.

The special-purpose bulk freighter shown here was named for Calgary, Alberta and had the fleet suffix "DOC" in its name. Calgary is a city on the western edge of the Great Plains and is about forty miles from the foothills of the Rocky Mountains. It has a population of about 350,000 persons.

The city was founded as Fort Calgary by the Northwest Mounted Police in 1875. The Canadian Pacific Railway came through in 1883 and the location was incorporated as a town in 1884 and chartered as a city in 1893.

Wheat farming is important in the region around Calgary. The city is also the province's most important wholesale center and has flour mills, meat-packing facilities, distillery, oil refining capacity and potash manufacturing plants to its credit. It is Alberta's "cosmopolitan city."

Steamer CARTIERDOC (1)

OWNER: N. M. Paterson & Sons Limited
BUILT: Swan, Hunter & Wigham Richardson Limited, Wallsend-on-Tyne, England - 1928
HULL NO.: 1329
O. A. DIMENSIONS: 259' x 43'3" x 24'
FORMER DATA: Deepened 6' at St. Lawrence Dry Docks, Montreal, Quebec in 1949.

The canal size bulk freight Steamer CARTIERDOC (1) was active until being sold for demolition in 1961. It was stripped down but not cut up as it was sold for use in marine construction work in 1965.

Jacques Cartier, navigator and discoverer of the St. Lawrence River Valley, was the namesake of this ship. Cartier was born August 15, 1491 at St. Malo, France and received his education at the place. He joined with various trading expeditions of the day and acquired a reputation as an exceptional navigator by an early age. He was on trusted search commissioned by Frances I in 1534 when he sailed his ship into the Gulf of St. Lawrence via the Strait of Belle Isle. Francis I had sent him to find a northwest passage to the Spice Islands.

In 1535 he again visited Canada in search of the fabled mines of the Saguenay Indians. Various troubles and triumphs were with Cartier and his party throughout this period. Many interesting facets of his bravery are too lengthy to be told here, but make fascinating reading. Cartier established a fort at Cap Rouge in May, 1541 and soon found what he thought were gold fragments and diamonds. Contrary to orders, he left Canada with his "prize" in 1542.

Cartier's namesake is shown below at Iroquois, Ontario on October 24, 1956.

Barge COLLINGDOC (2)

OWNER: N. M. Paterson & Sons Limited
BUILT F. W. Wheeler & Company,
West Bay City, Michigan—1897
HULL NO.: 120
O. A. DIMENSIONS: 378' × 44' × 26'
FORMER DATA: Launched as W. LeBARON JENNEY. Renamed ALFRED in 1937. Renamed ALFRED J. in 1938. Renamed COLLINGDOC (2) in 1949.

The Barge COLLINGDOC is shown above in the St. Mary's River on August 24, 1951 under tow of one of the fleet's powered bulk freighters. This bulk freight barge remained in the fleet until it was sold to the Goderich Elevator & Transit Company in 1962. After its sale and relocation in Goderich, Ontario harbor, the barge was renamed K. A. POWELL (1) in honor of one of the directors of the firm. It was sold for scrap in 1973.

The namesake of this barge while in the Paterson fleet was the town of Collingwood, Ontario. This town is located in Simcoe County on Nottawasaga Bay, a part of Georgian Bay some 34 miles northwest of Barrie, Ontario. The site was originally a part of the territory of the Tobacco Indians and had its first white settler in 1835. The area became the terminus of the Ontario, Simcoe and Huron Railway in 1855. This line was renamed Northern Railway of Canada in 1858 and is now part of the Canadian National Railways System.

The main port activity of Collingwood centers around the large shipbuilding and repairing plant of the Canadian Shipbuilding & Engineering Limited and the grain elevator of Collingwood Terminals, Limited. This shipyard has consistently turned out vessels which rank among the largest ever built for the inland Canadian fleet.

Steamer COTEAUDOC (2)

OWNER: N. M. Paterson & Sons Limited
BUILT: Swan, Hunter & Wigham Richardson Limited, Wallsend-on-Tyne, England—1929
HULL NO.: 1395
O. A. DIMENSIONS: 259′ × 43′3″ × 20′
FORMER DATA: Launched as DAMIA. Given last name in 1954.

The canal size bulk freight Steamer COTEAUDOC utilized the familiar fleet suffix, DOC, in its name and took as its specific namesake Coteau Landing, Quebec. This place is the county seat of Soulanges County and is on the north shore of Lake St. Francis which today forms part of the St. Lawrence Seaway system.

Coteau Landing is located exactly at 45 degrees 15 minutes north latitude and 74 degrees 13 minutes west longitude at the northeast extremity of Lake St. Francis opposite the entrance of the former Soulanges Canal. This former artery of Great Lakes commerce was a vital link to the sea and the landing at the site was important in the early days of travel in the area.

Coteau du Lac, Quebec and Coteau Station, Quebec, both in Soulanges County, are in the vicinity and share in the common pioneer heritage of Coteau Landing.

This ship continued active until being sold for scrap in 1963. On July 18, 1940 this steamer cleared Ashtabula, Ohio with the first cargo of iron ore ever to leave that port by water. It was destined for Port Colborne, Ontario delivery and had come from Canada several years previously and was stored on the dock of the Pittsburgh Coal Company. The ship is seen here in the Welland Ship Canal between Locks 6 and 7 on November 24, 1956.

Motor Vessel FARRANDOC (2)

OWNER:	N. M. Paterson & Sons Limited
BUILT:	Federal Shipbuilding & Dry Dock Company, Kearney, New Jersey—1926
HULL NO.:	84
O. A. DIMENSIONS:	258'3" × 42'9" × 20'
FORMER DATA:	Launched as STEEL ELECTRICIAN. Renamed FARRANDOC in 1948.

The canal-size bulk freight Motor Vessel FARRANDOC has the common fleet suffix with other vessels in this fleet and takes its specific name from a former navigational point on the old St. Lawrence Seaway.

Farran's Point was a site on the old canal system about midway between Cornwall and Morrisburg, Ontario. It was at this site that a single lock existed which was used by vessels for the upbound, or westbound, passage almost entirely. This may seem like a strange arrangement, but downbound, or eastbound, vessels went past the point by drifting in the currents of the main St. Lawrence River channel. Swiftness of the current made it too dangerous and unnecessary for the majority of ships to use the lock when heading east.

The entire location is now under water since the opening of the new St. Lawrence Seaway flooded adjacent land areas in the vicinity of Farran's Point. The village that formerly existed at the site was moved farther north and only a memory of the place exists today.

The Motor Vessel FARRANDOC was sold for off-lakes use and renamed QUEBEC TRADER in 1964. It is shown in the photograph below at the Robin Hood Elevator in Humberstone, Ontario on October 31, 1953. It is being unloaded of a domestic grain cargo brought down from the Canadian Lakehead.

Steamer FORT WILLDOC

OWNER:	N. M. Paterson & Sons Limited
BUILT:	American Ship Building Conpany, Cleveland, Ohio—1900
HULL NO.:	403
O. A. DIMENSIONS:	436' × 50'3" × 28'
FORMER DATA:	Launched as JOHN J. ALBRIGHT. Renamed REGULUS in 1916. Given last name in 1927.

The bulk freight Steamer FORT WILLDOC is shown below in the Welland Ship Canal on June 24, 1963. It continued to serve on the Great Lakes until being sold for scrap in 1964.

Fort William, Ontario, now combined with Port Arthur and known as Thunder Bay, Ontario, was the namesake of this vessel. Fort William is built on valley land overlooked by Mount McKay on the south and follows the dredged-out estuary of the Kaministiquia River for about five miles.

It is believed the first white settlement in the area was Dulhut's fur-trading post in 1678. A more substantial French fort, Kaministiquia, was erected in 1717 but was abandoned during the Seven Years' War. When Montreal traders resumed activities after the war they used the Grand Portage-Pigeon River route south of Fort William. Between 1801 and 1805 British traders erected a fort on the site, naming it Fort William after William McGillivray, director of the North West Company.

Fort William was incorporated as town in 1892 with Mr. John McKellar as the first mayor. The McKellar River at the site honors his name. In 1907 Fort William was granted status as a city and the merger between it and Port Arthur occurred on January 1, 1970.

Steamer GANANDOC

OWNER:	N. M. Paterson and Sons Limited
BUILT:	Swan, Hunter & Wigham Richardson Limited, Wallsend-on-Tyne, England—1929
HULL NO.:	1383
O. A. DIMENSIONS:	259' × 43'3" × 24'
FORMER DATA:	Deepened 4' at Davie Shipbuilding, Limited, Lauzon, Quebec in 1954.

The canal-sized bulk freight Steamer GANANDOC was active on the Great Lakes until it was sold for off-lakes use in 1961. It is shown in the photograph below in the Welland Ship Canal, at Dain City, on October 12, 1957.

The namesake of this ship was the town of Gananoque, Ontario which is located on the St. Lawrence River in Leeds County at the mouth of the Gananoque River. It is on the Canadian National Railway System and situated about eighteen miles east of Kingston, Ontario by way of Highway #2.

The town is locally known as the "Gateway to the Thousand Islands" and has pleasure boat connections with a number of the points of interest in the area and with islands where cottages and resorts can be found.

During the years previous to the 1959 opening of the modern St. Lawrence Seaway, vessels of the size of this carrier used to frequent this port and others like in on the St. Lawrence. However, today little remains as a port except for fishing tugs and pleasure craft. The name Gananoque is of Indian origin and means "rocks rising out of the water." Indeed, this is a true description for the picturesque area of Gananoque.

Motor Vessel GASPEDOC

OWNER: N. M. Paterson & Sons Limited
BUILT: Dravo Corporation, Neville Island, Pittsburgh, Pennsylvania—1944
HULL NO.: 2276
O. A. DIMENSIONS: 327'9" × 50' × 24'6"
FORMER DATA: Launched as the Landing Ship, Tank vessel #885. Converted to a bulk freighter at Davie Shipbuilding & Repairing Company, Limited, Lauzon, Quebec in 1951. Given last name in 1953.

This bulk freight motor vessel served mostly in the newsprint trades of the Great Lakes until being sold in 1967 for off-lakes use. It was a familiar sight on the Chicago River at the Sun Times and Daily News docks and was also seen frequently in Milwaukee, Wisconsin, Detroit, Michigan and Toledo, Ohio.

Utilizing the familiar Paterson Fleet name suffix "DOC," this vessel took the Gaspe Peninsula as its specific namesake. This famous peninsula juts into the Gulf of St. Lawrence and comprises that part of eastern Quebec Province which lies between the St. Lawrence River and the Province of New Brunswick.

The area is sparsely populated but is known as a great tourist center because of its rugged and picturesque coastal scenery, its striking hills and excellent hunting and fishing. Lumbering and coastal fishing are the principle occupations, but there is also some mining of copper, zinc and lead and a small production of pulpwood for papermaking. The area's namesake is shown in the St. Mary's River on August 28, 1966.

Steamer HAMILDOC (2)

OWNER:	N. M. Paterson & Sons Limited
BUILT:	Smith's Dock Company Limited, South Bank-on-Tees, England—1928
HULL NO.:	837
O. A. DIMENSIONS:	258' × 42'3" × 20'6"
FORMER DATA:	Launched as DEEPWATER. Renamed KEYMONT in 1939. Given last name in 1947.

This steamer was sold for scrap in 1961, but the name is carried on in the fleet by a modern, fast motor vessel. The common fleet suffix, "DOC," is used in the name and the namesake of the ship is Hamilton, Ontario.

The city of Hamilton is named in honor of Mr. George Hamilton who bought land at the site in 1813. It was incorporated as a village in 1816, as a town in 1833 and as a city in 1846.

Today the city is a thriving lake port catering both to heavy industry and to saltwater shipping. There are two large steel plants located there with three separate unloading docks. In addition, there are five coal docks, nine stone, sand and bulk dry cargo docks, eight liquid cargo docks and four docks assigned primarily to general cargo and overseas traffic in the harbor.

A point of land comes into Lake Ontario from both the north and the south at Hamilton, forming a deep, natural harbor for safe shelter and local marine activity.

The Steamer HAMILDOC is shown in the photograph below at the Cardinal Canal on October 26, 1956. It is upbound with a cargo of iron ore for Lake Erie delivery.

Motor Vessel HAMILDOC (3)

OWNER: N. M. Paterson & Sons Limited
BUILT: Davie Shipbuilding, Limited, Lauzon, Quebec—1963
HULL NO.: 642
O. A. DIMENSIONS: 315' × 49' × 26'

Namesake of the Motor Vessel HAMILDOC is the fifth largest city of Canada—Hamilton, Ontario. Hamilton is situated in Wentworth County at the south west tip of Lake Ontario and is Canada's largest steel-making center. The port is also heavily engaged in general cargo import-export activity and in liquid cargo activity.

The city of Hamilton is named in honor of Mr. George Hamilton who bought a tract of land at the site in 1813. He subdivided the area and named its streets for members of his family in 1813. Hamilton was incorporated as a village in 1816, as a town in 1833 and as a city in 1846.

First settlers in the area came in 1778, though La Salle had explored it in 1669. With completion of the Burlington Canal in 1824, the area grew rapidly. Railways brought it further along the road to full development in the 1850's.

Hamilton, Ontario has a metropolitan area population of about 400,000 people and has over six hundred manufacturing plants and forty-five parks.

This bulk freighter sailed on its maiden voyage August 16, 1963 with general cargo from Montreal, Quebec to St. John's, Newfoundland. It is shown below in 1972 outbound from Thunder Bay, Ontario. It was sold for off-Lake use at noon E.S.T., March 21, 1977.

Motor Vessel HUMBERDOC

OWNER: N. M. Paterson & Sons Limited
BUILT: Great Lakes Engineering Works, River Rouge, Michigan - 1937
HULL NO.: 284
O. A. DIMENSIONS: 303' x 43' x 27'
FORMER DATA: Launched as NORFOLK (2). Shortened 44' deepened 7', and given last name at Canadian Vickers Limited, Montreal, Quebec in 1950. Lengthened 46' at Kingston Shipyards, Kingston, Ontario in 1960.

The bulk freight Motor Vessel HUMBERDOC had a namesake which is no longer a separate township, but is amalgamated into the city of Port Colborne, Ontario at the southern end of the Welland Ship Canal. Humberstone, Ontario was originally named after Humberston Village at Lincolnshire, England. Locally, it was sometimes known as Stonebridge.

This vessel was the first cargo ship to transit the Wiley-Dondero ship channel and locks of the St. Lawrence Seaway. This occurred July 3, 1958.

The primary incentive to name this ship for the small township was the location at the site of the mill and grain elevator of Robin Hood Multifoods Limited for whose account this fleet has carried much grain over the years. The plant and elevator still receive large quantities of grain during the navigation season.

The Motor Vessel HUMBERDOC was active on the Great Lakes until 1967 when it was sold for overseas scrapping. It laid idle at Brockville, Ontario for two years thereafter and went overseas in a tow in 1969. It is shown in this picture at Toronto, Ontario on July 15, 1959.

Barge KENORDOC (2)

OWNER: N. M. Paterson & Sons Limited
BUILT: Globe Iron Works, Cleveland, Ohio—1898
HULL NO.: 73
O. A. DIMENSIONS: 378' × 44' × 26'
FORMER DATA: Launched as DAVID Z. NORTON (1). Renamed SAGAMORE (2) in 1904. Given last name in 1947.

This bulk freight Barge KENORDOC was the second ship in the history of the Great Lakes to bear this name. An earlier vessel, a powered bulk freighter, was the first. The barge is shown here under tow in Lake St. Clair on August 25, 1951. It was sold for scrapping at Hamilton, Ontario in 1957.

The Kenora District of the province of Ontario was the namesake area of this barge. The province is divided into many different districts which are larger than counties but smaller than the average area of any one of the United States. The districts are more like political subdivisions of the province.

This district occupies the northwest extremity of Ontario and extends from the Rainy River District in the south to the shores of Hudson and James bays. On the west is the province of Manitoba. Thunder Bay District forms the east boundary as far north as Lake St. Joseph, source of the Albany River. From this point, the river, flowing due east to James Bay, separates the district from both Thunder Bay and Cochrane districts to the south.

The town of Kenora, located on the Lake of the Woods, is the district seat. This has a population of about 12,000 persons in the metropolitan area.

Barge KENORDOC (3)

OWNER: N. M. Paterson & Sons Limited
BUILT: Chicago Shipbuilding Company, Chicago, Illinois—1896
HULL NO.: 23
O. A. DIMENSIONS: 378' × 44' × 26'
FORMER DATA: Launched as GEORGE H. CORLISS. Renamed ETHEL in 1937. Renamed ETHEL J. in 1939. Renamed PORTADOC (2) in 1945. Renamed KENORDOC (3) in 1961.

This bulk freight Barge KENORDOC (3) was renamed in a shuffle of names in this fleet in 1961, but the vessel was sold in 1962 for use as a floating grain storage hull at Goderich, Ontario and saw no operational service under this name. When the Goderich Elevator & Transit Company acquired the vessel, they renamed it F. H. DUNSFORD in honor of one of the directors of the company. This hull did not operate under this name, however, and remained part of the floating elevator storage fleet in Goderich harbor until sold for scrap in 1973.

The namesake of this barge is the same as that of the Barge KENORDOC (2), this being the Kenora District of Ontario. This district of 153,220 square miles area is the largest district in the province. It is an extensive expanse of forest and lakeland and was the site of many trading posts in the great days of the Hudson's Bay and North West companies.

This barge is seen above at Goderich, Ontario during the summer of 1961. It remained largely in this position until its total deactivation as a harbor barge.

Steamer KINGDOC (1)

OWNER:	N. M. Paterson & Sons Limited
BUILT:	Swan, Hunter & Wigham Richardson Limited, Wallsend-on-Tyne, England—1927
HULL NO.:	1297
O. A. DIMENSIONS:	261' × 43'3" × 22'
FORMER DATA:	Deepened 2' at Western Engineering Service Limited, Fort William, Ontario in 1949.

A modern motor vessel in the Paterson fleet carries on this name today in honor of the city of Kingston, Ontario. This steamer is shown here while upbound in the Welland Ship Canal on July 10, 1952. This vessel was sold for scrap in 1961.

Kingston, Ontario is the seat of Frontenac County and is located on the north shoreline of Lake Ontario. It was formerly a very busy trans-shipping point for eastbound grain prior to the opening of the large St. Lawrence Seaway. This size vessel was an ever-present sight in the harbor.

Kingston was the sight of Fort Frontenac in 1674. After a series of barrages and rebuildings, it was used again in 1756 as the base for Montcalm's successful attack on Oswego, New York. It was incorporated as a town in 1838 and as a city in 1846.

The maiden voyage of this ship commenced May 14, 1927 from Wallsend-on-Tyne, England, light for Montreal, Quebec. On June 11, 1952, the Steamer KINGDOC delivered the first waterborne shipment of aluminum ever to come to Sandusky, Ohio. It was a cargo of 430 tons for Magnesium, Incorporated.

Steamer LABRADOC (1)

OWNER: N. M. Paterson & Sons Limited
BUILT: North of Ireland Shipbuilding Company, Londonderry, Ireland—1922
HULL NO.: 101
O. A. DIMENSIONS: 257' × 42'9" × 19'3"
FORMER DATA: Launched as NEW YORK NEWS (1). Renamed SHELTER BAY (1) in 1933. Given last name in 1958.

The Steamer LABRADOC was sold for scrap in 1961, but the vessel name is carried forward by a modern motor vessel that was built for this firm in 1966.

Namesake of the vessel is Labrador, the name given to the northeast portion of the Canadian mainland, north of the Gulf of St. Lawrence. It is bounded by Hudson Bay on the west, Hudson Strait on the north and the Atlantic Ocean on the east. Its populated area now is included in the province of Newfoundland.

This vessel name honors an area that has grown rapidly since the discovery of rich deposits of iron ore were first made. These have proven vastly significant to industry and have attracted hundreds of millions of dollars in investment over the past two decades. Over thirty million tons of iron ore are now shipped from the mines of the area on an annual basis.

Traditionally, the area had depended upon fishing and the fur industry for livelihood, but that is not the case any longer.

The bulk freight Steamer LABRADOC is shown below on October 11, 1958 in the Welland Ship Canal.

Motor Vessel LACHINEDOC (2)

OWNER: N. M. Paterson & Sons Limited
BUILT: Atlantic Shipbuilding Company, Newport, England—1956
HULL NO.: 5
O. A. DIMENSIONS: 259' × 43'9" × 22'6"

The Motor Vessel LACHINEDOC is named for the city of Lachine, Quebec and the Lachine Canal which formerly was the main bypass of the Lachine Rapids in the St. Lawrence River at Montreal, Quebec. The canal was closed to traffic in 1970.

Lachine, Quebec is located on the south shore of Montreal Island seven miles west of downtown Montreal, Quebec. The land was used by La Salle as the base point for his 1669 explorations. It had been granted to him in 1666 by the Sulpicians. It is thought that the name was given by La Salle's men who dreamed of finding China in their push westward. The French "La Chine" means China. First settlers came to the spot in 1675. In 1689 many were massacred by Iroquois Indians, but later Lachine became the local headquarters for the Hudson's Bay Company. Today it is an industrial center and residential community.

The Lachine Canal was constructed between 1821 and 1825 to bypass the rapids in the St. Lawrence River. These rapids are the first barrier to navigation enroute to the Great Lakes. The canal was enlarged between 1843 and 1848 and again by 1884. Each lock was 270 feet long by 45 feet wide by 14 feet in depth.

This vessel was towed across the Atlantic Ocean in the spring of 1956, arriving at Halifax, Nova Scotia May 17th. It sailed on its maiden trip May 22, 1956 light from Halifax to Cornerbrook, Newfoundland. The vessel was sold for off-Lakes use at 12:00 E.S.T., at Sorel, Quebec, July 25, 1975.

Steamer LAVALDOC

OWNER:	N. M. Paterson & Sons Limited
BUILT:	Swan, Hunter & Wigham Richardson Limited, Wallsend-on-Tyne, England—1928
HULL NO.:	1331
O. A. DIMENSIONS:	259' × 43'3" × 22'
FORMER DATA:	Deepened 4' at Port Arthur Shipbuilding Company, Port Arthur, Ontario in 1950.

The bulk freight Steamer LAVALDOC remained active in the trade patterns of this fleet on the Great Lakes until being sold for scrap in 1963. It met that fate in Montreal, Quebec in 1965. The ship is shown in this photograph at Port Colborne, Ontario on May 27, 1961.

This vessel also has the common Paterson fleet suffix in its name and took the town of Laval, Quebec as its specific namesake. Laval is a town with about 4,000 population in Nicolet County, Quebec. It is on the south shore of the St. Lawrence River directly across from Trois Rivieres, Quebec and is connected with that city by both ferry service and a highway bridge.

It is the northern terminus of the Canadian National Railways line from Victoriaville to Trois Rivieres and was named in reference to a former resident in the town who kept a boarding house for railroad workers. His last name happened to be the same as Francois Xavier de Laval de Montigny, 1st Bishop of Quebec.

The town is known among natives variously as Ste. Angele de Laval and Des Ormeaux. Very little waterborne commerce is carried on at Laval today. Most of the river activity relates to the ferry service to and from Trois Rivieres where all large quantity waterborne commerce is handled for the area and its hinterland.

Steamer LAWRENDOC (1)

OWNER:	N. M. Paterson & Sons Limited
BUILT:	Swan, Hunter & Wigham Richardson Limited, Wallsend-on-Tyne, England—1929
HULL NO.:	1385
O. A. DIMENSIONS:	259' × 43'3" × 24'
FORMER DATA:	Deepened 4'3" at Port Arthur Shipbuilding Company, Port Arthur, Ontario in 1948.

The Steamer LAWRENDOC takes its name from the St. Lawrence River through which most of its trips were made during its lifetime. The vessel also has the same common fleet suffix.

The St. Lawrence River is 1,900 miles in length extending from the eastern end of Lake Ontario to the Atlantic Ocean. It is the vital link, together with the St. Lawrence Seaway improvements, which enables the Great Lakes to become the North American continent's "fourth seacoast."

It is a fairly narrow river at the western end, but widens into the Gulf of St. Lawrence at its mouth. Millions of tons of commerce are carried on its waters annually.

This ship name is carried forward today by a modern motor vessel in the fleet. The Steamer LAWRENDOC was sold for conversion to a barge in 1961 after having served well since its maiden voyage across the Atlantic Ocean from builders yards in 1929.

This vessel is shown below in Lock 15 of the old St. Lawrence River canal at Cornwall, Ontario on October 25, 1956.

Steamer MANTADOC (1)

OWNER:	N. M. Paterson & Sons Limited
BUILT:	West Bay City Shipbuilding Company, West Bay City, Michigan—1903
HULL NO.:	611
O. A. DIMENSIONS:	436' × 50' × 28'
FORMER DATA:	Launched as FRANK W. GILCHRIST. Renamed CEPHEUS in 1913. Given last name in 1926.

This bulk freighter was sold in 1963 for use as a storage grain barge at Goderich, Ontario. Its name is carried forward today on the bow of a modern bulk freight vessel in the fleet. This former Steamer MANTADOC is shown here in the St. Mary's River on September 12, 1960.

The Province of Manitoba was this ship's namesake. It is located in central Canada and has an area of approximately 251,000 square miles with a population of 925,000 people. The usual suffix in the ship names of this fleet, "DOC," refers to the Dominion of Canada.

Manitoba's main focal point is the city of Winnipeg. It is the largest city in the province and is the main transportation hub of the surrounding area. It is also the location of the Winnipeg Grain Exchange, the headquarters for all grain trading in the Dominion.

Since this fleet and its owners have been identified so closely with the grain trade over the years, it is a fitting tribute to that relationship that this vessel and its successor should bear the name in reference to the grain trade's headquarters province.

Steamer MONDOC (2)

OWNER:	N. M. Paterson & Sons Limited
BUILT:	Furness Shipbuilding Company Limited, Haverton Hill-on-Tees, England—1928
HULL NO.:	138
O. A. DIMENSIONS:	259' × 43'3" × 20'
FORMER DATA:	Launched as WILLIAM SCHUPP. Given last name in 1945.

This vessel was sold for scrap in 1961, but its name lives on on the bow of a modern motor vessel in the Paterson fleet.

Namesake of this ship is the city of Montreal, Quebec which is the eastern operating headquarters of the owners. It is also the largest city in Canada and the second largest French speaking city in the world. It is located on Montreal Island at the confluence of the St. Lawrence and Ottawa Rivers. Mount Royal, at the center of the island rises 769 feet above sea level. The metropolitan area has a population of 2,350,000, some 65% of which are French.

Montreal was discovered by Jacques Cartier in 1535. He was welcomed by a large group of Huron Indians who took him to their stockade of Hochelaga where he held prayers with them and read to them from the Gospel of St. John. No other recorded visits occurred until Champlain came to the site in 1603. The first mission was set up there in 1642 by Jeanne Mance and development on the waterway followed shortly thereafter.

The Steamer MONDOC is seen in this picture on September 17, 1957 in the Welland Ship Canal upbound with a load of iron ore from the lower St. Lawrence River port of Seven Islands, Quebec.

Motor Vessel MONDOC (3)

```
     OWNER:  N. M. Paterson & Sons Limited
     BUILT:  Collingwood Shipyards,
             Collingwood, Ontario—1962
   HULL NO.: 173
O. A. DIMENSIONS: 291' × 45' × 24'
```

The Motor Vessel MONDOC is named for Montreal, Quebec which is the eastern operating headquarters of the owners. It is also the largest city in Canada and the second largest French speaking city in the world. It is located on Montreal Island at the confluence of the St. Lawrence and Ottawa Rivers. Mount Royal, at the center of the island, rises 769 feet above sea level. The metropolitan area has a population of 2,300,000, some 64.5% of which are French.

Montreal was discovered by Jacques Cartier in 1535. He was welcomed by a large group of Huron Indians who took him to their stockaded settlement of Hochelaga where he held prayers with them and read to them from the Gospel of St. John. No other visitors came until Samuel de Champlain in 1603.

On May 17, 1642 a mission station was founded there by Jeanne Mance. The American Revolution led to an unsuccessful attack on Montreal in 1775 by Ethan Allen and to the city's abandonment by Sir Guy Carleton. When Upper and Lower Canada reunited in 1840, Montreal became the capital for a short time. Steam navigation began in 1809 with the Steamer ACCOMMODATION being built by John Molson, noted banker and brewer. At confederation, in 1867, Montreal was already the metropolitan city of Canada. Its namesake vessel is shown below while upbound at Port Robinson, Ontario in the Welland Ship Canal on November 6, 1973. It was sold for off-Lakes use in 1979.

Steamer NEWBRUNDOC (2)

OWNER:	N. M. Paterson & Sons Limited
BUILT:	Swan, Hunter & Wigham Richardson Limited, Wallsend-on-Tyne, England—1928
HULL NO.:	1347
O. A. DIMENSIONS:	259' × 43'3" × 24'
FORMER DATA:	Deepened 4'3" at St. Lawrence Dry Docks Limited, Montreal, Quebec in 1949.

The canal-sized Steamer NEWBRUNDOC was an active bulk freighter on the Great Lakes and in the St. Lawrence Seaway System until 1963 when it was sold for scrap.

The namesake of this vessel was the province of New Brunswick in eastern Canada. It is one of the four original Canadian provinces of the Confederation of 1867 and encompasses an area of 28,354 square miles. It has a coast line of 600 miles along Chaleur Bay in the north, the Gulf of St. Lawrence and Northumberland Strait in the east and the Bay of Fundy in the south.

The area was first settled by the French in 1604 and for a time was part of the French province in Canada and later part of the British province of Nova Scotia. New Brunswick separated from Nova Scotia in 1784 because of the influx of Loyalists into the Saint John Valley. Largely, population has left New Brunswick for greater industrial opportunity in the west. Current population is about 650,000, but the provincial government has taken steps to attract industry in later years.

The vessel is shown here between Locks 1 and 2 of the Welland Ship Canal on November 12, 1955.

Steamer ONTADOC (1)

OWNER: N. M. Paterson & Sons Limited
BUILT: Chicago Shipbuilding Company, Chicago, Illinois—1903
HULL NO.: 62
O. A. DIMENSIONS: 436' × 50' × 28'
FORMER DATA: Launched as R. L. IRELAND. Renamed SIRIUS in 1913. Given last name in 1926.

The Steamer ONTADOC was named for the province of Ontario, home province of the company and owners' family.

Ontario is geographically and historically the keystone province of Canada. It is centrally located among the ten provinces and links east and west. It is also the province in which the Dominion's capital is located, the site of Ottawa being selected for this purpose by Queen Victoria in 1857.

The name is Iroquoian and applied to the lake as early as 1641, much later to the county east of Toronto and finally to the province when it joined Confederation in 1867.

The Welland Canal, first begun in 1824, is a crucial link in Great Lakes commerce and lies wholly within Ontario. The name this vessel bore aptly honored a vital commercial and residential part of the Dominion of Canada.

This bulk freighter is shown below at Lock 2 of the Welland Ship Canal on May 30, 1970. It was active until taking its final cargo of grain at Thunder Bay, Ontario for Quebec City, Quebec delivery in October, 1970. From Quebec City it was towed across the Atlantic Ocean to be scrapped.

Barge OWENDOC

OWNER:	N. M. Paterson & Sons Limited
BUILT:	Chicago Shipbuilding Company, Chicago, Illinois—1896
HULL NO.:	18
O. A. DIMENSIONS:	367'6" × 44' × 26'1"
FORMER DATA:	Launched as MARTHA. Renamed FLORENCE in 1937. Renamed MAUREEN H. in 1938. Renamed FLORENCE J. in 1939. Renamed OWENDOC in 1949.

The bulk freight Barge OWENDOC is shown above while under tow near Sault Ste. Marie, Michigan on August 17, 1956. This vessel was sold for use as a grain storage hull at Goderich, Ontario in 1962 and bore the name C. S. BAND until sold for sinking as a breakwater in 1975.

The namesake of this vessel while in operation was the city of Owen Sound, Ontario which is the seat of Grey County and is located on Owen Sound, an inlet of Georgian Bay at the outlet of the Sydenham and Pottawattomi rivers. It became a port of call for steamers plying between Port Sarnia and Sturgeon Bay in 1844 and was incorporated as a town in 1857, taking the name of the bay on which it was located as its namesake. The bay, or sound, had in turn been named for Captain W. F. Owen who had charted it in 1815. The town was granted status as a city in 1920 and has a population of about 20,000 residents.

Great Lakes commerce is still carried on at the port with grain, liquid cargo and coal being the chief receipts. It is also the headquarters city for both the Owen Sound Transportation Company and the Hindman Transportation Company Limited.

Steamer PORTADOC (3)

OWNER: N. M. Paterson & Sons Limited
BUILT: Globe Iron Works, Cleveland, Ohio—1899
HULL NO.: 79
O. A. DIMENSIONS: 436' × 50' × 28'
FORMER DATA: Launched as H. C. FRICK. Renamed E. A. S. CLARKE (1) in 1906. Renamed MARS (3) in 1916. Renamed CANADOC (1) in 1926. Given last name in 1961.

The bulk freight Steamer PORTADOC was active in the iron ore, coal and grain trades on the Great Lakes until being sold for scrap in 1967. It relinquished its second last name when a modern motor vessel was commissioned for this fleet which took that name.

As is common in the Paterson Fleet, the suffix "DOC" is appended to the specific namesake in the ship name. This suffix stands for Dominion of Canada.

Port Arthur, Ontario was the namesake city of this freighter. That place does not exist under that name today. On January 1, 1970, it and its sister city, Fort William, were combined to be called Thunder Bay, Ontario.

Port Arthur was part of an area known as the "Canadian Lakehead." The Canadian National and Canadian Pacific systems both serve the area. There are important gold mines in the tributory area, but the shipments of grain and iron ore are the most important local industries. In addition, extensive pulp and paper mills and lumbering provide employment for large numbers of the area's residents.

The Steamer PORTADOC is shown below at the Port Colborne, Ontario entrance to the Welland Ship Canal on April 16, 1966.

Steamer PRESCODOC (2)

OWNER: N. M. Paterson & Sons Limited
BUILT: Barclay, Curle & Company, Limited, Glasgow, Scotland—1929
HULL NO.: 632
O. A. DIMENSIONS: 259' × 43'3" × 24'
FORMER DATA: Launched as SIOUX. Deepened 6'3" at Muir Brothers Dry Dock Company, Limited, Port Dalhousie, Ontario in 1940. Given last name in 1946.

Sold for scrap in 1963, the bulk freight Steamer PRESCODOC was one of several ships that this company owned which were originally built for ownership in Canada, but had operating control in the United States. In this case, this vessel was owned originally by St. Lawrence Steamship Company of Welland, Ontario but was operated by E. S. Crosby & Company of Buffalo, New York.

The Steamer PRESCODOC had the usual fleet name suffix and took the city of Prescott, Ontario as its specific namesake. Prescott is located on the north shore of the St. Lawrence River opposite Ogdensburg, Ontario. A bridge connects the two cities. It is a city rich in lore. The first settler was Colonel Edward Jessup who surveyed the townsite in 1810 and named it Prescott in honor of General Robert Prescott, Governor-in-Chief of Canada from 1797 to 1807.

The first house was erected in 1812 and the first water-related business was begun by Mr. William Gilkinson who operated a warehouse and wharf in 1815. In 1834 Prescott became a police village and in 1851 it was incorporated as a town. The city's namesake is shown here below Lock 4 in the Welland Ship Canal on December 1, 1956.

Steamer PRINDOC (2)

OWNER:	N. M. Paterson & Sons Limited
BUILT:	American Ship Building Company, Lorain, Ohio—1902
HULL NO.:	318
O. A. DIMENSIONS:	400' × 50' × 28'
FORMER DATA:	Launched as HAROLD B. NYE. Renamed W. D. CALVERLEY, JR. in 1925. Given last name in 1948.

A modern motor vessel now carries this name in the Paterson fleet. This Steamer PRINDOC was sold for scrap in 1964.

Namesake of the ship is the smallest province in the Dominion of Canada—Prince Edward Island. It is the smallest province in both area and population and is located in the Gulf of St. Lawrence, separated from Nova Scotia and New Brunswick by the Northumberland Strait.

The island has an area of 2,184 square miles and a current population of one hundred-ten thousand persons. Its name originated in 1799 to honor Prince Edward, Duke of Kent and father of Queen Victoria who had once shown an interest in the fortification of the city of Charlottetown, the capital of the province.

Prince Edward Island is 120 miles in length and from 3 to 35 miles in width. It has irregular coastlines with large bays and long inlets all around. High cliffs and sandy beaches are characteristic of the shoreline. It is a favorite tourist area in the summer season.

This freighter is shown below in the Detroit River on June 17, 1958.

Steamer QUEDOC (1)

OWNER:	N. M. Paterson & Sons Limited
BUILT:	Globe Iron Works, Cleveland, Ohio—1890
HULL NO.:	31
O. A. DIMENSIONS:	362' × 40'3" × 24'6"
FORMER DATA:	Launched as MARISKA. Cut in two at Buffalo Dry Dock Company, Buffalo, New York in 1918. Rejoined at Canadian Vickers, Limited, Montreal, Quebec in 1918. Cut in two and lengthened 48' at Canadian Vickers, Limited, Montreal, Quebec in 1923. Rejoined at Great Lakes Engineering Works, Ashtabula, Ohio and renamed KAMARIS in 1923. Renamed QUEDOC in 1926.

The Steamer QUEDOC is shown in this picture at Victory Soya Mills elevator in Toronto, Ontario on June 5, 1957.

This ship had an interesting career as can be seen from the above, but from its arrival back on the Great Lakes on October 11, 1923 it was strictly a Great Lakes carrier. It was sold for conversion to the Barge H.S.&G. No. 1 in 1959 and was scrapped in 1961 at Hamilton, Ontario.

The namesake of this vessel is the largest French-speaking province of Canada. Its capital is also known as Quebec, but usually the word "City" follows that placename to differentiate the city from the province. The first visitor to Quebec was Jacques Cartier in 1534 when he landed on the Gaspe Peninsula and proclaimed it French territory. Samuel de Champlain founded Quebec City in 1608.

Motor Vessel SARNIADOC (2)

OWNER: N. M. Paterson & Sons Limited
BUILT: Collingwood Shipyards,
Collingwood, Ontario—1956
HULL NO.: 155
O. A. DIMENSIONS: 259' × 43'9" × 22'6"

The bulk freight Motor Vessel SARNIADOC takes its name from the city of Sarnia, Ontario and the common fleet suffix. It is one of several pre-Seaway dimension vessels still operating on the Great Lakes. At one time there was a fleet of several hundred ships of this size on the Great Lakes, but since the construction of the St. Lawrence Seaway they have steadily dwindled in number.

Sarnia, Ontario is the home of Canada's largest complete oil refinery, largest Fiberglas plant, only synthetic-rubber plant, first glycol plant and only carbon-black facility. All these operations make up Sarnia's famous "Chemical Valley" along the shores of the St. Clair River.

There are in addition general cargo docks and warehouses, a grain elevator and miscellaneous bulk dry cargo docks in the area. All these front on one of the world's busiest waterways—the St. Clair River.

The city grew rapidly once heavy industry was established and actually doubled in size between 1946 and 1953.

This vessel was active in the fleet through 1975's navigation season and was sold in 1976 for off-Lakes use. It is shown below upbound at Port Weller, Ontario bound for Wallaceburg, Ontario on November 16, 1975.

Steamer SASKADOC

OWNER:	N. M. Paterson & Sons Limited
BUILT:	Globe Iron Works, Cleveland, Ohio—1900
HULL NO.:	80
O. A. DIMENSIONS:	436' × 50' × 28'
FORMER DATA:	Launched as WILLIAM E. REIS. Renamed URANUS (4) in 1916. Given last name in 1926.

The province of Saskatchewan, Canada was the namesake of this bulk freighter. It also had the familiar fleet suffix on the ship name. This vessel was sold for scrapping overseas in 1967. It is shown here in the St. Mary's River, upbound on August 19, 1964.

Saskatchewan is a Cree Indian word meaning "rapid river." The province extends from the International Boundary with the United States on the south to 60 degrees north latitude, a distance of seven hundred and sixty miles. It lies between Manitoba on the east and Alberta on the west. Total area of the province is 251,700 square miles.

Agriculture is the primary activity, though mining and oil refining have become fast-rising activities of the people of the province. The southern third of the province is treeless prairie. Much of this land is rich and yields high acreage production of wheat. Livestock also thrives in this area where sufficient rainfall occurs.

Lignite coal, brick and china clay are mined in the south and gold and copper are mined in the north. In this northern part of the province, lakes, fish and furs are found in abundance. Hudson Bay traders penetrated Saskatchewan's interior in 1691 and French fur traders reached the area about 1750. It has a current population of about one million.

Steamer SOODOC (1)

OWNER: N. M. Paterson & Sons Limited
BUILT: American Ship Building Company, Lorain, Ohio—1902
HULL NO.: 320
O. A. DIMENSIONS: 436' × 50' × 28'
FORMER DATA: Launched as MOSES TAYLOR. Given last name in 1926.

The bulk freight Steamer SOODOC (1) continued active in Great Lakes commerce until being sold for scrap in 1967. It is shown here in Sault Ste. Marie Harbor on April 25, 1964.

This ship utilized the famous Paterson fleet suffix on its ship name, "DOC," and specifically took Sault Ste. Marie, Ontario and Sault Ste. Marie, Michigan as its namesakes. These twin sister cities comprise the metropolitan area surrounding the world famous Soo Locks.

Etienne Brule first arrived at the site in the early 1600's and named the place Sault De Gaston. The name was changed to Sault Sainte Marie in 1669 when a permanent mission was established by the French. From that time until the discovery of iron ore and copper on Michigan's Upper Peninsula, little real permanent growth took place in the area. Following the opening of the first lock in 1855, however, commerce between the Upper and Lower Lakes has kept both "Soos" very busy places.

Not only are the locks vital to commerce and heavy industry on the North American continent, they also provide allied employment and income to hundreds of other businesses and people. These are primarily in the way of tourist accommodation in the summer, fishing and hunting in the winter and year-around activity of many varied civic responsibilities for the permanent residents.

Steamer SORELDOC (2)

OWNER:	N. M. Paterson & Sons Limited
BUILT:	Swan, Hunter & Wigham Richardson Limited, Sunderland, England—1929
HULL NO.:	1367
O. A. DIMENSIONS:	259' × 43'6" × 24'
FORMER DATA:	Launched as PHENICIA. Renamed CHEYENNE in 1931. Deepened 4' at Muir Brothers Dry Dock Company Limited, Port Dalhousie, Ontario in 1940. Given last name in 1946.

The canal size bulk freight Steamer SORELDOC was sold for scrap in 1966 and is shown in the below photograph in the Welland Ship Canal upbound with a load of newsprint in 1962.

The namesake community of this vessel is Sorel, Quebec. Sorel is a city and port in Richelieu County located on the south shore of the St. Lawrence River about 40 miles east of Montreal and 32 miles west of Three Rivers, Quebec. It has a population of nearly 20,000 residents and is on the mainline of the Canadian National Railways from Montreal, Quebec to Halifax, Nova Scotia.

Sorel commemorates Pierre de Saurel who in 1672 obtained a concession of lands surrounding Fort Richelieu. A monument now marks the old fort. The town was granted city status in 1889. It is an important maritime city today, being the headquarters of the Canadian Government dredging fleet, site of a major shipyard and major grain trans-shipping elevator.

Steamer THORDOC (2)

OWNER:	N. M. Paterson & Sons Limited
BUILT:	Earles Shipbuilding & Engineering Company, Hull, England—1927
HULL NO.:	670
O. A. DIMENSIONS:	261' × 43'3" × 20'
FORMER DATA:	Launched as CASCO. Renamed THORDOC in 1955.

The canal-sized bulk freight Steamer THORDOC was sold for conversion to a barge in 1961 after having been in the Paterson fleet since 1955. It is still visible as a hulk at Point Edward, Ontario and was known as CHEMBARGE No. 2 in its latter days.

Its namesake was the city of Thorold, Ontario. That city is located in Welland County directly on the famous and busy Welland Ship Canal. The site was founded in 1788 and named for Sir John Thorold who was then British M. P. for Lincolnshire and who opposed the war with American colonies. He voted against the Constitutional Act of 1791.

Thorold was incorporated in 1875 and has a population of about 10,000 persons today. The city has a huge paper mill in its boundaries which belongs to the Ontario Paper Company. Since the early days of the Paterson fleet, the firm has been engaged in both the movement of pulpwood and the movement of newsprint. Since pulpwood is brought into the paper plant at Thorold and newsprint is shipped out, both by water and land means, management thought it would be a fitting tribute to the industry at Thorold to put that city's name on this vessel bow.

The ship is shown below at Lock 1 of the Welland Ship Canal on November 5, 1955. It is upbound and about to enter the lock.

Steamer TORONDOC (2)

OWNER:	N. M. Paterson & Sons Limited
BUILT:	Swan, Hunter & Wigham Richardson Limited, Wallsend-on-Tyne, England—1929
HULL NO.:	1397
O. A. DIMENSIONS:	259' × 43'3" × 24'
FORMER DATA:	Launched as SARACEN. Given last name in 1954.

The bulk freight Steamer TORONDOC utilizes the common fleet suffix in the ship name and had the city of Toronto, Ontario as its specific namesake.

Toronto is the second largest city in the Dominion of Canada with a current population in the metropolitan area of 2,500,000 persons. It has two rivers flowing through it, the Humber River on the west and the Don River on the east. Its harbor is a natural one and is among the largest on Lake Ontario. In 1853 the harbor's eastern gap was formed by a violent storm which washed away the land making an island out of what was formerly a peninsula. This area of the modern harbor is under expansion with landfill to form additional modern waterborne commerce dock facilities.

The operations of this fleet are not concentrated at Toronto, but ships of the line call here from time to time with coal, grain and newsprint. The city is famous as the home of the Canadian National Exhibition, the world's largest annual fair. It is held for three weeks in August and September and annually attracts visitors from across Canada and from the United States. The fair has been an annual event since 1879 and adopted its present name in 1912.

The Steamer TORONDOC was active on the Great Lakes until being sold for scrap in 1962. It is shown in this picture in the Welland Ship Canal. Ironically, this vessel was scrapped at its namesake port.

Steamer TROISDOC (2)

OWNER:	N. M. Paterson & Sons Limited
BUILT:	Barclay, Curle & Company Limited, Glasgow, Scotland—1929
HULL NO.:	631
O. A. DIMENSIONS:	259' × 43'3" × 24'
FORMER DATA:	Launched as ALGONQUINS. Deepened 6'3" at Muir Brothers Dry Dock Company Limited, Port Dalhousie, Ontario in 1940. Given last name in 1946.

The Steamer TROISDOC was one of the last canal-sized bulk freight vessels powered by steam to be operated by this fleet when it was sold for scrap in 1966. It too fell victim to more progressive tonnage on the Great Lakes.

Namesake of this ship is the city of Trois Rivieres, Quebec. This city is often referred to in Anglicized form and unofficially as Three Rivers, Quebec.

The city is located on the north shore of the St. Lawrence River eighty-five miles downstream from Montreal, Quebec at the confluence of the St. Lawrence and the St. Maurice Rivers. The name comes from the fact that the St. Maurice River has three outlets separated by delta islands. the harbor is deep and has facilities for bulk dry cargo, grain, liquid cargo and general cargo.

The Paterson fleet has carried many thousands of tons of newsprint from the city wharves over the years and deemed it fitting to christen this ship in honor of the port. The area was first settled in 1610 and was incorporated as a city in 1857.

The steamer is shown below running light upbound in the Detroit River on August 24, 1961.

Steamer VANDOC (1)

OWNER: N. M. Paterson & Sons Limited
BUILT: Globe Iron Works, Cleveland, Ohio—1898
HULL NO.: 74
O. A. DIMENSIONS: 430' × 50' × 28'
FORMER DATA: Launched as HENDRICK S. HOLDEN. Renamed ARGUS (2) in 1916. Given last name in 1927.

The bulk freight Steamer VANDOC served in the iron ore, coal and grain trades on the Great Lakes until being sold for scrap in 1966. It took as its namesake the city of Vancouver, British Columbia.

Vancouver is the largest city and most important seaport of Canada on the Pacific Coast. It is located at the mouth of the Fraser River delta and has a current population of about 500,000. It has recently been in the marine news headlines as a major coal exporting center because of the development of the gigantic Robert's Bank facility.

The city takes its name from Captain George Vancouver of the Royal Navy who explored the area in 1792. A small settlement started there in 1865, but real growth did not occur until the Canadian Pacific Railway from the East was completed in the 1880's. Vancouver was incorporated as a city in 1886. By 1910 the population had reached 100,000. It became a great seaport after the completion of the Panama Canal in 1915 because it gave access to exports of large tonnages of Western Canadian grain stocks to European markets.

Vancouver has one of the mildest climates in the Dominion of Canada. Instead of large snowfall during the winter months, mostly rain falls. The city boasts of a fine park, Stanley Park, and a metropolitan zoo. The University of British Columbia and Simon Fraser University are also located there.

Steamer WELLANDOC (2)

OWNER: N. M. Paterson and Sons Limited
BUILT: Fraser Brace Limited,
Three Rivers, Quebec - 1922
HULL NO.: 21
O. A. DIMENSIONS: 263' x 43'3" x 20'6"
FORMER DATA: Launched as EDWARD L. STRONG. Renamed SHERBROOKE in 1927. Renamed AROSA in 1946. Renamed IDA O. in 1951. Given last name in 1952.

The bulk freight Steamer WELLANDOC (2) was sold for scrap in 1961 and met that fate during the winter of 1963-1964. It is shown in the photograph below in the Soulanges Canal on October 22, 1958. This vessel was originally constructed as a conventional steam canaller, but was rebuilt for salt water service later in her career and retained that look until the end of her career.

The namesake of this vessel was the namesake city in Ontario of the Welland Ship Canal–Welland. This city has been a focal point of the canal for decades. It used to be divided in its downtown district by the canal.

Welland is a city of about forty thousand residents and is highly industrialized. Steel manufacturing plants and allied industries are located in the city and its former docks annually took in and shipped over one half million tons of cargo, most of this being bulk commodities and finished products.

Steamer WINDOC (1)

OWNER: N. M. Paterson & Sons Limited
BUILT: Globe Iron Works,
Cleveland, Ohio - 1899
HULL NO.: 77
O. A. DIMENSIONS: 430' x 50' x 28'
FORMER DATA: Launched as M. A. HANNA. Renamed HYDRUS (2) in 1916. Given last name in 1927.

The bulk freight Steamer WINDOC (1) continued in operation in this fleet until 1967 when it was sold for scrap. During the last forty years of its existence it honored the city of Winnipeg, Manitoba as its namesake.

Winnipeg is the fourth largest city in Canada and is the capital of the Province of Manitoba. It has a current population of about 325,000 and is situated at the confluence of the Red and Assiniboine rivers. The city name comes from the Cree Indian words "win," meaning muddy and "nipee," meaning water.

Among the first settlers in the area were the fur-traders who erected a fort under the direction of Pierre de la Verendrye in 1738. Fort Gibraltor was built by the North West Company in 1804 and Fort Garry by Hudson's Bay Company in 1821. The city grew as settlers pushed westward across the prairies towards the Pacific Ocean. Winnipeg had no direct communication with other distant centers until 1859 when steamboats passed up the Red River from the United States. In 1878 the first train entered Winnipeg from Minnesota and, in 1885, the Canadian Pacific Railway passed through connecting Winnipeg with eastern Canadian cities.

This vessel is shown on May 14, 1966 in the Welland Ship Canal.

Steamer PELEE

OWNER:	Pelee Shipping Company Limited
BUILT:	Collingwood Shipbuilding Company, Limited, Collingwood, Ontario—1914
HULL NO.:	41
O. A. DIMENSIONS:	145' × 24' × 11'3"

The passenger and automobile ferry Steamer PELEE served on the usual routes for this firm from Leamington and Kingsville, Ontario to Sandusky, Ohio, via Pelee Island, from its inaugural trip in 1914 until it was sold for scrap in 1966.

The namesake of both the owners and this vessel was Pelee Island, a part of Essex County, Ontario. It lies in Lake Erie about eight miles southwest of Point Pelee and just north of the International Boundary. It is the southernmost portion of Canada. Measuring about 8 by 3-1/2 miles, Pelee is the largest of a group of islands lying along the border.

The name PELEE is derived from the French *pelée*, meaning "bare" or "bald." Leased from the Indians by Mr. Thomas McKee in 1788, the island was purchased by Mr. William McCormick in 1823 for $500.00. In 1834 McCormick moved to the island to found an ancestral estate for his family. Later, parts of the island were sold by his descendants.

Today, soybeans are the leading product of the farms on the island and these are shipped by Great Lakes freighters into export. Grape and tobacco growing are also in evidence. The island has many year-round residents but also attracts many visitors in the summer months. A number of these visitors have cabins and lakeshore property on Pelee Island and come from both the United States and Canada.

Steamer ASHTABULA

OWNER: Pennsylvania—Ontario Transportation Company
BUILT: Great Lakes Engineering Works,
St. Clair, Michigan—1906
HULL NO.: 19
O. A. DIMENSIONS: 350' × 56' × 21'6"

The five-year interval without a loss of Great Lakes vessels due to navigational hazards was broken when this carferry sank in collision with the Steamer BEN MOREELL in the outer harbor at Ashtabula, Ohio on September 18, 1958. No casualties were involved and the hull was subsequently raised. Damage was too great, however, to warrant repairs and the ship was scrapped at Ashtabula, Ohio in 1959.

During its life on Lake Erie this vessel traded regularly between its namesake port and Port Burwell, Ontario handling railroad cars for interchange with Canadian roads. It was equipped with some icebreaking capability and usually ran late into the winter.

Ashtabula, Ohio was the ship's namesake. It was first settled in 1803 when visitors were sent there by the Connecticut Land Company. Mr. Matthew Hubbard came in 1804 and became the first principal in the town. The village was incorporated in 1831 and a city charter was granted in 1891. The name of the city is Indian which means, literally, "river of many fish." This refers to the Ashtabula River which flows into Lake Erie at the mouth of the harbor.

The harbor is full of modern docks today. Iron ore and stone, as well as general cargo, are unloaded and major quantities of coal are shipped into export annually. Nearby, large chemical plants and automotive forging plants exist.

Steamer FRANK BILLINGS

OWNER: Pioneer Steamship Company
BUILT: Great Lakes Engineering Works, Ecorse, Michigan—1910
HULL NO.: 72
O. A. DIMENSIONS: 465' × 56' × 30'
FORMER DATA: Launched as CHAMPLAIN (2). Given last name in 1915.

This bulk freighter was re-christened in 1915 to honor Mr. Frank Billings of Cleveland, Ohio. He was born at Hastings-on-the-Hudson, New York on September 27, 1853 and was educated in the public schools and the University of Chicago.

His family moved to Cleveland about the time he finished his education and he started his career there in the paint business. In 1883, with N. D. Chapin, he founded the Billings-Chapin Company. He then married into the Tod family and his father-in-law was president of the Tod-Stambaugh Company, iron ore merchants. Upon the death of his father-in-law in 1894, Mr. Billings became president of the Tod-Stambaugh Company. His ore interests extended all over the Great Lakes. He retired from the firm in the 1920's and died at Cleveland, Ohio on January 19, 1928.

Mr. Billings was a director of Union Trust Company and Guardian Trust Company in addition to various other civic and business affiliations. His namesake was sold for scrapping in 1962.

The Steamer FRANK BILLINGS is shown in this photograph upbound for a cargo of iron ore at the area of the Soo Locks at Sault Ste. Marie, Michigan on June 17, 1955.

Steamer PRICE McKINNEY

OWNER: Pioneer Steamship Company
BUILT: American Ship Building Company, Lorain, Ohio—1908
HULL NO.: 363
O. A. DIMENSIONS: 452' × 54' × 28'3"

Namesake of this ship, which was sold for scrap in 1961, was Mr. Price McKinney who was born near Hamilton, Ohio on May 1, 1862. He went to Cleveland and Toledo, Ohio after completing his education to sell domestic furnaces. In this line he became familiar with the steel business.

For a time he worked for the Hocking Valley Railroad in the purchasing department and, later, made trips to Mexico for Judge Burke to inspect his gold and silver mines. On return to Cleveland, he was receiver of the Corrigan, Ives & Company, steel manufacturers, which firm foundered in the panic of 1893. Following the receivership, the firm prospered and Mr. McKinney remained a power in the company. It had plants at Genesee, New York, Scottsdale, Pennsylvania and Cleveland, Ohio.

In 1910 Mr. McKinney formed the McKinney Steel Company out of several firms and remained as president of the company until May, 1925. He shot himself with a German Luger and died on April 13, 1926 after suffering ill health for about one year. He was regarded as an extremely shrewd independent steel operator and was wrapped up in the romance of bringing iron ore down the lakes and forging it into steel. He shunned the public spotlight, but did allow himself the pleasures of an ardent horseman.

This ship departed Cleveland, Ohio on June 26, 1908 on its maiden voyage carrying a cargo of coal for Escanaba, Michigan. The ship is shown below in the Cuyahoga River, Cleveland, Ohio on April 28, 1960.

Steamer JOHN S. MANUEL

OWNER: Pioneer Steamship Company
BUILT: Great Lakes Engineering Works,
Ecorse, Michigan - 1910
HULL NO.: 73
O. A. DIMENSIONS: 465' x 56' x 30'
FORMER DATA: Launched as ST. CLAIR (1). Renamed E. L. PIERCE in 1915. Given last name in 1924.

When the bulk freight Steamer JOHN S. MANUEL was given its last name, its namesake was senior partner and manager of the firm of W. S. & J. S. Manuel Company, forwarders of lake shipments of coal and he was also vice president of this owning company.

Mr. John Sutphin Manuel was born in Shandon, Ohio on June 14, 1873 and was educated at Miami University at Oxford, Ohio. He began working for his uncle in the Sunday Creek Coal Company upon graduation in 1894 and, later that year, joined the Turney and Jones Coal Company in Columbus, Ohio. In 1896 he was promoted to supervisor of the company at Conneaut, Ohio and in 1898 was manager of the firm's dock and properties at Ashland, Wisconsin.

Mr. Manuel came to Cleveland, Ohio in 1902 to join his brother in the above named company. When Mr. W. S. Manuel died in 1919, Mr. John S. Manuel took over as head of the concern and remained in that position until his death at Cleveland, Ohio on February 2, 1940. Among his other business activities were directorships in the Buckeye Steamship Company and the Central National Bank of Cleveland.

His namesake was active until sold for scrap in 1961 and is shown in the photograph below in the lower St. Mary's River on August 28, 1953. The vessel's maiden voyage commenced from Detroit, Michigan on May 24, 1910 light to Duluth, Minnesota for iron ore.

Steamer WILLIAM A. PAINE

OWNER:	Pioneer Steamship Company
BUILT:	American Ship Building Company, Cleveland, Ohio—1905
HULL NO.:	427
O. A. DIMENSIONS:	500' × 52' × 30'

Mr. William Alfred Paine is the namesake of this vessel. He was born at Merrimacport, Massachusetts on January 29, 1855 and was educated in the public schools. He began working as a clerk in the Blackstone National Bank in Boston, Massachusetts and showed such ability that he was made assistant cashier. In 1880 he resigned this post and, with Wallace A. Webber, established the investment banking firm of Paine, Webber & Company. He became senior partner in the firm and held that post until his death at Swampscott, Massachusetts on September 24, 1929.

He was active in financing companies engaged in the development of the copper deposits of northern Michigan and these investments yielded handsome profits. Mr. Paine acquired control of small copper companies which he merged into the Copper Range Company in 1898 and became its president. He was also president of Champion Paper Company, Copper Range Railway Company and an officer or director in several other firms.

The firm he founded is now known as Paine, Webber, Jackson and Curtis. His association with the Great Lakes area led this vessel to be named in his honor. The ship was sold for scrap in 1961. The Steamer WILLIAM A. PAINE's maiden voyage was from Ashtabula, Ohio on August 7, 1905 with a cargo of coal for Duluth/Superior Harbor. It had run from Cleveland to Ashtabula light to load the cargo. The vessel is shown below at Port Weller, Ontario on November 5, 1955.

Steamer JOHN STANTON

OWNER:	Pioneer Steamship Company
BUILT:	American Ship Building Company, Lorain, Ohio—1905
HULL NO.:	338
O. A. DIMENSIONS:	524' × 54' × 30'

The Steamer JOHN STANTON was sold for scrap in 1961 shortly before the liquidation of this company. Its namesake was Mr. John Stanton who was born on February 25, 1830 at Bristol, England. He came to the United States with his family in 1835 because his father was planning to invest heavily in the coal fields of Pennsylvania. The father also bought two iron mines in New Jersey. Mr. John Stanton received little formal education and was tutored mostly by his father who set him to work at the age of seventeen in managing the two iron mines.

The businesses prospered and, after successful development of copper deposits along the eastern seaboard and in the South, attention was turned to the copper deposits in northern Michigan. Mr. Stanton developed several valuable mines in the area which saw production for many years.

He was president of Wolverine Copper Mining Company, Mohawk Mining Company, Baltic Mining Company and Winona Copper Company. He was also one of the founders of the New York Mining Stock Exchange and was its president in 1876. Mr. Stanton continued active in his various business affairs until his death in New York City on February 23, 1906. His namesake made its maiden voyage on October 11, 1905 when it left Lorain, Ohio light for Duluth, Minnesota for a cargo of iron ore. It is shown below passing through Little Rapids Cut, St. Mary's River, on August 13, 1957.

Steamer JAMES P. WALSH

OWNER: Pioneer Steamship Company
BUILT: Craig Shipbuilding Company, Toledo, Ohio—1905
HULL NO.: 103
O. A. DIMENSIONS: 508'6" × 52' × 30'

The bulk freight Steamer JAMES P. WALSH honored Mr. James Pennington Walsh as its namesake. He was born in Cleveland, Ohio on August 5, 1861 and was educated in the public schools. In 1880 he joined his father in the family Walsh Coal Company as a clerk. He learned the coal business from living it. By 1883 he was named manager of the firm. When it was consolidated into Walsh-Upstill Coal Company in 1888 Mr. Walsh became a partner in the firm.

In 1889 he joined M. A. Hanna Company as sales manager and, in 1894, joined Pittsburgh Coal Company as general sales manager. It was with this firm that he was to make his career until near normal retirement age. He was elected vice president of sales in 1910 and continued in that position until 1922. This firm was the largest coal shipper on the Great Lakes for many years.

During World War I, Mr. Walsh served at $1.00 per year salary, in addition to his official duties, as vice coal administrator of the United States. He also served as secretary-treasurer and director of Becker Steamship Company and Carnegie Metals Company from the early 1920's until 1928. In addition, Mr. Walsh served on the board of directors of Jenkins, Pioneer and Midland Steamship Companies.

When this ship was launched on May 16, 1905 it flew an Irish sunburst from the forward mast to signal it being the first "Irish" ship on the Lakes, Mr. Walsh being an Irishman. It continued active until being sold for scrap in 1961 and is shown below in the St. Mary's River on June 19, 1956.

Steamer STARBELLE

OWNER: K. A. Powell (Canada) Limited
BUILT: Greenock & Grangemouth Dockyard Company, Limited, Grangemouth, Scotland—1913
HULL NO.: 351
O. A. DIMENSIONS: 259' × 43' × 21'
FORMER DATA: Launched as the tanker IMPEROYAL. Renamed IMPERIAL COBOURG in 1947. Converted to a bulk freighter at Muir Brothers Dry Dock Company, Limited, Port Dalhousie, Ontario and given last name in 1953.

The Steamer STARBELLE served its last owners for eleven years in the bulk grain trades of the Great Lakes before being sold for scrap in 1964.

The owners considered this vessel a sister ship to the Steamer STARBUCK which they owned and operated for seventeen years in the grain trades of the Lake Superior and lower lake areas. In fact, it was not a sister ship, per se, but more of a companion for the older vessel once it entered service as a bulk freighter in 1953.

When it came time to choose a name for this ship, Mr. Kenneth A. Powell, owner of the company and grain merchant in Winnipeg, Manitoba, decided that it would be fitting to choose a name that would indicate a "mate" for the present vessel that they owned. Thus, the name *STARBELLE*. Since the present ship was named in the male gender it was deemed appropriate to christen this vessel in the female gender.

The Steamer STARBELLE is seen below in the St. Mary's River, upbound for a grain cargo, on August 20, 1961.

Steamer STARBUCK

OWNER:	K. A. Powell (Canada) Limited
BUILT:	Cleveland Shipbuilding Company, Cleveland, Ohio—1888
HULL NO.:	2
O. A. DIMENSIONS:	280' × 38'3" × 24'6"
FORMER DATA:	Launched as the package freighter SCRANTON. Renamed TEN (1) in 1927. Renamed NINE in 1935. Converted to a bulk carrier at F. Woods & Sons Limited, Port Colborne, Ontario and given last name in 1942.

The Steamer STARBUCK was the last of a rare breed of ships to sail on the Great Lakes. It had the original engine and boilers throughout its life and was constructed with a compartment forward of the forward cabins. This was a small hold used for trimming the ship when loading light cargo or course grains.

From 1942 until the ship was sold for scrap in 1957, it was in this fleet and primarily used for the transport of grain between the Canadian Lakehead and Duluth/Superior Harbor and various Georgian Bay ports in the Canadian domestic grain grade. It is shown in this photograph upbound in the St. Mary's River in 1956.

The namesake of this vessel was the small town of Starbuck, Manitoba which is located about 20 miles southwest of Winnipeg, Manitoba. Mr. Kenneth A. Powell, president of this firm and a prominent grain merchant in Winnipeg, had a farm in the town and selected this name for the ship. Currently, the town has a population of about 300 persons. It is in the heart of the rich grain growing region and is on the mainline of Canadian railways serving the area. From many areas such as this grain is exported to places of consumption around the world.

Barge CONSTITUTION (2)

OWNER:	Pringle Barge Line Division, Oglebay Norton Company
BUILT:	American Steel Barge Company, West Superior, Wisconsin—1897
HULL NO.:	140
O. A. DIMENSIONS:	451'6" x 44' x 26'
FORMER DATA:	Launched as a 3-masted schooner bulk freight barge. Lengthened 72' and sails removed at Superior Shipbuilding Company, West Superior, Wisconsin in 1905. Converted to a self-unloading barge at Kraft Shipbuilding Company, Chicago, Illinois and Interlake Engineering Company, Cleveland, Ohio in 1926.

The Barge CONSTITUTION was the first barge in Great Lakes history to be lengthened. It served on its last run between Toledo, Ohio and Detroit, Michigan until being sold for scrap in 1966. It was also the first Great Lakes built vessel to be equipped with steam mooring winches.

Namesake of this vessel was the famous United States frigate of the United States Navy which is more popularly known as "Old Ironsides." This ship was built at Boston, Massachusetts between 1794 and 1797 and was of 2,200 tons displacement. Its hull was made of oak from Massachusetts, Maine and Georgia and the masts were of white pine. The hull was launched October 21, 1797.

The ship was a veteran of many battles. In the War of 1812 it fought and won a battle near Cape Race against the English warship GUERRIERE. The ship was decommissioned in 1830 but was rebuilt and restored to service in 1833. In 1855 it was laid up at Portsmouth Naval Yard only to be rebuilt and returned to service in 1877. In 1897 it was permanently retired and preserved as a memorial at the Boston Naval Shipyard.

The wheel of this famous old barge now reposes in the den of this writer.

Barge MAIDA

OWNER:	Pringle Barge Line Division, Oglebay Norton Company
BUILT:	American Steel Barge Company, West Superior, Wisconsin—1898
HULL NO.:	142
O. A. DIMENSIONS:	390' × 46' × 26'
FORMER DATA:	Launched as a bulk freight barge. Converted to a self-unloading barge at Interlake Engineering Company, Cleveland, Ohio in 1929.

The self-unloading Barge MAIDA was a daily visitor to the ports of Toledo, Ohio and Detroit, Michigan until being sold for scrap in 1968. It was originally built for the Minnesota Steamship Company and carried on that owner's theme of ship names as described fully in the story of the Barges MAGNA and MAIA in this book.

Maida, Italy was the namesake of this vessel. It is located at 38.51 degrees north latitude and 16.22 degrees east longitude. Currently, Maida has a population of about 4,000. It is situated in Catanzaro province in the region of Calabria of southern Italy.

At the time this vessel was converted to a 4-belt unloading system, it was acclaimed as the only vessel in the world so equipped. The system reduced cubic loss in the hold and increased cargo carrying capacity in net tons of coal.

This barge is shown downbound in the Detroit River headed for Toledo, Ohio on August 10, 1965.

Steamer GOUDREAU (2)

OWNER: Providence Shipping Company, Limited
BUILT: Great Lakes Engineering Works, Ecorse, Michigan—1906
HULL NO.: 20
O. A. DIMENSIONS: 552' × 56' × 31'
FORMER DATA: Launched as MICHIGAN (4). Given last name in 1966.

Sold for scrap in 1969, the bulk freight Steamer GOUDREAU took the Goudreau District of Ontario as its namesake. This area is rich in gold properties and is located north of Sault Ste. Marie, Ontario in Algoma Central Railway country. This railway was the owner, through this subsidiary, of this vessel. The Goudreau Gold Mines Limited contained the original gold property of the Goudreau District.

The Goudreau District became opened to development when the Algoma Central Railway, then known as the Lake Superior Corporation, constructed a rail line north from Hawk Junction to Franz, Ontario between 1910 and 1912. This area developed into a mining bonanza and open pit mining of pyrites was carried on east of Goudreau, Ontario during World War I. Gold mines operated in the Goudreau-Lochalsh area in the 1930's and the Cline Lake Mine operated until 1948.

There are numerous mines in the area, but they are not in operation at this time. Goudreau is connected by highway to Lochalsh, Ontario on the Canadian Pacific Railway system. Although Goudreau and Lochalsh were thriving communities during the 1930's they are very dormant now.

The Steamer GOUDREAU is shown in this photograph on October 29, 1966 in the Welland Ship Canal, upbound light for Lake Erie.

Steamer MICHIPICOTEN (2)

OWNER:	Providence Shipping Company, Limited
BUILT:	West Bay City Shipbuilding Company, West Bay City, Michigan - 1905
HULL NO.:	615
O. A. DIMENSIONS:	569' x 56' x 31'
FORMER DATA:	Launched as HENRY C. FRICK. Given last name in 1964.

The bulk freight Steamer MICHIPICOTEN was named in reference to the iron ore loading port and coal receiving port of Michipicoten Harbour, Ontario which is located some one hundred-forty miles north of Sault Ste. Marie, Ontario on Lake Superior. It is eight miles southwest of the Algoma Central Railway division point of Wawa, Ontario and is one of the oldest through trading routes in Canada. The area served as a main thoroughfare in early fur trading days.

It was a fort in 1750 and was subsequently operated by the North West Company and Hudson's Bay Company. Its location was recorded by Etienne Brule in 1622 and is shown on a map of Samuel de Champlain in 1632.

Providence Shipping Company, Limited was a subsidiary of Algoma Central Railway and operated two bulk freighters for about a decade. The firm was headquartered in The Bahamas. This ship operated through most of the 1972 season, then was sold for scrap. It is shown above in Sault Ste. Marie Harbor in 1971.

Barge EN-AR-CO

OWNER: Pyke Towing & Salvage Company Limited
BUILT: Delaware River Iron Shipbuilding & Engine Company, Chester, Pennsylvania — 1874
HULL NO.: 13
O. A. DIMENSIONS: 200' x 29' x 14' 4"
FORMER DATA: Launched as the powered bulk freighter BERKS. Renamed W. S. CALVERT in 1906. Converted to a tank barge at Polson Iron Works, Toronto, Ontario in 1909. Given last name in 1921. Converted to a bulk freight barge by Pyke Towing & Salvage Company Limited, Kingston, Ontario in 1935.

This vessel was launched April 29, 1874 amid fanfare as the East Coast's newest collier. From 1909 through 1934 it was owned on the Great Lakes by the National Refining Company of Toronto, Ontario. During an explosion on July 23, 1934, in which Mr. John E. Russell, famous vessel owner of the area was killed, the fate of this tanker was sealed. After the accident the hull was sold to these owners who used the converted hull as a bulk freight barge and lighter. It remained in the fleet until being cut-up for scrap in 1969.

The name of this vessel was derived from the literal spelling of the 1909-1934 owners, that is, National Refining Company. This firm was incorporated on July 6, 1906 in Ohio to operate and own refineries, pipe lines and oil wells in Ohio and Kansas. Later a Canadian subsidiary of the same name emerged and bought this vessel. Today the firm is part of Shell Canada Limited.

Barge HILDA (1)

OWNER: Pyke Towing and Salvage Company
BUILT: Polson Iron Works,
Toronto, Ontario – 1898
HULL NO.: 39
O. A. DIMENSIONS: 164' x 30' x 12'3"

The bulk freight Barge HILDA was originally operated on Lake Ontario in the stone, sand and gravel trades. After several changes of ownership, it became the property of these owners and was based at Kingston, Ontario. In its last years of use, the early 1950's, it was used to service shallow draft ports such as Napanee and Deseronto, Ontario. The vessel was scuttled in Lake Ontario on November 7, 1967.

Namesake of this barge was Hilda Marjorie Scanlon, daughter of Captain Joseph Scanlon, original principal of the firm that had this vessel built. Miss Scanlon was born on December 1, 1885 at Clipston, England and came to Canada with her parents in 1889. She attended the public schools near Waterloo, Ontario and graduated from high school in 1903.

In 1904 she married Mr. James Boyson of Hamilton, Ontario and served as homemaker and mother to the couple's three children. Her hobbies were gardening and raising grapes on nearby vineyards along Lake Ontario. Mrs. Boyson was never active in business affairs, but did do volunteer work in local hospitals and was a civic-minded person. She kept active until her death at Granby, Ontario on May 1, 1951. Her namesake is shown while under tow on June 22, 1951.

Motor Vessel BLACK RIVER

OWNER:	Quebec and Ontario Transportation Company, Limited
BUILT:	F. W. Wheeler Company, West Bay City, Michigan – 1896
HULL NO.:	118
O. A. DIMENSIONS:	382'6" x 44'6" x 26'
FORMER DATA:	Launched as the barge SIR ISAAC LOTHIAN BELL. Renamed BLANCHE H. in 1937. Renamed BLACK RIVER in 1949. Converted to a powered bulk freighter at Port Weller Dry Docks, Limited, St. Catharines, Ontario in 1952. Renamed TUXPAN-CLIFFE in 1979.

The diesel-powered Motor Vessel BLACK RIVER had an interesting history as a barge and a motor vessel. It was one of the smaller ships still operating in 1978 and it had a special purpose on the Great Lakes which was to move newsprint and other cargo for the owners which are part of the Chicago Tribune organization.

Namesake of this ship was the Black River of Ontario. It flows southward from Manitouwadge Lake north of Lake Superior into the Pic River which then empties into Lake Superior. The Black River is within the timber limits of the Ontario Paper Company and has been utilized for logging operations in that area by the company. It has a number of forks and is about forty-five miles in length. The area is largely wilderness and is very scenic.

The Motor Vessel BLACK RIVER is seen here downbound in the St. Mary's River on July 21, 1976. The ship was sold for off-lakes use in 1979.

Steamer HELEN EVANS

OWNER: Quebec & Ontario Transportation Company, Limited
BUILT: Great Lakes Engineering Works, Ecorse, Michigan—1906
HULL NO.: 16
O. A. DIMENSIONS: 552' × 56' × 31'
FORMER DATA: Launched as JAMES LAUGHLIN. Given last name in 1965.

Namesake of this ship is Mrs. Helen Evans, formerly Helen Hindman, daughter of Captain George Hindman who was the founder and manager of Hindman Transportation Company.

Mrs. Evans was born at Sarnia, Ontario on August 19, 1915 and was educated in the schools of Owen Sound, Ontario. She was the eldest of two children and soon became involved in the business of her father. She served on duties with Hindman Transportation Company and the Hindman Lumber Company before marrying Mr. Parker Evans in 1938.

Her efforts in behalf of the family companies are rewarded in her joys of her family and in this vessel bearing her name. As family and civic responsibilities grew, she left the work of the steamship and a lumber business to her husband and brother to concentrate on being a homemaker and mother.

For a period in the 1930's and early 1940's, Mrs. Evans actually was the manager of the Hindman interests, working from an office in her home. Her namesake vessel is shown below while tied-up in Toronto, Ontario on May 17, 1979. It was sold for scrap later that year.

Steamer HERON BAY (1)

OWNER: Quebec and Ontario Transportation Company Limited
BUILT: Collingwood Shipbuilding Company Limited, Collingwood, Ontario—1902
HULL NO.: 2
O. A. DIMENSIONS: 390' × 46' × 26'
FORMER DATA: Launched as the sailing barge AGAWA (1). Converted to a powered bulk freighter at Collingwood Shipbuilding Company Limited, Collingwood, Ontario in 1907. Renamed ROBERT P. DURHAM in 1929. Renamed HERON BAY (1) in 1940.

The bulk freight Steamer HERON BAY was sold for off-lakes use as a storage barge and renamed FEDERAL HUSKY in 1963. It was scrapped in 1965.

Namesake of this ship is a village on the north shore of Lake Superior which is the headquarters for the Ontario Paper Company's logging operations in the area. Heron Bay, Ontario is located six miles southeast of Peninsula Harbor and is nearly at the extreme northeast corner of Lake Superior. It is a station on the Canadian Pacific Railway's mainline from Toronto, Ontario to Winnipeg, Manitoba which skirts Lake Superior in a scenic vista along that part of the lake.

The Steamer HERON BAY is shown here with a typical cargo of pulpwood from its namesake port. The ship is below the Soo Locks at Sault Ste. Marie, Michigan on June 20, 1958.

Steamer LAC DES ILES

OWNER: Quebec and Ontario Transportation Company Limited
BUILT: Detroit Shipbuilding Company, Wyandotte, Michigan - 1905
HULL NO.: 159
O. A. DIMENSIONS: 545' x 55' x 31'
FORMER DATA: Launched as LYMAN C. SMITH. Renamed MARTHA HINDMAN in 1966. Given last name in 1979.

The Ontario Paper Company, headquartered at Thorold, Ontario, is the parent Canadian firm of this fleet of ships. It is a major Canadian forest products enterprise with newsprint, pulp, lumbering and chemical operations in Ontario and Quebec. It employs more than 4,550 personnel and is the fifth largest of Canadian newsprint producers.

Among the firm's earlier activities was a woodlands operation at Franquelin, Quebec. From the mid-1920's until the late 1950's this region was active. Cutting was carried out in the area near the site of the namesake of this bulk freighter. Wood was collected in the lake, then floated down the Franquelin River to the village of Franquelin and was there loaded into ships by a jack-ladder or flume-drop for transport to the newsprint mill at Thorold, Ontario. The operations ceased when the timberlands were exhausted until a new crop of forest products could come into being.

The bulk freight Steamer LAC DES ILES was among the oldest operating vessels in the bulk freight trades on the Great Lakes until her condition precluded repair in November, 1980, and the ship was sold for scrap. It is shown below loading coke at Cleveland, Ohio on September 12, 1979.

Motor Vessel COL. ROBERT R. Mc CORMICK

OWNER:	Quebec and Ontario Transportation Company, Limited
BUILT:	Atlantic Shipbuilding Company, Limited, Newport, England—1955
HULL NO.:	4
O. A. DIMENSIONS:	259' × 43'9" × 22'6"
FORMER DATA:	Launched as MANICOUAGAN (2). Given last name in 1955.

The canal-size bulk freighter Motor Vessel COL. ROBERT R. Mc CORMICK was sold for off-lakes use in 1967. It is shown here on December 3, 1966 below Lock 4 of the Welland Ship Canal at Thorold, Ontario.

Namesake of this ship is Colonel Robert Rutherford Mc Cormick who was born at Chicago, Illinois on July 30, 1880. He was educated in private schools, largely overseas, and graduated from Yale University with a B.A. degree in 1903 and from Northwestern University in 1906 with an Ll.B. degree.

He was admitted to the Illinois Bar in 1908 and began practicing law in 1909 as a founding member of the firm of Shepard, Mc Cormick & Thomason. He was also president of the Sanitary District Board at this time and directed the completion of the Chicago Drainage Canal, now a vital artery of commerce in the area.

He became president of The Tribune Company in March, 1911 and oversaw the expansion of that firm's various enterprises, one of which is this ship's owners in Canada. Col. Mc Cormick died in Wheaton, Illino;is on April 1, 1955.

Steamer MANITOULIN (4)

OWNER:	Quebec and Ontario Transportation Company, Limited
BUILT:	Swan, Hunter & Wigham Richardson Limited, Sunderland, England—1929
HULL NO.:	1383
O. A. DIMENSIONS:	259' × 43'3" × 20'
FORMER DATA:	Launched as IMARI. Renamed DELAWARE (4) in 1931. Renamed EMPIRE ROTHER in 1943. Renamed MANICOUAGAN (1) in 1949. Renamed WASHINGTON TIMES HERALD in 1951. Given last name in 1954.

The Steamer MANITOULIN was named in honor of Manitoulin Island, Lake Huron on which the Ontario Paper Company held woodland timber rights for a number of years. Some pulpwood still comes from the island, but major operations have shifted to the north and inland.

The name of the island is Algonkian and is applied by Indian tribes for "abode of the Great Spirit." According to Indian legend it is the dwelling place of both the good spirit "gitchi manitou" and the evil spirit "matchi manitou." This vessel was sold for scrap in 1961.

The Steamer MANITOULIN is shown below at Port Weller, Ontario on October 27, 1956. It is fully loaded with a cargo of pulpwood for the Thorold, Ontario mill of Ontario Paper Company. Note the athwartships pass-thru tunnel built into the deck load.

Steamer MARLHILL

OWNER:	Quebec and Ontario Transportation Company Limited
BUILT:	Great Lakes Engineering Works, Ecorse, Michigan - 1908
HULL NO.:	40
O. A. DIMENSIONS:	556'9" x 58' x 31'
FORMER DATA:	Launched as HARRY A. BERWIND. Renamed HARVEY H. BROWN (2) in 1917. Renamed PARKER EVANS in 1964. Given last name in 1979.

The namesake of this bulk freighter comes from a former subsidiary of the Ontario Paper Company which was known as Marlhill Mines Limited.

During World War II the pulp and paper industry sought substitutes, or extenders, for wood pulp because of the shortage of men to work in the woods due to serving in the Armed Forces of the day. Ontario Paper Company used calcium carbonate as a filler and this came from natural deposits on the north shore of Lake Ontario at Marlbank, near Kingston and Belleville, Ontario. The Marlhill Mines mined and processed this calcium carbonate. After processing, it was delivered to the newsprint mill at Thorold, Ontario by ship. The Marlhill operations continued from 1942 until the end of the war in 1945.

The Steamer MARLHILL has the distinction of being the only Great Lakes vessel to have sunk three other ships, all under its different ownerships. It is shown passing upbound in the St. Clair River on September 16, 1979. The vessel was sold for scrap in 1980.

Steamer NEW YORK NEWS (2)

OWNER: Quebec and Ontario Transportation Company, Limited
BUILT: Swan, Hunter & Wigham Richardson Limited, Wallsend-on-Tyne, England—1925
HULL NO.: 1269
O. A. DIMENSIONS: 261' × 43'6" × 25'
FORMER DATA: Launched as BELVOIR (1). Given last name in 1933.

The canal-sized Steamer NEW YORK NEWS was built with good cubic in its holds to accommodate its carriage of newsprint and pulpwood for the owners. The vessel was sold in 1962 for off-lakes use and was eventually abandoned.

The ship is named for the famous tabloid daily newspaper in New York City which is also part of The Tribune Company organization of Chicago, Illinois. The fleet is a subsidiary, through other subsidiaries, of this company.

The two high masts on deck of this vessel are called kingposts and are used to assist in cargo handling. They each have booms which can be swung out from the posts and which are used to raise or lower cargo from or into the hold.

The vessel is shown below approaching the Nicholson Fuel Dock on the Detroit River.

Steamer OUTARDE (1)

OWNER:	Quebec and Ontario Transportation Company Limited
BUILT:	Palmer's Shipbuilding & Iron Company Limited, Newcastle, England—1924
HULL NO.:	949
O. A. DIMENSIONS:	261' × 43' × 25'
FORMER DATA:	Launched as BRULIN. Given last name in 1940.

This ship name was carried on by a larger vessel after this vessel was sold for off lakes use in 1960. This Steamer OUTARDE became the J. J. BUCKLER and was wrecked in the Gulf of St. Lawrence on June 13, 1960.

Namesake of the vessel is Riviere-aux-Outardes, a river in Saguenay County, Quebec which provided power for the building of the city of Baie Comeau, Quebec and the Quebec North Shore Paper Company plant there.

The river is two hundred-seventy miles in length and flows southward from its origin to join the St. Lawrence River about fifteen miles west of Baie Comeau at Pointe-aux-Outardes. Its name is derived from the French word for geese—Outardes. Numerous wild geese are frequently found along the river and it is ideal as a hunting area.

In 1937 a 70,000 horsepower hydro-electric plant was built on the river to harness its flow and produce the power for area development. The area has seen major industrial development over the past two decades and even further growth is anticipated because the area is yet a frontier to many modern ways and is beautiful for its scenic splendor.

The Steamer OUTARDE is shown in the photograph below in the Welland Ship Canal on July 28, 1953.

Motor Vessel JOSEPH MEDILL PATTERSON

OWNER:	Quebec and Ontario Transportation Company, Limited
BUILT:	Atlantic Shipbuilding Company, Limited, Newport, England—1954
HULL NO.:	3
O. A. DIMENSIONS:	259' × 43'9" × 22'6"
FORMER DATA:	Launched as BAIE COMEAU. Given last name in 1955.

Mr. Joseph Medill Patterson was born at Chicago, Illinois on January 6, 1879 and graduated from Yale University in 1901 with a B.A. degree.

Mr. Patterson and his cousin, Col. McCormick, were the key instrumentalists in furthering the enterprises of The Tribune Company. Mr. Patterson went to work for the Chicago Tribune as a reporter. His father was editor and publisher of the paper. In 1903 he was elected to the Illinois House of Representatives and in 1905 he helped elect the mayor of Chicago. From 1906 to 1910 he wrote four books in retirement on the family farm, but when his father died in 1910 he assumed the co-editorship and co-publishing responsibilities with his cousin.

After serving in World War I, he returned to private life and on June 26, 1919 began publishing what is now the New York Daily News. He moved to New York City in 1925 to oversee this operation which was and still is part of the Tribune organization. Mr. Patterson remained active until his death on May 25, 1946. His namesake was sold for off-lakes use in 1967 along with her sister ship the Motor Vessel COL. ROBERT R. McCORMICK.

The Motor Vessel JOSEPH MEDILL PATTERSON is seen below in Lock Eight of the Welland Ship Canal on November 13, 1960.

Motor Vessel PIC RIVER

OWNER: Quebec and Ontario Transportation Company, Limited
BUILT: F. W. Wheeler Company, West Bay City, Michigan—1896
HULL NO.: 117
O. A. DIMENSIONS: 382'6" × 44'6" × 26'
FORMER DATA: Launched as the barge JAMES NASMYTH. Renamed MERLE H. in 1937. Given last name in 1949. Converted to a powered bulk carrier at Port Weller Dry Docks, Limited, St. Catharines, Ontario in 1953.

The Motor Vessel PIC RIVER is named after a river in the timber limits of the Ontario Paper Company near Heron Bay, Ontario. The river empties into Lake Superior at a point two miles eastward of Ogilvy Point. Although one to three fathoms of water exist in the river, only very light draft vessels can be assured of passage over the sandbar which extends across the mouth of the river about a quarter of a mile offshore.

The Pic River is about four hundred fifty feet wide for two and one-half miles, then narrows considerably. The shore in the vicinity of the Pic River mouth is sandy and conspicuous on an otherwise dark-colored coast line of Lake Superior.

The Ontario Paper Company is a parent and affiliate firm of this ship's owners and has had a policy, long-standing, of naming their ships after places or things prominent in the firm's affairs, hence, the name of this vessel. The company has floated timber on the Pic River and otherwise used it in Ontario operations for over forty years. This bulk vessel is shown below with a load of newsprint upbound in the Welland Ship Canal, above Lock 2, on September 27, 1978. The ship sailed barely a month after and was sold for scrap in October, 1978.

Steamer JOHN P. REISS

OWNER: Reiss Steamship Company
BUILT: American Ship Building Company, Lorain, Ohio—1910
HULL NO.: 377
O. A. DIMENSIONS: 524' × 54' × 30'

The bulk freight Steamer JOHN P. REISS was active through the 1970 navigation season and laid idle at Buffalo, New York during 1971. It was part of a sale of bulk vessels to Kinsman Marine Transit Company early in 1972 but never passed into their hands except for paper-signing functions and was immediately resold for scrap. This ship had sailed on its maiden voyage with a cargo of coal from Lorain, Ohio on April 15, 1910 to Escanaba, Michigan.

The namesake of this vessel was Mr. John Peter Reiss who was born at Sheboygan, Wisconsin on May 15, 1875. He was educated in the public schools and joined the family coal business after completing high school. He spent his first years learning different aspects of the business and in 1906 was elected a vice president of the C. Reiss Coal Company. He served in this capacity until his death on the morning of July 21, 1916. In his comparatively short life he demonstrated that he possessed a natural ability that spelled success.

When the Reiss Steamship Company was formed to operate the four steamers acquired from the Peavey Steamship Company, Mr. John P. Reiss was made vice president and treasurer of that company. In addition, Mr. Reiss was a director of the American Steamship Company of Cleveland, Ohio in the period 1910-1916. His namesake is shown below in Lake Nicolet on August 15, 1969.

Steamer OTTO M. REISS (2)

OWNER: Reiss Steamship Company
BUILT: West Bay City Shipbuilding Company, West Bay City, Michigan—1906
HULL NO.: 620
O. A. DIMENSIONS: 440' × 52'3" × 28'
FORMER DATA: Launched as JAMES S. DUNHAM. Renamed LYNFORD E. GEER in 1926. Given last name in 1934.

The bulk freight Steamer OTTO M. REISS was active on the Great Lakes, mostly in the grain trade, through the 1970 navigation season. It laid idle at Cleveland, Ohio during 1971 and was sold for scrap early in 1972. It passed into the hands of the Kinsman Marine Transit Company momentarily during the transfer of this firm's bulk freight vessels to Kinsman, but immediately was resold for scrap. The ship is shown in this photograph upbound on Lake Huron on July 26, 1970.

Mr. Otto Martin Reiss was this vessel's namesake. He was born in Sheboygan, Wisconsin on July 23, 1891 and attended the University of Wisconsin before joining the Reiss group of companies. Mr. Reiss showed promise of a life of great usefulness but was not able to fulfill it to the utmost. He entered the hospital for an operation for appendicitis and died at his home after the operation on May 4, 1917 at the age of twenty-five.

During his short life he had become manager of the Reiss Steamship Company and was secretary-treasurer and a director of the C. Reiss Coal Company. His namesake was one of two ships which operated in the grain trades into the decade of the 1970's.

Steamer SUPERIOR (4)

OWNER: Reiss Steamship Company
BUILT: Chicago Shipbuilding Company, Chicago, Illinois - 1901
HULL NO.: 49
O. A. DIMENSIONS: 450'6" x 50'3" x 28'6"
FORMER DATA: Launched as FRANK T. HEFFELFINGER. Renamed CLEMENS A. REISS (1) in 1917. Given last name in 1959.

The namesake of this bulk freighter was the largest of the five Great Lakes – Lake Superior.

The bold northern coast of Lake Superior is fringed with rocky islands, some of which rise to 1,300 feet above the water. The largest island is Isle Royale which is forty-four miles long and which is now Isle Royale National Park. There are no motor vehicles allowed on this island. Wild and beautiful trails through the wooded areas are the only means of getting around.

The southern coast of the lake is generally lower and more sandy with occasional ridges of limestone. Keweenaw Point projects into the lake and is the location of famous copper mines of Northern Michigan.

The Apostle Islands lie off-shore of Bayfield, Wisconsin and have recently been made a National Park. The waters of Lake Superior are singularly pure and transparent. The lake has never been known to freeze over completely.

This vessel remained active on the Great Lakes until being sold for scrap in 1961. It is shown here at Superior, Wisconsin in 1959.

Steamer CHARLES C. WEST

OWNER: Reiss Steamship Company
BUILT: Manitowoc Shipbuilding Company, Manitowoc, Wisconsin—1925
HULL NO.: 216
O. A. DIMENSIONS: 592' × 60' × 31'
FORMER DATA: Lengthened 122' at Manitowoc Shipbuilding Company, Manitowoc, Wisconsin in 1948.

Namesake of this self-unloader is Mr. Charles Cameron West who was born at Chicago, Illinois on September 22, 1877. He graduated from Cornell University with a mechanical engineering degree in 1900.

From school Mr. West went right into the shipbuilding business and was secretary-treasurer of Manitowoc Drydock Company by 1905. In due course he became president of the firm and also was a director or officer of other corporations. His namesake began its maiden voyage September 23, 1925, departing Manitowoc, Wisconsin light for Rockport, Michigan to load stone for Cleveland, Ohio.

The Steamer CHARLES C. WEST was especially designed for maneuverability in the smaller ports and channels. It had a cruiser stern to protect the rudders and was the only twin-screw self-unloader on the Great Lakes. When the ship came out it was the first bulk vessel in Great Lakes history to be so equipped. The vessel was sold for scrap in 1978 after several idle seasons and is shown above at South Chicago, Illinois on July 16, 1973.

Steamer SPRUCEDALE

OWNER:	Redwood Enterprises, Limited
BUILT:	Toledo Shipbuilding Company, Toledo, Ohio—1908
HULL NO.:	111
O. A. DIMENSIONS:	524' × 58' × 30'
FORMER DATA:	Launched as JOHN DUNN, JR. Given last name in 1961.

Like all of the vessels in the various fleets managed by Reoch interests, this vessel had the suffix "DALE," honoring Mr. William Coverdale who was a close, personal friend of Captain Norman Reoch. The prefix of the ship name is its specific namesake and the theme of forest-related names is carried onward. This vessel continued to serve on the Great Lakes until being sold for scrap in 1969.

The spruce is an important genus of evergreen trees in the pine family. There are about forty species native to the cold and temperate regions of the northern hemisphere. Spruce trees are distinguished from pines by solitary instead of fascicled leaves and are subject to severe damage by pests and deer.

North American spruce have light, soft, compact, straight-grained wood that is strong and easy to work with and low in resin content.

The Steamer SPRUCEDALE is shown below on May 2, 1964 at Port Weller, Ontario.

Steamer BROOKDALE (1)

OWNER: Reoch Steamship Company Limited
BUILT: Bertram Engineering Works, Limited, Toronto, Ontario—1902
HULL NO.: 36
O. A. DIMENSIONS: 256' × 43'3" × 25'6"
FORMER DATA: Launched as TADENAC. Renamed THE IROQUOIS in 1902. Renamed COLORADO (2) in 1920. Renamed DORNOCH in 1922. Renamed BROOKTON in 1922. Renamed GEORGE HINDMAN (1) in 1940. Given last name in 1952.

The Steamer BROOKDALE was the last of the canal-sized freighters to be scrapped in the Reoch fleet when it finally was disposed of in 1966. Because of its greater proportionate depth and carrying capacity it was able to serve as an economic unit longer than other similar size ships with these overall dimensions in length.

The specific namesake of this vessel is seen in reference to the ship name prefix, with the common fleet suffix having the general reference to Mr. Coverdale.

A brook conjures up thoughts of a stream flowing peacefully through wooded areas and relates well to the fleet theme of names having to do with forests and forest-related subjects. There are countless brooks in the world and no one specific brook is referred to. It is the general context of the word that is the namesake meaning for this bulk freighter. This vessel is shown below in the St. Mary's River on September 2, 1964. The vessel is upbound light headed for Port Arthur, Ontario.

Steamer FORESTDALE

OWNER: Reoch Steamship Company Limited
BUILT: Cleveland Shipbuilding Company, Cleveland, Ohio—1890
HULL NO.: 6
O. A. DIMENSIONS: 285' × 38'3" × 23'3"
FORMER DATA: Launched as LaSALLE (1). Renamed EASTRICH in 1928. Renamed HOWARD HINDMAN (1) in 1943. Given last name in 1952.

The bulk freight Steamer FORESTDALE is shown in this photograph while downbound in the St. Clair River in 1958. It was sold for scrap in 1961.

This is the only ship in the Reoch group of companies that was named with both the common suffix, *DALE*, and with a prefix in the vessel name embodying the general context of the theme for ship names in the fleet. Forest products and things related thereto form the basis for all other ship names except for the current flagship which is named in honor of the fleet's founder.

The term forest originally meant a tract of wooded land owned by the sovereign in England and used for game preservation and hunting. Today we think of the lush forest growth covering much of the western states of America and the provinces of Alberta and British Columbia in Canada. This vessel had something in common with forests in that it was nearly as old, proportionately, as many elder trees in the great forest stands of today.

Steamer AVONDALE (1)

OWNER:	Reoch Transports Limited
BUILT:	Swan, Hunter & Wigham Richardson Limited, Sunderland, England—1929
HULL NO.:	1387
O. A. DIMENSIONS:	259' × 43'3" × 20'
FORMER DATA:	Launched as STARWELL. Renamed JOHN A. FRANCE (1) in 1944. Given last name in 1959.

With many other "canallers" this vessel was sold for scrap in 1962 after the opening of the large St. Lawrence Seaway proved that size vessel to be uneconomic except for some specialized trades.

Later the Reoch fleets had another ship named AVONDALE which was a self-unloader formerly of United States registry. The namesake of both ships was the same. The fleet has the common "DALE" suffix on all ship names, honoring the late William Coverdale.

Specific namesake, therefore, is the prefix of the ship name, namely, AVON. This prefix is in reference to the various rivers named Avon which are found throughout the western world and particularly in England and Canada.

These rivers flow through fine wooded areas and are the prominent features of their surroundings. The Avon River of England was famous in early times as Shakespeare's river for it was on this river that he worked and lived his life. He was called the "Bard of Avon." There is also an Avon River in Ontario which takes its name from the one in England.

The Steamer AVONDALE is shown below in the St. Mary's River on August 1, 1961. The vessel is upbound, light to load a cargo of grain.

Steamer ELMDALE

OWNER:	Reoch Transports Limited
BUILT:	Great Lakes Engineering Works, Ecorse, Michigan - 1909
HULL NO.:	57
O. A. DIMENSIONS:	464' x 56' x 28'
FORMER DATA:	Launched as CLIFFORD F. MOLL. Renamed STANDARD PORTLAND CEMENT in 1933. Renamed ELMDALE in 1960.

The bulk freight Steamer ELMDALE is shown below while downbound in the St. Mary's River in 1972. It remained an active unit in this fleet until 1973 when it was sold for non-transportation use as a storage grain hull at Goderich, Ontario and renamed K. A. POWELL (2). Like other hulls in that harbour's fleet, it has been cut down to the main deck and is unrecognizable as the steamer shown here. This hull, in mid-1979, was towed to Thunder Bay, Ontario for scrapping.

This vessel shared the common ship name suffix in the fleet and took as its namesake, specifically, the elm tree. This is a beautiful large tree common across North America and is valued for its lumber and its shade. The tree often reaches one hundred feet in height and may grow to be as much as 200 years old. It is hardwood and light brown in color.

There are nineteen species of elm known to exist around the world. The genus of all is "Ulmus." Various minor differences among the species occur in nature, but to most untrained observers, the common elms all look very much alike.

Steamer FERNDALE (1)

OWNER: Reoch Transports Limited
BUILT: Barclay, Curle & Company Limited, Glasgow, Scotland—1929
HULL NO.: 630
O. A. DIMENSIONS: 259' × 43'3" × 20'
FORMER DATA: Launched as COTEAUDOC (1). Renamed MILVERTON in 1947. Renamed CLARY FORAN in 1949. Given last name in 1959.

This canal-sized bulk freighter was the first in the fleet to bear this name. The name was later carried on by a larger self-unloader that formerly was under United States registry.

The common "DALE" suffix in the fleet refers to Mr. William Coverdale who was a great friend of the former owner of the fleet. Specific namesake for the vessel, therefore, is the fern, a family of leafy perennial spore-bearing plants with slender horizontal, stout roots.

These plants form a very large family of widely differing habits and structure. There are over seven thousand species belonging to one hundred-seventy genera scattered all over the world. Nineteen genera with some eighty-three species are native to Canada.

Forest-affiliated growth and products have formed the basis for most ship names in the Reoch fleet. This ship was sold for scrap in 1963.

The Steamer FERNDALE is shown below in the Welland Ship Canal on June 2, 1962.

Steamer GROVEDALE (2)

OWNER: Reoch Transports, Limited
BUILT: American Ship Building Company, Lorain, Ohio—1905
HULL NO.: 339
O. A. DIMENSIONS: 545' × 55' × 31'
FORMER DATA: Launched as JOSEPH G. BUTLER, JR. Renamed DONALD B. GILLIES in 1935. Given last name in 1963.

The bulk freight Steamer GROVEDALE is shown in the photograph below about to enter the McArthur Lock at "The Soo" in 1969. This vessel remained active on the Great Lakes throughout the 1970 navigation season, but did not fit out in 1971 and was sold for use as a breakwater, arriving at Hamilton, Ontario on June 30, 1971.

The Reoch group of ships had the common suffix, DALE, referring to Mr. William Coverdale who was a personal friend of Captain Norman J. Reoch, founder of the fleet. The balance of the ship names had the common theme of forest products or growth, or things related thereto.

The namesake of this bulk freighter was a grove, as in a grove of trees in a forest or park. A grove may be defined as a cluster or grouping of trees. Most commonly the term is used in reference to a grove of fruit or nut trees. The terms, orchard, vale or park may also be used in description of a grove.

Steamer VALLEYDALE

OWNER: Reoch Transports Limited
BUILT: Swan, Hunter & Wigham Richardson Limited, Newcastle-on-Tyne, England—1927
HULL NO.: 1228
O. A. DIMENSIONS: 310' × 43'3" × 26'3"
FORMER DATA: Launched as KINLOCH. Renamed VALLEY CAMP (1) in 1927. Lengthened 49' at Port Weller Dry Docks Limited, St. Catharines, Ontario in 1951. Given last name in 1965.

When this ship was built it had the greatest depth of any canaller in service on the Great Lakes system. This was done so that high cubic footage could be obtained in the cargo holds since the ship was to serve as a coal carrier.

The namesake of this self-unloader was twofold. The first part of the ship name was in reference to the Valley Camp Coal Company of Canada, a subsidiary of the Valley Camp Coal Company of Cleveland, Ohio, which originally operated the ship and which provided tonnage for the vessel after its sale to these owners. The second part of the ship name is the standard Reoch fleet reference to Mr. William H. Coverdale for whom the founder of this fleet originally worked at Canada Steamship Lines Limited.

The Steamer VALLEYDALE operated but a short time in the Reoch fleet and was sold for scrap in 1966. The cargoes of coal it was bought to carry were then carried in larger units of the Reoch fleet. This self-unloader is shown in the above photograph at Port Colborne, Ontario on May 22, 1965. It sailed from Newcastle-on-Tyne, England April 28, 1927 on its maiden voyage, light for Port Colborne, Ontario.

Steamer WILLOWDALE

OWNER: Reoch Transports Limited
BUILT: Collingwood Shipbuilding Company Limited, Collingwood, Ontario—1918
HULL NO.: 50
O. A. DIMENSIONS: 259'3" × 43'9" × 25'
FORMER DATA: Launched as the tanker TALARALITE. Renamed IMPERIAL MIDLAND in 1947. Converted to a bulk freighter at Port Dalhousie Dry Docks Limited, Port Dalhousie, Ontario and given last name in 1953.

The bulk freight Steamer WILLOWDALE is shown here downbound in the Welland Ship Canal near Thorold, Ontario on August 15, 1960. It continued to serve in this fleet until being sold for scrap in 1963.

With the common fleet suffix, DALE, in reference to Mr. William H. Coverdale, the shipname specifically refers to the willow family of dioecious trees or shrubs. These forest growths have alternate and simple leaves.

The willow family of three genera and over three hundred species mainly appears in the temperate and arctic-alpine parts of the northern hemisphere. The wood of the family is valuable for plywood, excelsior or for mill work or cooperage. The groves where willows abound become very dense and grow rapidly. They are thus quite effective and valuable for erosion control.

About one hundred-ninety species of willow are native to Canada and can be found throughout the Dominion. This ship name honors a member of the forest that is both pleasant to behold and valuable to both industry and individual land owners.

Motor Vessel ROBERT BARNES FIERTZ

OWNER:	Republic Steel Corporation
BUILT:	McDougall-Duluth Company, Duluth, Minnesota—1921
HULL NO.:	52
O. A. DIMENSIONS:	254' × 36'3" × 14'
FORMER DATA:	Launched as I. L. I. 103. Given last name in 1936. Rebuilt with new midbody at Todd Shipyards, Incorporated, Hoboken, New Jersey in 1947.

The New York State Barge Canal-type bulk carrier shown below was active on the Great Lakes and east coast domestic trade until being sold for off-lakes use in 1962. This photograph of the ship was taken at Cleveland, Ohio on July 18, 1956.

Mr. Robert Eugene Fiertz was this vessel's namesake. He was the grandson of Mr. Julius H. Barnes, who built this vessel, and the family name of Barnes was utilized in the ship name because of the grandfather's wishes. Mr. Fiertz was born in New York, New York on August 11, 1929 and was a graduate of Dartmouth College in 1951 with a B.A. degree.

He began his career with the DuPont organization as part of the Central Engineering Department at Wilmington, Delaware in 1952. Later that year he moved to Circleville, Ohio where he remained until entering the Armed Services in 1954. He rejoined DuPont in 1956 at Starke, Florida and held engineering positions of ever-increasing stature with DuPont until he left that firm in 1965 to join Celanese Fibers Company at Charlotte, North Carolina as senior research engineer. By 1967 he transferred to Rome, Georgia for this firm as production superintendent and held that post when he resigned to join Enjay Fibers & Laminates Company in 1968 at Odenton, Maryland.

Steamer TOM M. GIRDLER

OWNER: Republic Steel Corporation
BUILT: Kaiser Company, Incorporated, Vancouver, Washington—1945
HULL NO.: 513
O. A. DIMENSIONS: 600'3" × 71'6" × 35'
FORMER DATA: Launched as the C-4 type carrier LOUIS McHENRY HOWE. Rebuilt, lengthened 80', converted to a bulk freighter and given last name at Maryland Drydock Company, Baltimore, Maryland in 1951.

This ship's namesake was Mr. Tom Mercer Girdler who was born at Clark County, Indiana on May 19, 1877 and was a graduate of Lehigh University in 1901 with a degree in mechanical engineering.

He began his career as a salesman with Buffalo Forge Company in London, England in 1901, thence was with Oliver Iron & Steel Company from 1902 to 1905 in Pittsburgh, Pennsylvania. From 1905 to 1907 he worked in Pueblo, Colorado for Colorado Fuel & Iron Company and from 1907 to 1914 was general superintendent of Atlantic Steel Company in Atlanta, Georgia.

Mr. Girdler joined Jones and Laughlin Steel Corporation in 1914 as assistant general superintendent at the Aliquippa Works and rose to the presidency by 1929. He then moved over to Republic Steel Corporation in 1930 as president and chairman of the board. He retained both titles until 1937, then was only chairman until his retirement in 1956.

This vessel sailed on its maiden Great Lakes voyage from Chicago, Illinois October 21, 1951, light for Escanaba, Michigan to load iron ore for Cleveland, Ohio delivery. It is shown here downbound in the St. Mary's River July 24, 1974. It was sold for scrap in mid-1980.

Steamer THOMAS F. PATTON

OWNER: Republic Steel Corporation
BUILT: Kaiser Company, Incorporated, Vancouver, Washington—1945
HULL NO.: 520
O. A. DIMENSIONS: 600'3" × 71'6" × 35'
FORMER DATA: Launched as the C-4 type carrier SCOTT E. LAND. Rebuilt, lengthened 80', converted to a bulk freighter and renamed TROY H. BROWNING (3) at Maryland Drydock Company, Baltimore, Maryland in 1951. Given last name in 1955.

The namesake of this ship was a spokesman for the steel industry and a familiar figure in community affairs in Cleveland. Mr. Thomas Francis Patton was born on December 6, 1903 in Cleveland, Ohio. He attended Ohio State University and received an Ll.B. degree in 1926. The same year he was admitted to the Ohio Bar and joined the firm of Belden, Young & Veach where he worked until 1932. In 1936 he became general counsel for Republic Steel Corporation. In 1943 he was elected a director of Republic Steel and in 1944 vice president and general counsel in which position he served until being elected assistant president and first vice president in 1953. He became president of Republic Steel in 1956, chief executive officer in 1960 and chairman of the board in 1963. He retired September 15, 1971.

He has received many honorary degrees including a Ll.D. degree from the Cleveland Marshall Law School in 1953. Mr. Patton is a director of several other corporations and has long been held in high regard in the business community for his efforts and achievements.

This vessel is pictured here while downbound in the St. Clair River, September 2, 1973. It was sold for scrap in mid-1980.

Steamer PETER ROBERTSON (1)

OWNER: Republic Steel Corporation
BUILT: Superior Shipbuilding Company, Superior, Wisconsin—1906
HULL NO.: 514
O. A. DIMENSIONS: 555' × 55' × 31'
FORMER DATA: Launched as E. J. EARLING. Renamed ROBERT B. WALLACE in 1924. Given last name in 1957.

This Steamer PETER ROBERTSON was sold for overseas scrapping in midsummer 1969, however another ship later bore the name in lakes' service.

Namesake of the vessel is Mr. Peter Robertson who was born at Glasgow, Scotland on September 5, 1907. He came to the United States after graduation from high school and enrolled in apprentice training at General Electric Company.

Mr. Robertson went to work for Republic Steel Corporation in 1934 as an industrial engineer. By 1938 he was assistant chief industrial engineer and he was named manager of the Truscon Division in 1944. He was assistant vice president in charge of Republic's manufacturing operations from 1948 to 1954 when he advanced to the position of vice president in charge of research and planning. He has acquired the reputation of being one of the most knowledgeable persons on Great Lakes transportation and iron ore and steel activities in the industry. Mr. Robertson retired in 1971.

This bulk freighter is shown below in the St. Mary's River on August 28, 1963.

Steamer J. E. UPSON

OWNER:	Republic Steel Corporation
BUILT:	American Ship Building Company, Cleveland, Ohio—1908
HULL NO.:	441
O. A. DIMENSIONS:	524' × 54' × 30'

The Steamer J. E. UPSON is shown in this photograph on September 2, 1962 while downbound in the St. Mary's River.

Namesake of this bulk freighter is Mr. Joseph Edwin Upson who was born on August 14, 1842 at Tallmadge, Ohio. He received his education at Tallmadge Academy and Eastman's Business College. Mr. Upson began working in the Waterbury, Connecticut Savings Bank but later was in the New York City office of Scovil Manufacturing Company. In 1863 he served briefly as a "squirrel hunter" when Morgain's Raiders crossed the Ohio River. In 1864 he enlisted as a private in Company "D," 164th Ohio Volunteer Infantry and saw four months' service.

He then worked as a clerk for W. Bingham & Company and later joined L. L. Lyon in the ship chandlery business. When Mr. Lyon died, Mr. Upson formed the partnership of Upson & Walton with J. W. Walton in 1871. Together they bought out the Chris Grover Ship Supply Company and the foundation for a growing concern was laid. Mr. Upson felt deeply about having adequate ship's supplies on hand. His belief brought the firm to the foremost ship chandlery business on the Great Lakes. Mr. Upson was an original director and president of Wilson Transit Company who named this ship for him and owned it for many years. The vessel was sold for scrap in 1969.

Steamer VALLEY CAMP (2)

OWNER: Republic Steel Corporation
BUILT: American Ship Building Company, Lorain, Ohio—1917
HULL NO.: 721
O. A. DIMENSIONS: 550' × 58' × 31'
FORMER DATA: Launched as LOUIS W. HILL. Given last name in 1955.

The bulk freight Steamer VALLEY CAMP is shown in this photograph downbound in Whitefish Bay, Lake Superior on June 18, 1963. It was sold in 1968 for a nominal fee to the historical group at Sault Ste. Marie, Michigan for use as a floating ship museum and is serving in that capacity now. Thousands of visitors get a chance to see what a freighter is like by being onboard when they visit this vessel. For many, it is a "first" in their experience.

The namesake of this vessel is the Valley Camp Coal Company of Cleveland, Ohio which has had a long business relationship with the former owners of the vessel. The company was incorporated in 1907 in the state of Pennsylvania to operate mines and merchandise coal from a location known as Valley Camp. In 1918 the operating and general headquarters were moved to Cleveland, Ohio to facilitate coordination of movements with Great Lakes shipping.

In 1919 the wholly-owned subsidiary Valley Camp Coal Company of Canada was set up and that firm acquired the Fort William Coal Dock Company. That subsidiary is now known as Valley Camp Limited. Through the years other firms were acquired. The total number of employees in the organization now is about 2,500. The firm was in the marine news late in the 1960's when it built and opened a new iron ore loading facility next to its coal dock at Thunder Bay, Ontario.

Steamer CHARLES M. WHITE

OWNER: Republic Steel Corporation
BUILT: Kaiser Company, Incorporated, Vancouver, Washington—1946
HULL NO.: 516
O. A. DIMENSIONS: 600'3" × 71'6" × 35'
FORMER DATA: Launched as the C-4 type carrier MOUNT MANSFIELD. Rebuilt, lengthened 80', converted to a bulk freighter and given last name at Maryland Drydock Company, Baltimore, Maryland in 1951.

Mr. Charles McElroy White was born in Oakland, Maryland on June 13, 1891 and graduated from the University of Maryland in 1913 with a B.S. degree. He attended Carnegie Institute of Technology from 1914 to 1917 and also received numerous honorary degrees later in life.

Mr. White began his business career as a millwright's helper in 1913 with Jones and Laughlin Steel Corporation. He rose to become assistant to the general superintendent of the Monongahela Connecting Railroad in 1919 and from 1920 to 1929 was assistant superintendent and superintendent of Jones and Laughlin's Aliquippa Works.

He then joined Republic Steel Corporation serving as assistant vice president from 1930 to 1935, vice president of operations from 1935 to 1945 and was elected president of Republic in 1945 serving in that post until 1956. Mr. White was chairman of the board of Republic until retiring in 1960.

This vessel is shown here in the West Neebish Channel, St. Mary's River on May 24, 1979. It was sold for scrap in mid-1980.

Barge LILLIAN

OWNER: Roen Steamship Company
BUILT: American Ship Building Company, Cleveland, Ohio – 1910
HULL NO.: 450
O. A. DIMENSIONS: 350' x 56' x 19' 6"
FORMER DATA: Launched as the powered carferry MARQUETTE & BESSEMER NO. 2. Renamed MOSES CLEVELAND in 1938. Renamed MARQUETTE & BESSEMER NO. 2, for the second time, in 1939. Converted to a barge at Holthe Marine Construction Company, Manistee, Michigan in 1944. Given last name in 1948.

The bulk freight, crane-equipped Barge LILLIAN honored the wife of Mr. Marquis Roen, son of the late Captain John Roen. Captain Roen was the founder and president of this line until his death in 1970. This lady is the former Miss Lillian Engblom who was born in Norway, Michigan on September 2, 1919.

Miss Engblom completed her education at Norway, Michigan and worked as a clerk at H. C. Prange Company of Green Bay, Wisconsin. She rose to become auditor of the firm when she met Mr. Marquis Roen. The couple was married on December 12, 1943 and settled at Sturgeon Bay, Wisconsin.

Mrs. Lillian Roen did not hold any active position in the Roen affiliated companies, but rather was busy with life as a homemaker. Her namesake is shown above in the St. Mary's River on August 18, 1957. It was sold in 1972 for use as a shipyard workfloat at Sturgeon Bay, Wisconsin after a number of years of idleness at that port.

Barge RESOLUTE (2)

OWNER:	Roen Steamship Company
BUILT:	Chicago Shipbuilding Company, Chicago, Illinois—1896
HULL NO.:	17
O. A. DIMENSIONS:	366' × 44'3" × 26'3"
FORMER DATA:	Launched as the barge MANDA. Converted to a wrecking lighter at Great Lakes Towing Company, Cleveland, Ohio and given present name in 1928. Re-converted to a barge at Filer Fibre Company, Manistee, Michigan in 1942.

The crane-equipped Barge RESOLUTE had been used as a salvage barge, construction barge and as a wood-carrying barge in the Roen fleet. It was the oldest piece of equipment in the fleet when sold for final scrapping in 1972 at Green Bay, Wisconsin.

The namesakes of this barge were the several Navy ships of the world bearing the same name. When Great Lakes Towing Company acquired and converted this vessel to a wrecking lighter, they searched for a name that would signify their resolve in mastering whatever job they undertook in salvage work. No better name could have been chosen.

By definition, resolute means, "having a fixed purpose, being determined and constant in pursuing a purpose." Another definition explains, "steady and firm, of convincing manner, as in a resolute commander who is unable to be shaken."

This barge is shown above fully loaded with coal at Amherstburg, Ontario in the lower Detroit River in the 1950's.

Barge MARQUIS ROEN (2)

OWNER: Roen Steamship Company
BUILT: Chicago Shipbuilding Company, Chicago, Illinois - 1900
HULL NO.: 40
O. A. DIMENSIONS: 461' x 50'3" x 29'6"
FORMER DATA: Launched as the powered bulk freighter ROBERT W. E. BUNSEN. Converted to a barge at Sturgeon Bay Shipbuilding Company, Sturgeon Bay, Wisconsin and renamed MARQUIS ROEN in 1954. Converted to a combination self-unloader and crane-equipped barge at Sturgeon Bay Shipbuilding Company, Sturgeon Bay, Wisconsin in 1957.

The namesake of this unique bulk freight barge is Mr. Marquis John Roen who was born in Charlevoix, Michigan on July 12, 1917. He attended Lawrence College at Appleton, Wisconsin and Green Bay Business College, Green Bay, Wisconsin before joining the United States Coast Guard in 1939. Mr. Roen served in Lake Michigan waters during World War II and went to the east coast for his father in 1945 to manage the Charlevoix Transit Company's fleet of fishing trawlers. He returned to the Great Lakes area in 1947 and began sailing on the firm's vessels in the Detroit-Toledo coal trade, rising to earn his master's papers by 1954.

Mr. Roen then returned to Sturgeon Bay, Wisconsin to look after the shoreside affairs of the fleet and was appointed vice president of Roen Steamship Company in 1960. His namesake continued active until being sold for off-Lakes use in 1973. It is shown above on a typical trip while underway.

Barge SOLVEIG

OWNER:	Roen Steamship Company
BUILT:	Bethlehem Steel Company, Quincy, Massachusetts - 1944
HULL NO.:	1582
O. A. DIMENSIONS:	325' x 50' x 25'3"
FORMER DATA:	Launched as the Landing Ship, Tank Vessel #1006. Converted to a crane-equipped bulk freight barge at Sturgeon Bay Shipbuilding Company, Sturgeon Bay, Wisconsin and given last name in 1951.

The 4,050 gross ton carrying capacity, crane-equipped barge shown above was named in honor of the second wife of the late Captain John Roen, famed salvor of Great Lakes ships. Mrs. Roen was the former Miss Solveig Veseth and was born in Bergen, Norway on October 14, 1906. She completed her education in that country.

After high school she worked in several secretarial positions and met Captain Roen on one of his visits to Norway in 1932. The couple were married July 1, 1933 and she returned to the United States with her husband that year, settling in Sturgeon Bay, Wisconsin.

During intervening years Mrs. Roen served as an official of the family firms, but more importantly, she was a homemaker and mother of two children.

Her late husband became reknown in 1944 when he successfully raised the 600' Steamer GEORGE M. HUMPHREY (1) in the Straits of Mackinac. The Barge SOLVEIG is shown underway with a full load of pulpwood in the St. Mary's River in 1954. The barge was sold for scrap in 1973.

Steamer ERIE QUEEN

OWNER: Myles J. Rosenthal
BUILT: Rice Bros. Corporation, East Boothbay, Maine – 1922
HULL NO.: 17
O. A. DIMENSIONS: 152' x 31' x 21'
FORMER DATA: Launched as the combination passenger and package freight vessel BAINBRIDGE. Renamed ALGOMAH II in 1936. Converted to a passenger vessel and reduced in depth 6'4" at Defoe Boat and Motor Works, Bay City, Michigan in 1940. Renamed ERIE QUEEN in 1962.

This passenger vessel is shown above in its latest operating colors off Cleveland, Ohio in 1962. Following a series of owners after an unsuccessful operating life in the Cleveland area, which ended in 1963, the above named owner acquired the ship and, in 1968, sold it to New York interests who took the vessel off the lakes to become a restaurant in New York City.

The three-deck passenger Steamer ERIE QUEEN had a capacity of 300 persons and prior to coming to Cleveland operated for over twenty years in the Straits of Mackinac. Before that it served largely Lake Michigan ports once it became a Great Lakes ship. This vessel was a hand-fired coal burning ship and labor costs to operate quickly became prohibitive. Besides that, the ship was damaged in Cleveland by a saltwater vessel which struck her and repairs far outweighed the value of the vessel.

Namesake of this vessel was the last lake she operated on – Lake ERIE and, when originally commissioned to this use, the owners, WASAC Waterways, Inc., believed she would become the QUEEN of the lake.

Steamer HARRY L. ALLEN

OWNER: S. & E. Shipping Corporation
BUILT: American Ship Building Company, Lorain, Ohio – 1910
HULL. NO.: 379
O. A. DIMENSIONS: 545' x 58' x 31'
FORMER DATA: Launched as JOHN B. COWLE (2). Given last name in 1969.

The bulk freight Steamer HARRY L. ALLEN was one of the smallest U. S. flag vessels on the Great Lakes when its end came. While moored along the Capital 4 grain elevator in Duluth, Minnesota for the winter, a fire broke out in the elevator which demolished it and, in the process, parts of the elevator fell upon the ship and burned its superstructure and scorched its hull so badly that it was a total loss and was sold for scrap. The fire occurred on January 21-22, 1978. The vessel is shown in its bicentennial dress while downbound in the West Neebish Channel, St. Mary's River on July 19, 1976.

Namesake of this ship was Mr. Harry Lee Allen who was born in Cleveland, Ohio on July 16, 1908. He attended Case Institute of Technology and the University of Alabama and began work in 1933 for a predecessor firm of Republic Steel Corporation. In 1943 he was named open hearth superintendent and, in 1952, was named manager of Republic's Buffalo, New York plant.

Mr. Allen became vice president of operations in 1960 and vice president and general manager in 1966. From 1972 until retirement on January 31, 1973, he was senior vice president - operations.

Steamer CHICAGO TRADER

OWNER: S. & E. Shipping Corporation
BUILT: American Ship Building Company, Lorain, Ohio—1911
HULL NO.: 391
O. A. DIMENSIONS: 545' × 58' × 31'
FORMER DATA: Launched as THE HARVESTER. Given last name in 1965.

Honoring the home port and operating headquarters of the original owning company, the Steamer CHICAGO TRADER takes its name from Illinois' largest city—Chicago. The city and surrounding area comprise a major commercial and industrial complex and the greatest transportation center on Earth. With an aggregate population of eight million in this area, it is by far the largest port cities complex on the Great Lakes.

The original owners of this ship, International-Harvester Company, are headquartered in Chicago. The subsequent owners, Gartland, were also headquartered there, though are now a wholly-owned subsidiary of a larger eastern fleet. As an independent fleet, Gartland made many trades and had many varied trade routes to follow. It followed that when this vessel was acquired a fitting name be chosen and the current name was settled upon.

This ship was the third vessel built on the Great Lakes on the Isherwood longitudinal design. It began its maiden voyage with a cargo of coal from Lorain, Ohio on August 21, 1911 bound for Duluth, Minnesota. It is seen here downbound in the West Neebish Channel, St. Mary's River on September 3, 1973. It was sold for scrap in March, 1977.

Steamer KINSMAN ENTERPRISE (1)

OWNER: S. & E. Shipping Corporation
BUILT: Chicago Shipbuilding Company, Chicago, Illinois - 1906
HULL NO.: 70
O. A. DIMENSIONS: 601' x 58' x 32'
FORMER DATA: Launched as NORMAN B. REAM. Given last name in 1965.

The first word in the bulk freighter Steamer KINSMAN ENTERPRISE's name was in reference to the operating company title. The second word of the ship name was reference to the fact that through enterprise and systematic purposeful activity the fleet grew.

A definition of the word enterprise is "a project or undertaking that is difficult, complicated or risky." The Kinsman Marine Transit Company was an independent fleet, not having ownership controlled by any steel company or other large organization that could furnish a ready supply of cargoes. Through management effort and initiative the firm prospered under these conditions at a time when most other independent companies engaged in bulk cargo transportation on the Great Lakes were waning or going out of business.

The name of this ship, therefore, was a memorial to the survival of the Kinsman organization in Great Lakes transportation. The company is however, now a wholly-owned subsidiary of the American Ship Building Company. This bulk freighter is shown while downbound in Little Rapids Cut, St. Mary's River on August 17, 1970. It was sold for use as a grain storage hull at Port Huron, Michigan in May, 1979.

Steamer HENRY STEINBRENNER (3)

OWNER: S. & E. Shipping Corporation
BUILT: Superior Shipbuilding Company, Superior, Wisconsin—1907
HULL NO.: 517
O. A. DIMENSIONS: 601' × 58' × 32'
FORMER DATA: Launched as GEORGE F. BAKER. Given last name in 1965.

Mr. Henry Steinbrenner was born in Cleveland, Ohio on May 20, 1849 and was the eldest of four children. He was educated in the public schools and then read law for two years in the offices of Grannis & Henderson. Law did not have lasting appeal, however, and at the age of twenty-four he left it to go into the real estate business for himself.

In time, he married Sophia Minch who was the daughter of Captain Philip Minch, one of the largest shipowners on the Great Lakes. When Captain Minch died in 1887, Mr. Steinbrenner left the real estate field to take over his father-in-law's vessel firm. In 1901, he constructed his first vessel and named it Steamer HENRY STEINBRENNER. In 1905 he formed the Kinsman Transit Company and served as its head until his death on May 29, 1929. The firm had a capitalization of $1,500,000 when it was formed.

A quotation at the time said, "He carved his name deeply upon the commercial history of Cleveland and the straightforward policy he has followed in his business career commends him to the confidence and good will of all with whom he has come in contact." His namesake was the first ship to use the new West Neebish channel, St. Mary's River when it opened on August 16, 1908. It is shown here passing downbound in the West Neebish Channel, St. Mary's River, on August 11, 1978. The ship was sold for scrap in May, 1979.

Steamer PAUL L. TIETJEN

OWNER: S. & E. Shipping Corporation
BUILT: American Ship Building Company, Cleveland, Ohio - 1907
HULL NO.: 437
O. A. DIMENSIONS: 552' x 56' x 31'
FORMER DATA: Launched as MATTHEW ANDREWS (1). Renamed HARRY L. FINDLAY in 1933. Given last name in 1965.

The man for whom this ship is named is Mr. Paul Lindhorst Tietjen who was born in Cleveland, Ohio on July 28, 1911. He graduated from the University of Michigan in 1934 with a degree in Naval Architecture and Marine Engineering.

Mr. Tietjen began his career with Toledo Shipbuilding Company and then was with Pittsburgh Steamship Company in Cleveland, Ohio from 1936 to 1941, in the construction department. He joined Jones & Laughlin Steel Corporation in 1941 and in 1942 was appointed marine manager of Interstate Steamship Company which was a subsidiary of the steel company. He served as president of Interstate Steamship from 1949 to 1952 at which time he became manager of traffic and transportation of the parent company. Mr. Tietjen held that post until 1958 when he was made general manager of traffic and transportation until 1961. He served as vice president of Jones & Laughlin Steel Corporation until retiring February 29, 1972.

His namesake ship is shown below while upbound in the St. Mary's River on July 18, 1977 destined to load what was to be its last cargo. The ship was laid-up at Toledo, Ohio after discharge and was sold for scrap in 1978.

Steamer CARROLLTON

OWNER:	Saginaw Dock and Terminal Company
BUILT:	Buffalo Dry Dock Company, Buffalo, New York—1904
HULL NO.:	206
O. A. DIMENSIONS:	255' × 43' × 21'6"
FORMER DATA:	Launched as the special-loading bulk freighter MARQUETTE & BESSEMER NO. 1. Converted to a conventional bulk freighter at Buffalo Dry Dock Company, Buffalo, New York in 1928. Given last name in 1937.

The Steamer CARROLLTON remained in the bulk freight trades of pig iron and sand on the Great Lakes until being sold for scrap in 1958. It subsequently was partially demolished at Duluth, Minnesota and part of its hull existed as a hulk until 1969.

This vessel was unique in its initial appearance and had a square stern much like many carferry vessels. Indeed, it used carferry slips for loading its coal cargoes when it ran in collier service on Lake Erie prior to 1928 when the rails on the ship's afterend were burned off to make a conventional freighter on deck. It laid idle during the Depression years but was returned to service in 1935. It is shown while underway in June, 1956.

The namesake of this vessel was the unincorporated village into which it regularly traded—Carrollton, Michigan. This is a city of about 7,000 people today and is a residential and commercial suburb of Saginaw, Michigan located at the head of deep-water navigation on the Saginaw River. The township was organized in 1866 and the village organized in 1869. It is named for Judge Carroll who first entered the land in official ledgers.

Motor Vessel SECOLA

OWNER: Secola Shipping Limited
BUILT: Marine Industries, Limited, Sorel, Quebec – 1951
HULL NO.: 197
O. A. DIMENSIONS: 290'10" x 43'6" x 20'
FORMER DATA: Launched as CEDARBRANCH (2). Lengthened 30' at Marine Industries, Limited, Sorel, Quebec in 1965. Given present name in 1978.

The 29,900 barrel capacity tank Motor Vessel SECOLA was an ideal vessel for this firm when acquired in 1978. Its good capacity at shallow draft made it economically usable in numerous wayports that could not be served by larger units of other fleets.

This tanker had become excess capacity in the Branch Lines fleet because of that fleet's expansion program of the late 1960's and 1970's. This firm was formed to own and operate this tanker. It is affiliated with Johnstone Shipping and its parent firm of which Mr. Rod Smith is president. Formerly, the affiliated firms have operated other tankers in the Great Lakes trade, but had no active vessels when this ship was acquired.

Namesake of both the tanker and the owning company is found in three words, these being: SEa, COast and LAke. This name was chosen because of the trade routes expected for this vessel, namely, the sea in an around the Maritimes, the coastal ports of the lower St. Lawrence River and the Great Lakes. The vessel is shown between Locks 6 and 7, Welland Ship Canal, on October 8, 1978. It was sold for off-lakes use late in 1979.

Steamer SHASTA

OWNER:	Shasta Steamship Company
BUILT:	American Ship Building Company, Lorain, Ohio—1902
HULL NO.:	315
O. A. DIMENSIONS:	400' × 50' × 28'
FORMER DATA:	Launched as C. W. WATSON. Given last name in 1929.

The small bulk freight Steamer SHASTA was sold for scrap in 1956 and is shown in the photograph below upbound in the St. Clair River on June 23, 1951. It has unloaded at Buffalo, New York and is upbound, light for Duluth, Minnesota and another cargo of grain.

This steamer was given its last name while under the management of Mr. George Ashley Tomlinson who had a theme of vessel names in his various fleets in which the ship name began with the letter "S" and ended with the letter "A" There were exceptions to this theme, but most ship names in Great Lakes history which had this commonality were at one time or another managed by Mr. Tomlinson and, in most cases, the subsequent owners kept the same name on the bow.

In the case of this vessel, the name referred to a Hokan-speaking group of North American Indians who live on and south of the Klamath River of California east of Mount Shasta. Culturally they stand between the northwestern tribes, such as the Yurok and Hupa, and the Maidu and other central Californian tribes. When first seen by white men in the 19th century, these people lived largely on salmon and also relied on roots and seeds for their food.

Motor Vessel BAYSHELL (1)

OWNER: Shell Canada Limited
BUILT: Bethlehem Shipbuilding & Drydock Company, Sparrows Point, Maryland—1930
HULL NO.: 4271
O. A. DIMENSIONS: 209'3" × 38' × 14'6"
FORMER DATA: Launched as JUSTINE C. ALLEN. Given last name in 1950.

The small tank Motor Vessel BAYSHELL was deleted from the operating Great Lakes fleet of these owners in 1967 and has since served in off-lakes use. The tanker is shown in the photograph above at Toronto, Ontario in August, 1952.

The namesake of this motor vessel is not specific, but, rather, the system of bays and inlets that surround the Great Lakes and tributary waters. A bay is commonly referred to or defined as an indentation of land that borders a lake or ocean. Some bays are called estuaries or fiords or rias. None of these specifically is the namesake, but all bays in general.

The suffix of the ship name, SHELL, refers to the owning firm name and is common to most of the Great Lakes tankers in the fleet of this company. The vessels of this fleet are engaged in transporting company products from refineries along the Great Lakes and St. Lawrence River to distribution terminals located at various ports throughout the Great Lakes, connecting channels and Maritimes.

Steamer FUEL MARKETER (2)

OWNER: Shell Canada Limited
BUILT: Marine Industries Limited, Sorel, Quebec—1944
HULL NO.: 142
O. A. DIMENSIONS: 259' × 43'9" × 20'
FORMER DATA: Launched as EGLINTON PARK. Renamed JOHN IRWIN (2) in 1945. Renamed WHITE ROSE II in 1956. Renamed WHITE ROSE in 1957. Given last name in 1970.

The Royal Dutch/Shell Group is the parent firm of a number of subsidiary or affiliated companies around the world. Among these, the Weaver Coal Company and its affiliated companies in Canada are a part. One of the affiliates is Canadian Fuel Marketers Limited of Toronto, Ontario.

The Steamer FUEL MARKETER takes its name from the second and third words in the corporate title of Canadian Fuel Marketers Limited, dropping the plural of the third word. The tanker is busily engaged in the Lake Ontario, Lake Erie and St. Lawrence River trades. It services the company-owned facilities and also carries out customer needs for others.

The name is quite applicable because fuel and fuel products are the type of liquid cargo carried. Also, to market or be a marketer may be defined as the act of bringing to a selling place or a buying place goods which are to be sold or delivered. This vessel was sold for scrap in 1978 and is shown discharging gasoline at Kingston, Ontario on October 2, 1976.

Motor Vessel RIVERSHELL (2)

OWNER:	Shell Canada Limited
BUILT:	Marine Industries Limited, Sorel, Quebec—1940
HULL NO.:	76
O. A. DIMENSIONS:	259' × 43'9" × 20'3"
FORMER DATA:	Launched as LAKESHELL (2). Given last name in 1969.

The tank vessel RIVERSHELL was sold for scrap in 1969 and never saw much service under its last name. The modern Motor Vessel LAKESHELL was commissioned by this company in 1969 and this elder carrier was retired.

This vessel had the common fleet suffix standing in recognition of the owners. Shell Oil Canada was incorporated as the Shell Company of Canada Limited on August 7, 1925 succeeding another firm of the same name. It acquired Canadian Oil Companies Limited in January, 1963 and took its present name in July of that year.

The prefix of this ship name pays honor to the river system of the Great Lakes region. No specific river is the namesake, but all the important tributaries to the Great Lakes-Seaway system. The most frequented river for the fleet, however, is the St. Lawrence.

The vessel is shown at the Shell Dock in Toronto, Ontario on April 22, 1969. When this ship was launched in May, 1940, it was the largest all-welded tanker ever built in the Dominion of Canada. It sailed on its maiden voyage from Toronto, Ontario July 31, 1940 with a cargo of crude oil for Montreal, Quebec delivery.

Steamer G. G. POST

OWNER:	Silloc, Limited
BUILT:	Chicago Shipbuilding Company, Chicago, Illinois—1902
HULL NO.:	54
O. A. DIMENSIONS:	366' × 48' × 28'
FORMER DATA:	Launched as the bulk freighter LUZON. Renamed JOHN ANDERSON in 1924. Given last name in 1933. Converted to a crane ship at American Ship Building Company, Cleveland, Ohio in 1936.

The crane-equipped vessel shown above was named in honor of Mr. George Gilbert Post by the owners of the Morrow Steamship Company. This firm was affiliated with the Valley Camp Coal Company in the 1930's and did considerable coal business with Mr. Post's utility company in Milwaukee, Wisconsin. Subsequent owners of the ship never saw fit to change the name.

Mr. Post was born on his father's farm three miles west of Madison, Wisconsin on September 15, 1881. He was educated at the University of Wisconsin and graduated in 1904 with a degree in electrical engineering. In 1906 he joined the Wisconsin Electric Power Company and in 1912 was named head of the firm's power distribution. He was elected vice president of the company in 1927 and retained that position until retirement in 1947.

Mr. Post resided in Milwaukee, Wisconsin until his death early in 1971. The power company he worked for has primary coal-receiving plants at Oak Creek, Milwaukee and Port Washington, Wisconsin. This vessel was sold for scrap in 1970 but the deal fell through and the vessel was again sold for scrap in 1971. The boat is shown above in its last colors at Hamilton, Ontario on May 7, 1966.

Motor Vessel SINCLAIR MILWAUKEE

OWNER: Sinclair Refining Company
BUILT: New York Shipbuilding Corporation, Camden, New Jersey—1924
HULL NO.: 290
O. A. DIMENSIONS: 259' × 40' × 22'
FORMER DATA: Launched as PROVIDENCE SOCONY. Rebuilt with new midbody at Brewer Dry Dock Company, New York, New York in 1943. Renamed BERT REINAUER (2) in 1952. Given last name in 1956.

The tank Motor Vessel SINCLAIR MILWAUKEE was sold for off-lakes use in 1964 and actually served for barely a full decade in Great Lakes service exclusively.

The first word of the ship name refers to the owning company which controlled the ship before that firm's merger into Atlantic Richfield Company in 1968. The second word in the ship name is the specific namesake and is in honor of the city of Milwaukee, Wisconsin where the firm has a large liquid cargo installation for receipt of Great Lakes cargoes.

Milwaukee, Wisconsin is the largest city in the state and is one of the world's leading producers of heavy machinery and mining equipment. Of course, it is even more famous as the "Brewing Capital of the World."

The name comes from the Algonkian Indian word "millioke" which means good land. Indeed, good land abounds in the area and has made Wisconsin famous as the nation's dairy state.

Steamer TRAVERSE CITY SOCONY

OWNER: Socony-Mobil Oil Company
BUILT: Manitowoc Shipbuilding Company, Manitowoc, Wisconsin—1938
HULL NO.: 299
O. A. DIMENSIONS: 300' × 49'6" × 20'6"

The tank Steamer TRAVERSE CITY SOCONY hailed from East Chicago, Indiana where the owners have a huge refinery and from which port more petroleum products move annually in Great Lakes commerce than any other port. Due to the extension of pipelines to areas formerly served by this fleet of tankers, this ship was sold for off-lakes use in 1962.

The namesake of this vessel is actually in two parts. The first part is the county seat of Grand Traverse County known as Traverse City, Michigan. It is 150 miles north of Grand Rapids, Michigan on Grand Traverse Bay of Lake Michigan. Two liquid cargo receiving docks are located at the port and this vessel was a frequent caller at one of them.

Traverse City was first settled in 1846 and the community was chartered as a village in 1881. It was granted status as a city in 1895. Current population is about 20,000, but this is swelled in the summer by visitors to the scenic areas around the bay area. The region is famous for its cherry crop as well as for other fruits. Principal manufactures include canned and frozen cherries, apples, light metal working, machine tools and dies.

The second part of this namesake is the former first word of the company name. This company is now known as Mobil Oil Corporation, having taken that name on May 17, 1966. The firm was founded on August 10, 1882. Several corporate names were used between then and the adoption of the name shown above in 1955.

Steamer PIERSON INDEPENDENT

OWNER: The Soo River Company
BUILT: Great Lakes Engineering Works, Ecorse, Michigan — 1906
HULL NO.: 22
O. A. DIMENSIONS: 550' x 56' x 31'
FORMER DATA: Launched as J. H. SHEADLE (1). Renamed F. A. BAILEY in 1924. Renamed LA SALLE (2) in 1930. Renamed MEAFORD (3) in 1966. Given last name in 1979.

The bulk freight Steamer PIERSON INDEPENDENT was one of the smaller such classed vessels in operation of the Great Lakes-Seaway system. While being an "extra boat" to its previous owners, it suited a definite need in this fleet which characterizes itself as an "independent" fleet. That is, this fleet is not involved with long-term contracts with very large shippers of bulk commodities. Rather, The Soo River Company had grown from a one-boat fleet at the beginning of 1975 to a fleet of over a half dozen ships with the acquisition of this freighter.

From the beginning, the fleet was to be a "people company," meaning a very personal interest was taken by the owner, Mr. Robert Scott Pierson, in the furtherance of the fleet's objectives in concert with those of the employees aboard ship.

Since the fleet was to offer its services to all customers in a variety of trades, it was truly to be an independent firm, and hence the choice of this vessel name. The ship is shown below at Port Huron, Michigan on August 25, 1979. It grounded, unfortunately, near Brockville, Ontario in the fall of 1979 and was badly damaged. It was sold, therefore, for scrap in 1980.

Steamer STEEL PRODUCTS

OWNER:	Steel Products Steamship Corporation
BUILT:	American Ship Building Company, Lorain, Ohio—1901
HULL NO.:	307
O. A. DIMENSIONS:	366' × 48' × 28'
FORMER DATA:	Launched as the bulk freighter VENUS (1). Converted to a crane ship at Toledo Shipbuilding Company, Toledo, Ohio in 1927. Given last name in 1958.

The crane-equipped Steamer STEEL PRODUCTS honored the name of the company which was formed at the time of its sale in 1958 from the Ore Navigation Corporation, a subsidiary of Bethlehem Steel Corporation, to the Steel Products Steamship Company, a subsidiary of Lake Shore, Incorporated of Iron Mountain, Michigan. The new company bore a name that reflected the heavy industrial activity of the parent firm which had bought the ship to assist in its marketing program to ports on the Great Lakes.

The whole operation was shortlived, however, and this vessel was sold for scrap in 1961. Enroute to Port Colborne, Ontario for scrapping, the tow line broke and this ship ran hard aground near Point Abino in Lake Erie. It has been mostly dismantled by scrappers since then, but parts of the hull still remain on the scene.

The name of this vessel also bore direct relationship to the business it was about. Handling of products of steel was the primary activity of this hull ever since she was first converted to a crane ship in 1927.

Motor Vessel TOLEDO SUN

OWNER: Sun Oil Company
BUILT: S. B. A. Shipyards, Incorporated, Jennings, Louisiana – 1968
HULL NO.: 187
O. A. DIMENSIONS: 300' x 43' x 21'6"

The vessel shown above may occasionally be called a "self-propelled barge." Actually this tank vessel was self-contained as to its power plant and served on the Great Lakes only a short while, running between the Toledo, Ohio refinery and the East Coast via the New York State Barge Canal. It was sent into off-lakes service for these owners in 1971 and is shown above on its trial runs in the Louisiana bayous.

This vessel has a double namesake. The first name refers to Toledo, Ohio in which city the company has a 1,500,000 barrel capacity refinery. This facility forwards into Great Lakes shipment such items as gasoline and # 1, 2 and 6 fuel oil. The city is at the western tip of Lake Erie at the mouth of the Maumee River. It has a population of about 325,000 and is one of the greatest coal shipping ports in the world.

The second word in this ship name refers to the owning company. Sun Oil Company was incorporated in New Jersey May 2, 1901 as Sun Company and Sun Oil Company of Ohio was formed in 1890. The name was changed to Sun Oil Company on December 15, 1922.

Steamer NORMAN P. CLEMENT

OWNER: Tank Truck Transport Limited
BUILT: J. Samuel White & Company,
East Cowes, Isle of Wight, England—1924
HULL NO.: 1604
O. A. DIMENSIONS: 261' × 43' × 20'
FORMER DATA: Launched as a bulk freighter. Converted to a sulphuric acid tanker at Tank Truck Transport Limited, Sarnia, Ontario in 1962.

After this vessel suffered an explosion at Collingwood, Ontario it was taken out into Georgian Bay and scuttled on October 23, 1968. This accident ended the service of the only acid tank steamer on the Great Lakes.

Mr. Norman Parsons Clement was the namesake of this ship. He was born at Buffalo, New York on April 12, 1885 and graduated from Yale University in 1907 with a B.A. degree and began working at the Marine National Bank of Buffalo, New York. From 1917 to 1919 he served in military service and then joined Citizen's Trust Company at Buffalo.

Mr. Clement soon became president of the Citizen's Trust and also of Genesee Properties, Incorporated. The latter firm was a real estate enterprise which Mr. Clement owned. In addition, he was a director and vice president of Eastern Grain, Mill and Elevator Corporation.

This ship had the distinction of being the first to load at the Iron Ore Company of Canada's Contrecoeur, Quebec facility on May 27, 1955. It took onboard 2,235 gross tons of iron ore for Toledo, Ohio delivery. It had sailed from Liverpool, England on April 3, 1924 with a cargo of manganese ore for Sault Ste. Marie, Ontario on its maiden voyage.

Steamer TEXACO-BRAVE (1)

OWNER: Texaco Canada Limited
BUILT: Furness Shipbuilding Company, Limited, Haverton Hill-on-Tees, England – 1929
HULL NO.: 145
O. A. DIMENSIONS: 258' x 43'3" x 24'3"
FORMER DATA: Launched as JOHN IRWIN (1). Renamed CYCLO-BRAVE in 1940. Given last name in 1947.

The tank Steamer TEXACO-BRAVE is shown above while downbound in the Rock Cut, St. Mary's River on May 24, 1972. It worked faithfully for forty-six seasons before finally being sold for scrap in early 1975. When retired, this vessel was the last steam canal tanker on the Great Lakes that was built as a tanker. Two other vessels remained, but they had been converted to tankers and were originally bulk freighters.

Namesake of this carrier was twofold. First the name of the owning company was honored by the first word of the ship name. The second word in the ship name refers to the Indian usage of the word brave.

For many years this firm operated as the McColl-Frontenac Oil Company, Limited. As that firm's corporate symbol was an Indian Chief, management felt the theme should be carried through in the vessel names. While a brave is of lesser importance in a tribe than the chief, he is nonetheless an integral part of a tribe. In this context, this vessel was viewed as an integral part of the Texaco fleet in Canada in the movement of petroleum products throughout the Great Lakes-Seaway distribution system.

Steamer TEXACO MICHIGAN

OWNER: Texaco, Incorporated
BUILT: Chicago Shipbuilding Company, Chicago, Illinois—1902
HULL NO.: 53
O. A. DIMENSIONS: 390' × 48' × 28'
FORMER DATA: Launched as the bulk freighter HORACE S. WILKINSON (1). Renamed BELGIUM in 1916. Converted to a tanker and renamed MICHIGAN (7) at Toledo Shipbuilding Company, Toledo, Ohio in 1942. Given last name in 1960.

The tank Steamer TEXACO MICHIGAN served under this name until it was sold for off-lakes use in 1963. It was actually renamed TRINA before it left the lakes. The new owners tried to beat the Seaway deadline by taking on a grain cargo in the lakes for Gulf of Mexico delivery in December, 1963, but failed to get the ship out in time and the vessel laid at Kingston, Ontario for the winter. Financial troubles mounted and the vessel was auctioned, eventually getting to off-lakes service in 1964.

On the Great Lakes this ship honored its owners, formerly known as The Texas Company and originally organized in 1902. The corporate name shown above was adopted in May, 1959. This firm has grown through the years by merger and acquisition to become one of the world's major oil refining and pipeline companies.

The second word of this ship's name honored the state of Michigan which is the most fully aligned with the Great Lakes of all lake states. It has more shoreline on the Great Lakes than any other state and is one of the most heavily dependent on Great Lakes commerce.

Steamer CUYLER ADAMS

OWNER: Tomlinson Fleet Corporation
BUILT: American Ship Building Company, Lorain, Ohio—1904
HULL NO.: 331
O. A. DIMENSIONS: 497' × 52' × 29'
FORMER DATA: Launched as SAHARA. Given last name in 1913.

A distinguished mining engineer was the namesake of this bulk freighter which was sold for scrap in 1960. He was Mr. Cuyler Adams who was born in Canton, Illinois on August 20, 1852. He was educated in New York City and went to Minnesota in 1870.

Mr. Adams was a land examiner with the Northern Pacific when the financial panic of 1873 hit and through astute thinking turned his financial holdings in the railroad into real estate lands in North Dakota. With outside help from Philadelphia, Pennsylvania he acquired large holdings of land and practiced bonanza farming. In addition he prospected for other wealth near Deerwood, Minnesota and noticed, on one of his trips with his St. Bernard dog Una, that the compass needle swung wildly when he passed over a certain area. This was in 1890 and was the discovery of iron ore in the location that now bears the name Cuyuna Range.

By 1911 the first ore was shipped from the range and Mr. Adams became a legend in his own time. He was president of the Cuyuna Iron Range Railway and the Biwango Mining Company in addition to his other interests. He died November 29, 1932 at his winter home in Tryon, North Carolina.

His namesake is shown below while upbound with a cargo of coal at Port Huron, Michigan as seen from the Blue Water Bridge.

Steamer BALL BROTHERS

OWNER: Tomlinson Fleet Corporation
BUILT: American Ship Building Company, Lorain, Ohio—1905
HULL NO.: 333
O. A. DIMENSIONS: 500' × 52' × 30'

Sold for overseas scrapping in 1963, the bulk freight Steamer BALL BROTHERS honored the five brothers of the Ball family as its namesakes.

These gentlemen were, in order of birth: Lucius Lorenzo Ball, born March 29, 1850, William Charles Ball, born August 13, 1852, Edmund Burke Ball, born October 27, 1855, Frank Clayton Ball, born November 24, 1857 and George Alexander Ball, born November 5, 1862. All were born at Greensburg, Ohio.

The connection between the Ball family and the Tomlinson organization dates from very early times. Lucius Ball's wife was the aunt of Laura Tomlinson, wife of George Ashley Tomlinson, founder of the fleet. The younger brothers were interested in the fleet and were investors in it during its beginnings.

The Ball brothers were interested in a wide range of business ventures including the Ball Brothers Glass Manufacturing Company, now known as Ball Corporation. Ladies throughout the world are familiar with the Ball glass containers since they have been a hallmark of canning excellence for decades.

Mr. Edmund F. Ball, nephew of Frank C. Ball, was the last remaining Ball family representative on the board of directors of the Tomlinson Fleet Corporation. This streamer is shown in the St. Mary's River near Lime Island on August 20, 1958.

Steamer JAMES E. DAVIDSON

OWNER: Tomlinson Fleet Corporation
BUILT: Great Lakes Engineering Works, Ecorse, Michigan—1905
HULL NO.: 5
O. A. DIMENSIONS: 524' × 54' × 30'

Mr. James Edward Davidson was born at Buffalo, New York on December 7, 1865. He was educated at Hillsdale College and received a B.A. degree in 1887. That same year he joined his father, Captain James Davidson, in the family business interests at Bay City, Michigan.

He learned management of the various Davidson enterprises including shipbuilding, shipping and banking and, in 1929, on the death of his father assumed full direction of the companies. He continued in these activities until his death at White Sulphur Springs, West Virginia on July 25, 1947.

Mr. Davidson was chairman of the board of Hillsdale County National Bank and president of the Peoples Commercial & Savings Bank, Davidson Building Company, Bay Trust Company, Globe Steamship Company, Duluth Steamship Company, Triton Steamship Company, Inter-Ocean Steamship Company and Continental Steamship Company as well as an officer of American Ship Building Company, Robert Gage Coal Company and Rock County Sugar Company. He also held numerous directorships in other firms.

His namesake was sold for scrapping in 1963. It is shown below in the St. Mary's River below Sault Ste. Marie, Michigan on June 19, 1956. The vessel is downbound with a cargo of iron ore for Cleveland, Ohio delivery.

Steamer CHARLES E. DUNLAP

OWNER: Tomlinson Fleet Corporation
BUILT: American Ship Building Company, Lorain, Ohio—1920
HULL NO.: 777
O. A. DIMENSIONS: 600' × 60' × 32'
FORMER DATA: Launched as L. M. BOWERS. Given last name in 1935.

After seven years of inactivity, the Steamer CHARLES E. DUNLAP was sold for trade-in and subsequent scrapping in 1968.

Namesake of this bulk freighter was Mr. Charles Edward Dunlap who was born at Philadelphia, Pennsylvania on December 3, 1888. He received a B.A. degree from Harvard University in 1911 and began working that year for the Berwind-White Coal Mining Company.

Mr. Dunlap served in various capacities, gradually assuming more responsibility and administrative functions. In 1928 his hard work was rewarded with the appointment as a vice president of the firm. He was elected president of the company in 1930 and served in that capacity until retiring in the early 1960's.

The Steamer CHARLES E. DUNLAP is seen in the photograph below on July 10, 1960 downbound at Port Huron, Michigan. The vessel is heading towards Lake Erie with an early loaded cargo of winter storage grain for holding at Buffalo, New York. The vessel began its maiden trip July 31, 1920 light from Lorain, Ohio to Superior, Wisconsin to load iron ore.

Steamer RUFUS P. RANNEY (2)

OWNER: Tomlinson Fleet Corporation
BUILT: Superior Shipbuilding Company, Superior, Wisconsin—1908
HULL NO.: 520
O. A. DIMENSIONS: 440' × 52' × 28'6"

This bulk freight Steamer RUFUS P. RANNEY was the second Great Lakes ship to bear this name. The first was a wooden freighter built in the last century and named in honor of this man's grandfather, the famous jurist from the state of Ohio.

The man for whom this ship was named was Mr. Rufus Percival Ranney who was born on May 24, 1874 at Cleveland, Ohio. He attended the local schools and was a graduate of the University of Michigan with an Ll.B. degree.

Mr. Ranney went directly into the practice of law at Cleveland, Ohio and became associated with vessel and coal interests of the family. He financed the construction of this bulk vessel for the Triton Steamship Company which was later absorbed into the Tomlinson fleet. He was also head of the Ranney Coal Company and supplied much upbound cargo for this vessel and others of the fleet.

Mr. Ranney was stricken with a sudden attack of appendicitis and died on November 13, 1920. His namesake, having fulfilled its usefulness, was sold for scrap in 1960. It is shown below at Port Weller, Ontario on July 28, 1953 enroute to Lake Erie. The previous day it had completed unloading a grain cargo from Duluth, Minnesota at Oswego, New York and had left that port.

Motor Vessel JULIUS H. BARNES

OWNER:	Toth Motorship, Incorporated
BUILT:	Charleston Shipbuilding & Dry Dock Company, Charleston, South Carolina—1940
HULL NO.:	5500
O. A. DIMENSIONS:	290' × 42'3" × 18'

The New York State Barge Canal-size Motor Vessel JULIUS H. BARNES was a combination bulk and package freight vessel. It was sold for off-lakes use in 1962 and lately has been in service in the Caribbean Sea. The ship is shown here in Lock Five of the Welland Ship Canal on November 4, 1956.

Namesake of this vessel was Mr. Julius Howland Barnes who was born on February 2, 1873 at Little Rock, Arkansas. He moved to Duluth, Minnesota with his family in 1883 and began working as an office boy in the wheat brokerage office of Mr. Ward Ames in 1889. By 1895 he had left the Ames firm and went into business for himself as a grain merchant and exporter.

By 1917, Mr. Barnes had achieved the distinction of being the largest grain exporter in the United States and he served as president of the Food Administration Grain Corportation from 1917 to 1919. He was also United States Wheat Director in 1919 and 1920.

He served in various official national capacities in ensuing years as well as being chairman of the board of Klearflax Linen Looms, Inc., president of Barnes-Duluth Shipbuilding Company, Erie & St. Lawrence Corporation, National St. Lawrence Association and several other firms. Mr. Barnes died at Duluth, Minnesota on April 17, 1959. His namesake carried nitrate of soda from Norfolk, Virginia to Toronto, Ontario and Cleveland, Ohio on its maiden voyage which began September 20, 1940. It was the largest ship ever to pass through the New York State Barge Canal on that trip.

Steamer HERON BAY (2)

OWNER: Trico Enterprises, Limited
BUILT: Chicago Shipbuilding Company, Chicago, Illinois—1906
HULL NO.: 68
O. A. DIMENSIONS: 601' x 58' x 32'
FORMER DATA: Launched as J. PIERPONT MORGAN. Given last name in 1966.

Operated by the Quebec & Ontario Transportation Company Limited, the Steamer HERON BAY was named after the village of the same name which was the headquarters for the Ontario Paper Company's logging operations on the north shore of Lake Superior.

Heron Bay, Ontario is located six miles southeast of Peninsula Harbor and is nearly at the extreme northeast corner of Lake Superior. It is a station on the Canadian Pacific Railway's mainline from Toronto to Winnipeg which skirts Lake Superior in a scenic vista along that part of Lake Superior.

The harbor used to be the scene of much waterborne commerce in the log and lumber business, but now it has little commerce except fisherman and pleasure craft who visit the area for its scenic beauty.

This bulk freighter is shown below while downbound in the West Neebish Channel, St. Mary's River on July 3, 1978. The ship was sold for scrap in November, 1978.

Steamer SHELTER BAY (2)

OWNER: Trico Enterprises, Limited
BUILT: American Ship Building Company, Cleveland, Ohio - 1907
HULL NO.: 438
O. A. DIMENSIONS: 552' x 58' x 31'
FORMER DATA: Launched as JAY C. MORSE. Given last name in 1965.

The Steamer SHELTER BAY (2) was named for a former pulpwood cutting plant of the Quebec North Shore Paper Company located about midway between Baie Comeau and Seven Islands, Quebec. The village is now amalgamated with Port Cartier, Quebec but supplied pulpwood from 1920 to 1962. Ships of this fleet were frequent callers at the port.

Shelter Bay is now known as Port-Cartier-Quest. It is situated at the mouth of Riviere-aux-Roches, five miles west from Pointe Ste-Marguerite. The docks in the port are now partially silted in and barely eleven feet of water remains alongside.

The area is not forgotten in current commerce, however, because Port Cartier is a major new iron ore loading port of the Quebec Cartier Mining Company, a subsidiary of the United States Steel Corporation. It is also the site of a large, modern export grain elevator owned by Louis Dreyfus Canada Limited.

Though the original pulpwood port is abandoned, area residents are reminded of the busy port days goneby when only pulpwood and occasional general cargo ships entered their port. This bulk freighter is shown in the West Neebish Channel, St. Mary's River, on May 29, 1978. It was sold late that year for non-transportation use as a grain storage barge at Goderich, Ontario and for scrap in 1983.

Steamer WILLIAM EDENBORN

OWNER: Pittsburgh Steamship Division, United States Steel Corporation
BUILT: West Bay City Shipbuilding Company, West Bay City, Michigan—1900
HULL NO.: 40
O. A. DIMENSIONS: 497' × 52' × 30'

Mr. William Edenborn was born at Westphalia, Prussia on March 20, 1848 and was educated there, apprenticing to a manufacturer of steel wire and awls. At the end of his apprenticeship he came to the United States in 1867.

He began his career here as a wire drawer in Pittsburgh, Pennsylvania and Cincinnati, Ohio before going to work in association with Frank M. Ludlow to erect the first wire mill in St. Louis, Missouri in 1870. He organized the St. Louis Wire Mill Company in 1877 and in 1882 began making barbed wire. In 1886 he added wire nails to the line.

He was president of his St. Louis firm until this company and others were merged in 1898 to form the American Steel & Wire Company. He then became a vice president and member of the executive committee of the larger company and served in that capacity until 1901 when he was named a member of the executive and advisory committees of United States Steel Corporation, on its formation. He held these posts when he retired in 1904. Mr. Edenborn died on May 14, 1926.

His namesake was sold for use as a breakwater in 1961 after serving many profitable years carrying iron ore, coal and stone. It is shown here in the St. Mary's River below Sault Ste. Michigan on August 19, 1957.

Steamer ISAAC L. ELLWOOD

OWNER:	Pittsburgh Steamship Division, United States Steel Corporation
BUILT:	West Bay City Shipbuilding Company, West Bay City, Michigan—1900
HULL NO.:	39
O. A. DIMENSIONS:	497' × 52' × 30'

The bulk freight Steamer ISAAC L. ELLWOOD was sold for scrap in 1961 after over a half-century of faithful service in the United States Steel Corporation's Great Lakes fleet.

Namesake of this ship was Mr. Isaac Leonard Ellwood who was born at Salt Springville, New York on August 3, 1833. He finished his education and became interested, with J. F. Glidden, in the manufacture and sale of barbed wire. In 1876 Glidden sold his interest to Washburn and Moen Manufacturing Company and the business was carried on under the name of I. L. Ellwood and Company.

Mr. Ellwood became managing partner of the operation and, later, sole owner of large manufacturing establishments at De Kalb, Illinois. An affiliate firm was named Ellwood Wire & Nail Company. Both of these companies were sold to American Steel & Wire Company when it was organized in 1898 and Mr. Ellwood held management positions in the new, enlarged firm. He died in 1910 after seeing his ideas prosper and his business become very successful.

His namesake was one of four fleet ships that had "submarine" after quarters. The ship is shown at Cleveland, Ohio on August 10, 1957.

Steamer JOHN W. GATES

OWNER:	Pittsburgh Steamship Division, United States Steel Corporation
BUILT:	American Ship Building Company, Lorain, Ohio—1900
HULL NO.:	37
O. A. DIMENSIONS:	497' × 52' × 30'

Mr. John Warne Gates was the namesake of this bulk freighter. He was born near Turner Junction, Illinois on May 8, 1855 and was educated at North-Western College at Naperville, Illinois where he received commercial courses. Upon completing his schooling, he left the farm and bought one-half interest in a hardware store in Turner Junction.

In 1878 Mr. Gates sought out Mr. I. L. Ellwood and offered to take a partnership in his wiremaking concern. Mr. Ellwood was receptive to the idea and hired him and sent him to Texas as a salesman of Ellwood's new barbed wire products. Mr. Gates did such a good job selling these new products he resigned from Ellwood's employ and set up his own business in St. Louis, Missouri in 1880. This was known as the Southern Wire Company and later Braddock Wire Company.

Mr. Gates' business thrived. He had several other firms and re-organized companies which he sold in 1898 on the formation of the American Steel & Wire Company. This firm later became a subsidiary of United States Steel Corporation. Mr. Gates continued in business supervising his many interests and holdings in railroads and industrial firms. He died on August 9, 1911. This ship was sold for scrap in 1961. It is shown here downbound with iron ore in the St. Clair River in 1957.

Steamer JAMES J. HILL

OWNER:	Pittsburgh Steamship Division, United States Steel Corporation
BUILT:	American Ship Building Company, Lorain, Ohio—1900
HULL NO.:	38
O. A. DIMENSIONS:	497' × 52' × 30'

Referred to as the "Empire Builder," Mr. James Jerome Hill was born at Guelph, Ontario on September 16, 1838 and was educated at Rockwood Academy. He left his father's farm after finishing school and went to Minnesota to seek a career in business. Mr. Hill began as a clerk in steamship offices in St. Paul, Minnesota in 1856 and remained there until 1865.

In 1869 he set up his own fuel company and transportation business known as Hill, Griggs & Company. In 1870 he established the Red River Transportation Company to become the first direct link between St. Paul and Winnipeg, Manitoba. After these successful ventures, he organized a syndicate to acquire control of the St. Paul & Pacific Railroad and renamed it St. Paul, Minneapolis & Manitoba Railway Company. He served as general manager from 1879 to 1881, vice president in 1881-1882 and president from then until 1890 when it became part of the Great Northern Railway System.

Mr. Hill was president until 1907 and chairman of the board until July 7, 1912. He died at St. Paul, Minnesota on May 29, 1916 after having seen his dream of a through rail line to Puget Sound become a reality. His namesake was sold in 1961 and sunk as a breakwater at Cleveland, Ohio. It is shown below in the Detroit River on July 18, 1957.

Steamer CARL D. BRADLEY (2)

OWNER: Michigan Limestone Division, United States Steel Corporation
BUILT: American Ship Building Company, Lorain, Ohio—1927
HULL NO.: 797
O. A. DIMENSIONS: 638' × 65'2" × 33'

This self-loader set a record for limestone cargoes when it cleared Calcite, Michigan on July 29, 1927 for Buffington, Indiana with 14,627 gross tons on its maiden trip. It continued to hold the record, with larger cargoes through the years, until that honor went to another large self-unloader on September 9, 1952.

Namesake of this ship was Mr. Carl David Bradley who was born in Chicago, Illinois on September 12, 1860. He was educated in that city and began working as an iron founder. In due course he was managing several small foundries. In the late 1890's he moved to New York City where he took the position of an engineer with a consulting firm.

Mr. Bradley was sent to Chicago, Illinois in 1911 as manager of the newly formed Michigan Limestone & Chemical Company. In February, 1912 he moved to Rogers City, Michigan to be on hand for the expansion of the quarry operations. Mr. Bradley continued as general manager of the firm until being named its president in 1920. He was also president of Bradley Transportation Company which was the steamship arm of the enterprise. Mr. Bradley died in Pasadena, California on March 19, 1928.

His namesake was the victim of a foundering off Gull Island, Lake Michigan in a violent storm on November 18, 1958. Only two members of the crew of 35 were saved. The ship is shown above on Lake St. Clair August 25, 1951.

Steamer CALCITE

OWNER: Michigan Limestone Division, United States Steel Corporation
BUILT: Detroit Shipbuilding Company, Wyandotte, Michigan—1912
HULL NO.: 188
O. A. DIMENSIONS: 436' × 54'3" × 29'

The Steamer CALCITE was the first self-unloader built and operated by the United States Steel Corporation. It was through the subsidiary Michigan Limestone Division that the vessel spent its last operating days.

Namesake of the vessel is Calcite, Michign. It is the largest limestone quarry in the world and is adjacent to United States Steel's shipping and port facilities at Rogers City, Michigan on the western shore of Lake Huron about sixty-five miles below the Straits of Mackinac.

The limestone layers of this property were deposited during the Devonian period of geologic time. It is limestone of high calcium and of unusual purity compared to ordinary limestone. More than fifteen million net tons of this product are shipped annually from the Calcite quarry.

This self-unloader spent its entire career as a unit of United States Steel Corporation, so it was a fitting departure for the vessel in 1961 when it was sold to the P. & C. Dock Company of Conneaut, Ohio for cutting up and scrapping. That dock company operates the various facilities in the Conneaut harbor and is also a United States Steel subsidiary.

The Steamer CALCITE is shown above in the Lower St. Mary's River at Sault Ste. Marie, Michigan on August 19, 1954. Its maiden trip began June 15, 1912 with a cargo of stone from its namesake port to Buffalo, New York.

Steamer EUGENE J. BUFFINGTON

OWNER: United States Steel Corporation Great Lakes Fleet
BUILT: American Ship Building Company, Lorain, Ohio—1909
HULL NO.: 366
O. A. DIMENSIONS: 601' × 58' × 32'

Mr. Eugene Jackson Buffington was born on March 14, 1863 at Guyandotte, West Virginia and was educated at Chickering Institute and Vanderbilt University. He began his career in business as treasurer of the American Wire & Screw Nail Company at Covington, Kentucky in 1883. This firm evolved into the American Wire & Nail Company of Anderson, Indiana and he served as treasurer and secretary-treasurer of that organization until 1898.

Mr. Buffington left this firm to become president of Illinois Steel Company in 1899 and stayed in that post until 1932. During this time he was also president of Indiana Steel Company and the Gary Land Company.

When Illinois Steel became a subsidiary of United States Steel Corporation in 1901 and the need for another steel plant became apparant, Mr. Buffington was given the assignment to plan and supervise construction of the new plant. This new plant was built on the marsh lands of northern Indiana and was the world's largest and most modern steel facility. The name Gary, Indiana was given to the new plant and industrial city, in honor of Judge Elbert H. Gary, then chairman of the board of United States Steel. Mr. Buffington was a director of this company until his death on December 9, 1937. His namesake began its maiden trip May 6, 1909 from Lorain, Ohio, light to Two Harbors, Minnesota to load iron ore. It is shown below in the West Neebish channel, St. Mary's River on August 19, 1973 and was sold for scrap in 1980.

Steamer CEDARVILLE

OWNER:	United States Steel Corporation Great Lakes Fleet
BUILT:	Great Lakes Engineering Works, River Rouge, Michigan—1927
HULL NO.:	255
O. A. DIMENSIONS:	603'9" × 60' × 32'
FORMER DATA:	Launched as the bulk freighter A. F. HARVEY (2). Converted to a self-unloader at Defoe Shipbuilding Company, Bay City, Michigan and given last name in 1957.

The self-unloading Steamer CEDARVILLE began its career when it sailed from Detroit, Michigan upbound, light on May 17, 1927 for Duluth, Minnesota for a cargo of iron ore. Its career was ended on May 7, 1965 when it was sunk in the Straits of Mackinac as a result of a collision with the Norwegian Motor Vessel TOPDALSFJORD. This accident occurred during heavy fog and the Steamer CEDARVILLE sank about two miles east of the Mackinac Bridge, at about 9:50 AM. Ten crew members from the CEDARVILLE were lost, while survivors were rescued by the German Motor Vessel WEISSENBURG.

Cedarville, Michigan is the namesake of this ship. It was developed by the United States Steel Corporation as a shipping port for limestone and is also known as Port Dolomite. Cedarville is located in Mackinac County, Michigan on the south shore of the Upper Peninsula between St. Ignace and Detour. Many localities in this area are named for French explorers and Jesuit missionaries who were the first white men to settle the area.

The Steamer CEDARVILLE is shown above near Sault Ste. Marie, Michigan on June 15, 1962.

Steamer D. M. CLEMSON (2)

OWNER: United States Steel Corporation Great Lakes Fleet
BUILT: American Ship Building Company,
Lorain, Ohio—1917
HULL NO.: 716
O. A. DIMENSIONS: 600' × 60' × 32'

The Isherwood design Steamer D. M. CLEMSON is named in honor of Mr. Daniel Melancthon Clemson who was born on the family farm near Bellefonte, Pennsylvania on May 23, 1853. After early work on the farm he became a blacksmith's helper and at the age of eighteen went to work at the Scotia ore mines of Carnegie Brothers & Company near Bellefonte.

From 1880 to 1889 he was superintendent of Scotia mines and the Latimer Coke Works. In 1889 he was appointed general manager of the Carnegie Natural Gas Company and in 1897 became president and managing director of that company. He continued in that post until his retirement in 1921.

He was associated with United States Steel Corporation as director of Carnegie Steel Company and all of its subsidiaries and president of Oliver Mining Company and Pittsburgh Steamship Company from 1901 to 1904.

After his retirement he gave much of his time to charitable welfare organizations and served many of these as director. Mr. Clemson died on April 7, 1936. His namesake was nearly ready for service in mid-December, 1916 but because of the nearness of the close of navigation the vessel did not get finished and go into service until it left Lorain, Ohio on its maiden voyage April 24, 1917. It went light to Duluth, Minnesota to load iron ore. The ship is shown below while upbound in the St. Mary's River on August 4, 1971 and was sold for scrap in 1980.

Steamer THOMAS F. COLE

OWNER: United States Steel Corporation Great Lakes Fleet
BUILT: Great Lakes Engineering Works, Ecorse, Michigan—1907
HULL NO.: 27
O. A. DIMENSIONS: 605'6" × 58' × 32'

Mr. Thomas Frederick Cole was born on July 19, 1862 at his parents home near Phoenix, Keweenaw County, Michigan. His father died when he was very young and this young lad went to work at the age of eight around the Phoenix and Cliffs copper mines in the area. At the age of fifteen he became a brakeman on the Hecla & Torch Lake Railroad and in 1884 was a clerk for the Calumet & Hecla Company at Calumet, Michigan.

From 1886 to 1889, Mr. Cole was chief clerk and cashier for the Chapin Mine at Iron Mountain, Michigan. He then became general manager of the Ferdinand Schlessinger Iron Mines at Negaunee, Michigan. In 1896 he took the post of manager of mines for Oliver Mining Company, then a subsidiary of Carnegie Steel Company and later United States Steel Corporation. He and Mr. N. P. Hulst obtained leases or bought properties for the company in Minnesota which proved so successful that Mr. Cole was made vice president and later president of Oliver Mining.

Mr. Cole resigned his presidency at Oliver Mining in 1909 to devote full time to copper interests he founded and was president of in Montana. He later acquired silver and gold holdings in California and Nevada and was responsible for their development. His namesake is shown upbound in the St. Mary's River. It was sold for scrap in 1980.

Steamer GEORGE G. CRAWFORD

OWNER: United States Steel Corporation Great Lakes Fleet
BUILT: American Ship Building Company, Lorain, Ohio — 1907
HULL NO.: 347
O. A. DIMENSIONS: 605'9" x 60' x 32'
FORMER DATA: Launched as Le GRAND S. de GRAFF. Given last name in 1911.

Mr. George Gordon Crawford was born at Madison, Georgia on August 24, 1869 and graduated from Georgia Institute of Technology in 1890 with a B.S. degree. After further study in Germany, he began as a chemist and draftsman at the Edgar Thompson Works of Carnegie Steel Company in 1892. He became assistant superintendent of those Works in 1895.

From 1897 to 1899 he was superintendent of blast furnaces and steel works at National Tube Company in McKeesport, Pennsylvania and from 1899 to 1901 was superintendent at the Edgar Thompson Works. From 1901 to 1907 he was manager of the national department of National Tube Company involved in planning and plant rebuilding. He was chairman of the coke committee while on this assignment and showed the feasibility of using by-product coke in blast furnaces. This success led to his being named president of the subsidiary Tennessee Coal & Iron & Railroad Company in 1907 at Birmingham, Alabama. He held this post until 1930 when he resigned from United States Steel Corporation to become president of Jones & Laughlin Steel Corporation. He resigned from that post in 1935 and returned to live in Alabama. His namesake was sold for scrap in 1974 and is shown while upbound in the St. Mary's River in 1969.

Steamer ALVA C. DINKEY

OWNER:	United States Steel Corporation Great Lakes Fleet
BUILT:	American Ship Building Company, Lorain, Ohio—1909
HULL NO.:	365
O. A. DIMENSIONS:	601' × 58' × 32'

The bulk freight Steamer ALVA C. DINKEY is named in honor of Mr. Alva Clymer Dinkey who was born on February 20, 1866 at Weatherly, Pennsylvania and who was educated in the public schools.

He began his career in the steel industry as a water boy at the Edgar Thompson Works of Carnegie Steel Company on May 21, 1879 and was made telegraph operator in 1885. That year he left to become a machinist at Pittsburg Locomotive Works and left that firm in 1889 to be an expert machinist and electrician with McTighe Electric Company.

He rejoined Carnegie Steel in 1893 as electrician of the Homestead Works and rose through several positions to be named superintendent of that plant in 1901. He became general manager of Carnegie Steel in 1903 and served in that capacity until resigning in 1915 to become president of the Midvale Steel & Ordinance Company. He was serving as president of this company when it was acquired in 1923 by Bethlehem Steel Corporation and remained in executive posts until his death on August 11, 1931. His namesake's maiden trip was commenced April 27, 1909 light for iron ore from Cleveland, Ohio to Duluth, Minnesota. It was the first freighter to use the then new Davis Lock at the Soo, passing upbound light at 3:00 PM on October 22, 1914. The vessel is shown below while downbound in the Rock Cut, St. Mary's River on August 7, 1973. It was sold for scrap in 1980.

Steamer JAMES A. FARRELL

OWNER: United States Steel Corporation Great Lakes Fleet
BUILT: American Ship Building Company, Lorain, Ohio—1913
HULL NO.: 397
O. A. DIMENSIONS: 600' × 58' × 32'

Shown here in the St. Mary's River on August 11, 1971, the Steamer JAMES A. FARRELL honors Mr. James Augustine Farrell who was born at New Haven, Connecticut February 15, 1863. He was educated in the public schools and began work at 16 in the Pittsburg Wire Company mill. He later became superintendent and manager of that company.

Mr. Farrell organized a wire company at Braddock, Pennsylvania which became part of the American Steel & Wire Company, a subsidiary of United States Steel Corporation. He was general manager of exports of that firm in 1903 when he was elected president of United States Steel Products Export Company, serving in that post until 1911. He built a fleet of ocean steamers to carry the company products to all parts of the world.

The leadership and ability he displayed in foreign development coupled with his years of steel manufacturing experience led to his election as president of United States Steel Corporation in 1912. His namesake was the first of this fleet to have large guest quarters beneath the pilot house as seen in this photograph. Mr. Farrell died on March 28, 1943. His namesake sailed on its maiden trip April 22, 1913 light from Cleveland, Ohio to Two Harbors, Minnesota to load iron ore. It was the first freighter to pass through the then new Davis Lock at the Soo with cargo. This occurred at 4:00 PM October 22, 1914 and the cargo amounted to 11,745 gross tons of iron ore. The ship was sold for scrap in 1978.

Steamer WILLIAM J. FILBERT

OWNER: United States Steel Corporation Great Lakes Fleet
BUILT: American Ship Building Company, Lorain, Ohio—1907
HULL NO.: 348
O. A. DIMENSIONS: 605'9" × 60' × 32'
FORMER DATA: Launched as WILLIAM M. MILLS. Given last name in 1911.

Namesake of this bulk freighter is Mr. William Jennings Filbert who was born at Palatine, Illinois on November 4, 1865 and was educated in the public schools.

Mr. Filbert began his career in the railroad industry working in the purchasing department and later in the accounting division of the Chicago & North Western Railroad. He became chief accountant before leaving to join the Federal Steel Corporation as assistant auditor. He rose through the financial end of the steel business to become president of Federal Steel in 1898 and was serving as president when it was merged into United States Steel Corporation in 1901. In the new organization he served as assistant controller in 1901 and 1902, then controller from late 1902 to 1933 and chairman of the finance committee from then until retiring on January 1, 1936.

He was a director in many subsidiary companies including Pittsburgh Steamship Company, Oliver Mining Company, National Tube Company and many others. He died on February 4, 1944.

Mr. Filbert's namesake is shown below while downbound with iron ore in the lower St. Mary's River in the summer of 1970. It was sold for scrap in 1976 after five idle seasons.

Steamer CLIFFORD F. HOOD

OWNER: United States Steel Corporation Great Lakes Fleet
BUILT: West Bay City Shipbuilding Company, West Bay City, Michigan—1902
HULL NO.: 605
O. A. DIMENSIONS: 434' x 50' x 28'
FORMER DATA: Launched as the bulk freighter BRANSFORD. Renamed JOHN H. McLEAN in 1916. Given last name in 1943. Converted to a crane ship at American Ship Building Company, Cleveland, Ohio in 1944.

Namesake of this ship is Mr. Clifford Firoved Hood who was born in Monmouth, Illinois on February 8, 1894. He was graduated with a B. S. degree from the University of Illinois in 1915 and later in life received many honorary degrees.

Mr. Hood began as a technical apprentice and later was a sales engineer with Packard Electric Company. In 1917 he joined American Steel & Wire Company as a clerk and by 1928 had progressed to manager, which post he held until 1935. He then became vice president of operations in 1935 and in 1937 was elected executive vice president. He served as president from 1938 to 1940. Mr. Hood became president of Carnegie Illinois Steel Company in 1950 and executive vice president of the parent United States Steel Corporation in 1951. He served as president of United States Steel from 1953 until retirement in 1959. Mr. Hood died on November 9, 1978 at Palm Beach, Florida. His namesake is shown while upbound in the St. Mary's River on August 6, 1970, its last season of operation. It was sold for scrap in 1974.

Steamer D. G. KERR (2)

OWNER: United States Steel Corporation Great Lakes Fleet
BUILT: American Ship Building Company, Lorain, Ohio—1916
HULL NO.: 714
O. A. DIMENSIONS: 600' × 60' × 32'

Mr. David Garrett Kerr is the namesake of this ship and was born at Conemaugh, Pennsylvania on February 13, 1864. He received a B.E. degree from Lehigh University in 1884, but prior to that had worked as a laboratory boy at the Homestead Works of Carnegie-Phipps Steel Company. His career with that firm thus started on July 1, 1882.

Mr. Kerr visited Sweden in 1889 and came back to the United States with new ideas for the manufacture of steel. In 1897 he was promoted to assistant vice president in charge of raw materials at Carnegie Steel and in 1909 was named vice president of mining and transportation for United States Steel Corporation in New York City. He retained that position until retiring in 1932. Carnegie Steel Company was one of the primary firms merged into United States Steel on its formation in 1901.

He was also president of Pennsylvania & Lake Erie Dock Company and Pittsburgh & Conneaut Dock Company when he retired. Mr. Kerr was a bachelor and shunned publicity during his life. He had amassed a $10,000,000 fortune by the time of his death in Pittsburgh, Pennsylvania October 18, 1948. His namesake began its maiden trip June 29, 1916 when it departed Lorain, Ohio light to load iron ore at Duluth, Minnesota. It is shown below in the Rock Cut, St. Mary's River on August 11, 1969. It was sold for scrap in 1980.

Steamer GOVERNOR MILLER

OWNER: United States Steel Corporation Great Lakes Fleet
BUILT: American Ship Building Company, Lorain, Ohio—1938
HULL NO.: 810
O. A. DIMENSIONS: 610'9" × 60' × 32'6"

Mr. Nathan Ell Miller was born at Solon, New York on October 10, 1868 and received his Ll.D. degree through studies at Columbia, Syracuse, Colgate and Union Universities. During these studies he taught school from 1887 to 1889 and in 1893 was admitted to the New York Bar. From 1894 to 1900 he was school commissioner of the First District, Cortland County, New York.

Mr. Miller became a corporate counsel in 1901, state comptroller in New York in 1902 and Justice of the New York Supreme Court in 1907 and held other judicial posts until 1915 when he resumed private law practice in Syracuse, New York. He was retained by Solvay Process Company and later was with Crucible Steel Company.

Mr. Miller ran for governor of New York in 1921 and was elected, serving until 1923. He then joined the board of directors of United States Steel Corporation in 1926 and in 1927 and 1928 was its general counsel as well as a director and member of its finance committee. He was senior partner in the firm of Steele and Otis and its succeeding companies concurrently until resigning in 1939. Mr. Miller died on June 26, 1953. His namesake sailed light from Lorain, Ohio June 8, 1938 on its maiden trip to Duluth, Minnesota to load iron ore. It is shown here while downbound in the St. Mary's River on August 11, 1973 and was sold for scrap in mid-1980.

Steamer J. P. MORGAN, JR.

OWNER: United States Steel Corporation Great Lakes Fleet
BUILT: American Ship Building Company, Lorain, Ohio—1910
HULL NO.: 373
O. A. DIMENSIONS: 601' × 58' × 32'

Namesake of the Steamer J. P. MORGAN, JR. was the son of the famous financier of the nineteenth century. Mr. John Pierpont Morgan, Jr. was born at Irvington, New York on September 7, 1867 and received his B.A. degree at Harvard University in 1889.

He started at the bottom of the employment ladder and worked very hard with the result that at an early age he was promoted to responsible positions in the Morgan Bank. His first great achievement was when the United States Government asked the Morgans to arrange for the payment to the French Panama Canal Company of $40,000,000 in gold for the right to take over and complete the canal which had been left in ruin by Ferdinand de Lesseps. He accomplished this without the least disturbance in delicate international exchange.

When his father died in 1913 there was no doubt in anyone's mind that the son could and would take over. During World War I he was the master of financial loan and aid arrangements to assist foreign countries with dollar totals running to nearly one billion dollars. Literally billions of dollars passed through the firm per year. Mr. Morgan, Jr. was chairman of the board of United States Steel Corporation as well as of his own firm until 1932. He died on March 13, 1943.

This bulk freighter's maiden trip began April 15, 1910 from Lorain, Ohio and was upbound, light to Duluth, Minnesota to load iron ore. The vessel is shown here shortly after resuming activity following several seasons in lay-up status. It is downbound at the Rock Cut, St. Mary's River on September 7, 1973. It was sold for scrap in 1980.

Steamer WILLIAM P. PALMER (2)

OWNER: United States Steel Corporation Great Lakes Fleet
BUILT: Great Lakes Engineering Works, Ecorse, Michigan—1910
HULL NO.: 76
O. A. DIMENSIONS: 601' × 58' × 32'

The Steamer WILLIAM P. PALMER is named for Mr. William Pendleton Palmer who was born on June 17, 1861 at Pittsburgh, Pennsylvania and graduated from public high school in 1878.

Mr. Palmer began his career with Carnegie, Phipps & Company and was secretary of that firm in 1887. He left that company to become general sales agent with Carnegie Steel Company in 1888, serving until 1894 when he was named assistant to the president. Mr. Palmer was elected president of Carnegie Steel in 1895 and served one year before being named second vice president of Illinois Steel Company in 1896. He became general manager and president of American Steel & Wire Company in 1899 and served in that position until his death on December 17, 1927. The latter three firms were eventually all subsidiaries of the United States Steel Corporation.

In addition to these posts, Mr. Palmer served as president of the Newburgh & South Shore Railroad and American Mining Company. He was also a director of several financial institutions and the H. C. Frick Coke Company.

The Steamer WILLIAM P. PALMER was the first vessel built on the Great Lakes to use the Isherwood system of longitudinal design in construction of its framing. Mr. J. W. Isherwood came to the builder's yard to personally inspect the use of his technique and patent on November 5, 1910. The vessel was accepted by the owners in mid-December, however, it did not sail on its maiden trip until departing from Cleveland, Ohio April 24, 1911, light for Duluth, Minnesota to load ore. It had sailed from Detroit to Cleveland for owner's inspection in mid-December, 1910 and wintered in that port. It is shown below in the Detroit River. It was sold for scrap in 1978.

Steamer HENRY PHIPPS

OWNER: United States Steel Corporation Great Lakes Fleet
BUILT: West Bay City Shipbuilding Company, West Bay City, Michigan—1907
HULL NO.: 623
O. A. DIMENSIONS: 601' × 58' × 32'

The Steamer HENRY PHIPPS was named in honor of Mr. Henry Phipps who was born at Philadelphia, Pennsylvania on September 27, 1839. He was educated in the public schools of Allegheny City, Pennsylvania.

Mr. Phipps began work as an office boy and bookkeeper for Dillworth and Bidwell, spike manufacturers, in 1856. He stayed there until 1861 when he left to form his own company, Bidwell & Phipps, which was agent for the DuPont Powder Company. He was also a partner in a small iron mill known as Kloman & Phipps.

He eventually became associated with Thomas M. and Andrew Carnegie in the iron and steel business and he gained the confidence of Mr. Andrew Carnegie who had him handle his finances. Mr. Phipps became an officer in Carnegie Steel Company and was one of the 24 original directors of United States Steel Corporation when it was formed on April 1, 1901 since Carnegie Steel was one of the principal entities in the make up of United States Steel. Mr. Phipps was quite a philanthropist and gave large sums of money to health research. He died on September 22, 1930.

The Steamer HENRY PHIPPS is shown below while upbound at Six Mile Point, St. Mary's River on July 22, 1974. It was sold for scrap in 1976 after having spent the 1975 season in idleness.

Steamer PERCIVAL ROBERTS, JR.

```
          OWNER:  United States Steel Corporation Great Lakes Fleet
          BUILT:  American Ship Building Company,
                  Lorain, Ohio—1913
       HULL NO.:  398
O. A. DIMENSIONS: 600' × 58' × 32'
```

Namesake of this bulk freighter is Mr. Percival Roberts, Jr. who was born at Philadelphia, Pennsylvania on July 15, 1857 and who was a graduate of Haverford College in 1876. That year he joined Pencoyd Iron Company as a clerk but in 1877 returned to school to take graduate work in metallurgy.

The Pencoyd Iron Company was being run by his father at the time and Mr. Roberts, Jr. rose through various positions to become general manager, vice president and was named president of the firm in the 1890's. This concern merged with the American Bridge Company and Mr. Roberts, Jr. became president of the merged company.

In 1901 when American Bridge was merged into United States Steel Corporation on its formation, Mr. Roberts, Jr. was an original director and a member of the executive committee. He served as a director of United States Steel for thirty-four years before retiring in 1935. He was the last survivor of the original board of twenty-four men of United States Steel Corporation when he died on March 6, 1943.

Mr. Roberts, Jr. was a world recognized authority on bridge work and structural steel. Judge Gary called him "the greatest practical steel man in the world." His namesake cleared Lorain, Ohio April 25, 1913 on its maiden voyage, light to load iron ore at Two Harbors, Minnesota. The ship was sold for scrap in 1978.

Steamer HENRY H. ROGERS

OWNER: United States Steel Corporation Great Lakes Fleet
BUILT: Chicago Shipbuilding Company, Chicago, Illinois – 1906
HULL NO.: 69
O. A. DIMENSIONS: 601' x 58' x 32'

Mr. Henry Huddleston Rogers was the namesake of this bulk freighter. He was one of the country's foremost captains of industry and was one of the original 24 men who formed the board of directors in 1901 on the incorporation of United States Steel Corporation.

Mr. Rogers was born in Fairhaven, Massachusetts on January 29, 1840 and was educated in the public schools. After clerking in grocery stores, he left the area in 1859 for Pennsylvania to seek his fortune in the oil fields. He and a friend built a refinery at McClintockville, Pennsylvania in 1861 and in 1863 Mr. Rogers invented an improved still for refining petroleum which later was adopted, with improvements, the world over.

By 1872 he and his associates joined what came to be the Standard Oil Trust and Mr. Rogers was chairman of its manufacturing committee. Through this relationship he was closely allied with Mr. John D. Rockefeller. Mr. Rogers served as president of Standard Oil until his death on May 19, 1909.

His namesake was the victim of a grounding accident in mid-July, 1973 at Gary, Indiana and is shown here on July 3, 1973, its second last trip in operation, in the West Neebish Channel, St. Mary's River, downbound with iron ore. It was sold for scrap in 1974.

Steamer WILLIAM B. SCHILLER

OWNER: United States Steel Corporation Great Lakes Fleet
BUILT: American Ship Building Company, Lorain, Ohio - 1910
HULL NO.: 372
O. A. DIMENSIONS: 601' x 58' x 32'

The name on this ship's bow had remained the same for over sixty years. Mr. William Bacon Schiller was its namesake and was born on July 7, 1859 in Pittsburgh, Pennsylvania. He was educated in Pittsburgh public schools.

Mr. Schiller began his career in business as an office boy with R. W. Hitchcock Company at Youngstown, Pennsylvania in 1876. From 1879 to 1883 he was a bookkeeper at the Second National Bank and from 1883 to 1886 was secretary of Brier Hill Iron & Coal Company. Mr. Schiller joined Youngstown Coal and Coke Company Limited and Bessemer Limestone Company in 1886 as treasurer and general manager, serving until 1889 when he became general manager of Monongahela Furnace Company. When that firm was merged with National Tube Works Company in 1892, he became manager of blast furnaces. He served in that capacity until organization of the National Tube Company in 1899, in which firm he rose to the presidency by 1902.

He was a director of Union Trust Company, Mellon National Bank, H. C. Frick Coal Company, Pittsburgh & Lake Erie Railroad and the West Penn Railways. His namesake started on its maiden trip April 15, 1910 proceeding upbound, light to Duluth, Minnesota for iron ore and is shown below underway in the Detroit River. The vessel was sold for scrap in 1978.

The vessel had the distinction of loading the first full cargo of sintered taconite concentrate when it took aboard 12,152 G.T. at D.M. & I.R., Railway Dock No. 6 in Duluth, Minnesota on May 3, 1954.

Steamer RICHARD TRIMBLE

OWNER: United States Steel Corporation Great Lakes Fleet
BUILT: American Ship Building Company, Lorain, Ohio—1913
HULL NO.: 707
O. A. DIMENSIONS: 600' × 58' × 32'

Mr. Richard Trimble who was born in New York, New York on March 26, 1858 is the namesake of this bulk freighter. He graduated from Harvard University with a B.A. degree in 1880 and decided to find his activity in the West.

Mr. Trimble went to Wyoming and sought work. He was successful and for several years was in the cattle business in that state. But the eastern business world really was appealing to him and he left Wyoming to return there. He joined Federal Steel Corporation and served in various capacities while rising to the post of treasurer. Then he served as ensign in the Spanish-American War in 1898. After that service he became associated with J. Pierpont Morgan who was active in the formation of the United States Steel Corporation.

Mr. Trimble was still treasurer of Federal Steel and when that firm was merged into the new United States Steel Corporation in 1901, he became its new secretary-treasurer. He served in that capacity for 21 years before retiring in 1923. His namesake departed Lorain, Ohio July 12, 1913 on its maiden voyage, light for Duluth, Minnesota to load ore. It is shown here while upbound in the St. Mary's River on August 11, 1970. The ship was sold for scrap in 1978.

Steamer PETER A. B. WIDENER

> OWNER: United States Steel Corporation Great Lakes Fleet
> BUILT: Chicago Shipbuilding Company, Chicago, Illinois - 1906
> HULL NO.: 71
> O. A. DIMENSIONS: 601' x 58' x 32'

Later to become a financier, Mr. Peter Ariel Brown Widener was born at Philadelphia, Pennsylvania on November 13, 1834 and was educated in the public schools. He began working in butcher stores and learned the meat business, eventually having his own retail and wholesale operation. He later became prominent in Republican politics and in 1873 was appointed to serve out the term of Mr. Joseph F. Mercer as city treasurer of Philadelphia.

After his political life he turned his attention to the developing interurban railway and street railway systems of America. He was largely interested in these in Philadelphia, Atlanta, Omaha, Minneapolis, Reading, and other cities. Mr. Widener invested heavily in these ventures and lived to see them flourish.

He took part in the organization of the United States Steel Corporation and was on its board of directors in 1901. He also helped organize the International Mercantile Marine Company and the American Tobacco Company. He was a director or officer of Cresson & Clinchfield Coal Company, Philadelphia & Reading Coal & Iron Company, Lehigh Valley Railroad and others. Mr. Widener died on November 6, 1915. His namesake is shown while downbound in the West Neebish Channel, St. Mary's River on July 8, 1974. In April, 1980 it was sold for non-transportation use as a grain storage hull after five years of idleness. The use proved unsuccessful, however, and the vessel was sold for scrap in 1986.

Barge GREAT WESTERN (2)

OWNER: United Towing and Salvage Company Limited
BUILT: Henry Jenkings, Walkerville, Ontario - 1867
HULL NO.: None assigned.
O. A. DIMENSIONS: 245' x 40'2" x 10'
FORMER DATA: Launched as a powered carferry. Reduced in depth 3' and converted to a bulk freight barge at Merlo, Merlo & Roy Limited, Ford, Ontario in 1923. Converted to a crane-equipped bulk freight barge at Wallaceburg Sand & Gravel Company, Windsor, Ontario in 1929.

This iron-hulled vessel remained active on the Great Lakes for nearly a century. It is shown above in a very rare photograph at the Gravel River Sand Pit, Nipigon Bay, Lake Superior on June 2, 1953. Following service in the St. Lawrence Seaway construction project, it was finally scrapped at Sorel, Quebec in 1962.

The namesake of this vessel was the Great Western Railway of Canada which opened for traffic between Suspension Bridge, Ontario and Windsor, Ontario in 1854. This was the first railway to reach the Detroit-Windsor area from the East. At a cost of $190,000, this vessel was fabricated at Barclay, Curle and Company, Glasgow, Scotland in 1866 and shipped in 10,878 pieces to Windsor, Ontario to be assembled. Launching took place on September 6th and the maiden trip took place January 1, 1867 with 14 railroad cars aboard. The route was across the Detroit River to the foot of Brush Street. This area of operation continued until the ship was sold and converted in 1923.

Steamer EDWIN T. DOUGLASS

OWNER: Upper Lakes and St. Lawrence Transportation Company, Limited
BUILT: Napier & Miller Limited, Old Kilpatrick, Scotland—1923
HULL NO.: 240
O. A. DIMENSIONS: 258'6" × 43'3" × 20'

The canal-size bulk freighter discussed here was named in honor of Mr. Edwin Thomas Douglass who was born on February 23, 1868 at Troy, New York. He was educated in the local schools and began his career as an office boy in the Buffalo, New York office of the Western Transit Company in 1885. This firm later became known as the Rutland Transit Company.

In 1895, Mr. Douglass moved to the New York City headquarters of the line as assistant manager, but he returned to Buffalo in 1902 to become vice president and general manager when his father died. He remained with the firm during its absorption in the Great Lakes Transit Corporation in 1915, but resigned on April 30, 1916 to join the Eastern Grain Milling and Elevator Corporation at Buffalo, New York as director. Concurrently, he also served as president of the Douglass Agency Corporation. He was head of the grain concern when he died at Buffalo, New York, January 18, 1944.

This vessel continued to serve in the Great Lakes fleet long after it passed into Canadian registry in 1936, being active until 1959 when it was sold for use as a lighter. The maiden voyage of this ship began on May 9, 1923 from Glasgow, Scotland with a cargo of scrap iron for Buffalo, New York where it arrived on June 1, 1923. The vessel is shown here in Soulanges Canal on October 22, 1958.

Steamer GROVEDALE (1)

OWNER: Upper Lakes and St. Lawrence Transportation Company, Limited
BUILT: Buffalo Dry Dock Company, Buffalo, New York - 1903
HULL NO.: 204
O. A. DIMENSIONS: 254'9" x 41' x 23'
FORMER DATA: Launched as ROBERT WALLACE (2). Renamed TREGASTEL in 1916. Renamed GLENDOWAN in 1921. Renamed CHANDLER in 1926. Renamed ASPENLEAF in 1942. Renamed HELEN HINDMAN (1) in 1949. Given last name in 1952. Deepened 5' at Port Dalhousie Dry Docks, Limited, Port Dalhousie, Ontario in 1953.

This ship name was a holdover name when the last owners acquired the vessel from the Reoch interests in 1956. It continued on the bow until the vessel was scrapped at Port Weller, Ontario in 1959. The name, however, continued into the 1970's on the bow of a larger ship in the Reoch fleet.

The common Reoch fleet suffix, "DALE," is applied to this ship name, with the specific namesake being a grove as one that might be found in a forest or orchard. The forest-related series of ship names is carried on by this connection.

A grove may be a clustering of trees or may refer to vast stands of tall timber such as in the Redwoods of California. Vale and park are words that occasionally are interchanged for the word grove.

The Steamer GROVEDALE (1) is shown in the photograph below at Port Weller, Ontario on May 4, 1957.

Steamer NORMAN B. MACPHERSON

OWNER:	Upper Lakes and St. Lawrence Transportation Company, Limited
BUILT:	Napier & Miller Limited, Old Kilpatrick, Scotland—1925
HULL NO.:	247
O. A. DIMENSIONS:	258' × 43'3" × 20'

The bulk freighter shown below was named in honor of Mr. Norman Barclay Macpherson who was born September 29, 1883 at Thorold, Ontario. After completing his education he moved to Buffalo, New York in 1900 and began his career stacking books at the Buffalo Public Library.

In 1905 he moved to San Diego, California for health reasons and was secretary of the Young Men's Christian Association in that city by 1908. He returned to Buffalo, New York in 1914 and joined the Eastern Grain Elevator Corporation in the position of assistant in the traffic department.

Through various promotions, Mr. Macpherson became president and treasurer of the corporation in 1938 and headed the firm until its dissolution in 1945. He had been elected secretary-treasurer in 1925 and a vice president in 1929. He was also a director of Eastern Steamship Company which built this vessel. Mr. Macpherson died in Rochester, New York on the second day of his second honeymoon on June 2, 1946. His namesake was sold for off-lakes use in 1959.

This vessel's maiden voyage commenced on April 2, 1925 when it departed Partington, England with a cargo of fluorspar for Sault Ste. Marie, Ontario delivery. This vessel is shown departing Lachine Lock near Montreal, Quebec on August 10, 1958. This hull returned for use as a scow in 1971 as ILE D'ORLEANS in the Quebec Harbor dredging Project.

Steamer L. A. McCORQUODALE

OWNER:	Upper Lakes Shipping Limited
BUILT:	Great Lakes Engineering Works, Ecorse, Michigan—1905
HULL NO.:	7
O. A. DIMENSIONS:	402'6" × 50'3" × 30'
FORMER DATA:	Launched as the package freighter SUPERIOR (5). Renamed RALPH BUDD in 1926. Converted to a combination package freight and automobile carrier at Buffalo Dry Dock Company, Buffalo, New York in 1928. Converted to a package freighter and bulk carrier at Collingwood Shipbuilding Company, Collingwood, Ontario in 1930. Given last name in 1959.

During its last days this ship was enhanced with small derrick cranes on deck for the purpose of handling light package freight cargo. These were installed at Port Weller Dry Docks Limited, St. Catharines, Ontario in 1963 but the trade for their use or further use of the vessel did not develop and the hull was sold for scrap in 1966. It is shown above on its last run, on December 7, 1963 in the Welland Ship Canal.

The namesake of this ship was Mr. Lorne Alvin McCorquodale who was born in Wakopa, Manitoba on March 7, 1905. He was educated in Winnipeg, Manitoba and joined Maple Leaf Milling Company at Winnipeg in 1920. Mr. Corquodale rose in the firm through all phases of grain operations at Winnipeg and became a member of the Winnipeg Grain Exchange, remaining a member when he moved to the firm's Toronto, Ontario headquarters as assistant manager for grain in 1961. He returned to Winnipeg in 1967 as grain manager and retained that position until his retirement in February, 1971.

Steamer PARKDALE (1)

OWNER: Upper Lakes and St. Lawrence Transportation Company, Limited
BUILT: Detroit Shipbuilding Company, Wyandotte, Michigan - 1903
HULL NO.: 151
O. A. DIMENSIONS: 254'9" x 41' x 23'
FORMER DATA: Launched as the crane-equipped bulk freighter S. N. PARENT. Renamed VEULETTES in 1916. Renamed GLENARM in 1921. Renamed CAMROSE in 1926. Renamed PALMLEAF in 1942. Renamed BLANCHE HINDMAN (1) in 1949. Given last name in 1952. Deepened 5' at Port Dalhousie Dry Docks, Limited, Port Dalhousie, Ontario in 1953.

The canal-sized Steamer PARKDALE (1) was scrapped by these owners in 1959 and had carried the name given it by Reoch interests under its last ownership which began in 1956. The name carried on in the 1960's on the hull of a six hundred foot bulk freighter until it was sold for scrap in 1970.

The common fleet suffix of DALE, with reference to Mr. William Coverdale, is used in this ship name. The specific namesake, therefore, is the prefix "PARK." A park is a tract of land which often includes lawns, trees, and wooded area, such as found in a city. Or, it may be a forest park, such as Glacier National Park or Yellowstone National Park. These are vast wooded areas protected by the Department of the Interior for the use and enjoyment of all visitors and for animal wildlife living in the parks. The forest-related theme is carried out in this ship name.

The Steamer PARKDALE (1) is shown below approaching Lock Four of the Welland Ship Canal at Thorold, Ontario on May 25, 1957.

Steamer JOHN B. RICHARDS

OWNER:	Upper Lakes and St. Lawrence Transportation Company, Limited
BUILT:	Napier & Miller Limited, Old Kilpatrick, Scotland—1925
HULL NO.:	248
O. A. DIMENSIONS:	263' × 43'3" × 20'

The canal-size bulk freight Steamer JOHN B. RICHARDS was named in honor of one of Buffalo, New York's best known and able admiralty lawyers. Mr. John Bunn Richards was born in Lock Haven, Pennsylvania on November 4, 1874 and received a Ph.B. degree from Cornell University in 1896. He graduated from the Cornell Law School in 1897 and passed the bar.

Mr. Richards practiced with the Buffalo law firm of Bissell, Carey & Cooke until 1906 when he joined in a partnership with Harvey L. Brown and Fred W. Ely to form the firm of Brown, Ely & Richards. This partnership was dissolved on December 1, 1943 and Mr. Richards formed a new law firm with Laurence E. Coffey and was active in it until his death on September 8, 1946 at Buffalo, New York.

He handled a number of important marine cases for ship owners and grain demurrage cases for Buffalo grain merchants. He represented consignees of the grain cargoes of some forty ships in the widely-publicized demurrage cases of 1922 when the vessels were tied up in Buffalo harbor.

His namesake was sold for off-lakes use in 1959. It is shown below at Lock Seventeen of the old St. Lawrence Canals at Cornwall, Ontario on October 25, 1956.

Steamer SHELTON WEED

OWNER:	Upper Lakes and St. Lawrence Transportation Company, Limited
BUILT:	Earle's Shipbuilding & Engineering Company, Limited, Hull, England—1925
HULL NO.:	650
O. A. DIMENSIONS:	263' × 43'3" × 20'

The bulk freight Steamer SHELTON WEED was sold for scrap in 1959 after having served under the Canadian flag on the Great Lakes for over thirty-four years.

Its namesake was a former director of the Eastern Steamship Company which originally built the vessel. Mr. Weed was born in Buffalo, New York on June 15, 1873. He was educated at Heathcote School For Boys at Buffalo, New York and entered the firm of Weed and Company in 1891. He learned the business the hard way, attaining promotion only when earned and he served in many departments of the business.

In 1903 he was elected vice president of the firm and continued in that capacity until his father died in 1915, at which time he was elected president of Weed and Company. He served in this capacity until his death on February 1, 1946.

Mr. Weed was active in various social and civic activities in his native city and he was a close friend and confidant of the Boland & Cornelius group who controlled Eastern Steamship Company.

The Steamer SHELTON WEED is shown in the photograph below at Lock Three of the Welland Ship Canal, St. Catharines, Ontario on July 22, 1954.

Barge 137

OWNER:	Upper Lakes Shipping Limited
BUILT:	American Steel Barge Company, West Superior, Wisconsin—1896
HULL NO.:	137
O. A. DIMENSIONS:	360' × 45' × 26'

Before being sold for scrap in 1965, Barge 137 served as a grain storage hull for a period of several years. Prior to that it ran in regular Upper Lakes service in the grain trade.

When these "whaleback" barges were being built in the mid-to-late 1890's, they were literally being turned out like sausages. Demand for vessel capacity was so great because of the prompt rise of steel-making capacity around the shores of the Great Lakes that Mr. Alexander McDougall, originator and inventor of the "whaleback" ship was building hulls as fast as the yard could produce them.

Some of these hulls were given names, per se, but this characteristic was generally reserved for "whaleback" steamers while "whaleback" barges were just assigned numbers. These numbers corresponded to their hull numbers. Thus, the namesake of this bulk freight barge was its hull number.

When this hull passed into Pittsburgh Steamship Company in 1901, the same number was kept on the bow. Along with this barge that firm acquired scores of others, all with a different number.

This bulk freight barge is shown above while upbound at Sarnia, Ontario on July 6, 1948.

Motor Vessel BLUE RIVER

OWNER:	Upper Lakes Shipping Limited
BUILT:	Canadian Vickers Limited, Montreal, Quebec—1930
HULL NO.:	116
O. A. DIMENSIONS:	260' × 43'6" × 20'
FORMER DATA:	Launched as the barge REDCHIEF. Converted to a powered bulk freighter at Muir Brothers Dry Dock Company, Limited, Port Dalhousie, Ontario and given last name in 1934.

The canal-size bulk freight Motor Vessel BLUE RIVER was originally a member of the fleet of barges known as the Red Barge Line of Montreal, Quebec. The ships were painted red in color to easily identify them and to keep the name of the fleet evident on the hulls.

In 1934 this ship was sold from the fleet and the new owners elected to repaint the hull and rename the vessel after its conversion to power. Without any specific idea in mind except to be sure that the usage of the word red was not in evidence, the first word of this ship name was chosen to indicate the opposite color from red. Thus, *BLUE* was chosen. Concurrently, the company became known as Blue Line Motorships, Ltd.

The second word of the ship name, *RIVER*, identifies no specific river, but all rivers in general. It is interesting to note that a former sister ship of this vessel was named REDRIVER and was still in the Red Barge Line fleet at the time this ship was sold. The Motor Vessel BLUE RIVER was sold for scrap in 1968 after having lain idle at Toronto, Ontario as a grain storage barge for six years.

The vessel is shown below leaving Lock Twenty at Cornwall, Ontario on the old St. Lawrence River Canal System on October 25, 1956.

Steamer BROWN BEAVER

OWNER:	Upper Lakes Shipping Limited
BUILT:	Smith's Dock Company, Limited, South Bank-on-Tees, England—1929
HULL NO.:	871
O. A. DIMENSIONS:	259' × 43'9" × 20'6"
FORMER DATA:	Launched as FULTON. Given last name in 1932.

The canal-sized bulk freight Steamer BROWN BEAVER took the familiar rodent mammal, the beaver, as its namesake. This name was not given the ship by these owners, however, but was applied the year prior by the Beaver Industries, Limited of Glasgow, Scotland. This firm was an affiliate of the Smith's Dock Company which repossessed this ship and a sister ship, on the default action of the former Mathews Steamship Company. In 1933 the vessels were sold to a predecessor firm of Upper Lakes Shipping Limited.

The first word in this ship name refers to the most common beaver species. It also refers to one of the two colors that were used to identify Beaver Industries' products. The beaver is an aquatic mammal by nature and is widely known for its various architectural devices. The building of dams by placement of chewed-down trees is probably the most famous activity of this animal.

This steamer served the last few years of its life as a grain storage unit at Toronto, Ontario and was sold for scrap in 1965. It is shown here at Detour, Michigan on June 20, 1954.

Barge BRYN BARGE

OWNER:	Upper Lakes Shipping Limited
BUILT:	Chicago Shipbuilding Company, Chicago, Illinois—1900
HULL NO.:	41
O. A. DIMENSIONS:	412' × 50' × 27'2"
FORMER DATA:	Launched as BRYN MAWR. Given last name in 1940.

With other old barges in this fleet, the Barge BRYN BARGE was sold for use as a breakwall in 1968 after having served for about five years as a grain storage hull at Goderich, Ontario and at Toronto, Ontario. It is shown above on October 19, 1962 upbound for a load of grain in the St. Mary's River below Sault Ste. Marie, Michigan.

This vessel was originally a unit in the Pittsburgh Steamship Company fleet which was owned from 1901 onward by the United States Steel Corporation. It was built at the time when naming of ships took the theme of colleges, particularly those in the eastern part of the United States.

This particular vessel was named for Bryn Mawr College, a private non-sectarian institution of higher education for women located at Bryn Mawr, Pennsylvania. The college is also open to male students at the graduate level. Bryn Mawr College was founded by Dr. Joseph Taylor, a Quaker physician, in 1885 and originally was associated with the Society of Friends. Since 1893, however, it has been non-sectarian.

Degrees are offered in the liberal arts and sciences at the undergraduate and graduate levels. Enrollment is purposely limited to ensure quality of education. The upper limit of enrollment is about 1,500 students, including about 550 graduate students.

Steamer JAMES B. EADS

OWNER: Upper Lakes Shipping Limited
BUILT: Globe Iron Works, Cleveland, Ohio—1894
HULL NO.: 53
O. A. DIMENSIONS: 417'9" × 42'3" × 28'
FORMER DATA: Launched as the package freighter GLOBE. Converted to a bulk freighter, lengthened 72' and given last name at Globe Iron Works, Cleveland, Ohio in 1899.

The venerable bulk freighter shown here was named in honor of Mr. James Buchanan Eads who was one of a gallery of famous inventors, engineers and pioneers who had Great Lakes ships named for them.

Mr. Eads was born at Lawrenceburg, Indiana on May 23, 1820 and was educated in the public schools. He became a partner in a steamship salvaging firm in 1842 and invented the diving bell.

He built the Eads Bridge across the Mississippi River at St. Louis, Missouri between 1867 and 1874 and was instrumental in improving harbor facilities at Toronto, Ontario, Liverpool, England and in Mexico. Mr. Eads received numerous awards for his contributions to marine and allied interests prior to his death at Nassau, The Bahamas on March 16, 1887. His namesake was demolished for scrap in 1967. Though it was equipped with a small cargo crane at Port Weller Dry Docks Limited, Port Weller, Ontario in 1961, and another in 1962 at the same yard, for the purpose of handling some package freight, it never saw much service in that trade and always retained its class as a bulk freighter from 1899 on. It is shown below at Toronto, Ontario on May 17, 1961.

Steamer JOHN ERICSSON

OWNER:	Upper Lakes Shipping Limited
BUILT:	American Steel Barge Company, West Superior, Wisconsin—1896
HULL NO.:	138
O. A. DIMENSIONS:	405' × 48'3" × 27'

After several years of inactivity and grain storage use this ship was sold for scrapping in 1968. Efforts to save her as a museum failed and her passing left no other bulk freight "whaleback" steamers on the Great Lakes.

Namesake of the ship is Mr. John Ericsson who was born on July 31, 1803 at Langbanshyttan, Sweden. He was educated in the public schools and became interested in machinery and ships. He went to London, England in 1826 and built a locomotive engine in partnership with John Braithwaite for the Liverpool and Manchester Railway in 1829.

He worked out a plan for placing marine engines entirely below the water line and took out a patent for a screw propeller in 1836. This was first tried on the FRANCIS B. OGDEN in 1837 and proved successful.

Mr. Ericsson died at New York City on March 8, 1889. His namesake is shown in this photograph downbound with a load of grain at Sault Ste. Marie, Michigan on June 18, 1953. When this vessel passed downbound in the Welland Ship Canal at 8:00 AM, December 5, 1930, it was the largest ship ever to have transited that waterway. It had a cargo of rye and wheat from Fort William, Ontario aboard bound for Toronto, Ontario.

Barge JOHN FRITZ

OWNER: Upper Lakes Shipping Limited
BUILT: F. W. Wheeler & Company, West Bay City, Michigan—1898
HULL NO.: 125
O. A. DIMENSIONS: 450' × 50' × 28'7"

Namesake of this bulk freight barge was Mr. John Fritz who was born on August 21, 1822 in Londonderry Township, Pennsylvania. He attended the local schools and began working as a blacksmith's apprentice at Parkesburg, Pennsylvania in 1838.

In 1844 he obtained a job as mechanic in the Moore & Hooven Iron Works at Norristown, Pennsylvania. This firm made boiler iron, nails and bar iron. Mr. Fritz became general foreman of the mill in 1846 but left in 1849 to take a job at Safe Harbor, Pennsylvania with Reeves, Abbott & Company when they were erecting a new iron works. In 1854 he became general superintendent of Cambria Iron Works at Johnstown, Pennsylvania and showed his genius for remodeling and rebuilding steel plants.

He supervised and engineered the building of Bethlehem Iron Works at Bethlehem, Pennsylvania in 1860 and became highly esteemed by Mr. Andrew Carnegie. The John Fritz gold medal was awarded him on his 80th birthday by his friends in the iron and steel industry. Mr. Fritz died at Pittsburgh, Pennsylvania on February 13, 1913.

His namesake was sold for use as a breakwall in 1968 after having served as a storage grain hull for a number of years. It is shown above entering Neebish Rock Cut of the St. Mary's River on June 18, 1953.

Barge GLENBOGIE

OWNER:	Upper Lakes Shipping Limited
BUILT:	Buffalo Drydock Company, Buffalo, New York—1902
HULL NO.:	202
O. A. DIMENSIONS:	380' × 44' × 26'
FORMER DATA:	Launched as ALEXANDER MAITLAND. Given last name in 1925.

The bulk freight Barge GLENBOGIE was active until being retired to storage grain use at Goderich, Ontario in 1964. It then was scrapped in 1968.

The namesake of this vessel was a small community located about thirteen miles northeast of Glasgow, Scotland in Lanarks County. Glenbogie is only one and one-half miles from the large steel works at Gartcosh and many of its inhabitants are workers for that mill.

Glenbogie is the principal junction point for trains from the south, via Carstairs, going to Glasgow and northern points. The scenery around this town is beautiful as one moves away from industrialized Glasgow. This is especially true as one goes into the Campsie Fells and the Kilsyth Hills areas.

Glenbogie itself has a large brickworks as its principal industry. The town of about 5,000 population has changed little during the past half-century even though it is nearby some of the most highly industrialized areas of the British Isles.

The barge is shown above at Toronto, Ontario on October 28, 1957.

Steamer GREY BEAVER

OWNER:	Upper Lakes Shipping Limited
BUILT:	Smith's Dock Company, Limited, South Bank-on-Tees, England—1929
HULL NO.:	872
O. A. DIMENSIONS:	259' × 43'9" × 20'6"
FORMER DATA:	Launched as SOUTHTON. Given last name in 1932.

This bulk freighter was a sister ship to the Steamer BROWN BEAVER, also of this fleet. The color grey was one of the two main product identification colors of Beaver Industries, Limited of Glasgow, Scotland. The other color was brown. These two vessels shared the role of identifying the Beaver Industries' colors in their ship names. Both also took the first word of that firm's corporate title in their names. This word was, in fact, based upon the animal known around the world as the beaver.

There is a strain in the species of beavers which occurs more rarely than the common brown beaver. That strain produces a beaver with a grey underside and this animal is properly known as the grey beaver. The beaver is usually about thirty inches long with a broad, flat and scaly tail which is an additional ten inches in length. Its body is plump, the back is arched, the neck thick, the hind feet webbed and the toes clawed.

Its front teeth on either jaw are like those of other rodents and are sharpened from wear so as to have a chisel-like edge.

This ship was used as a storage grain hull at Toronto, Ontario until being sold for scrap in 1965. It is shown below at Port Weller, Ontario on October 30, 1954.

Barge ALEXANDER HOLLEY

OWNER:	Upper Lakes Shipping Limited
BUILT:	American Steel Barge Company, West Superior, Wisconsin—1896
HULL NO.:	139
O. A. DIMENSIONS:	376' × 46' × 26'

The "whaleback" bulk freight Barge ALEXANDER HOLLEY served on the Great Lakes in regular service until the early 1960's. It then served as a grain storage barge at Goderich, Ontario until being sold for scrap in 1965.

Throughout its career it changed hands several times, but no owner saw fit to rename this venerable hull and it continued to the last to honor Mr. Alexander Lyman Holley as its namesake. He was born in Lakeville, Connecticut on July 20, 1832 and graduated from Brown University in 1853 with a degree in engineering. In that year he joined Corliss Engine Works at Providence, Rhode Island. In 1855 he left to join the New Jersey Locomotive Works, staying there until 1857 when he went to Europe to study locomotive engineering and practice for three years.

On returning to the United States in 1860 he entered consulting work and, in 1863, again went to Europe to purchase rights to the Bessemer process of steelmaking for the Corning, Winslow & Company. Mr. Holley meshed this process with the Kelly process, producing the American Bessemer process in 1865 when it was first used at the steel plant in Troy, New York. From then on he supervised the building of steel plants at Harrisburg and Pittsburgh, Pennsylvania and at Joliet and Chicago, Illinois. He also worked actively for the betterment of the steel industry as a trustee of Rensselaer Polytechnic Institute until his death at Brooklyn, New York on January 29, 1882.

His namesake barge is shown above leaving Sarnia, Ontario in June, 1960.

Steamer DOUGLASS HOUGHTON

OWNER:	Upper Lakes Shipping Limited
BUILT:	Globe Iron Works, Cleveland, Ohio—1899
HULL NO.:	78
O. A. DIMENSIONS:	475' × 50'3" × 29'

The Steamer DOUGLASS HOUGHTON was sold in 1969 for use as part of a breakwall near Toronto, Ontario. Its cabins were cut down and the vessel was sunk and filled with stone. It was one of the few Great Lakes ships that had served under the same name for seventy years.

Namesake of this ship is Mr. Douglass Houghton who was born at Troy, New York on September 21, 1809. He graduated from Rensselaer Polytecnic Institute in 1829 and began his varied career by teaching biology, geology and chemistry. In 1831 he was appointed surgeon and botanist in Henry Schoolcraft's expedition to find the source of the Mississippi River and from 1832 to 1837 was a practicing surgeon in Detroit, Michigan.

Mr. Houghton was a brilliant physician. He also discovered some of Michigan's chief copper deposits in 1840 and discovered salt beds in the Saginaw River Valley. For two years, 1842-43, he served as mayor of Detroit, Michigan. In addition, he taught geology and mineralogy at the University of Michigan and was on one of his many junkets to the copper areas of Michigan when he died by drowning in Lake Superior on October 13, 1845. He was one of the early, important prospectors of the area.

His namesake is shown below at Port Weller, Ontario on June 6, 1964.

Steamer MAUNALOA II

OWNER:	Upper Lakes Shipping Limited
BUILT:	Chicago Shipbuilding Company, Chicago, Illinois—1899
HULL NO.:	37
O. A. DIMENSIONS:	452' × 50'3" × 28'6"
FORMER DATA:	Launched as MAUNALOA. Given last name in 1945.

When this bulk freighter changed hands in 1945 the new owners felt the name should be retained for its mystic beauty but added "II" to the name because there already was another vessel under Canadian registry with the name MAUNALOA.

The Steamer MAUNALOA II was named for the historic volcanic mountain on the island of Hawaii. Mauna Loa rises 16,680 feet above the sea and is in Hawaii National Park. A large crater called Mokuaweoweo is at its summit and Kilauea, one of the world's largest active craters, is on its southeast slope.

Mauna Loa averages one eruption every three years. The longest eruption lasted eighteen months and occurred in 1855-56. Approximately 600,000,000 cubic yards of lava was produced from eruptions in 1859 and 1950. The city of Hilo, which is located nearby, is sometimes threatened by the lava flows.

The Steamer MAUNALOA II was active on the Great Lakes until mid-1971 when it was sold for scrap. It is shown in this photograph on a typical trip where grain has been loaded at Thunder Bay, Ontario for the line's elevator at Goderich, Ontario. This photograph was taken in the St. Mary's River on August 26, 1966.

Steamer JOHN S. PILLSBURY

OWNER:	Upper Lakes Shipping Limited
BUILT:	Earle's Shipbuilding & Engineering Company, Limited, Hull, England—1926
HULL NO.:	668
O. A. DIMENSIONS:	261' × 43'3" × 20'

This canal-sized bulk freighter was sold for scrap in 1964 after the opening of the St. Lawrence Seaway proved her to be uneconomical in modern trading.

Namesake of this ship is Mr. John Sargent Pillsbury who was born in Sutton, New Hampshire on July 29, 1828. He was educated in the local schools and, after learning the printer's trade and finding it unsuitable, formed a partnership with Walter Harriman, later a governor of New Hampshire.

In 1853 Mr. Pillsbury went into the west and northwest hunting opportunity. He located a hardware operation at St. Anthony Falls, Minnesota in June, 1855. He was successful and elected a member of city council in 1858, holding that post until 1864. He was one of the original sponsors of the founding of the C. A. Pillsbury Company in 1864 which firm has become one of the major movers of grain on the Great Lakes.

He also served as governor of the State of Minnesota in 1876-82. Mr. Pillsbury died on October 18, 1901. His namesake steamer is shown in the photograph below in the Welland Ship Canal at Port Weller, Ontario on April 16, 1955.

Steamer RIDGETOWN

OWNER: Upper Lakes Shipping Limited
BUILT: Chicago Shipbuilding Company, Chicago, Illinois—1905
HULL NO.: 67
O. A. DIMENSIONS: 569' × 56' × 31'
FORMER DATA: Launched as WILLIAM E. COREY. Given last name in 1963.

Ridgetown is a small community in Kent County, Ontario 44 miles southwest of St. Thomas and 5 miles north of the northern shore of Lake Erie. It was the hometown of Mr. and Mrs. Gordon C. Leitch, parents of the current president of Upper Lakes Shipping Limited. The name for this ship was chosen to honor the community for that reason.

Ridgetown itself is named for the ridge on which it stands and which divides the north and south watersheds of the county. It is the location of a potato co-operative and an agricultural school and experimental farm aside from being in the heart of a rich farming and tobacco-growing district.

The population of Ridgetown is about 2,700 and industry includes canning, book binding, tool-and-die making and metal working plants.

The Steamer RIDGETOWN departed Chicago, Illinois on August 12, 1905 on its maiden voyage light to Duluth, Minnesota to load iron ore. It is shown here upbound in the St. Mary's River heading towards Lake Superior. This ship was active until being sold in 1970 for sinking as part of a cofferdam at Nanticoke, Ontario.

Barge JOHN A. ROEBLING

OWNER: Upper Lakes Shipping Limited
BUILT: F. W. Wheeler & Company, West Bay City, Michigan—1898
HULL NO.: 126
O. A. DIMENSIONS: 450' × 50' × 28'7"

The bulk freight Barge JOHN A. ROEBLING was used for several years as a storage grain hull before being sold for use as a breakwall in 1968. Advent of larger ships and the demise of huge quantities of grain in the trans-shipment trade caused this barge and others like her to become uneconomical.

Mr. John Augustus Roebling was born in Muhlhausen, Prussia on June 12, 1806. He received a B.S. degree in civil engineering at Royal Polytechnic School in Berlin, Germany in 1826 and worked in the service of the State until 1829 as superintendent of public works in Westphalia. Mr. Roebling came to the United States in 1831 and purchased a tract of land near Pittsburgh, Pennsylvania which he began to develop and build up.

He continued his civil engineering pursuits in navigation projects and also began the first practical application of wire rope usage in bridges in the United States. He had been fond of this concept since college. He built the famous Suspension Bridge at Niagara Falls in 1855 and also designed the Brooklyn Bridge. He never saw the latter completed, however, as he died at Brooklyn, New York on July 22, 1869. The bridge was completed under the supervision of his son.

The Barge JOHN A. ROEBLING is shown above in the St. Mary's River on August 16, 1956. She is downbound with grain for Owen Sound, Ontario.

Steamer HOWARD L. SHAW

OWNER: Upper Lakes Shipping Limited
BUILT: Detroit Shipbuilding Company, Wyandotte, Michigan—1900
HULL NO.: 136
O. A. DIMENSIONS: 451'6" × 51'6" × 28'

The useful life of this vessel spanned nearly seven decades. It was sold for sinking as part of a breakwater in 1969.

Mr. Howard Lanridge Shaw was born at Port Ryerse, Ontario on September 29, 1866 but moved to Bay City, Michigan with his family in 1868. He lived in that city the remainder of his life. At the age of seventeen he left high school to take a job on one of the freighters of the Eddy-Shaw firm. His father was a captain in the line at that time.

In 1889 he received his master's papers and took command of one of the first steel hulled freighters on the Great Lakes. Captain Shaw continued sailing until the death of his father in 1895 at which time he went ashore to work for the family interests in the Eddy-Shaw firm. This activity remained his primary business interest well into the current century until his retirement. He died at Bay City, Michigan on October 8, 1936.

This vessel was never renamed when it passed into other ownership several times. This was a fine testimony to a man who was a Great Lakes man all of his life and who was a managing partner in the firm which built the vessel originally. The vessel is shown here on a typical passage through the Soo Locks area on October 16, 1963.

Steamer JAMES STEWART

OWNER:	Upper Lakes Shipping Limited
BUILT:	Napier & Miller Limited, Old Kilpatrick, Scotland—1926
HULL NO.:	256
O. A. DIMENSIONS:	261' × 43'3" × 20'

The canal-sized bulk freighter shown below honored Mr. James Stewart as its namesake. He was born in Kinlocheil, Scotland on December 11, 1881 and attended school there until moving to Canada with his family in 1893. He completed his education in the Fort William, Ontario school system.

In June, 1906 Mr. Stewart joined the Canadian Pacific Railway as an accountant at Winnipeg, Manitoba, but he left that firm in November, 1906 to enter the grain business as a merchant with the Western Elevator Company.

In 1917 he became president of the Wheat Export Company and in August, 1919 was named chairman of the Canadian Wheat Board in which position he oversaw the contracting and merchandising of Canada's wheat crop. He returned to private business in 1920 and formed the James Stewart Grain Corporation. Through the 1920's he concurrently headed many firms including Maple Leaf Milling Company, Canadian Bakeries Limited, Alberta Pacific Grain Company, Limited and Federal Grain Limited. Mr. Stewart resigned as predident of Alberta Pacific Grain Company and as managing director of Federal Grain on August 18, 1930, but continued to head his own firms until his death at Winnipeg, Manitoba on December 1, 1941.

His namesake was sold for scrap in 1960 and is shown here at Lock Two of the Welland Ship Canal on November 1, 1958.

Steamer SHIRLEY G. TAYLOR

OWNER:	Upper Lakes Shipping Limited
BUILT:	Earle's Shipbuilding & Engineering Company, Limited, Hull, England—1925
HULL NO.:	649
O. A. DIMENSIONS:	263' × 43'3" × 20'

The bulk freight steamer shown in the photograph below was named in honor of Mr. Shirley Grey Taylor who was born on March 31, 1878 at Buffalo, New York. He was to become a great friend of the Boland & Cornelius partnership and they honored that friendship when this vessel took his name. It was originally built to order for the Eastern Steamship Company of Buffalo, New York.

Mr. Taylor attended local schools and Yale University until his father died in 1899. At that time he left school to return to Buffalo and enter the firm of Taylor and Crate, Incorporated which had been started by his father and Mr. Crate in 1865. The firm was engaged in the lumber and cotton business.

He began in ordinary jobs but assumed management status in the early 1900's and was elected vice president of the company by 1910. He continued to serve in that capacity until retiring in 1944. Mr Taylor died in March, 1968 at Buffalo, New York.

His namesake continued to serve in the active Great Lakes fleet until 1959 and was then relegated to standby status and use as a floating grain storage ship at Toronto, Ontario. It was sold for scrap in 1960.

The Steamer SHIRLEY G. TAYLOR is shown in the photograph below at Lock One of the Welland Ship Canal, Port Weller, Ontario on April 16, 1955.

Steamer THORNHILL

OWNER: Upper Lakes Shipping Limited
BUILT: Great Lakes Engineering Works, Ecorse, Michigan—1906
HULL NO.: 21
O. A. DIMENSIONS: 552' × 56' × 31'
FORMER DATA: Launched as ISHPEMING (2). Given last name in 1966.

Thornhill, Ontario, a suburb of Toronto, Ontario, was the namesake for this steamer. It is a village about five miles north of Toronto and is named after an early merchant in the area, Mr. Benjamin Thorne.

The connection between Upper Lakes Shipping Limited and Thornhill is through the experimental research farm for agricultural products and feeds for animals that is located there and is also connected with Maple Leaf Mills Limited. The two principals of the farm are closely related in business and the farm has been the scene of many breakthroughs in the feed business. Newer and more nutritious farm feeds are tested there before being placed on the market for general sale.

This bulk freighter took on the initial cargo of iron ore pellets from the Atikokan, Ontario plant of Steep Rock Iron Mines Limited when it departed Port Arthur, Ontario September 24, 1967 with 10,591 gross tons for Sault Ste. Marie, Ontario delivery. It is shown here in the Welland Ship Canal on October 29, 1966. The ship was sold for scrap in mid-1976.

Steamer VICTORIOUS

OWNER: Upper Lakes Shipping Limited
BUILT: Chicago Shipbuilding Company, Chicago, Illinois—1895
HULL NO.: 14
O. A. DIMENSIONS: 472' × 48' × 28'
FORMER DATA: Launched as VICTORY. Lengthened 72' at Superior Shipbuilding Company, West Superior, Wisconsin in 1905. Given last name in 1940.

When this steamer took to the water in 1895 it was the first ship on the Great Lakes to be constructed to the four hundred-foot length. When it was sold for sinking as part of a breakwater at Toronto, Ontario in 1969 it was among the smaller ships of "upper lake" class still existing on the Great Lakes and was the oldest bulk freighter in existance on the Great Lakes. The ship is shown below in Mud Lake, lower St. Mary's River, on August 22, 1965.

The namesake of this vessel was the famous race horse owned by the noted Mr. Joseph E. Seagram, distiller, horseman and political figure in Ontario until 1919. VICTORIOUS was the first champion Mr. Seagram had, but it started a chain of eight successive victories for him.

This race is the oldest stake race in North America and was known as the King's Plate when first run in the province of Ontario in 1836. The race changes between King's Plate and Queen's Plate, depending upon which sex is the ruling monarch in Great Britain at the time. The race has been run every year since 1860 with the trophy being a foot-high gold cup.

Steamer WIARTON (2)

OWNER: Upper Lakes Shipping Limited
BUILT: Chicago Shipbuilding Company, Chicago, Illinois—1907
HULL NO.: 73
O. A. DIMENSIONS: 601' × 58' × 32'
FORMER DATA: Launched as THOMAS LYNCH. Given last name in 1965.

The bulk freight Steamer WIARTON was active on the Great Lakes through the 1970 season and was sold for scrap in mid-1971. It is shown below during its last season of operation.

This vessel was named in honor of the small town of Wiarton, Ontario in which a number of sailors and officers of the Upper Lakes fleet reside.

Wiarton has a population of 2,000 people and is at the head of Colpoys Bay, an inlet running nine miles inland from the southwest extremity of White Cloud Island which, together with Hay Island, shelters the inlet from the heavier seas of Georgian Bay.

The town is the terminus of a Canadian National Railways branch line and is 140 miles northwest of Toronto, Ontario. It was the site of Indian mission stations as early as 1680. The town is named after Wiarton Place in Kent, England. This was the birthplace of Sir Edmund Walker Head who succeeded Lord Elgin as Governor General of Canada. It was first settled in 1866 and was incorporated as a village in 1880. It was granted status as a town in 1893.

Steamer GRAND HAVEN

OWNER: USCAN Transport Bahamas, Limited
BUILT: Craig Shipbuilding Company, Toledo, Ohio—1903
HULL NO.: 92
O. A. DIMENSIONS: 320' × 54' × 20'

The Steamer GRAND HAVEN honored its original home port even though it served in off-lakes service from 1945 until 1964 when it returned for use in trans-Lake Erie transportation of truck trailers. Grand Haven, Michigan was the namesake of this veteran ship until it was towed out of Cleveland, Ohio for the scrap heap in December, 1969. It is seen above at Brockville, Ontario in November, 1964.

This ship was originally built for the Grand Trunk Railway as an extension across Lake Michigan of its rail lines from Grand Haven, Michigan to Milwaukee, Wisconsin. This provided the railway with competing transportation across the lake with the Ann Arbor Rail Road and the Pere Marquette Railroad Company. The subsidiary firm which operated the ferry went bankrupt and this ship was sold at auction to the parent Grand Trunk Railway System on November 7, 1905.

Grand Haven, Michigan is a port of entry and the seat of Ottawa County on the eastern shore of Lake Michigan at the mouth of the Grand River. It is a popular summer resort town and has a fine lake-front beach for recreational sports. It is also the local center for extensive fishing, fruit and celery growing interests.

Steamer MICHAEL G. BROWNING

OWNER:	Wayne Steamship Company
BUILT:	Detroit Shipbuilding Company, Wyandotte, Michigan—1907
HULL NO.:	172
O. A. DIMENSIONS:	440' × 54'2" × 28'
FORMER DATA:	Launched as EDWIN N. OHL. Renamed MICHAEL GALLAGHER (1) in 1923. Given last name in 1956.

The namesake of this bulk freighter was ten years old when his father, Mr. L. D. Browning, chose to name the vessel for him. Mr. Michael Gorry Browning is the oldest son in the family and was born at Detroit, Michigan on May 27, 1946.

He attended Notre Dame University for his higher education and graduated in 1968 with a B.A. degree. During his years in college he was active in many affairs and was president of the Student Union in his senior year.

Following college he entered the United States Army and eventually saw service in Vietnam. He returned to the United States on June 23, 1970 and subsequently found gainful employment in the business world. He has imagination and talent and will probably follow his father and uncle, Mr. Troy H. Browning, as a successful man in his chosen career.

The Steamer MICHAEL G. BROWNING was sold for grain storage use at the port of Buffalo, New York in 1959 and was subsequently resold for scrap. It is shown in the picture below while upbound, light in the St. Mary's River near Sault Ste. Marie, Michigan on August 17, 1957.

Steamer PARKDALE (2)

OWNER: International Cruising Company, Limited
BUILT: American Ship Building Company, Lorain, Ohio - 1910
HULL NO.: 387
O. A. DIMENSIONS: 600' x 58' x 32'
FORMER DATA: Launched as WILLIAM C. MORELAND. New forward section of 346' joined to salvaged stern section and renamed SIR TREVOR DAWSON in 1916. Renamed CHARLES L. HUTCHINSON (2) in 1921. Renamed GENE C. HUTCHINSON in 1951. Given last name in 1963.

On its fifth trip after being commissioned, the bulk freight Steamer WILLIAM C. MORELAND ran on Sawtooth Rocks at Eagle River Reef, Lake Superior on October 18, 1910. The Reid Salvage & Wrecking Company of Sarnia, Ontario won the salvage contract and succeeded in saving the stern section in 1911. This 254' section of the ship was towed to port on September 1, 1911 by the tugs MANISTIQUE and CORA A. SHELDON. Machinery and 11 hatches of the cargo hold were saved.

On September 9, 1916, the forward 346' portion of this vessel was launched at Superior Shipbuilding Company, Superior, Wisconsin. The two sections were joined and entered service for American Interlake Line, a subsidiary of Canada Steamship Lines, as SIR TREVOR DAWSON.

The namesake of this vessel was a park, though none in particular, but all in general in the Great Lakes region.

This vessel continued active on the Great Lakes until being sold for scrap in 1970. It is shown below downbound in the St. Mary's River on May 31, 1964. It had made its maiden voyage on September 1, 1910, light to Superior, Wisconsin from Lorain, Ohio for iron ore.

Steamer AVONDALE (2)

OWNER: Westdale Shipping Limited
BUILT: Great Lakes Engineering Works,
St. Clair, Michigan - 1908
HULL NO.: 53
O. A. DIMENSIONS: 489' x 52' x 28'
FORMER DATA: Launched as the bulk freighter ADAM E. CORNELIUS (1). Lengthened 48', converted to a self-unloader at Manitowoc Shipbuilding Company, Manitowoc, Wisconsin and renamed DETROIT EDISON (1) in 1947. Renamed GEORGE F. RAND (2) in 1954. Given last name in 1962.

The bulk self-unloading Steamer AVONDALE (2) is shown above inbound at Port Colborne, Ontario on June 23, 1963. Following hull deterioration which was discovered late in 1975, the ship was sold for scrap in 1976.

In keeping with the fleet theme of names, the common suffix dale is used and the specific namesake is the Avon River of England. The name is also applied to rivers in various parts of the western world.

These rivers flow through wooded areas and are the prominent features of their surroundings. The Avon River of England was famous in early times as Shakespeare's river for it was along this river that he lived and worked. He was known as the "Bard of Avon." Cities called Stratford exist on the river both in England and Canada.

Steamer BROOKDALE (2)

OWNER: Westdale Shipping Limited
BUILT: American Ship Building Company, Lorain, Ohio - 1909
HULL NO.: 371
O. A. DIMENSIONS: 524' x 54' x 30'3"
FORMER DATA: Launched as the bulk freighter J. S. ASHLEY. Converted to a self-unloader at American Ship Building Company, Lorain, Ohio in 1937. Renamed FRED A. MANSKE (2) in 1962. Given present name in 1976.

The bulk freight self-unloading Steamer BROOKDALE (2) became part of this fleet in the spring of 1976. As a unit of the fleet of the American Steamship Company, its former owners, it laid idle during 1975 at Chicago, Illinois. Its surplus capacity in the American Steamship fleet was nicely coordinated with the need for such a vessel in the Westdale fleet, hence the transfer.

The namesake of this vessel can be seen in reference to the ship name prefix. The common fleet suffix, DALE follows.

Not one specific brook, but all brooks of the woodlands together are honored by this ship name. This name follows on the fleet idea of names germane to woods and forest-related products. It also utilizes a name which formerly was on the Great Lakes for the first time when this firm acquired the BROOKDALE (1) in 1952. This bulk carrier was of canal dimensions and was eventually sold for scrap in 1966.

The Steamer BROOKDALE is shown above in the Welland Ship Canal in September 1976, and was sold for scrap in 1980 after losing its boom in a fierce wind and rain storm at Ojibway, Ontario while loading a salt cargo.

Steamer FERNDALE (2)

OWNER: Westdale Shipping Limited
BUILT: Great Lakes Engineering Works, Ashtabula, Ohio—1912
HULL NO.: 95
O. A. DIMENSIONS: 524' × 56' × 30'
FORMER DATA: Launched as the bulk freighter LOUIS R. DAVIDSON. Converted to a self-unloader at American Ship Building Company, Lorain, Ohio and renamed DIAMOND ALKALI (1) in 1932. Renamed DOW CHEMICAL (2) in 1939. Given last name in 1964.

This ship is named for the fern, a family of leafy perenial spore-bearing plants with slender horizontal, stout roots. It is a very large family of widely differing habit and structure existing among over seven thousand species belonging to one hundred-seventy genera scattered all over the world. Nineteen genera with some eighty-three species are native to Canada.

The latter part of the vessel name—"dale" refers to a gentlemen, Mr. William Coverdale, who was a great friend and business associate of Mr. Norman J. Reoch, original founder of this and several other Great Lakes steamship companies.

The Steamer FERNDALE is shown at Welland, Ontario on May 30, 1970. It was the first steel steamer ever built at Ashtabula, Ohio and was launched April 6, 1912. It sailed on its maiden trip with coal loaded at Buffalo, New York May 30, 1912 for Ashland, Wisconsin delivery. It was sold for scrap in 1974 when repairs to keep it in shape were too great.

Steamer LEADALE (1)

OWNER: Westdale Shipping Limited
BUILT: Great Lakes Engineering Works,
St. Clair, Michigan—1910
HULL NO.: 77
O. A. DIMENSIONS: 524' × 56' × 30'
FORMER DATA: Launched as the bulk freighter HARRY YATES (1). Converted to a self-unloader at American Ship Building Company, Lorain, Ohio and renamed CONSUMERS POWER (2) in 1934. Renamed FRED A. MANSKE (1) in 1958. Given last name in 1962.

The Steamer LEADALE shares the common fleet suffix to ship names but has a prefix for its namesake that connotes pleasant scenery or location like that found in a countryside. A lea is a grassland or pasture area not used for any specific thing but, rather, left idle or used for grazing for the beauty of the beholder.

The name was chosen because of the wondrous nature and environment one beholds in transiting the forested areas of the Great Lakes shores. Vast acres of primitive and beautiful scenery can be seen along the shorelines of the Great Lakes. Captain Reoch was appreciative of these sights when he sailed the Great Lakes and thought it was a fitting name for this vessel when he acquired it.

This vessel was active through 1977 and was sold for scrap in 1978. It is shown above while outbound in the Cuyahoga River at Cleveland, Ohio on June 4, 1977.

Steamer PINEDALE

OWNER: Westdale Shipping Limited
BUILT: Detroit Shipbuilding Company, Wyandotte, Michigan – 1906
HULL NO.: 162
O. A. DIMENSIONS: 524' x 54' x 30'3"
FORMER DATA: Launched as the bulk freighter E. D. CARTER. Renamed WILLIAM T. ROBERTS in 1916. Converted to a self-unloader at American Ship Building Company, Lorain, Ohio and renamed DOW CHEMICAL (1) in 1932. Renamed NORMAN J. KOPMEIER in 1939. Given last name in 1961.

This vessel carried through the theme of vessels' names in the fleet and was named for the pine tree. Pines are a family of resinous, cone-bearing evergreen trees with needle-like leaves. They furnish valuable lumber and pulpwood in the Northern Hemisphere. The tree is beautiful in appearance and fragrant in scent. Anyone who has experienced a visit into a forest knows the unique way in which the pine tree rustles in the wind, making the sound of an onrushing train. Some kinds of pine are: Norway pine, Jack pine, White pine, Red pine and Ponderosa pine.

The Steamer PINEDALE is shown above at Iroquois, Ontario on June 22, 1969 while upbound, light. The vessel ran through the 1976 navigation season but was found to be in need of too many repairs for further service and it was sold for non-transportation use in 1977 and for scrap in 1980.

Steamer WESTDALE (1)

OWNER:	Westdale Shipping Limited
BUILT:	Swan, Hunter & Wigham Richardson Limited, Wallsend-on-Tyne, England—1929
HULL NO.:	1373
O. A. DIMENSIONS:	259' × 43'3" × 20'
FORMER DATA:	Launched as RALPH GILCHRIST. Renamed E. P. MURPHY in 1944. Given last name in 1959.

In the Reoch fleets a later ship also bore this ship name, but it was a larger eleven thousand ton carrier. This Steamer WESTDALE was a canal-size bulk freighter and was sold for scrap in 1962.

This vessel name is in the theme of names for the fleet, but only in an indirect way. Forest products and affiliated growth provide the reference for the majority of the fleet's ship names so far as the prefix is concerned. The common "DALE" suffix then follows.

This ship name refers to the direction west, but not for its own sake. Rather, it is because in the western parts of this continent lay the majority of large forest stands and timber reserves. The states of Washington, Oregon and California, as well as the provinces of British Columbia and Alberta are primary producers of the continent's lumber. Since the theme of names refers to forestry items, the reference to the westerly direction where these stands exist, as opposed to some other direction where they are not so prominent, is germane to this fleet.

The ship is shown below at Thorold, Ontario on April 23, 1960.

Steamer HILLSDALE

OWNER:	Winona Steamships Limited
BUILT:	West Bay City Shipbuilding Company, West Bay City, Michigan—1908
HULL NO.:	173
O. A. DIMENSIONS:	524' × 54' × 30'
FORMER DATA:	Launched as CALDERA. Renamed A. T. KINNEY in 1918. Given last name in 1961.

The bulk freight Steamer HILLSDALE was sold for overseas scrapping in 1968 after having been in lay-up status for a short while. Prior to its acquisition by the Reoch interests, it sailed the Wilson Marine Transit Company flag for many years.

The common fleet suffix to vessel names is again used in the case of this steamer. It is in reference to Mr. William Coverdale who was a close friend to Captain Norman Reoch who founded this company.

The balance of the ship name, HILLS, refers to the many hills that surround the valleys of the St. Lawrence River and Great Lakes basin. No specific hill or group of them is intended by the reference.

A hill may be defined as "a rounded natural elevation of land lower than a mountain." The scenic hills of the lower St. Lawrence are found to abound in forest products and, since the fleet has the forestry theme in its ship names, it was a natural follow through on that theme to christen this ship with this name on the bow.

The Steamer HILLSDALE is shown below in the St. Mary's River on August 26, 1966 downbound with a cargo of grain for St. Lawrence River delivery.

Steamer ROBERT L. IRELAND (2)

OWNER:	Wilson Transit Company
BUILT:	American Ship Building Company, Lorain, Ohio—1914
HULL NO.:	709
O. A. DIMENSIONS:	524' × 54' × 30'2"

Mr. Robert Livingston Ireland is the namesake of this bulk freighter. He was born at Stratford, Connecticut on August 20, 1867 and was a graduate of Yale University in the class of 1890.

He began his career as an employee of the Cleveland Hardware Company. But his first business venture on his own was in the organization of Hackney Bicycle Company in 1892 and Mr. Ireland became its secretary-treasurer. In 1894 he went with Globe Iron Works Company and was made vice president in 1898. In 1899 he assisted in the large consolidation of shipbuilding interests on the Great Lakes to form the American Ship Building Company. He remained with the new company as vice president until resigning in October, 1903.

He then went with M. A. Hanna Company and became a partner in January, 1904. He retired from active participation on August 20, 1917 and died on February 17, 1928 at the Hotel Seymour in New York City. During his career he had become a potent spokesman of Great Lakes coal, iron ore and shipping interests.

Mr. Ireland's namesake was sold in 1957 after having been declared a constructive total loss. It was reduced to a 434' floating drydock the following year at Duluth, Minnesota. The ship's maiden trip was from Lorain, Ohio on April 30, 1914 with coal for Duluth, Minnesota. It is shown below downbound in Lake St. Clair on August 4, 1951.

Steamer CHARLES S. HEBARD

OWNER: Wilson Marine Transit Company
BUILT: American Ship Building Company, Cleveland, Ohio—1906
HULL NO.: 430
O. A. DIMENSIONS: 524' × 54' × 30'

This bulk freighter's namesake was a good friend of Mr. Joseph Wood, president of Wilson Transit Company, and also was a substantial stockholder of the line. This vessel continued to serve on the Great Lakes trade routes of the company until being sold for use as a breakwater in 1964.

Mr. Charles Samuel Hebard was born in Williamsport, Pennsylvania on December 6, 1860 and received his college education at Yale University, graduating in the class of 1881. He remained in the East to attend college while his family moved to Pequaming, Michigan in 1877. His father established a flourishing lumber business in Baraga County, Michigan with headquarters at Pequaming and young Charles Hebard entered the business with his brother Daniel.

The firm became known as Charles Hebard and Sons Company in 1882 with the father being president and young Charles serving as general manager. The senior Hebard died on June 11, 1902 and the brothers incorporated the business in 1905, changing the name of the firm to Charles Hebard & Sons, Incorporated. They continued to operate the firm until selling it to Mr. Henry Ford on September 9, 1923.

Charles Samuel Hebard lived in retirement until he died on May 1, 1931 at Philadelphia, Pennsylvania.

This ship was the first of its size to navigate as far east as Ogdensburg, New York when it arrived safely there on October 20, 1933 with 356,000 bushels of corn from Milwaukee, Wisconsin.

Steamer CHARLES HUBBARD

OWNER: Wilson Marine Transit Company
BUILT: Toledo Shipbuilding Company, Toledo, Ohio—1907
HULL NO.: 109
O. A. DIMENSIONS: 458′ × 52′ × 28′

The bulk freight Steamer CHARLES HUBBARD was an original member of the Great Lakes Steamship Company fleet on its formation out of an amalgamation of several predecessor firms. Mr. Charles Wells Hubbard had a financial interest in one of these lines and was a close personal friend of Mr. Horace S. Wilkinson who was a moving force in Great Lakes Steamship Company.

Mr. Hubbard was born at Newton, Massachusetts on February 24, 1856 and was a graduate of Harvard University in the Class of 1878. In that year he entered the employ of Ludlow Manufacturing Company. His grandfather had founded this firm years earlier. It was a concern engaged in the manufacture of linen and jute carpet yarns, upholsterers webbing, jute bagging for covering cotton and of hemp twines.

Mr. Hubbard rose quickly and was named treasurer of the firm in 1887 and he held that post until 1912 when he retired to devote his talents to other interests. Concurrent with his office at Ludlow Manufacturing, he was a trustee of the Franklin Savings Bank of Boston and was the founder and major supporter of several eastern preparatory schools. It was in this field that he spent his later years. Mr. Hubbard remained active in civic and business affairs until his death on May 22, 1933 in Weston, Massachusetts.

His namesake passed into this fleet in 1957 upon the liquidation of Great Lakes Steamship Company. It was sold for scrap in 1961 and is shown below in Little Rapids Cut of the St. Mary's River on June 18, 1959.

Steamer B. F. JONES (2)

OWNER:	Wilson Marine Transit Company
BUILT:	West Bay City Shipbuilding Company, West Bay City, Michigan—1907
HULL NO.:	621
O. A. DIMENSIONS:	540' × 54' × 31'
FORMER DATA:	Launched as GENERAL GARRETSON. Renamed E. J. KULAS (1) in 1935. Renamed POWHATAN in 1936. Renamed CHARLES A. PAUL in 1937. Given last name in 1956.

The bulk freighter B. F. JONES was named for Mr. Benjamin Franklin Jones who was born in Washington County, Pennsylvania on August 8, 1824. He was educated in the public schools and began his career as a clerk in a local transportation firm in 1843.

The namesake of this vessel is the same as that of the Steamer B. F. JONES (1) shown and described on a previous page. Re-telling of the same narrative seems unnecessary. The first paragraph, therefore, is provided to plainly identify the same namesake for both vessels.

When the Steamer B. F. JONES (1) met with disaster in 1955, these owners felt obliged to rename another of their carriers in Mr. Jones' honor since they had a prime iron ore floating contract with Jones and Laughlin Steel Corporation, the nation's fourth largest steel producer. In the spring of 1956 this vessel was renamed to carry on the traditional name on the Great Lakes.

Economics finally brought this ship to its end. The vessel took its last cargo, wheat from Duluth/Superior to Buffalo, New York in the early fall of 1971 and laid idle during the 1972 navigation season. It was sold for scrap in early 1973. It is shown below upbound in the middle Neebish Channel at the "dark hole" on August 17, 1970.

Steamer EDWARD S. KENDRICK

OWNER:	Wilson Marine Transit Company
BUILT:	West Bay City Shipbuilding Company, West Bay City, Michigan—1907
HULL NO.:	622
O. A. DIMENSIONS:	540' × 54' × 31'
FORMER DATA:	Launched as H. P. McINTOSH. Given last name in 1934.

The namesake of this bulk freighter was Mr. Edward Stillman Kendrick who was born in Atlanta, Georgia on April 12, 1886. He was educated in the public schools and came to the Great Lakes area in 1910 at which time he formed the Kendrick Coal and Dock Company in Minneapolis, Minnesota. Concurrently, he formed the Edward S. Kendrick Company in Cincinnati, Ohio. He was president of both firms and served as a coal forwarder on the southern Great Lakes and as a receiver and distributor on the northern Great Lakes.

In 1920, Mr. Kendrick affiliated with Inland Coal and Dock Company in Minneapolis and North American Coal Corporation in Cleveland, Ohio and served as president. Mr. Kendrick served in these capacities until retiring on November 5, 1936. Thereafter, he served as a director of these firms.

His namesake vessel is shown below at Cleveland, Ohio inbound with a cargo of iron ore for Republic Steel Corporation. This vessel continued active in the Wilson fleet until late 1970. It was sold for scrap in 1973.

Barge A. E. NETTLETON

OWNER:	Wilson Marine Transit Company
BUILT:	Detroit Shipbuilding Company, Wyandotte, Michigan – 1908
HULL NO.:	176
O. A. DIMENSIONS:	545' x 55' x 31'
FORMER DATA:	Launched as a powered bulk freighter. Converted to a barge at Oldman Boiler Works, Buffalo, New York and Port Weller Dry Docks, Limited, St. Catharines, Ontario in 1971.

This bulk freight barge was utilized briefly in 1971 and 1972 under charter by these owners to Escanaba Towing Company. Upon sale of this firm's equipment to Kinsman Marine Transit Company early in 1973, this unit was immediately sold for scrap. It is shown above while under tow beneath the Blue Water Bridge at Port Huron, Michigan in August, 1971.

The namesake of this vessel was Mr. Albert Edward Nettleton who at one time was vice president and a director of the Great Lakes Transportation Company, a predecessor company to the former Great Lakes Steamship Company which owned the unit until 1957.

Mr. Nettleton was born at Fulton, New York on October 29, 1850 and was educated in the public schools and Falley Seminary, graduating in 1869. He was the son of the founder of a shoe and boot business and opened a store in Fulton in 1872. In 1879 he went to Syracuse, New York and formed a partnership with Wickcliffe A. Hill. In 1907 he incorporated his father's business as the A. E. Nettleton Shoe Company and served as its president until 1916. He died at Syracuse, New York on November 3, 1939.

Barge LANSDOWNE

OWNER: Windsor Detroit Barge Line Limited
BUILT: Detroit Shipbuilding Company, Wyandotte, Michigan — 1884
HULL NO.: 66
O. A. DIMENSIONS: 319' x 41'3" x 13'
FORMER DATA: Launched as a powered carferry. Converted to a barge carfloat at Romeo Machine Shop Limited, Windsor, Ontario in 1970.

The Barge LANSDOWNE is shown in the photograph above being pushed across the Detroit River by the pusher-tug MARGARET YORKE in 1972. It saw very little service after that and was laid-up for several seasons until being sold for non-transportation use in 1978. Just prior to conversion to a barge in 1970, this vessel was the only remaining side-wheel unit on the Great Lakes.

This ship was named for Mr. Henry Charles Keith Petty-Fitzmaurice, 5th Marquess of Lansdowne who was Governor General of Canada from 1883 through 1888. He was born in London, England on January 14, 1845 and was educated at Eton and Oxford Universities. He succeeded to the peerage and to one of the largest estates in England in 1866 when he took his seat in the House of Lords.

He was junior lord of the treasury from 1869 to 1872, under secretary of war from 1872 to 1874 and also held several other posts between then and 1883 when he was appointed Governor General and took office on October 23rd.

Steamer WYANDOTTE (3)

OWNER:	Wyandotte Transportation Company
BUILT:	Great Lakes Engineering Works, Ecorse, Michigan—1908
HULL NO.:	54
O. A. DIMENSIONS:	364′ × 45′3″ × 24′
FORMER DATA:	Lengthened 60′ at Great Lakes Engineering Works, Ecorse, Michigan in 1910.

The Steamer WYANDOTTE was the first self-unloader ever built as such on the Great Lakes and was constructed on the design of Mr. George B. Palmer, chief engineer for the parent firm, Wyandotte Chemicals Corporation. He had developed the concept in an effort to speed delivery of products at the plant without the need of expensive shore-based machinery. His concept has withstood the test of time. Mr. Palmer would undoubtedly be pleased to know that more and more self-unloaders are being built in the modern Great Lakes era.

This ship's namesake was the owning company which, in turn, was owned by Wyandotte Chemicals Corporation of Wyandotte, Michigan. The port of ship registry was also Wyandotte, Michigan. Sailors on the Great Lakes used to refer to this vessel as, "the WYANDOTTE of Wyandotte of Wyandotte of Wyandotte."

The chemical company was incorporated under its present name on December 30, 1942 as a consolidation of Michigan Alkali Company and J. B. Ford Company. It is a firm producing basic heavy chemicals, cleaning and sanitizing products for industrial and institutional use.

This vessel was sold for scrap in 1966 and is shown here in the Lower St. Clair River in the early 1950's. It made its maiden trip August 5, 1908 from Sandusky, Ohio to Alpena, Michigan with a cargo of coal.

Steamer MANCOX

OWNER:	Yankcanuck Steamships, Limited
BUILT:	Superior Shipbuilding Company, Superior, Wisconsin - 1903
HULL NO.:	508
O. A. DIMENSIONS:	254' x 40'9" x 18'3"
FORMER DATA:	Launched as the crane-equipped bulk freighter H. G. DALTON. Renamed COURSEULLES in 1916. Renamed GLENDOCHART in 1921. Renamed CHATSWORTH in 1927. Renamed BAYLEAF in 1942. Converted to a crane ship at Marine Industries, Limited, Sorel, Quebec and given last name in 1951.

The Steamer MANCOX had two namesakes, but because the prefix of the ship name refers to Captain Filicano Manzzuttti who is discussed on the next page, only the second part of the ship name will be explained here.

The suffix of the vessel name, "COX," is in honor of Mrs. Manzzutti, the former Eleanor Cox, who was born at Marinette, Wisconsin on August 11, 1915. She received her education in the local schools and met Captain Manzzutti one winter when the steamer on which he was serving wintered at Marinette after discharging its lumber cargo.

In due course the couple decided to get married and did so onboard the former composite-hulled Steamer YANKCANUCK at Midland, Ontario on December 9, 1944. Mrs. Manzzutti became active in the family business and served as secretary-treasurer of Manzzutti Enterprises, Limited at Sault Ste. Marie, Ontario for a number of years. Her namesake was sold for scrap in 1970.

The vessel is shown above while upbound in the lower St. Mary's River, light for the Algoma Steel Corporation plant at Sault Ste. Marie, Ontario where another cargo of finished steel was awaiting her.

Steamer MANZZUTTI

OWNER: Yankcanuck Steamships, Limited
BUILT: Buffalo Dry Dock Company, Buffalo, New York - 1903
HULL NO.: 203
O. A. DIMENSIONS: 254' x 40'9" x 18'
FORMER DATA: Launched as the crane-equipped bulk freighter J. S. KEEFE. Renamed PARAME in 1916. Renamed GLENFARN in 1921. Renamed CANMORE in 1927. Renamed ASHLEAF in 1942. Converted to a crane ship at Marine Industries, Limited, Sorel, Quebec and given last name in 1951.

The namesake of this crane vessel is Captain Filicano Manzzutti, more popularly known as Frank Manzzutti. He was born at Udine, Italy on July 27, 1910 and came to Canada in 1912 with his mother to join his father at Sault Ste. Marie, Ontario. His father had preceded them to the area in 1911.

Captain Manzzutti was educated in the public schools and started his sailing career with A. B. McLean in 1928. He then went to the Windsor, Ontario area and worked for Cadwell Sand & Gravel Company on their sand ships for four years. In 1934 he joined the Tree Line and, in 1936, with his master's papers, began sailing for Canada Steamship Lines on the passenger ships of the Upper Lakes.

Captain Manzzutti came ashore in 1946 and founded his own company at Sault Ste. Marie, Ontario and acquired this vessel and its sister ship in 1951. Both ships were sold for scrap in 1970. These vessels are probably unique in that they were both built in 1903 and largely followed each other in trade patterns and ownership over the intervening years.

The Steamer MANZZUTTI is shown above on a clear day while it is approaching the Sault Ste. Marie area in the lower St. Mary's River.

Steamer YANKCANUCK (1)

OWNER: Yankcanuck Steamships Limited
BUILT: Detroit Dry Dock Company, Wyandotte, Michigan—1889
HULL NO.: 91
O. A. DIMENSIONS: 256'9" × 42' × 23'3"
FORMER DATA: Launched as the bulk freighter MANCHESTER. Renamed JOSEPH W. SIMPSON in 1921. Shortened 41'1" at Manitowoc Shipbuilding Company, Manitowoc, Wisconsin in 1922. Converted to a crane vessel at Buffalo Dry Dock Company, Buffalo, New York in 1928. Renamed MINDEMOYA in 1938. Given last name in 1946.

The crane vessel Steamer YANKCANUCK has been superceded in modern times by a larger motor vessel of the same name. This ship served its various owners well, however, until it was sold for scrap in 1959. At that time it was the last of the famous "composite" hull Great Lakes vessels. Its hull was made of oak timber and charcoal iron.

The name of this carrier was derived from the fact that the owning company had its origination as a husband and wife business venture with Captain Frank Manzzutti being a Canadian and Mrs. Manzzutti being an American.

The prefix "YANK" is a term of unknown origin which is short for Yankee, meaning a resident or native of the United States. The suffix "CANUCK" is a nickname for a Canadian. It can be used as an adjective as well as a noun. Though its origin is also obscure, it is thought by some to be a corruption of Connaught, a name given by French-speaking Canadians to the Irish.

This venerable ship is shown above in the Little Rapids Cut of the St. Mary's River, near its home port of Sault Ste. Marie, Ontario, on June 21, 1953.

INDEX

VESSEL	PAGE	VESSEL	PAGE
A		Augustus, A. A.	266
		Avondale (1)	493
Acadialite	392	Avondale (2)	596
Acadian (2)	85		
Acton	352	**B**	
Adams, Avery C.	255		
Adams, Cuyler	531		
Adriatic (2)	276	B. A. Sentinel	290
Agassiz, R. L.	389	Baffin Transport	245
Agawa (1)	477	Baie Comeau	484
Agawa (2)	1	Bailey, F. A.	525
Agnew, William C.	10	Bainbridge	510
Ailes, John W.	173	Baker, George F.	514
Alabama	150	Ball Brothers	532
Albright, John J.	426	Baltic (3)	173
Alfred	423	Band, C. S.	444
Alfred J.	423	Barclay, David	354
Algocen (1)	2	Barlum, John J. (2)	2
Algomah II	510	Barlum, Thomas	5
Algonac	192	Barnes, Julius H.	536
Algonquins	455	Barnum, George G.	217
Algorail (1)	3	Barrie	87
Algosoo (1)	4	Bartow, J. H.	401
Algosteel (1)	5	Basing Creek	237
Algoway (1)	6	Battleford	88
Allen, Harry L.	511	Bay Transport (1)	229
Allen, Justine C.	519	Bay Transport (2)	246
Allen, Martha E.	167	Bayanna	19
Alpena (1)	206	Baybranch	41
Altadoc (2)	419	Bayfair	20
American	191	Bayfax	22
Ames, Ward	339	Baygeorge	21
Amherst	170	Bayleaf	611
Amoco Michigan	8	Bayquinte	22
Anderson, Edward H.	341	Bayshell (1)	519
Anderson, John	522	Bayton	355
Andrews, Matthew (1)	515	Bayusona	396
Angeline	348	Beatty, Charles	396
Ann Arbor No. 3	80	Beaumont Parks	160
Ann Arbor No. 4	341	Beaverton (2)	89
Ann Arbor No. 5	16	Becker, W. H.	62
Ansell, C. A.	353	Belgium	530
Anticosti	264	Bell, Sir Isaac Lothian	475
A. O. G. 21	414	Belvoir (1)	482
Applebranch	40	Belvoir (2)	382
Aragon	19	Bennett, C. A.	356
Arcturus	277	Bennett, Viscount	356
Argus (2)	456	Berks	473
Arosa	457	Berry, B. F.	356
Arrowhead	260	Berry, Nixon	357
Ashcroft	86	Berryton	356
Ashleaf	612	Berwind, Harry A.	481
Ashley, J. S.	597	Bethlehem (2)	32
Ashtabula	460	Biessard	133
Aspenleaf	566	Billings, Frank	461
Assiniboia	137	Birchton	223

VESSEL	PAGE	VESSEL	PAGE
Bixby, W. K.	209	Burlington (3)	90
Black River	475	Butler, Hazen	407
Black, Herbert F.	156	Butler, Jr., Joseph G.	496
Blanche H.	475	Byers, A. M.	210
Block, Joseph	307		
Blue Comet	335		
Blue Cross	288	**C**	
Blue Laker	39		
Blue River	573	Cabatern	245
Boland, John J. (1)	13	Cadillac (3)	260
Boland, John J. (2)	304	Calcite	544
Boland, Jr., John J.	6	Caldera	602
Booth, Edwin L.	171	Calgadoc (2)	421
Bope, H. P.	299	Calgarian (2)	91
Boston Socony	287	Callender, D. E. (2)	178
Bowers, L. M.	534	Calumet	139
Bradley, Carl D. (2)	543	Calvert, W. S.	473
Bradley, M. A.	362	Calverley, Jr., W. D.	447
Brampton	358	Calvin, Ben W.	10
Bransford	553	Cambria (3)	30
Breckling, A. G.	202	Campbell, J. A.	295
Bricoldoc	420	Campbell, Peter G.	290
Brignogan	395	Camrose	569
Britamlube	229	Canadian (2)	92
Britamoco	240	Canadiana	193
Britamoil	231	Canadoc (1)	445
Britamolene	236	Canmore	612
Britt, Thomas (1)	234	Canopus	393
Britt, Thomas (2)	171	Cape Transport	247
Brookdale (1)	491	Captain Sam	381
Brookdale (2)	597	Cardinal (2)	366
Brookton	491	Cardinal (3)	9
Brower, A. G.	178	Carl, George M. (1)	360
Brown Beaver	574	Carport/G1	140
Brown, Fayette (2)	278	Carrington	262
Brown, Frank H.	359	Carrollton	516
Brown, Harvey H. (2)	481	Carter, E. D.	600
Brown, J. J. H.	52	Cartierdoc (1)	422
Brown, William L.	328	Casco	453
Brown, W. W.	173	Caulkins, Ralph S.	215
Browning, L. D.	54	Cayuga (1)	144
Browning, Michael G.	594	Cedarbay	168
Browning, Troy H. (1)	56	Cedarbranch (2)	517
Browning, Troy H. (2)	54	Cedarton	224
Browning, Troy H. (3)	501	Cedarville	546
Brulin	483	Cementkarrier	84
Bryn Barge	575	Cemico	338
Bryn Mawr	575	Cemico-Erie	201
Buck, Robert J.	115	Cepheus	439
Buckeye, (1)	171	Champlain (2)	461
Buckeye Monitor	295	Chandler	566
Buckeye State (2)	212	Charpentier	168
Buckler, J. J.	483	Chatsworth	611
Budd, Ralph	568	Chembarge No. 2	453
Buffington, Eugene J.	545	Chemong	363
Bulkarier	83	Cheyenne	452
Bunsen, Robert W. E.	508	Chicago Socony	380
Burke, Joseph P.	368	Chicago Trader	512

VESSEL	PAGE
Christopher	234
City of Alpena (2)	410
City of Alpena II	410
City of Cheboygan	341
City of Cleveland (4)	194
City of Cleveland III	194
City of Detroit	195
City of Detroit III	195
City of Green Bay (2)	17
City of Hamilton (2)	93
City of Kingston	94
City of Montreal (2)	95
City of Munising	342
City of Petoskey	343
City of Saginaw 31	145
City of Saugatuck	410
City of Toronto	96
City of Windsor (3)	97
Clark Milwaukee	152
Clarke, E. A. S. (1)	445
Clarke, E. A. S. (2)	299
Clarkson, Worrell	261
Clayton	361
Clearwater	319
Cleet, George S.	21
Clemson, D. M. (2)	547
Clement, Norman P.	528
Clement, Stephen M.	304
Cleveland, Moses	506
Coalfax	230
Coalhaven	20
Coastal Carrier	246
Coastal Cascades	168
Coastal Cliff	169
Coastal Creek	237
Cole, Thomas F.	548
Collier (2)	180
Collier (3)	98
Collier No. 1	98
Collingdoc (2)	423
Collingwood	99
Colorado (2)	491
Comet	159
Cometa	159
Congar (1)	288
Congar (2)	289
Coniscliffe Hall (1)	352
Coniscliffe Hall (3)	248
Conneaut (2)	188
Connelly, William M.	114
Constitution (2)	469
Consumers Power (1)	12
Consumers Power (2)	599
Conway, Carle C.	389
Cooke, Delos W.	403
Coralia	54
Cordova (1)	204
Cordova (2)	262

VESSEL	PAGE
Corey, William E.	585
Corliss, George H.	433
Cornelius, Adam E. (1)	596
Cornelius, Jr., Adam E.	56
Cornell	291
Corrigan, James	300
Coteaudoc (1)	495
Coteaudoc (2)	424
Coulby, Harry (1)	305
Courseulles	611
Cove Transport	249
Cowee	312
Cowle, John B. (2)	511
Crawford, George G.	549
Crawford, William D.	265
Creek Transport	237
Crescent City	57
Crete (2)	279
Croft, Harry W.	284
Cuddy, Loftus	308
Cyclo-Brave	529
Cyclo-Chief	239
Cyclo-Warrior	252
Cypress	255
Cytacki, Alfred	37

D

Dalrymple	110
Dalton, H. G.	611
Dalton, Henry G.	285
Dalton, Jack	198
Damia	424
Daniels, William H.	346
Davidson, James	172
Davidson, James E.	533
Davidson, Louis R.	598
Davin, John W.	349
Dawson, Sir Trevor	595
Deepwater	429
de Graff, Le Grand S.	549
Delaware (4)	480
Delkote	262
Denmark	326
Desgagnes, Roland	253
Detroit (2)	345
Detroit Edison (1)	596
Diamond Alkali (1)	598
Dick, Charles	388
Dick, O'Connor	334
Dinkey, Alva C.	550
Dolomite	323
Donaldson, John A.	29
Donnacona (2)	100
Donnelly, Charles	394
Donner, William H.	31
Dornoch	491

VESSEL	PAGE
Douglas, S. M.	38
Douglass, Edwin T.	565
Dow Chemical (1)	600
Dow Chemical (2)	598
Drumahoe	359
Dunbar, K. H.	201
Dunham, James S.	487
Dunlap, Charles E.	534
Dunn, Jr., John	490
Dunsford, F. H.	433
Durham, Robert P.	477
Durston, J. F.	327
Dustin, Alton C.	295
Du-Val	201

E

VESSEL	PAGE
Eads, James B.	576
Eaglescliffe Hall (1)	354
Eaglescliffe Hall (2)	250
Earling, E. J.	502
Eastcliffe Hall	238
Eastern Shell (1)	37
Eastern States	196
Eastrich	492
Eaton, George L. (2)	370
Edenborn, William	539
Edgewater	162
Edmonton	101
Eels, Jr., Howard P.	178
Eglinton Park	520
Elba	32
Elgin	102
Elliott, James R.	418
Ellwood, Isaac L.	540
Elmbranch	42
Elmdale	494
Elphicke, Mary C.	330
Empire City	323
Empire Maldon	289
Empire Rother	480
Empire Stickleback	47
Empire Tadpole	237
En-Ar-Co	473
England, R. W.	11
Ericsson, John	577
Erie (2)	214
Erie Queen	510
Eskimo	132
Ethel	433
Ethel J.	433
Eurochemist	245
Evans, Helen	476
Evans, Parker	481
Everetton	362
Ewig, Harry T.	173

F

VESSEL	PAGE
Fairbairn, Sir William	64
Fairlake	353
Fairmount (2)	103
Fairriver	375
Farr, Merton E.	357
Farrandoc (1)	361
Farrandoc (2)	425
Farrell, James A.	551
Fawcett, Donald F.	363
Federal Husky	477
Fellowcraft (2)	395
Ferndale (1)	495
Ferndale (2)	598
Fernie	104
Ferris, James E.	296
Fiertz, Alden Barnes	246
Fiertz, Robert Barnes	499
Filbert, William J.	552
Findlay, Harry L.	515
Fink, George R. (1)	60
Fink, George R. (2)	261
Finland	305
Firbranch	43
Fitzgerald, Edmund	174
Fitzgerald, W. E.	216
Florence	444
Florence J.	444
Fontana (2)	11
Foran, Clary	495
Ford, Emory L.	158
Forestdale	492
Fort Willdoc	426
Fosna	245
Foster, Parks	412
Foster, Sparkman D.	58
Foy, Norman W.	59
France, John A. (1)	493
Frankcliffe Hall (1)	253
Franklin	163
Franquelin (2)	199
Freja	255
French, G. Watson	6
Frick, H. C.	445
Frick, Henry C.	472
Fritz, John	578
Frontenac (4)	154
FS-231	39
Fuel Marketer (1)	37
Fuel Marketer (2)	520
Fuel Transport	239
Fuel Transporter	239
Fulton	574

VESSEL	PAGE
G	
Gallagher, Michael (1)	594
Gallagher, Michael (2)	349
Ganandoc	427
Garretson, General	606
Gary	200
Gary, Elbert H.	309
Gaspedoc	428
Gates, John W.	541
Geer, Lynford E.	487
Geistman, John P.	419
Gilbert	313
Gilchrist, Frank W.	439
Gilchrist, Ralph	601
Gillies, Donald B.	496
Girdler, Tom M.	500
Glenarm	569
Glenbogie	579
Glencalvie	108
Glenclova	264
Glencorrie	125
Glendochart	611
Glendowan	566
Glenelg	105
Glenellah	91
Glenfarn	612
Glengeldie	102
Gleniffer (2)	86
Glenisla	119
Glenledi	120
Glenmavis	85
Glenmohr	111
Glenross	88
Glenshee	1
Globe	576
Goderich (1)	1
Golden Sable	392
Good Hope	290
Good Star	126
Goudreau (2)	471
Goulder, Harvey D.	179
Grainmotor	106
Grammer, G. J.	56
Grand Haven	593
Grand Island (2)	155
Grand Rapids	76
Great Lakes	18
Great Western (2)	564
Greater Detroit	197
Gréeur	134
Grey Beaver	580
Griffin (1)	208
Grovedale (1)	566
Grovedale (2)	496
Gulf Sentinel	290
Gulf Transport	240
Gunnell, E.	170

VESSEL	PAGE
H	
Hagarty	107
Hagarty, J. H. G.	107
Halfueler	133
Hamildoc (2)	429
Hamildoc (3)	430
Hancock, W. Wayne	60
Hanna, Leonard C.	35
Hanna, M. A.	458
Hanna, Jr., Howard M. (1)	1
Hanna, Jr., Howard M. (2)	175
Harmony	225
Hartwell, Fred G. (1)	284
Harvard	65
Harvey, A. F. (2)	546
Hastings	108
Hawgood, Arthur H.	307
Hawgood, William A.	389
Hay, John C.	61
Hazard, F. R.	296
Hebard, Charles S.	604
Hecker, Frank J.	400
Heffelfinger, Frank T.	488
Hemlock	141
Hennipen (2)	217
Heron Bay (1)	477
Heron Bay (2)	537
Hewitt, Fred L. (1)	362
Hewitt, Fred L. (2)	55
Hilda (1)	474
Hilda (2)	77
Hill, James J.	542
Hill, Louis W.	504
Hillsdale	602
Hindman, Blanche (1)	569
Hindman, Blanche (2)	263
Hindman, Elizabeth	264
Hindman, George (1)	491
Hindman, George (2)	264
Hindman, George (3)	265
Hindman, Helen (1)	566
Hindman, Howard (1)	492
Hindman, Howard (2)	266
Hindman, Martha	478
Hindman, Ruth	267
Holden, Hendrick S.	456
Holley, Alexander	581
Hood, Clifford F.	553
Hoover & Mason	58
Hosford, Harry Wm.	66
Houghton, Douglass	582
House, Francis E.	297
Houson, C. H.	367
Howe, Louis McHenry	500
Hoyt, James H.	420
H. S. & G. No. 1	448
Hubbard, Charles	605

VESSEL	PAGE
Hudson, A. A.	411
Hudson, Bruce	169
Humberdoc	431
Huron (4)	176
Hutchcliffe Hall	241
Hutchinson, Charles L. (1)	278
Hutchinson, Charles L. (2)	595
Hutchinson, Gene C.	595
Hutchinson, J. T.	408
Hydro	203
Hydrus (2)	458

I

VESSEL	PAGE
Ida O.	457
I'Le Aux Coudres	241
I'Le De Montreal	237
I. L. I. 103	499
I. L. I. 104	246
I. L. I. 105	340
Imari	480
Imperial Cobourg	467
Imperial Cornwall	392
Imperial Halifax	289
Imperial Hamilton	271
Imperial La Have	272
Imperial Midland	498
Imperial Ottawa (1)	272
Imperial Sarnia (1)	271
Imperial Simcoe	273
Imperial Welland	274
Imperial Whitby	21
Imperial Windsor	9
Imperoyal	467
Inca	337
Ingalls, George H.	328
Inkster, Walter	351
Inland, The	251
Inland Transport	251
International Waterways Line Incorporated 105	340
Iocoma	21
Ireland, R. L.	443
Ireland, Robert L. (2)	603
Ironwood	396
Irwin, J. G.	364
Irwin, John (1)	529
Irwin, John (2)	520
Iselin, Adrian	397
Ishpeming (2)	590
Island Transport (1)	231
Isle Royale (2)	242
Ivey, T. A.	214

J

VESSEL	PAGE
Jean-Talon	199
Jenkins, Charles O.	349
Jenks, J. M.	215
Jenny, W. Le Baron	423
Jodrey, Roy A.	7
John, J. B. (2)	202
Johnson, E. E.	419
Johnson, Ernest R.	62
Joliet (2)	156
Jones, B. F. (2)	606
Jones, Harry R.	142
Joynt, Robert N.	329
Jupiter (2)	143

K

VESSEL	PAGE
Kamaris	448
Keefe, J. S.	612
Keewatin (2)	138
Kelley Island	292
Kendrick, Edward S.	607
Kenefick, Judge	286
Kennedy, Hugh	207
Kennedy, John McCartney	180
Kenora	109
Kenordoc (2)	432
Kenordoc (3)	433
Kensington	177
Kernan, Robert P.	87
Kerr, D. G. (1)	142
Kerr, D. G. (2)	554
Kerr, William B.	297
Keybar	314
Keybell	315
Keydon	316
Keymont	429
Keynor	317
Keyport	318
Keyshey	319
Keystate	320
Keyvive	321
Keywest (2)	322
Kingdoc (1)	434
Kinloch	497
Kinmount (2)	110
Kinney, A. T.	602
Kinsman Enterprise (1)	513
Kinsman Independent (1)	297
Kinsman Venture	298
Kinsman Voyager	299
Koenig, Peter	170
Kopmeier, Norman J.	600
Kopp, Jacob T.	12
Kotcher, Charles W.	221
Krupp, Alfred	383
Kulas, E. J. (1)	606

VESSEL	PAGE
L	
L. C. T. 516	205
L. S. T. 1063	164
La Belle	293
La Salle (1)	492
La Salle (2)	525
Labradoc (1)	435
Lac Des Iles	478
Lachinedoc (1)	372
Lachinedoc (2)	436
Lackawanna (2)	301
Lady Hamilton	260
Lagonda	417
Lake Transport (1)	288
Lake Transport (2)	252
Lakeshell (1)	37
Lakeshell (2)	521
Laketon (1)	365
Lakewood (1)	192
La Liberte, Henry	300
Land, Scott E.	501
Lansdowne	609
Latimer, J. L.	287
Laughlin, James	476
Lavaldoc	437
Lawrendoc (1)	438
Leadale (1)	599
Lebanon	34
Leecliffe Hall (1)	249
Leecliffe Hall (2)	232
Lemoyne (1)	111
Leona	410
Leslie, Alexander	408
Lethbridge	112
Lil' Rock	205
Lillian	506
Linn, William R.	63
Lio	287
Livingstone, William	182
Lockwell	366
Londonderry	325
Lubrolake	311
Luzon	522
Lynch, Thomas	592
M	
McAlpine, James E.	53
McCarren, Charles	200
McCarthy,, T. J.	330
McColl, B. B.	345
McCool, Daniel	202
McCormick, Col. Robert R.	479
McCorquodale, L. A.	568
McCullough, Jr., C. H.	339
McDougall, John A.	37

VESSEL	PAGE
McFarland, O. S.	177
McGean, W. H.	213
McIntosh, H. P	607
McKellar, John O. (1)	364
McKinney, Price	462
McLean, John H.	553
McManus, H. J.	286
McNamara, Robert S.	213
McWatters, J. N. (1)	366
Mack, William S.	3
Macoubrey, J. H.	29
Macpherson, Norman B.	567
Madison	78
Magna	67
Maia	68
Maida	470
Maine (2)	163
Maitland No. 1	79
Maitland, Alexander	579
Makaweli	312
Malietoa	413
Malta	47
Manchester	613
Mancox	611
Manda	507
Manicouagan (1)	480
Manicouagan (2)	479
Manila	69
Manion, Paul	367
Manistee (2)	80
Manitoba (2)	409
Manitoulin (4)	480
Manske, Fred A. (1)	599
Manske, Fred A. (2)	597
Mantadoc (1)	439
Manuel, John S.	463
Manzzutti	612
Maplebay	134
Mapleheath	113
Marcia	268
Maricopa	419
Marine Fuel	338
Marinsal	305
Mariska	448
Markham, General	165
Marlhill	481
Marquette (2)	157
Marquette (3)	1
Marquette & Bessemer No. 1	516
Marquette & Bessemer No. 2 (2)	506
Mars (3)	445
Marsala	70
Marshall, Albert M.	395
Marshall, R. H.	368
Martha	444
Martian (2)	114
Maryland	300
Massey, F. V.	384

VESSEL	PAGE	VESSEL	PAGE
Mataafa	398	Morgan, Jr., J. P.	556
Mathewston	369	Morrell, Daniel J.	81
Mathiott, E. G. (2)	178	Morris, Effingham B.	34
Maunaloa	583	Morrow, Joe S.	303
Maunaloa II	583	Morse, Jay C.	538
Maureen H.	444	Mount Mansfield	505
Meacham, Daniel B.	301	Mudge, Edmund W.	390
Mead, George W.	331	Munro, Josiah G.	34
Meadcliffe Hall	371	Murphy, E. P.	601
Meaford (2)	115	Murphy, Simon J. (2)	71
Meaford (3)	525		
Mercury (1)	311		
Mercury (2)	160	*N*	
Merle H.	485		
Metcalfe	103	#137	572
Meteor (2)	161	#885	428
Mexoil (2)	50	#1006	509
Meyers, Carl W.	57	Narragansett	121
M. I. L. 461	40	Nasmyth, James	485
M. I. L. 462	41	National Trader	371
M. I. L. 464	45	Nelson, William	186
M. I. L. 465	46	Neptune	114
Michigan (4)	471	Nereus	334
Michigan (6)	340	Nettleton, A. E.	608
Michigan (7)	530	Newbrundoc (2)	442
Michipicoten (2)	472	New York News (1)	435
Midland Prince	116	New York News (2)	482
Midvale	33	Newbold, Arthur E.	300
Miller, Governor	555	Niagara Mohawk	304
Miller, J. Clare	179	Nienaber, C. B.	178
Miller, P. P.	180	Nine	468
Millican Park	43	Norco	337
Mills, D. O.	187	Norfolk (2)	431
Mills, William M	552	Norgoma	415
Millsop, Thomas E. (1)	60	Norisle	416
Milverton	495	Normac	418
Minch, Philip (2)	302	Normania	185
Mindemoya	613	Normil	410
Minneapolis Husky	152	North American	136
Misener, Lt. John	376	Northcliffe Hall (1)	247
Misener, Ralph S. (1)	353	Northcliffe Hall (2)	253
Misener, Ralph S. (2)	369	Norton, David Z. (1)	432
Misener, Scott (1)	360	Norton, David Z. (2)	181
Mitschfibre	268	Norway (2)	267
Mobil Albany	379	Norwood Park	42
Mobil Chicago	380	Nye, Harold B.	447
Mobil New York	381		
Mohawk Deer	385		
Moll, Clifford F.	494	*O*	
Moloney, D. A.	56		
Mondoc (2)	440	Oag, J. M.	386
Mondoc (3)	441	Oglebay, Crispin (1)	182
Moody, R. E.	180	Ohl, Edwin N.	594
Moore, F. W.	370	Oil Transport	233
Mooremack	204	Oil Transporter	233
Morden, W. Grant	100	Olau Mark	256
Moreland, William C.	595	Olcott, William J.	306
Morgan, J. Pierpont	537	Olivebranch	44

VESSEL	PAGE
Oliver, Henry W.	90
Ontadoc (1)	443
Ontario (4)	296
Orefax	242
Orion (3)	162
Osborn, Frank C.	22
Osler	118
Osler, E. B.	118
Oswego Socony	166
Otco Bayway	414
Ottawalite	272
Otterburn Park	48
Outarde (1)	483
Outarde (2)	189
Owana	214

P

Vessel	Page
Pabjune	126
Paine, William A.	464
Paisley, Robert J. (2)	234
Palmbranch	45
Palmer, William P. (2)	557
Palmleaf	569
Panay	186
Parame	612
Paratex	226
Parent, S. N.	569
Parkdale (1)	569
Parkdale (2)	595
Parks, Sheldon	59
Parsons, Lionel	1
Patmore, A. J.	345
Patterson, Joseph Medill	484
Patton, Thomas F.	501
Paul, Charles A.	606
Peachbranch	46
Pearson, Jay A.	204
Peavey Pioneer	304
Peerless (2)	202
Pelee	459
Penetang	117
Pennsylvania (1)	214
Pennsylvania (2)	398
Penobscot (2)	399
Pere Marquette 14	146
Pere Marquette 17	343
Pere Marquette 18 (2)	147
Pere Marquette 19	77
Pere Marquette 20	342
Pere Marquette 21	148
Pere Marquette 22	149
Perseus	400
Petman, R. O.	118
Phenicia	452
Phipps, Henry	558
Pic River	485

VESSEL	PAGE
Pickands, Colonel James	280
Picton (3)	371
Pientre	133
Pierce, Daniel	51
Pierce, E. L.	463
Pierson Independent	525
Pillsbury Barge	218
Pillsbury, John S.	584
Pinebranch	47
Pinedale	600
Pioneer (2)	401
Pioneer (3)	44
Platt, Jr., Henry R. (1)	218
Platt, Jr. Henry R. (2)	219
Plattsburgh Socony	379
Pleiades	163
Polaris	164
Poling Bros. No. 10	338
Pollock, W. G.	350
Poplarbay	133
Port de St. Malo	396
Portadoc (2)	433
Portadoc (3)	445
Porter, H. H.	391
Portwell	376
Post, G. G.	522
Poughkeepsie Socony	381
Powell, K. A. (1)	423
Powell, K. A. (2)	494
Powhatan	606
Prescodoc (2)	446
Prescott (2)	119
Price, John H.	235
Prince Ungava	199
Princeton	72
Prindoc (2)	447
Providence Socony	523
Puloe Brani	345

Q

Vessel	Page
Quebec (1)	325
Quebec Trader	425
Quedoc (1)	448
Queenston	372
Quinnebaug	254

R

Vessel	Page
Radiant	165
Rahane	411
Rammacher, John J.	347
Rand, George F. (1)	10
Rand, George F. (2)	596
Randall, Clarence B. (2)	275
Ranney, Rufus P. (2)	535

VESSEL	PAGE	VESSEL	PAGE
Rapprich, William F.	244	Rockwood	204
Real Gold	88	Roebling, John A.	586
Ream, Norman B.	513	Roen, Marquis (2)	508
Redchief	573	Rogers, Henry H.	560
Redcloud	23	Rosemount (2)	237
Redfern	24	Roslyn	396
Redhead	288	Rotary	345
Redriver	25	Royalite	274
Redstar	24	Royalton (1)	378
Redwing (1)	26	Royston	414
Redwood	26	Russel, George H.	393
Reeb, M. A.	177		
Regent	227		
Regulus	426	**S**	
Reinauer, Bert (1)	200		
Reinauer, Bert (2)	523	St. Clair (1)	463
Reinauer, Franklin	201	St. Lawrence (2)	122
Reinauer, Peggy	345	Sable Island	83
Reis, William E.	450	Sagamore (2)	432
Reiss, Clemens A. (1)	488	Sahara	531
Reiss, Clemens A. (2)	210	Sainte Marie (2)	336
Reiss, J. L.	209	Sandland	27
Reiss, John P.	486	Saracen	454
Reiss, Otto M. (1)	218	Sargent	178
Reiss, Otto M. (2)	487	Sarniadoc (2)	449
Reiss, Peter	153	Sarnolite	271
Reiss, Raymond H.	158	Saskadoc	450
Renown	160	Saskatoon (1)	237
Renvoyle (2)	120	Saskatoon (2)	123
Republic-Pittsburgh	152	Saturn (1)	4
Resolute (2)	507	Saturn (3)	298
Restigouche (2)	334	Saugatuck	410
Reynolds, Walter B. (1)	117	Saunders, Jr., Edward N. (1)	189
Reynolds, Walter B. (2)	373	Saunders, Jr., Edward N. (2)	62
Rhodes, Joshua W.	407	Savage, J. E.	234
Richards, John B.	570	Saxona	365
Richardson, R. R.	215	Schiller, William B.	561
Richardson, W. C. (2)	183	Schneider, A. E. R.	386
Richelieu (2)	121	Schoellkopf, Jr., J. F.	207
Riddle, J. Q.	60	Schupp, William	440
Ridgetown	585	Schwartz, K. V.	192
River Transport	254	Scobell, Joseph S.	208
Risacua	264	Scotiacliffe Hall	255
Rivershell (1)	290	Scott Mark	346
Rivershell (2)	521	Scranton	468
Rivershell (3)	290	Sea Transport (1)	243
Riverton	385	Sea Transport (2)	256
Robbins, Francis L.	331	Sea Transporter	243
Robbins, S. H.	90	Secola	517
Roberts, Jr., Percival	559	Secord, Captain C. D.	386
Roberts, William T.	600	Seedhouse, George E.	306
Robertson, Peter (1)	502	Seither, Frank (1)	11
Robertson, Peter (2)	305	Seither, Frank (2)	407
Robinson, C. S.	308	Selkirk (3)	124
Rock, H. A.	408	Sellwood, Joseph	281
Rockcliffe Hall (1)	374	Sequatchie	414
Rockefeller, Frank	161	Servitor, H. M. S.	345
Rocket (2)	165	Shasta	518

VESSEL	PAGE	VESSEL	PAGE
Shaughnessy, Sir Thomas	387	Stearn, Abraham	189
Shaw, Howard L.	587	Steel Chemist	251
Shaw, Quincy A.	390	Steel Electrician	425
Sheadle, J. H. (1)	525	Steel King (2)	403
Shelter Bay (1)	435	Steel Products	526
Shelter Bay (2)	538	Steinbrenner, George M. (1)	298
Sherbrooke	457	Steinbrenner, George M. (2)	307
Sherwin, John (1)	298	Steinbrenner, Henry (2)	409
Shiercliffe Hall	257	Steinbrenner, Henry (3)	514
Shikellamy	51	Stephenson, George	74
Shiras, Mac Gilvray	294	Sterncliffe Hall	258
Sidney M.	334	Stewart, James	588
Sierra	184	Stewart, Robert W.	8
Simcoe (1)	125	Stifel, William F.	185
Simcolite	273	Stone, Amasa	282
Simpson, Joseph W.	613	Stonefax	244
Sinaloa	244	Strong, Edward L.	457
Sinclair, E. W.	51	Sullivan Brothers (1)	218
Sinclair Gary	200	Sullivan Brothers (2)	220
Sinclair Great Lakes	18	Sullivan, J. J.	275
Sinclair Milwaukee	523	Sultana	404
Sinclair Power	200	Sumatra	323
Sioux	446	Sunchief	351
Sirius	443	Superior (2)	412
Slick, Edwin E.	301	Superior (4)	488
Smeaton, John	73	Superior (5)	568
Smith, Edmund P.	12	Supertest	44
Smith, Home	3	Supreme	228
Smith, Hurlbut W.	332	Surewater	322
Smith, L. C.	333	Sweden	333
Smith, Lyman C.	478	Swederope (2)	269
Smith, Jr., Sidney E. (1)	206	Swiftwater	316
Smith, Jr., Sidney E. (2)	209	Syracuse (1)	192
Snyder, Harris N.	13	Syracuse Socony	201
Socapa	217		
Solveig	509	*T*	
Sonoma	55		
Sonora (2)	402	Tadenac	491
Soodoc (1)	451	Tadoussac (3)	127
Soreldoc (2)	452	Talaralite	498
Sotteville	134	Tampico	405
South American	151	Taplin, Frank E.	221
South Park	161	Tate, Ben E.	186
Southcliffe Hall	242	Taurus (2)	166
Southton	580	Taylor, J. Frater	4
Spaulding, Jesse	204	Taylor, Moses	451
Sprucebranch	48	Taylor, Shirley G.	589
Sprucedale	490	Teakbay	128
Squire, F. B.	66	Tellico	243
Stackhouse, Powell	36	Ten (1)	468
Stadacona (1)	213	Tewksbury, Baird	265
Standard Portland Cement	494	Tewksbury, Michael K.	189
Stanton, John	465	Texaco-Brave (1)	529
Starbelle	467	Texaco Chief (1)	239
Starbuck	468	Texaco Michigan	530
Starmount	126	Texaco Warrior (1)	252
Starucca	403	The Harvester	512
Starwell	493	The Iroquois	491

VESSEL	PAGE	VESSEL	PAGE
The Straits of Mackinac	344	**V**	
Thomas, Sidney G.	269		
Thompson, Alexis W.	62	Vacationland	198
Thompson, Carmi A.	190	Valley Camp (1)	497
Thompson, David P.	15	Valley Camp (2)	504
Thompson, Smith	329	Valleydale	497
Thordoc (2)	453	Van Hise, Charles R.	386
Thornhill	590	Vandoc (1)	456
Thorold (3)	190	Venus (1)	526
Thunder Bay (1)	47	Venus (2)	167
Thunder Bay Quarries (1)	14	Vernon	168
Thunder Bay Quarries (2)	13	Verona	409
Tietjen, Paul L.	515	Veulettes	569
Toiler (1)	113	Victory	591
Toledo Sun	527	Victorious	591
Tomlinson, G. A. (1)	219	Vigilant	270
Tomlinson, G. A. (2)	187	Vindal	204
Torondoc (2)	454	Virginia	338
Townsend, Edward Y.	82	Virginia, Joan	168
Transbay	170		
Transea	243		
Transinland	251	**W**	
Transiter	135		
Translake	133	Wabash	17
Transoil	233	Wainwright	183
Transpan	254	Waldo, L. C.	385
Transriver	134	Wallace, E. L.	157
Transtream	135	Wallace, James C.	283
Traverse City Socony	524	Wallace, Robert (2)	566
Tregastel	566	Wallace, Robert B.	502
Tremaine, Morris S.	330	Wallaceburg	347
Trenora	319	Walsh, James P.	466
Trenton	373	Walton, J. S.	374
Trimble, Richard	562	Warren, William C.	28
Trina	530	Washington Times Herald	480
Troisdoc (2)	455	Watson, C. W.	518
Troxel, David S.	55	Watson, Walter H.	391
Troy (2)	394	Watt, James	406
Troy Socony	335	Wave Transport	236
Truesdale, William H.	53	Way, S. B. (1)	178
Turner, J. J.	60	Way, S. B. (2)	386
Turret Cape	351	Way, S. B. (3)	182
Tuxpancliffe	475	Webster, R. E.	309
		Weed, Shelton	571
U		Weir, David M.	59
		Weir, Ernest T. (1)	261
Uhlmann Brothers (1)	409	Weldon, D. B.	419
Uhlmann Brothers (2)	308	Wellandoc (1)	358
Uhrig, Edward A.	59	Wellandoc (2)	457
Umbria	294	Wells, Frederick B.	218
Union	255	Wells, J. P.	407
United States Gypsum (1)	304	Werner, Henry P.	6
United States Gypsum (2)	14	Wescoat, L. S.	63
Upson, Andrew S.	75	West, Charles C.	489
Upson, J. E.	503	Westcliffe Hall (1)	377
Uranus (4)	450	Westcliffe Hall (2)	259
Usona	396	Westdale (1)	601
Utley, E. H.	30	Western Shell	37

VESSEL	PAGE	VESSEL	PAGE
Western Star	119	Windsolite	9
Westmount (2)	129	Winnipeg (3)	131
Weyburn	130	Wirt, Jack	210
Wheaton	377	Witcroix	169
White Flash	200	Witsupply	135
White, Charles M.	505	Wolf, William H. (2)	222
White, Peter	61	Wolvin, Augustus B.	310
White Rose	520	Wood, James B.	277
White Rose II	520	Wood, Joseph	220
White Star (2)	38	Woodruff, Graham C.	362
Whitney, D. M.	171	Wyandotte (3)	610
Whitney, David M.	171	Wyandotte (4)	188
Whitney, David Marshall	171	Wyatt, H. L.	376
Wiarton (2)	592		
Wickwire, Theodore H.	263	**Y**	
Wickwire, Jr., Theodore H.	14		
Widener, Peter A. B.	563		
Widlar, Francis	355	Yankcanuck (1)	613
Wilkinson, Frank	375	Yates, Harry (1)	599
Wilkinson, Horace S. (1)	530	Yates, Harry (2)	12
Wilkinson, Horace S. (2)	211	Yates, Harry (3)	263
Williams, John C.	189	Young, Colonel E. M.	58
Williamsport	29	Young, E. M.	58
Willowbranch (1)	237	Young, Joseph S. (2)	15
Willowbranch (2)	49	Youngstown	391
Willowdale	498		
Wilpen	15	**Z**	
Wilson, G. N. (1)	171		
Wilson, G. N. (2)	12		
Wiltranco	211	Zebrula	39
Wiltranco I	211	Zenave	24
Windoc (1)	458	Zimmerman, Eugene	155